曾智明"曾子学术基金"科研成果

山东大学曾子研究所科研成果

曾子研究院科研成果

儒家文明协同创新中心（山东大学）研究成果

曾子文化丛书

《孟子》通解

曾振宇 主编

刘单平 注译

MengZi
Tongjie

人民出版社

责任编辑:宫　共
封面设计:胡欣欣

图书在版编目(CIP)数据

《孟子》通解/曾振宇 主编;刘单平 注译. —北京:人民出版社,2023.11
ISBN 978-7-01-026035-8

Ⅰ.①孟… Ⅱ.①曾… ②刘… Ⅲ.①《孟子》-研究 Ⅳ.①B222.55

中国国家版本馆 CIP 数据核字(2023)第 200327 号

《孟子》通解

MENGZI TONGJIE

曾振宇　主编
刘单平　注译

人民出版社 出版发行

(100706　北京市东城区隆福寺街 99 号)

北京汇林印务有限公司印刷　新华书店经销

2023 年 11 月第 1 版　2023 年 11 月北京第 1 次印刷
开本:710 毫米×1000 毫米 1/16　印张:39.25　字数:563 千字

ISBN 978-7-01-026035-8　定价:160.00 元

邮购地址 100706　北京市东城区隆福寺街 99 号
人民东方图书销售中心　电话 (010)65250042　65289539

| 曾振宇 |

　　中国著名儒学专家，儒学研究领域"泰山学者"。山东省社会科学名家。山东大学二级教授，山东大学儒学高等研究院教授、博士生导师、史学博士，山东大学儒学高等研究院原副院长、曾子研究院院长。山东省第 9、10、11 届政协委员。美国康涅狄格大学访问学者、布莱恩特大学访问学者。中国哲学史学会曾子研究会会长，国际儒联理事。专业为儒学与中国思想史。

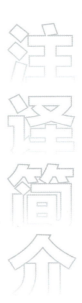

| 刘单平 |

　　1982 年生，山东东平人，历史学博士，毕业于山东大学历史文化学院，现就职于潍坊学院文史学院，研究方向为先秦思想史。

序　言

　　"四书"是国学经典。所谓"经典"，意味着时间的长河慢慢将文本中有永恒意义的东西筛选出来，并将非本质的成分滤除。简言之，经典永远具有现代性价值。从汉代开始，《论语》便成为人人诵读的蒙学教材。第一部由外国人翻译的《论语》英译本，由拉丁文转译而来，初版于康熙三十年（1691）；马歇曼（Joshua Marshman，1768—1837）于1809年出版的《论语》英文节译本，乃第一部直接由中文直译的《论语》英译本；第一部中国人翻译的英译本，则是辜鸿铭于1898出版的译本。迄至今日，"四书"英译本已不下十余种。

　　不同的哲学与文化形态需要沟通与互鉴。相互学习、"美美与共"，各民族历史文化传统中优秀成分才能升华为全世界人人共享的文明成果。在各种英译本"四书"基础上，让全世界各国读者对"四书"的理解有进一步的提升，是本丛书的努力方向，也是本丛书特点所在。我们分别择选出几种有代表性的"四书"译本，从概念、文句和翻译风格等等方面加以比较、分析和点评，冀望读者在阅读过程中，对"四书"的领悟与把握有所深化。譬如，在《论语》一书中，众多弟子问"什么是仁?"孔子的回答都不一致。在大多数语境中，孔子立足于伦理学与工夫论层面讨论"为仁之方"，而非逻辑学意义上的"仁是什么?"但是，在逻辑学和道德哲学层面，孔子自己是否对"仁是什么"存在一个哲学的思考和逻辑上的定义？这是我们今天颇感兴趣的话题。实际上，孔子仁论不属于认识论层面的概念，也不仅仅是道德论层面的概念，而应该将其视为审美境界的概念。孔子仁学重心不在于从认识论维度界说"仁是什么"，也不单纯在道德层面表述"应该""如何"，而是更多地关注心与性合一、身与心合一。换言之，天与人合一。这种审美境界的仁学，对外在客观必然性已有所超越，其中蕴含自由与自由意志的色彩。由此而来，也给历代学者如何准确翻译"仁"这一核心概念产生了很大的挑战。理雅各将"仁"译为"true virtue"（真正的美德），辜鸿铭将"仁"译为"moral character"（符合道德的性格）。读者不仅仅是阅读者，也是文本创作者。在阅读作者研究成果的同时，必然提升对"四书"思想的整体认识。

六朝时期的鸠摩罗什曾经感叹道："但改梵为秦，失其藻蔚，虽得大意，殊隔文体。有似嚼饭与人，非徒失味，乃令呕哕也。"①鸠摩罗什的感叹蕴涵诸多困惑与无奈，"依实出华"是译者矻矻以求的奋斗目标，也是阅读者期望之所在。

是为序。

曾振宇
2023 年 7 月 25 日于山东大学

---

① 慧皎撰、汤用彤校注：《高僧传》卷二，中华书局 1992 年版，第 53 页。

目　录

卷　一

梁惠王章句上

【原文】1.1　孟子见梁惠王[1]。王曰："叟[2]！不远千里[3]而来，亦将有以利[4]吾国乎？"孟子对曰："王何必曰利？亦有仁义[5]而已矣。王曰，'何以利吾国？'大夫曰，'何以利吾家[6]？'士庶人曰，'何以利吾身？'上下交征利而国危矣。万乘[7]之国，弑[8]其君者，必千乘之家；千乘之国，弑其君者，必百乘之家。万取千焉，千取百焉，不为不多矣。苟为后义而先利，不夺不餍。未有仁而遗其亲者也，未有义而后其君者也。王亦曰仁义而已矣，何必曰利？"

【译文】孟子去拜见梁惠王。梁惠王说："老先生！你不远千里而来，将会给我的国家带来什么利益呢？"孟子回答说："大王为什么非要说利呢？我只有仁义而已。如果君王说，'怎样对我的国家有利？'大夫说，'怎样对我的封地有利？'士人和老百姓说，'怎样对我自己有利？'就会导致上下相互争夺利益，从而使国家陷入危险之中！在拥有上万辆兵车的国家里，以下犯上杀掉国君的必定是拥有上千辆兵车的大夫；在拥有上千辆兵车的国家里，以下犯上杀掉国君的必定是拥有上百辆兵车的大夫。在国君拥有上万辆兵车的国家里，大夫可以拥有一千辆兵车；在国君拥有上千辆兵车的国家里，大夫可以拥有一百辆兵车。这些大夫拥有的不能说不多。如果重利轻义，把义放在利之后，那些大夫不全部夺走君主的东西就永远不会满足。重仁的人不会抛弃自己的父母，重义的人不会怠慢自己的君主。大王也是只讲仁义就行了，何必要谈利益呢？"

【英译】① Mencius went to see king Hûi of Liang. The king said，'Venerable sir，since you have not counted it far to come here，a distance of a thousand lî，may I presume that you are provided with counsels to profit my kingdom？' Mencius replied，'Why must your Majesty use that word "profit？" What I am provided with，are counsels to benevolence and righteousness，and these are my only topics. If your Majesty say，"What is to be done to profit my kingdom？" the great officers will say，"What is to be done to profit our families？" and the inferior officers and the common people will say，"What is to be done to profit our persons？" Superiors and inferiors will try to snatch this profit the one from the other，and the kingdom will be endangered. In the kingdom of ten thousand chariots，the murderer of his sovereign shall be the chief of a family of a thousand chariots. In a kingdom of a thousand chariots，the murderer of his prince shall be the chief of a family of a hundred chariots. To have a thousand in ten thousand，and a hundred in a thousand，cannot be said to be a large allotment，but if righteousness be put last，and profit be put first，they will not be satisfied without snatching all. There never has been a benevolent man

---

① 本书中的英文译文采用的是理雅各（James Legge）的《孟子》英译本（James Legge，*The Works of Mencius*，New York：Dover Pub.，Inc，1970.），试图通过将该译本同刘殿爵（D. C. Lau）、伦纳德·赖发洛（Leonard A. Lyall）、大卫·亨顿（David Hinton）以及赵甄陶主译的《孟子》英译本进行对比研究，彰显孟子多维度诠释的空间。理雅各的译本早在1861 年就已经出现，当时用威妥玛式拼音翻译中国的地名、人名在中国和国际上都很流行，因而他的译文既体现了威妥玛式拼音的特点，又沿袭了前人使用送气符号来表示声母的办法，便于我们了解中国人名、地名外译的历史。他的译文也体现了英国人在对话中喜用单引号的特点。

who neglected his parents. There never has been a righteous man who made his sovereign an after consideration. Let your Majesty also say, "Benevolence and righteousness，and let these be your only themes." Why must you use that word–"profit?"'

【注释】

[1] 战国时期魏国的国君魏惠王，因建都大梁，所以被称作"梁惠王"。孟子在周游诸侯国时，虽然是晚年到魏国，却将与梁惠王的对话放在首篇，因为本章直接阐释了孟子的义利观。

[2] "叟"，是对老者、长者的称呼。古代因年长而受到尊敬的人被称为叟，类似于我们今天的老先生。春秋战国时期，诸侯为表示尊重，通常称有才能的人为夫子或者先生。从他对孟子的称呼中可以看出，梁惠王并不认为孟子是有治国之才的人，这也从《史记·孟子荀卿列传》"梁惠王不果所言，则见以为迂远而阔于事情"可窥一斑。刘殿爵将之翻译为"Sir"，突出对男性的尊重。理雅各和赵甄陶将之译为"Venerable sir"，强调是因年长、智慧或者品德而受到尊敬。

[3] "里"，是中国古代特有的长度计量单位，一里等于五百米。刘殿爵采取音译的方法，将之译为"li"，理雅各、赵甄陶等译者在翻译的时候也采取这一翻译策略。在翻译"里"时，赖发洛和亨顿则选择用外国人比较熟悉的"mile"翻译。

[4] 此处的"利"特指富国强兵之利。"利"是梁惠王首要关注的问题，所以一见孟子，来不及含蓄，就直奔主题，从而引出了孟子的义利观。义利观是孟子思想的核心，孟子将之概括为"何必曰利? 亦有仁义而已矣"。要准确理解孟子的义利观，应抓住两点：一是针对梁惠王治国之问，孟子主张要以仁义治国，不应以利治国，否则会导致整个国家求利之心膨胀，导致国家危亡；二是在义和利的关系上，义是首位的，利的获得要限制在道德和正义的范围之内。纵观《孟子》全文，孟子并非反对所有利，而是反对通过发动战争、压榨百姓而获得的短期之利。

[5]"仁"和"义"是儒家思想的核心概念。对于其翻译,译者们见仁见智。首先看"仁"的翻译。在《孟子》中,刘殿爵和赵甄陶基本上把"仁"都翻译为"benevolence",理雅各则根据上下文,有时将之译为"benevolence",有时译为"perfect virtue";赖发洛选择用"love"翻译"仁",辜鸿铭将其译作"moral sense"。陈荣捷在《儒学之"仁"的意义演变》中列举了"仁"的众多英译词:benevolence、love、altruism、kindness、charity、compassion、magnanimity、perfect、virtue、goodness、true manhood、manhood at its best、human-heartedness、humanness、humanity、man-to-man-ness。学界之所以难以统一对"仁"的翻译,与其内涵的丰富性密切相关。孟子的"仁"含义丰富,包含亲亲、仁民、爱物三个层次,在西方词汇中难以找到内涵和外延相当的对等词。其次看"义"的翻译。"义"是《孟子》的又一核心概念,内涵丰富。《礼记·中庸》指出:"义者,宜也。"孔颖达疏:"宜谓于事得宜。"可见,"义"就是做适宜的事情。在《孟子》中,"义"出现了一〇八次,主要是指符合正确的道理、符合规律、符合礼仪、符合道德的事情。理雅各和刘殿爵则倾向于根据文意,翻译"义"的不同内涵。在他们的译文中,"义"有 right、righteous、rightness、duty、dutiful 等多种含义。亨顿将之翻译为"duty",莱尔将之翻译为"right"。儒家核心概念内涵的丰富性决定了在翻译这些儒家核心概念时,音译加注不失为一种有益的尝试。音译可以确保对这些核心概念的翻译前后保持一致,使读者尤其是外国读者明白这些核心概念在原文中的位置及出现的频率。通过注释对这一概念在文中的具体含义作出解释,有助于读者感受到这些核心概念所蕴含的丰富的文化内涵,进而更全面地理解原文。

[6]"家",此处特指古代执政大夫的封邑。理雅各的译文"family"更强调家庭成员,莱尔、亨顿的译文"house"更突出住宅、建筑。相比较而言,刘殿爵的"vassal"指诸侯、封臣,更能清楚、准确地翻译出其内涵。

[7]"乘",在春秋战国时期多指兵车。"一乘"通常包括一车四马和三名甲士。刘殿爵和理雅各将"乘"译为"chariot",基本上能体现其内涵。

赖发洛将之译为"car"，容易使人联想到在街上奔驰的日常交通工具。

[8]"弑"，指古代臣子杀死君主，子女杀死父母等卑幼杀死尊长的大不敬行为。刘殿爵的"regicide"很好地翻译出了其内涵。赵甄陶的"killer"、亨顿的"kill"，以及理雅各和莱尔的"murder"都不能完美再现"弑"的内涵。

【原文】1.2　孟子见梁惠王。王立于沼上，顾鸿雁麋鹿，曰："贤者[1]亦乐此乎?"孟子对曰："贤者而后乐此，不贤者虽有此，不乐也[2]。《诗》[3]云：'经始灵台，经之营之，庶民攻[4]之，不日成之。经始勿亟，庶民子来。王[5]在灵囿，麀鹿攸伏，麀鹿濯濯，白鸟鹤鹤。王在灵沼，於牣鱼跃。'文王以民力为台为沼，而民欢乐之，谓其台曰灵台，谓其沼曰灵沼，乐其有麋鹿鱼鳖。古之人与民偕乐，故能乐也。《汤誓》[6]曰：'时日害丧，予及女偕亡。'[7]民欲与之偕亡，虽有台池鸟兽，岂能独乐哉?"

【译文】孟子去拜见梁惠王。梁惠王站在池塘边上，一边观赏着鸿雁麋鹿等飞禽走兽，一边问孟子："道德高尚的贤能之人也以此为快乐吗?"孟子回答说："只有道德高尚的贤能之人才会有这种快乐，不贤的人即使拥有这些飞禽走兽，也无法享受其中的乐趣。正如《诗经》所说：'(文王)开始建筑灵台，细心筹谋安排，百姓一起努力，很快便建成。虽然文王说大家不要急，但是百姓更加努力。王来灵苑参观，母鹿祥和安卧。母鹿肥美，闪耀光泽。白鸟洁净，羽毛柔顺。王站在灵沼上，满池的鱼儿欢喜跳跃。'虽然文王是用百姓的力量建造高台深池，可是百姓却非常高兴，称他搭建的高台为'灵台'，他挖掘的池沼为'灵沼'，并很高兴他能拥有大群的鸿雁、麋鹿和鱼鳖。像文王那样的古代圣王能够与民一同享受这些快乐，所以能够真正拥有这些快乐。(相反，百姓对于自称太阳的暴君夏桀的怨恨)正如《汤誓》所记载的那样：'这个太阳啊，你到底什么时候毁灭呢? 我宁愿和你一起灭亡。'百姓要和暴君同归于尽，即使他拥有高台深池和遍地鸟兽，又怎能独自快乐地享受这些呢？"

【英译】Mencius another day, saw king Hûi of Liang. The king went and stood with him by a pond, and, looking round at the large geese and deer, said, 'Do wise and good princes also find pleasure in these things?' Mencius replied, 'Being wise and good, they have pleasure in these things. If they are not wise and good, though they have these things, they do not find pleasure. It is said in the Book of Poetry, "He measured out and commenced his marvelous tower; He measured it out and planned it. The people addressed themselves to it, and in less than a day completed it. When he measured and began it, he said to them-Be not so earnest: but the multitudes came as if they had been his children. The king was in his marvelous park; the does reposed about, the does so sleek and fat: and the white birds shone glistening. The king was by his marvelous pond; how full was it of fishes leaping about!" King wǎn used the strength of the people to make his tower and his pond, and yet the people rejoiced to do the work, calling the tower "the marvelous tower," calling the pond "the marvelous pond," and rejoicing that he had his large deer, his fishes, and turtles. The ancients caused the people to have pleasure as well as themselves, and therefore they could enjoy it. In the Declaration of T'ang it is said. "O sun, when wilt thou expire? We will die together with thee." The people wished for Chieh's death, though they should die with him. Although he had towers, ponds, birds, and animals, how could he have pleasure alone?'

【注释】

[1] 据统计，"贤"在《孟子》中总共出现了68次，主要意思是品德

高、能力强。理雅各将"贤者"翻译为"wise and good princes",刘殿爵翻译为"a good and wise man"。这两个译本皆体现了"贤者"德才兼备的特点。赖发洛将其翻译为"men of worth"稍显笼统,未能体现出"贤"字的内涵。赵甄陶将之翻译为"virtuous men",只强调了贤者在道德品质方面的突出特点。和刘殿爵以及其他译者认为此处的"贤者"泛指所有的人不同,理雅各认为是特指贤明的君主。纵观孟子和梁惠王的谈话,多围绕君主应该如何治理国家展开,不仅如此,下文引文王之"贤"和夏桀之"不贤"作对比,以突出本节"与民同乐"的宗旨以及后面举的文王和纣王的例子看,理雅各的翻译更准确。

[2] 孟子在此处首次提出了与民同乐的观点,这既是本章的主旨,又是孟子仁政思想的重要组成部分。孟子认为,只有成为贤者,与民同乐,才能享受这种快乐。否则,即使暂时有了鸿雁麋鹿之乐,也难以享受和维持这种快乐。理雅各将之翻译为"Being wise and good, they have pleasure in these things. If they are not wise and good,though they have these things,they do not find pleasure",他严格按照原文句型结构直译,再现了原文风格。刘殿爵将之翻译为"'Only if a man is good and wise,'answered Mencius,'is he able to enjoy them. Otherwise he would not,even if he had them'",他的译文则更符合英语表达习惯,便于西方读者理解。

[3] 《诗》是中国古代最早的一部诗歌总集,收集了西周初年至春秋中叶的 305 篇诗歌。西汉时被尊为儒家经典,始称《诗经》。刘殿爵将之翻译为"The Book of Odes","Odes"的含义是颂歌集,但《诗经》包含《风》《雅》《颂》三个部分,因而理雅各和赵甄陶的译文"the Book of Poetry"更准确。

[4] "攻"是致力于建造的意思。刘殿爵的"worked at",理雅各的"addressed to"和赖发洛的"toiled",都能表现出百姓辛勤劳作,共同努力建造灵台的情景。

[5] 根据下文,此处的"王"指的是周文王,与其他译者将之翻译为

"The king" 不同，刘殿爵选择将之翻译为 "The King"，通过大写以突出其含义的特殊性。

[6] 汤是商代的开国君主，也是孟子推崇的古代圣王。他在率领军队征伐夏代暴君桀时，在决战开始之前，为鼓舞士气，一举消灭夏桀，作《汤誓》以鼓舞士气。理雅各和赵甄陶皆选择用 "Declaration" 翻译。"Declaration" 多指官方、正式的宣告，基本能表达《汤誓》的内涵。赖发洛将之翻译为 "The oath of T'ang"，"oath" 多指公开的承诺，不甚准确。与其他译者不同，刘殿爵选择音译《汤誓》来凸显其独特性。笔者认为，在英译的基础上，通过增加注释的方式，帮助读者了解其含义不失为翻译中国特有文化词语的好方法。

[7] 关于"时日害丧，予及女偕亡"的含义，古来有两种注释。清焦循在《孟子正义》中引赵岐注曰："言是日当大丧亡，我及女俱往亡也。害，大也。"即这个太阳到了大丧亡的时候了，我们一起去将它灭亡吧。另一说见宋代朱熹的《孟子集注》："时，是也。日，指夏桀。害，何也。桀尝自言，吾有天下，如天之有日，日亡吾乃亡耳。民怨其虐，故因其自言而目之曰，此日何时亡乎？若亡则我宁与之俱亡，盖欲其亡之甚也。"即这个太阳到底什么时候灭亡啊？即使和它俱亡，我也在所不惜。笔者认为，朱熹的注释更符合文义。孟子在此处主要论证与民同乐的重要性。在上文他援引《诗经》称文王为贤者，他能与民同乐，故能得到人民的拥护，保有其乐。下文他引用《汤誓》说明夏桀不贤，失民心，百姓宁愿和他一起灭亡。刘殿爵选择用 "perish" 翻译"丧"，该词多强调暴力、武力毁灭，和汤出师伐桀这一史实相符合。理雅各和赵甄陶选择用 "expire" 翻译，强调因时间到了而失效，更加突出天命靡常的含义。刘殿爵对本句的翻译更能表达人们对夏桀的憎恨、厌恶之情。他的译文是："O Sun, when wilt thou perish? We care not if we have to die with thee." 即"太阳啊，你什么时候毁灭？即使我们不得不和你一起灭亡，我们也不在乎。"译文将人们对夏桀的厌恶之情表达得淋漓尽致。赖发洛的译文是："Let this sun be destroyed and I and thou will die

together with him."即"让这个太阳毁灭吧，我们一起和他同归于尽。"译文用祈使句的形式，表达了人们渴望暴君夏桀毁灭的心愿。理雅各的翻译"O sun, when wilt thou expire? We will die together with thee."即"太阳啊，你什么时候毁灭？我们将会和你一起灭亡。"译文虽能准确表达原文之意，但没有传达原文所蕴含的感情色彩。

【原文】 1.3 梁惠王曰："寡人[1]之于国也，尽心焉耳矣[2]。河内[3]凶，则移其民于河东[4]，移其粟于河内。河东凶亦然。察邻国之政，无如寡人之用心者。邻国之民不加少，寡人之民不加多，何也？"孟子对曰："王好战，请以战喻。填然鼓之，兵刃既接，弃甲曳兵而走。或百步而后止，或五十步而后止。以五十步笑百步[5]，则何如？"曰："不可，直不百步耳，是亦走[6]也。"曰："王如知此，则无望民之多于邻国也。不违农时，谷不可胜食也；数罟不入洿池，鱼鳖不可胜食也；斧斤以时入山林，材木不可胜用也。谷与鱼鳖不可胜食，材木不可胜用[7]，是使民养生丧死无憾也[8]。养生丧死无憾，王道之始也。五亩[9]之宅，树之以桑，五十者可以衣帛矣。鸡豚狗彘[10]之畜，无失其时[11]，七十者可以食肉矣。百亩之田，勿夺其时，数口之家可以无饥矣。谨庠序[12]之教，申之以孝悌之义[13]，颁白者不负戴于道路矣。七十者衣帛食肉，黎民不饥不寒，然而不王者，未之有也。狗彘食人食而不知检[14]，途有饿莩而不知发；人死，则曰'非我也，岁也'，是何异于刺人而杀之，曰'非我也，兵也'。王无罪岁，斯天下之民至焉。"

【译文】 梁惠王说："在治理国家方面，我真是尽心尽力了。如果河内闹饥荒，我就会把难民迁移到河东，同时把河东的粮食运到河内。如果河东遭遇灾荒，我也会这样做。再看看周围国家的国君，在治理国家时没有像我一样尽心的。为什么邻国的百姓没有因此而减少，我的百姓也没有因此增多？"孟子回答说："您喜欢战争，请允许我用战争打个比方吧。战鼓敲响，双方士兵刚一交战，就有士兵丢盔弃甲，拖着兵器落荒而逃。有的士兵跑了一百步才停下，有的跑了五十步就停下了。那些逃跑了五十步的士兵是否可以嘲笑跑了一百步的士兵？"梁惠王说："不行，虽然没有跑到一百步，但是也逃跑了。"孟子说："既然您懂得这个道理，就不要期望您的百姓要比邻国多了。如果不违背农时，确保百姓有足够的时间耕作，则粮食便会吃不完。如果不用有细密网眼的渔网去池沼捕鱼，鱼鳖也会吃不完。如果按照时令砍伐树木，木材也用不完。粮食和鱼鳖吃不完，木材用不尽，就能够使人们在赡养和丧葬方面没有什么遗憾了。在生养死葬方面没有遗憾和不满是王道的开端。在五亩大的宅院周围种植上桑树，年满五十岁的人可以穿丝绸衣服了。鸡狗猪等家畜都按时喂养，七十岁的人就可以吃肉了。拥有百亩农田的人家，如果不去妨碍他们的生产劳动，好几口人都可以吃得饱饱的。努力办好各级学校，并用孝敬父母、敬爱兄长的道理教导他们，就不会出现年龄大的人背负着重物在路上行走的现象。如果能够做到确保七十岁的老人有丝绸穿，有肉吃，并且普通百姓不冷不饿，但是仍然不能成为天下归服的王者，是从来没有过的。现在的君主看到猪狗吃百姓的粮食却不知道制裁和限制，看到道路上有饿死的人，却不知道开仓赈灾，等到人死了，却说'不是我杀的，是年成不好'，这和杀了人却说'不是我，是兵器杀的'有什么区别呢？所以国君千万不要责怪年成不好，（而要从自己身上找原因）这样，别的国家的百姓就会来投奔你了。"

【英译】King Hûi of Liang said, 'Small as my virtue is, in the government of my kingdom, I do indeed exert my mind to the most. If the year be bad on the inside of the river, I remove as many of the people as I can to the east of the river, and convey grain to the country in the inside. When the year is bad on the east of the river, I act on the same plan. On examining the government of the neighbouring kingdoms, I do not find that there is any prince who exerts his mind as I do. And yet the people of the neighbouring kingdoms do not decrease, nor do my people increase. How is this?' Mencius replied, 'Your Majesty is fond of war; -let me take an illustration from war.-The soldiers move forward to the sound of the drums; and after their weapons have been crossed, on one side they throw away their coasts of mail, trail their arms behind them, and run. Some run a hundred paces and stop; some run fifty paces and stop. What would you think if those who run fifty paces were to laugh at those who run a hundred paces?' the king said, 'They should not do so. Though they did not run a hundred paces, yet they also run away.' 'Since your Majesty knows this,' replied Mencius, 'you need not hope that your people will become more numerous than those of the neighbouring kingdoms. If the seasons of husbandry be not interfered with, the grain will be more than can be eaten. If close nets are not allowed to enter the pools and ponds, the fishes and turtles will be more than can be consumed. If the axes and bills enter the hills and forests only at the proper time, the wood will be more than can be used. When the grain and fish and turtles are more than can be eaten, and there is more wood than can be used, this enables the people to nourish their living and mourn for their dead, without any feeling against any. This condition, in which the people nourish their living and bury their dead without any feeling against any, is the first step of royal government. Let mulberry trees be planted about the homesteads with their five mâu, and persons of fifty years may be clothed with silk. In keeping fowls, pigs, dogs, and swine, let not their times of breeding be neglected, and persons of seventy years may eat flesh. Let there not be taken away the time that is proper for the cultivation of the farm with its hundred mâu, and the family of several mouths that is supported by it shall not suffer from hunger. Let careful attention be paid to education in schools，inculcating in it especially the filial and fraternal duties，and grey-haired men will not be seen upon the roads，carrying burdens on their backs or on their heads. It never has been that the ruler of a State，where such results were seen，-persons of seventy wearing silk and eating flesh，and the black-haired people suffering neither from hunger nor cold，-did not attain to the royal dignity. Your dogs and swine eat the food of men，and you do not make any restrictive arrangements. There are people dying from famine on the roads，and you do not issue the stores of your granaries for them. When people die，you say，"It is not owing to me；it is owing to the year." In what does this differ from stabbing a man and killing him，and then saying- "It was not I；it was the weapon?" Let your Majesty cease to lay the blame on the year，and instantly from all the nation the people will come to you.'

【注释】

[1] "寡人"，古代诸侯的自称，后来成为君主的谦称。《礼记·曲礼下》说："诸侯见天子，曰'臣某侯某'。其与民言自称曰'寡人'。"孔颖达疏曰："寡人者，言己是寡德之人。"可见，"寡人"是古代王侯的一种谦称。理雅各将之译为"Small as my virtue is，in the government of my kingdom"，这种解释性翻译能够准确再现"寡人"的含义。刘殿爵、赵甄陶等译者选择直接用"I"翻译，未能体现中国特色文化词语"寡人"的内涵。

[2] "焉耳矣"，用在这里是为了强调"尽心"。陈器之对此做过详细的论述："焉耳矣是语气词连用，重点在'矣'字上，用于陈述句，表示十分肯定的语气，可译为'啦'或'了啊'。"理雅各在翻译时，用"do indeed"对"尽心"作了强调，再现了本句的强调语气。刘殿爵的译文虽然准确再现了尽心的含义，但没有对此作出突出强调。

[3] 此处的"河"专指黄河。在先秦文献中有关黄河的记载都称为"河"。据现有资料记载,"黄河"一词最早出现在《汉书》中。"河内"在古代指河南省黄河以北地区,也就是现在的济源一带,战国时是魏国的领土。理雅各将"河内"翻译为"the inside of the river"(河流的内侧),这一翻译过于笼统、模糊。刘殿爵则采用音译法,将"河内"翻译为"Ho Nei",以突出其作为中国特有地名的独特性。但只有音译,没有注释不便于读者理解其确切含义。赵甄陶则将之译为"north of the Yellow River",准确再现了原文内涵。

[4] 黄河自北而南流经山西省,故山西省境内黄河以东的地区,也就是今山西运城一带,战国时期也是魏国的领土,被称为"河东"。理雅各将之直译为"the east of the river",不能完整再现"河东"的内涵。刘殿爵选择将之音译为"Ho Tung",虽能突出其独特性,但表意不明确。若能采取注释的形式,对其进行进一步解释说明,更能完整传递河东包含的地理信息。相比较而言,赵甄陶将之译为"east of the Yellow River"更准确。

[5] 我们常用的成语"五十步笑百步"就是出自于此处。孟子通过举作战的时候,逃跑了五十步的人嘲笑逃跑了一百步人的故事,告诫梁惠王他的"尽心"只是"五十步笑百步",不能真正解决问题。梁惠王并没有真正实施仁政,因而也不能期望自己的国家比邻国更加强大。在古代,举足一次叫跬(半步),两足各跨一次叫步。理雅各、赵甄陶和刘殿爵都将"百步"翻译为"a hundred paces",赖发洛将之翻译为"a hundred steps",不论"pace"还是"step"皆可以表示一步的距离。亨顿将之翻译为"a hundred feet",不准确。

[6] 在古代,行、步、趋、走的使用是根据行进速度进行划分的,正如汉代刘熙在《释名·释姿容》中所说:"徐行曰步,疾行曰趋,疾趋曰走。"可见,此处的"走"其实相当于现代汉语中的跑,因而译者都选用"run"翻译。

[7] "谷与鱼鳖不可胜食"与"材木不可胜用"采用的是排偶句式,

给人整齐匀称的美感。刘殿爵将之译为"When the people have more grain,more fish and turtles than they can eat, and more timber than they can use",他的译文很好地再现了排偶句的优势,起到了反复强调,增强语势的表达效果。赖发洛将之翻译为"the grain, fish and turtle are more than can be eaten,and the wood and timber are more than can be used",他的译文也达到了同样的效果,可以很好地再现原文的文采。理雅各的译文也能够准确传递原文之意,但两种不同句式的使用不能再现原文句式特点。

[8] 对"是使民养生丧死无憾也"的翻译,不同译者所表达的侧重点不同。刘殿爵的译文表明,他认为谷、鱼鳖和材木的富足能使百姓在赡养父母和办理父母丧事上不会因为该做而未能做到而有所遗憾。理雅各将之翻译为"This condition, in which the people nourish their living and bury their dead without any feeling against any"。可见,他认为谷、鱼鳖和材木的富足可以使君主免遭百姓的怨恨,赢得民心。赖发洛的译文是"To feed the living and bury the dead without fretting",即人们在供养生人和安葬死者上没有烦恼。他强调的是"王政"给百姓带来的好处——谷、鱼鳖和材木的富足会使人民生活快乐无忧。清焦循在《孟子正义》中指出:"憾,恨也。"显然,他的注解和理雅各的百姓生活富足就不会对君主有所怨恨相一致,是在强调王政给君主带来的积极影响,即"王道"可以得民心,故理雅各的翻译更符合原文之意。

[9] "亩"是中国古代特有的计量单位,在英语中没有对等词。刘殿爵和理雅各在翻译时采取音译加注的方法,很好地向读者介绍了中国古代这一土地计量单位的内涵。赖发洛试图在英语中找对等词翻译"亩",并最终选择了"rood"(路德),虽然很容易让英国读者理解,但不能准确传递"亩"的内涵。

[10] "豚"是小猪,"彘"指大猪。杨伯峻指出:"豚是小猪,但只能杀以祭祀,正如王筠在《说文释例》所说的,'古人之豕,非大不食,小豕惟以致祭也'。所以这里既言'彘',又言'豚'。"可见,孟子在此处将

"豚"和"彘"分开来说，含有深意。刘殿爵将"豚"和"彘"统一译为"pigs"不妥。理雅各将之译为"pigs"和"swine"，赖发洛翻译为"pigs and sows"，两位译者虽看到了豚、彘的不同，但未能将其内涵翻译准确。

[11] 刘殿爵、理雅各、赖发洛、赵甄陶等译者都将"时"翻译为"breeding seasons"，即繁殖期。但结合上文的豚（小猪）和下文的"勿夺其时"，此处的"时"指喂养的时间更准确。

[12] "庠序"是古代的地方学校。陈器之指出："商朝叫序，周朝叫庠"。译者在翻译"庠序"时都采取意译的策略，但在准确性上差别较大。其中，刘殿爵将"庠序"翻译为"village schools"，赵甄陶翻译为"local schools"，都能准确体现"庠序"的含义。理雅各选择用"shools"翻译，则略显宽泛。赖发洛的"schools and colleges"很容易让人联想到学校和大学，这与原文之意相差甚远。

[13] "孝悌"是儒家的伦理道德思想之一。《论语·学而》中有"其为人也孝悌"。朱熹注曰："善事父母为孝，善事兄长为悌。"可见，"孝"是子女要孝顺父母，"悌"指弟弟对兄长要敬重、顺从。理雅各将"孝"翻译为"filial"（子女的，孝顺的）是准确的。但他将"悌"翻译为"fraternal duties"（兄弟间的义务）不确切，扩大了"悌"的内涵。赖发洛将"孝"译为"piety"，将"悌"翻译为"modesty"（谦虚）。在英语世界里，"piety"指虔诚的状态或性质，尤指宗教中人对上帝的爱和尊敬，在此处翻译"孝"不合适。而用"modesty"（谦虚）来翻译"悌"过于笼统。刘殿爵通过解释性翻译准确清楚地传递了"孝悌"的含义，即子女和弟弟应尽的义务。

[14] 对于"狗彘食人食而不知检"，古今注家对此句的理解不尽相同。赵岐注曰："言人君但养犬彘，使食人食，不知以法度检敛也。"清初阎若璩赞同此说。他在《四书释地三续》中说："古虽丰穰，未有以人食予狗彘者。'狗彘食人食'即下章'庖有肥肉'意，谓厚敛于民以养禽兽者耳。"富金壁、牟维珍不赞同此说。他们在《王力〈古代汉语〉注释汇考》中指出："在丰年'狗彘食人食'是正常的。今北方农村在丰收时，仍不限制马牛等

吃禾穗，应是古代习俗的遗留。'庖有肥肉'云云是孟子的另一层意思。阎说实不可从。"另一种解释由颜师古提出。他在注《汉书·食货志赞》"《孟子》亦非'狗彘食人食而不知检'"时说："言岁丰熟，菽粟饶多，狗彘食人之食，此时可敛之也。"即收成好的时候，为了防止谷贱伤农，国家应当采取经济手段，平价收购粮食，以免用来饲养狗彘。这两种解释的根本区别在于：第一种解释把"狗彘食人食"和下文的"庖有肥肉"放在同一时空之下，与"途有饿莩"作对比，指责统治者实行虐政残害人民。而后一种解释则认为"狗彘食人食"和"途有饿莩"指的是在丰年和灾年出现的两种不同的社会现象，而"检"和"发"是统治者采取的不同经济措施。在《汉书·食货志赞》中，孟子的这句话和当时盛行的一系列经济政策并排列举，《汉书·食货志赞》："《易》称'裒多益寡，称物平施'，《书》云'楙迁有无'，周有泉府之官，而《孟子》亦非'狗彘食人之食不知敛，野有饿莩而弗知发'。故《管氏》之轻重，李悝之平籴，弘羊均输，寿昌常平，亦有从徕。"故引用的《孟子》语句也应是当时实行的一种经济政策。清钱大昕在《十驾斋养新录》卷三，对"发敛之法"做过精确的解释："丰岁则敛之于官，凶岁则粜之于民。"可见孟子所谓的"检"应指政府在丰年时采取的经济措施。刘殿爵将之译为"Now when food meant for human being is so plentiful as to be thrown to dogs and pigs，you fail to realize that it is time for garnering."他在翻译时采取解释性翻译的策略，认为当粮食非常充裕的时候，人们用它喂猪狗，而你（统治者）却没意识到此时应当储备粮食。这一译文既能让外国读者很容易明白"狗彘食人食"的现象发生在丰年之时，又能让他们对中国古代统治者在丰年时采取的经济措施有所了解。理译本将之翻译为"Your dogs and swine eat the food of men，and you do not make any restrictive arrangements"，他的译文是对统治者虐政的指责，认为人君应当制止夺人口粮以养猪狗的现象，不能为了满足自己的口腹之欲，而置民众生死于不顾。笔者认为这一理解与《孟子》原意有出入。赖发洛的翻译非常简洁。他采取模糊策略，译为"Dogs and sows eat man's food，and no one knows what to do"，即"猪狗在吃人的口粮，而没有人知道应当怎么办"。这就轻而易举地回避了注家们的分歧。但从忠于原文、传播中国文化的角度讲，这是不可取的。

【原文】 1.4　梁惠王曰："寡人愿安承教[1]。"孟子对曰："杀人以梃与刃，有以异乎？"曰："无以异也。""以刃与政，有以异乎？"曰："无以异也。"曰："庖有肥肉，厩有肥马，民有饥色，野有饿莩，此率兽而食人也[2]。兽相食，且人恶之。为民父母，行政不免于率兽而食人，恶在其为民父母也？仲尼曰：'始作俑者[3]，其无后乎！'为其象人而用之也。如之何其使斯民饥而死也？"

【译文】 梁惠王说："我很乐意听您的指教。"孟子问道："用木棒杀人和用刀子杀人，有什么不同吗？"梁惠王说："没有什么不同。"（孟子）说："用刀杀人和为政害人有什么不同吗？"梁惠王回答说："没有什么不同。"孟子说："厨房里有肥美的肉，马厩里有健壮的马，但是百姓面露饥色，野外有饿死的人，这就是率领着禽兽去吃人。禽兽之间自相残食，人尚且厌恶，作为百姓的父母，在治理国家时却难以避免率禽兽去吃肉的行为，那又如何体现他是百姓的父母呢？正如孔子所说：'最先用人形木偶陪葬的人，大概不会有后代吧！'这是因为他用像人的木偶去陪葬，（像人尚且不可）又怎能让这些百姓因饥饿而死呢？"

【英译】 King Hûi of Liang said, 'I wish quietly to receive your instructions.' Mencius replied, 'Is there any difference between killing a man with a stick and with a sword?' The king said, 'There is no difference.' 'Is there any difference between doing it with a sword and with the style of government?' 'There is no difference,' was the reply. Mencius then said, 'In your kitchen there is fat meat; in your stables there are fat horses. But your people have the look of hunger, and on the wilds there are those who have died of famine. This is leading on beasts to devour men. Beasts devour one another，and men hate them for doing so. When a prince，being the parent of his people，administers his government so as to be chargeable with leading on beasts to devour men，where is his parental relationship to the people?' Chung-ni said，'Was he not without posterity who first made wooden images to bury with the dead? So he said，because that man made the semblances of men，and used them for that purpose：-what shall be thought of him who causes his people to die of hunger?'

【注释】

[1] 孟子紧承上章，从反面论证了施行仁政的必要性。他首先通过两个设问，使梁惠王意识到用棍棒、刀剑杀人与用暴政杀人没有什么区别，接着通过鲜明强烈的对比，给梁惠王描绘了现实政治中只顾个人享乐、不顾人民死活的行政方式给人民带来的巨大痛苦，从而凸显实行仁政，关心百姓疾苦的重要性。梁惠王一句"寡人愿安承教"则展示出了谦虚、恭敬的态度。刘殿爵根据上下文，将"安"翻译为"ready to"（愿意、乐意）是准确的。理雅各将之翻译为"quietly"，赖发洛翻译为"in peace"，二人按照"安"的字面意思将之直译为"安静"不准确。

[2] 在"庖有肥肉，厩有肥马，民有饥色，野有饿莩，此率兽而食人也"中，孟子通过简短却形象鲜明的对比句指责君主纵一己私欲、不顾人民死活是率兽食人。刘殿爵的译文不仅符合英语语言的表达习惯，还完整再现了原文鲜明的对比技巧。但他将"率"翻译为"show"，译此句为"This is to show animals the way to devour men"，即这是向禽兽展示吃人的方法，这一理解和前面对比句的逻辑联系较弱，在达意上稍逊一筹。"此率兽而食人也"是对前面对比句所表达意思的总结。从句意上看，孟子此段话的意思是，厨房里有肥肉，马厩里有肥马，这说明禽兽都得到了你很好的照顾，而百姓却因你的忽视在挨饿、甚至饿死，这简直就是带领禽兽吃人啊。因而理雅各和赖发洛都将"率"译为"leading"，将此句分别翻译为"leading on

beasts to devour men" 和 "leading beasts to eat men"，即带领禽兽吃人，可以很好地再现原文的意思。

[3] "俑" 是古代用以殉葬的偶人，一般为木制或陶制。赵岐注曰："俑，偶人也，用之送死。" 刘殿爵将之翻译为 "the inventor of burial figures in human form"，他的译文将 "俑" 的外形、作用完美呈现。赵甄陶将之翻译为 "wooden or clay figures to bury with the dead"，理雅各的翻译亦与之相类，他们的译文突出了 "俑" 的制作材料和作用，但未强调其外形像人。结合下文可以看出，孔子之所以批判始作俑者就是因为俑的外形像人，因而刘殿爵的翻译更准确。他采用肯定句，将孔子对第一个制作木偶来殉葬的人的厌恶、鄙视和咒骂之情传神地表达了出来。

【原文】 1.5 梁惠王曰："晋国，天下[1]莫强焉，叟之所知也。及寡人之身，东败于齐，长子死焉；西丧地于秦七百里；南辱于楚。寡人耻之，愿比死者一洒之[2]，如之何则可？" 孟子对曰："地方百里[3]而可以王[4]。王如施仁政于民，省刑罚，薄税敛，深耕易耨[5]；壮者以暇日修其孝悌忠信，入以事其父兄，出以事其长上，可使制梃以挞秦楚之坚甲利兵矣。彼夺其民时，使不得耕耨以养其父母。父母冻饿，兄弟妻子离散。彼陷溺其民，王往而征之，夫谁与王敌？故曰：'仁者无敌。'[6]王请勿疑！"

【译文】 梁惠王说："就像您老人家所知道的那样，晋国是当时天下强大的国家。但是到我执政时，在东边和齐国交战大败，我的大儿子也在战争中阵亡；在西边和秦国战争，又败给秦国，割让河西之地七百里；在南边和楚国战争，也被迫割让大片土地。我对这些失败感到耻辱，想要替战死的人报仇雪恨，我应该如何做呢？" 孟子回答说："拥有方圆百里国土的君主也可以成为统一天下的王者。您如果能够在治理国家时对百姓施行仁政，减轻刑罚，减少赋税，让百姓能够深耕细作，除去杂草但不伤及谷根；还在闲暇时间反复向那些年轻力壮的人讲孝顺父母、敬爱兄长、对待他人尽心竭力、与人交往诚实守信的道理，那么他们就可以在家里侍奉父母兄长，在外尊重长辈上级，这样，即使他们手拿木棒，也可以打败那些拥有坚甲利刃的秦、楚军队了。（因为）他们占用百姓的生产耕种时间，使得百姓不能依靠耕种赡养父母。（士兵的）父母挨饿受冻，兄弟、妻子儿女流离失所。秦王和楚王这样做是使百姓陷入痛苦的深渊，这个时候您去讨伐他们，又有谁会抵抗您呢？所以说'实行仁政的君主没有对手'，请您不要怀疑我的话。"

【英译】King Hûi of Liang said，"There was not in the nation a stronger State than Tsin，as you，venerable Sir，know. But since it descended to me，on the east we have been defeated by Ch'i，and then my eldest son perished，on the west we have lost seven hundred lî of territory to Ch'ĭn；and on the south we have sustained disgrace at the hands of Ch'û. I have brought shame on my departed predecessors，and wish on their account to wipe it away，once for all. What course is to be pursued to accomplish this?' Mencius replied，'With a territory which is only a hundred lîsquare，it is possible to attain to the royal dignity. If your Majesty will indeed dispense a benevolent government to the people，being sparing in the use of punishments and fines，and making the taxes and levies light，so causing that the fields shall be ploughed deep，and the weeding of them be carefully attended to，and that the strong-bodied，during their days of leisure，shall cultivate their filial piety，fraternal respectfulness，sincerity，and truthfulness，serving thereby，at home，their fathers and elder brothers，and，abroad，their elders and superiors，-you will then have a people who can be employed，with sticks which they have prepared，to oppose the strong mail and sharp weapons of the troops of Ch'ĭn and Ch'û. The rulers of those states rob their people of their time，so that they cannot plough and weed their fields，in order to support their parents. Their parents suffer from cold and hunger. Brothers，wives，and children are separated and scattered abroad. Those rulers as it were，drive their people into pit-falls，or drown them. Your Majesty will go to punish them. In such a case，who will oppose your Majesty？ In accordance with this is the saying， —— "The benevolent has no enemy." I beg your Majesty not to doubt what I say.'

【注释】

[1] 在古代"天下"的内涵极其丰富，可以从政治、空间等多角度理解。此处取"天下"的地理空间意义，特指战国时期各诸侯国和周天子生活的地域，是古代中国的版图，而非世界上所有的国家。刘殿爵将之翻译为"Empire"，既能体现诸侯国之间的关系，又通过大写来突出其内涵的独特性，可以很好传递天下的含义。赵甄陶翻译为"the world"，但是古人眼中的天下和现在的世界有很大不同。理雅各将之翻译为"nation"，泛指国家，亦可。

[2] 关于"比"的含义，古代学者如朱熹、焦循认为是介词，是"为""代"的意思。今人杨伯峻等学者也认可"比"在此处取"为""替""代"之意。但刘殿爵受 W.Simon 教授的影响，认为将"比"训作"及其时"甚具说服力。 他指出："按照 Simon 的说法，本句可解为'我为此感到羞耻，并希望在我死前能够洗雪此辱'。"他也肯定前代学者孙奭和俞樾将"比"解为"近"，认为本句也可以理解为"我为此感到羞耻，并希望（我）这濒临死亡的人能够洗雪此辱"。刘殿爵指出："从《孟子》文本考察，'比'可以从上述任何一种诠释方式去理解。"刘殿爵受上述学者的影响，对本句进行了创新性翻译。根据他的译文，本句可理解为"我感到非常羞愧，并希望在我简短的有生之年能够彻底洗雪此辱"。理雅各将其译为"I have brought shame on my departed predecessors，and wish on their account to wipe it away，once for al.l"，即"我给先人带来了耻辱，希望能为他们彻底雪耻。"显然，

他受朱熹影响，认为"比"是介词"为"。理雅各在翻译时不仅改变了原文句型，还对句意作了适当补充。理雅各将"之"理解为"先人"，并认为"先人"和"死者"都是指"晋国强大时的那些国君"。赖发洛的译文是"I am ashamed, and wish, for the sake of the dead, to wash it all away"，即"我感到耻辱，希望能为死者报仇雪恨"。他的译文也认为"比"是"为"，不过赖发洛将"耻之"理解为"以这些事为耻"，将"死者"理解为"战死沙场的人"。笔者认为，这几种解释都有足够的证据作为支撑，虽然表达的侧重点不同，但都可以从不同的角度反映原文之意。

[3]"里"是中国特有的计量单位，在英语中难以找到对等词，因而刘殿爵选择音译，理雅各亦如此。而赖发洛则选择用英国人熟悉的"mile"（英里）翻译，虽然这样容易使西方读者理解，但不能准确传达"里"的含义。

[4] 孟子此处的"王"特指用仁政统一全中国的圣王，刘殿爵选择将"King"大写，以突出其含义的特殊性，并以"true"进行修饰，来表明此处的王并非一般意义上的王，而是真正的王者。理雅各将"王"翻译为"the royal dignity"，赖发洛译为"rule the kingdom"，二者的译文能体现"王"的某一方面的特征。在翻译"地方百里而可以王"时，理雅各的译文突出的是虽然国家狭小，仍然有获得王位的可能性。刘殿爵译为"With a territory which is only a hundred lî square, it is possible to attain to the royal dignity"，他认为这句话是说即使是小国，仍然可以成为真正的王者。这一理解与孟子的"仁者无敌"，即不论国家大小，只要实行仁政，就可以成为统一天下的王者是一致的。赖发洛的译文是"A land of a hundred square miles may rule the kingdom"，即"一百平方英里的国土可以统治整个王国"。这一翻译略显僵硬，不便于读者理解"地方百里而可以王"的确切含义。根据上下文，孟子指的是一个小国的君主，也可以通过实行仁政，成为统一中国的圣王。

[5]"易耨"究竟为何意，历来众说纷纭。学者任俊华、赵清文曾在《大学·中庸·孟子正宗》中对古今学者的注释进行过系统归纳，根据他们的研究，"易耨"共有四种含义："一说为芸苗宜浅，赵岐注、宋张栻《癸

巳孟子说》均持'芸苗令简易也'之说。……盖深耕则土疏通而苗易发达，浅耨则但去草而不伤谷根。一说为芸苗而使之疏。如阎若璩《四书释地》中说：'愚谓即朱虚侯刘章为高后言"田立苗欲疏"之意，与上深耕字相对。'……一说为'易，治也。耨，耘也'，'易耨'即尽力耕耘之意。朱熹《集注》中持此说。……一说'易'为疾、速之意，杨伯峻《孟子译注》中持此说。"显然刘殿爵的理解同杨伯峻相类，将"易耨"翻译为"weed promptly"，即迅速锄草。理雅各将之译为"the weeding of them be carefully attended to"即"尽心锄草"，他的理解受朱熹影响较大。朱熹训"易"为"治"，取尽力耕耘之意。赖发洛则给出了另外一种新的理解。他的译文是"there were shifts of hoers"，即"锄者轮作"，显然他对"易"的理解和其他学者不同。他认为此处的"易"和"以小易大，彼恶知之"（《孟子·梁惠王上》）相类，取"交换"之意，而"耨"的本义为"锄草的农具"，在此处代指"锄地者"。"深耕易耨"是施仁政于民的君主支持的耕种方式，这种方式顺应和有利于农作物的生长，因而在深耕的基础上"浅耨"，即"除去杂草但不伤谷根"更准确。

　　[6] 纵观不同译者的翻译，他们关于"无敌"有多种理解，如刘殿爵将"仁者无敌"翻译为"The benevolent man has no match"，即"仁爱的人没有对手"。理雅各则译为"The benevolent has no enemy"即"仁爱的人没有敌人"。赖发洛的译文是"Love has no one against it"，即"没有人反对仁"。"故曰：'仁者无敌'"是对前文的总结，结合前文的"可使制梃以挞秦楚之坚甲利兵矣"和"王往而征之，夫谁与王敌"，可以看出，孟子劝说梁惠王实行仁政，认为这样可以打败所有的对手统一中国，因而这儿的"无敌"是没有"对手"而非"没有敌人。"

　　【原文】1.6　孟子见梁襄王[1]，出，语人曰："望之不似人君，就之而不见所畏焉。卒然[2]问曰：'天下恶乎定[3]？'吾对曰：'定于一。''孰能一之？'对曰：'不嗜杀人者能一之。''孰能与之[4]？'

对曰：'天下莫不与也。王知夫苗^[5]乎？七八月^[6]之间旱，则苗槁矣。天油然作云，沛然下雨，则苗浡然兴之矣。其如是，孰能御之？今夫天下之人牧，未有不嗜杀人者也，如有不嗜杀人者，则天下之民皆引领而望之^[7]矣。诚如是也，民归之，由水之就下，沛然谁能御之？'"

【译文】 孟子去拜见梁襄王，出来后告诉别人说："远看他不像国君的样子，走近了，也看不见他的威严。他突然问我'天下怎样才能安定？'我回答说：'天下统一了就会安定。'他又问：'谁能统一天下？'我回答说：'不喜欢杀人的国君，可以统一天下。'他又问：'谁又能去追随他呢？'我回答说：'天下没有人不会追随他。你见过禾苗吧？七八月间遇到干旱，禾苗就会枯萎。如果天上突然乌云密布，大雨倾盆，禾苗又会茂盛地生长。如果是这样，谁又能阻挡呢？现在管理国家的君主，没有不喜欢杀人的。如果有不喜欢杀人的君主，天下百姓就会伸长脖子盼望他的到来。确实是这样，百姓归附他，就像水往下奔流一样，谁又能阻挡得住呢？'"

【英译】 Mencius went to see the king Hsiang of Liang. On coming out from the interview, he said to some persons, 'When I looked at him from a distance, he did not appear like a sovereign; when I drew near to him, I saw nothing venerable about him. Abruptly he asked me, "How can the kingdom be settled?" I replied, "It will be settled by being united under one sway." "Who can so unite it?" I replied, "He who has no pleasure in killing men can so unite it." "Who can give it to him?" I replied, "All the people of the nation will unanimously give it to him. Does your Majesty understand the way of growing grain? During the seventh and eighth mouths, when drought prevails, the plants become dry. Then the clouds collect densely in the heavens, they send down torrents of rain and the grain erects itself, as if by a shoot.

When it does so，who can keep it back? Now among the shepherds of men throughout the nation，there is not one who does not find pleasure in killing men. If there were one who did not find pleasure in killing men，all the people in the nation would look towards him with outstretched necks. Such being indeed the case，the people would flock to him，as water flows downwards with a rush，which no one can repress." '

【注释】

[1] 梁襄王是梁惠王的儿子。本章生动地记载了孟子与梁襄王首次会面的情景。这次会面给孟子留下了不好的印象，孟子认为襄王无论在仪态上还是在说话时都不具备王者风范。在描写二人对话时，孟子通过襄王问话时曰字的省略，来表达说话者的急迫，和"卒然问曰"相对应，使襄王"不似人君"的形象跃然纸上。

[2] 刘殿爵、理雅各和赵甄陶选择用"abruptly"翻译"卒然"，赖发洛和亨顿则选择用"suddenly"。虽然"abruptly"和"suddenly"都有突然、出乎意料的含义，但前者突出语言或者行为莽撞、令人不快，正如焦循在《孟子正义》中对"卒然"做的进一步解释："不由其次，即无渐也。"因而"abruptly"更准确。

[3] 此处的"定"是安定、稳定，没有战乱和纠纷的意思。理雅各和刘殿爵选择用"settle"翻译，突出纷争的结束，更能形象地体现出天下由战乱到安定的变化过程。赖发洛译为"be brought to rest"（使……停下来）不准确。

[4] 理雅各和刘殿爵对"孰能与之"的理解相同，都将之翻译为"Who can give it to him"，即"谁能给他？"但是刘殿爵后来在《孟子杂志》中指出："此文问题既然是'孰能与之'而却以'孰能御之'、'谁能御之'作答，令人颇觉奇怪。由此看来，问题中'与'似误，原来的提问当为'孰能御之'。因此，孟子便以原来的问题作回应，以达至反问的修辞效果。"笔

者认为，孟子在下文中举"孰能御之""谁能御之"的例子旨在说明"民归之，由水之就下"，即人民追随实行仁政的君主，就像水往下流一样，因而"天下莫不与也"指的是"天下人没有不追随他的"，故问题"孰能与之"应指"谁能追随他"而非"谁能给他""谁能抵御他"。赵甄陶将之翻译为"Who will be his follower"，即"谁会是他的追谁者"更准确。

[5] 此处的"苗"特指农作物禾苗。《说文解字》："禾，嘉谷。"未吐穗的禾被称作苗。理雅各和赵甄陶将之翻译为"grain"，泛指谷物，多指谷类幼苗。赖发洛将之译为"young corn"，但是"corn"多指玉米。玉米大约在1550年左右才传入中国。刘殿爵将之译为"rice"（水稻）。《汉书》卷二九《沟洫志》记载："邺有贤令兮为史公，决漳水兮灌邺旁，终古舄卤兮生稻粱。"可见，虽然史书有关于魏国种植水稻的记载，但也无法断定此处的苗特指大米。相比较而言理雅各和赵甄陶的谷类更准确。

[6] 此处的"七八月"是用的周代的历法，相当于夏历的五六月，这一时期正是禾苗生长急需雨水的时期。

[7] "引领而望之"表明了人们对实行仁政之君的盼望之情。理雅各的译文以及刘殿爵的"crane their necks to watch for him coming"（伸长脖子期待他的到来），都能很好地体现出人们的热切盼望之情。赖发洛的译文是"stretch their necks to see him"（伸长脖子去看他），未能体现出期盼之情。

【原文】1.7 齐宣王[1]问曰："齐桓、晋文[2]之事可得闻乎？"孟子对曰："仲尼之徒无道桓、文之事者，是以后世无传焉，臣[3]未之闻也。无以，则王乎？"曰："德何如则可以王矣？"曰："保民而王，莫之能御也。[4]"曰："若寡人者，可以保民乎哉？"曰："可。"曰："何由知吾可也？"曰："臣闻之胡龁曰，王坐于堂上，有牵牛而过堂下者[5]，王见之，曰：'牛何之？'对曰：'将以衅钟[6]。'王曰：'舍之！吾不忍其觳觫，若无罪而就死地。'对曰：'然则废衅钟与？'曰：'何可废也？以羊易之！'不识有诸？"曰：

"有之。"曰："是心足以王矣。百姓皆以王为爱[7]也，臣固知王之不忍也。"王曰："然。诚有百姓者[8]。齐国虽褊小，吾何爱一牛？即不忍其觳觫，若无罪而就死地，故以羊易之也。"曰："王无异于百姓之以王为爱也。以小易大，彼恶知之？王若隐其无罪而就死地，则牛羊何择焉？"王笑曰："是诚何心哉？我非爱其财而易之以羊也[9]。宜乎百姓之谓我爱也。"曰："无伤也，是乃仁术[10]也，见牛未见羊也。君子之于禽兽也，见其生，不忍见其死；闻其声，不忍食其肉。是以君子[11]远庖厨[12]也。"王说曰："《诗》云：'他人有心，予忖度之。'夫子之谓也。夫我乃行之，反而求之，不得吾心。夫子言之，于我心有戚戚焉。此心之所以合于王者，何也？"曰："有复于王者曰：'吾力足以举百钧[13]，而不足以举一羽；明足以察秋毫[14]之末，而不见舆薪。'则王许之乎？"曰："否。""今恩足以及禽兽，而功不至于百姓者，独何与？然则一羽之不举，为不用力焉；舆薪之不见，为不用明焉；百姓之不见保，为不用恩焉。故王之不王，不为也，非不能也。"曰："不为者与不能者之形何以异？"曰："挟太山以超北海，语人曰：'我不能。'是诚不能也。为长者折枝[15]，语人曰：'我不能。'是不为也，非不能也。故王之不王，非挟太山以超北海之类也；王之不王，是折枝之类也。老吾老，以及人之老；幼吾幼，以及人之幼[16]，天下可运于掌。《诗》云：'刑于寡妻，至于兄弟，以御于家邦。'言举斯心加诸彼而已。故推恩[17]足以保四海[18]，不推恩无以保妻子。古之人[19]所以大过人者，无他焉，善推其所为而已矣。今恩足以及禽兽，而功不至于百姓者，独何与？权，然后知轻重；度，然后知长短。物皆然，心为甚。王请度之！抑王兴甲兵，危士臣，构怨于诸侯，然后快于心与？[20]"王曰："否，吾何快于是？将以求吾所大欲也。"曰："王之所大欲可得闻与？"王笑而不言。曰："为肥甘不足于口与？轻暖不足于体与？抑为采色不足视于目与？声音不足听于耳与？便嬖不足使令于前与？王之诸臣皆足以供之，而王岂为是哉？"曰："否。吾不为是也。"曰："然则王之所大欲可知已，欲辟土地，朝秦楚，莅中国而抚四夷[21]也。以若所为求若所欲，犹缘木而求鱼也。"王曰："若是其甚与？"曰："殆有甚焉。缘木求鱼，虽不得鱼，无后灾。以若所为求若所欲，尽心力而为之，后必有灾。"曰："可得闻与？"曰："邹人与楚人战，则王以为孰胜？"曰："楚人胜。"曰："然则小固不可以敌大，寡固不可以敌众，弱固不可以敌强。海内之地方千里者九，齐集有其一。以一服八，何以异于邹敌楚哉？盖亦反其本矣。今王发政施仁，使天下仕者皆欲立于王之朝，耕者皆欲耕于王之野，商贾[22]皆欲藏于王之市，行旅皆欲出于王之途，天下之欲疾其君者皆欲赴愬于王。其若是，孰能御之？"王曰："吾惛，不能进于是矣。愿夫子辅吾志，明以教我。我虽不敏，请尝试之。"曰："无恒产而有恒心者，惟士[23]为能。若民，则无恒产，因无恒心。苟无恒心，放辟邪侈，无不为已。及陷于罪，然后从而刑之，是罔民也。焉有仁人在位罔民而可为也？是故明君制民之产，必使仰足以事父母，俯足以畜妻子，乐岁终身饱，凶年免于死亡；然后驱而之善，故民之从之也轻。今也制民之产，仰不足以事父母，俯不足以畜妻子；乐岁终身苦，凶年不免于死亡。此惟救死而恐不赡，奚暇治礼[24]义哉？王欲行之，则盍反其本矣：五亩之宅，树之以桑，五十者可以衣帛矣。鸡豚狗彘之畜，无失其时，七十者可以食肉矣。百亩之田，勿夺其时，八口之家可以无饥矣。谨庠序之教，申之以孝悌之义，颁白者不负戴于道路矣。老者衣帛食肉，黎民不饥不寒，然而不王者，未之有也。"

【译文】齐宣王问道："齐桓公、晋文公称霸的事迹，你可以给我讲讲吗？"孟子回答说："孔子的学生都没有谈及齐桓公、晋文公的事迹，所以没有传给后世，我也没有听说过。如果一定要讲的话，我可以说说如何成为统一天下的王者。"齐宣王问："品德如何才能成为统一天下的王者?"孟子回答说:"爱护百姓就可以成为统一天下的王者,没有人能够阻挡。""像我这样,可以爱护、安抚百姓吗?"齐宣王接着问。孟子说:"当然可以。"齐宣王问:"你怎么知道我可以呢?"孟子说:"我从您的近臣胡龁那里听说有一次您坐在堂上,有人牵着牛从堂下经过,您问:'要牵牛去哪里?'那人回答说:'要去屠宰牛,用他的血祭钟。'王说:'放了它吧,我不忍心看到它被吓得哆哆嗦嗦的样子,就像没有犯罪却要被处死一样。'那人问道:'那么,我们要废除祭钟的仪式吗?'王说:'怎么能废除呢,用羊代替牛!'不知道有这件事吗?"齐宣王说:"确实有这件事。"孟子说:"这种仁爱之心足可以使您成为统一天下的王。不过百姓都以为您是吝啬,只有我知道您是不忍心。"齐宣王说:"是的,确实有百姓这么认为。虽然我们齐国不大,我也不会吝啬一头牛,因为我是不忍心看到它吓得哆哆嗦嗦,就像没有犯罪却要被处死一样,所以用羊换了牛。"孟子说:"您也不要奇怪百姓会认为您吝啬。用小的换大的,他们怎么会知道其中的深意呢。您要是可怜它没有罪却被杀死,那么杀牛和杀羊又有什么不同呢?"齐宣王笑着说:"我到底心里是怎么想的我自己都不知道了。我确实不是因为吝惜钱财才用羊代替牛的。怪不得百姓会认为我吝啬。"孟子回答说:"百姓这么想也没有关系。您的不忍之心正是仁爱啊,因为您看到了牛,没有看见羊。君子对于禽兽,看见它们活着,就不忍心看到它们被杀死;听到它们悲鸣的声音,就不忍心吃它们的肉,因而君子会把厨房建到离自己比较远的地方。"齐宣王说:"《诗》说:'别人的存心,我能揣摩到。'您就是这样啊!虽然我自己做了这样的事情,如果反过来问自己为什么这么做,却说不出所以然来,先生正说到我心坎上了。不过为什么这样的心适合成为统一天下的王呢?"孟子说:"假如有人对王说:'我能够举起千斤的重量,但却举不起一片羽毛;我能看见秋天小鸟身上细小的绒毛,却看不见眼前的满车柴火。'您能相信吗?"齐宣王说:"不会相信。"孟子说:"现在您的仁爱之心可以惠及动物,却不能让百姓享受恩惠,那又是为什么呢？如果一片羽毛都举不起来，是没有用力举；满车的柴火看不见，是没有用眼睛看；不能爱护安抚百姓，是没有施恩百姓。您没有成为统一天下的王者，是不去做，而非不能做啊！"齐宣王说："不去做和不能做有什么不同呢？"孟子回答说："夹着泰山跳过北海，告诉别人说：'我办不到。'这确实是办不到。替老人按摩关节，告诉人说：'这个我办不到。'这是不愿意做，而不是不能做。您不行仁政不是夹着泰山跳北海一类的办不到，而是替老人按摩关节一类的不愿意做。尊敬我们家里的老人，然后推广到尊敬别人的老人；爱护我们家里的孩子，然后推广到爱护别人家的孩子。（用这种推恩之心）治理天下就会像在手里转东西一样容易，正如《诗》所说：'给妻子做榜样，然后推广到兄弟，再推广到封邑和国家。'就是说的把这种仁爱之心推广开来。所以说推恩可以保有四海，不推恩，甚至连妻儿都保护不了。古代的圣王之所以远远超过其他人，没有别的原因，就是因为他们善于推广自己的善行罢了。现在您的恩惠足以惠及禽兽，却不能让百姓受益，这是为什么呢？称一下，才能知道物体的轻重；量一量，才能知道物体的长短。什么东西都是这样，人心更是如此。请您考虑一下吧！难道您要兴师动众，使得百姓、大臣陷入危险之中，和其他诸侯结怨才心里痛快吗？"齐宣王说："不，我怎么会这样做才痛快呢？我是想要满足我最大的欲望。"孟子问："我可以听听你的最大欲望是什么吗？"齐宣王笑着不回答。孟子说："难道是因为肥美甘甜的食物不够吃吗？还是因为轻薄温暖的衣服不够穿呢？还是因为美妙的音乐不够听呢？还用因为伺候的人不够用？您的臣属都可以满足您的这些需求。难道您真是为了这些？"齐宣王说："不，这些都不是。"孟子说："那么您最大的欲望我知道了。您想扩张土地，使秦、楚等国来朝贡，成为天下的君主，使四夷安抚。您以这样的方式去实现您最大的欲望，就如同爬到树上去逮鱼一样。"王说："真的有这么严重？"孟子说："甚至比这还要严重。爬到树上捉鱼，虽然抓不着，但没有祸害。如果用这样的方式实现您的欲望，即使费力去做，也难以实现，还会带来灾难。"齐宣王说："能再说说为什么吗？"孟子问："如果邹国和楚国发生战争，您觉得谁会赢？"齐宣王说："楚国人会胜。"孟子说："所以小国不可以与大国为敌，人口稀少的国家不能与人口众多的国家为敌。现在天下土地方圆千里的国家有九个，齐国全部土地加起来只不过占其中之一，以一敌八，和邹国与楚国发动战争又有什么区别呢？为何不回到根本上呢？如果您现在实行仁政，那么天下想要做官的士人都愿来您的朝堂做官；农民都愿意来您的田野耕种；行商坐贾都愿意来您的国家做买卖，来往的行人也都愿意来齐国取道，那些痛恨本国国君的人也都愿意来您这里诉说他们的委屈。如果是这样，谁又能抵挡呢？"齐宣王说："我头脑昏聩，不能实现这些，还希望您能辅佐我、明明白白地教导我，实现这些目标。我虽然不聪明，但是也想试一试。"孟子说："只有士人能做到，没有固定产业却有稳定向上的志向。至于普通百姓，如果没有固定的产业，就不会有稳定向善的志向。如果没有稳定向善的志向，就会胡作非为，无恶不作。等他们犯了罪，就去处罚他们，这是陷害百姓啊。哪有仁德的人在掌握权力的时候会去做陷害百姓的事情呢？所以，贤明的君主在规定人们产业的时候，都会让他们既能够赡养父母，又可以抚养妻儿；年成好的时候，丰衣足食，收成不好的时候，也不会饿死。然后再去教导他们向善，所以百姓也很容易追随他。现在规定的百姓产业，既不能满足他们赡养父母的需要，也不够他们抚养妻儿。年成好的时候，终身忙碌，仍然难免困苦；年成不好的时候，也免不了饿死。他们连保命都来不及，哪里顾得上去学习礼义？如果大王要行仁政，为什么不回到根本上去呢。分给每家五亩的住宅，在周围种上桑树，五十岁的人就可以穿丝制品的衣服了；鸡狗猪等家畜，不错过饲养、繁殖的时间，七十岁的人就可以吃肉了。分配给每家百亩耕地，不占用他们耕种生产的时间，八口之家也能免于饥荒。办好各类学校，并反复教导他们孝顺父母，尊敬兄长的道理，那么，头发斑白的老人也不会背着、顶着重物在路上行走了。老年人能穿丝织品做成的衣物，能吃上肉，普通人不挨饿受冻，这样的国君如果还不能成为统一天下的王者，这是从来未有过的事情。”

【英译】The king Hsüan of Chî asked, saying, 'May I be informed by you of the transactions of Hwan of Chî, and Wǎn of Tsin?' Mencius replied, 'There were none of the disciples of Chung-nî who spoke about the affairs of Hwan and Wǎn, and therefore they have not been transmitted to these after-ages; -your servant has not heard them. If you will have me speak, let it be about royal government.' The king said, 'What virtue must there be in order to attain to royal sway?' Mencius answered, 'The love and protection of the people; with this there is no power which can prevent a ruler from attaining to it.' The king asked again, 'Is such an one as I competent to love and protect the people?' Mencius said, 'Yes.' 'How do you know that I am competent for that?' 'I heard the following incident from H ǔ Ho: — "The king," said he, "was sitting aloft in the hall, when a man appeared, leading an ox past the lower part of it. The king saw him, and asked, Where is the ox going? The man replied, We are going to consecrate a bell with its blood. The king said, Let it go. I cannot bear its frightened appearance, as if it were an innocent person going to the place of death. The man answered, Shall we then omit the consecration of the bell? The king said, How can that be omitted? Change it for a sheep." I do not know whether this incident really occurred.' The king replied, 'It did,' and then Mencius said, 'The heart seen in this is sufficient to carry you to the royal sway. The people all supposed that your Majesty grudged the animal, but your servant knows surely, that it was your Majesty's not being able to bear the sight, which made you do as you did.' The king said, 'You are right. And yet there really was an appearance of what the people condemned. But though Chî be a small and narrow State, how should I grudge one ox? Indeed it was because I could not bear its frightened appearance, as if it were an innocent person going to the place of death, that therefore I changed it for a sheep.' Mencius pursued, 'Let not your Majesty deem it strange that the people should think you were grudging the animal. When you changed a large one for a small, how should they know the true reason? If you felt pained by its being led without guilt to the place of death, what was there to choose between an ox and a sheep?' The king laughed and said, 'What really was my mind in the matter? I did not grudge the expense of it, and changed it for a sheep! —There was reason in the people's saying that I grudged it.' 'There is no harm in their saying so,' said Mencius. 'Your conduct was an artifice of benevolence. You saw the ox, and had not seen the sheep. So is the superior man affected towards animals, that, having seen them alive, he cannot bear to see them die; having heard their dying cries, he cannot bear to eat their flesh. Therefore he keeps away from his slaughter-house and cook-room.' The king was pleased, and said, 'It is said in the Book of Poetry, "The minds of others, I am able by reflection to measure; "—this is verified, my Master, in your discovery of my motive. I indeed did the thing, but when I turned my thoughts inward, and examined into it, I could not discover my own mind. When you, Master, spoke those words, the movements of compassion began to work in my mind. How is it that this heart has in it what is equal to the royal sway?' Mencius replied, 'Suppose a man were to make this statement to your Majesty: —"My strength is sufficient to lift three thousand catties, but it is not sufficient to lift one feather; —my eyesight is sharp enough to examine the point of an autumn hair, but I do not see a waggon-load of faggots; " would your Majesty allow what he said?' 'No,' was the answer, on which Mencius proceeded, 'Now here is kindness sufficient to reach to animals, and no benefits are extended from it to the people.—How is this? Is an exception to be made here? The truth is, the feather is not lifted, because strength is not used; the waggon-load of firewood is not seen, because the eyesight is not used; and the people are not loved and protected, because kindness is not employed. Therefore your Majesty's not exercising the royal sway, is because you do not do it, not because you are not able to do it.' The king asked, 'How may the difference between the not doing a thing, and the not being able to do it, be represented?' Mencius replied, 'In such a thing as taking the T'âi mountain under your arm, and leaping over the north sea with it, if you say to people— "I am not able to do it," that is a real case of not being able. In such a matter as breaking off a branch from a tree at the order of a superior, if you say to people— "I am not able to do it," that is a case of not doing it, it is not a case of not being able to do it. Therefore your Majesty's not exercising the royal sway, is not such a case as that of taking the T'âi mountain under your arm, and leaping over the north sea with it. Your Majesty's not exercising the royal sway is a case like that of breaking off a branch from a tree. Treat with the reverence due to age the elders in your own family, so that the elders in the families of others shall be similarly treated; treat with the kindness due to youth the young in your own family, so that the young in the families of others shall be similarly treated: —do this, and the kingdom may be made to go round in your palm. It is said in the Book of Poetry, "His example affected his wife. It reached to his brothers, and his family of the State was governed by it." —The language shows how king Wăn simply took his kindly heart, and exercised it towards those parties. Therefore the carrying out his kindness of heart by a prince will suffice for the love and protection of all within the four seas, and if he do not carry it out, he will not be able to protect his wife and children. The way in which the ancients came greatly to surpass other men, was no other but this: —simply that they knew well how to carry out, so as to affect others, what they themselves did. Now your kindness is sufficient to reach to animals, and no benefits are extended from it to reach the people.—How is this? Is an exception to be made here? By weighing, we know what things are light, and what heavy. By measuring, we know what things are long, and what short. The relations of all things may be thus determined, and it is of the greatest importance to estimate the motions of the mind. I beg your Majesty to measure it. You collect your equipments of war, endanger your soldiers and officers, and excite the resentment of the other princes; —do these things cause you pleasure in your mind?' The king replied, 'No. How should I derive pleasure from these things? My object in them is to seek for what I greatly desire.' Mencius said, 'May I hear from you what it is that you greatly desire?' The king laughed and did not speak. Mencius resumed, 'Are you led to desire it, because you have not enough of rich and sweet food for your mouth? Or because you have not enough of light and warm clothing for your body? Or because you have not enough of beautifully coloured objects to delight your eyes? Or because you have not voices and tones enough to please your ears? Or because you have not enough of attendants and favourites to stand before you and receive your orders? Your Majesty's various officers are sufficient to supply you with those things. How can your Majesty be led to entertain such a desire on account of them?' 'No,' said the king; 'my desire is not on account of them.' Mencius added, 'Then, what your Majesty greatly desires may be known. You wish to enlarge your territories, to have Ch'in and Ch'û wait at your court, to rule the Middle Kingdom, and to attract to you the barbarous tribes that surround it. But doing what you do to seek for what you desire is like climbing a tree to seek for fish.' The king said, 'Is it so bad as that?' 'It is even worse,' was the reply. 'If you climb a tree to seek for fish, although you do not get the fish, you will not suffer any subsequent calamity. But doing what you do to seek for what you desire, doing it moreover with all your heart, you will assuredly afterwards meet with calamities.' The king asked, 'May I hear from you the proof of that?' Mencius said, 'If the people of Tsâu should fight with the people of Ch'û, which of them does your Majesty think would conquer?' 'The people of Ch'û would conquer.' 'Yes; —and so it is certain that a small country cannot contend with a great, that few cannot contend with many, that the weak cannot contend with the strong. The territory within the four seas embraces nine divisions, each of a thousand lî square. All Ch'in together is but one of them. If with one part you try to subdue the other eight, what is the difference between that and Tsâu's contending with Ch'û? For, with such a desire, you must turn back to the proper course for its attainment. Now if your Majesty will institute a government whose action shall be benevolent, this will cause all the officers in the kingdom to wish to stand in your Majesty's court, and all the farmers to wish to plough in your Majesty's fields, and all the merchants, both travelling and stationary, to wish to store their goods in your Majesty's market-places, and all travelling strangers to wish to make their tours on your Majesty's roads, and all throughout the kingdom who feel aggrieved by their rulers to wish to come and complain to your Majesty. And when they are so bent, who will be able to keep them back?' The king said, 'I am stupid, and not able to advance to this. I wish you, my Master, to assist my intentions. Teach me clearly; although I am deficient in intelligence and vigour, I will essay and try to carry your instructions into effect.' Mencius replied, 'They are only men of education, who, without a certain livelihood, are able to maintain a fixed heart. As to the people, if they have not a certain livelihood, it follows that they will not have a fixed heart. And if they have not a fixed heart, there is nothing which they will not do, in the way of self-abandonment, of moral deflection, of depravity, and of wild license. When they thus have been involved in crime, to follow them up and punish them; —this is to entrap the people. How can such a thing as entrapping the people be done under the rule of a benevolent man? Therefore an intelligent ruler will regulate the livelihood of the people, so as to make sure that, for those above them, they shall have sufficient wherewith to serve their parents, and, for those below them, sufficient wherewith to support their wives and children; that in good years they shall always be abundantly satisfied, and that in bad years they shall escape the danger of perishing. After this he may urge them, and they will proceed to what is good, for in this case the people will follow after it with ease. Now, the livelihood of the people is so regulated, that, above, they have not sufficient wherewith to serve their parents, and, below, they have not sufficient wherewith to support their wives and children. Notwithstanding good years, their lives are continually embittered, and, in bad years, they do not escape perishing. In such circumstances they only try to save themselves from death, and are afraid they will not succeed. What leisure have they to cultivate propriety and righteousness? If your Majesty wishes to effect this regulation of the livelihood of the people, why not turn to that which is the essential step to it? Let mulberry-trees be planted about the homesteads with their five mâu, and persons of fifty years may be clothed with silk. In keeping fowls, pigs, dogs, and swine, let not their times of breeding be neglected, and persons of seventy years may eat flesh. Let there not be taken away the time that is proper for the cultivation of the farm with its hundred mâu, and the family of eight mouths that is supported by it shall not suffer from hunger. Let careful attention be paid to education in schools, ——the inculcation in it especially of the filial and fraternal duties, and grey-haired men will not be seen upon the roads, carrying burdens on their backs or on their heads. It never has been that the ruler of a State where such results were seen, ——the old wearing silk and eating flesh, and the black-haired people suffering neither from hunger nor cold, ——did not attain to the royal dignity.'

【注释】

[1] 齐宣王是齐国国君，在位时间为公元前 319—前 301 年。孟子见梁襄王后，认识到他能实行仁政，于是离开，到齐国后和齐宣王围绕如何成为王者进行了深入交流，从而使本章成为《孟子》一书中最长的一篇。在本篇中，齐宣王提出"德何如则可以王矣"的疑问，孟子的回答是"保民而王，莫之能御"。孟子围绕"保民而王"这一宗旨，详细论述了"保民而王"的条件——仁心、仁术；做法——推恩及民；具体施政措施——制民恒产，先

养后教。

[2] 齐桓即齐桓公，姜姓，名小白，为春秋时期齐国国君，最先称霸，为春秋五霸之首。晋文公，名重耳，是春秋时期晋国的君主，是春秋五霸中第二位霸主。齐桓公与晋文公并称"齐桓晋文"。刘殿爵选择用"Duke"翻译，但是该词通常指公爵，尤指旧时欧洲部分地区小公国的君主，容易引起歧义，不如赖发洛和理雅各直接音译准确。

[3] "臣"，刘殿爵直接将之翻译为"I"（我），不能体现君臣之间的等级关系，相比较而言，理雅各的"your servant"和赖发洛的"your liege"更能体现出敬意。

[4] 本文的宗旨是"保民而王莫之能御"。理雅各的译文强调爱护和保护人民，刘殿爵则从当时诸侯混战、民不聊生的社会现实出发，将"保民"翻译为"bringing peace to the people"，他认为只有结束战争，给人民带来和平的君主才能成为真正的王者。他进一步强调任何人都不能阻止这样的君主成为王者。赵甄陶的译文是"protection of the people"，他认为"保民"就是保护人民。从孟子的整个思想体系看，他反对争夺土地和百姓的争霸战争，主张安民、富民的仁政，而仁政的第一步就是要结束战争，让百姓有生产和受教育的条件，因而刘殿爵对"保民"的翻译更准确。

译者们对此处"王"的内涵的理解也各不相同，赵甄陶通过解释性翻译将之理解为"统一世界的统治者"，理译本认为"royal sway/government"更符合孟子"王"的含义。在他的理解中，孟子的"王"是统一国家中具有至高无上权力的帝王。赖发洛则将"王"笼统地翻译为"king"（国王、君主），未翻译出孟子的"王"的准确含义。刘译本把"王"翻译为"真正的君主"，并将 King 大写，以突出其含义的特殊性。孟子口中的"王"的具体含义究竟是什么？我们可以从孟子生活的时代和孟子思想中寻求答案。战国时期，各诸侯国试图通过兼并战争来统一天下，对百姓横征暴敛。孟子对这一社会现实极度不满，强调以仁政来统一天下，提出了自己的仁政、王道观。纵观《孟子》全书，可以看出孟子所谓的"王"应具备以下含义：首先要富民、爱民，也就是所谓的保民；二是反对兼并战争，通过仁政来统一天下。可见，试图从现有英语词汇中找出一个和孟子推崇的"王者"相似的英文词汇非常困难，因而刘殿爵的适度异化策略，将"King"大写，来突出其含义的特殊性更准确。

[5]"有牵牛而过堂下者"，根据理雅各的译文，君主和牵牛者同在大厅，一个高高坐在大厅上方，一个从大厅下方牵牛走过。赖发洛的译文是"The King was sitting in the hall above and when a man passed below the hall dragging an ox."根据他的译文，二人所处的空间不同，齐宣王坐在高高的厅堂之内，在厅堂之外有数个台阶与地面相连，牵牛者是从厅堂之外的地上走过。笔者认为赖发洛的译文更准确。中国古代重要的建筑物，比如说宫殿，通常是建在一个离地面很高的地板上的，需要经过一个宽宽的楼梯才能上去，而牵牛者是从厅堂之外的地上走过。不仅如此，中国自古就是一个注重礼仪的国家，对君臣之礼规定得尤为详细，不可能允许在君主休息或办公的厅堂之内有人或者牛羊来回走动，否则这与集市有何区别。

[6]"衅钟"是古代的一种血祭方式，具体做法就是杀生取血涂物以祭。理雅各的译文较为全面地介绍了衅钟的含义。赖发洛的译文是"He is going to the bell sacrifice"，即"他要去参加祭钟"。但是这一翻译容易引起歧义，即牛只参与祭钟的仪式还是自己被杀死用来祭钟？

[7]此处的"爱"是吝啬的意思，译者基本都能翻译出其含义，但对"爱"的对象的认识存在些许差异。刘殿爵认为是吝惜祭钟的花费，理雅各进一步缩小范围，认为是吝惜祭祀用的动物，而赵甄陶直接指出是"grudged the ox"（吝惜祭祀用的牛）。从下文齐宣王的"齐国虽褊小，吾何爱一牛"可知，赵甄陶的译文更准确。

[8]"诚有百姓者"，刘殿爵选择用反问句"How could there be such people?"（怎么会有这样的人呢）将齐宣王的疑惑和不满之情刻画得惟妙惟肖。理雅各的译文则是表述了一个事实，即齐宣王确实也听到有人好像这么评价他，但是没有体现过多的感情色彩。赖发洛则用一个感叹句，即"there

really were such people！"表达了他的震惊和不满。从孟子接下来的答话"王无异于百姓之以王为爱也"可以推测出齐宣王对百姓认为他吝啬感到奇怪和反感，因而孟子开解他，故刘殿爵的译文更能体现原文的意思。

[9] 对于"我非爱其财而易之以羊也"，刘殿爵将之断为"我非爱其财，而易之以羊也"。根据这一断句，"非"仅仅否定"爱其财"，"而"在句中表转折，相当于"然而"。在这一新的断句下，原句可理解为"我并不是吝啬钱财，然而，我确实用羊换了牛"。这就和后文的"百姓认为我是吝啬也是应该的"浑然一体。理雅各的译文是"I did not grudge the expense of it, and changed it for a sheep"，即"我用羊替换牛不是因为吝啬花费"，这就和后面"百姓认为我是吝啬的也是应该的"存在逻辑冲突。

[10] "仁术"，朱熹《四书集注》指出："术，谓法之巧者。盖杀牛既所不忍，衅钟又不可废，于此无以处之，则此心虽发而终不得施矣。然见牛则此心已发而不可遏，未见羊，则其理未形而无所妨，故以羊易牛，则二者得以两全而无害，此所以为仁之术也。"刘殿爵选择用"way"（方法）翻译，该词是中性词，在传意上略显逊色。理雅各的"artifice"和赖发洛的"sleight"都有技巧的意思和人工的含义，相比较而言，赵甄陶的"act"更准确。

[11] "君子"的本义是对有地位的男子的统称，与"小人"或"野人"相对，并不含有道德含义在里面。《诗经·魏风·伐檀》中"彼君子兮，不素餐兮！"但是在儒家那里，"君子"则成为对那些德才出众的人的称呼。在孔孟的言论中，虽然"君子"有时还是指有地位的统治者，但在大多时候是指那些有道德的人。译者通常把"君子"翻译为"gentleman"（绅士）。应当指出的是，虽然君子和绅士在外在形象上相似，但不能把二者对等。绅士是地位的象征，君子是德行的体现，二者有本质区别。值得注意的是，在此处孟子是为齐宣王分析"以羊易牛"出于何心，因而此处的"君子"特指居于高位的统治者，刘殿爵采用归化译法，将"君子"翻译为"gentleman"更便于读者理解。理雅各根据上下文，将"君子"翻译为"superior man"（居

上位者）也是合适的。

[12]"庖厨"是同义词连用，指厨房。刘殿爵准确翻译出了"庖厨"的含义，但是理雅各将之翻译为"slaughter-house and cook-room"，赖发洛的译文是"slaughter-house and kitchen"，二人认为庖厨指屠宰场和厨房，扩大了词义。刘殿爵将"远"理解为"远离，不靠近"，而赖发洛翻译为"puts far away"（安置在很远的地方），从文意上看，自觉选择远离、不靠近更准确。

[13]"钧"是中国古代的重量单位，相当于今天的三十斤。刘殿爵在翻译中国特有的度量单位时，往往采取异化译法，他用汉语拼音翻译"钧"来突出其特殊性。在翻译"百钧"时，理雅各采取意译的方法，译为"three thousand catties"（三千斤）。"cattie"指斤，是东南亚尤指中国的度量单位。理雅各的翻译既便于读者理解，又译出了"百钧"的准确重量。赖发洛译为"a hundred bushels"（一百蒲式耳）。蒲式耳是英国人熟悉的体积或容量单位，用它翻译"钧"虽便于读者理解，但容易给读者造成误解，将蒲式耳和钧等同起来。

[14]"秋毫"，指的是鸟兽秋天新长出来的细毛。此处是形容人目光敏锐能看清楚任何细微的东西。刘殿爵将"秋毫"译为"a tiny hair"（细微的毛发），既便于读者理解，又准确地翻译出了原文的深层含义。理雅各和赖发洛都将"秋毫"直译为"autumn hair"。何为秋天的毛发？为什么能看清秋天的毛发就说明人目光敏锐？恐怕读者需要细细思量了。

[15]"为长者折枝"的注解，历来存在歧义。据焦循《孟子正义》记载，"折枝"古来有三种含义：其一，赵岐注曰："折枝，案摩折手节解罢枝也。少者耻是役。是不为耳，非不能也。"其二，《音义》引陆善经云："折草树枝。"其三，《文献通考》载陆筠解为："磬折腰肢，盖犹今拜揖也。刘殿爵的译文取"折枝"的第一种含义，即"为老人按摩关节"。理雅各受朱熹"以长者之命，折草木之枝"的影响，将之翻译为"breaking off a branch from a tree at the order of a superior"（根据老者的要求，为他折树枝）。其他

译者，如赖发洛、赵甄陶等皆取"折取树枝"之意。笔者认为，"为长者折枝"是"不为者"的代表，指的是那些很容易做但年轻人却不愿意做的事情。在中国古代，年轻人见到老人弯腰行礼是当然之事，应循之礼，不存在是否愿意做的问题，因而应排除在外。"为长者"三字放到"折枝"前是为了强调尊老之意，然而根据长者的要求，折取树枝不足以表达此意，亦应排除。孟子在这里是为齐宣王解释"不为者与不能者的区别"，而"替老人按摩关节"对年轻人来说是很容易做到但不愿意做的事情，因而刘殿爵的译文更准确。

[16]"老吾老，以及人之老；幼吾幼，以及人之幼"中，第一个"老"为动词，即以敬老之礼侍奉老人。第一个"幼"也是动词，即爱护儿童。刘殿爵的译文准确体现了儒家的推恩思想。他强调要以敬老之礼对待自己家的老人，并把它推广到对待别人家的老人；用爱幼之心对待自己家的孩子，并把它推广到爱护别人家的孩子。他的译文更加突出强调通过推己及人的方法，将"老吾老""幼吾幼"的血亲情感普遍地推广到他人。理雅各强调以敬老之礼对待自己家的老人，那么别人家的老人也将会受到同样的对待；以爱幼之心对待自己的孩子，那么别人家的孩子也会受到同样的对待。根据理雅各的翻译，尊敬自己家的老人、爱护自己的孩子是尊敬别人家老人，爱护别人家孩子的前提。理雅各强调"老吾老"的重要性，他的译文和儒家"爱有差等"的思想是一致的。赖发洛的译文是"If our reverence for our old folk spreads to the old folk of other men, and our care for our young folk spreads to the young folk of other men."（如果我们把对自己家老人的尊敬推广到对别人家的老人，把对自己家孩子的爱推广到对别人家的孩子）很明显，他的译文没有体现儒家的爱有差等思想，和孟子强调的"亲亲而仁民，仁民而爱物"的思想不一致。

[17]"推恩"，刘殿爵将之理解为"推广恩惠"，他认为"推广恩惠的人可以给四海带来和平"。这一译文和下文的"善推其所为而已矣"相呼应，突出推恩的重要性。理雅各则提出另外一种理解。他将本句翻译为

"Therefore the carrying out his kindness of heart by a prince will suffice for the love and protection of all within the four seas."（因此君主如果能把他的仁慈之心付诸行动的话，就可以保有四海）理雅各将"推恩"理解为推行、实践仁慈之心，与前文"百姓之不见保，为不用恩焉"相呼应，强调此句是针对君主是否有为而言。这一翻译也能很好地呼应前文。赖发洛的译文是"Thus if mercy multiplies, it will suffice to ward the four seas."（因此，如果仁慈增加就足以保有四海）他将"推恩"机械翻译为"增加仁慈"，令读者不知所云。

[18] "四海"是中国古书中常用的词语，多指整个国家。理雅各和赖发洛将之直译为"the four seas"，刘殿爵通过将"Four Seas"大写以突出其含义的特殊性，相比较而言，赵甄陶的"the whole world"更能准确反映"四海"的内涵。

[19] 刘殿爵将"古之人"翻译为"the ancients"，即"古代的人"。赖发洛、理雅各和亨顿等译者也持这一观点。笔者认为，在上文中，孟子以文王为例，指出推恩的重要性，所以此处"古之人"应指古代圣人。此外，从逻辑上看，并不是所有古代的人都是"大过人"之人，因而赵甄陶将"古之人"翻译为"the ancient sages"（古代圣人）更确切。

[20] 刘殿爵在翻译本句时，将"抑"理解为选择连词，他的理解是"或者只有在发动战争，使你的臣民处于危险之中，并且招致其他诸侯的怨恨才能使你快乐？"他的译文没有表达出明显的感情色彩，仅仅提供了一种可能的选择。庄荣贞在《杨伯峻〈孟子译注〉指瑕》中亦提出一种类似的观点。他指出："'抑'是选择连词，当对译作'抑或'、'还是'从上文的对话中明显可见，是孟子摆出两种做法之后，再请宣王任选其中的一种做法，使之权衡对比其利弊。"理雅各将之翻译为"You collect your equipments of war, endanger your soldiers and officers, and excite the resentment of the other princes；—do these things cause you pleasure in your mind?"即"收集武器，使士兵和大臣处于危险中，激起其他诸侯的怨恨，这些事情会给你带来快乐吗？"较之刘殿爵的译文，他选择用一般疑问句表达自己的疑惑。赖发洛

则用反问的语气指责这是一种错误的行为。他将此句翻译为"Must you raise men in mail，endanger knights and lieges，and pick a quarrel with the feudal lords，before your heart is happy，King"，即"一定要让人们处于战争状态，使士兵和大臣处于危险中，寻衅诸侯才能使你的心感到快乐吗?"从整个篇章看，孟子一直在用循循善诱的方式劝说齐宣王行王政，而非咄咄逼人，因而刘殿爵的翻译更准确。

[21] "四夷"是古代华夏族对四周少数民族的统称，含有轻蔑的意味。赖发洛按字面意思直译"四夷"为"the four tribes"（四个部落），既没有体现出原文的轻蔑，也错误传递了"四夷"的内涵。"抚四夷"即安抚四周的少数民族，刘殿爵从当时的社会现实出发，将之意译为"bring peace to the barbarian tribes on the four borders"（给四方的野蛮部落带来和平）是准确的。赖发洛翻译为"lay hand on the four tribes"（统治四个部落）则和孟子推崇的仁政思想不符。

[22] 在古代，行商为商，坐商为贾。理雅各将之翻译为"all the merchants，both travelling and stationary"（包含行商和坐商在内的所有商人），准确再现了"商贾"的含义。

[23] "士"起初是指贵族出身的武士，到春秋末期主要是指知识分子阶层。刘殿爵把"士"翻译为"Gentleman"。他在注释中对此做了如下说明："在本书中'Gentleman'用来翻译'士'，'gentleman'用来翻译'君子'。士是最低的统治阶层，君子指居上位的人或者是具有高尚道德的人。用同一个词翻译这两类人并非是完全随意的，因为在墨子和荀子那里，'士'和'君子'是通用的。"虽然刘殿爵对这种译法做了解释，但是"Gentleman"不能准确表达"士"的含义。理雅各将"士"翻译为"men of education"（受过教育的人）符合原文的意思。赖发洛将"士"译为"knight"（骑士、武士），这一异化的翻译方法便于读者理解，但不能完全传达"士"的内涵。

[24] 在儒家思想中，"礼"的内涵非常丰富，既包含规定人们日常行

为准则的礼仪制度，也包括典礼仪式。此处的"礼"指的是行为方式符合礼仪规定。刘殿爵将之译为"rite"，该词主要指宗教性的礼仪或礼节，用在此处不妥。理雅各将之译为"propriety"（文明社会中所规定的行为方式），赖发洛译为"courtesy"（有礼貌的举止行为），他们的译文只能体现"礼"的某一方面，用来翻译中国特有文化词语不准确。

卷 二

梁惠王章句下

【原文】2.1　庄暴见孟子，曰："暴见于王[1]，王语暴以好乐，暴未有以对也。"曰："好乐何如？"孟子曰："王之好乐甚，则齐国其庶几乎[2]！"他日，见于王曰："王尝语庄子以好乐，有诸？"王变乎色[3]，曰："寡人非能好先王之乐也，直好世俗之乐耳。"曰："王之好乐甚，则齐其庶几乎！今之乐由古之乐也[4]。"曰："可得闻与？"曰："独乐乐，与人乐乐，孰乐？[5]"曰："不若与人。"曰："与少乐乐，与众乐乐，孰乐？"曰："不若与众。""臣请为王言乐[6]。今[7]王鼓乐于此，百姓闻王钟鼓之声，管籥之音，举疾首蹙额而相告曰：'吾王之好鼓乐，夫何使我至于此极也？父子不相见，兄弟妻子离散。'今王田猎于此，百姓闻王车马之音[8]，见羽旄之美，举疾首蹙额而相告曰：'吾王之好田猎，夫何使我至于此极也？父子不相见，兄弟妻子离散。'此无他，不与民同乐也。今王鼓乐于此，百姓闻王钟鼓之声，管籥之音，举欣欣然有喜色而相告曰：'吾王庶几无疾病与，何以能鼓乐也？'今王田猎于此，百姓闻王车马之音，见羽旄之美，举欣欣然有喜色而相告曰：'吾王庶几无疾病与，何以能田猎也？'此无他，与民同乐也。今王与百姓同乐，则王矣[9]。"

【译文】齐国的大臣庄暴去见孟子，并告诉他："我去朝见大王的时候，大王告诉我他爱好音乐，我不知道怎么回答。"他接着问："爱好音乐好不好？"孟子回答说："大王非常爱好音乐，那么齐国基本上可以治理好了！"过了几天，孟子去拜见齐王，问道："您曾经告诉庄暴爱好音乐，对吗？"齐王不好意思地说："我不是爱好古代先王的音乐，只是爱好当下流行的音乐罢了。"孟子回答说："您特别爱好音乐，那么齐国基本上可以治理好了！今天的流行音乐和古代先王的音乐都是一样的。"齐王说："能进一步说说其中的道理吗？"孟子说："独自一人欣赏音乐快乐，还是和别人一起欣赏音乐快乐呢？"齐王说："大家一起欣赏音乐更快乐。"孟子说："和少数人一起欣赏音乐快乐还是和很多人一起欣赏音乐快乐？"齐王说："和很多人一起欣赏音乐更快乐。"孟子接着说："请让我和您谈谈快乐的道理吧。假设您在这里奏乐，百姓听到鸣钟击鼓的乐声和吹箫奏笛的声音，都觉得头疼，并且愁眉苦脸地互相抱怨说：'我们的君主爱好音乐，为什么让我们沦落到如此困顿的地步呢？！父子不能相见，兄弟妻儿流离失散！'假设您在这里狩猎，百姓听到车马的声音，看见华丽的旗帜，却都觉得头疼，并且愁眉苦脸地互相抱怨：'我们的君主爱好狩猎，为什么让我们沦落到如此困顿的地步呢？！父子不能相见，兄弟妻儿流离失散！'这没有别的原因，就是因为不能和百姓共同享受快乐的缘故。假设您在这儿奏乐，百姓听到鸣钟击鼓的乐声和吹箫奏笛的声音，都眉开眼笑地互相转告说：'我们的君主应该很健康吧，要不怎么能奏乐呢？假设您在这里狩猎，百姓听到车马的声音，看见华丽的旗帜，都眉开眼笑地互相转告说：'我们的君主应该很健康吧，要不怎么能狩猎呢？'这没有别的原因，就是因为能和百姓共同享受快乐的缘故。如果你能和百姓一起享受快乐，就可以成为统一天下的王。"

【英译】 Chwang Pâo，seeing Mencius，said to him，'I had an interview with the king. His Majesty told me that he loved music，and I was not prepared with anything to reply to him. What do you pronounce about that love of music?' Mencius replied, 'If the king's love of music were very great, the kingdom of Ch'î would be near to a state of good government!' Another day, Mencius, having an interview with the king, said, 'Your Majesty, I have heard, told the officer Chwang, that you love music—was it so?' The king changed colour, and said, 'I am unable to love the music of the ancient sovereigns; I only love the music that suits the manners of the present age.' Mencius said, 'If your Majesty's love of music were very great, Ch'î would be near to a state of good government! The music of the present day is just like the music of antiquity, as regards effecting that.' The king said, 'May I hear from you the proof of that?' Mencius asked, 'Which is the more pleasant, —to enjoy music by yourself alone, or to enjoy it with others?' 'To enjoy it with others,' was the reply. 'And which is the more pleasant, —to enjoy music with a few, or to enjoy it with many?' 'To enjoy it with many.' Mencius proceeded, 'Your servant begs to explain what I have said about music to your Majesty. Now, your Majesty is having music here.—The people hear the noise of your bells and drums, and the notes of your fifes and pipes, and they all, with aching heads, knit their brows, and say to one another, "That's how our king likes his music! But why does he reduce us to this extremity of distress? Fathers and sons cannot see one another. Elder brothers and younger brothers, wives and children, are separated and scattered abroad." Now, your Majesty is hunting here.—The people hear the noise of your carriages and horses, and see the beauty of your plumes and streamers, and they all, with aching heads, knit their brows, and say to one another, "That's how our king likes his hunting! But why does he reduce us to this extremity of distress? —

Fathers and sons cannot see one another. Elder brothers and younger brothers, wives and children, are separated and scattered abroad." Their feeling thus is from no other reason but that you do not allow the people to have pleasure as well as yourself. Now, your Majesty is having music here. The people hear the noise of your bells and drums, and the notes of your fifes and pipes, and they all, delighted, and with joyful looks, say to one another, "That sounds as if our king were free from all sickness! If he were not, how could he enjoy this music?" Now, your Majesty is hunting here.—The people hear the noise of your carriages and horses, and see the beauty of your plumes and streamers, and they all, delighted, and with joyful looks, say to one another, "That looks as if our king were free from all sickness! If he were not, how could he enjoy this hunting?" Their feeling thus is from no other reason but that you cause them to have their pleasure as you have yours. If your Majesty now will make pleasure a thing common to the people and yourself, the royal sway awaits you.'

【注释】

[1] "庄暴见孟子"是庄暴主动去拜见孟子，而"暴见于王"则是庄暴被王召见。刘殿爵的译文完美再现了这一差异。理雅各和赖发洛将之翻译为"Chuang Pao saw Mencius, and said, When the King saw me"，译文只是陈述了"我和王见过面"这一事实，但究竟是我主动去见王，还是王召见我，没有翻译出来，因而在翻译此句时，准确性不够。赵甄陶将之译为"Zhuang Bao (an official in the State of Qi—tr.) went to see Mencius, 'I was given an interview by the king'"，译文不仅准确再现了原文的句型和句意，还对庄暴的身份做了注解，指出他是齐国官员。

[2] "庶几"是大概、差不多的意思。刘殿爵、亨顿和赵甄陶等译者皆将之翻译为"齐国或许会有希望"。他们的译文突出了爱好音乐的积极

意义。赖发洛选择用"be little amiss",即"不会有什么差错"翻译。他的译文在达意上略显保守。理雅各为了将此句话的含义翻译清楚,对译文做了适当补充,将之译为"the kingdom of Ch'îwould be near to a state of good government!"他的译文更便于读者理解。

[3]"变色",理雅各和赖发洛都直译为"changed colour"(改变脸色),译者并没有告诉读者齐王为什么而变色。赵岐认为是"因恼怒而变色",朱熹指出是"因惭愧而变色"。刘殿爵选择用"blush"翻译,他认为齐王是因羞愧而变色。赵甄陶的译文"blushed with shame"则进一步明确了齐王变色的原因。

[4]"今之乐由古之乐也",朱熹指出:"其实今乐、古乐何可同也?但与民同乐之意,则无古今之异耳……"可见,孟子之所以认为古代雅乐和流行音乐差不多,是看到了音乐在启发君主与民同乐上的作用。理雅各受朱熹影响,将原文中的隐含之意完整表达了出来。刘殿爵、赵甄陶、亨顿等则按照字面意思,选择用"make no difference"(没有什么不同)来翻译。

[5]关于"乐乐",有两种理解。梁涛认为:"前一乐字指喜好;后一乐字指快乐。"刘殿爵的译文基本持这种观点。理雅各、赖发洛和亨顿则认为后一个"乐"特指"音乐",并将之翻译为"enjoy music"。两种理解皆通。

[6]关于"言乐"之"乐",译者的理解也存在差异。理雅各、赖发洛和赵甄陶将之翻译为"music",亨顿和刘殿爵将之翻译为"enjoyment"。笔者认为,本章从爱好音乐谈起,进而说明与民同享快乐的道理,"乐"的范围是不断扩大的,由享受音乐的快乐,扩展到田猎的快乐,进而扩展到实现仁政与民同乐的快乐,因而刘殿爵、亨顿的译文更符合原文的意思。

[7]孟子以"今"开头举了两个例子,向齐王说明"与民同乐"的道理。理雅各按字面意思将"今"翻译为"Now",赖发洛将之译为"to-day"。杨树达在《词诠》中指出:"'今'为假设连词",他还引用王念孙的"今犹若也"作为支撑。刘殿爵和赵甄陶将"今"翻译为"suppose"(假设)更符合原文的意思。不仅如此,由于此处的两个例子是假设的情况而非真实的存

在，故刘殿爵和赵甄陶使用过去时态在达意上更准确。

[8]"音"即声音，中性词。理雅各和赵甄陶选择用"noise"翻译，突出了车马的嘈杂之声。相比较而言，亨顿和刘殿爵的"sound"更准确。

[9]孟子经过论述，总结说，如果齐王能够做到与百姓同乐，就可以成为统一天下的王者。对于"则王矣"的内涵，译者有不同的认识。理雅各采用解释性翻译的策略将之译为"the royal sway awaits you"。他的译文更强调获得君王的权力。赖发洛的译文是"the kingdom would now be yours"，他的译文突出对王国的所有权。刘殿爵的译文是"a true King"，即真正的王，突出和现在的诸侯君主不同，但没有明确真正的王者到底是什么样子的。赵甄陶的译文是"be able to unify the world"，即统一天下的王者。他的译文立足当时诸侯割据混战的现状而发，更符合孟子"王者"的含义。

【原文】2.2　齐宣王问曰[1]："文王之囿[2]方七十里，有诸?"孟子对曰："于传[3]有之。"曰："若是其大乎[4]?"曰："民犹以为小也。"曰："寡人之囿方四十里，民犹以为大，何也?"曰："文王之囿方七十里，刍荛者往焉，雉兔者往焉，与民同之。民以为小，不亦宜乎? 臣始至于境，问国之大禁[5]，然后敢入。臣闻郊关[6]之内有囿方四十里，杀其麋鹿者如杀人之罪，则是方四十里为阱于国中。民以为大，不亦宜乎?"

【译文】齐宣王问孟子："听说文王的狩猎场方圆七十里，对吗?"孟子回答说："史书上是这么记载的。"齐宣王接着问："如果是这样，是不是太大了啊?"孟子回答说："百姓仍然认为小呢。"齐宣王说："我的狩猎场才四十里，百姓还觉得大呢，为什么呢?"孟子回答说："文王的狩猎场方圆七十里，割草砍柴的人可以去，打鸟捕兔的人也可以去，他和百姓共同使用。百姓认为小，不应当吗? 我刚到齐国边境的时候，首先打听齐国最严厉的禁令，然后才敢进入。我听说郊外有狩猎场方圆四十里，杀死麋鹿的人犯的罪和杀人一样。这是在国内布置了个四十里的陷阱啊。百姓认为大，不应该吗?"

【英译】The king Hsüan of Ch'î asked，'Was it so，that the park of king Wǎn contained seventy square li?' Mencius replied，'It is so in the records.' 'Was it so large as that?' exclaimed the king. 'The people，'said Mencius，'still looked on it as small.' The king added，'My park contains only forty square li，and the people still look on it as large. How is this?' 'The park of king Wǎn，'was the reply，'contained seventy square li，but the grass-cutters and fuel-gatherers had the privilege of entrance into it；so also had the catchers of pheasants and hares. He shared it with the people，and was it not with reason that they looked on it as small? When I first arrived at the borders of your kingdom，I inquired about the great prohibitory regulations，before I would venture to enter it；and I heard，that inside the barrier-gates there was a park of forty square lî，and that he who killed a deer in it，was held guilty of the same crime as if he had killed a man.—Thus those forty square lî are a pitfall in the middle of the kingdom. Is it not with reason that the people look upon them as large?'

【注释】

[1] 本章通过记载百姓对文王和齐宣王狩猎场的不同看法来说明"与民同之"的重要性。文王的狩猎场虽然方圆七十里，但与民同享，百姓仍认为它太小；齐宣王的狩猎场仅方圆四十里，但用严刑峻法禁止人们狩猎，因而人们认为它太大了。

[2] 朱熹认为"囿"是"蓄育鸟兽之所"，即古代畜养鸟兽的园林。赵甄陶和亨顿将之翻译为"the hunting ground"，理雅各和刘殿爵则直接翻译为"the park"。

[3] "传"在这儿是名词，指的是古代书籍。理雅各将其译为"records"（历史记载），不管是在词性还是在意思上都符合"传"的含义。赖发洛将

"传"译为"Chronicles"。"Chronicles"是一个专有名词,指的是《圣经·旧约》历代记,用它来翻译中国古代书籍不合适。刘殿爵将"传"翻译为"It is so recorded",虽然改变了词性,但也能准确传递原文的含义。赵甄陶进一步明确是史书上有这样的记载,并将之翻译为"recorded in history"。

[4] 理雅各在翻译此句时运用了"exclaimed"(惊叫)一词,将齐王的惊异之情形象地表达了出来。赖发洛、亨顿、刘殿爵和赵甄陶的译文体现得更多的是疑问,而非惊叹。

[5]"大禁"通常指法令、习俗或道德上最禁忌的事情。理雅各将之译为"the great prohibitory regulations"。他的译文和刘殿爵相似,认为"大禁"是"重要的禁令"。赖发洛将之翻译为"chiefly forbidden",亨顿将之译为"the great prohibitions",赵甄陶译为"major prohibitions",即"主要的忌讳"。相比较而言,理雅各和刘殿爵仅仅凸显了"大禁"法令层面上的含义,没有体现习俗和道德忌讳。

[6]"郊关",朱熹注:"国外百里为郊,郊外有关。"刘殿爵和赵甄陶将之译为"outskirts of the capital"(国都的郊外),以突出"郊关"和国都密切相关的特点。理雅各将其翻译为"barrier-gates",赖发洛翻译为"the gates of the marches",即"边界的大门"。他们认为此处的"郊关"是古代城邑四郊起拱卫防御作用的关门,也就是梁涛所谓的"四郊之门"。

【原文】2.3 齐宣王问曰[1]:"交邻国[2]有道乎?"孟子对曰:"有。惟仁者为能以大事小,是故汤事葛,文王事昆夷。惟智者为能以小事大,故大王事獯鬻,勾践事吴。以大事小者,乐天者也;以小事大者,畏天者也。乐天者保天下,畏天者保其国。《诗》[3]云:'畏天之威,于时保之。'[4]"王曰:"大哉言矣!寡人有疾,寡人好勇。"对曰:"王请无好小勇。夫抚剑疾视曰:'彼恶敢当我哉!'此匹夫之勇,敌一人者也。王请大之!《诗》云:'王赫斯怒,爰整其旅,以遏徂莒,以笃周祜,以对于天下。'此文王之勇也。文王一怒而安天下之民。《书》曰：'天降下民[5]，作之君，作之师，惟曰其助上帝宠之。四方有罪无罪惟我在[6]，天下曷敢有越厥志[7]？一人衡行[8]于天下，武王耻之。此武王之勇也。而武王亦一怒而安天下之民。今王亦一怒而安天下之民，民惟恐王之不好勇也。"

【译文】齐宣王问："和邻国交往有什么原则和方法吗？"孟子回答说："有。只有仁德的人能以大国的身份服侍小国，因而商汤能服侍葛伯，文王能服侍昆夷。只有智慧的人能以小国的身份服侍大国，所以太王服事獯鬻，勾践服事吴王。以大国服事小国，是乐于听从天命的人；以小国侍奉大国，是敬畏天命的人。乐于听从天命的人能够保有天下，敬畏天命的人能够保存自己的国家。《诗》说：'敬畏上天的威严，才能得到安定。'"齐宣王说："您说得太好了！不过我有个毛病，我喜欢勇敢。"孟子说："请您不要喜好小勇。一个人手拿刀剑瞪着眼睛说：'他怎么敢抵挡我呢！'这是匹夫之勇，只能抵挡一个人。请您将勇气扩大。《诗》上说：'文王勃然发怒，整顿军队，挡住侵犯莒国的敌人，增强周国的威望，不辜负天下的期望'，这是文王的勇。文王一发怒，就使得天下的百姓得到安定。《书经》说：'上天降生百姓，也为他们降生了君主和老师，并让君主和老师协助上天爱护百姓。四方是否有罪由我决定，天下哪有人敢超越他的本分？'有一个人敢在天下横行，武王感到羞耻，这就是武王的勇。武王一生气，使得天下百姓得到安宁。如果您也一生气而使天下百姓得到安定，那么百姓还唯恐您不喜爱勇敢呢。"

【英译】The king Hsüan of Ch'î asked, saying, 'Is there any way to regulate one's maintenance of intercourse with neighbouring kingdoms?' Mencius replied, 'There is. But it requires a perfectly virtuous prince to be able, with a great country, to serve a small one, —as, for instance, T'ang served Ko, and king Wǎn served the Kwǎn barbarians. And it requires a wise prince to be able, with a mall country, to serve a large one, —as the king T'âi served the Hsün-yü, and Kâu-ch'ien served Wû. He who with a great State serves a small one, delights in Heaven. He who with a small State serves a large one, stands in awe of Heaven. He who delights in Heaven, will affect with his love and protection the whole kingdom. He who stands in awe of Heaven, will affect with his love and protection his own kingdom. It is said in the Book of Poetry, "I fear the Majesty of Heaven, and will thus preserve its favouring decree."' The king said, 'A great saying! But I have an infirmity;—I love valour.' 'I beg your Majesty,' was the reply, 'not to love small valour. If a man brandishes his sword, looks fiercely, and says, "How dare he withstand me?" —this is the valour of a common man, who can be the opponent only of a single individual. I beg your Majesty to greaten it. It is said in the Book of Poetry, "The king blazed with anger, and he marshalled his hosts, to stop the march to Chü, to consolidate the prosperity of Châu, to meet the expectations of the nation." This was the valour of king Wăn. King Wăn, in one burst of his anger, gave repose to all the people of the kingdom. In the Book of History it is said, "Heaven having produced the inferior people, made for them rulers and teachers, with the purpose that they should be assisting to God, and therefore distinguished them throughout the four quarters of the land. Whoever are offenders, and whoever are innocent, here am I to deal with them. How dare any under heaven give indulgence to their refractory wills?" There was one man pursuing a violent and disorderly course in the kingdom, and king Wû was ashamed of it. This was the valour of king Wû. He also, by one display of his anger, gave repose to all the people of the kingdom. Let now your Majesty also, in one burst of anger，give repose to all the people of the kingdom. The people are only afraid that your Majesty does not love valour.'

【注释】

[1] 在本章中，孟子首次提出了他对"勇"的看法。他将"勇"划分为"大勇"和"小勇"，并推崇以"安天下之民"为己任、拯救人民于水深火热之中的大勇，反对逞一人之威、恃强凌弱的小勇。

[2] 此处齐宣王向孟子请教与邻国的交往之道。理雅各将之译为"regulate one's maintenance of intercourse with neighbouring kingdoms"，即"与邻国保持交往"，而刘殿爵、赖发洛、赵甄陶等译者则将之理解为"推进和邻国的友好的关系"。从下文孟子所举几个"交邻国有道"的例子可以看出，这儿的"交"仅仅是保持交往，尚未上升到"交好"和"推进友好关系"的层面，因而理雅各的译文更符合原文的意思。

[3] 作为中国最早的一部诗歌总集，《诗》在西汉时期被奉为儒家经典，始称《诗经》。赵甄陶、理雅各将之翻译为"the Book of Poetry"，这也是《诗经》最常见的翻译。刘殿爵将之翻译为"The Book of Odes"。据《现代英汉大词典》记载，"The Book of Odes"也被翻译为"中国的《诗经》"。此外，《诗经》还被翻译为"The songs""Shijing"等。

[4] "畏"在此处是指"敬畏"，理雅各和赖发洛都把它翻译成"fear"，该词侧重指面临危险或灾祸时内心所引起的恐惧心情，当表示"敬畏"时，往往指对神的敬畏，含有宗教意味。刘殿爵和赵甄陶选择用"in awe of"翻译更准确。因为此处的"畏"是和"天"相连，正如梁启雄所言，"天"在《孟子》一书中，"主宰性的、宗教性的天道思想的成分很少，而客观性的、法则性的天道思想成分很多"。

[5] 此处的"天降下民"与孟子在后面章节中提到的"天生蒸民，有物有则"的含义非常相近，"降"和"生"应是同义词。理雅各将之翻译为"Heaven having produced the inferior people"，显然他认为上天制造了下等人。相比较而言，刘殿爵的译文"Heaven created people on earth"更准确。

[6] 译者对"惟曰其助上帝宠之四方"的理解不同。刘殿爵的译文同焦循，将原文断句为"惟曰其助上帝宠之。四方有罪无罪惟我在"。理雅各则将之翻译为"they should be assisting to God，and therefore distinguished them throughout the four quarters of the land." 显然他的译文受朱熹"惟曰其助上帝，宠之四方"的影响。赖发洛的译文是"they might help the Lord Above and be honoured in the four region." 他的断句和理雅各一致。结合下文"一人衡行于天下"可知，刘殿爵的"四方有罪无罪惟我在"更符合原文之意。

[7] "厥"的用法同"其"，但是"其"指代的是上天的意志，还是普通百姓的心志，或者是君师的意志，译者有不同的看法。朱熹注："我既在此，天下何敢有过越其心志而作乱者乎。"受其影响，理雅各将之翻译为"How dare any under heaven give indulgence to their refractory wills"，即"天下人谁敢放任心志胡作非为？"赵甄陶则给出了另外一种理解，即"no one would dare disobey Heaven's will"，显然他认为没有人敢违背上天的意志。刘殿爵的译文没有明确指出"厥"到底是谁，而是选择用"himself"翻译，让读者自己体会。

[8] 朱熹注："衡，与横同，衡行，谓作乱也"。刘殿爵改变原文结构，直接用"one bully"（恃强凌弱者）翻译，抓住了"衡行"者的特点。理雅各采取解释性翻译策略将之翻译为"one man pursuing a violent and disorderly course"，即"从事任性、残暴行为的人"。两位译者皆认为此处的"一人"为泛指。赵甄陶将之翻译为"a tyrant who bullied people everywhere"，显然他认为此处的"一人"专指欺凌百姓的暴君。梁涛进一步指出："一人指殷纣王。"

【原文】2.4　齐宣王见孟子于雪宫[1]。王曰："贤者[2]亦有此乐乎？"孟子对曰："有。人不得，则非其上矣。不得而非其上者，非也；为民上而不与民同乐者，亦非也。乐民之乐者，民亦乐其乐；忧民之忧者，民亦忧其忧^[3]。乐以天下，忧以天下^[4]，然而不王者，未之有也。昔者齐景公问于晏子曰：'吾欲观于转附、朝儛，遵海而南，放于琅邪，吾何修而可以比于先王观也？'晏子对曰：'善哉问也！天子适诸侯曰巡狩。巡狩者，巡所守也。诸侯朝于天子曰述职。述职者，述所职也。无非事者。春省耕而补不足，秋省敛而助不给。夏谚曰："吾王不游，吾何以休^[5]？吾王不豫，吾何以助？一游一豫，为诸侯度。"今也不然：师行而粮食，饥者弗食，劳者弗息。睊睊胥谗，民乃作慝。方命虐民，饮食若流。流连荒亡，为诸侯忧^[6]。从流下而忘反谓之流，从流上而忘反谓之连，从兽无厌谓之荒，乐酒无厌谓之亡。先王无流连之乐，荒亡之行。惟君所行也。'景公悦，大戒^[7]于国^[8]，出舍于郊^[9]。于是始兴发补不足。召大师曰：'为我作君臣相说之乐！'盖《徵招》《角招》^[10]是也。其诗曰：'畜君^[11]何尤？'畜君者，好君也。"

【译文】齐宣王在雪宫里接见孟子。齐宣王问："有道德的贤能之人也有这种快乐吗？"孟子回答："有的。人们得不到这种快乐，就会埋怨他们的国君。得不到这种快乐就埋怨国君，是不对的。作为国君但不同百姓一同享受这种快乐，也是不对的。国君以百姓的快乐为快乐，百姓也会以国君的快乐为快乐；国君以百姓的忧愁为忧愁，百姓也会以国君的忧愁为忧愁。君主能够和天下人同乐，和天下人同忧，这样还不能成为统一天下的王者，是从来不曾有过的。以前齐景公问晏子说：'我想到转附、朝儛两个山上去巡游，然后沿着海向南走，一直到琅邪。我该怎样做才能够和过去圣王的巡游相比呢？'晏子答道：'问得好！天子到诸侯的国家巡游叫巡狩。巡狩就是巡视诸侯所守的疆土。诸侯去朝见天子叫述职。述职就是汇报他的职责工作。没有不和工作相关的。春天里巡视耕种情况，补助贫穷的农户；秋天里考察收获情况，救济歉收的农户。夏朝的谚语说："我王不出来巡游，我哪能得到休息？我王不出来视察，我哪会得到补助？我的王经常巡狩，足以作为诸侯的法度。"现在的巡游却不是这样，大队伍出动，到处筹备粮食，饥饿的人没饭吃，劳累的人不能休息。人们无不切齿侧目，怨声载道，百姓被迫为非作歹。这种巡游违背天命，虐待百姓，大吃大喝如流水。这种流连荒亡的行为，使诸侯感到忧愁。从上游向下游的游乐忘返叫流，从下游向上游的游乐忘返叫连，不知厌倦地打猎叫荒，不加节制地喝酒叫亡。古代的圣王没有这种流连荒亡的行为。您自己来决定选择哪种巡游吧。'景公特别高兴，在城内做好准备，然后搬到郊外去居住。他开仓放粮，救济那些穷苦的人。景公召来乐官，告诉他：'为我做君臣同乐的乐曲'。即《徵招》《角招》，其中有歌词说：'匡正君主的过失有什么不对的么？'匡正君主的过失就是爱护君主啊！"

【英译】The king Hsüan of Ch'î had an interview with Mencius in the Snow palace, and said to him, 'Do men of talents and worth likewise find pleasure in these things?' Mencius replied, 'They do; and if people generally are not able to enjoy themselves, they condemn their superiors. For them, when they cannot enjoy themselves, to condemn their superiors is wrong, but when the superiors of the people do not make enjoyment a thing common to the people and themselves, they also do wrong. When a ruler rejoices in the joy of his people, they also rejoice in his joy; when he grieves at the sorrow of his people, they also grieve at his sorrow. A sympathy of joy will pervade the kingdom; a sympathy of sorrow will do the same: —in such a state of things, it cannot be but that the ruler attain to the royal dignity.' Formerly, the duke Ching of Ch'î asked the minister Yen, saying, "I wish to pay a visit of inspection to Chwan-fû, and Châo-wû, and then to bend my course southward along the shore, till I come to Lang-yê. What shall I do that my tour may be fit to be compared with the visits of inspection made by the ancient sovereigns?" The minister Yen replied, "An excellent inquiry! When the Son of Heaven visited the princes, it was called a tour of inspection, that is, he surveyed the States under their care. When the princes attended at the court of the Son of Heaven, it was called a report of office, that is, they reported their administration of their offices. Thus, neither of the proceedings was without a purpose. And moreover, in the spring they examined the ploughing, and supplied any deficiency of seed; in the autumn they examined the reaping, and supplied any deficiency of yield. There is the saying of the Hsiâ dynasty, —If our king do not take his ramble, what will become of our happiness? If our king do not make his excursion, what will become of our help? That ramble, and that excursion, were a pattern to the princes. Now, the state of things is different. —A host marches in attendance on the ruler, and stores of provisions are consumed. The hungry are deprived of their food, and there is no rest for those who are called to toil. Maledictions are uttered by one to another with eyes askance, and the people proceed to the commission of wickedness. Thus the royal ordinances are violated, and the people are oppressed, and the supplies of food and drink flow away like water. The rulers yield themselves to the current, or they urge their way against it; they are wild; they are utterly lost: —these things proceed to the grief of the inferior princes. Descending along with the current, and forgetting to return, is what I call yielding to it. Pressing up against it, and forgetting to return, is what I call urging their way against it. Pursuing the chase without satiety is what I call being wild. Delighting in wine without satiety is what I call being lost. The ancient sovereigns had no pleasures to which they gave themselves as on the flowing stream; no doings which might be so characterized as wild and lost. It is for you，my prince，to pursue your course."' The duke Ching was pleased. He issued a proclamation throughout his State，and went out and occupied a shed in the borders. From that time he began to open his granaries to supply the wants of the people，and calling the Grand music-master，he said to him— "Make for me music to suit a prince and his minister pleased with each other."And it was then that the Chî-shâo and Chio-shâo were made，in the words to which it was said，"Is it a fault to restrain one's prince?" He who restrains his prince loves his prince.'

【注释】

[1] 在本章，孟子继续向齐宣王宣扬他的"与民同忧乐"的思想。孟子认为，一个统治者只有把人民的生活放在优先考虑的地位，关心人民的疾苦，才能得到人民的拥护，永远保有天命，成为统一全中国的王者。

[2] "贤者"指的是德才兼备的人。刘殿爵的译文表明他认为"贤者"的特征是聪明而有美德。理雅各将之译为"men of talents and worth"，也突出了"贤者"德才兼备的特征。赵甄陶将之译为"a virtuous man"，强调了"贤者"道德品性高尚的一面。亨顿将之译为"the sage"，突出了"贤者"睿智的一面。

[3] 刘殿爵认为"乐民之乐者，民亦乐其乐；忧民之忧者，民亦忧其忧"适用于所有人。理雅各和赵甄陶则认为此句话是针对统治者而发。从孟子的王政思想和本章"与民同忧乐"的宗旨看，理雅各和赵甄陶的补充性翻译更准确。

[4] 本句是对前面"乐民之乐者，民亦乐其乐；忧民之忧者，民亦忧其忧"的强调总结。这儿的"天下"指的是"天下的百姓"。本句话的意思是"以天下人的快乐为快乐，以天下人的忧愁为忧愁"，因而赵甄陶的译文"If a ruler shares joys and sorrows with the people of the world"能够准确传达原文之意。理雅各将之翻译为"A sympathy of joy will pervade the kingdom；

a sympathy of sorrow will do the same"，即"共同的快乐将会遍及这个国家，共同的忧伤也是如此"亦通。

[5]"休"，刘殿爵、赖发洛、赵甄陶将之译为"rest"，即休息。只有理雅各将其翻译为"happiness"，即幸福、福禄。从字义上看，"休"确实有"福禄"的意思，如《左传·襄公二十八年》"以礼承天之休"中，"休"的意思就是"福禄"。但是从下文"饥者弗食，劳者弗息"可知，将之翻译为"休息"更准确。

[6]刘殿爵认为上面提到的那些"流连荒亡"的行为是诸侯的行为，这些行为令人担忧。赵甄陶也持这一观点，将之译为"These excesses prevailing among the feudal princes cause worry and grief"，即"诸侯中存在的这些荒淫行为令人担心和忧伤"。理雅各则认为是统治者（流连荒亡）的行为给下级诸侯带来麻烦，将之翻译为"these things proceed to the grief of the inferior princes"。赖发洛也持这种观点，将之译为"Drifting, stubbornness, wildness and deadness are a sorrow to the feudal lords"，即"流连荒亡令诸侯忧伤"。晏子将古代天子巡游和今天的国君巡游作对比，指出天子巡游是为了帮助百姓，这为诸侯做了榜样，而今天的国君出游是为了个人享乐，给所到之处的地方官员带来了无休止的麻烦，使百姓不得安宁。因而此处的"诸侯"指的是地方官员或附庸，"忧"是给他们带来困扰。刘殿爵和赵甄陶的译文是从另一个角度理解。古代天子巡游都带有明确的目的性，是为了帮助百姓，因而受到百姓的欢迎。但今天的诸侯国君出游时的浪费奢侈行为给百姓带来了巨大负担，令百姓不满，这一状况值得担忧。可见，这两种译文从不同的角度翻译了原文。

[7]"戒"，赵岐注曰："备也。"杨伯峻认为此处并非戒备之意，而是"准备"之意。刘殿爵和赵甄陶的译文皆持此说。但是理雅各将之译为"issued a proclamation"，即"发布公告"，显然他的译文受朱熹"戒，告命也"的影响。赖发洛则将之翻译为"A great warning"，即"发出警告"。结合下文景公开仓放粮，救济穷苦人可知，此处的"大戒"理解为"做好充分

的准备"更佳。

[8] "国"最初并非指国家，而是指都城，因而刘殿爵和赵甄陶将之译为"capital"。理雅各将之翻译为"State"，赖发洛将之翻译为"land"，不准确。

[9] 先秦时期的"郊"一般指国都之外的郊区。刘殿爵和赵甄陶译为"outskirts"，基本能体现其含义。理雅各和赖发洛取"边界"之意，将之分别翻译为"the borders"和"the marches"。从文意上看，齐景公"出舍于郊"的目的是体恤民情，救济穷苦人，他至多去国都之外的郊区居住，而不可能跑到边界去。

[10] 《徵招》《角招》是古代的乐曲名，在英语中没有对等甚至相类的词，译者都选用音译的办法，包括一贯追求用英文读者熟悉的词语翻译中国特有文化词语的译者赖发洛。

[11] "畜君"，朱熹注："孟子释之，以为臣能蓄止其君之欲，乃是爱其君者也。"刘殿爵和赖发洛将之翻译为"curbing the lord"（约束君主），亨顿翻译为"guiding the sovereign"（引导君主），理雅各翻译为"restrain one's prince"（限制君主）。四位译者皆认为"畜君"是匡正君主之意。赵甄陶则将之翻译为"supporting the ruler"，即"奉养国君"。孟子在本次谈话中力劝齐王"与百姓同忧乐"，他还引用晏子规劝其君的例子来说明匡正君主的重要性，因而此处取"畜君"的"劝止、匡正君主"之意更佳。

【原文】2.5 齐宣王问曰："人皆谓我毁明堂[1]，毁诸？已乎？"孟子对曰："夫明堂者，王者之堂[2]也。王欲行王政，则勿毁之矣。"王曰："王政可得闻与？"对曰："昔者文王之治岐也，耕者九一[3]，仕者世禄，关市讥而不征，泽梁无禁，罪人不孥[4]。老而无妻曰鳏，老而无夫曰寡，老而无子曰独，幼而无父曰孤。此四者，天下之穷民而无告者。文王发政施仁，必先斯四者。诗云：'哿矣富人，哀此茕独！'"王曰："善哉言乎！"曰："王如善之，则何为不行?"王曰:"寡人有疾,寡人好货。"对曰:"昔者公刘好货,《诗》云:'乃积乃仓,乃裹糇粮,于橐于囊,思戢用光。弓矢斯张,干戈戚扬,爰方启行。'故居者有积仓,行者有裹囊也,然后可以爰方启行。王如好货,与百姓同之,于王何有?"王曰:"寡人有疾,寡人好色。"对曰:"昔者太王好色,爱厥妃。诗云:'古公亶父,来朝走马,率西水浒,至于岐下,爰及姜女,聿来胥宇。'当是时也,内无怨女,外无旷夫[5]。王如好色,与百姓同之,于王何有?"

【译文】齐宣王问:"别人都建议我拆掉明堂。是拆掉呢,还是不拆呢?"孟子回答说:"明堂是能统一天下的王者的殿堂。您如果要实行王政,就不要毁掉它。"齐宣王说:"可以给我讲一下王政吗?"孟子回答道:"从前周文王治理岐周时,对耕种土地的人实行九分抽一的税率,对做官的人实行世代承袭的俸禄,对关口和市场,只是稽查,不征税,不禁止人们在湖泊捕鱼;犯罪的人,只对本人实行刑罚,不牵连妻子儿女。没有妻室的老年男子叫作鳏夫,没有丈夫的老年女人叫作寡妇,没有儿女的老人叫作独老,没有父亲的儿童叫作孤儿。这四种人是全天下最穷苦无靠的人。周文王实行仁政,一定首先想到他们。《诗》上说:'富人是可以过得去的了,可怜那些孤单无依的人吧!'"宣王说:"说得真好呀!"孟子说:"如果您认为这话好,为什么不实行呢?"宣王说:"我有个毛病,我喜好钱财。"孟子回答说:"以前的公刘也喜爱钱财,《诗》上说:'粮食装满仓,备好充足的干粮,装满橐,装满囊。团结和睦争荣光。箭上弦,弓开张,干戈斧钺都上场,然后浩浩荡荡向前行。'因此,留在家里的人有粮食,行军的人有干粮,这才能率领军队前行。如果王喜爱钱财,能让百姓也有钱财,那么实行王政又有什么困难呢?"齐宣王又说:"我有个毛病,我喜欢女色。"孟子说:"从前太王也喜爱女色,非常爱他的妃子。《诗》上说:'古公亶父,清早骑马奔驰,沿着西边河岸,来到岐山脚下。带着他的妻子姜氏女,视察住处好安家。'那个时候，没有嫁不出去的女子，也没有娶不上妻子的单身汉。王如果喜爱女色，能和百姓一道，那对于实行王政又有什么困难呢?"

【英译】The king Hsüan of Ch'î said, 'People all tell me to pull down and remove the Hall of Distinction. Shall I pull it down, or stop the movement for that object?' Mencius replied, 'The Hall of Distinction is a Hall appropriate to the sovereigns. If your Majesty wishes to practise the true royal government, then do not pull it down.' The king said, 'May I hear from you what the true royal government is?' 'Formerly,' was the reply, 'king Wăn's government of Ch'î was as follows: The husbandmen cultivated for the government one-ninth of the land; the descendants of officers were salaried; at the passes and in the markets, strangers were inspected, but goods were not taxed: there were no prohibitions respecting the ponds and weirs; the wives and children of criminals were not involved in their guilt. There were the old and wifeless, or widowers; the old and husbandless, or widows; the old and childless, or solitaries; the young and fatherless, or orphans: —these four classes are the most destitute of the people, and have none to whom they can tell their wants, and king Wăn, in the institution of his government with its benevolent action, made them the first objects of his regard, as it is said in the Book of Poetry, "The rich may get through life well; but alas! for the miserable and solitary!"' The king said, 'O excellent words!' Mencius said, 'Since your Majesty deems them excellent, why do you not practise them?' 'I have an infirmity,' said the king; 'I am fond of wealth.' The reply was, 'Formerly, Kung-liû was fond of wealth. It is said in the Book of Poetry, "He reared his ricks, and filled his granaries, he tied up dried provisions and grain, in bottomless bags, and sacks, that he might gather his people together, and glorify his State. With bows and arrows all-displayed, with shields, and spears, and battle-axes, large and small, he commenced his march." In this way those who remained in their old seat had their ricks and granaries, and those who marched had their bags of provisions. It was not till after this that he thought he could begin his march. If your Majesty loves wealth, give the people power to gratify the same feeling, and what difficulty will there be in your attaining the royal sway?' The king said, 'I have an infirmity; I am fond of beauty.' The reply was, 'Formerly, king T'âi was fond of beauty, and loved his wife. It is said in the Book of Poetry, "Kû-kung T'an-fû, came in the morning, galloping his horse, by the banks of the western waters, as far as the foot of Ch'î hill, along with the lady of Chiang; they came and together chose the site for their settlement." At that time, in the seclusion of the house, there were no dissatisfied women, and abroad, there were no unmarried men. If your Majesty loves beauty, let the people be able to gratify the same feeling, and what difficulty will there be in your attaining the royal sway?'

【注释】

[1] "明堂"是中国古代天子宣明政教的地方。齐国仅仅是一个诸侯国，为什么会有"明堂"呢？我们可以从赵岐的注解中找到答案。赵岐注："泰山下明堂，本周天子东巡狩朝诸侯之处也，齐侵地而得有之。人劝齐宣王，诸侯不用明堂，可毁坏，故疑而问于孟子当毁之乎。"刘殿爵和赵甄陶将"明堂"翻译为"The Hall of Light"，取"明亮"之意。理雅各将之译为"The Hall of Distinction"，取"显赫、声望和级别"之意，以突出"明堂"的与众不同。

[2] "王者之堂"是对"明堂"的进一步解释。对于何为"王者"，刘殿爵选择用"a true King"（真正的王）翻译，何为真正的王，则是让读

者自己去体会。赵甄陶则采取解释性的翻译策略，将之翻译为"a unifier of the whole world"，即"结束诸侯混战，统一天下的王者"。理雅各的"sovereigns"（最高统治者）体现了"王"的一个方面的特征，而赖发洛的翻译"kings"则略显笼统。

[3]"九一"指井田制度，是孟子推崇的理想的土地制度。井田制将一里划分为九区，每区一百亩，共九百亩，形如"井"字。外面八个区域由八家各自耕种，中央区域为公田，由八家共同耕种。这种土地制度的特点是九分土地而税其一。刘殿爵用简明的译文，翻译出了井田制的特点，"tillers of land were taxed one part in nine"，即"耕地者被收取九分之一的税"。理雅各将之译为"The husbandmen cultivated for the government one-ninth of the land"，即"农民为政府耕种九分之一的土地"。这一翻译比较准确地表述出了井田制的内容。赵甄陶将之译为"tillers of land had to cultivate for the government only one ninth of the land with the rest belonging to themselves"。他的译文完整传递了井田制的内涵。

[4]"孥"，妻子和儿女，此处用作动词。"不孥"，指不牵连妻子和儿女。刘殿爵、赵甄陶、理雅各的"惩罚不殃及罪犯的妻儿"，准确再现了原文之意。赖发洛将之译为"the children of criminal were sackless"，他将"不孥"理解为"罪犯的孩子是无害的"不准确。

[5] 在中国古代，一般是女主内，男主外，因而"内"通常会与女相连，而"外"也常和男同用，此处"内""外"的含义可以不译出。本句是针对好色与百姓同之而发，因而"怨女"指的是到了婚嫁的年龄而没有找到合适的配偶的女子。"旷夫"指的是到了娶亲的年龄而未找到合适的配偶的男子。理雅各翻译为"in the seclusion of the house, there were no dissatisfied women, and abroad, there were no unmarried men"，即"在偏室里没有不满意的妇女，在室外没有未婚的男人"。赖发洛翻译为"there were no grumbling maids within, and no lonely men without"，即"在屋内没有抱怨的女人，在屋外没有孤独的男人"。二人皆按字面意思直译，未能体现出"怨

女”“旷夫”在此处的确切含义。

【原文】2.6　孟子谓齐宣王曰[1]：“王之臣有托其妻子于其友而之楚游者，比其反也，则冻馁其妻子[2]，则如之何？”王曰：“弃之。”曰：“士师[3]不能治士，则如之何？”王曰：“已之。”曰：“四境之内不治，则如之何？”王顾左右[4]而言他。

【译文】孟子对齐宣王说：“如果您有位大臣把妻子儿女付托给朋友照顾，自己去楚国游历，等他回来的时候，发现他的妻子儿女却在挨饿受冻，应该怎样对待这样的朋友呢？”齐王说：“和他绝交。”孟子说：“如果管刑罚的长官不能管理好他的下级，应该怎样办呢？”齐宣王说：“罢免他。”孟子说：“如果一个国家治理得不好，那该怎样办呢？”齐王环顾左右，把话题扯到别处去了。

【英译】Mencius said to the king Hsüan of Ch'î, 'Suppose that one of your Majesty's ministers were to entrust his wife and children to the care of his friend, while he himself went into Ch'û to travel, and that, on his return, he should find that the friend had let his wife and children suffer from cold and hunger; —how ought he to deal with him?' The king said, 'He should cast him off.' Mencius proceeded, 'Suppose that the chief criminal judge could not regulate the officers under him, how would you deal with him?' The king said, 'Dismiss him.' Mencius again said, 'If within the four borders of your kingdom there is not good government, what is to be done?' The king looked to the right and left, and spoke of other matters.

【注释】

[1] 以小见大、从小推大是孟子惯用的辩论技巧。在本章中，孟子同样从小事说起，进而论及治理国家的道理。孟子试图用简单的例子向齐宣王说明每个人，不论他是君主还是普通人，都承担着一定的责任和义务。要想

取得别人的尊重和拥护，就要出色地完成自己的职责。任何人，即使是君主不能完成自己的职责，也有被罢免和遗弃的危险。孟子的提问咄咄逼人，步步紧逼，令宣王"顾左右而言他"。

[2] 要准确翻译此句，首先要弄清楚其所蕴含的感情色彩。大臣因信任朋友，故在出门远游时将妻儿托付给朋友照顾，以使他们免除挨饿受冻之苦。没想到在他回来的时候，竟然发现他的妻儿在挨饿受冻，可见本句蕴含着"出乎意料、极其震惊"的含义。刘殿爵的译文将原文蕴含的感情色彩非常传神地表达了出来。不仅如此，"则"在此处表明"冻馁"的情况已经存在，《词诠》卷六："则，承接连词，于初发见一事之已然状态时用之。"理雅各的译文既能体现出吃惊的意思，又能表现出"已经"存在的含义。赖发洛的译文是"when he came back his wife and child were cold and starved"，这一翻译只是将原文的表面意思翻译了出来，没能表现出原文蕴含的感情色彩。

[3] "士师"是掌管刑狱的官，朱熹注曰："士师，狱官也。其属有乡士、遂士之官，士师皆当治之。"理雅各将"士师"翻译为"the chief criminal judge"，赵甄陶将之译为"the chief judge"。这两种翻译基本能体现"士师"的主要特征。刘殿爵的译文"Marshal of the Guards"、赖发洛的"the Chief Knight"，略显笼统，不能准确再现"士师"的内涵。

[4] "左右"，刘殿爵将之理解为"随从人员"，将"王顾左右而言他"理解为"王转向随从，开始说其他事情"。显然刘殿爵认为，齐王不愿意和孟子继续这一话题，因而借吩咐左右随从办其他事情以终止这一谈话。理雅各、赖发洛、赵甄陶等译者都将"左右"理解为"左边、右边"，将"王顾左右"翻译为"the king looked to the right and left"，即"王左看看右看看，把话题引到其他事情上"。根据他们的翻译，王借左看右看，不与孟子对视来表明不愿意继续讨论这一问题的态度。两种翻译皆通。

【原文】2.7 孟子见齐宣王，曰："所谓故国[1]者，非谓有乔木之谓也，有世臣[2]之谓也。王无亲臣[3]矣，昔者所进，今日不知其亡也。"王曰："吾何以识其不才而舍之？"曰："国君进贤，如不得已，将使卑逾尊，疏逾戚，可不慎与？[4]左右皆曰贤，未可也；诸大夫[5]皆曰贤，未可也；国人皆曰贤，然后察之；见贤焉，然后用之。左右皆曰不可，勿听；诸大夫皆曰不可，勿听；国人皆曰不可，然后察之；见不可焉，然后去之。左右皆曰可杀，勿听；诸大夫皆曰可杀，勿听；国人皆曰可杀，然后察之；见可杀焉，然后杀之。故曰，国人杀之也。如此，然后可以为民父母。"

【译文】孟子拜见齐宣王，对他说："平常我们说的'故国'，并不是因为那个国家有高大的树木，而是因为有世代建立功勋的老臣。现在您没有亲信的大臣啦，以前任用的人现在都不知道哪里去了。"王问："我怎么才能识别无才能的人而不任用他们呢？"孟子回答："国君选拔贤才，如果不得已要把卑贱者提拔到尊贵者之上，把疏远的人提拔到亲近者之上，能不慎重吗？左右亲近的人都说贤能，不行；众位大臣都说贤能，也不行；全国的人都说贤能，然后去了解，发现他真的贤能，然后再任用他。左右亲近的人都说不好，不要听信；众位大臣都说不好，也不要听信；全国的人都说不好，然后去了解，发现他真不好，然后再罢免他。左右亲近的人都说可杀，不要听；众位大臣都说可杀，也不要听；全国的人都说可杀，然后去了解，发现他该杀，再杀他。所以说，是全国人杀的他。这样，才可以做百姓的父母。"

【英译】Mencius, having an interview with the king Hsüan of Ch'î, said to him, 'When men speak of "an ancient kingdom," it is not meant thereby that it has lofty trees in it, but that it has ministers sprung from families which have been noted in it for generations. Your Majesty has no intimate ministers even. Those whom you advanced yesterday are gone to-day, and you do not know it.' The king said, 'How shall I know that they have not ability, and so avoid employing them at all？' The reply was, 'The ruler of a State advances to office men of talents and virtue only as a matter of necessity. Since he will thereby cause the low to overstep the honourable，and distant to overstep his near relatives，ought he to do so but with caution? When all those about you say, — "This is a man of talents and worth," you may not therefore believe it. When your great officers all say, — "This is a man of talents and virtue," neither may you for that believe it. When all the people say, — "This is a man of talents and virtue," then examine into the case，and when you find that the man is such, employ him. When all those about you say, — "This man won't do," don't listen to them. When all your great officers say, — "This man won't do," don't listen to them. When the people all say, — "This man won't do," then examine into the case，and when you find that the man won't do, send him away. When all those about you say, — "This man deserves death," don't listen to them. When all your great officers say, — "This man deserves death," don't listen to them. When the people all say, — "This man deserves death," then inquire into the case，and when you see that the man deserves death，put him to death. In accordance with this we have the saying, "The people killed him." You must act in this way in order to be the parent of the people.'

【注释】

[1] "故国"，刘殿爵强调国家的传统悠久，将之译为 "state of established traditions"。其他三位译者则突出年代久远，如赵甄陶将之翻译为 "old country"，赖发洛翻译为 "an old kingdom"，理雅各翻译为 "an ancient kingdom"。译者基本都能翻译出 "故国" 含义，但是结合下文孟子的进一步解释，刘殿爵的译文更准确。

[2] "世臣"，朱熹注曰："累世勋旧之臣，与国同休戚者也。" 刘殿爵

的译文将"世臣"的特征，即"家族数代一直在这个国家任职的大臣"准确翻译了出来。理雅各认为"世臣"的一个显著特征就是"那些大臣的家族在本国数代以来一直处于显贵地位"，因而将之译为"ministers sprung from families which have been noted in it for generations." 他的译文也能准确再现"世臣"的含义。赖发洛将之译为"lines of ministers"，译文虽简洁，但不便于读者了解"世臣"的真实含义。

[3] "亲臣"，朱熹认为是"君所亲信之臣"，受其影响，刘殿爵和赵甄陶都将之翻译为"值得信任的大臣"。理雅各将之翻译为"intimate minister"，强调君主和大臣关系亲密。赖发洛的译文是"near ministers"，亨顿的译文是"old family bonds between you and your ministers"，二人的译文强调君主和大臣之间的亲属、血缘关系。

[4] 孟子生活的时代虽然奴隶主贵族土地所制已经土崩瓦解，封建地主土地所有制正在形成，但任用官员时注重门第和出身的情况仍然存在，使"卑逾尊，疏逾戚"是一件需要慎重对待的大事，但这并不意味着孟子反对"尚贤"。相反，孟子多次强调"尊贤使能""立贤无方"的重要性。理雅各的译文表明，国君提拔贤能的人是"不得已"，不得不办的事情。赖发洛的译文是"The lord of a kingdom promotes men of worth when there is no help for it."很明显他认为，中国古代的君主一般不会提拔贤能的人，除非他遇到一些特殊情况，只能靠提拔贤能的人才能解决问题。刘殿爵认为，"如不得已"不是用来限制"国君进贤"，而是限制"卑逾尊，疏逾戚"的情况，因而将之翻译为"When there is no choice, the ruler of a state, in advancing good and wise men, may have to promote those of low position over the heads of those of exalted rank and distant relatives over near ones"。春秋战国时期，尚贤之风盛行，各诸侯国竞相启用贤能之才，以实现富国强兵的目的。因而提拔贤能的人并非国君的无奈之举，而是诸侯国君大力推崇的政策，国君需要谨慎的仅仅是"使卑逾尊，疏逾戚"的情况。

[5] "大夫"，古代官职。先秦诸侯国中，在国君之下设卿、大

夫、士三级。理雅各将之翻译为"great officers"，赵甄陶将之译为"high officialsf"，二位译者基本上能体现"大夫"作为古代高级官员的基本内涵。刘殿爵将之翻译为"the Counsellors"，突出"大夫"在国君做决策时提供建议的特点，赖发洛将之翻译为"the great men"，不准确。

【原文】2.8　齐宣王问曰："汤放桀，武王伐[1]纣，有诸？"孟子对曰："于传有之。"曰："臣弒[2]其君，可乎？"曰："贼仁者谓之'贼'，贼义者谓之'残'。残贼之人谓之'一夫'[3]。闻诛一夫纣矣，未闻弒君也。"

【译文】齐宣王问孟子："商汤流放了夏桀，武王讨伐商纣，有这回事吗？"孟子回答："史书上有记载。"宣王问："臣子以下犯上杀死君主，可以吗？"孟子回答说："残害仁的人被称作'贼'，残害义的人被称作'残'。残贼的人被称作'独夫'。我只听说过诛杀独夫纣的，没有听说过以下犯上杀死君主的。"

【英译】The king Hsüan of Chʻî asked, saying, 'Was it so, that Tʻang banished Chieh, and that king Wû smote Châu?' Mencius replied, 'It is so in the records.' The king said, 'May a minister then put his sovereign to death?' Mencius said, 'He who outrages the benevolence proper to his nature, is called a robber; he who outrages righteousness, is called a ruffian. The robber and ruffian we call a mere fellow. I have heard of the cutting off of the fellow Châu, but I have not heard of the putting a sovereign to death, in his case.'

【注释】

[1]"伐"的甲骨文写作用戈砍人头，其本义为砍杀，多用于诸侯之间的公开宣战。孟子曾指出讨和伐的不同："天子讨而不伐，诸侯伐而不讨。"（《孟子·告子下》）焦循在《孟子正义》中进一步解释说："讨者，上伐下也，伐者，敌国相征伐也。"后因常和"征"连用，逐渐有了褒义。武王继

承文王的遗志，推翻暴君纣王的统治，解救百姓于水火之中，是正义战争。理雅各和赖发洛将之翻译为"smote"，该词有侵袭之义，感情色彩与"伐"不同。亨顿将之翻译为"overthrew"，即"用武力推翻"，体现了"伐"的本义。刘殿爵的译文仅仅表明是进军，没有明显的感情色彩。

[2] "弑"和下文的"诛"都有杀的意思，但二者褒贬意不同。"弑"指地位卑下者违背礼制杀死尊者、长者，而"诛"则是正义者诛杀无道者。理雅各将"弑"翻译为"put to death"（杀死），赖发洛翻译为"slay"（谋杀），都没有准确翻译出"弑"的特殊含义。刘殿爵翻译为"regicide"（弑君），准确翻译出了"弑"的含义。

[3] "一夫"指的是那些残害"仁义"、众叛亲离、人人唾弃的人。理雅各按字面意思理解"一夫"为"仅仅是一个人"，赖发洛翻译为"churls"（粗野的人），刘殿爵翻译为"outcast"（被抛弃的人）。理雅各的译文过于照字面意思直译，没有体现出"一夫"的含义。赖发洛和刘殿爵的译文从不同的侧面体现了"一夫"的特征。相比较而言，赵甄陶的译文"a despot forsaken by all"准确翻译出了"一夫"的含义。

【原文】2.9　孟子见齐宣王[1]，曰："为巨室，则必使工师[2]求大木。工师得大木，则王喜，以为能胜其任也[3]。匠人斫而小之，则王怒，以为不胜其任矣。夫人幼而学之，壮而欲行之，王曰：'姑舍汝所学而从我。'则何如？今有璞玉于此，虽万镒[4]，必使玉人雕琢之。至于治国家，则曰：'姑舍汝所学而从我。'则何以异于教玉人之雕琢玉哉？"

【译文】孟子去拜见齐宣王，说道："如果要建造一所大房子，一定会命令工师去寻找大木料。工师找到大木料，王就会高兴，认为他能胜任工作。如果木匠将木料砍小了，那么王就会发怒，认为他不能胜任工作。有人从小就学一种本领，长大了想要运用，大王却说：'暂且放下你学的，听我的吧。'这能行吗？假设这里有未经雕琢的玉石，虽然价值极高，也一定会请玉石工匠去雕琢。到了治理国家，却说：'暂且放下你学的，听我的吧。'这和教玉石工匠如何雕琢玉石又有什么区别呢？"

【英译】Mencius, having an interview with the king Hsüan of Ch'î, said to him, 'If you are going to build a large mansion, you will surely cause the Master of the workmen to look out for large trees, and when he has found such large trees, you will be glad, thinking that they will answer for the intended object. Should the workmen hew them so as to make them too small, then your Majesty will be angry, thinking that they will not answer for the purpose. Now, a man spends his youth in learning the principles of right government, and, being grown up to vigour, he wishes to put them in practice; — if your Majesty says to him, "For the present put aside what you have learned, and follow me," what shall we say? Here now you have a gem unwrought, in the stone. Although it may be worth 240, 000 taels, you will surely employ a lapidary to cut and polish it. But when you come to the government of the State, then you say, — "For the present put aside what you have learned, and follow me." How is it that you herein act so differently from your conduct in calling in the lapidary to cut the gem?'

【注释】

[1] 本章通过在工师斫大木和玉人琢璞玉之间作类比，来说明术业有专攻，外行不应瞎指挥，指导内行如何行事。治理国家更应如此。君主不仅要善于选拔治国之才，更要礼遇、信任这些人才。礼遇、信任人才不仅仅是指言行举止上的恭敬，更重要的是要接受他们的正确意见，让他们可以放开手脚去做事，而不是处处束缚人才，限制人才，使他们不能展露才能，有所作为。

[2]"工师"是古代官名，指百工之长，即管理工匠的官员。理雅各将"工师"翻译为"Master of the workmen"（掌管工匠的人），赖发洛翻译为"master workman"（工匠管理者）。两位译者都翻译出了"工师"的基本含义。刘殿爵和赵甄陶则从孟子"求大木，为巨室"出发，将"工师"分别翻译为"the master carpenter"（木匠管理者）和"the master builder"（建筑大师）。

[3]对"以为能胜其任"有两种理解。一种认为"其"是指大木，将本句理解为"认为大木能承担建巨室的大任"；一种认为"其"是指工师，"认为工师能很好地履行他的责任"。理雅各和赖发洛的译文持第一种观点，即"大木可以实现建造巨室的大任"。刘殿爵和赵甄陶的译文支持第二种观点，认为是"工师能胜任他的工作"。从文意上看，如何利用大木建筑巨室是工师的强项，而王却凭借自己的认识妄加批判工师的行为是否称职，这无异于教玉人雕琢玉，教善于治国之人如何治理国家。因而刘殿爵和赵甄陶的译文更符合原文的意思。

[4]"镒"是古代的重量单位，一说二十两为一镒；一说二十四两为一镒。理雅各将"万镒"翻译为"240000 taels"（240000两）。显然，他认为"镒"为二十四两。由于"镒"在英文中没有对等词，而外国读者对"两"（taels）较为熟悉，因而他将"镒"换算成"两"来表达。赖发洛选择了外国人熟悉的"pounds"（磅）来翻译"镒"，虽然便于理解，但二者存在很大差异。刘殿爵音译"镒"为"yi"，以表明这是中国古代特有的重量单位，在英语中没有对等词。赵甄陶则根据文意将之意译为"great value"，即"很大的价值"。相比较而言，音译加注即保留了中国特有文化词的独特性，又能通过注解便于读者理解，不失为翻译中国特有文化词的较好选择。

【原文】2.10 齐人伐燕[1]，胜之。宣王问曰："或谓寡人勿取[2]，或谓寡人取之。以万乘之国伐万乘之国，五旬而举之，人力不至于此。不取，必有天殃。取之，何如？"孟子对曰："取之而燕

民悦，则取之。古之人有行之者，武王是也。取之而燕民不悦，则
勿取。古之人有行之者，文王是也。以万乘之国伐万乘之国，箪^[3]
食壶浆^[4]以迎王师，岂有他哉？避水火也。如水益深，如火益热，
亦运而已矣^[5]。"

【译文】齐国攻打燕国取得了胜利。齐宣王问孟子："有人劝我占
领燕国，有人劝我不要占领它。拥有万辆兵车的国家去攻打同样拥有万
辆兵车的国家，用了五十天就攻打下来了，仅凭人力是做不到的。不占
领的话，必然会受到上天的惩罚。占领它怎么样？"孟子回答说："占
领它，如果燕国百姓高兴，那就占领它。古人有这样做的，那就是周
武王。占领它，如果燕国百姓不高兴，那就不要占领它。古人有这样做
的，那就是周文王。拥有一万辆兵车的大国去攻打同样拥有一万辆兵车
的大国，被攻打国家的百姓却用筐盛着干饭，用壶盛着美酒去欢迎进攻
者，难道会有别的意思吗？只不过是想逃避他们正过着的水深火热的苦
日子。如果水更深，火更热，他们只好转向其他人求助了。"

【英译】The people of Ch'î attacked Yen，and conquered it. The
king Hsüan asked，saying，'Some tell me not to take possession of it
for myself，and some tell me to take possession of it. For a kingdom
of ten thousand chariots，attacking another of ten thousand chariots，
to complete the conquest of it in fifty days，is an achievement beyond
mere human strength. If I do not take possession of it，calamities
from Heaven will surely come upon me. What do you say to my taking
possession of it?' Mencius replied，'If the people of Yen will be
pleased with your taking possession of it，then do so.——Among the
ancients there was one who acted on this principle，namely king Wû.
If the people of Yen will not be pleased with your taking possession of
it，then do not do so.——Among the ancients there was one who acted on
this principle，namely king Wǎn. When，with all the strength of your

country of ten thousand chariots，you attacked another country of ten thousand chariots，and the people brought baskets of rice and vessels of congee，to meet your Majesty's host，was there any other reason for this but that they hoped to escape out of fire and water？If you make the water more deep and the fire more fierce，they will in like manner make another revolution.'

【注释】

[1] 孟子的政治思想具有鲜明的民本特色。他一贯主张君主应当把是否得到人民的支持和拥护作为自己行政和做出决定的依据，因为民意是天命的体现，"天视自我民视，天听自我民听"（《尚书·泰誓》）。

[2] 此处"取"的含义是占领、吞并。刘殿爵、赵甄陶和亨顿选择用"annex"翻译，理雅各选择用"take possession of"翻译，皆能体现"取"的含义。赖发洛选择用"keep"翻译，过于宽泛。

[3] "箪"是古代用竹或者苇编成的，用来盛饭的圆形器具。理雅各、刘殿爵和赵甄陶都将之翻译为"baskets"。他们的译文凸显了"Baskets"与"箪"的共同之处，即用竹子编织而成的圆形盛器。赖发洛将"箪"翻译为"trays"（盘、碟）则是关注二者在用途上的一致性，即都是盛饭的器皿。

[4] "浆"，是古代用米熬成的一种解渴的微酸饮品，用以代酒。刘殿爵和赵甄陶将之翻译为"drink"（饮品），基本能体现其含义。理雅各将之翻译为"congee"（粥），赖发洛翻译为"broth"（清汤或肉汤），不能体现"浆"的本质。

[5] 对"亦运而已矣"的理解存在分歧。一种以朱熹为代表，他在《四书集注》中解为"民将转而望救于他人"。杨伯峻不同意朱熹的注解，他认为"这一理解与'亦'和'而已矣'所表示的语气不合，恐未当"。他将此句解释为"那只是统治者由燕转为齐罢了"。笔者认为，从孟子的回答可以看出，孟子认为人民的意愿是君主决策的重要根据。人民之所以"箪食壶浆以迎王师"是为了"避水火"，如果"水益深，火益热，亦运而已矣"。

因而从篇章主旨和逻辑关系上看，"亦运而已矣"的主语是人民。朱熹的理解更符合原文的意思。理雅各将此句翻译为"they will in like manner make another revolution"（他们将会以同样的方式再一次转向他人）。理雅各将"亦"理解为"也"。为了便于读者理解，他根据文意增加了"another"，以表明与前面一样再一次"箪食壶浆以迎王师"。赖发洛的译文是"they will only turn once more"，他将"亦"理解为"只能"，将本句理解为"他们只能再一次转向（他人）"。赖发洛严格按照原文句子结构翻译，未对原文省略之处做出必要的添加。刘殿爵的译文也将"亦"理解为"只能"，不过根据文意对原文省略的地方做了适当添加，他的译文表明，百姓们别无选择，只能转向他处寻求援助。赵甄陶将之翻译为"they will have no other choice but to flee again"，即"他们将别无选择，只好再次逃跑"。相比较而言刘殿爵的"转向他处寻求帮助"更能体现百姓的主观能动性和人心向背的重要性，而"再次逃跑"之意略显消极。

【原文】2.11　齐人伐燕[1]，取之。诸侯将谋救燕。宣王曰："诸侯多谋伐寡人者[2]，何以待之？"孟子对曰："臣闻七十里为政于天下者[3]，汤是也。未闻以千里畏人者也。《书》曰：'汤一征，自葛始。'天下信之，东面而征，西夷怨；南面而征，北狄怨[4]，曰：'奚为后我？'民望之，若大旱之望云霓[5]也。归市者不止，耕者不变，诛其君而吊其民，若时雨降。民大悦。《书》曰：'徯我后，后来其苏。'今燕虐其民，王往而征之，民以为将拯己于水火之中也，箪食壶浆以迎王师。若杀其父兄，系累其子弟，毁其宗庙，迁其重器[6]，如之何其可也？天下固畏齐之强也，今又倍地而不行仁政，是动天下之兵也。王速出令，反其旄倪，止其重器，谋于燕众，置君而后去之，则犹可及止也。"

【译文】齐国人攻打燕国，并且吞并了它。其他诸侯国谋划着救助燕国。宣王说："很多国家谋划着要攻打我，我应该怎么办？"孟子回答说："我听说过凭借方圆七十里的土地统治天下的人，就是商汤。但是我没有听说过凭借方圆千里的国土还害怕别人的。《尚书》说：'商汤初次征伐，从葛国开始。'天下的百姓都相信他，他去东方征伐，西方的百姓就会抱怨；去南方征伐，北方的百姓就会抱怨，他们说：'为什么要把我们放在后面？'百姓盼望他，就像久旱的人盼望乌云和虹霓一样。赶集的人像往常一样赶集，种庄稼的像往常一样下地。（他）诛杀暴君，安抚那些受迫害的百姓，就像及时雨一样。老百姓非常高兴。《尚书》说：'等待我们的君王，他来了我们可以重获新生！'现在燕国的君主虐待百姓，您去征伐，百姓认为您要解救他们于水火之中，都用筐盛着食物，用壶盛着饮品来欢迎您的军队。如果杀掉他们的父兄，捆绑他们的子弟，毁坏他们的宗庙，搬走他们的传国宝器，这怎么可以呢？天下本来就担心齐国强大，现在齐国的土地又扩大了一倍，但是却不实行仁政，这是挑动各国出兵啊。您赶快发布命令，放回老人和孩子，停止搬运燕国的宝器，再和燕国的人们商议，选立一位燕王，然后从燕国撤兵，这样还来得及阻止其他国家出兵。"

【英译】The people of Ch'î, having smitten Yen, took possession of it, and upon this, the princes of the various States deliberated together, and resolved to deliver Yen from their power. The king Hsüan said to Mencius, 'The princes have formed many plans to attack me: —how shall I prepare myself for them?' Mencius replied, 'I have heard of one who with seventy lî exercised all the functions of government throughout the kingdom. That was T'ang. I have never heard of a prince with a thousand lî standing in fear of others. It is said in the Book of History, As soon as T'ang began his work of executing justice, he commenced with Ko. The whole kingdom had confidence in him. When he pursued his work in the east, the rude tribes on the west murmured. So did those on the north, when he was engaged in the south. Their cry was— "Why does he put us last?" Thus，the people looked to him，as we look in a time of great drought to the clouds and rainbows. The frequenters of the markets stopped not. The husbandmen made no change in their operations. While he punished their rulers，he consoled the people. His progress was like the falling of opportune rain，and the people were delighted. It is said again in the Book of History，"We have waited for our prince long；the prince's coming will be our reviving！" Now the ruler of Yen was tyrannizing over his people，and your Majesty went and punished him. The people supposed that you were going to deliver them out of the water and the fire，and brought baskets of rice and vessels of congee，to meet your Majesty's host. But you have slain their fathers and elder brothers，and put their sons and younger brothers in confinement. You have pulled down the ancestral temple of the State，and are removing to Ch'î its precious vessels. How can such a course be deemed proper？ The rest of the kingdom is indeed jealously afraid of the strength of Ch'î；and now，when with a doubled territory you do not put in practice a benevolent government；—it is this which sets the arms of the kingdom in motion. If your Majesty will make haste to issue an ordinance，restoring your captives，old and young，stopping the removal of the precious vessels，and saying that，after consulting with the people of Yen，you will appoint them a ruler，and withdraw from the country；—in this way you may still be able to stop the threatened attack.'

【注释】

[1] 春秋战国时期，诸侯国之间战争不断。当时的许多思想家都发表自己对战争的看法。例如墨子的"非攻"思想，以及兵家的"慎战"主张。从孟子的言谈中可以看出，他反对为了一己私利，置百姓安危于不顾的战

争，支持诛无道、安百姓的正义战争。

[2] 刘殿爵认为此处的"多"是限定"诸侯"的，即"大多数诸侯正在考虑和我作战"。但是理雅各则认为"多"是用来限定"谋"的，指的是许多计划和策略。结合下文"动天下之兵也"可以看出，此句话应指许多诸侯在谋划，而非诸侯制定了许多计划。

[3] "臣"是古人的自称，表示自谦。《礼记·典礼》记载："夫礼者，自卑而尊人。"理雅各和刘殿爵将之翻译为"I"，赖发洛翻译为"Your liege"（您的臣民），两种译文从不同的侧面体现了"臣"的含义。"七十里为政于天下者"强调的是凭借仅仅方圆七十里的小国仍然可以成为统治整个天下的王。孟子举这个例子旨在说明，国土的大小并不是决定一个君主能否统一天下的决定因素，即使小国家的君主也可以统一天下。刘殿爵的译文"one who gained ascendancy over the Empire from the modest beginning of seventy lî square"准确再现了原文的内涵。

[4] 孟子通过反复和对仗，将人们对正义战争的期盼表现得淋漓尽致。刘殿爵的译文保留了原文的这一句式特点，而理雅各的译文则更符合英文的表达习惯。

[5] "云"是乌云，"霓"是虹霓，出于西方，是下雨的先兆。和刘殿爵直接用"a rainbow"翻译不同，其他译者多将"云霓"翻译为"clouds and rainbows"，而亨顿则将之意译为"rain"。

[6] 理雅各和刘殿爵分别将"重器"译为"precious vessels"（贵重的器皿）和"valuable vessels"（宝贵的器皿），赖发洛按字面意思直译为"heavy ware"（沉重的器皿）。"重器"指的是国家宝器，"重"在此处表达的是珍贵、宝贵的含义，因而理雅各和刘殿爵的译文更准确。

【原文】2.12　邹与鲁哄[1]。穆公问曰："吾有司死者三十三人，而民莫之死也[2]。诛之，则不可胜诛；不诛，则疾视其长上之死而不救[3]，如之何则可也？"孟子对曰："凶年饥岁，君之民老弱转乎沟壑，壮者散而之四方者，几千人矣[4]；而君之仓廪实，府库充，有司莫以告，是上慢而残下也。曾子曰：'戒之戒之！出乎尔者，反乎尔者也。'夫民今而后得反之也。君无尤焉。君行仁政，斯民亲其上，死其长矣[5]。"

【译文】邹国同鲁国发生了争斗。邹穆公问道："我的官吏在争斗中死了三十三人，但老百姓却没有一个为他们死的。杀了他们吧，人数太多；不杀吧，又恨他们眼睁睁地看着长官被杀却不去营救，怎么办才好呢？"孟子回答说："在灾荒年岁，您的百姓，年老体弱的被弃尸荒野，年轻体壮的四处逃荒，这样的人将近千人吧，但是您的谷仓中堆满了粮食，库房里装满了财宝，相关的官吏没有报告给您，这是官员怠慢渎职和残害百姓啊。曾子说：'警惕，警惕！你怎样去对待别人，别人也会怎样对待你。'现在是百姓报复的时刻了。您不要责备百姓了！您如果实行仁政，百姓就会爱护长官，并情愿为他们去效命。"

【英译】There had been a brush between Tsâu and Lû, when the duke Mû asked Mencius, saying, 'Of my officers there were killed thirty-three men, and none of the people would die in their defence. Though I sentenced them to death for their conduct, it is impossible to put such a multitude to death. If I do not put them to death, then there is the crime unpunished of their looking angrily on at the death of their officers, and not saving them. How is the exigency of the case to be met?' Mencius replied, 'In calamitous years and years of famine, the old and weak of your people, who have been found lying in the ditches and water-channels, and the able-bodied who have been scattered about to the four quarters, have amounted to several thousands. All the while, your granaries, O prince, have been stored with grain, and your treasuries and arsenals have been full, and not one of your officers has told you of the distress. Thus negligent have the superiors in your

State been，and cruel to their inferiors. The philosopher Tsǎng said，
"Beware，beware. What proceeds from you，will return to you again."
Now at length the people have paid back the conduct of their officers to
them. Do not you，O prince，blame them. If you will put in practice a
benevolent government，this people will love you and all above them，
and will die for their officers.'

【注释】

[1] 孟子在本章再次强调实行仁政的重要性。他认为统治者只有用仁
爱之心对待百姓，关心百姓疾苦，才能得到百姓的拥护和支持。否则，就会
众叛亲离，无人为之效命。"出乎尔者，反乎尔者"还告诉我们一个亘古不
变的真理：你想让别人如何对你，你就首先要这样对别人。"邹与鲁哄"是
孟子的母国邹国与鲁国在边界上发生的争斗，刘殿爵的译文"border clash"
（边界冲突），为读者准确明白地传递当时的历史事实。理雅的"brush"（小
冲突）和赖发洛的"brawl"（斗殴）也能翻译出"哄"的字面意思。

[2] 在翻译"民莫之死"时，理雅各、刘殿爵、赵甄陶都理解为"民
莫肯为之死"，即"没有一个百姓愿意为保卫（有司）而送命"。赖发洛则将
之翻译为"but none of the people died"，即"没有一个百姓丧命"。很明显，
赖发洛将本句和前面一句理解为对比关系，"虽然有三十三个长官丢了命，
但是没有一个百姓丧命"。但是从后文"疾视其长上之死而不救"和"君无
尤焉"可以看出，理雅各、刘殿爵和赵甄陶的翻译更符合原文的意思。

[3] 对于这句话有两种理解，一种以朱熹为代表，认为是"民怨其上，
故疾视其死而不救也"。即百姓对长官充满怨恨，所以满怀敌意地看着他们
的长官被杀而不营救。刘殿爵、赵甄陶、理雅各、赖发洛等译者皆持这种观
点。一种以杨伯峻为代表，他指出："'疾'是主要动词，相当于论语卫灵公
第十五的'君子疾没世而名不称焉'和季氏第十六的'君子疾夫舍曰欲之而
必为之辞'的'疾'，'视其长上之死而不救'一句作为'疾'的宾语。"杨
伯峻将之译为"他们瞪着两眼看着长官被杀却不去营救，实在可恨"。从后

文的"君无尤焉"可以看出，穆公是在指责百姓不为长上效命，因而杨伯峻的观点更符合原文的意思。

[4] 在翻译"几千人矣"时，理雅各和赖发洛都将"几"理解为数词，理雅各翻译为"several thousands"（几千人），赖发洛翻译为"thousands of"（数千人）。刘殿爵将"几"理解为"副词，几乎，差不多"，翻译为"close on a thousand"。

[5] 理雅各认为"上"指"君主和一般官员"，"长"指"一般官员不包括君主"。赖发洛将"上"翻译为"those over them"（地位高于他们的人），将"长"翻译为"chiefs"（长官），虽然在用词上和理雅各略有差异，但内涵基本一致。刘殿爵和赵甄陶则认为"上"和"长"内涵一致，都指"上级"。

【原文】2.13　滕文公问曰[1]："滕，小国也，间于齐、楚。事[2]齐乎？事楚乎？"孟子对曰："是谋[3]非吾所能及也。无已，则有一焉：凿斯池也，筑斯城也，与民守之，效死而民弗去[4]，则是可为也。"

【译文】滕文公问道："滕国是一个小国，处在齐国和楚国之间，是服事齐国呢，还是服事楚国呢？"孟子回答道："这样的谋略我想不出来。一定要我谈谈，就有一个主意：挖深护城河，筑牢城墙，和百姓一起守卫，百姓宁肯献出生命，也不愿意离开，这样就有办法了。"

【英译】The duke Wǎn of Tʻǎng asked Mencius, saying, 'Tʻǎng is a small kingdom, and lies between Chʻî and Chʻû. Shall I serve Chʻî? Or shall I serve Chʻû?' Mencius replied, 'This plan which you propose is beyond me. If you will have me counsel you, there is one thing I can suggest. Dig deeper your moats; build higher your walls; guard them as well as your people. In case of attack, be prepared to die in your defence, and have the people so that they will not leave you；—this is a proper course.'

【注释】

[1]　在本章中，滕文公向孟子提出一个当时各诸侯国普遍关心的问题，即在诸侯争战不断、弱肉强食的战国时期如何保全国家，免遭灭国之灾。孟子以推行、实践仁政为己任，对如何侍奉强国之类的问题不屑关注，因而回答"是谋非吾所能及"。尽管如此，对于滕文公的礼遇他还是报之以李，提出了自己的应对之策，即增强防御力量，与民同仇敌忾，共同捍卫国家。

[2]　此处的"事"是动词，含义是"依附"。理雅各、赖发洛和赵甄陶都译为"serve"（侍候），刘殿爵翻译为"be subservient to"（屈从、依附）。译文都能体现出原文的意思。

[3]　"是谋非吾所能及也"是对"事齐乎？事楚乎？"的回答，因而刘殿爵和赵甄陶都选择用"question"翻译"谋"。赖发洛则选择用"plots"翻译，但该词多指阴谋诡计，用在此处不妥。

[4]　"效死而民弗去"，理雅各的译文能翻译出其含义，但过于冗长。赖发洛将之翻译为"If in face of death the people do not flee"。他的译文虽然简洁，但只是突出了人们的勇敢，临危不惧，未能体现百姓与王同仇敌忾之意。刘殿爵的译文"If they would rather die than desert you"，则表现了百姓宁死不屈，和君主共同捍卫国家的决心。

【原文】 2.14　滕文公问曰[1]："齐人将筑薛，吾甚恐，如之何则可？"孟子对曰："昔者大王居邠，狄人侵之[2]，去之岐山之下居焉。非择而取之，不得已也。苟为善，后世子孙必有王者矣[3]。君子[4]创业垂统[5]，为可继也。若夫成功，则天也。君如彼何哉？强为善而已矣。"

【译文】 滕文公问："齐国人将要加强薛地的城池，我特别担心，怎么办呢？"

孟子回答："以前太王居住在邠地，狄人侵犯该地。他就离开，搬到岐山下居住。这不是主动选择，实在是不得已。如果能实行善政，后代子孙一定会有成为统一天下的王者。君子创立功业，并传给子孙后代，就是为了能代代相传。至于能否成功，则由天命决定。您怎样去对付齐国呢？只有努力推行善政罢了。"

【英译】The duke Wǎn of T'ǎng asked Mencius, saying, 'The people of Ch'î are going to fortify Hsieh. The movement occasions me great alarm. What is the proper course for me to take in the case?' Mencius replied, 'Formerly, when king T'âi dwelt in Pin, the barbarians of the north were continually making incursions upon it. He therefore left it, went to the foot of mount Ch'î, and there took up his residence. He did not take that situation, as having selected it. It was a matter of necessity with him. If you do good, among your descendants, in after generations, there shall be one who will attain to the royal dignity. A prince lays the foundation of the inheritance, and hands down the beginning which he has made, doing what may be continued by his successors. As to the accomplishment of the great result, that is with Heaven. What is that Ch'î to you, O prince? Be strong to do good. That is all your business.'

【注释】

[1] 孟子在本章强调"善"的重要性。孟子认为"善政"对君主至关重要。君主推行"善政"，关心百姓疾苦，就会得到好的回报，长期保有并传承自己的基业。

[2] "狄"是我国古代北部的少数民族。理雅各和赖发洛在翻译时采取意译的方式，分别将之翻译为"the barbarians of the north"（北方的野蛮民族）和"the northern hordes"（北方的游牧部落）。刘殿爵则采取音译的方法。意译便于读者理解，音译能突出中国古代文化的特殊性。在翻译中国特有文化词语时可以将它们结合起来，用音译加注的方法翻译。在翻译"侵之"时，

理雅各译为"continually making incursions upon it"（不断侵袭它），赖发洛翻译为"harassed him"（反复袭击令他疲惫），刘殿爵译为"invaded Pin"（侵略邠）。很明显，理雅各和赖发洛认为"侵"是反复侵略、骚扰，而刘殿爵的译文仅陈述了一个入侵的事实。结合后面章节"事之以皮币，不得免焉；事之以犬马，不得免焉；事之以珠玉，不得免焉"可知，狄人是反复袭击邠地，并非单独一次侵略，因而理雅各和赖发洛的译文更准确。

[3]"苟为善，后世子孙必有王者矣"省略了主语，刘殿爵认为是泛指，理雅各则选择用第二人称"you"作主语，并用"shall be"句型将原文中的肯定和允诺之情表达了出来。"shall be"表将来时一般用于第一人称，在第一人称之外使用时，通常包含强烈的感情色彩，有强烈的鼓动和允诺的意味，很容易使听者为之所动，有助于说服滕文公行善政。

[4]理雅各将"君子"译为"A prince"（君主）。他认为在《孟子》一书中，"君子"一般指"君主"。从文意上看，虽然本章中的"君子"可以理解为"君主"，但认为《孟子》中的"君子"一般指"君主"不妥。在儒家思想中，"君子"虽然有时候指居上位的统治者，但在大多情况下是指那些品德高尚的人。赖发洛和刘殿爵都将"君子"翻译为"gentleman"（绅士）。在西方文化中，"绅士"是地位的象征，而中国的"君子"更侧重于德行方面，因而以"绅士"为"君子"的对等词不妥。但此处的"君子"指有地位的统治者，与"绅士"具有相似性。赵甄陶也根据文意将"君子"翻译为"a man of position"（有地位的人）。

[5]理雅各将"统"翻译为"beginning"（开端）。很明显，他的翻译受朱熹影响较深。朱熹认为："统，绪也。""绪"又有"开端"之意，因而理雅各将之翻译为"开端"。笔者认为，理雅各对"统"的翻译过于拘泥于字面意思。根据《高级汉语词典》，"统"有"世代相继的系统"之意，因而可以将"统"意译为"后世子孙"，"君子创业垂统，为可继也"可以翻译为"君子创立基业并把它传给子孙是为了能够世代相承"。这在文意上更清楚、更符合逻辑。赖发洛将"统"翻译为"clew"（线索、线团），取"统"

的本义"丝的头绪"之意。在希腊神话中，"clew"特指引领西修斯走出迷宫的线团。可见用"clew"翻译"统"的本义是恰当的。但正如前面所说，此处取"统"的引申义"后世子孙"更符合文意。刘殿爵将"统"翻译为"tradition"（传统）。这一翻译是对前代译文的创新。根据刘殿爵的译文，本句强调的重点是传统，而很明显，孟子在此处旨在强调"为可继也"。因而，从准确体现原文的意思上讲，译文的创新存在缺陷。相比较而言，赵甄陶的翻译"The reason why a man of position starts an enterprise is that he hopes it can be carried on by future generations."更为准确。

【原文】 2.15　滕文公问曰[1]："滕，小国也；竭力以事[2]大国[3]，则不得免焉，如之何则可？"孟子对曰："昔者大王居邠，狄人侵之。事之以皮币[4]，不得免焉；事之以犬马，不得免焉；事之以珠玉，不得免焉。乃属其耆老而告之曰：'狄人之所欲者，吾土地也。吾闻之也：君子[5]不以其所以养人者害人。二三子[6]何患乎无君？我将去之。'去邠，逾梁山，邑于岐山之下居焉。邠人曰：'仁人也，不可失也。'从之者如归市。或曰：'世守也，非身之所能为也。[7]效死勿去。'君请择于斯二者。"

【译文】 滕文公问道："滕国是个弱小的国家，尽力去服事大国，也免不了祸害，应该怎么办呢？"孟子回答："以前太王居住在邠地，狄人来侵略。送给他们毛皮和缯帛，也没有免于侵犯；送给他们狗和马，也没有免于侵犯；送给他们珍珠宝玉，也没有免于侵犯。于是便召集长老并告诉他们：'狄人想要的是我们的土地。我听说过：君子不能用养人之物祸害人。你们不必担心没有君主，我准备离开这儿。'太王离开邠地，越过梁山，在岐山下建造了一个城邑居住。邠人说：'这是位仁德的人，不能失去他。'追随他的人就像赶集一样。也有人说：'这是世代相传，应该守护的基业，不是我能擅自作主的。我宁可丢掉性命也不会离去。'您请从两者选一个。"

【英译】The duke Wăn of T'ăng asked Mencius, saying, 'T'ăng is a small State. Though I do my utmost to serve those large kingdoms on either side of it, we cannot escape suffering from them. What course shall I take that we may do so?' Mencius replied, 'Formerly, when king T'âi dwelt in Pin, the barbarians of the north were constantly making incursions upon it. He served them with skins and silks, and still he suffered from them. He served them with dogs and horses, and still he suffered from them. He served them with pearls and gems, and still he suffered from them. Seeing this, he assembled the old men, and announced to them, saying, "What the barbarians want is my territory. I have heard this, —that a ruler does not injure his people with that wherewith he nourishes them. My children, why should you be troubled about having no prince? I will leave this." Accordingly, he left Pin, crossed the mountain Liang, built a town at the foot of mount Ch'î, and dwelt there. The people of Pin said, "He is a benevolent man. We must not lose him." Those who followed him looked like crowds hastening to market. On the other hand, some say, 'The kingdom is a thing to be kept from generation to generation. One individual cannot undertake to dispose of it in his own person. Let him be prepared to die for it. Let him not quit it." I ask you, prince, to make your election between these two courses.'

【注释】

[1] 孟子在本章提出了他对土地的认识。他指出土地等生产资料的重要性，在于它们可以养民，使百姓的生活更加富足。当统治者为了争夺土地不惜牺牲百姓的生命时，土地也就失去了它应有的价值。而当时统治者却不能理解这一点。他们为了争城夺地，不顾百姓的生死，在孟子看来这是不明智的做法，是"以其所以养人者害人"。

[2] 理雅各和赖发洛都将"事"翻译为"serve"（侍奉）。笔者认为，"serve"一般指仆人对主子、臣下对君主的效忠和服侍，在此处用来形容小国对大国的态度不妥。战国时期，虽然诸侯国林立，但没有一个力量能统一全中国，因而当时国与国之间也仅仅是依附、联合的关系，而非臣属关系。刘殿爵将"事"翻译为"please"（取悦），将小国为求自保，依附、献媚，竭力取悦大国的形态体现得淋漓尽致。

[3] 赖发洛、刘殿爵、赵甄陶认为，此处的"大国"是泛指当时所有比滕国大的国家。在前文中，滕文公已经问过孟子，位于齐、楚之间的滕国，应当侍奉齐国还是楚国？因而理雅各认为"大国"指与滕国接壤的两大国。

[4] 此处的"币"并非今天人们所熟悉的钱币，而是指丝帛。正如朱熹在《集注》所说："皮，谓虎豹麋鹿之皮也。币，帛也。"

[5] 理雅各认为此处的"君子"特指统治者，赖发洛则统一翻译为"gentleman"，而刘殿爵的译文则习惯根据"君子"在不同语句中的不同含义，采用不同的词进行翻译。他认为此处的"君子"指的是有地位的人，因而将之翻译为"a man in authority"（当权者）。

[6] "子"是我国古代对男子的统称，"二三子"相当于今天的"你们诸位"。理雅各和赖发洛都将之翻译为"My children"。结合前文"属其耆老"可知，他召集的人是族内德高望重的老人，因而这一翻译不准确。刘殿爵将之翻译为"you，my friends"（阁下），赵甄陶翻译为"gentlemen"，基本能体现原文的意思。

[7] 孟子在本章列举了两种对待国土的情况，一种是为了使百姓免受战乱之苦而舍弃土地；另一种与之相反，认为国土是世代相传的基业，个人不能擅自舍弃。中国古籍用词言简意赅，为了使译文准确达意，译者在翻译时或意译，或根据上下文，对译文作恰当补充。刘殿爵在翻译"世守也，非身之所能为也"时采取意译策略，将之译为"This is the land of our forbears. It is not a matter for us to decide"，即"这是我们祖先的土地。我们并不能决定它的归属。"赖发洛将之译为"For generations we have been on guard. This

is not the work of one lifetime"（数代以来，我们一直在守护。这不是一个人用一生就可以完成的工作）。赖发洛的译文则突出了守卫国土的艰辛。

【原文】 2.16　鲁平公将出[1]，嬖人臧仓者请曰："他日君出，则必命有司所之。今乘舆[2]已驾矣，有司未知所之，敢请[3]。"公曰："将见孟子。"曰："何哉，君所为轻身以先于匹夫者？以为贤乎？[4]礼[5]义由贤者出，而孟子之后丧逾前丧。君无见焉[6]！"公曰："诺。"乐正子入见，曰："君奚为不见孟轲也？"曰："或告寡人曰：'孟子之后丧逾前丧。'是以不往见也。"曰："何哉，君所谓逾者？前以士，后以大夫；前以三鼎[7]，而后以五鼎与？"曰："否；谓棺椁衣衾之美也。"曰："非所谓逾也，贫富不同也。"乐正之见孟子，曰："克告于君，君为来见也。嬖人有臧仓者沮君，君是以不果来也。"曰："行，或使之；止，或尼之。行止，非人所能也。吾之不遇鲁侯，天也[8]。臧氏之子焉能使予不遇哉？"

【译文】 鲁平公准备出门，他宠幸的人臧仓请示道："您以前出去的时候，一定会告诉相关的官员去什么地方。现在车马已经都准备好了，管事的人还不知道您要去哪里，因此冒昧地来请示。"平公说："我准备去见孟子。"臧仓说："您不顾忌身份先去拜访一个普通人，为什么呢？您以为他是贤德的人吗？贤德的人遵循礼义，而孟子母亲的丧事超过了父亲的丧事，您不要去见他！"平公说："好。"乐正子进来拜见平公，问道："您为什么不去见孟轲呢？"平公说："有人告诉我：'孟子母亲的丧事超过了父亲的丧事。'所以不去见他了。"乐正子问："您所说的超过，是什么意思呢？是先前办父亲的丧事用士礼，后来办母亲的丧事用大夫礼吗？是先前用三个鼎，后来用五个鼎吗？"平公说："不，我指的是棺椁衣物的精美。"乐正子说："这不叫'超过'，只是前后贫富不同罢了。"乐正子去见孟子，说："我告诉鲁君，他打算来看您。可是他宠幸的小臣臧仓阻止了他，鲁君所以就不来了。"孟子说："来，是有一种力量在促使；不来，也是一种力量在阻止。来与不来，不是人力所能决定的。我不能和鲁侯相见，是天意。姓臧的那个小子，怎么能使我不和鲁侯相见呢?"

【英译】The duke P'ing of Lû was about to leave his palace, when his favourite, one Tsang Ts'ang, made a request to him, saying, 'On other days, when you have gone out, you have given instructions to the officers as to where you were going. But now, the horses have been put to the carriage, and the officers do not yet know where you are going. I venture to ask.' The duke said, 'I am going to see the scholar Măng' 'How is this?' said the other. 'That you demean yourself, prince, in paying the honour of the first visit to a common man, is, I suppose, because you think that he is a man of talents and virtue. By such men the rules of ceremonial proprieties and right are observed. But on the occasion of this Măng's second mourning, his observances exceeded those of the former. Do not go to see him, my prince.' The duke said, 'I will not.' The officer Yo-chăng entered the court, and had an audience. He said, 'Prince, why have you not gone to see Măng K'o?' The duke said, 'One told me that, on the occasion of the scholar Măng's second mourning, his observances exceeded those of the former. It is on that account that I have not gone to see him.' 'How is this!' answered Yo-chăng. 'By what you call "exceeding," you mean, I suppose, that, on the first occasion, he used the rites appropriate to a scholar, and, on the second, those appropriate to a great officer; that he first used three tripods, and afterwards five tripods.' The duke said, 'No; I refer to the greater excellence of the coffin, the shell, the grave-clothes, and the shroud.' Yo-chăng said, 'That cannot be called "exceeding." That was the difference between being poor and being rich.' After this, Yo-chǎng saw Mencius, and said to him, 'I told the prince about you, and he was consequently coming to see you, when one of his favourites, named Tsang Ts‘ang, stopped him, and therefore he did not come according to his purpose.' Mencius said, 'A man's advancement is effected, it may be, by others, and the stopping him is, it may be, from the efforts of others. But to advance a man or to stop his advance is really beyond the power of other men. My not finding in the prince of Lû a ruler who would confide in me, and put my counsels into practice, is from Heaven. How could that scion of the Tsang family cause me not to find the ruler that would suit me?'

【注释】

[1] 本章体现了孟子的天命观以及积极乐观的处世原则。孟子虽然认识到自己不能见鲁平公、进而实施自己的仁政思想是天命所定，但他不沮丧、不气馁，继续周游列国推广自己的政治思想。这也体现了儒家以天下为己任，知其不可为而为之的入世思想。

[2] 在古代，"乘舆"特指天子和诸侯所乘坐的车子。杨伯峻引贾谊《新书·等齐》篇说："'天子车曰乘舆，诸侯车曰乘舆，乘舆等也。'他虽然说的是汉初当时的制度，但必本于先秦。"理雅各和刘殿爵都将"乘舆"翻译为"carriage"（马车）。"乘舆"是古代中国文化中的特有词语，是乘车者身份的象征，在英语中没有对等词。虽然"carriage"不能完全再现"乘舆"的含义，但二者具有极大的相似性，因而用它翻译是合适的。而赖发洛将"乘舆"翻译为"car"。正如前文提到的，西方人看见"car"容易联想到拥有四个轮子在街上奔驰的汽车。

[3] "敢"是表示敬意的副词，没有实际意义。理雅各将之翻译为"I venture to ask"（我斗胆请示），赖发洛翻译为"made bold to ask"（我冒昧请示）。二人的译文不仅保留了原文句型，还体现了原文所含的谦卑之意。刘殿

爵的译文虽然也能体现原文的意思，但未能体现原文的句型和包含的谦卑之意。

[4] "何哉，君所为轻身以先于匹夫者？以为贤乎？"有两种断句。一种如本文所示，受到杨伯峻等国内学者的支持。杨伯峻认为："这是一倒装句，'君所为轻身以先于匹夫者'为主语，后置，'何'以疑问词作谓语，先置。"另一种断句是"何哉？君所为轻身以先于匹夫者，以为贤乎？"理雅各的译文同第一种断句，根据他的译文，臧仓只是询问国君首先去会见孟子的原因，未等国君回答，紧接着又提出了自己的推测。刘殿爵将之译为"I am amazed! Is it because you think him a good and wise man that you lower yourself in taking the initiative towards a meeting with a common fellow?"在他的译文中，"何哉？"不是用来表疑问，而是用来表示说话者的惊异之情。根据他的译文，臧仓的惊讶来自两个方面。首先，他对鲁平公去见孟子感到非常吃惊。当时的等级森严，礼仪繁杂，一般都是臣下去拜见君主，或接受君主召见，而君主首先去会见臣下的例子实属罕见，因而他对国君首先去见孟子感到吃惊。其次，他联系到当时在各诸侯国君中盛行的礼贤之风做出大胆推测，鲁平公有可能是因为孟子的贤德才主动去会见他。臧仓对此也感到惊讶，从后文的论述中可以看出，在他心里，孟子并非是一个贤者。虽然这两种断句都能传达出原文的意思，但是笔者认为，与理雅各的译文相比，刘殿爵的译文将臧仓对孟子的轻视、诋毁之情体现得更淋漓尽致。

[5] 译者对"礼"的翻译侧重点各不相同。理雅各将之翻译为"rules of ceremonial proprieties"（仪式上应遵循的礼仪准则）。根据译文可以看出，他认为此处的"礼"指等级社会的典章制度，规定在重大场合上应当遵循的基本礼节和程序。赖发洛翻译为"Good form"（有礼貌的态度）。显然，他认为"礼"是发自内心的尊敬和敬意在外表和行动上的体现。刘殿爵翻译为"rites"（仪礼，典礼）。"rites"强调在重大仪式和场合应遵循的基本形式和惯例。从后文臧仓对孟子"后丧逾前丧"的指责可以看出，此处的"礼"指的是对在丧葬等重大仪式上应当遵循的基本形式和程序的规定，因而理雅各和刘殿爵对"礼"的翻译更准确。

[6]"君无见焉"是臧仓对鲁平公的建议和请求。从身份上看，他是一个受君主宠爱、身份卑下的小人。在向君主提出建议时，他不可能像刚正不阿的忠贞之臣那样，为避免君主犯错，严词告诫、指责君主不要去做某事。理雅各翻译为"Do not go to see him, my prince."（不要去见他，君主）这一翻译从语气上讲过于强势，有较强的告诫之意。赖发洛翻译为"My lord ought not to see him."（君主不应该去见他）则暗含有指责之意。刘殿爵的译文是"My lord, I beg you not to go to see him"（君主啊，我请求您不要去见他），他的译文更符合臧仓的身份。

[7]"鼎"原为古代的炊器，又为祭祀时用来盛动物类祭品的礼器和墓葬的冥器，三足两耳。按照古代的礼制，身份不同祭祀时所用鼎的数量也不同。《春秋公羊传》桓公二年何休注云："礼祭，天子九鼎，诸侯七，卿大夫五，元士三也。"孟子的父亲去世时，孟子的身份为士，因此祭祀父亲时用三鼎；等到他母亲去世时，孟子已成为大夫，所以祭祀母亲用五鼎。理雅各将"鼎"翻译为"tripods"。"tripod"指的是有三条腿的物品，理雅各用它来翻译"鼎"是因为二者在外形上具有"三足"的相似性，但未能准确介绍其作用。赖发洛将"鼎"翻译为"urns"。"urns"通常有脚架或底座的容器，如瓮、缸和水壶等，和鼎具有很大差距，不能准确再现中国古代特有物品"鼎"。刘殿爵翻译为"tripods of offerings"。如前面所说，"tripod"指的是有三条腿的物品，和"鼎"在外形上具有相似性。"offering"有祭品之意，体现了鼎的功能。因而刘殿爵对"鼎"的翻译可谓形神兼备，向读者准确介绍了中国特有物品。

[8]"吾之不遇鲁侯，天也。"理雅各的译文不仅翻译出了字面意思，还翻译出了本句所包含的暗含之意。"不遇鲁侯"不仅仅是指此次会面未能成行，还指鲁侯不能得到孟子的辅助，成为统一天下的王。孟子认为，鲁侯不能成为相信他、支持他实现政治抱负的君主是由上天决定的。刘殿爵的译文仅翻译出了原文的字面意思，即"It is due to Heaven that I failed to meet the Marquis of Lu"（不能和鲁侯会面是由上天决定的）。

卷 三

公孙丑章句上

【原文】3.1 公孙丑问曰[1]："夫子当路于齐，管仲、晏子之功，可复许乎？"孟子曰："子诚齐人也。知管仲、晏子而已矣。或问乎曾西曰：'吾子[2]与子路孰贤？'曾西蹙然曰：'吾先子[3]之所畏也。'曰：'然则吾子与管仲孰贤？'曾西艴然[4]不悦，曰：'尔何曾比予于管仲？管仲得君如彼其专也，行乎国政如彼其久也，功烈如彼其卑也，尔何曾比予于是？'"曰："管仲，曾西之所不为也，而子为我愿之乎？"曰："管仲以其君霸，晏子以其君显。管仲、晏子犹不足为与？"曰："以齐王，由反手也。"曰："若是，则弟子之惑滋甚。且以文王之德，百年而后崩，犹未洽于天下；武王、周公继之，然后大行。今言王若易然，则文王不足法与？"曰："文王何可当也？由汤至于武丁，贤圣之君六七作，天下归殷久矣，久则难变也。武丁朝诸侯，有天下，犹运之掌也。纣之去武丁未久也，其故家遗俗，流风善政，犹有存者；又有微子、微仲、王子比干、箕子、胶鬲，皆贤人也，相与辅相之，故久而后失之也。尺地，莫非其有也；一民，莫非其臣也；然而文王犹方百里起，是以难也。齐人有言曰：'虽有智慧，不如乘势；虽有镃基，不如待时。'今时则易然也。夏后、殷、周之盛，地未有过千里者也，而齐有其地矣；鸡鸣狗吠相闻，而达乎四境，而齐有其民矣。地不改辟矣，民不改

聚矣，行仁政而王，莫之能御也。且王者之不作，未有疏于此时者
也；民之憔悴于虐政，未有甚于此时者也。饥者易为食，渴者易为
饮。孔子曰：'德之流行，速于置邮[5]而传命。'当今之时，万乘之
国行仁政，民之悦之，犹解倒悬也。故事半古之人，功必倍之，惟
此时为然。"

【译文】公孙丑问道："如果您在齐国当政，管仲、晏子的功业可
以再度兴起吗？"孟子说："你真是一个齐国人。只知道管仲、晏子。有
人曾经问曾西说：'先生您和子路谁更贤能？'曾西不安地说道：'他是
我父亲所敬畏的人。'那人又问：'那么，你和管仲相比，谁更贤能？'
曾西非常不高兴地说道：'你为何竟然拿我跟管仲相比？管仲得到君主
的信任是那样地专一，掌握国家的政权那样长久，而功绩却那样地微
小。你为什么竟拿我跟他相比？'"孟子说："管仲是曾西都不愿意效仿
的人，你以为我愿意吗？"公孙丑说："管仲使他的君主称霸天下，晏子
使他的君主显名诸侯。难道管仲、晏子不值得效仿吗？"孟子说："对齐
王来说，易如反掌。"公孙丑说："要是这样，学生更加迷惑了。像文王
如此高的德行，活了将近一百岁才去世，仍然没有使天下和洽，武王、
周公继承了他的事业，然后王道才广泛推行。现在你说齐王统一天下很
容易，那么，文王也不值得效法吗？"孟子说："怎么能和文王比呢？从
汤到武丁，贤明的君主有六七个，天下的百姓归服殷朝也很长时间了，
时间长了就很难变化。武丁使诸侯归顺，治理天下，就像在手中运转东
西一样。纣王统治的时期离武丁时期并不太久，当时的世家和习俗、遗
风和善政仍有存蓄；又有微子、微仲、王子比干、箕子、胶鬲等贤德的
人一同辅助，所以用了好长的时间才亡国。当时没有一尺土地不归纣王
所有，没有一个百姓不是纣王的臣民。然而文王仅仅从方圆百里的国土
起步，所以很难。正如齐国人所说：'虽然有智慧，不如借形势；虽然
有锄头，不如待农时。'在现在的形势下要王天下非常容易：即使在夏、
商、周兴盛的年代，国土也没有超过方圆千里，而齐国有辽阔的土地；

鸡鸣狗叫的声音，从边界都能听到，而齐国有这么多的百姓。土地不需要再开拓，百姓不需要再增加，通过行仁政而成为统一天下的王，没有人能够抵抗。而且统一天下的王者不出现的时间，从来没有这么长过；百姓被暴政折磨的困顿，也没有比现在更厉害的。挨饿的人不挑食物，受渴的人不挑饮品。孔子说：'德政的流行，比设立驿站传递命令还要迅速。'现在这个时候，拥有万辆兵车的大国实行仁政，百姓会非常高兴，就像倒挂的人被解救了一样。所以，'事半功倍'就在此时啊。"

【英译】Kung-sun Ch'âu asked Mencius, saying, 'Master, if you were to obtain the ordering of the government in Ch'î, could you promise yourself to accomplish anew such results as those realized by Kwan Chung and Yen?' Mencius said, 'You are indeed a true man of Ch'î. You know about Kwan Chung and Yen, and nothing more. Some one asked Tsǎng Hsî, saying, "Sir, to which do you give the superiority, —to yourself or to Tsze-lû?" Tsǎng Hsî looked uneasy, and said, "He was an object of veneration to my grandfather." "Then," pursued the other, "Do you give the superiority to yourself or to Kwan Chung?" Tsǎng Hsî, flushed with anger and displeased, said, "How dare you compare me with Kwan Chung? Considering how entirely Kwan Chung possessed the confidence of his prince, how long he enjoyed the direction of the government of the State, and how low, after all, was what he accomplished, —how is it that you liken me to him?"' 'Thus,' concluded Mencius, 'Tsǎng Hsî would not play Kwan Chung, and is it what you desire for me that I should do so?' Kung-sun Ch'âu said, 'Kwan Chung raised his prince to be the leader of all the other princes, and Yen made his prince illustrious, and do you still think it would not be enough for you to do what they did?' Mencius answered, 'To raise Ch'î to the royal dignity would be as easy as it is to turn round the hand.' 'So!' returned the other. 'The perplexity of your disciple is hereby very much increased. There was king Wăn, moreover, with all the virtue which belonged to him; and who did not die till he had reached a hundred years; —and still his influence had not penetrated throughout the kingdom. It required king Wû and the duke of Châu to continue his course, before that influence greatly prevailed. Now you say that the royal dignity might be so easily obtained; —is king Wăn then not a sufficient object for imitation?' Mencius said, 'How can king Wăn be matched? From T'ang to Wû-ting there had appeared six or seven worthy and sage sovereigns. The kingdom had been attached to Yin for a long time, and this length of time made a change difficult. Wû-ting had all the princes coming to his court, and possessed the kingdom as if it had been a thing which he moved round in his palm. Then, Châu was removed from Wû-ting by no great interval of time. There were still remaining some of the ancient families and of the old manners, of the influence also which had emanated from the earlier sovereigns, and of their good government. Moreover, there were the viscount of Wei and his second son, their Royal Highnesses Pî-kan and the viscount of Ch'î, and Kâo-ko, all men of ability and virtue, who gave their joint assistance to Châu in his government. In consequence of these things, it took a long time for him to lose the throne. There was not a foot of ground which he did not possess. There was not one of all the people who was not his subject. So it was on his side, and king Wăn at his beginning had only a territory of one hundred square li. On all these accounts, it was difficult for him immediately to attain to the royal dignity. The people of Ch'î have a saying— "A man may have wisdom and discernment, but that is not like embracing the favourable opportunity. A man may have instruments of husbandry，but that is not like waiting for the farming seasons." The present time is one in which the royal dignity may be easily attained. In the flourishing periods of the Hsiâ，Yin，and Châu dynasties，the royal domain did not exceed a thousand lî，and Ch'î embraces so much territory. Cocks crow and dogs bark to one another，all the way to the four borders of the State：—so Ch'î possesses the people. No change is needed for the enlarging of its territory：no change is needed for the collecting of a population. If its ruler will put in practice a benevolent government，no power will be able to prevent his becoming sovereign. Moreover，never was there a time farther removed than the present from the rise of a true sovereign：never was there a time when the sufferings of the people from tyrannical government were more intense than the present. The hungry readily partake of any food，and the thirsty of any drink. Confucius said，"The flowing progress of virtue is more rapid than the transmission of royal orders by stages and couriers." At the present time，in a country of ten thousand chariots，let benevolent government be put in practice，and the people will be delighted with it，as if they were relieved from hanging by the heels. With half the merit of the ancients，double their achievements is sure to be realized. It is only at this time that such could be the case.'

【注释】

[1] 通过孟子与公孙丑的对话可以看出，孟子认为社会治理方式有王道和霸道两种。他周游列国，致力于推行王道，对霸道所取得的成绩持否定态度，这从他对管仲的评价中可以看出来。管仲是春秋时期著名的政治家和思想家，他辅佐齐桓公改革内政外交，使齐国成为当时最强大的诸侯国。但孟子却对管仲的成就持蔑视态度。他认为在管仲所处的时代，实行"王道"

是轻而易举的事情，而管仲却为君主谋求眼前利益，置"王道"于不顾，这是不明智也是不值得推崇的。

[2]"吾子"在此处是敬语，可译为"先生您"，亨顿将之翻译为"you"（你），没有体现出问话者对曾西的尊敬之情。问话者将曾西和子路相提并论，可见他对曾西是非常尊敬的。理译本和刘译本体现了原文中所蕴含的尊敬之情。

[3] 译者对"先子"的含义认识不同。理译本将"吾先子"理解为"我的祖父"，认为曾西为曾参之孙。东汉赵岐和南宋朱熹亦持此种观点。但此说很早便遭到人们质疑。宋代王应麟在《困学纪闻》卷八中指出："曾西，《注》以为曾子之孙，《集注》因之。《经典序录》：曾申，字子西，曾参之子。子夏以《诗》传曾申，左丘明作《传》以授曾申。楚斗宜申、公子申，皆字子西，则曾西之为曾申无疑。"明代陈耀文《经典稽疑》、胡爌《拾遗录》、清代阎若璩《古文尚书疏证》与《四书释地》、陆陇其《四书讲义困勉录》、毛奇龄《四书剩言》、朱彝尊《经义考》与《孔子门人考》等著作中均赞同此说。可见，"先子"应是古代对亡父的称呼。正如焦循《正义》所说："称'先子'者，谓父，非谓祖父也。"杨伯峻亦指出："这里的'先子'指其父亲曾参（孔子弟子，与子路为同学，但年辈晚于子路）。"亨顿、刘殿爵和赵甄陶都译"先子"为"父"，他们的译文准确再现了原文的含义。

[4]"艴然"，恼怒、生气的样子，将孟子不愿意和管仲相提并论的感情体现得淋漓尽致。理雅各受赵岐注"愠怒色"的影响，将之翻译为"flushed with anger"（气得满脸通红），形神兼备地再现了孟子当时恼怒的情景。刘殿爵的译文能体现"艴然"的意思，但是在传神和表达的恼怒程度上略显不足。

[5]"置"，多解释为驿站。朱熹注曰："置，驿也。邮，音尤，驿也。所以传命也。"理雅各将之翻译为"stages and couriers"。虽然他也认为"置"和"邮"都是驿站，但在翻译中突出了二者的区别，即"以马传递为置，以人传递为邮"。刘殿爵和赵甄陶则统一译为"posting stations"。显然，三位

译者都认为"置邮"为驿站。但是刘殿爵在后来的文章中又提出一种新的理解："'置'是动词，而'置邮'应释为'设立驿站。'"刘士红也在2007年发文指出："汉代以前'置'没有'驿站'之意……'置邮而传命'中的'置'不是'驿站'而应该像其它绝大部分汉代以前出现的'置'一样解释为'设置'。"

【原文】3.2　公孙丑问曰[1]："夫子加齐之卿相，得行道焉，虽由此霸王，不异矣。如此，则动心[2]否乎？"孟子曰："否；我四十不动心。"曰："若是，则夫子过孟贲远矣。"曰："是不难，告子先我不动心。"曰："不动心有道乎？"曰："有。北宫黝之养勇也：不肤桡，不目逃，思以一豪挫于人，若挞之于市朝[3]；不受于褐宽博，亦不受于万乘之君；视刺万乘之君，若刺褐夫；无严诸侯，恶声至，必反之。孟施舍之所养勇也，曰：'视不胜犹胜也；量敌而后进，虑胜而后会，是畏三军[4]者也。舍岂能为必胜哉？能无惧而已矣。'孟施舍似曾子，北宫黝似子夏。夫二子之勇，未知其孰贤，然而孟施舍守约也。昔者曾子谓子襄曰：'子好勇乎？吾尝闻大勇于夫子矣：自反而不缩，虽褐宽博，吾不惴焉[5]；自反而缩，虽千万人，吾往矣。'孟施舍之守气，又不如曾子之守约也。"曰："敢问夫子之不动心与告子之不动心，可得闻与？""告子曰：'不得于言，勿求于心，不得于心，勿求于气。'[6]不得于心，勿求于气，可；不得于言，勿求于心，不可。夫志，气之帅也；气，体之充也。夫志至焉，气次焉[7]；故曰：'持其志，无暴其气。'""既曰'志至焉，气次焉'，又曰'持其志，无暴其气'者，何也？"曰："志壹则动气，气壹则动志也。今夫蹶者趋者，是气也，而反动其心。""敢问夫子恶乎长？"曰："我知言，我善养吾浩然之气[8]。""敢问何谓浩然之气？"曰："难言也。其为气也，至大至刚，以直养而无害，则塞于天地之间。其为气也，配义与道；无是，馁也。是集义所生者，非义袭而取之也。行有不慊于心，则馁矣。我故曰，告子未尝知义，以其外之也。必有事焉，而勿正[9]，心勿忘，勿助长也。无若宋人然：宋人有闵其苗之不长而揠之者，芒芒然归，谓其人曰：'今日病矣！予助苗长矣！'其子趋而往视之，苗则槁矣。天下之不助苗长者寡矣。以为无益而舍之者，不耘苗者也；助之长者，揠苗者也，非徒无益，而又害之。""何谓知言？"曰："诐辞知其所蔽，淫辞知其所陷，邪辞知其所离，遁辞知其所穷。生于其心，害于其政；发于其政，害于其事。圣人复起，必从吾言矣。""宰我、子贡善为说辞，冉牛、闵子、颜渊善言德行。孔子兼之，曰：'我于辞命，则不能也。'然则夫子既圣矣乎？"曰："恶！是何言也！昔者子贡问于孔子曰：'夫子圣矣乎？'孔子曰：'圣则吾不能，我学不厌而教不倦也。'子贡曰：'学不厌，智也；教不倦，仁也。仁且智，夫子既圣矣。'夫圣，孔子不居，是何言也？""昔者窃闻之，子夏、子游、子张皆有圣人之一体，冉牛、闵子、颜渊则具体而微。敢问所安？"曰："姑舍是。"曰："伯夷、伊尹何如？"曰："不同道。非其君不事，非其民不使；治则进，乱则退，伯夷也。何事非君，何使非民；治亦进，乱亦进，伊尹也。可以仕则仕，可以止则止，可以久则久，可以速则速，孔子也。皆古圣人也，吾未能有行焉。乃所愿，则学孔子也。""伯夷、伊尹于孔子，若是班乎？"曰："否，自有生民以来，未有孔子也。"曰："然则有同与？"曰："有。得百里之地而君之，皆能以朝诸侯，有天下；行一不义、杀一不辜而得天下，皆不为也，是则同。"曰："敢问其所以异？"曰："宰我、子贡、有若，智足以知圣人，污不至阿其所好。宰我曰：'以予观于夫子，贤于尧舜远矣。'子贡曰：'见其礼[10]而知其政，闻其乐而知其德。由百世之后，等百世之王，莫之能违也。自生民以来，未有夫子也。'有若曰：'岂惟民哉？麒麟之于走兽，凤凰之于飞鸟，太山之于丘垤，河海之于行潦，类也；圣人之于民，亦类也。出于其类，拔乎其萃。自生民以来，未有盛于孔子也。'"

【译文】公孙丑问道："如果老师做了齐国的卿相，可以实现自己的主张，由此成就了霸业和王业，也不奇怪。如果是这样，您是否会动心呢？"孟子说："不，我四十岁开始就不再动心了。"公孙丑说："这样的话老师比孟贲厉害多了。"孟子说："这并不难，告子比我还早做到了不动心。"公孙丑说："有什么方法可以做到不动心吗？"孟子说："有。北宫黝在培养勇气的时候，肌肤被刺也不退缩，眼睛被戳也不逃避。他认为受一点点挫折，就好像在大庭广众之下挨鞭打一样。他不受百姓的侮辱，也不受大国君主的侮辱。把刺杀大国君主看作和刺杀普通百姓一样。不畏惧诸侯，被骂了一定反击。孟施舍是这样培养勇气，他说：'我把不能战胜的看作是可以战胜的。如果先估量敌人的强弱才前进，先考虑胜败才交锋，这是畏惧强大的敌人啊。我哪能一定打胜仗呢？只是能够无所畏惧罢了。'孟施舍像曾子，北宫黝像子夏。这两个人（培养）勇气，不知道哪个更好，但是孟施舍抓住了关键。以前曾子对子襄说：'你喜欢勇敢吗？我曾经从老师孔子那里听到过何为大勇：自我反省，如果我理亏的话，看到普通人我也会害怕；自我反省，如果理在我，虽然有千万人，我也勇往直前。'孟施舍在守气方面，又不如曾子抓住了关键。"公孙丑说："请问老师的不动心和告子的不动心，可以让我听听吗？"孟子说："告子说：'如果你不能理解语言，不要在内心中去寻求；如果（一些东西）在心里难以理解，不要在气中寻求满足。'心里难以理解，不要在气中寻求满足是可以的。不能理解语言，不要在内心中去探求是不对的。志是气的主帅，气则充满身体。志到了哪里，气也会随之而来。所以说：'要坚定自己的志，不要滥用气。'公孙丑说："您既说'志到了哪里，气也会随之而来'，又说'要坚定自己的志，不要滥用气'。这是为什么？"孟子说："志若专一，就会鼓动气，气若专一，也会影响到志。那些跌倒和奔跑的人，是气专一而影响到心。"公孙丑问："请问老师在哪方面擅长？"孟子说："我能了解别人的言辞，也擅长培养浩然之气。"公孙丑问："请问什么是浩然之气？"孟子说："很难用语言说。那种气，最伟大，最刚强。用义去培养它而不去伤害，就会充满天地之间。那种气，必须用义和道培养，如果不是这样，就会丧失力量。那种气，是由义积聚而产生，不是偶然的义的行为就可以获得的。行为只要愧于心，就会气馁。所以我说，告子不懂义，因为他认为义是外在的。一定要培养它，但不要有预期的目的，不要忘记它，但也不能帮助它生长。不要像宋国人那样。宋国有个人担心禾苗不长而去把它拔高，十分疲倦地回去，对家人说：'今天累坏了，我帮助禾苗生长了！'他儿子跑去一看，禾苗都枯萎了。天下不帮助禾苗生长的人很少。认为培养没有什么好处而不去干的，是种庄稼不锄草的人；帮助它生长的人是拔苗的人。（这种助长行为）不仅没有好处，反而会伤害它。"公孙丑问："怎么样才算知言呢？"孟子说："片面的言辞知道它片面的地方；浮夸的言辞知道它失真的地方；不合正道的言辞知道它背离正道的地方；躲闪的言辞知道它理屈的地方。这四种言辞，从心中产生，必会对政治产生危害；在政治中出现，必会危及国家的具体工作。如果圣人复出，肯定会认可我的话。"公孙丑说："宰我、子贡擅长言语，冉牛、闵子、颜渊擅长德行，孔子兼而有之，但他说：'在言辞方面，我太不擅长。'那么，先生您已经是圣人了吧？"孟子说："哎，说的什么话！以前子贡问孔子说：'老师已经是圣人了吧？'孔子说：'圣人，我还不能做到；我不过是学习不感到满足，教人不嫌疲倦罢了。'子贡说：'学习不感到满足，这是智慧；教人不嫌疲倦，这是仁。仁且智，老师您已经是圣人了。'圣人，连孔子都不敢自居，（你却这么说我）这是什么话呢？"公孙丑说："以前我私下里听说，子夏、子游、子张都各有圣人的一个方面的长处；冉牛、闵子、颜渊大体近于圣人，但略逊一筹。您是属于哪一种？"孟子说："暂且不谈这个。"公孙丑问："伯夷和伊尹怎么样？"孟子说："他们不相同。不认可的君主不去服事，不认可的百姓不去使唤；天下太平就出来做官，天下昏乱则隐居，这是伯夷。任何君主都可以去服事，任何百姓可以去使唤；天下太平去做官，不太平也做官，这就是伊尹。该做官就做官，该辞职就辞职，该长久就长久，该短暂就短暂，这就是孔子。他们都是古代的圣人，我都不能做到。我的愿望是能学习孔子。"公孙丑问："伯夷、伊尹与孔子是一样的吗？"孟子答："不！从有人类以来没有人能比得上孔子。"公孙丑问："那么，他们有相同的地方吗？"孟子说："有。如果有方圆百里的土地，让他们为君主，他们都能够让诸侯来朝，统一天下。如果做一件不义的事，杀一个无辜的人，才能得到天下，他们都不会做。这方面他们相同。"公孙丑说："请问，他们不同的地方有哪些？"孟子说："宰我、子贡、有若三人，他们的智慧足以了解圣人，虽然身份地位低下，但也不会吹捧他们喜欢的人。宰我说：'依我看，老师比尧舜强多了。'子贡说：'看到一个国家的礼制，就能知道它的政治；听到一个国家的音乐，就能知道这个国家的德教。百代以后去评价百代以来的君王，也没有违离孔子的主张。从有人类以来，没有能比过孔子的。'有若说：'难道仅仅是人类有不同吗？麒麟对于走兽，凤凰对于飞鸟，泰山对于土堆，黄河和大海对于小溪，都是同类；圣人对于百姓，也是同类。虽然是同类，但远远高出了同类。自有人类以来没有比孔子更伟大的。"

【英译】Kung-sun Châu asked Mencius, saying, 'Master, if you were to be appointed a high noble and the prime minister of Ch'î, so as to be able to carry your principles into practice, though you should thereupon raise the ruler to the headship of all the other princes, or even to the royal dignity, it would not be to be wondered at.—In such a position would your mind be perturbed or not?' Mencius replied, 'No. At forty, I attained to an unperturbed mind.' Châu said, 'Since it is so with you, my Master, you are far beyond Mǎng Pǎn.' 'The mere attainment,' said Mencius, 'is not difficult. The scholar Kâo had attained to an unperturbed mind at an earlier period of life than I did.'

Châu asked, 'Is there any way to an unperturbed mind?' The answer was, 'Yes. Pî-kung Yû had this way of nourishing his valour: —He did not flinch from any strokes at his body. He did not turn his eyes aside from any thrusts at them. He considered that the slightest push from any one was the same as if he were beaten before the crowds in the market-place, and that what he would not receive from a common man in his loose large garments of hair, neither should he receive from a prince of ten thousand chariots. He viewed stabbing a prince of ten thousand chariots just as stabbing a fellow dressed in cloth of hair. He feared not any of all the princes. A bad word addressed to him he always returned. Măng Shih-Shê had this way of nourishing his valour: —He said, "I look upon not conquering and conquering in the same way. To measure the enemy and then advance; to calculate the chances of victory and then engage: —this is to stand in awe of the opposing force. How can I make certain of conquering? I can only rise superior to all fear." Măng Shih-Shê resembled the philosopher Tsăng. Pî-kung Yû resembled Tsze-hsiâ. I do not know to the valour of which of the two the superiority should be ascribed, but yet Măng Shih-Shê attended to what was of the greater importance. Formerly, the philosopher Tsăng said to Tsze-hsiang, "Do you love valour? I heard an account of great valour from the Master. It speaks thus: — 'If, on self-examination, I find that I am not upright, shall I not be in fear even of a poor man in his loose garments of hair-cloth? If, on self-examination, I find that I am upright, I will go forward against thousands and tens of thousands.'" Yet, what Măng Shih-Shêmaintained, being merely his physical energy, was after all inferior to what the philosopher Tsăng maintained, which was indeed of the most importance. Kung-sun Châu said, 'May I venture to ask an explanation from you, Master, of how you maintain an unperturbed mind, and how the philosopher Kâo does the same?' Mencius answered, ' Kâo says, —What is not attained in words is not to be sought for in the mind; what produces dissatisfaction in the mind, is not to be helped by passion-effort." This last, —when there is unrest in the mind, not to seek for relief from passion-effort, may be conceded. But not to seek in the mind for what is not attained in words cannot be conceded. The will is the leader of the passion-nature. The passion-nature pervades and animates the body. The will is first and chief, and the passion-nature is subordinate to it. Therefore I say, — Maintain firm the will, and do no violence to the passion-nature.' Châu observed, 'Since you say— "The will is chief, and the passion-nature is subordinate," how do you also say, "Maintain firm the will, and do no violence to the passion-nature?"' Mencius replied, 'When it is the will alone which is active, it moves the passion-nature. When it is the passion-nature alone which is active, it moves the will. For instance now, in the case of a man falling or running, that is from the passion-nature, and yet it moves the mind." 'I venture to ask,' said Châu again, 'wherein you, Master, surpass Kâo.' Mencius told him, 'I understand words. I am skilful in nourishing my vast, flowing passion-nature.' Châu pursued, 'I venture to ask what you mean by your vast, flowing passion-nature!' The reply was, 'It is difficult to describe it. This is the passion-nature: —It is exceedingly great, and exceedingly strong. Being nourished by rectitude, and sustaining no injury, it fills up all between heaven and earth. This is the passion-nature: —It is the mate and assistant of righteousness and reason. Without it, man is in a state of starvation. It is produced by the accumulation of righteous deeds; it is not to be obtained by incidental acts of righteousness. If the mind does not feel complacency in the conduct, the nature becomes starved. I therefore said, " Kâo has never understood righteousness, because he makes it something external." There must be the constant practice of this righteousness, but without the object of thereby nourishing the passion-nature. Let not the mind forget its work, but let there be no assisting the growth of that nature. Let us not be like the man of Sung. There was a man of Sung, who was grieved that his growing corn was not longer, and so he pulled it up. Having done this, he returned home, looking very stupid, and said to his people, "I am tired to-day. I have been helping the corn to grow long." His son ran to look at it, and found the corn all withered. There are few in the world, who do not deal with their passion-nature, as if they were assisting the corn to grow long. Some indeed consider it of no benefit to them, and let it alone: —they do not weed their corn. They who assist it to grow long, pull out their corn. What they do is not only of no benefit to the nature, but it also injures it.' Kung-sun Châu further asked, 'What do you mean by saying that you understand whatever words you hear?' Mencius replied, 'When words are one-sided, I know how the mind of the speaker is clouded over. When words are extravagant, I know how the mind is fallen and sunk. When words are all-depraved, I know how the mind has departed from principle. When words are evasive, I know how the mind is at its wit's end. These evils growing in the mind, do injury to government, and, displayed in the government, are hurtful to the conduct of affairs. When a Sage shall again arise, he will certainly follow my words.' On this Châu observed, 'Tsâi Wo and Tsze-kung were skilful in speaking.

Zan Niû, the disciple Min, and Yen Yüan, while their words were good, were distinguished for their virtuous conduct. Confucius united the qualities of the disciples in himself, but still he said, "In the matter of speeches, I am not competent." —Then, Master, have you attained to be a Sage?' Mencius said, 'Oh! what words are these? Formerly Tsze-kung asked Confucius, saying, "Master, are you a Sage?" Confucius answered him, "A Sage is what I cannot rise to. I learn without satiety, and teach without being tired." Tsze-kung said, "You learn without satiety—that shows your wisdom. You teach without being tired—that shows your benevolence. Benevolent and wise: — Master, you ARE a Sage." Now, since Confucius would not allow himself to be regarded as a Sage, what words were those?' Châu said, 'Formerly, I once heard this: —Tsze-hsiâ, Tsze-yû, and Tsze-chang had each one member of the Sage. Zan Niû, the disciple Min, and Yan Yüan had all the members, but in small proportions. I venture to ask, —With which of these are you pleased to rank yourself?' Mencius replied, 'Let us drop speaking about these, if you please.' Châu then asked, 'What do you say of Po-î and Î Yin?' 'Their ways were different from mine,' said Mencius. 'Not to serve a prince whom he did not esteem, nor command a people whom he did not approve; in a time of good government to take office, and on the occurrence of confusion to retire: —this was the way of Po-î. To say— "Whom may I not serve? My serving him makes him my ruler. What people may I not command? My commanding them makes them my people." In a time of good government to take office, and when disorder prevailed, also to take office—that was the way of Î Yin. When it was proper to go into office, then to go into it; when it was proper to keep retired from office, then to keep retired from it; when it was proper to continue in it long, then to continue in it long; when it was proper to withdraw from it quickly, then to withdraw quickly: —that was the way of Confucius. These were all sages of antiquity, and I have not attained to do what they did. But what I wish to do is to learn to be like Confucius.' Châu said, 'Comparing Po-î and Î Yin with Confucius, are they to be placed in the same rank?' Mencius replied, 'No. Since there were living men until now, there never was another Confucius.' Châu said, 'Then, did they have any points of agreement with him?' The reply was, — 'Yes. If they had been sovereigns over a hundred lî of territory, they would, all of them, have brought all the princes to attend in their court, and have obtained the throne. And none of them, in order to obtain the throne, would have committed one act of unrighteousness, or put to death one innocent person. In those things they agreed with him.' Châu said, 'I venture to ask wherein he differed from them.' Mencius replied, 'Tsâi Wo, Tsze-kung, and Yû Zo had wisdom sufficient to know the sage. Even had they been ranking themselves low, they would not have demeaned themselves to flatter their favourite. Now, Tsâi Wo said, "According to my view of our Master, he was far superior to Yâo and Shun." Tsze-kung said, "By viewing the ceremonial ordinances of a prince, we know the character of his government. By hearing his music, we know the character of his virtue. After the lapse of a hundred ages I can arrange, according to their merits, the kings of a hundred ages; —not one of them can escape me. From the birth of mankind till now, there has never been another like our Master." Yû Zo said, "Is it only among men that it is so? There is the Chî -lin among quadrupeds, the Făng-hwang among birds, the

T'âi mountain among mounds and ant-hills，and rivers and seas among rain-pools. Though different in degree，they are the same in kind. So the sages among mankind are also the same in kind. But they stand out from their fellows，and rise above the level，and from the birth of mankind till now，there never has been one so complete as Confucius."'

【注释】

[1] 本章被学术界公认为最难理解的一章。古往今来，学术界对本章的争论不断。由于本章主要谈论了知言和养气问题，所以又被称为"知言养气章"。

[2] 赵岐以"畏难自恐"释"动心"，朱熹在此义的基础上又增加了"疑惑"之义。理雅各和赵甄陶都将之译为"mind be perturbed"。"perturbed"指"使疑惑不解、使不安"，与朱熹的理解基本相类。赖发洛译为"heart throb"。译文仅仅是描述心脏快而剧烈地跳动的状态。刘殿爵的译文"stirring in your heart"则强调心因激动而猛烈跳动。结合原文，公孙丑对"动心"进行提问的前提是假设孟子已经实现了政治抱负。对于普通人来说，伟大的政治抱负得以实现，会因激动、兴奋而使心猛烈跳动，无法保持平静，因而刘殿爵的翻译更准确。

[3] 古文中"市朝"常连言，但重点在市，指人流密集的集市。顾炎武《日知录》卷七"市朝"条目中说："'若挞之于市朝'即《书》所言'若挞于市'。古者朝无挞人之事，市则有之。"理雅各等译者将之翻译为"market-place"（集市）是准确的。

[4] 根据周朝的建军制度，大诸侯国设"三军"。《周礼·夏官司马》中说："凡制军，万有二千五百人为军，王六军、大国三军，次国二军，小国一军。"可见，"三军"具有表数功能，原指三万七千五百人，后来泛指人数众多的军队。理雅各将"三军"译为"the opposing force"（敌军），赖发洛直译为"three lines of battle"（三行作战队形）。从文意上看，孟施舍认为，

要做的不惧怕敌人并不难，难的是在敌我力量悬殊的情况下，仍保持不畏惧的心态，理雅各和赖发洛的译文不能体现"三军"所蕴含的数量众多之义。相比较而言赵甄陶的"the superior force"（优势力量）更准确。

[5] 杨伯峻指出："'惴'是使动用法，是'使他惊惧之意'。"刘殿爵对此提出异议："首先，既然'惴'不属于他动词，通常不带宾语，那么，很难看得出'惴'在这里会充当使动词。第二，否定句式通常要求宾语前置，但'吾不惴焉'则否。"阎若璩也反对把"吾不惴焉"当作否定句看待，认为此处的"不"相当于"岂不也。犹经传中'敢'为'不敢'，'如'为'不如'之类。"理雅各、赖发洛、赵甄陶对"不"的理解与阎若璩相类，选择用"shall I not be"翻译，并将"吾不惴焉"译为"难道我不会害怕吗?"刘殿爵反对将"不"理解为"岂不也"。他指出："在《孟子》一书中，其他的'不'字亦无此用法，因而对'吾不惴焉'唯一合理的解释，是'不'为'必'之误。"因而刘殿爵将"吾不惴焉"翻译为"one is bound to tremble with fear"（这个人必定害怕得发抖）。

[6] 虽然告子做到"不动心"的方法仅仅有十六个字，但译者、历代注释家和研究者对其内涵的认识仍未达成一致。朱熹将"不得于言，勿求于心，不得于心，勿求于气"注解为："告子谓于言有所不达，则当舍置其言，而不必反求其理于心；于心有所不安，则当力制其心，而不必更求其助于气，此所以固守其心而不动之速也。"理雅各的译文和朱熹相类。杨伯峻则提出了一种新的理解："不得乃不能得胜之意。这几句都是讲养勇之事，故以胜负言。旧注皆未得其义。'不得于言'谓人家能服我之口却未能服我之心。"赵甄陶受其影响，将之译为"If you fail to win by words, do not resort to your thoughts; if you fail to win by your thoughts, do not resort to your vital energy."刘殿爵译为"If you fail to understand words, do not worry about this in your heart; and if you fail to understand in your heart, do not seek satisfaction in your ch'i."他的译文旨在强调如何保持内心平静，确保心不受外界干扰。梁涛则结合告子的"义外"说指出："'言'实际上是一种思想学说。告子

将'言'置于心之前，实际上是让思想无条件地服从外在的主义和学说，是一种典型的'义外'说。"学者们从不同的角度和重点出发，阐释了他们对"不得于言，勿求于心，不得于心，勿求于气"的看法。从上下文的逻辑关系看，本句是对告子如何做到不动心的回答，应围绕如何摆脱外界干扰，确保内心平静来论述，因而笔者认为刘殿爵的译文更准确、清楚。

[7]"志至焉，气次焉"体现了孟子对"志"和"气"关系的认识。赵岐认为："志为至要之本，气为其次。"受其影响，理雅各将之译为"The will is first and chief, and the passion-nature is subordinate to it."（志是首要的、主要的，气从属于志）他的译文突出了"志"的重要性，可以很好地呼应前文的"夫志，气之帅也"。赖发洛将之译为"The will is highest, the spirits come next."（志是至高无上的，气仅次于它）他的译文和朱熹的"故志固为至极，而气即次之"相类，强调"志"和"气"都很重要，可以用来说明为什么孟子要强调"持其志，无暴其气"。刘殿爵将之翻译为"The ch'i halts where the will arrives."（志到了哪里，气就停在哪里）这一翻译和毛奇龄《逸诗笺》"志之所至，气即随之而止"的理解一致。"志至焉，气次焉"强调的是"志"统帅和决定着"气"。因而刘殿爵的译文可以很好地体现"志"和"气"的关系。

[8]"气"是中国特有的哲学概念，内涵极其丰富。根据孟子的论述，它首先是身体的一部分，是"体之充"，具有自然属性。其次，"气"是需要后天修养的道德状态，只有经过长期正义行为的积累方能发展为"浩然之气"。理雅各将之译为"passion-nature"。"nature"表明"气"是"身体的运作或功能"，可以很好地体现"气"所具备的"体之充"的特征。但"passion"指深沉的、压倒一切的感情，尤指爱、恨、怒等，不能表明"气"是"集义所生"的道德精神状态。赖发洛译为"spirit"，即"精神、生气或勇气"。他的译文过于笼统和模糊，不能体现孟子气论所蕴含的道德意义。赵甄陶将之翻译为"energy"，该词虽内涵较为丰富，但更容易引起读者不必要的联想，诚如学者刘翌和包通法所指出的："'energy'一词体现的是

一种科学化、物理化的概念"。虽然刘殿爵不赞同音译,但对于中国特有的哲学概念"气",他仍采用威妥玛拼音译法将之译为"ch'i"。他在《刘殿爵教授谈翻译问题》中给出了这么翻译的原因:"因为'气'字牵涉到中国人对宇宙的看法,而这概念西方是没有的。"如果他进一步对"气"作出解释的话,会更有利用读者理解,正如冯友兰将"浩然之气"翻译为"Hao Jan Chih Ch'i,a term which I translate as the 'Great Morale'"。

[9] 学界关于"正"的认识大体有三种,一是赵岐将"正"解为"止"的变体。陈器之支持这种观点,认为"必须先有集义的事却不停止"。赵甄陶的译文与之相类,将"正"翻译为"keep at it"(坚持不放弃);二是朱熹解"正"为"预期",受其影响,理雅各将"正"翻译为"the object of thereby nourishing the passion-nature"(要把养气作为预定的目标);三是刘殿爵将"正"翻译为"let it out of mind"(忘),但是没有给出如此翻译的依据。

[10] "礼"是儒家的核心价值观念,既具有广泛的外延,又具备丰富的内涵。理雅各将"礼"翻译为"ceremonial ordinances"(礼仪制度),缩小了其内涵。赖发洛和刘殿爵选择用"rite"翻译"礼"。根据《牛津词典》,"rite"的含义是"a ceremony performed by a particular group of people, often for religious purposes",可见该单词带有明显的宗教色彩。

【原文】3.3 孟子曰:[1]"以力[2]假仁者霸[3],霸必有大国;以德[4]行仁者王,王不待大——汤以七十里,文王以百里。以力服人者,非心服也,力不赡也;以德服人者,中心悦而诚服也,如七十子之服孔子也。《诗》云:'自西自东,自南自北,无思不服。'此之谓也。"

【译文】孟子说:"依靠武力并假借仁义的君主可以成就霸业,所以要成就霸业必须是大国;依靠道德推行仁政的君主可以成为统一天下的王,成为王者不必是大国——汤以方圆七十里,文王以方圆百里(为王)。用武力使人服从,并不是真心臣服,只是力量不够;用道德使人臣服，是心悦诚服，就像七十多位贤能弟子服从孔子一样。正如《诗经》所说：'从西到东，从南到北，没有不服从的。'正是这个意思。"

【英译】Mencius said, 'He who, using force, makes a pretence to benevolence is the leader of the princes. A leader of the princes requires a large kingdom. He who, using virtue, practises benevolence is the sovereign of the kingdom. To become the sovereign of the kingdom, a prince need not wait for a large kingdom. T'ang did it with only seventy lî, and king Wăn with only a hundred. When one by force subdues men, they do not submit to him in heart. They submit, because their strength is not adequate to resist. When one subdues men by virtue, in their hearts' core they are pleased, and sincerely submit, as was the case with the seventy disciples in their submission to Confucius. What is said in the Book of Poetry, "From the west, from the east, from the south, from the north, there was not one who thought of refusing submission," is an illustration of this.'

【注释】

[1] 孟子针对当时各国只重视富国强兵，而忽视德行培养的弊政，指出霸业和王政的区别在于是"以力服人"还是"以德服人"。他认为虽然采取这两种不同的方式都可以达到服人的目的，但是效果不同。前者的服人只是暂时的，当被征服者力量强大后就会起来反抗，最终将会导致无休止的厮杀。而依靠道德的力量感化别人，使人心悦诚服，不仅可以避免战争，而且可以成为统一天下的王。

[2] 理雅各和刘殿爵都将"力"翻译为"force"，而赖发洛翻译为"strength"。"strength"尤指身体、精神或道德上的坚强力量，而"force"主要是指武力和军队的影响力。根据孟子对王霸之道的论述可以看出，他认为霸道的一个主要特征是依靠武力和战争征服对手，因而理雅各和刘殿爵的译文更准确。

[3]　在中国古代，"霸"指诸侯之长。理雅各将之翻译为"the leader of the princes"是准确的，而赖发洛将之翻译为"power"（强国）则略显模糊。

[4]　"德"，理雅各和刘殿爵分别将之翻译为"virtue"（美德）和"morality"（道德）。根据《美国传统词典》，"morality"通常指符合正确的或好的行为标准的品质。可见，二位译者都认为此处的"德"指的是良好的品德。而赖发洛持反对意见。他认为："最初'德'指的是精神的力量，与体力相对，因为精神的力量一般都是好的，所以可以指美德、德行，即'virtue'。但是在许多时候，孟子都未指美德，因而都用'mind'来翻译德。"但是纵观《孟子》文本，本书中提到的"德"在绝大多数情况下都是指"美德"，是君子孜孜以求的高尚品行。

【原文】3.4　孟子[1]曰："仁则[2]荣，不仁则辱；今恶辱而居不仁，是犹恶湿而居下也。如恶之，莫如贵德而尊士，贤者[3]在位，能者在职；国家闲暇，及是时，明其政刑。虽大国，必畏之矣。《诗》云：'迨天之未阴雨，彻彼桑土，绸缪牖户。今此下民，或敢侮予?'孔子曰：'为此诗者，其[4]知道[5]乎！能治其国家，谁敢侮之?'今国家闲暇[6]，及是时，般乐怠敖，是自求祸也。祸福无不自己求之者。《诗》云：'永言配命[7]，自求多福。'《太甲》曰：'天作孽，犹可违；自作孽，不可活。'[8]此之谓也。"

【译文】孟子说："实行仁政就会带来荣耀，不行仁政，就会带来耻辱。如今厌恶耻辱，却居于不仁之地，就好比厌恶潮却居住在低洼之地。如果厌恶耻辱，不如贵德和尊敬士人，使贤德的人担任官位，使有才能的人担任职务；国家无内忧外患，趁着这个时候，修明政治法典。即使是大国，也必定会害怕（行仁政的国家）。《诗经》上说：'趁着天晴没下雨，从桑树根上剥些皮，补好门和窗。下面的人，谁还敢来把我欺?'孔子说：'做这首诗的人，大概懂得道呀！能够治理好自己的国家，谁敢侮辱?'现在国家没有内忧外患，这个时候，纵情作乐，到处游玩，这是自招祸害啊。祸害或者幸福都是自己找来的。《诗经》说：'永远想着与天命相配，自己去寻求更多的幸福。'《太甲》说：'天降下灾害，还可以躲避，自己作孽，就无处可逃。'正是这个意思。

【英译】Mencius said, 'Benevolence brings glory to a prince, and the opposite of it brings disgrace. For the princes of the present day to hate disgrace and yet to live complacently doing what is not benevolent, is like hating moisture and yet living in a low situation. If a prince hates disgrace, the best course for him to pursue, is to esteem virtue and honour virtuous scholars, giving the worthiest among them places of dignity, and the able offices of trust. When throughout his kingdom there is leisure and rest from external troubles, let him, taking advantage of such a season, clearly digest the principles of his government with its legal sanctions, and then even great kingdoms will be constrained to stand in awe of him. It is said in the Book of Poetry, "Before the heavens were dark with rain, I gathered the bark from the roots of the mulberry trees, and wove it closely to form the window and door of my nest; Now, I thought, ye people below, perhaps ye will not dare to insult me." Confucius said, "Did not he who made this ode understand the way of governing?" If a prince is able rightly to govern his kingdom, who will dare to insult him? But now the princes take advantage of the time when throughout their kingdoms there is leisure and rest from external troubles, to abandon themselves to pleasure and indolent indifference—they in fact seek for calamities for themselves. Calamity and happiness in all cases are men's own seeking. This is illustrated by what is said in the Book of Poetry, — "Be always studious to be in harmony with the ordinances of God, so you will certainly get for yourself much happiness;" and by the passage of the Tâi Chiah, — "When Heaven sends down calamities, it is still possible to escape from them; when we occasion the calamities ourselves, it is not possible any longer to live."'

【注释】

[1] 在本章中，孟子继续强调行仁贵德的重要性，并指出"祸福无不自己求之"。他试图以此来告诫统治者修德明政、尊贤使能的重要性。

[2] "则"，《词诠》卷六记载："承接连词，表因果关系。则字以上文为原因，以下文为结果。"刘殿爵的译文"Benevolence brings honour, cruelty, disgrace."不仅体现了因果关系，而且生动再现了原文简洁的风格。

[3] 在《孟子》中，"贤者"一般指"德才兼备的人"，但在"贤者在位，能者在职"中，"能者"被单列出来，因而此处的"贤者"更侧重于德行的高尚，否则就有重复啰唆之嫌。理雅各和赖发洛都看到了"贤者"和"能者"的区别，将之分别译为"高尚的人"和"有能力的人"。

[4] "其"是副词，相当于大概，表推测。理雅各用反义疑问句"Did not he understand"来表肯定，强调作诗的人一定懂得治国之道。赖发洛用"seems to"表推测，"seem"是根据表面现象作出的判断，这种判断往往接近事实。刘殿爵的"must have done"是对过去事情肯定的推测，表示一定做过某事。虽然三位译者表肯定的程度存在差异，但都体现原文所包含的推测、肯定之意。

[5] "道"，理雅各将之译为"the way of governing"（治国之道），赖发洛和刘殿爵都将之翻译为"Way"。对于儒家"道"的含义，刘殿爵曾经做过如此论述："孔子所赋予'道'的重要性，可以从他'朝闻道，夕死可矣'的话中看到。在这个意义上使用的'道'似乎涵盖了有关宇宙和人类真理的总和。不仅对个人而言，对国家来说也是同样，要么有'道'，要么无'道'……如此说来，'道'是一个非常具有感情色情的用语，它和西方哲学、宗教著作中可以找到的'真理'概念非常接近。"尽管"道"和"真理"非常接近，但二者绝不是对等词，若用"真理"对译"道"容易引起读者对东

西方哲学概念的混淆。因而刘殿爵和赖发洛都选择用大写的"Way"来翻译"道"以突出其含义的特殊性。理雅各则翻译出了"道"在此段文字中的具体含义。纵观全文，孟子在此处主要是向国君阐述为政之道。而后面孔子的评价也是针对君主治理国家而发，因而理雅各的译文也是准确的。

[6] "闲暇"，赵岐以"无邻国之虞"释之，受其影响，理雅各将之翻译为 "leisure and rest from external troubles"（当国家安定空闲，没有外来忧患）。但是杨伯峻持反对意见，他引《国语·晋语》指出："无内乱也可谓之闲暇。"焦循亦指出："国家闲暇，谓不用兵戈。无论外患内乱，战攻则不得休息。"受其影响，赖发洛和刘殿爵将"闲暇"分别翻译为 "quiet spells"（安定期）和 "times of peace"（和平时期），这两种翻译更准确。

[7] "命"，理雅各将之翻译为 "ordinances of God"，赖发洛的翻译是 "Bidding"，刘殿爵的译文是 "Heaven's Mandate"。此处的"命"是"天命"，朱熹注曰："配，合也。命，天命也。"而理雅各将"天"翻译为 "God"（上帝），这在无意中暴露了他基督教传教士的身份。虽然"ordinance"有命令的意思，但当它和"God"连用时，通常指基督教仪式。退一步讲，即使"ordinance"在这里的含义是"命令"，"ordinances of God"的意思就是上帝的旨意。因而用 "ordinances of God" 翻译"命"不妥。从赖发洛将"福"翻译为 "bliss"（福佑、天堂）可知，他亦将"命"理解为"圣训"或"上帝的戒律"。与其他两位译者明显的基督教倾向相比，刘殿爵的 "Heaven's Mandate"（上天的命令）更准确，尽管 "Heaven" 通常指"天国、天堂"，也具有一定的基督教倾向。

[8] 关于"活"有两种理解。一种以朱熹为代表，认为"活，生也"。理雅各受其影响，将本句翻译为 "it is not possible any longer to live"（不可能再继续存活）。一种认为"活"犹"逜"也。如杨伯峻指出，"此处的'活'字当是'逜'之借字。郑玄《注》云：'逜，逃也。'"刘殿爵和赖发洛皆选择"活"的"逃避"之意。

【原文】3.5 孟子[1]曰："尊贤使能，俊杰在位，则天下之士皆悦，而愿立于其朝矣；市，廛而不征，法而不廛[2]，则天下之商皆悦，而愿藏于其市矣；关，讥而不征，则天下之旅皆悦，而愿出于其路矣；耕者，助而不税[3]，则天下之农皆悦，而愿耕于其野矣；廛，无夫里之布[4]，则天下之民皆悦，而愿为之氓矣。信能行此五者，则邻国之民仰之若父母矣。率其子弟，攻其父母，自有生民以来未有能济者也。如此，则无敌于天下。无敌于天下者[5]，天吏也。然而不王者，未之有也。"

【译文】孟子说："尊重贤德的人，使用有才能的人，俊杰都担任官职，那么，天下的士人都会很高兴，愿意在朝廷担任官职；市场上，只是对存储货物的宅舍收租，但不征收货物税，或者依法进行管理，而不对存储货物的宅舍收租。那么，天下的商人都会很高兴，愿意把货物存放在市场上；关卡，只稽查但不征税，那么，天下的旅行者都会很高兴，愿意从他的道路走；耕田的人，只是助耕公田，但不征税，那么，天下的农民都会很高兴，愿意在他的田野上耕种；居所没有劳务税和地税，那么，天下的百姓都会很高兴，愿意成为他的居民。真能做到这五样，那么邻国的百姓就会像对待父母一样爱慕他。率领他的子女去攻打他们的父母，从有人类以来没有能成功的。如果是这样，那么就会无敌天下。无敌天下的人是'天吏'。如果不能成为统一天下的王，是从来没有过的。"

【英译】Mencius said, 'If a ruler give honour to men of talents and virtue and employ the able, so that offices shall all be filled by individuals of distinction and mark—then all the scholars of the kingdom will be pleased, and wish to stand in his court. If, in the market-place of his capital, he levy a ground-rent on the shops but do not tax the goods, or enforce the proper regulations without levying a ground-rent;—then all the traders of the kingdom will be pleased, and wish to store their goods in his market-place. If, at his frontier-passes, there be an inspection of persons, but no taxes charged on goods or other articles, then all the travellers of the kingdom will be pleased, and wish to make their tours on his roads. If he require that the husbandmen give their mutual aid to cultivate the public field, and exact no other taxes from them; —then all the husbandmen of the kingdom will be pleased, and wish to plough in his fields. If from the occupiers of the shops in his market-place he do not exact the fine of the individual idler, or of the hamlet's quota of cloth, then all the people of the kingdom will be pleased, and wish to come and be his people. If a ruler can truly practise these five things, then the people in the neighbouring kingdoms will look up to him as a parent. From the first birth of mankind till now, never has any one led children to attack their parent, and succeeded in his design. Thus, such a ruler will not have an enemy in all the kingdom, and he who has no enemy in the kingdom is the minister of Heaven. Never has there been a ruler in such a case who did not attain to the royal dignity.'

【注释】

[1] 在本章中孟子列举了五项治理国家的大纲，认为君主如果能依此而行，就可以成为统一中国、无敌天下的王者。

[2] "市，廛而不征，法而不廛"主要讲古代市场的管理制度。"廛"用作名词的时候，指的是国家为商人建造的储藏、堆积货物的栈房。商人只需交租金，不需要交货物税，如郑玄注《礼记·王制》"市，廛而不税"说："廛，市物邸舍。税其舍，不税其物。"此处用作动词，指对储存货物的宅舍征租。理雅各将之译为"levy a ground-rent on the shops"。他的译文和刘殿爵的"premises are taxed"皆能准确翻译出此处"廛"的内涵。但二人对"法"的理解不同。朱熹《集注》引张子曰："治之以市官之法，而不赋其廛。"理

雅各受其影响，将"法"翻译为"enforce the proper regulations"。刘殿爵则受赵岐"当以什一之法征其地耳，不当征其廛宅"影响，将之翻译为"当征收土地税时，就不征收廛宅税"。大中华文库版《孟子》则将之译为"if goods are purchased by the state according to law when unsalable"，即"国家根据法律购买那些（市场上）滞销的货物"。这一译文受郑司农"其有货物久滞于廛而不售者，官以法为居取之"的影响，译者虽然理解存在差异，但都能将市场管理中"廛而不征，法而不廛"的优越性体现出来。

[3]"助而不税"是我国古代与井田制相关的一项经济政策。孟子在《孟子·滕文公》上对此做过详细论述，"方里而井，井九百亩，其中为公田。八家皆私百亩，同养公田；公事毕，然后敢治私事"。可见井田制的显著特征就是耕者不必交纳土地税，只是共同耕作公田。刘殿爵的译文将中国古代"助而不税"的农业政策的精髓"农夫帮助耕种公田，不需要因使用土地而付税"准确地译介给了外国读者。

[4]"夫里之布"，朱熹注曰："周礼：'宅不毛者有里布，民无职事者，出夫家之征。'郑氏谓：'宅不种桑麻者，罚之使出一里二十五家之布；民无常业者，罚之使出一夫百亩之税，一家力役之征也。'"可见，"夫里之布"是对所有人都适用的赋税、徭役规定。刘殿爵采取解释性翻译策略，准确翻译出了夫里之布的内涵，即"代替劳役和植桑树的税金"。理雅各的"the fine of the individual idler, or of the hamlet's quota of cloth"（对游手好闲者征收的罚金和乡里应交布匹的份额）亦可。

[5]"无敌于天下者"指能够结束战国时期中国境内四分五裂的状态，统一全中国的人。由于他能够行仁政，得民心，因而没有人有能力与之抗衡，因而刘殿爵的"no match"（无可匹敌者）准确翻译出了其含义。理雅各的"no enemy"和赖发洛的"on one against him"不准确，结合前文"自有生民以来未有能济者也"，可以看出来，天吏不是没有敌人，而是没有能击败他，和他匹敌的敌人。

【原文】3.6　孟子曰：[1]"人皆有不忍人之心[2]。先王有不忍人之心，斯有不忍人之政矣。以不忍人之心，行不忍人之政，治天下可运之掌上。所以谓人皆有不忍人之心者，今人乍见孺子将入于井，皆有怵惕恻隐之心[3]——非所以内交于孺子之父母也，非所以要誉于乡党朋友也，非恶其声而然也[4]。由是观之，无恻隐之心，非人也；无羞恶之心，非人也；无辞让之心，非人也；无是非之心，非人也。恻隐之心，仁之端也；羞恶之心，义之端也；辞让之心，礼之端也；是非之心，智之端也。人之有是四端[5]也，犹其有四体也。有是四端而自谓不能者，自贼者也；谓其君不能者，贼其君者也。凡有四端于我者，知皆扩而充之矣，若火之始然，泉之始达。苟能充之，足以保四海；苟不充之，不足以事父母。"

【译文】孟子说："人都有不忍他人受苦的怜悯心。先王因为有不忍他人受苦的怜悯心，然后有了怜悯的政治。凭借怜悯心，实行怜悯的政治，治理天下就像在手掌来回传递小物品一样简单。之所以说人都有不忍他人受苦的怜悯心，是因为如果有人突然看见有个小孩要掉入井中，都会有震惊和怜悯同情的心，这并不是因为要和孩子的父母交朋友，不是为了在朋友乡亲那里为自己赢得好名声，不是厌恶他的哭声才这样做。因此可以看出来，没有恻隐之心，不是人；没有羞恶之心，不是人；没有辞让之心，不是人；没有是非之心，不是人。恻隐之心是仁的萌芽；羞恶之心是义的萌芽；辞让之心是礼的萌芽；是非之心是智的萌芽。人有这四种萌芽，就像人有四肢一样。有这四种萌芽却说自己不行的人，是自暴自弃的人；说自己的君主不行的，是暴弃君主的人。凡是有这四中萌芽，并知道扩充它们，就像火开始燃烧，泉水开始外涌一样。如果能扩充这四种萌芽，可以安定天下；如果不能扩充它们，连父母都不能赡养。"

【英译】Mencius said, 'All men have a mind which cannot bear to see the sufferings of others. The ancient kings had this commiserating mind, and they, as a matter of course, had likewise a commiserating government. When with a commiserating mind was practised a commiserating government, to rule the kingdom was as easy a matter as to make anything go round in the palm. When I say that all men have a mind which cannot bear to see the sufferings of others, my meaning may be illustrated thus: —even now-a-days, if men suddenly see a child about to fall into a well, they will without exception experience a feeling of alarm and distress. They will feel so, not as a ground on which they may gain the favour of the child's parents, nor as a ground on which they may seek the praise of their neighbours and friends, nor from a dislike to the reputation of having been unmoved by such a thing. From this case we may perceive that the feeling of commiseration is essential to man, that the feeling of shame and dislike is essential to man, that the feeling of modesty and complaisance is essential to man, and that the feeling of approving and disapproving is essential to man. The feeling of commiseration is the principle of benevolence. The feeling of shame and dislike is the principle of righteousness. The feeling of modesty and complaisance is the principle of propriety. The feeling of approving and disapproving is the principle of knowledge. Men have these four principles just as they have their four limbs. When men, having these four principles, yet say of themselves that they cannot develop them, they play the thief with themselves, and he who says of his prince that he cannot develop them plays the thief with his prince. Since all men have these four principles in themselves, let them know to give them all their development and completion, and the issue will be like that of fire which has begun to burn, or that of a spring which has begun to find vent. Let them have their complete

development，and they will suffice to love and protect all within the
four seas. Let them be denied that development，and they will not
suffice for a man to serve his parents with.'

【注释】

[1] 孟子本章主要介绍了他的"四端"说，该学说是孟子性善论和道德修养以及推行仁政的前提，在孟子思想体系中占有重要地位。

[2]《说文解字》云："恻，痛也。"朱熹注曰："隐，痛之深也。"可见"恻隐之心"是对他人的悲惨遭遇而产生的哀痛、怜悯之情。理雅各的译文虽然能体现"恻隐"的含义，但是将"心"翻译为"mind"不妥。"Mind"和脑有关，多偏向思维，具有较强的逻辑性。相比较而言，以"heart"翻译"心"更准确。赖发洛将之翻译为"a heart that pities others"（同情他人的心）。"pity"是对他人的不幸遭遇产生的怜悯和悲哀之情，和"恻隐"的内涵相似。

[3] "怵惕恻隐之心"，将人们突然看见孩子要跌入井里时，在瞬间由惊慌到同情的感情变化描绘得生动逼真。"乍见"表明事情发生得非常突然，是在人们的预料之外，因而给人造成的第一感觉首先是惊慌，其次才是同情。尽管感情变化有可能是在瞬间完成，但肯定存在先后关系。理雅各的译文较好体现了"乍见"后人的感情变化。

[4] 对"非恶其声而然也"的理解有二：一种以刘殿爵为代表，认为"声"指"哭声"，译为"nor because the child's cries hurt him"（也不是因为他厌恶孩子的哭声）。一种以理雅各为代表，认为"声"指"名声"，将之译为"nor from a dislike to the reputation of having been unmoved by such a thing"（不是因为厌恶背上对此事冷漠的名声）。笔者认为，前文的"乍见孺子"表明，事情发生得非常突然，人们在没有任何心理准备的情况下做出了"怵惕恻隐"的本能反应，完全是人真实情感的呈现，不掺杂任何利益得失的考虑。而三个"非"则是在排除对自身利益考虑的种种假设，"非所以要誉于乡党朋友也"已经和名声相关，故此处理解为"哭声"令人厌烦更具说

服力。

[5] 朱熹《集注》曰："端，绪也。"《说文》曰："耑，物初生之题也，上象生形，下象其根也。"可见"端"的含义是萌芽，开端。理雅各将"端"翻译为"principle"（起源），认为"四心"是仁、义、礼和智的来源，符合孟子对四心的认知。赖发洛用"seed"译"端"。"seed"有"萌芽、开端"之意，形神兼备地翻译出了古汉语中"端"的含义。

【原文】3.7　孟子曰[1]："矢人岂不仁于函人哉？矢人唯恐不伤人，函人唯恐伤人。巫匠[2]亦然。故术不可不慎也。孔子曰：'里仁为美。择不处仁，焉得智？'夫仁，天之尊爵也，人之安宅也。莫之御而不仁，是不智也。不仁、不智，无礼、无义，人役也。人役而耻为役，由弓人而耻为弓，矢人而耻为矢也。如耻之，莫如为仁。仁者如射：射者正己而后发；发而不中，不怨胜己者，反求诸己而已矣。"

【译文】孟子说："造箭的人难道不如造铠甲的人仁慈吗？造箭的人只是担心自己造的箭不能射伤人，造铠甲的人只是担心伤到人。巫医和做棺材的工匠也是这样。所以在选择谋生手段时，不得不谨慎。孔子说：'住在仁者居住的地方是好的。在可以选择的时候不与仁人相处，哪能说是聪明的呢？'仁是天下最尊贵的爵位，是人最安稳的住宅。没有人阻挡的时候而行不仁，是不明智的。不仁、不智，无礼、无义的人只能做别人的奴仆。是奴仆但却以被人奴役为耻，这和造弓的人以造弓为耻，造箭的人以造箭为耻一样。如果觉得耻辱，不如去行仁。行仁就好像射箭一样：射箭的人先端正自己然后再射箭；如果射不中，也不去怨恨胜过自己的人，只是从自身找原因罢了。"

【英译】Mencius said, 'Is the arrow-maker less benevolent than the maker of armour of defence? And yet, the arrow-maker's only fear is lest men should not be hurt, and the armour-maker's only fear is lest men should be hurt. So it is with the priest and the coffin-maker. The choice of a profession, therefore, is a thing in which great caution is required. Confucius said, "It is virtuous manners which constitute the excellence of a neighbourhood. If a man, in selecting a residence, do not fix on one where such prevail, how can he be wise?" Now, benevolence is the most honourable dignity conferred by Heaven, and the quiet home in which man should dwell. Since no one can hinder us from being so, if yet we are not benevolent;—this is being not wise. From the want of benevolence and the want of wisdom will ensue the entire absence of propriety and righteousness;—he who is in such a case must be the servant of other men. To be the servant of men and yet ashamed of such servitude, is like a bowmaker's being ashamed to make bows, or an arrow-maker's being ashamed to make arrows. If he be ashamed of his case, his best course is to practise benevolence. The man who would be benevolent is like the archer. The archer adjusts himself and then shoots. If he misses, he does not murmur against those who surpass himself. He simply turns round and seeks the cause of his failure in himself.'

【注释】

[1] 孟子认为，人在生来就具备的善性上没有什么区别，但由于后天选择的谋生手段不同，使人性呈现出不同的发展态势，故而发出了"术不可不慎也"的感慨。

[2] 中国古代巫医不分。最初的"巫"从事祈祷、卜筮、星占，并兼用药物为人求福、却灾、治病。春秋以后，医道才逐渐从巫术中分离出来，但民间仍有许多专门用巫术为人祈祷治病者。东汉许慎《说文解字·匚部》说："匠，木工也。"此处的巫和匠是对举而言，"匠"应特指制造棺材的人，这样才能和治病的巫医形成对比。刘殿爵的译文准确再现了"巫匠"的内

涵。理雅各将"巫匠"翻译为"priest and the coffin-maker"（牧师和制造棺材的人）。他看到了"巫"在祈祷求福中的作用，但未注意到"巫"作为医生在治病上的作用，因而将"巫"翻译为"牧师"不准确。不过他对"匠"的翻译十分恰当。赖发洛译为"leech and the wright"（医生和工匠）。他看到了"巫"在救人上的作用，但未看到此处的"匠"特指制造棺材的人，因而译文没有再现原文强烈的对比效果。

【原文】3.8 孟子[1]曰："子路，人告之以有过，则喜。禹闻善言，则拜。大舜有大焉，善与人同，舍己从人[2]，乐取于人以为善。自耕稼、陶、渔以至为帝，无非取于人者。取诸人以为善，是与人为善者也[3]。故君子莫大乎与人为善。"

【译文】孟子说："子路，当别人告诉他他的过错的时候，就会很开心。大禹听到善言，就会拜谢。舜更伟大，在行善上乐于和他人共享。抛弃自身不好的，学习别人的优点，快乐地向别人学习行善。从耕种庄稼、制作陶瓷、捕鱼到成为天子，没有一处不是从别人那里学来的。从别人那里学习行善，是帮助别人一起行善啊。所以君主最大的德行就是帮助别人一起行善。"

【英译】Mencius said, 'When any one told Tszŭ-lû that he had a fault, he rejoiced. When Yü heard good words, he bowed to the speaker. The great Shun had a still greater delight in what was good. He regarded virtue as the common property of himself and others, giving up his own way to follow that of others, and delighting to learn from others to practise what was good. From the time when he ploughed and sowed, exercised the potter's art, and was a fisherman, to the time when he became emperor, he was continually learning from others. To take example from others to practise virtue, is to help them in the same practice. Therefore, there is no attribute of the superior man greater than his helping men to practise virtue.'

【注释】

[1] 孟子通过列举子路、禹和舜的例子来强调与人为善的重要性，并认为与人为善是君子应具备的最大德行。

[2] 刘殿爵对"舍己从人"采用了字面直译法，容易让读者误以为大舜是一个没有原则，盲目追随别人的人。从上下文看，"舍己从人"的意思应是"舍己之非，从人之是"，因而赵甄陶的译文"giving up his own incorrect opinions for their correct propositions"，即"放弃自己的错误观点，听取别人的正确建议"更准确。

[3] "与"，朱熹注曰："犹许也，助也。取彼之善而为之于我，则彼益劝于为善矣，是我助其为善也。"刘殿爵受其影响，将之翻译为"to help them do good"（帮助别人做好事）。理雅各的译文亦与之相类。焦循提出另外一种理解："是取人为善，即是与人同为此善也。"两种理解皆通。

【原文】 3.9　孟子曰[1]："伯夷[2]，非其君，不事；非其友，不友[3]。不立于恶人之朝，不与恶人言；立于恶人之朝，与恶人言，如以朝衣朝冠坐于涂炭。推恶恶之心，思与乡人立，其冠不正，望望然去之，若将浼焉。是故诸侯虽有善其辞命而至者，不受也。不受也者，是亦不屑就已。柳下惠[4]不羞污君，不卑小官；进不隐贤，必以其道[5]；遗佚而不怨，厄穷而不悯。故曰：'尔为尔，我为我，虽袒裼裸裎于我侧，尔焉能浼我哉？'故由由然与之偕而不自失焉，援而止之而止。援而止之而止者，是亦不屑去已。"孟子曰："伯夷隘[6]，柳下惠不恭。隘与不恭，君子不由也。"

【译文】 孟子说："伯夷不是他认可的君主，不去侍奉；不是他理想的朋友，不去结交。不去坏人的朝廷做官，不和坏人说话；在坏人的朝廷做官，和坏人说话就像穿着朝衣带着朝冠坐在污泥和炭灰上一样。将厌恶坏人的心推广，他认为和乡下人站在一起，如果那个人的帽子没有戴正，也会不高兴地离开，好像自己要被玷污似的。所以，虽然有诸侯用好言好语来聘请他，他也不会接受。不接受是因为不屑于接近。柳下惠不以侍奉坏君为耻辱，也不认为小官卑下，做官的时候不隐藏自己的贤能，但一定要按照自己的原则处理政事；被遗弃也不怨恨，身处穷困，也不忧愁。所以他说：'你是你，我是我，即使赤身露体在我身边，你怎么能玷污我呢？'所以他可以悠然自得地与别人在一起也不会丧失自我。拉住他，让他留下，他就留下。要他留就留下，也是因为他不屑离开罢了。"孟子说："伯夷太狭隘，柳下惠太不严肃。狭隘和太不严肃，君子都不会做。"

【英译】Mencius said, 'Po-î would not serve a prince whom he did not approve, nor associate with a friend whom he did not esteem. He would not stand in a bad prince's court, nor speak with a bad man. To stand in a bad prince's court, or to speak with a bad man, would have been to him the same as to sit with his court robes and court cap amid mire and ashes. Pursuing the examination of his dislike to what was evil, we find that he thought it necessary, if he happened to be standing with a villager whose cap was not rightly adjusted, to leave him with a high air, as if he were going to be defiled. Therefore, although some of the princes made application to him with very proper messages, he would not receive their gifts.—He would not receive their gifts, counting it inconsistent with his purity to go to them. Hûi of Liû hsiâ was not ashamed to serve an impure prince, nor did he think it low to be an inferior officer. When advanced to employment, he did not conceal his virtue, but made it a point to carry out his principles. When neglected and left without office, he did not murmur. When straitened by poverty, he did not grieve. Accordingly, he had a saying, "You are you, and I am I. Although you stand by my side with breast and aims bare, or with your body naked, how can you defile me?" Therefore, self-possessed, he companied with men indifferently, at the same time not losing himself. When he wished to leave, if pressed to remain in office, he would remain. He would remain in office, when pressed to do so, not counting it required by his purity to go away.' Mencius said, 'Po-î was narrow-minded, and Hûi of Liû hsiâ was wanting in self-respect. The superior man will not manifest either narrow-mindedness, or the want of self-respect.'

【注释】

[1] 在本章中孟子举了伯夷和柳下惠的例子来说明，君子处世既不能器量太小，也不能太不严肃，要坚持中庸之道，无过无不及。

[2] "伯夷"是孟子较为推崇的历史人物。伯夷是商朝末年孤竹国君的长子。孤竹国国君在世时，以次子叔齐为王位的继承人。他死后二子互相让位，后都投奔周。因反对武王伐纣不食其粟饿死在首阳山。孟子赞伯夷为"圣之清者"。

[3] "非其君，不事；非其友，不友"，表明伯夷是一个清高的人，不是他认可的君主，就不会去侍奉；不是他理想的朋友就不去结交。刘殿爵的译文"仅辅佐正当的君主，只和正直的人作朋友"，将伯夷的形象完满再现。赖发洛将之译为"Po-yi served none but his own lord, he was friends with none but his own friends"（伯夷只辅佐他自己的君主，只和自己的朋友交朋友），他的译文过于直白，不便于读者理解。

[4] "柳下惠"是春秋时期鲁国人，"柳下"是他的食邑，"惠"是他的谥号。关于他"坐怀不乱"的故事被广为传颂。孟子称他为"圣之和者"。孟子认为他和伯夷是"百世之师"。尽管对二人赞誉有加，但是孟子认为伯夷过于清高，无容人之量，而柳下惠处世太不严肃，都非君子正道。

[5] "必以其道"，理雅各认为，此处的"道"是个中性词，特指柳下惠的做事原则，将之翻译为"carry out his principles"。赖发洛也持这种观点，

将之译为"held his own way"（坚持自己的方法）。刘殿爵选择用"Way"来翻译"道"，即"符合规律和正义的普遍准则"。

[6]"隘"是孟子对伯夷的评价。孟子认为伯夷时刻考虑的是自己会不会被别人玷污，无容人之量。理雅各将之翻译为"narrow-minded"，侧重于心胸狭窄，小肚鸡肠；刘殿爵将之译为"straight-laced"，侧重于道德观念上过于古板，不变通。相比较而言，刘殿爵的译文更能体现出孟子对伯夷的认识。

卷　四

公孙丑章句下

【原文】 4.1　孟子曰：[1]"天时[2]不如地利，地利不如人和。三里之城，七里之郭[3]，环而攻之而不胜。夫环而攻之，必有得天时者矣；然而不胜者，是天时不如地利也。城非不高也，池非不深也，兵革非不坚利也，米粟非不多也；委而去之，是地利不如人和也。故曰：域民不以封疆之界，固国不以山溪之险。威天下不以兵革之利。得道者多助，失道者寡助。寡助之至，亲戚[4]畔之；多助之至，天下顺之。以天下之所顺，攻亲戚之所畔，故君子[5]有不战，战必胜矣。"

【译文】 孟子说："天时不如地利，地利不如人和。（有个小城）内城边长三里，外城七里，被围攻但不能取胜。能够围攻，一定有天时之利，但没有取胜，是因为天时不如地利；城墙不是不高，护城河也不是不深，兵器和皮革不是不锋利坚固，粮食不是不多，但是却弃城逃跑，是因为地利不如人和啊！所以我说，限制百姓不用疆界，保护国家不用依靠山川险峻，在天下诸侯那里获得威信不用凭借兵器的锐利。得道者就会有很多人帮助他，失道者很少有人帮助。帮助的人少到极点，亲戚和朋友都会背叛他；多道的人达到顶峰，全天下的人都会归顺。凭借全天下的人都归顺的力量去攻打亲戚都背叛的人，那么君子或许不去战斗，如果战斗一定会胜利。"

【英译】Mencius said, 'Opportunities of time vouchsafed by Heaven are not equal to advantages of situation afforded by the Earth, and advantages of situation afforded by the Earth are not equal to the union arising from the accord of Men. There is a city, with an inner wall of three lî in circumference, and an outer wall of seven.—The enemy surround and attack it, but they are not able to take it. Now, to surround and attack it, there must have been vouchsafed to them by Heaven the opportunity of time, and in such case their not taking it is because opportunities of time vouchsafed by Heaven are not equal to advantages of situation afforded by the Earth. There is a city, whose walls are distinguished for their height, and whose moats are distinguished for their depth, where the arms of its defenders, offensive and defensive, are distinguished for their strength and sharpness, and the stores of rice and other grain are very large. Yet it is obliged to be given up and abandoned. This is because advantages of situation afforded by the Earth are not equal to the union arising from the accord of Men. In accordance with these principles it is said, "A people is bounded in, not by the limits of dykes and borders; a State is secured, not by the strengths of mountains and rivers; the kingdom is overawed, not by the sharpness and strength of arms." He who finds the proper course has many to assist him. He who loses the proper course has few to assist him. When this, —the being assisted by few, —reaches its extreme point, his own relations revolt from the prince. When the being assisted by many reaches its highest point, the whole kingdom becomes obedient to the prince. When one to whom the whole kingdom is prepared to be obedient, attacks those from whom their own relations revolt, what must be the result? Therefore, the true ruler will prefer not to fight；but if he do fight，he must overcome.'

【注释】

[1] 孟子从当时诸侯征战的社会现实出发，探讨了天、地、人三者在军事战争中的关系，并一针见血地指出"人和"的重要性。

[2]"天时"，朱熹注曰："时日支干、孤虚、王相之属也。"理雅各将之翻译为"Opportunities of time vouchsafed by Heaven"（上天赋予的时机），他的译文具有较强的神秘主义色彩。相比较而言，刘殿爵的"Heaven's favorable weather"（有利的气候条件）更准确。

[3] 在古代都邑四周都有用作防御的高墙，里面的叫"内城"，内城的外围加筑的城墙叫"郭"。理雅各的译文虽然看到了"城"和"郭"的区别，但在翻译"三里之城，七里之郭"时，错误地认为三里和七里分别指城墙的周长。刘殿爵将之译为"a city with inner walls measuring，on each side，three lǐ and outer walls measuring seven li"（有一座城邦，它的内城墙每边长三里，外城墙每边长七里）。他的译文不仅体现了城、郭之别，还将"三""七"分别指"边长"准确翻译了出来。

[4]"亲戚"，在古代有三种含义：一是父母，二是父母兄妹，三是和自己有血亲和姻亲的人。刘殿爵将之翻译为"his own flesh and blood"（血肉至亲），以突出"寡助之至"的危害。理雅各则取第三种含义，将之翻译为"relations"。"relations"指因血缘或婚姻而发生关联的人。这两种理解皆可。赖发洛的"kith and kin"（亲朋好友）将朋友也纳入其中，扩大了"亲戚"的范围。

[5]"君子"内涵丰富，且在不同的篇章中含义不同。本章从论述作战说起，最后引申到以仁政治国，显然此处的"君子"特指得人心的统治者。理雅各和赵甄陶根据上下文，将之翻译为"the true ruler"（真正的统治者）和"a good ruler"（好的统治者）。赖发洛和刘殿爵将之翻译为"gentleman"，他们更关注对孟子中核心词汇翻译的统一性。

【原文】 4.2 孟子将朝王[1]，王使人来曰："寡人如[2]就见者也，有寒疾，不可以风。朝，将视朝，不识可使寡人得见乎？"对曰："不幸而有疾，不能造朝。"明日，出吊于东郭氏。公孙丑曰："昔者辞以病，今日吊，或者不可乎？"曰："昔者疾，今日愈，如之何不吊？"王使人问疾，医来。孟仲子对曰："昔者有王命，有采薪之忧[3]，不能造朝。今病小愈，趋造于朝，我不识能至否乎？"使数人要于路，曰："请必无归，而造于朝！"不得已而之景丑[4]氏宿焉。景子曰："内则父子，外则君臣，人之大伦也。父子主恩，君臣主敬。丑见王之敬子也，未见所以敬王也。"曰："恶！是何言也！齐人无以仁义与王言者，岂以仁义为不美也？其心曰，'是何足与言仁义也。'云尔，则不敬莫大乎是。我非尧舜之道，不敢以陈于王前，故齐人莫如我敬王也。"景子曰："否，非此之谓也。《礼》曰：'父召，无诺[5]；君命召，不俟驾。'固将朝也，闻王命而遂不果，宜与夫礼若不相似然。"曰："岂谓是与？曾子曰：'晋楚之富，不可及也；彼以其富，我以吾仁；彼以其爵，我以吾义，吾何慊乎哉？'夫岂不义而曾子言之？是或一道也。天下有达尊三：爵一，齿一，德一。朝廷莫如爵，乡党莫如齿，辅世长民莫如德。恶得有其一以慢其二哉？故将大有为之君，必有所不召之臣；欲有谋焉，则就之。其尊德乐道，不如是，不足与有为也。故汤之于伊尹，学焉而后臣之，故不劳而王；桓公之于管仲，学焉而后臣之，故不劳而霸[6]今天下地丑[7]德齐，莫能相尚，无他，好臣其所教，而不好臣其所受教。汤之于伊尹，桓公之于管仲，则不敢召。管仲且犹不可召，而况不为管仲者乎？[8]"

【译文】 孟子准备去拜见齐王，王正好派人来传话："我本打算来看您，但是着了风寒，不能吹风。早晨我要临朝听政，不知道可以在朝堂上看到您吗？"孟子回答说："我也不幸得病，不能上朝。"第二天，孟子要去东郭大夫家吊丧。公孙丑说："昨天以生病为由推辞召见，今天去吊丧，大概不好吧？"孟子回答说："昨天生病了，今天好了，为什么不去吊丧呢？"齐王派人问孟子的病情，并且有医生陪同。孟仲子回答说："昨天君主下令，正好生病，不能上朝。今天病好了一点，就急匆匆去上朝了，我不知道是不是已经到达了？"派了好几个人在路上拦截，说："千万不要回家，赶紧去朝堂。"孟子没办法，只好住宿在景丑氏家。景丑说："在家里有父子，在外有君臣，是最大的伦理。父子之间以恩情为主，君臣之间以尊敬为主。我看到君主尊敬您了，但是没见到您尊敬君主啊！"孟子说："哎，说的什么话啊！齐国人没有向王讲仁义的道理的，难道是因为仁义不好吗？他们心里面说：'这个王哪值得和他讲仁义啊。'这才是对王最大的不敬呢！我除了尧舜之道不敢向王讲别的，所以齐国人中没有一个比我更尊敬王的。"景丑说："不，我不是说这个。《礼》上记载：'父亲召唤，"唯"一声就起身，不说"诺"，君主召唤，不等车马驾好就先走。'你本来准备去朝见，听到王召见就不去了，似乎和礼的规定不符合吧。"孟子说："原来说的是这个啊！曾子说：'晋国和楚国的富有，很难达到；他们有财富，我有仁；他们有爵位，我有义，我有什么比不上他们呢？'如果这些话不对，曾子会说吗？应该是有些道理。天下被普遍认为是尊贵的东西有三种：一种是爵位，一种是年龄，一种是道德。在朝廷中，爵位最尊贵；在乡里中，年龄最尊贵；在辅助君主统治百姓方面，道德最尊贵。他只有一个爵位，怎么可以怠慢有两个达爵的人呢？所以大有作为的君主，一定有不能召唤的臣子。如果他想商量请教事情，就会亲自去拜访。这才是崇尚道德，乐行天道。如果不是这样，就不值当和他一起大有作为。所以汤对伊尹，就是先向他学习，然后以他为臣，于是不费力气就成就王业。桓公对于管仲，也是先向他学习，然后以他为臣，于是不费力气就称霸诸侯。现在，各个诸侯国的土地大小相差不大，君主德行相差不多，谁也不能超过谁，没有别的原因，因为他们喜欢用那些受他们教导的人为臣，不喜欢用那些教导他们的人为臣。商汤对于伊尹，桓公对于管仲，就不敢召唤。管仲尚且不可以被召唤，何况不屑做管仲那样的人呢？"

【英译】As Mencius was about to go to court to see the king，the king sent a person to him with this message：—'I was wishing to come and see you. But I have got a cold，and may not expose myself to the wind. In the morning I will hold my court. I do not know whether you will give me the opportunity of seeing you then.'Mencius replied，'Unfortunately，I am unwell，and not able to go to the court.'Next day，he went out to pay a visit of condolence to some one of the Tung-kwŏh family，when Kung-sun Ch'âu said to him，'Yesterday，you declined going to the court on the ground of being unwell，and to-day you are going to pay a visit of condolence. May this not be regarded as improper？''Yesterday，'said Mencius，'I was unwell；to-day，I am better：—why should I not pay this visit？'In the mean time，the king sent a messenger to inquire about his sickness，and also a physician. Măng Chung replied to them，'Yesterday，when the king's order came，he was feeling a little unwell，and could not go to the court. To-day he was a little better，and hastened to go to court. I do not know whether he can have reached it by this time or not.'Having said this，he sent several men to look for Mencius on the way，and say to him，'I beg that，before you return home，you will go to the court.'On this，Mencius felt himself compelled to go to Ching Ch'âu's，and there stop the night. Mr. Ching said to him，'In the family，there is the relation of father and son；abroad，there is the relation of prince and minister. These are the two great relations among men. Between father and son the ruling principle is kindness. Between prince and minister the ruling principle is respect. I have seen the respect of the king to you，Sir，but I have not seen in what way you show respect to him.' Mencius replied, 'Oh! what words are these? Among the people of Ch'î there is no one who speaks to the king about benevolence and righteousness. Are they thus silent because they do not think that benevolence and righteousness are admirable? No, but in their hearts they say, "This man is not fit to be spoken with about benevolence and righteousness." Thus they manifest a disrespect than which there can be none greater. I do not dare to set forth before the king any but the ways of Yâo and Shun. There is therefore no man of Ch'î who respects the king so much as I do.' Mr. Ching said, 'Not so. That was not what I meant. In the Book of Rites it is said, "When a father calls, the answer must be without a moment's hesitation. When the prince's order calls, the carriage must not be waited for." You were certainly going to the court, but when you heard the king's order, then you did not carry your purpose out. This does seem as if it were not in accordance with that rule of propriety.' Mencius answered him, 'How can you give that meaning to my conduct? The philosopher Tsǎng said, "The wealth of Tsin and Ch'û cannot be equalled. Let their rulers have their wealth: —I have my benevolence. Let them have their nobility: —I have my righteousness. Wherein should I be dissatisfied as inferior to them?" Now shall we say that these sentiments are not right? Seeing that the philosopher Tsǎng spoke them, there is in them, I apprehend, a real principle.—In the kingdom there are three things universally acknowledged to be honourable. Nobility is one of them; age is one of them; virtue is one of them. In courts, nobility holds the first place of the three; in villages, age holds the first place; and for helping one's generation and presiding over the people, the other two are not equal to virtue. How can the possession of only one of these be presumed on to despise one who possesses the other two? Therefore a prince who is to accomplish great deeds will certainly have ministers whom he does not call to go to him. When he wishes to consult with them, he goes to them. The prince who does not honour the virtuous, and delight in their ways of doing, to this extent, is not worth having to do with. Accordingly, there was the behaviour of T'ang to Î Yin:—he first learned of him, and then employed him as his minister; and so without difficulty he became sovereign. There was the behaviour of the duke Hwan to Kwan Chung:—he first learned of him, and then employed him as his minister; and so without difficulty he became chief of all the princes. Now throughout the kingdom, the territories of the princes are of equal extent, and in their achievements they are on a level. Not one of them is able to exceed the others. This is from no other reason, but that they love to make ministers of those whom they teach, and do not love to make ministers of those by whom they might be taught. So did T'ang behave to Î Yin, and the duke Hwan to Kwan Chung, that they would not venture to call them to go to them. If Kwan Chung might not be called to him by his prince, how much less may he be called, who would not play the part of Kwan Chung!'

【注释】

[1] 本章记载了弟子、齐王之臣景子关于孟子是否应该去见王的辩论。孟子在争论中表明了他喻警齐王，使他明"大有为之君，必有所不召之臣"之理的良苦用心。

[2] "如"，理雅各将之翻译为"wish"（想要），赖发洛翻译为"meant to"（本打算），刘殿爵将之翻译为"I was to have come to see you"（本应去）。"有寒疾"是齐王给出的自己不去见孟子的理由，孟子意识到齐王没有认识到礼贤下士的重要性，所以也找借口拒绝上朝拜见齐王。如果将"如"理解

为"本应去",则表明齐王已经认识到不去见孟子是不符合礼贤下士之礼，那么孟子也不用煞费苦心地喻警齐王"大有为之君，必有所不召之臣"的道理了。

[3]"采薪之忧"的本义是生病不能去砍柴，后引申为生病。赖发洛将之直译为"humble worries"，不便于读者理解，不如刘殿爵的"ill"和理雅各的"a little unwell"简明扼要。

[4]"景丑"是齐王的大夫，对他做出注释，才能深刻揭示孟子欲警齐王的良苦用心。孟子当时是以宾师而非齐王之臣的身份在齐国。齐王召见他是失礼的表现，但齐王并未认识到这一点，因而孟子出吊东郭氏，以暗示齐王自己没有病，是因为他的召见不符合礼。但弟子并不明白孟子的良苦用心，为孟子编造理由，使齐王不能明白自己的过失，因而孟子到齐王大夫景丑家住宿，希望他能向齐王转达自己的不满。

[5]《礼记·曲礼》："父召无诺，先生召无诺，唯而起。"东汉郑玄的注："敬词唯恭于诺。"可见，应答之词"诺"有怠慢之意，"唯"比"诺"更显恭敬。根据《礼》的规定，"父召无诺"指当父亲召唤的时候，应毫不怠慢，"唯"一声就起身，不说"诺"。刘殿爵将"父召无诺"翻译为"When summoned by one's father, one should not answer, I am coming"（当父亲召唤的时候，不能回答"我就来"）。"我就来"含有"怠慢地答应"之意，与古代应答之词"诺"相似，故刘殿爵在翻译此句时做到了与原文"形神兼备"。赖发洛将之直译为"When thy father calls do not answer"（当父亲叫你的时候，不要答应）。这一翻译与《礼》的规定背道而驰。

[6] 在孟子思想中，"王"和"霸"有着显著的区别。王道是以德服人，凭借仁政统一天下的人，也就是孟子所谓的"以德行仁者王"。（《孟子·公孙丑》）而霸道则是通过武力、假装仁义而成为诸侯之长，也就是孟子所谓的"以力假仁者霸"（《孟子·公孙丑》）。理雅各和刘殿爵选择用"a true King"（一个真正的王）突出"王"的独特性，用"a leader of the feudal lords"（诸侯之长）将"霸"的内涵准确地体现了出来。

[7] 此处的"丑"指"相同",而非译者赖发洛的"unsightly"（难看的）。据《方言》记载："丑，同也，东齐曰丑。"理雅各将之翻译为"equal extent"，刘殿爵翻译为"equal in size"，两位译者皆准确翻译出了"丑"的含义。

[8]"管仲且犹不可召，而况不为管仲者乎?"为我们刻画了一个自重而略带些狂傲之气的孟子的形象。管仲是春秋时期著名的政治家和思想家，他辅佐齐桓公改革内政外交，使齐国成为当时最强大的诸侯国。但孟子却对管仲的成就持蔑视态度。在言谈中几次表示自己不愿意成为像管仲那样的人。如《孟子·公孙丑上》："管仲，曾西之所不为也，而子为我愿之乎?"因而此处的"不为管仲者"指"不屑为管仲者"。理雅各和刘殿爵的译文都将孟子的态度准确传递了出来。

【原文】 4.3　陈臻问曰：[1]"前日于齐，王馈兼金[2]一百，而不受；于宋，馈七十镒而受；于薛，馈五十镒而受。前日之不受是，则今日之受非也；今日之受是，则前日之不受非也。夫子必居一于此矣。"孟子曰："皆是也。当在宋也，予将有远行，行者必以赆；辞曰：'馈赆。'予何为不受? 当在薛也，予有戒心[3]；辞曰：'闻戒，故为兵馈之。'予何为不受? 若于齐，则未有处也。无处而馈之，是货之也[4]。焉有君子而可以货取乎?"

【译文】 陈臻问道："以前在齐国，齐王赠送您上等金一百镒，您不接受；在宋国，宋王赠送您七十镒，您接受了；在薛国时，您也接受了赠金五十镒。如果以前不接受是对的，那现在接受便是错的；如果现在接受是对的，那过去不接受是错的。二者中您必有一个是做错了的。"孟子说："都是对的。在宋国的时候，我将要有远行。对远行的人应该送些盘费，他说：'送点盘费。'我为什么不接受呢? 在薛地的时候，我有戒备的打算，他说：'听说准备戒备，送您点钱买兵器吧。'我为什么不接受呢? 至于在齐国，馈赠就没有什么缘由了。没有什么缘由却赠送我钱，是用金钱收买我。哪有君子可以被收买的？"

【英译】Ch'ǎn Tsin asked Mencius, saying, 'Formerly, when you were in Ch'î, the king sent you a present of 2，400 taels of fine silver, and you refused to accept it. When you were in Sung, 1，680 taels were sent to you, which you accepted; and when you were in Hsieh, 1，200 taels were sent, which you likewise accepted. If your declining to accept the gift in the first case was right, your accepting it in the latter cases was wrong. If your accepting it in the latter cases was right, your declining to do so in the first case was wrong. You must accept, Master, one of these alternatives.' Mencius said, 'I did right in all the cases. When I was in Sung, I was about to take a long journey. Travellers must be provided with what is necessary for their expenses. The prince's message was, "A present against travelling-expenses." Why should I have declined the gift? When I was in Hsieh, I was apprehensive for my safety, and taking measures for my protection. The message was, "I have heard that you are taking measures to protect yourself, and send this to help you in procuring arms." Why should I have declined the gift? But when I was in Ch'î, I had no occasion for money. To send a man a gift when he has no occasion for it, is to bribe him. How is it possible that a superior man should be taken with a bribe?'

【注释】

[1] 孟子在本章中再一次阐释了他的义利观。他虽然认为义利并重，但强调先义后利，并鲜明地表达了他对金钱的态度——君子不可以货取，这和"富与贵是人之所欲也，不以其道得之，不处也；贫与贱是人之所恶也，不以其道得之，不去也"（《论语·里仁》）的认识具有一致性。

[2] "兼金"，赵岐注："好金也。其价兼倍于常者。"理雅各将之翻译

为"fine silver"（好银子）。但刘殿爵和赵甄陶翻译时则将"兼金"翻译为"gold of superior quality"（优质黄金）和"high-quality gold"（高质量的黄金）。陈器之在《孟子通译》中指出："古代所说的金多指黄铜，有别于现在的黄金；一说指银子。"

[3]"戒心"，赵岐注："戒备不虞之心也。时有恶人欲害孟子，孟子戒备。"理雅各的译文准确体现了"戒心"的含义。赖发洛将之翻译为"my heart misgave me."（我的心忧虑不安）译文不仅没有翻译出"戒心"的含义，而且与孟子"我四十不动心"的话相矛盾。根据梁涛的《孟子行年考》："孟子离开宋国，回到邹的时间是公元前325年，在途中曾经路过薛。"那时孟子已经过了四十岁，进入了"不动心"的境界。

[4]"无处而馈之，是货之也"，刘殿爵采用意译法，将之翻译为"To accept a gift without justification is tantamount to being bought"（在没有正当理由时接受别人的礼物，等于被收买）。他的译文更关注接受礼物者的态度，更能凸显孟子的金钱观。理雅各则完全按照原文的句式结构进行翻译。

【原文】4.4　孟子之平陆[1]，谓其大夫曰："子之持戟之士，一日而三失伍[2]，则去之[3]否乎？"曰："不待三。""然则子之失伍也亦多矣。凶年饥岁，子之民，老羸转于沟壑，壮者散而之四方者，几千人矣。"曰："此非距心之所得为也。"曰："今有受人之牛羊而为之牧之者，则必为之求牧与刍矣。求牧与刍而不得，则反诸其人乎？抑亦立而视其死与？"曰："此则距心之罪也。"他日，见于王曰："王之为都者，臣知五人焉。知其罪者[4]，惟孔距心。"为王诵之。王曰："此则寡人之罪也。"

【译文】孟子在平陆的时候，对当地的大夫（孔距心）说："如果你的战士，一天三次掉队，你会开除他吗？"（孔距心）回答说："不用等到三次。"孟子说："那么你失职的地方多了。灾荒年岁，你的百姓，年老体弱的被抛尸山谷中的，年轻力壮的逃到四方的，接近千人。"（孔距心）回答说："这不是我的力量能做到的。"孟子说："如果有人接受了别人的牛羊并替人家放牧，那一定要去寻找牧场和草料。如果找不到牧场和草料，是把牛羊退还给人家呢？还是站在那里看着它们死去？"（孔距心）回答说："这确实是距心的错。"过了几天，孟子朝见齐王，说道："王的封邑长官，我认识五位。知道自己有过错的，只有孔距心。"他把和孔距心的谈话给齐王重复了一遍。齐王说："在这方面我也有错！"

【英译】Mencius having gone to P'ing-lû, addressed the governor of it, saying, 'If one of your spearmen should lose his place in the ranks three times in one day, would you, Sir, put him to death or not?' 'I would not wait for three times to do so,' was the reply. Mencius said, 'Well then, you, Sir, have likewise lost your place in the ranks many times. In bad calamitous years, and years of famine, the old and feeble of your people, who have been found lying in the ditches and water-channels, and the able-bodied, who have been scattered about to the four quarters, have amounted to several thousand.' The governor replied, 'That is a state of things in which it does not belong to me Chü-hsin to act.' 'Here,' said Mencius, 'is a man who receives charge of the cattle and sheep of another, and undertakes to feed them for him; —of course he must search for pasture-ground and grass for them. If, after searching for those, he cannot find them, will he return his charge to the owner? or will he stand by and see them die?' 'Herein,' said the officer, 'I am guilty.' Another day, Mencius had an audience of the king, and said to him, 'Of the governors of your Majesty's cities I am acquainted with five, but the only one of them who knows his faults is K'ung Chü-hsin.' He then repeated the conversation to the king, who said, 'In this matter,

I am the guilty one.'

【注释】

[1] 孟子在说理时善于以小喻大，通过放牧牛羊、战士掉队、地方长官治理地方政事来说明每个人在社会上都承担着一定的责任，人们都应当把自己分内的事做好。

[2]"失伍"，赵岐注曰："失其行伍。"理雅各将之翻译为"lose his place in the ranks"，赖发洛翻译为"missing from the ranks"。二人都认为"失伍"是"掉队"。刘殿爵则将之意译为"failed three times in one day to report for duty"（一天三次失职）。根据孟子接下来对距心"失伍"的指责来看，此处取"失职"之意亦可。

[3]"去之"，刘殿爵取"解职"之意，将之翻译为"dismiss"，理雅各将其翻译为"put him to death"（处死）。结合下文距心的回答"不待三"可知，"去之"作为一种惩罚手段，并没有严峻到"处死"的程度，因而取"解职"之义更佳。

[4]"知其罪者，惟孔距心。"表明孟子对平陆大夫勇于承认错误是肯定的，这与孔子"过则勿惮改"的思想一致。此处的"罪"指的是未认识到失职之过，因而理雅各和刘殿爵将之翻译为"fault"（过错、过失）是准确的。

【原文】 4.5　孟子谓蚳鼃曰[1]："子之辞灵丘而请士师，似也，为其可以言也。今既数月矣，未可以言与？"蚳鼃谏于王而不用，致为臣而去[2]。齐人曰："所以为蚳鼃则善矣；所以自为，则吾不知也。"公都子以告。曰："吾闻之也：有官守者，不得其职则去；有言责者，不得其言[3]则去。我无官守，我无言责也，则吾进退，岂不绰绰然有余裕哉[4]？"

【译文】 孟子对蚳鼃说："你辞去灵丘的长官，去做治狱官，好像有道理，因为可以向齐王进言。现在过去了好几个月了，还不能进言吗？"蚳鼃向王进谏，但是王不听，所以辞官离开。齐国有人说："孟子给蚳鼃的建议不错，但是怎么为自己打算的，我就不知道了。"公都子把话告诉孟子。孟子说："我听说过：有官职的人，如果不能尽职，就应离开；有进言之责的人，进言不听就应该离开。我既没有官职，又没有进言的责任，那我的进退，难道不是有很大的余地吗？"

【英译】Mencius said to Ch'î Wâ, 'There seemed to be reason in your declining the governorship of Ling-ch'iû, and requesting to be appointed chief criminal judge, because the latter office would afford you the opportunity of speaking your views. Now several months have elapsed, and have you yet found nothing of which you might speak?' On this, Ch'î Wâ remonstrated on some matter with the king, and, his counsel not being taken, resigned his office and went away. The people of Ch'î said, 'In the course which he marked out for Ch'î Wâ he did well, but we do not know as to the course which he pursues for himself.' His disciple Kung-tû told him these remarks. Mencius said, 'I have heard that he who is in charge of an office, when he is prevented from fulfilling its duties, ought to take his departure, and that he on whom is the responsibility of giving his opinion, when he finds his words unattended to, ought to do the same. But I am in charge of no office; on me devolves no duty of speaking out my opinion: —may not I therefore act freely and without any constraint, either in going forward or in retiring?'

【注释】

[1] 孟子在本章阐发了"不在其位，不谋其政"（《论语·泰伯》）的道理。孟子在齐，无官守、无言责，因而进退比较自由。而为臣者，应进臣道，否则就应辞官而退。

[2] "谏于王而不用，致为臣而去"体现了古代礼制对为臣之道的规

定。《礼记·曲礼下》："为人臣之礼，不显谏。三谏而不听，则逃之。"刘殿爵将之译为"Ch'ih Wa offered advice to the King and tendered his resignation when this was not followed."（蚳鼃向齐王提出建议但是没有被接纳，于是辞职）他的译文准确再现了古代的为臣之道。

[3]"不得其言"，刘殿爵认为是"不能提出建议"，因而将之翻译为"he is unable to give it（advice）"。笔者认为，此处的"不得其言"和前文"蚳蛙谏于王而不用"的含义一致，因而"得"指的是建议被王采纳，而非"不能提出建议"。因而赵甄陶的译文"his remonstrances with a ruler are rejected"更准确。

[4]"绰"和"裕"都指宽。宽则自由、没有限制，因而刘殿爵将之意译为"have plenty of scope"（有很大的空间）。理雅各则严格按照原文行文特点，通过同义反复，突出没有官守、言责的孟子行动自由，不受任何约束。

【原文】4.6　孟子[1]为卿于齐，出吊于滕，王使盖大夫王驩为辅行。王驩朝暮见[2]，反齐滕之路，未尝与之言行事也。公孙丑曰："齐卿之位，不为小矣；齐滕之路，不为近矣，反之而未尝与言行事，何也？"曰："夫既或治之，予何言哉？"[3]

【译文】孟子在齐国为卿，去滕国吊丧，齐王还派了盖邑的地方官王驩作副手同行。王驩和孟子朝夕相处，在往返齐、滕两国的路上，孟子却没有和他探讨过公事。公孙丑说："齐国的卿位，不算小了，齐、滕之间的距离，也不算近，但来回的路上却没有和他讨论过公事，为什么呢？"孟子说："他已经一个人独断专行了，我还能说什么？"

【英译】Mencius, occupying the position of a high dignitary in Ch'î, went on a mission of condolence to T'ǎng. The king also sent Wang Hwan, the governor of Kâ as assistant-commissioner. Wang Hwan, morning and evening, waited upon Mencius, who, during all the way to T'ǎng and back，never spoke to him about the business of their mission. Kung-sun Ch'âu said to Mencius，'The position of a high dignitary of Ch'î，is not a small one；the road from Ch'î to T'ǎng is not short. How was it that during all the way there and back，you never spoke to Hwan about the matters of your mission?' Mencius replied，'There were the proper officers who attended to them. What occasion had I to speak to him about them?'

【注释】

[1] 子曰："道不同，不相为谋。"(《论语·卫灵公》)孟子曾和王驩共同出使滕国，但王驩自恃受宠于齐王，事事独断专行，不与孟子商量。孟子也不悦他善于逢迎的为人，虽与他早晚见面，但也从不讨论吊亡之事。

[2] "朝暮见"指王驩和孟子每天都会见面，理雅各将之译为"Wang Hwan，morning and evening，waited upon Mencius"(王驩每天早晚都会去侍候孟子)。仅从译文看，王驩是一个知礼、谦逊的人，这和孟子下文提到的独断专行有出入。赵甄陶将之翻译为"Wang Huan saw Mencius mornings and evenings"，他的译文仅仅陈述一个事实，即两人早晚见面，朝夕相处，但并不一定是王驩去主动拜见孟子。

[3] "夫既或治之，予何言哉?"体现了孟子对王驩的不满和厌恶。孟子一再强调不在其位不谋其政，而王驩作为辅行却越俎代庖，令孟子不满，因而孟子"不与之言行事"以示抗议。刘殿爵将之翻译为"He has managed the whole affair. What was there for me to say."(他已经把整个事情都做好了，我还能说什么)他的译文形象再现了孟子的不满。

【原文】 4.7　孟子自齐葬于鲁，反于齐，止于嬴。充虞请曰："前日不知虞之不肖，使虞敦匠事。严，虞不敢请。今愿窃有请也：木若以美然[1]。"曰："古者棺椁无度，中古棺七寸，椁称之。[2]自天子达于庶人，非直为观美也，然后尽于人心。不得[3]，不可以为悦；无财，不可以为悦。得之为有财，古之人皆用之，吾何为独不然？且比[4]化者无使土亲肤，于人心独无恔乎？吾闻之也：君子不以天下俭其亲。"

【译文】 孟子从齐国回到鲁国埋葬母亲，又返回齐国，在嬴县停留下来。充虞请教道："前段时间您不嫌弃我无能，让我监理棺椁的制造工作，当时时间紧，我不敢请教。现在请教一下：棺椁好像太华丽了吧？"孟子说："上古时对于棺椁的厚度没有规定，中古时，规定棺厚七寸，椁的厚度要与之相当。从天子到普通百姓都是这样，不仅是为了好看，而是这样才能尽孝子之心。为礼制所限制，不能用上等棺椁，就会不称心；没有财力，也不称心。礼制允许，财力又可以负担，古人都用了，我为什么不能呢？而且棺椁可以保护死者的尸体避免和泥土接触，对孝子来说不是很称心吗？我听说过：君子不会为了天下节俭财物而在父母身上省钱。"

【英译】 Mencius went from Chʻî to Lû to bury his mother. On his return to Chʻî, he stopped at Ying, where Chʻung Yü begged to put a question to him, and said, 'Formerly, in ignorance of my incompetency, you employed me to superintend the making of the coffin. As you were then pressed by the urgency of the business, I did not venture to put any question to you. Now, however, I wish to take the liberty to submit the matter. The wood of the coffin, it appeared to me, was too good.' Mencius replied, 'Anciently, there was no rule for the size of either the inner or the outer coffin. In middle antiquity, the inner coffin was made seven inches thick, and the outer one the same. This was done by all, from the sovereign to the common people, and not simply for the beauty of the appearance, but because they thus satisfied the natural feelings of their hearts. If prevented by statutory regulations from making their coffins in this way, men cannot have the feeling of pleasure. If they have not the money to make them in this way, they cannot have the feeling of pleasure. When they were not prevented, and had the money, the ancients all used this style. Why should I alone not do so? And moreover, is there no satisfaction to the natural feelings of a man, in preventing the earth from getting near to the bodies of his dead? I have heard that the superior man will not for all the world be niggardly to his parents.'

【注释】

[1] 孟子的学生充虞认为孟子在安葬母亲时，所用棺木太奢侈浪费，因而提出"木若以美然"的疑问。在翻译此句时，应看到虽然原文使用的是疑问语气，但却表现了说话者对棺木过于奢华的感慨和不认同。刘殿爵和理雅各都改变了原文的句型结构，刘殿爵将之翻译为"The wood seemed to be excessively fine in quality"（木头的质量似乎过于上乘了）。理雅各将之翻译为"The wood of the coffin, it appeared to me, was too good"（我觉得棺木太上等了）。二人的译文体现出了充虞对棺木过于奢华的不认同。

[2] "古者棺椁无度，中古棺七寸，椁称之。"简要概括了我国古代丧葬礼制的发展史。中国传统上将古代划分为上古、中古和近古三个阶段。刘殿爵将"上古"和"中古"分别翻译为"high antiquity"和"middle antiquity"，体现了二者在时间上的延续性。理雅各和赖发洛分别选择用不同的词语翻译，不能体现上古和中古的关系。不仅如此，赖发洛选择用"the Middle Ages"翻译"中古"，这一翻译容易在西方人中引起误解，将他们历史上的"中世纪"等同于中国的"中古"时期。实际上朱熹认为"中古"是"周公制礼时也"。"称之"指的是椁的厚度应与棺相称。理雅各认为二者厚度一致不准确。刘殿爵将之译为"the inner coffin was to be seven inches thick with the outer coffin to match."（棺厚七寸，椁的厚度与之相当）他的译文准确体现了棺和椁的关系。

[3] "不得"，朱熹注曰："谓法治所不当得"。受其影响理雅各将之

翻译为"If prevented by statutory regulations from making their coffins in this way"。刘殿爵和赵甄陶则翻译为"if such wood (coffins) is not available",即"找不到这样的棺木"。两种理解皆通。梁涛还提出一种解释："为礼制所不允许。"

[4] "比",传统观点一般训为"为了"。朱熹注云："比,犹为也。"杨伯峻也认为："比,为也。"杨树达《词诠》："比,介词,亦读去声,义同'为'。"理雅各的译文受传统观点的影响,也将"比"理解成"为了",虽然这一理解从文意上可以讲通,但是不符合古代语法结构。尹洁在《〈孟子〉"比化者"献疑》一文中对此做过详细的论述,她认为："如果将'比'理解为介词'为了',那么'比化者无使土亲肤'的句法结构可分析为:介宾短语＋否定副词＋'使'+n+vp。"尹洁对《十三经》中"否定副词＋'使'"的句子进行考察后发现："否定副词＋'使'的句式,共得23例,均表示'使役''使令'之义,但是对于介宾短语＋否定副词＋'使'的句式,除《孟子·公孙丑下》中该句以外,未见他例。"赖发洛在此处选择了"比"的另一层含义"及其时",西方学者W.Simon教授也认可这种理解："此处的'比'当训作'及其时'"。这一认识也受到刘殿爵的认可。刘殿爵将本句翻译为"to be able to prevent the earth from coming into contact with the dead who is about to decompose"(能够阻止泥土接近将要腐烂的尸体)。这种创新性理解,丰富了原文的内涵。

【原文】4.8 沈同以其私[1]问曰："燕可伐与?"孟子曰："可。子哙不得与人燕,子之不得受燕于子哙。有仕于此,而子悦之,不告于王而私与之吾子之禄爵;夫士也,亦无王命而私受之于子,则可乎?——何以异于是?"齐人伐燕。或问曰："劝齐伐燕,有诸?"曰："未也。沈同问'燕可伐与',吾应之曰:'可。'彼然而伐之也。彼如曰:'孰可以伐之?'则将应之曰:'为天吏[2],则可以伐之。'今有杀人者,或问之曰:'人可杀与?'则将应之曰:'可。'彼如曰：'孰可以杀之？'则将应之曰：'为士师，则可以杀之。'今以燕伐燕[3]，何为劝之哉？"

【译文】 沈同以个人身份问道："可以讨伐燕国吗？"孟子回答："可以。燕王哙不能够把燕国让给别人，他的相国子之也不能够从燕王哙那里接受燕国。如果这儿有个人，你很欣赏他，便不向王请示而私自把你的俸禄和官位都给他；那个人呢，也没有得到国王的任命而是私下从你那里接受了俸禄官位，这样可以吗？私下让国和这个又有什么区别？"齐国去讨伐燕国。有人问孟子："（你）劝说齐国讨伐燕国，有这回事吗？"孟子说："没有。沈同曾经问我：'可以讨伐燕国吗？'我回答说：'可以。'他们就去打燕国了。如果他再问：'谁可以去讨伐？'我便会说：'只有天吏才可以去讨伐。'假设这里有个杀人犯，有人问我：'可以杀死这人吗？'我会说：'可杀。'他如果再问：'谁可以杀他？'我将会告诉他：'只有治狱官可以杀他。'现在是一个类似燕国的国家去讨伐燕国，我为什么要劝他呢？"

【英译】 Shǎn T'ung, on his own impulse, asked Mencius, saying, 'May Yen be smitten?' Mencius replied, 'It may. Tsze-k'wâi had no right to give Yen to another man, and Tsze-chih had no right to receive Yen from Tsze-k'wâi. Suppose there were an officer here, with whom you, Sir, were pleased, and that, without informing the king, you were privately to give to him your salary and rank; and suppose that this officer, also without the king's orders, were privately to receive them from you:—would such a transaction be allowable? And where is the difference between the case of Yen and this?' The people of Ch'î smote Yen. Some one asked Mencius, saying, 'Is it really the case that you advised Ch'î to smite Yen?' He replied, 'No. Shǎn T'ung asked me whether Yen might be smitten, and I answered him, "It may." They accordingly went and smote it. If he had asked me— "Who may smite it?" I would have answered him，"He who is the minister of Heaven may smite it." Suppose the case of a murderer，and that one asks me—"May this man be put to death?" I will answer him，—"He may." If he ask me—"Who may put him to death?" I will answer him，—"The chief criminal judge may put him to death." But now with one Yen to smite another Yen：—how should I have advised this?'

【注释】

[1] 此处突出"以其私"是因为沈同是齐国的大臣，他不是代表国家来向孟子请教国事，而是以个人身份向孟子请教。因此理雅各在翻译时如果像赵甄陶那样"Shen Tong (minister of Qi) asked Mencius in a private capacity"，对沈同的身份作进一步解释，更便于读者理解。

[2] "天吏"，通常指奉天之命，治理百姓的人，也就是孔子所谓"礼乐征伐自天子出"的天子。在《孟子》中，"天吏"主要指凭借仁政统一天下的王者。刘殿爵的"Heaven-appointed officer"（天指定的官员）基本上能体现其含义。

[3] "以燕伐燕"体现了孟子对齐国伐燕的态度。他认为虽然无道的燕国应当被讨伐，但不应该受同为诸侯国的齐国征讨。刘殿爵将之译为"it is just one Yen marching on another Yen"（这就好比是一个燕国正在讨伐另外一个燕国）。他的译文能准确再现原文的暗含之意。

【原文】 4.9　燕人畔[1]。王曰："吾甚惭于孟子[2]。"陈贾曰："王无患焉。王自以为与周公孰仁且智？"王曰："恶！是何言也！"曰："周公使管叔监殷，管叔以殷畔；知而使之，是不仁也；不知而使之，是不智也。仁智，周公未之尽也，而况于王乎？贾请见而解之[3]。"见孟子，问曰："周公何人也？"曰："古圣人[4]也。"曰："使管叔监殷，管叔以殷畔也，有诸？"曰："然。"曰："周公知其将畔而使之与？"曰："不知也。""然则圣人且有过与？"曰："周公，弟也；管叔，兄也。周公之过，不亦宜乎？且古之君子，过则改之；今之君子，过则顺之。古之君子，其过也，如日月之食，民皆见之；及其更也，民皆仰之。今之君子[5]，岂徒顺之，又从为之辞。"

【译文】燕国人群起反抗。齐王说："我对孟子感到非常惭愧。"陈贾说："王不要担心。您觉得和周公相比，在仁和智方面，谁更强一些？"王说："哎，说的是什么话！"陈贾说："周公让管叔监视殷国遗民，管叔却率领殷国遗民造反，如果周公早就预见到这个结果，仍任用管叔，那是不仁；如果周公没有预见到而任用管叔，那是他不明智。仁和智，周公也没有完全做到，何况王呢？我请求您让我去见孟子，并说服他。"陈贾去见孟子，问道："周公是什么样的人？"孟子回答说"古代的圣人。"陈贾说："让管叔监视殷国遗民，管叔却率领殷国遗民造反，有这回事吗？"答道："有的。"问道："周公预见到管叔会造反，仍然任命他去的吗？"答道："周公没有预见。"陈贾说："那么圣人也会有过错吗？"孟子说："周公是弟弟，管叔是哥哥，周公的过错不也是合情合理吗？况且，古代的君子有了过错，就会改正；今天的君子，有了过错，竟一直错下去。古代的君子，他的过错就像日食月食一样，百姓都能看见；当他改正的时候，百姓也都仰望着。今天的君子，不仅将错就错，还要为错误辩解。"

【英译】The people of Yen having rebelled, the king of Ch'î said, 'I feel very much ashamed when I think of Mencius.' Ch'ǎn Chiâ said to him, 'Let not your Majesty be grieved. Whether does your Majesty consider yourself or Châu-kung the more benevolent and wise?' The king replied, 'Oh！what words are those?' 'The duke of Châu,' said Chiâ, 'appointed Kwan-shû to oversee the heir of Yin, but Kwan-shû with the power of the Yin State rebelled. If knowing that this would happen he appointed Kwan-shû, he was deficient in benevolence. If he appointed him, not knowing that it would happen, he was deficient in knowledge. If the duke of Châu was not completely benevolent and wise, how much less can your Majesty be expected to be so! I beg to go and see Mencius, and relieve your Majesty from that feeling.' Ch'ǎn Chiâ accordingly saw Mencius, and asked him, saying, 'What kind of man was the duke of Châu?' 'An ancient sage,' was the reply. 'Is it the fact, that he appointed Kwan-shû to oversee the heir of Yin, and that Kwan-shû with the State of Yin rebelled?' 'It is.' 'Did the duke of Châu know that he would rebel, and purposely appoint him to that office?' Mencius said, 'He did not know.' 'Then, though a sage, he still fell into error?' 'The duke of Châu,' answered Mencius, 'was the younger brother. Kwan-shû was his elder brother. Was not the error of Châu-kung in accordance with what is right? Moreover, when the superior men of old had errors, they reformed them. The superior men of the present time, when they have errors, persist in them. The errors of the superior men of old were like eclipses of the sun and moon. All the people witnessed them, and when they had reformed them, all the people looked up to them with their former admiration. But do the superior men of the present day only persist in their errors? They go on to apologize for them likewise.'

【注释】

[1] 孔子曾提出过对待错误的态度："过则勿惮改"。(《论语·学而》) 孟子继承并发展了这一思想，认为君子一生中难免会犯错误，犯了错误能够敢于改正，会继续得到百姓的支持和仰慕，而将错就错、掩饰错误是不可取的。

[2] 齐王因不听取孟子的意见而陷入燕人叛的僵局，感到无颜面对孟子，因而发出"吾甚惭于孟子"的感叹。理雅各的译文表明，齐王想到孟子就会感到很惭愧。他没有给出齐王惭愧的原因。赵甄陶在翻译时做了进一

步的解释，"I am very much ashamed to see Mencius for my not listening to his advice"，更便于读者理解。

[3]"见而解之"的对象是孟子。理雅各却认为是把君主从愧疚中解脱出来，笔者认为这种解释与后文脱节。赖发洛的译文是"Let me see Mencius，pray，and explain this."（请让我去见孟子，向他解释这件事）但是从下文二人的谈话可以看出，他并没有试图向孟子解释，而是想要说服孟子。因而刘殿爵的译文"May I be permitted to go and disabuse Mencius's mind?"（请允许我去见孟子，纠正他的观点）更准确。

[4]"圣人"是中国文化独有的内容。《说文解字》云："圣，通也。"《尚书·洪范》篇说："于事无不通谓之圣。"孟子认为"圣人，人伦之至也。"（《孟子·离娄上》）可见，圣人是人中之杰，是儒家理想人格的最高境界。理雅各、刘殿爵、赵甄陶都将"圣人"翻译为"sage"。在英语中，"sage"的含义是贤哲、智者，主要强调人的睿智。睿智可与年龄俱增，因而"sage"更侧重于指那些年高望重的人。"sage"只代表了"圣人"的某一项突出品质，但不能体现它的全部内涵。赖发洛将"圣人"翻译为"A holy man"，"holy"的含义是"神的，神圣的"，和宗教有着密切的联系，用它翻译儒家的理想人格不妥。

[5]结合文意，此处的"君子"应专指那些居上位者，而非儒家所推崇的理想人格。理雅各的译文能准确体现出此处"君子"的含义。刘殿爵将"君子"翻译为"gentlemen"，未能体现此处的特殊含义。

【原文】4.10 孟子致为臣而归[1]。王就见孟子，曰："前日愿见而不可得，得侍同朝[2]，甚喜；今又弃寡人而归，不识可以继此而得见乎？"对曰："不敢请耳，固所愿也。"他日，王谓时子曰："我欲中国[3]而授孟子室，养弟子以万钟[4]，使诸大夫国人皆有所矜式。子盍为我言之！"时子因陈子而以告孟子，陈子以时子之言告孟子。孟子曰："然；夫时子恶知其不可也？如使予欲富，辞十万而受万，是为欲富乎？季孙曰：'异哉子叔疑！使己为政，不用，则亦已矣，又使其子弟为卿。人亦孰不欲富贵？而独于富贵之中，有私龙断[5]焉。'古之为市也，以其所有易其所无者，有司者治之耳。有贱丈夫焉，必求龙断而登之，以左右望，而罔市利。人皆以为贱，故从而征之。征商自此贱丈夫[6]始矣。"

【译文】孟子辞去官职准备返回家乡，齐王前往孟子家中相见，说道："过去想见您，却见不着；后来您来我的朝堂为官，我非常高兴；现在您又离开我回去了，不知道以后还可以见到您吗？"孟子回答说："只是不敢请求罢了，这个也是我很希望的。"过了几天，齐王对时子说："我想在临淄城中给孟子一座房子，用万钟之粟来养他的弟子，使官吏和百姓都有效法的对象。你何不替我向孟子说说！"时子便托陈子告诉孟子，陈子就把时子的话告诉了孟子。孟子说："嗯，时子怎么知道这样做不可呢？如果我想要富贵，辞去十万钟的俸禄来接受一万钟的赏赐，这难道是想求富贵吗？季孙说过：'奇怪啊，子叔疑！自己想要做官，不能被任用，也就算了；却又让自己的儿子、兄弟去做卿大夫。哪有人不想要富贵呢？但是他却想要独占富贵之利。'古代经商，是用自己有的东西去交换别人没有的，同时有相关部门管理。却有一个卑鄙的男人，一定要找到独立的高地登上去，左望望，右望望，恨不得把市场上所有的好处都捞尽。人们都觉得这个人卑鄙，于是向他征税。所以向商人征税便从这个卑鄙的男人开始了。"

【英译】Mencius gave up his office, and made arrangements for returning to his native State. The king came to visit him, and said, 'Formerly, I wished to see you, but in vain. Then, I got the opportunity of being by your side, and all my court joyed exceedingly along with me. Now again you abandon me, and are returning home. I do not know if hereafter I may expect to have another opportunity of seeing you.' Mencius replied, 'I dare not request permission to visit you at any particular time, but, indeed, it is what I desire.' Another day, the king said to the officer Shih, 'I wish to give Mencius a house, somewhere in the middle of the kingdom, and to support his disciples with an allowance of 10, 000 chung, that all the officers and the people may have such an example to reverence and imitate. Had you not better tell him this for me?' Shih took advantage to convey this message by means of the disciple Ch'ǎn, who reported his words to Mencius. Mencius said, 'Yes; but how should the officer Shih know that the thing could not be? Suppose that I wanted to be rich, having formerly declined 100, 000 chung, would my now accepting 10, 000 be the conduct of one desiring riches? Chî-sun said, "A strange man was Tsze-shû Î. He pushed himself into the service of government. His prince declining to employ him, he had to retire indeed, but he again schemed that his son or younger brother should be made a high officer. Who indeed is there of men but wishes for riches and honour? But he only, among the seekers of these, tried to monopolize the conspicuous mound." Of old time, the market-dealers exchanged the articles which they had for others which they had not, and simply had certain officers to keep order among them. It happened that there was a mean fellow, who made it a point to look out for a conspicuous mound, and get up upon it. Thence he looked right and left, to catch in his net the whole gain of the market. The people all thought his conduct mean, and therefore they proceeded to lay a tax upon his wares. The taxing of traders took its rise from this mean fellow.'

【注释】

[1] 孟子曾经对齐王抱有厚望，希望他能施行仁政，成为统一天下的王者。而齐王不仅不能行孟子之道，还试图以利引诱孟子留在齐国，因而孟

子举贱丈夫试图垄断市利的例子来表明自己不为利诱，坚守道义的决心。

[2]"得侍同朝甚喜"，理雅各将之翻译为"I got the opportunity of being by your side，and all my court joyed exceedingly along with me"（然后有机会在你身边，我和整个朝廷的人都非常高兴）。显然，他将此句断为"得侍。同朝甚喜"。杨伯峻认为："此读实误。孔广深《经学卮言》云：'得侍同朝'者谦词，言与孟子得为君臣而同朝也。'甚喜'，王自言甚喜也。俗读'得侍'绝句者，谬。"刘殿爵的译本同杨伯峻，将本句断为"得侍同朝，甚喜"。

[3]"中国"指的是国都之中央，即"临淄城中"。"中"，《词诠》卷五视为"方所介词"，可译为"在……中央"。"国"既可以指"国都"，也可以指"全国"。理雅各的译文取"国家中央"，但从下文使"诸大夫国人皆有所矜式"来看，刘殿爵译为"in the most central part of my capital"（齐国都城正中央）更准确。

[4]"钟"是中国古代的容量单位。《古代汉语词典》记载："一钟相当于六石四斗。万钟即六万四千石。一斗约合近代两升。"在英语中，没有与之相对应的词，理雅各将之音译为"chung"，并在注释中对它作了说明。赖发洛用英国谷物计量单位"bushels"翻译"钟"。刘殿爵则采取意译法，将"钟"翻译为"measures of rice"（谷物的计量标准）。

[5]"龙断"的本义指独立的高地。陈器之指出："'龙'通'垄'，亦作'陇'，土山高起而四面削落的，叫作'垄断'。"理雅各的译文取其本义"突出的土丘"，不便于读者理解。赖发洛将之译为"Dragon Crag"，并未对此做任何注释，令人不知所云。刘殿爵取其引申意，将之译为"a vantage point"（有利的位置），更方便读者理解。

[6]"贱丈夫"指的是那些行为卑鄙，想独占市利的人。理雅各将之翻译为"a mean fellow"（吝啬刻薄的人），不如刘殿爵的"a despicable fellow"（卑劣的人）更能体现出卑鄙的含义。赖发洛将之译为"a cheap fellow"（卑鄙的人）。"贱"的本义是"价格低"，而"cheap"的基本含义是"不值钱"。

"贱"用来形容人，指人格卑鄙，而"cheap"修饰人时也有"可鄙"之意。

【原文】4.11　孟子去齐[1]，宿于昼。有欲为王留行者，坐[2]而言。不应，隐几而卧。客不悦曰："弟子齐宿[3]而后敢言，夫子卧而不听，请勿复敢见矣。"曰："坐！我明语子。昔者鲁缪公无人乎子思之侧，则不能安子思；泄柳、申详无人乎缪公之侧，则不能安其身。子为长者虑，而不及子思；子绝长者乎？长者绝子乎？[4]"

【译文】孟子离开齐国，在昼县过夜。有个想替齐王挽留孟子的人，坐着同孟子说话。孟子却不答应，靠着几案躺着。客人很不高兴，说道："我提前一天斋戒后才敢和您说话，您却躺着不听我说，以后我再也不敢和您相见了。"孟子说："坐下！我明白地告诉你。以前，鲁缪公要是没有派人在子思身边服侍，就不能够使子思安心；泄柳、申详要是没有人在鲁缪公身边进言，就不能使自己安心。你为我这个长辈考虑，却连鲁缪公怎样对待子思都做不到，是你跟我绝交呢，还是我跟你绝交呢？"

【英译】Mencius, having taken his leave of Ch'î, was passing the night in Châu. A person who wished to detain him on behalf of the king, came and sat down, and began to speak to him. Mencius gave him no answer, but leant upon his stool and slept. The visitor was displeased, and said, 'I passed the night in careful vigil, before I would venture to speak to you, and you, Master, sleep and do not listen to me. Allow me to request that I may not again presume to see you.' Mencius replied, 'Sit down, and I will explain the case clearly to you. Formerly, if the duke Mû had not kept a person by the side of Tsze-sze, he could not have induced Tsze-sze to remain with him. If Hsieh Liû and Shǎn Hsiang had not had a remembrancer by the side of the duke Mû, he would not have been able to make them feel at home and remain with him. You anxiously form plans with reference to me, but you do not treat me as Tsze-sze was treated. Is it you，Sir，who cut me？ Or is it I who cut you？'

【注释】

[1] 孟子认为"恭敬而无实，君子不可虚拘。"(《孟子·尽心》) 对待贤才首先要发自内心地尊敬，如果既不尊重贤者的政见，又不能像鲁缪公对待子思那样真心实意，君子是不会被那些虚假的礼文所留住的。

[2] 古人席地而坐，有两种坐法。一曰"危坐"(跪坐)，即两膝着地，腰和大腿伸直，前文的"坐而言"，就是"客危坐而言"；一曰"安坐"，即两膝着地，屁股落在脚后跟上，坐下来比较舒服。"坐！我明语子"的"坐"是"安坐"。理雅各和赖发洛在翻译时，没有发现"危坐"和"安坐"的区别，都统一翻译为"sit down"(坐下)，给读者前后重复的感觉。而刘殿爵对中国传统文化比较熟悉，看到了"坐"在不同语境下的不同意思，分别将"坐而言"和"坐！我明语子"翻译为"sat upright"(端坐)和"Be seated"(安坐)。

[3] "齐宿"，朱熹注曰："斋戒越宿也。"陈器之指出："齐，同'斋'，指斋戒。斋戒：沐浴更衣，不饮酒，不吃荤。"理雅各将"齐宿"翻译为"passed the night in careful vigil"。"vigil"的含义是宗教节日的前夕，通过虔诚的守夜来庆祝。用他来翻译"齐宿"给中国传统文化增添了西方的宗教色彩。赖发洛翻译为"spent the night in abstinence"。"abstinence"，有禁酒、禁食的含义，这和"斋戒"有相似之处，但也不能完全翻译出它的含义。相比较而言，刘殿爵的译文"observing a day's fast"更准确。

[4] "长者"是孟子的自称，赵岐《注》曰："长者，老者也。孟子年老，故自称长者。""子"是古代对男子的通称，孟子在此处以长者自称，故"子"没有尊称的含义，而是长者对年轻人的称呼。理雅各和赖发洛都将"子"翻译为大写的"Sir"，以表明孟子对留行者的尊敬，不如刘殿爵的"my son"准确。此处的"son"非指"儿子"，而是长者对年轻人的称呼。

【原文】4.12　孟子去齐[1]。尹士语人曰:"不识王之不可以为汤武,则是不明也;识其不可,然且至,则是干泽也。千里而见王,不遇[2]故去。三宿而后出昼,是何濡滞也?士则兹不悦。"高子以告。曰:"夫尹士恶知予哉?千里而见王,是予所欲也;不遇故去,岂予所欲哉?予不得已也。予三宿而出昼,于予心犹以为速,王庶几改之[3]!王如改诸,则必反予。夫出昼,而王不予追也,予然后浩然[4]有归志。予虽然,岂舍王哉?王由足用为善[5];王如用予,则岂徒齐民安,天下之民举安。王庶几改之!予日望之!予岂若是小丈夫[6]然哉?谏于其君而不受,则怒,悻悻然见于其面,去则穷日之力而后宿哉?"尹士闻之,曰:"士诚小人也。"

【译文】孟子离开了齐国,尹士和别人说:"不知道齐王不能够成为商汤、周武王那是不明智;知道他不行,然而还要来,那就是为了求取富贵。不远千里来见齐王,不相融洽就离去。在昼县住了三晚才离开,为什么那样迟缓呢?我对这种情况很不满意。"高子把这些话告诉给孟子。孟子说:"尹士哪能理解我呢?不远千里来见齐王,这是我愿意的;不相融洽而离开,难道也是我愿意的吗?是我不得已啊。我在昼县住了三夜后离开,我心里还以为太快了。王或许会改变态度;王如果改变态度,就一定会召回我。离开昼县后,王还是没有来追我,我才毅然有了回乡的念头。虽然是这样,我难道肯抛弃齐王吗?齐王还是可以有所作为的。齐王如果用我,不仅仅齐国的百姓可以得到安定,天下的百姓也都可以得到安定。齐王或许会改变态度!我天天盼望着啊!我难道要像小气量的人那样吗?向君主进谏,未被接受,就会生气,脸上露出不高兴的神色,离开时非得走到精疲力竭才肯休息吗?"尹士听到这些话,说:"我真是个小人啊。"

【英译】When Mencius had left Ch'î, Yin Shih spoke about him to others, saying, 'If he did not know that the king could not be made a T'ang or a Wû, that showed his want of intelligence. If he knew that he could not be made such, and came notwithstanding, that shows he was seeking his own benefit. He came a thousand lî to wait on the king; because he did not find in him a ruler to suit him, he took his leave, but how dilatory and lingering was his departure, stopping three nights before he quitted Châu! I am dissatisfied on account of this.' The disciple Kâo informed Mencius of these remarks. Mencius said, 'How should Yin Shih know me! When I came a thousand lî to wait on the king, it was what I desired to do. When I went away because I did not find in him a ruler to suit me, was that what I desired to do? I felt myself constrained to do it. When I stopped three nights before I quitted Châu, in my own mind I still considered my departure speedy. I was hoping that the king might change. If the king had changed, he would certainly have recalled me. When I quitted Châu, and the king had not sent after me, then, and not till then, was my mind resolutely bent on returning to Tsâu. But, notwithstanding that, how can it be said that I give up the king? The king, after all, is one who may be made to do what is good. If he were to use me, would it be for the happiness of the people of Ch'î only? It would be for the happiness of the people of the whole kingdom. I am hoping that the king will change. I am daily hoping for this. Am I like one of your little-minded people? They will remonstrate with their prince, and on their remonstrance not being accepted, they get angry; and, with their passion displayed in their countenance, they take their leave, and travel with all their strength for a whole day, before they will stop for the night.' When Yin Shih heard this explanation, he said, 'I am indeed a small man.'

【注释】

[1] 儒家以安天下为己任，积极入世的态度在本章体现得淋漓尽致。

为了实现自己的政治主张，孟子不远千里来到齐国。在得知齐王不能实行仁政后，不受利益诱惑，决定离去。在遭遇挫折时，他仍未舍弃安齐民、安天下民的政治抱负，濡滞而归，以期齐王能改变态度。

[2]"不遇"，刘殿爵翻译为"he met with no success"（他们的会面不成功）略显模糊。理雅各采取解释性翻译策略，将之翻译为"he did not find in him a ruler to suit him，he took his leave"（他发现齐王不是适合他的君主，所以离开），这一翻译虽能体现原文的意思，但略显冗长。孟子离开齐国的原因是齐王不能听取他的建议，这在前面章节中已明确体现，所以赵甄陶的译文"left owing to divergence of opinion"（因为意见分歧而离开）更准确。

[3]"王庶几改之"反映了孟子期望齐王能够改变态度的迫切心情。理雅各的译文准确再现了孟子盼望齐王改变的殷切心情。

[4]朱熹注曰："浩然，如水之流不可止。""浩然有归志"表明孟子要毅然离开的决心。理雅各取"浩然"的引申义，将之翻译为"my mind resolutely bent on returning to Tsâu."（我坚决要返回邹）赖发洛的译文是"Then the wish to be home came sweeping over me."（回家的愿望向我袭来）这一翻译再现了"浩然"所蕴含的"水之流不可止"的意象。刘殿爵的"surged up"不仅体现了水的汹涌澎湃，也反映了回家的希望急剧增长的动态过程。

[5]"王由足用为善"，《词诠》记载："'由'，副词，尚也。亦假作'犹'字用。"本句可以理解为"齐王仍然可以做一番善事"，即齐王有做善事的能力。赖发洛将之译为"The King may yet be brought to do good."（仍然可以劝服齐王行善）显然，他认为齐王是被动接受者，能否做善事取决于贤者的引导。理雅各的译文与之相似。刘殿爵则认为，本句强调的是"齐王仍然具备做好事的能力"，因而将之翻译为"The King is still capable of doing good."笔者认为，孟子之所以迟迟不愿离开齐国，就是看到了齐王"足用为善"的能力，因而刘殿爵的译文更准确。

[6]从孟子的描述可以看出，"小丈夫"指的是那些心胸狭窄的人，

他们会因建议不被采纳而显怒于面，愤然离去。理雅各将之翻译为"little-minded people"（气量小的人），准确体现了"小丈夫"的含义。赖发洛的"small fellow"（小人物）更侧重于地位不高，无足轻重，不准确。刘殿爵的"petty man"（小心眼的人）也能准确体现其含义。

【原文】4.13　孟子去齐[1]，充虞路问曰："夫子若有不豫色然。前日虞闻诸夫子曰：'君子不怨天，不尤人。'"曰："彼一时，此一时也[2]。五百年必有王者兴，其间必有名世者[3]。由周而来，七百有余岁矣。以其数，则过矣；以其时考之，则可矣。[4]夫天未欲平治天下也；如欲平治天下，当今之世，舍我其谁也？吾何为不豫哉？"

【译文】孟子离开齐国，充虞在路上问道："老师好像有些不高兴。前几天我从您那里听到：'君子不抱怨天，不怪罪人。'"孟子说："那是一个时候，现在又是一个时候。五百年必定会有圣王兴起，其间必定有闻名于世的贤者出现。从周朝到现在有七百多年了，从年数上看，已经超过了；就时势而言，现在应该有圣贤出现。老天大概还是不想使天下太平吧。如果想使天下太平，在今天这个社会，除了我，还会有谁呢？我为什么会不高兴呢？"

【英译】When Mencius left Ch'î Ch'ung Yü questioned him upon the way, saying, 'Master, you look like one who carries an air of dissatisfaction in his countenance. But formerly I heard you say,—"The superior man does not murmur against Heaven, nor grudge against men.'" Mencius said, 'That was one time, and this is another. It is a rule that a true royal sovereign should arise in the course of five hundred years, and that during that time there should be men illustrious in their generation. From the commencement of the Châu dynasty till now, more than seven hundred years have elapsed. Judging numerically, the date is past. Examining the character of the present time，we might expect the rise of such individuals in it. But Heaven does not yet wish that the kingdom should enjoy tranquillity and good order. If it wished this，who is there besides me to bring it about? How should I be otherwise than dissatisfied?'

【注释】

[1]"不怨天，不尤人"是孔子自述之语，孟子引用它是为了教育学生遇事要保持平常心，不患得患失，怪天责人。

[2] 焦循《正义》曰："近通解以'彼一时'为充虞所闻君子不怨天不尤人之时，'此一时'为今孟子去齐之时。"可见"彼一时"指的是通常情况下人们的处世态度，而"此一时"指的是特殊时期，即百姓需要王者统一天下，而自诩为有"名世"之才的孟子却不能得到圣君重用之时。理雅各和刘殿爵的译文只是按照字面意思翻译，不如亨顿的译文"That was then"和"This is now"准确。

[3] 关于"名世"的含义，历来歧义很多。赵岐注："名世，次圣之才，物来能名，正于一世者，生于圣人之间也。"朱熹注曰："名世，谓其人德业闻望，可名于一世者，为之辅佐。"杨伯峻认为："'名世'疑即后代之'命世'，'名'与'命'古本通用，焦循《正义》已言之。孟子所谓'其间必有名世者'，恐系指辅佐'王者'之臣而言。孟子一匹夫，无所凭籍，自不敢自居于'王者'，但为周公则未尝不可。《三国志·魏志·武帝纪》云：'天下将乱，非命世之才不能济也。'孟子所谓'名世者'疑即此意。"刘殿爵的译文"one from whom an age takes its name"准确翻译出了"名世者"的含义。

[4] 根据孟子总结出来的人类社会发展规律，每隔五百年就会出现王者和命世之才，但由周而来，已有七百余岁，从时间上看，已经超过了五百年；从社会状况上看，时机已经具备。因而孟子说"以其数，则过矣；以其时考之，则可矣"。理雅各在翻译时按字面意思直译，不方便读者理

解。刘殿爵采用意译法，根据上下文将本句翻译为"The five hundred mark is passed；the time seems ripe."（五百年的标准已经达到了，时机似乎也成熟了）他的翻译紧紧围绕篇章主旨，使译文成为一个有机整体。

【原文】4.14　孟子去齐，[1]居休[2]。公孙丑问曰："仕而不受禄，古之道乎？"曰："非也。于崇，吾得见王，退而有去志，不欲变，故不受也。继而有师命，[3]不可以请。久于齐，非我志也。"

【译文】孟子离开齐国，暂住在休地。公孙丑问："做官但不接受俸禄，合乎古道吗？"孟子说："不是。在崇，我见了齐王，回来便想离开，不想改变，所以不接受。接着齐国出现战事，不可以请求离开。长久地留在齐国，不是我的心愿。"

【英译】When Mencius left Chʻî，he dwelt in Hsiû. There Kung-sun Chʻâu asked him，saying，'Was it the way of the ancients to hold office without receiving salary?' Mencius replied，'No；when I first saw the king in Chʻung，it was my intention，on retiring from the interview，to go away. Because I did not wish to change this intention，I declined to receive any salary. Immediately after，there came orders for the collection of troops，when it would have been improper for me to beg permission to leave. But to remain so long in Chʻî was not my purpose.'

【注释】

[1]《孟子·公孙丑下》的最后几章记录了孟子离开齐国时的所作所为，为我们展示了君子的进退之道。孟子和子思在受禄上的态度一脉相承，子思说："事君三违而不出竟，则利禄也；人虽曰不要，吾弗信也。"（《礼记·表记》）

[2]"居休"，理雅各和赖发洛都将之翻译为"dwelt in Hsiu"（居住在休），而刘殿爵翻译为"stayed at Hsiu"（暂住在休），赵甄陶翻译为"stopped

at Xiu"（在休逗留）。从孟子的游历经历看，他在休地仅仅是暂住，而非长久居住。从孟子的整个思想体系看，他一直以平治天下为己任，即使在齐国遭遇挫折，显露出"不豫色"，仍没有放弃"如欲平治天下，当今之世，舍我其谁也"的凌云壮志，而非受到些许打击，就退居休地，隐藏自己的治世之才，因而"暂住、逗留"更符合孟子作为儒家的代表人物，积极入世的形象。

[3]"继而有师命，不可以请"是孟子陈述的自己不受禄的原因。理雅各将之翻译为"there came orders for the collection of troops, when it would have been improper for me to beg permission to leave."（紧接着传来了召集军队的命令，这时如果我请求离开是不合礼的）他将本句话放在儒家的思想体系下进行理解，认为儒家重礼，要求进退出处都要符合礼的规定。刘殿爵的翻译是"It so happened that war broke out and I had no opportunity of requesting permission to leave."（碰巧爆发了战争，我没有机会请求离开）他突出了战争爆发的偶然性，表明自己"不受禄"是特殊原因造成的，并非"古之道"。译文紧扣公孙丑的问题，再现了原文紧凑的结构。

卷　五

滕文公章句上

【原文】 5.1　滕文公为世子，将之楚，过宋而见孟子。孟子道性善[1]，言必称尧舜[2]。世子自楚反，复见孟子。孟子曰："世子疑吾言乎？夫道一而已矣。成覸谓齐景公曰：'彼[3]，丈夫也；我，丈夫也；吾何畏彼哉？'颜渊曰：'舜，何人也？予，何人也？有为者亦若是。'公明仪曰：'文王，我师也。周公岂欺我哉？'[4]今滕，绝长补短，将五十里也，犹可以为善国。《书》曰：'若药不瞑眩，厥疾不瘳。'"

【译文】 滕文公做太子的时候，要去楚国，路过宋国时和孟子相见。孟子同他讲了性善的道理，谈话的内容也都围绕着尧舜展开。太子从楚国回来，又去见孟子。孟子说："太子怀疑我的话吗？道就只有一个。成覸对齐景公说：'他是个男子汉，我也是个男子汉，我为什么要害怕他？'颜渊说：'舜是什么样的人，我也是什么样的人，有作为的人也都是这样。'公明仪说：'文王是我的老师。周公也不会骗我。'现在的滕国，长短折算下来，方圆近五十里，仍然可以治理成一个好国家。《书经》说：'如果吃的药物不能使人头晕目眩，那种病就不会痊愈。'"

【英译】 When the prince, afterwards duke Wǎn of T'ǎng, had to go to Ch'û, he went by way of Sung, and visited Mencius. Mencius discoursed to him how the nature of man is good, and when speaking, always made laudatory reference to Yâo and Shun. When the prince was returning from Ch'û, he again visited Mencius. Mencius said to him, 'Prince, do you doubt my words? The path is one, and only one. Ch'ǎng Chi'en said to duke King of Ch'î, "They were men. I am a man. Why should I stand in awe of them?" Yen Yüan said, "What kind of man was Shun? What kind of man am I? He who exerts himself will also become such as he was." Kung-ming Î said, "King Wǎn is my teacher. How should the duke of Châu deceive me by those words?" Now, Tǎng, taking its length with its breadth, will amount, I suppose, to fifty lî It is small, but still sufficient to make a good State. It is said in the Book of History, "If medicine do not raise a commotion in the patient, his disease will not be cured by it."'

【注释】

[1] 在本章中首次出现孟子的性善论。孟子仅"道性善",但并未详细论及性善的含义。理雅各将之翻译为"Mencius discoursed to him how the nature of man is good"(孟子告诉他为什么人性是善的)。梁涛对此种理解持批判态度,他曾指出:"很多学者将'孟子道性善'理解为'孟子认为人性是善的',实际上《孟子》一书中只说'孟子道性善'、'言性善',而'道性善'、'言性善'是宣传、言说关于性善的一种学说、理论,不能直接等同于'人性是善的'。'人性是善的'是一个命题,是对人性的直言判断,而'性善'则是孟子对人性的独特理解,是基于孟子特殊生活经历的一种体验与智慧,是一种意味深长、富有启发意义的道理。理解孟子性善论,固然要重视孟子提出的种种理由与根据,但更为重要的则是要对孟子'道性善'的深刻意蕴有一种'觉悟',而这种深刻意蕴绝不是'人性是善的'这样一个命题所能表达的。"可见,刘殿爵的译文"Mencius who talked to him about the goodness of human nature"(孟子和他谈性善)更准确表达了"道性善"的含义。

[2] 朱熹注："性者，人所禀于天以生之理也，浑然至善，未尝有恶。人与尧舜初无少异，但众人汩于私欲而失之，尧舜则无私欲之蔽，而能充其性尔。故孟子与世子言，每道性善，而必称尧舜以实之。欲其知仁义不假外求，圣人可学而至，而不懈于用力也。"根据朱熹的解释，此处的"称"有"称引""援引"尧舜以证实之意。刘殿爵亦持这种观点。赖发洛和理雅各则取"称"的"赞颂"之意，将之分别翻译为"Mencius always praised Yao and Shun"和"always made laudatory reference to Yâo and Shun"。从逻辑关系上看，刘殿爵的译文更准确。

[3] 译者对"彼"的理解不同。一种观点认为泛指那些有大丈夫之气的人，如刘殿爵将"彼"翻译为"he"，认为是泛指；一种说法认为特指齐景公等显贵者，如焦循认为："彼，尊贵者，盖指景公言"；一说认为特指尧舜等圣人。朱熹注："彼，谓圣贤也。"理雅各将"彼"翻译为"they"，并在注释中指出，"彼"指的是圣人。赖发洛也持这种观点，他亦将"彼"翻译为"they"，强调"彼"指尧和舜。

[4]"公明仪曰：'文王，我师也，周公岂欺我哉?'"有两种理解，一种认为"文王，我师也"是公明仪引用的周公的话，而"周公岂欺我哉?"是他对这句话的评价，认为周公这句话是真实无妄的。朱熹的《四书集注》就持这一观点："文王我师也，盖周公之言。公明仪亦以文王为必可师，故诵周公之言而叹其不我欺也。"另一种观点认为，公明仪为贤能之人，他师文王信周公。如焦循的《孟子正义》就认为："公明仪贤者也。师文王信周公，言其知所法则也。"这两种解释皆通。理雅各的理解同朱熹，赖发洛的译文是"King Wen is my teacher；would the Duke of Chou cheat me?"（文王是我的老师，周公会欺骗我吗）他的逐字直译掩盖了译文前后两句的逻辑关联，使文意晦涩难懂。刘殿爵的译文亦同朱熹，将本句翻译为"When he said that he modeled himself on King Wen, the Duck of Chou was only telling the truth."（当周公说他以文王为师时，他只是在陈述一个事实）笔者认为，由于中西两种语言存在较大差异，有时候在汉语语言环境中通过简短的词语

可以清楚表达的含义，在翻译成英语时需要作出必要的添加才能说清楚，因而译者如果过于拘泥于原文，反而不容易让读者理解。

【原文】 5.2 滕定公薨[1]，世子谓然友曰："昔者孟子尝与我言于宋，于心终不忘。今也不幸至于大故[2]，吾欲使子问于孟子，然后行事。"然友之邹问于孟子。孟子曰："不亦善乎！亲丧，固所自尽也[3]。曾子曰：'生，事之以礼；死，葬之以礼，祭之以礼，可谓孝矣。'诸侯之礼，吾未之学也。虽然，吾尝闻之矣。三年之丧，齐疏之服，飦粥之食[4]，自天子达于庶人，三代共之。"然友反命，定为三年之丧。父兄百官皆不欲，曰："吾宗国鲁先君莫之行，吾先君亦莫之行也，至于子之身而反之，不可。且《志》曰：'丧祭从先祖。'曰：'吾有所受之也。'[5]"谓然友曰："吾他日未尝学问，好驰马试剑。今也父兄百官不我足也，恐其[6]不能尽于大事，子为我问孟子！"然友复之邹问孟子。孟子曰："然，不可以他求者也。孔子曰：'君薨，听于冢宰。歠粥，面深墨，即位而哭，百官有司莫敢不哀，先之也。'上有好者，下必有甚焉者矣。君子之德，风也；小人之德，草也。草尚之风，必偃。[7]是在世子。"然友反命。世子曰："然；是诚在我。"五月居庐，未有命戒。百官族人可，谓曰知[8]。及至葬，四方来观之，颜色之戚，哭泣之哀，吊者大悦。

【译文】 滕定公去世了，太子对然友说："以前孟子在宋国，给我谈了许多，我的心里一直没有忘记。今天不幸遭遇父丧，我想请您去问问孟子，然后再办丧事。"然友去邹国问孟子。孟子说："不也很好呀！父母的丧事，本就应该尽心竭力。曾子说：'父母在世的时候，依礼侍奉他们；去世了，依礼去埋葬，依礼去祭祀，可以说是孝顺了。'诸侯的礼，我没有学过，即使这样，但也听说过。丧期三年，穿粗布缉边的衣服、吃稀粥，从天子到老百姓，夏，商、周三代都是这样。"然友回国复命，太子决定丧期三年。滕国的宗室官吏都不愿意，说："我们的宗国鲁国的历代君主都没有实行过，我们的历代君主也没有实行过，到你这里便改变先前的做法，不可以。而且《志》说：'丧礼祭礼都遵循祖先的规矩。'意思是说，'我们是这样传承下来的'。"太子便对然友说："我以前不好学问，只喜欢跑马舞剑。现在宗室、官吏们都对我不满意，恐怕他们在丧礼上不能够尽心竭力，你替我去问问孟子！"然友再次去邹国问孟子。孟子说："是的！这事不能够要求别人。孔子说：'君主死了，政务交给宰相，喝稀粥，面色深黑，走到孝子之位便哭，大小官吏没有敢不悲哀的，因为太子带头啊。'居上位的人爱好什么，下面的人一定会爱好得更厉害。'君子的德像风，小人的德像草，风吹到草上，草就会倒下。'这事取决于太子。"然友返回向太子复命。太子说；"对，这确实取决于我。"在丧庐中居住了五个月，也没有发布过任何命令和禁令。官员和同族的人都很认可，称赞他知礼。等到葬礼的时候，四面八方的人都来观礼。太子容色悲戚，哭的哀痛，吊丧的人都很满意。

【英译】When the duke Ting of T'ǎng died, the prince said to Yen Yû, 'Formerly, Mencius spoke with me in Sung, and in my mind I have never forgotten his words. Now, alas! this great duty to my father devolves upon me; I wish to send you to ask the advice of Mencius, and then to proceed to its various services' Zan Yû accordingly proceeded to Tsâu, and consulted Mencius. Mencius said, 'Is this not good? In discharging the funeral duties to parents, men indeed feel constrained to do their utmost. The philosopher Tsǎng said, "When parents are alive, they should be served according to propriety; when they are dead, they should be buried according to propriety; and they should be sacrificed to according to propriety: —this may be called filial piety." The ceremonies to be observed by the princes I have

not learned, but I have heard these points: —that the three years'
mourning, the garment of coarse cloth with its lower edge even, and
the eating of congee, were equally prescribed by the three dynasties,
and binding on all, from the sovereign to the mass of the people.'
Zan Yû reported the execution of his commission, and the prince
determined that the three years' mourning should be observed. His aged
relatives, and the body of the officers, did not wish that it should be
so, and said, 'The former princes of Lû, that kingdom which we
honour, have, none of them, observed this practice, neither have
any of our own former princes observed it. For you to act contrary to
their example is not proper. Moreover, the History says, — "In the
observances of mourning and sacrifice, ancestors are to be followed,"
meaning that they received those things from a proper source to hand
them down.' The prince said again to Zan Yû, 'Hitherto, I have not
given myself to the pursuit of learning, but have found my pleasure
in horsemanship and sword-exercise, and now I don't come up to
the wishes of my aged relatives and the officers. I am afraid I may not
be able to discharge my duty in the great business that I have entered
on; do you again consult Mencius for me.' On this, Zan Yû went
again to Tsâu, and consulted Mencius. Mencius said, 'It is so, but
he may not seek a remedy in others, but only in himself. Confucius
said, "When a prince dies, his successor entrusts the administration to
the prime minister. He sips the congee. His face is of a deep black. He
approaches the place of mourning, and weeps. Of all the officers and
inferior ministers there is not one who will presume not to join in the
lamentation, he setting them this example. What the superior loves,
his inferiors will be found to love exceedingly. The relation between

superiors and inferiors is like that between the wind and grass. The grass must bend when the wind blows upon it." The business depends on the prince.' Zan Yû returned with this answer to his commission, and the prince said, 'It is so. The matter does indeed depend on me.' So for five months he dwelt in the shed, without issuing an order or a caution. All the officers and his relatives said, 'He may be said to understand the ceremonies.' When the time of interment arrived, they came from all quarters of the State to witness it. Those who had come from other States to condole with him, were greatly pleased with the deep dejection of his countenance and the mournfulness of his wailing and weeping.

【注释】

[1] 本章详细记录了孟子对丧葬之礼的理解，并指出在道德教化中统治者要充分发挥榜样的作用，以身作则，才会上行下效，实现教化的目的。儒家的创始人孔子早就认识到统治者在道德教化中的作用，指出："政者，正也。子帅以正，孰敢不正。"（《论语颜渊》）孟子继承了孔子的认识，强调"上有好者，下必有甚焉者矣。"

[2] 古代经常用"大故"一词指称君主或父母去世等不幸的事情。如《汉书·匈奴传下》中有："自黄龙、竟宁时，单于朝中国辄有大故。"颜师古注曰："大故，谓国之大丧。"刘殿爵的译文"the misfortune to lose my father"（不幸失去了父亲）准确翻译出了"大故"的含义。理雅各将"大故"翻译为"this great duty to my father devolves upon me"（对我父亲应尽的重大义务），这一翻译略显隐晦，不便于读者理解。赖发洛的"Now that the great matter has come upon me"（那件大事落在了我身上）未能体现出"大故"在此处所蕴含的父丧之意。

[3] "亲"指的是"父母双亲"，而非赖发洛翻译的"kinsman"。"kinsman"指的是男性亲戚或同族者。孝子出于内心对父母的爱，竭尽全力

为他们尽的最后的孝体现在丧葬之礼上就是"固所自尽也"。刘殿爵将之译为"The funeral of a parent is an occasion for giving of one's utmost"（父母的葬礼是尽心竭力孝敬他们的机会）准确表达了孟子重视丧葬之礼的原因。

[4] 孟子介绍了古代的丧葬之礼，即"三年之丧，齐疏之服，飦粥之食"。朱熹注曰："齐，衣下缝也。……疏，粗也，粗布也。"可见古代丧服的特征是粗布并且缉边。理雅各的译文准确翻译出了"齐疏之服"和"飦粥之食"的含义，将古代丧葬之礼完整、准确地翻译了出来。

[5] 在翻译"曰：'吾有所受之也'"时，理雅各的译文是"meaning that they received those things from a proper source to hand them down."（也就是说，他们认可的上述事情是通过正确的渠道传承下来的）显然，理雅各认为这句话是反对三年之丧的"父兄百官"对自己的反对理由所做的进一步解释。刘殿爵的译文是"I have authority for what I do."（我这样做是有依据的）他认为这句话是文公对"父兄百官"的反对做出的辩解，指出自己这样做是向贤者孟子请教的结果。笔者认为，将本句话理解为父兄百官对自己反对意见的进一步解释更准确。《词诠》卷九："'曰'为外动词，亦言义。惟用以解释上文，在今语与'他的意思是说'相同。"

[6] 杨伯峻指出，"'恐其不能尽于大事'的'其'字固可以看作世子自称之词，古人本有藉第三人称代词以自指之例，赵岐注以为指父兄百官，亦通。"理雅各将"其"理解为文公自称，刘殿爵同赵岐，翻译为"I am afraid they may not give of their best in this matter."（我担心他们在这件事上恐不能尽心尽力）而赖发洛又提出了一种新的理解："Now my uncles and cousins and the hundred officers think little of me and are afraid that I shall fall short in this great business."（父兄百官担心我不能做好这一大事）从文意上看，这一理解也是可以接受的。文公认为自己从前沉迷于骑马练剑，不好学问，导致父兄百官对他不满意，因而担心他不能做好丧葬之事。

[7] "君子之德，风也；小人之德，草也。草尚之风，必偃"，表明统治者对百姓的教化作用，犹如风吹在草上，草必随之倒下。刘殿爵选择用

"virtue"翻译"德"。虽然在《孟子》中出现的"德"绝大多数情况下都是指"美德"，是君子孜孜以求的高尚品行，但傅佩荣指出："在此'德'是指人的言行表现所形成的特色或作风，与善恶无关。"赖发洛选择用"mind"（意识、意愿）翻译。"Mind"是中性词，仅仅是表明人的思想特点，翻译此处的"德"更准确。

[8] 对"百官族人可谓曰知"有两种断句方法：一是杨伯峻提出的"百官族人可，谓曰知。"即"官吏同族都很赞成，认为知礼。"一是陈器之的"百官族人，可谓曰知。"即"大小官吏和同族的人，才肯说为知礼。"同时陈器之指出："百官态度与前不同，故'可'当译为'肯'，《说文》：'可，肯也。'曰，《词诠》卷九：'不完全内动词，为也，''曰'字用于'谓'字之下，可合译为'说为'。"这两种断句从文义上看都能说得过去，是可以接受的。刘殿爵在翻译时支持第一种断句，将之翻译为"The officials and his kinsmen approved of his actions and thought him well-versed in the rites."（百官和亲族都赞成他的行为，认为他精通礼仪）他认为"知"是对"知礼"的省略，在翻译时做了必要的补充，使句意更加完整。理雅各支持第二种断句方法，将之翻译为"All the officers and his relatives said, 'He may be said to understand the ceremonies."（百官和亲人说："可以称他懂的礼仪"）这一翻译符合英语表达习惯，也便于读者理解。

【原文】5.3　滕文公问为国[1]。孟子曰："民事不可缓也。《诗》云：'昼尔于茅，宵尔索绹；亟其乘屋[2]，其始播百谷。'民之为道也，有恒产者有恒心，无恒产者无恒心。苟无恒心，放辟邪侈，无不为已。及陷乎罪，然后从而刑之，是罔民也。焉有仁人在位罔民而可为也？是故贤君必恭俭礼下，取于民有制。阳虎曰：'为富不仁矣，为仁不富矣。'夏后氏五十而贡，殷人七十而助，周人百亩而彻[3]，其实皆什一也。彻者，彻也；助者，籍也。龙子曰：'治地莫善于助，莫不善于贡。'贡者，校数岁之中以为常。乐岁，粒米狼戾[4]，多取之而不为虐，则寡取之；凶年，粪其田而不足，则必取盈焉。为民父母，使民盻盻然，将终岁勤动，不得以养其父母，又称贷而益之，使老稚转乎沟壑，恶在其为民父母也？夫世禄，滕固行之矣。诗云：'雨我公田，遂及我私。'惟助为有公田。由此观之，虽周亦助也。设为庠序学校[5]以教之。庠者，养也；校者，教也；序者，射也。夏曰校，殷曰序，周曰庠；学则三代共之，皆所以明人伦也。人伦明于上，小民亲于下。有王者起，必来取法，是为王者师也。《诗》云：'周虽旧邦，其命惟新。'文王之谓也。子力行之，亦以新子之国！"使毕战问井地。孟子曰："子之君将行仁政，选择而使子，子必勉之！夫仁政，必自经界始。经界不正，井地不钧，谷禄不平，是故暴君污吏必慢其经界。经界既正，分田制禄，可坐而定也。夫滕，壤地褊小，将为君子焉，将为野人焉。无君子，莫治野人；无野人，莫养君子。请野九一而助，国中什一使自赋。卿以下必有圭田[6]，圭田五十亩；余夫[7]二十五亩。死徙无出乡，乡田同井，出入相友，守望相助，疾病相扶持，则百姓亲睦。方里而井[8]，井九百亩，其中为公田。八家皆私百亩，同养公田；公事毕，然后敢治私事，所以别野人也。此其大略也，若夫润泽之，则在君与子矣。"

【译文】 滕文公问孟子治理国家的事情。孟子说："百姓的事刻不容缓。《诗经》上说：'白天去割茅草，晚上搓好绳索，赶紧上房修屋，按时播种谷物。'百姓有一个特点，就是有固定的产业收入就有一定的道德观念，没有固定的产业收入就没有固定的道德观念。如果没有固定的道德观念，就会胡作非为，什么事都干。等犯了罪，然后去处罚他们，这是陷害百姓。哪有仁人掌权却做陷害老百姓的事呢？所以贤能的君主一定要恭敬节俭，有礼貌地对待下属，从百姓那里征税要有定制。阳虎说：'要发财就不能仁爱，要仁爱就不能发财。'夏代以五十亩地为单位实行'贡法'，商朝以七十亩地为单位实行'助'法，周朝以一百亩地为单位实行'彻'法。他们的税率其实都是十分之一。'彻'是'抽取'的意思，'助'是'借助'的意思。龙子说：'管理土地没有比助法更好的，没有比贡法更坏的。'贡法是比较若干年的收成取一个平均数。收成好的时候，到处是谷物，多征收也不算苛暴，却收的少；灾荒年月，即使给田地多施肥，粮食也不够吃，但也要按规定的数足额征收。作为百姓的父母，国君使百姓终年辛劳，但也不能养活父母，还得靠借贷来凑足赋税，最终使得老小抛尸山沟，这怎么能说是百姓的父母呢？为官的人有可以子孙相传的田租收入，滕国已经实行了。《诗经》说：'雨下到公田里，然后再落到私田！'只有助法有公田的说法，从这可以看出，就是周朝，也实行助法。要建立'庠''序''学''校'去教育他们。'庠'是养的意思，'校'是教导的意思，'序'是射箭的意思。夏代叫'校'，商代叫'序'，周代叫'庠'；至于学，三代的叫法都一样。它们都是为了教导百姓明白人与人之间的各种关系。人与人之间的关系和行为准则，掌权者都明白了，百姓就会亲密团结。有王者兴起，一定会来学习，这样便可以成为王者的老师了。《诗经》上说：'歧周虽是一个古老的邦家，国运中充满新机。'这是说的文王。你努力实行吧，使你的国家焕然一新！"

滕文公又让毕战问井田制的事情。孟子说："你的君主准备行仁政，让你来问我。你一定要好好努力。仁政一定要从划分田界开始。田界划分不正确，井田的大小就不均匀，谷物的收入就不公平合理，所以暴君和贪官污吏必定要破坏田界。田间正确了，分配田地，制定俸禄，都可以毫不费力地确定。虽然滕国的土地狭小，却也要有管理者和劳动者。没有管理者，就不能管理劳动者；没有劳动者，也不能养活管理者。请在郊野用九分抽一的助法，在城市用十分抽一的贡法。公卿以下的官吏一定要有用于祭祀的圭田，每家五十亩。家里剩余的劳动力，每人再给二十五亩。埋葬和搬家都不离开乡土。同一井田的乡邻，平时出入，互相友爱；防御盗贼，互相帮助；疾病时互相扶持，那么百姓间就会亲爱和睦。每一方里的土地为一个井田，每个井田九百亩，中间为公田，周围八家各有私田百亩，大家共同耕种公田。先耕种完公田，再耕种私田，这就是区别官吏和劳动者的方法。这只是一个大概情况，怎样再进一步改进完善，那就靠君主和你了。"

【英译】The duke Wăn of T'ăng asked Mencius about the proper way of governing a kingdom. Mencius said，'The business of the people may not be remissly attended to. It is said in the Book of Poetry，"In the day-light go and gather the grass，and at night twist your ropes；then get up quickly on the roofs；soon must we begin sowing again the grain." The way of the people is this：—If they have a certain livelihood，they will have a fixed heart；if they have not a certain livelihood，they have not a fixed heart. If they have not a fixed heart，there is nothing which they will not do in the way of self-abandonment，of moral deflection，of depravity，and of wild license. When they have thus been involved in crime，to follow them up and punish them：—this is to entrap the people. How can such a thing as entrapping the people be done under the rule of a benevolent man？Therefore，a ruler who is endowed with talents and virtue will be gravely complaisant and economical，showing a respectful politeness to his ministers，and taking from the people only in accordance with regulated limits. Yang Hû said，"He who seeks to be rich will not be benevolent. He who wishes to be benevolent will not be rich." The sovereign of the Hsiâ dynasty enacted the fifty mâu allotment，and the payment of a tax. The founder of the Yin enacted the seventy mâu allotment，and the system of mutual aid. The founder of the Châu enacted the hundred mâu allotment，and the share system. In reality，what was paid in all these was a tithe. The share system means mutual division. The aid system means mutual dependence. Lung said, "For regulating the lands, there is no better system than that of mutual aid, and none which is not better than that of taxing. By the tax system, the regular amount was fixed by taking the average of several years. In good years, when the grain lies about in abundance, much might be taken without its being oppressive, and the actual exaction would be small. But in bad years, the produce being not sufficient to repay the manuring of the fields, this system still requires the taking of the full amount. When the parent of the people causes the people to wear looks of distress, and, after the whole year's toil, yet not to be able to nourish their parents, so that they proceed to borrowing to increase their means, till the old people and children are found lying in the ditches and water-channels: —where, in such a case, is his parental relation to the people?" As to the system of hereditary salaries, that is already observed in T'ăng. It is said in the Book of Poetry, "May the rain come down on our public field, and then upon our private fields!" It is only in the system of mutual aid that there is a public field, and from this passage we perceive that even in the Châu dynasty this system has been recognised. Establish hsiang, hsü, hsio, and hsiâo, — all those educational institutions, —for the instruction of the people. The name hsiang indicates nourishing as its object; hsiâo, indicates teaching; and hsü, indicates archery. By the Hsiâ dynasty the name hsiâo was used; by the Yin, that of hsü; and by the Châu, that of hsiang. As to the hsio, they belonged to the three dynasties, and by that name. The object of them all is to illustrate the human relations. When those are thus illustrated by superiors, kindly feeling will prevail among the inferior people below. Should a real sovereign arise, he

will certainly come and take an example from you; and thus you will
be the teacher of the true sovereign. It is said in the Book of Poetry,
"Although Châu was an old country, it received a new destiny." That
is said with reference to king Wăn. Do you practise those things with
vigour, and you also will by them make new your kingdom. The duke
afterwards sent Pî Chan to consult Mencius about the nine-squares
system of dividing the land. Mencius said to him, 'Since your prince,
wishing to put in practice a benevolent government, has made choice
of you and put you into this employment, you must exert yourself
to the utmost. Now, the first thing towards a benevolent government
must be to lay down the boundaries. If the boundaries be not defined
correctly, the division of the land into squares will not be equal, and
the produce available for salaries will not be evenly distributed. On this
account, oppressive rulers and impure ministers are sure to neglect
this defining of the boundaries. When the boundaries have been defined
correctly, the division of the fields and the regulation of allowances
may be determined by you, sitting at your ease. Although the territory
of T'ăng is narrow and small, yet there must be in it men of a superior
grade, and there must be in it country-men. If there were not men of a
superior grade, there would be none to rule the country-men. If there
were not country-men, there would be none to support the men of
superior grade. I would ask you, in the remoter districts, observing the
nine-squares division, to reserve one division to be cultivated on the
system of mutual aid, and in the more central parts of the kingdom, to
make the people pay for themselves a tenth part of their produce. From
the highest officers down to the lowest, each one must have his holy
field, consisting of fifty mâu. Let the supernumerary males have their

twenty-five mâu. On occasions of death, or removal from one dwelling to another, there will be no quitting the district. In the fields of a district, those who belong to the same nine squares render all friendly offices to one another in their going out and coming in, aid one another in keeping watch and ward, and sustain one another in sickness. Thus the people are brought to live in affection and harmony. A square lî covers nine squares of land, which nine squares contain nine hundred mâu. The central square is the public field, and eight families, each having its private hundred mâu, cultivate in common the public field. And not till the public work is finished, may they presume to attend to their private affairs. This is the way by which the country-men are distinguished from those of a superior grade. Those are the great outlines of the system. Happily to modify and adapt it depends on the prince and you.'

【注释】

[1] 通过向滕文公讲述治国之道，孟子详细阐述了自己的政治理想：重视民事，使民有恒产，并以此为基础兴办学校，教育百姓。

[2] "亟其乘屋"，理雅各取"乘"的本义"登，升"，将之翻译为"Then get up quickly on the roofs"（很快爬上屋顶）。这一翻译容易割裂诗句前后的联系，不便于读者理解。"乘"，《诗》郑《笺》云："治也"。刘殿爵将之翻译为"They hasten to repair the roof"（赶紧修葺屋顶），准确翻译出了其含义。

[3] "贡、助和彻"是孟子提及的夏商周三代的土地和赋税政策。这些政策年代久远，早已废弃不用，今天的中国人都很难理解。朱熹注曰："夏时一夫授田五十亩，而每夫计其五亩之入以为贡。商人始为井田之制，以六百三十亩之地，画为九区，区七十亩。中为公田，其外八家各授一区，但借其力以助耕公田，而不复税其私田。周时一夫授田百亩。乡隧用贡法，十

夫有沟。都鄙用助法，八家同井。耕则通力而作，收则计亩而分，故谓之彻。"可见，"贡、助和彻"是中国古代社会特有的租税制度。理雅各分别将之翻译为"the payment of a tax"（交税）、"mutual aid"（互助制度）和"the share system"（共享制度）。这些翻译仅仅抓住了"贡、助和彻"的某个显著特征，不能准确涵盖它们丰富的内涵，容易导致以偏概全，产生误解。赖发洛也存在类似的缺陷，将之分别译为"was taxed"（征税）、"gave aids"（提供帮助）和"tithed"（什一税）。在西方国家，"tithed"通常和宗教捐税相关，容易引起不必要的联想。刘殿爵对这些文化词语的处理比较好。他在翻译时采用音译法，以突出其含义的特殊性。同时为了便于读者了解中国传统文化，又在注释或索引中对之做出详细的解释。

[4]"狼戾"，赵岐《注》曰："犹狼藉也"。即非常充足，因而散乱堆放，不很珍惜。理雅各翻译为"lies about in abundance"（非常充裕，到处都是），取"狼""散乱堆积、纵横交错之意"。刘殿爵取其引申意，意译为"so plentiful that it goes to waste"（非常丰富，以至于浪费掉了）。从上下文看，"乐岁"和"凶年"，"狼戾"和"不足"相对举而言，故"狼戾"取充裕之意。"狼戾"不仅表明谷物非常充裕，还传达了散乱堆放、到处皆是的杂乱意象。这两种翻译都充分准确地传递了"狼戾"的含义。

[5]"庠、序、学、校"都是我国古代的教育机构。综合各家注释，概括来说，"庠、序、校"是乡学，分别以养老、习射和教民为义，而"学"则指国学。这些教育机构在英语中没有对等词，刘殿爵在翻译时采取音译的方式，笔者认为这是翻译中国古代社会习俗制度的最佳方式。

[6]"圭田"，朱熹注："圭，洁也。所以奉祭祀也。"可见，"圭田"是卿、大夫因洁行受赐以供祭祀的田地。理雅各认为"圭田"象征圣洁，将之翻译为"holy field"；刘殿爵强调"圭田"的作用，将之翻译为"land for sacrifice purposes"（祭祀用的田地）。理雅各的翻译体现了"圭田"的象征意，刘殿爵的译文重在强调其用途，虽然二者的侧重点不同，但都能将"圭田"的含义说清楚。

　　[7]"余夫"，赵岐注曰："余夫者，一家一人受田，其余老小尚有余力者，受二十五亩，半于圭田，谓之余夫也。"朱熹注曰："程子曰：'一夫上父母，下妻子，以五口八口为率，受田百亩。如有弟，是余夫也。年十六，别受田二十五亩，俟其壮而有室，然后更受百亩之田。愚按：此百亩常制之外，又有余夫之田，以厚野人也。"理雅各的"supernumerary males"基本上能体现"余夫"的含义。

　　[8]"井"，理雅各采取解释性翻译策略，根据自己对"井田制"的理解，将之译为"nine squares of land"（九个正方形的土地），赖发洛将"井"翻译为"Well"（水井），并推测"井田制"这一名称的出现或许是因为田地中间有一个井。但是笔者认为英文"Well"和中国的"井田"似乎没有任何联系。刘殿爵在翻译"井"时采用音译法，将之翻译为"ching"，并在索引中对它做了详细的解释，因而更准确。

【原文】5.4　有为神农[1]之言者许行，自楚之滕，踵门而告文公曰："远方之人闻君行仁政，愿受一廛而为氓。"文公与之处。其徒数十人，皆衣褐[2]，捆屦织席以为食。陈良之徒陈相与其弟辛负耒耜而自宋之滕，曰："闻君行圣人之政，是亦圣人也，愿为圣人氓。"陈相见许行而大悦，尽弃其学而学焉。陈相见孟子，道许行之言曰："滕君则诚贤君也；虽然，未闻道[3]也。贤者与民并耕而食，饔飧而治。今也滕有仓廪府库，则是厉民而以自养也，恶得贤？"孟子曰："许子必种粟而后食乎？"曰："然。""许子必织布而后衣乎？"曰："否，许子衣褐。""许子冠乎？"曰："冠。"曰："奚冠？"曰："冠素。"曰："自织之与？"曰："否，以粟易之。"曰："许子奚为不自织？"曰："害于耕。"曰："许子以釜甑爨，以铁耕乎？"曰："然。""自为之与？"曰："否，以粟易之。""以粟易械器者，不为厉陶冶；陶冶亦以其械器易粟者，岂为厉农夫哉？且许子何不为陶冶，舍皆取诸其宫中而用之？何为纷纷然与百工交易？何许子

之不惮烦?"曰:"百工之事固不可耕且为也。""然则治天下独可耕
且为与? 有大人之事,有小人之事。且一人之身,而百工之所为
备^[4],如必自为而后用之,是率天下而路^[5]也。故曰,或劳心^[6],
或劳力;劳心者治人,劳力者治于人;治于人者食人,治人者食于
人,天下之通义也。当尧之时,天下犹未平,洪水横流,泛滥于天
下,草木畅茂,禽兽繁殖,五谷不登,禽兽逼人,兽蹄鸟迹之道交
于中国。尧独忧之,举舜而敷治焉。舜使益掌火,益烈山泽而焚
之,禽兽逃匿。禹疏九河,瀹济、漯而注诸海;决汝、汉,排淮、
泗而注之江,然后中国可得而食也。当是时也,禹八年于外,三过
其门而不入,虽欲耕,得乎? 后稷教民稼穑,树艺五谷;五谷熟而
民人育。人之有道^[7]也,饱食、暖衣、逸居而无教,则近于禽兽。
圣人有忧之,使契为司徒,教以人伦,——父子有亲,君臣有义,
夫妇有别,长幼有序,朋友有信。放勋曰:'劳之来之,匡之直之,
辅之翼之,使自得之,又从而振德^[8]之。'圣人之忧民如此,而暇
耕乎? 尧以不得舜为己忧,舜以不得禹、皋陶为己忧。夫以百亩之
不易为己忧者,农夫也。分人以财谓之惠,教人以善谓之忠,为
天下得人者谓之仁。是故以天下与人易,为天下得人难。孔子曰:
'大哉,尧之为君! 惟天为大,惟尧则之。荡荡乎民无能名焉! 君
哉舜也! 巍巍乎有天下而不与焉!'尧舜之治天下,岂无所用其心
哉? 亦不用于耕耳。吾闻用夏变夷者,未闻变于夷者也。陈良,楚
产也,悦周公、仲尼之道,北学于中国。北方之学者,未能或之先
也。彼所谓豪杰之士也。子之兄弟事之数十年,师死而遂倍之! 昔
者孔子没,三年之外,门人治任将归,入揖于子贡,相向而哭,皆
失声,然后归。子贡反,筑室于场,独居三年,然后归。他日,子
夏、子张、子游以有若似圣人,欲以所事孔子事之,强曾子。曾子
曰:'不可;江汉以濯之,秋阳以暴之,皞皞乎不可尚已。'今也南
蛮鴃舌之人^[9],非先王之道^[10],子倍子之师而学之,亦异于曾子

矣！吾闻出于幽谷迁于乔木者，末闻下乔木而入于幽谷者。《鲁颂》曰：'戎狄是膺，荆舒是惩[11]。'周公方且膺之，子是之学，亦为不善变矣。""从许子之道，则市贾不贰，国中无伪；虽使五尺之童适市，莫之或欺。布帛长短同，则贾相若；麻缕丝絮轻重同，则贾相若；五谷多寡同，则贾相若；屦大小同，则贾相若。"曰："夫物之不齐，物之情也；或相倍蓰，或相什百，或相千万。子比而同之，是乱天下也。巨屦小屦[12]同贾，人岂为之哉？从许子之道，相率而为伪者也，恶能治国家？"

【译文】有个叫许行的人研究神农学说，从楚国来到滕国，拜见文公说："我在遥远的地方听说您实行仁政，希望您能给我提供一个住所，让我成为您的百姓。"文公给了他房屋。他有几十个门徒，都穿着粗麻衣服，以编草鞋织席子谋生。

陈良的门人陈相和他的弟弟陈辛背着农具，从宋国来到滕国，对文公说："听说您实行圣人的政治，您也是圣人了，愿意做圣人的百姓。"陈相见了许行后非常高兴，完全丢掉了他以前所学而向许行学习。陈相去见孟子，告诉他许行所说的话："滕国的君主确实是个贤明的君主，但是也还没有听说过真正的治国之道。贤人要和百姓一道耕种来获得粮食养活自己，一边做饭，一边治理国家。现在滕国有储备粮食财物的仓库，这是损害百姓来奉养自己，怎么能说他贤明呢？"孟子说："许子一定自己种粮食然后再吃饭吗？"答："是。""许子一定自己织布然后再穿衣服吗？""不！许子只穿粗麻衣服。""许子戴帽子吗？"答道："戴。"孟子问："戴什么帽子？"答道："戴生丝织的帽子。"孟子问："自己织的吗？"答道："不，用谷米换的。"孟子问："许子为什么不自己织？"答道："因为耽误庄稼活。"孟子问："许子也用锅烧火做饭，用铁器耕田吗？"答道："是的。""自己做的吗？"答道："不，用谷米换的。""用谷米换取锅甑和农具，不算是损害瓦匠铁匠；瓦匠铁匠用锅甑和农具来换取谷米，难道说是损害了农夫吗？而且许子为什么不亲自去烧窑冶铁，所有东西都储备在家中随时取用？为什么要一件件地和各种工匠交换？为什么许子不怕麻烦？"答道："各种工匠的工作本来就不能一边耕种一边同时干。""那么，难道管理国家可以一边耕种一边干吗？有官吏的工作，有百姓的工作。况且一个人需要的东西，需要各种工匠的成品才能完备，如果每件东西都要自己制造然后再使用，这是率领天下的人疲于奔命。所以说，有人劳心，有人劳力；劳心的人统治人，劳力的人被统治；被统治的人养活别人，统治者靠人养活，这是天下通行的原则。""在尧那个时候，天下还没有平定，大水四处泛滥，草木非常茂盛地生长，禽兽大量繁殖，谷物却没有收成；禽兽危害人类，到处都是它们的足迹。尧为此忧虑，提拔舜进行全面治理。舜命令伯益掌管火，益用烈火烧毁山野沼泽地的草木，使禽兽到处逃匿。大禹又疏通了多条河道，治理济水、漯水，导入大海，挖掘汝水、汉水，疏通淮水、泗水，引流入长江，这样中原地区才可以耕种。那个时候，禹八年在外，三次经过自己的家门前都不进去，虽然想种地，可以吗？后稷教导百姓种庄稼，栽培谷物。谷物成熟了，百姓便得到了养育。人有自己的特点，吃饱穿暖了，住得安逸却不进行教育，这和禽兽差不多。圣人又为此感到忧虑，命令契做司徒，教给百姓处理人与人之间关系的道理：父子之间有亲情，君臣之间有道义，夫妻之间有内外之别，长幼之间有尊卑之序，朋友之间有诚信。放勋说：'慰劳他们，纠正他们，帮助他们，使他们各得其所。然后帮助他们提升品德。'圣人如此担忧百姓，哪有时间耕种呀？尧因为找不着舜这样的人感到忧虑，舜因为找不着禹和皋陶这样的人感到忧虑。以耕种不好自己的地感到忧虑的，那是农夫。把钱财分给别人叫作惠，教导别人善良叫作忠，替天下找到人才叫作仁。所以说把天下让给别人比较容易，为天下找到人才比较难。孔子说：'真伟大啊，尧做天子！只有天最伟大，只有尧能够效法天。他的圣德广阔无边，百姓找不到合适的词赞美他！舜真是了不得的君主！多么崇高啊！有天下却不独占它！'尧、舜治理天下，难道不用心吗？只是不用在耕种上罢了。我只是听说过用中原华夏民族的先进文化去改变周边少数民族的落后文化，没有听说过用周边少数民族的落后文化改变中原文化的。陈良是楚国人，喜好周公、孔子的学说，由南到北来中原学习，北方的读书人还没有超过他的，他真是豪杰之士。你们兄弟跟他学习了几十年，他死后竟然背叛了他。以前，孔子去世，三年之后，学生收拾行李准备离开，走进子贡处作揖告别。他们面对面地哭，都泣不成声，然后离去。子贡又回到墓地重新筑屋，独自住了三年，才回去。过了些日子，子夏、子张、子游认为有若长得有点像孔子，想要用侍奉孔子的礼数来待他，他们想劝说曾子同意。曾子说：'不行。好像用江汉之水洗涤过，好像六月骄阳暴晒过，真是洁白的无人能比！'现在南蛮之人怪腔怪调地非议先代圣王，你们却背叛老师向他学，也是和曾子不同。我听说'飞出幽暗的山沟，迁往高大树木'，没有听说过离开高大树木飞入幽暗山沟的。《鲁颂》说：'攻击戎狄，惩罚荆舒。'周公还要打击它，你却向他学，这是越学越坏。""如果按照许子的学说，那么市场上就不会有两种价格，城里也不会有欺诈，即使让小孩子去市场，也没有人欺骗他。布匹、丝绸的长短一样，价钱就一样；麻线、丝绵的轻重相同，价钱便一样；谷米的重量一样，价钱也一样；鞋子的大小一样，价钱也一样。"孟子说："物品不一样，价格不一样，这是自然的。有的相差一倍五倍，有的相差十倍百倍，有的相差千倍万倍；你要它们完全相同，这是扰乱天下。好鞋和坏鞋一样价钱，人们难道愿意吗？听从许子的学说，是率领大家做伪劣的东西，怎么能治理国家呢？"

【英译】There came from Ch'û to T'ǎng one Hsü Hsing, who gave out that he acted according to the words of Shǎn-nǎng. Coming right to his gate, he addressed the duke Wǎn, saying, 'A man of a distant region, I have heard that you, Prince, are practising a benevolent government, and I wish to receive a site for a house, and to become one of your people.' The duke Wǎn gave him a dwelling-place. His disciples, amounting to several tens, all wore clothes of haircloth, and made sandals of hemp and wove mats for a living. At the same time, Ch'ăn Hsiang, a disciple of Ch'ăn Liang, and his younger brother, Hsin, with their plough-handles and shares on their backs, came from Sung to T'ăng, saying, 'We have heard that you, Prince, are putting into practice the government of the ancient sages, showing that you are likewise a sage. We wish to become the subjects of a sage.' When Ch'ăn Hsiang saw Hsü Hsing, he was greatly pleased with him, and, abandoning entirely whatever he had learned, became his disciple. Having an interview with Mencius, he related to him with approbation the words of Hsü Hsing to the following effect: — 'The prince of T'ăng is indeed a worthy prince. He has not yet heard, however, the real doctrines of antiquity. Now, wise and able princes should cultivate the ground equally and along with their people, and eat the fruit of their labour. They should prepare their own meals, morning and evening, while at the same time they carry on their government. But now, the prince of T'ăng has his granaries, treasuries, and arsenals, which is an oppressing of the people to nourish himself. How can he be deemed a real worthy prince?' Mencius said, 'I suppose that Hsü Hsing sows grain and eats the produce. Is it not so?' 'It is so,' was the answer. 'I suppose also he weaves cloth, and wears his own manufacture. Is it not so?' 'No. Hsü wears clothes of haircloth.' 'Does he wear a cap?' 'He wears a cap.' 'What kind of cap?' 'A plain cap.' 'Is it woven by himself?' 'No. He gets it in exchange for grain.' 'Why does Hsü not weave it himself?' 'That would injure his husbandry.' 'Does Hsü cook his food in boilers and earthenware pans, and does he plough with an iron share?' 'Yes.'

'Does he make those articles himself?' 'No. He gets them in exchange for grain.' Mencius then said, 'The getting those various articles in exchange for grain, is not oppressive to the potter and the founder, and the potter and the founder in their turn, in exchanging their various articles for grain, are not oppressive to the husbandman. How should such a thing be supposed? And moreover, why does not Hsü act the potter and founder, supplying himself with the articles which he uses solely from his own establishment? Why does he go confusedly dealing and exchanging with the handicraftsmen? Why does he not spare himself so much trouble?' Ch'ǎn Hsiang replied, 'The business of the handicraftsman can by no means be carried on along with the business of husbandry.' Mencius resumed, 'Then, is it the government of the kingdom which alone can be carried on along with the practice of husbandry? Great men have their proper business, and little men have their proper business. Moreover, in the case of any single individual, whatever articles he can require are ready to his hand, being produced by the various handicraftsmen—if he must first make them for his own use, this way of doing would keep all the people running about upon the roads. Hence, there is the saying, "Some labour with their minds, and some labour with their strength. Those who labour with their minds govern others; those who labour with their strength are governed by others. Those who are governed by others support them; those who govern others are supported by them." This is a principle universally recognised. In the time of Yâo, when the world had not yet been perfectly reduced to order, the vast waters, flowing out of their channels, made a universal inundation. Vegetation was luxuriant, and birds and beasts swarmed. The various kinds of grain could not be grown. The birds and beasts pressed upon men. The paths marked by the feet of beasts and prints of birds crossed one another throughout the Middle Kingdom. To Yâo alone this caused anxious sorrow. He raised Shun to office, and measures to regulate the disorder were set forth. Shun committed to Yî the direction of the fire to be employed, and Yî set fire to, and consumed, the forests and vegetation on the mountains and in the marshes, so that the birds and beasts fled away to hide themselves. Yü separated the nine streams, cleared the courses of the Zû and Han and led them all to the sea. He opened a vent also for the Hwâi and Sze, and regulated the course of the Hwâi and Sze, so that they all flowed into the Chiang. When this was done, it became possible for the people of the Middle Kingdom to cultivate the ground and get food for themselves. During that time, Yü was eight years away from his home, and though he thrice passed the door of it, he did not enter. Although he had wished to cultivate the ground, could he have done so? The Minister of Agriculture taught the people to sow and reap, cultivating the five kinds of grain. When the five kinds of grain were brought to maturity, the people all obtained a subsistence. But men possess a moral nature; and if they are well fed, warmly clad, and comfortably lodged, without being taught at the same time, they become almost like the beasts. This was a subject of anxious solicitude to the sage Shun, and he appointed Hsieh to be the Minister of Instruction, to teach the relations of humanity: —how, between father and son, there should be affection; between sovereign and minister, righteousness; between husband and wife, attention to their separate functions; between old and young, a proper order; and between friends, fidelity. The high meritorious sovereign said to him,

"Encourage them; lead them on; rectify them; straighten them; help them; give them wings: —thus causing them to become possessors of themselves. Then follow this up by stimulating them, and conferring benefits on them." When the sages were exercising their solicitude for the people in this way, had they leisure to cultivate the ground? What Yâo felt giving him anxiety was the not getting Shun. What Shun felt giving him anxiety was the not getting Yü and Kâo Yâo . But he whose anxiety is about his hundred mu not being properly cultivated, is a mere husbandman. The imparting by a man to others of his wealth, is called "kindness." The teaching others what is good, is called "the exercise of fidelity." The finding a man who shall benefit the kingdom, is called "benevolence." Hence to give the throne to another man would be easy; to find a man who shall benefit the kingdom is difficult. Confucius said, "Great indeed was Yâo as a sovereign. It is only Heaven that is great, and only Yâo corresponded to it. How vast was his virtue! The people could find no name for it. Princely indeed was Shun! How majestic was he, having possession of the kingdom, and yet seeming as if it were nothing to him!" In their governing the kingdom, were there no subjects on which Yâo and Shun employed their minds? There were subjects, only they did not employ their minds on the cultivation of the ground. I have heard of men using the doctrines of our great land to change barbarians, but I have never yet heard of any being changed by barbarians. Ch'an Liang was a native of Ch'û. Pleased with the doctrines of Châu-kung and Chung-nî, he came northwards to the Middle Kingdom and studied them. Among the scholars of the northern regions, there was perhaps no one who excelled him. He was what you call a scholar of high and distinguished qualities. You and your brother followed him some tens of years, and when your master died, you forthwith turned away from him. Formerly, when Confucius died, after three years had elapsed, his disciples collected their baggage, and prepared to return to their several homes. But on entering to take their leave of Tsze-kung, as they looked towards one another, they wailed, till they all lost their voices. After this they returned to their homes, but Tsze-kung went back, and built a house for himself on the altar-ground, where he lived alone other three years, before he returned home. On another occasion, Tsze-hsiâ, Tsze-chang, and Tsze-yû, thinking that Yû Zo resembled the sage, wished to render to him the same observances which they had rendered to Confucius. They tried to force the disciple Tsăng to join with them, but he said, "This may not be done. What has been washed in the waters of the Chiang and Han, and bleached in the autumn sun:—how glistening is it! Nothing can be added to it." Now here is this shrike-tongued barbarian of the south, whose doctrines are not those of the ancient kings. You turn away from your master and become his disciple. Your conduct is different indeed from that of the philosopher Tsăng. I have heard of birds leaving dark valleys to remove to lofty trees, but I have not heard of their descending from lofty trees to enter into dark valleys. In the Praise-songs of Lû it is said, "He smote the barbarians of the west and the north, he punished Ching and Shû." Thus Châu-kung would be sure to smite them, and you become their disciple again; it appears that your change is not good.' Ch'an Hsiang said, 'If Hsü's doctrines were followed, then there would not be two prices in the market, nor any deceit in the kingdom. If a boy of five cubits were sent to the market, no one would impose on him;

linen and silk of the same length would be of the same price. So it would be with bundles of hemp and silk，being of the same weight；with the different kinds of grain，being the same in quantity；and with shoes which were of the same size.' Mencius replied，'It is the nature of things to be of unequal quality. Some are twice，some five times，some ten times，some a hundred times，some a thousand times，some ten thousand times as valuable as others. If you reduce them all to the same standard，that must throw the kingdom into confusion. If large shoes and small shoes were of the same price，who would make them? For people to follow the doctrines of Hsü，would be for them to lead one another on to practise deceit. How can they avail for the government of a State?'

【注释】

[1] 孟子在本章中提出"劳心者治人，劳力者治于人；治于人者食人，治人者食于人，天下之通义也。"这一论断曾一度被认定为为剥削者的剥削行为辩护的证据，给孟子招致无尽的批判，但纵观全章可以清楚地看到，它是孟子在驳斥农家否认社会分工的必要性和合理性的基础上提出来的，实际上是在强调社会分工的重要性。在战国时期，诸家多依托古代圣贤来增加自己学说的可信度，如孟子"言必称尧舜"，农家托神农以自重。神农是传说中的太古帝王，是三皇之一，相传他教导百姓务农，如《吕氏春秋爱类篇》："神农之教曰：'士有当年而不耕者，则天下或受其饥矣；女有当年而不织者，则天下或受其寒矣。'故身亲耕，妻亲织，所以见致民利也。"可见，劝耕桑以足衣食是农家的基本主张。在诸侯混战的战国时期，主张重农桑虽有积极意义，但忽视其他行业，否认社会分工则是不可取的。在翻译"有为神农之言"时，理雅各将之翻译为"he acted according to the words of Shǎn-nǎng"，赖发洛翻译为"who carried out Shen-nung's words"。显然二人都认为许行是"神农学说的践行者"。刘殿爵翻译为"preached the teaching of Shen Nung"

（宣扬神农学说）。前者突出许行是行动家，实践者，以自己的行动感召别人，使之成为神农学说的拥护者。而后者将许行塑造为一个传道者，通过鼓吹、宣言神农学说，为自己的学派寻找更多的信徒。

[2]"衣褐"是农家学派门徒在着装上的一个重要特征。赵岐注"褐"曰："以毳为之，若今马衣者也；或曰，褐，集衣也；一曰，粗布衣也。"杨伯峻据此指出："褐有三义，一为用细兽毛做的衣服，像汉朝的所谓马衣（短褂；后代马褂一词来源是否本此，代考）；二为以未织之麻所制成的短衣；三为粗布衣。但据陈相对孟子的答语（否；许字衣褐），似乎褐不必织而后成，则此处宜取第一或者第二义。"显然，此处"褐"的一个显著特征是无须经过纺织。理雅各和刘殿爵分别取赵岐注的第一、二意，基本能体现"褐"的含义。

[3]"道"是儒家哲学思想的重要概念之一，含义非常丰富。在不同的语境下，其侧重点不同。例如在"未闻道"中，结合下文"贤者与民并耕而食，饔飧而治"，可以推测出"道"的含义更倾向于"一种正确的治国方法"。理雅各将之翻译为"the real doctrines of antiquity"，基本再现了此处"道"的含义。刘殿爵则直接将之译为"the Way"，让读者自己体会"道"的含义。

[4]对"且一人之身，而百工之所为备"的理解有两种：一种以理雅各和刘殿爵为代表，认为一个人要生活，需要利用各种工匠的成品；另一种以赖发洛为代表，将之翻译为"if one man is to learn the whole of a hundred crafts himself"，即一个人应当集百工技能为一身。笔者认为，孟子在此处强调社会分工的必要性，认为人的精力有限，必须有所为有所不为，否则就会"率天下而路"，陷于疲于奔命的困境。孟子并不否定一个人可以具备多种技能，他仅反对农家轻视社会分工，认为治理国家可以"耕且为"，故理雅各和刘殿爵的理解更符合原文的意思。

[5]"路"，赵岐注曰："谓导人赢困之路"。显然，他取"路"形容人形体疲惫瘦弱，生活潦倒之意。朱熹则认为："路，谓奔走道路，无时休息

也。"理雅各受朱熹影响，将之翻译为"this way of doing would keep all the people running about upon the roads"（使所有人奔走于路）。这种翻译虽然比较形象，但不能再现原文所包含的疲于奔命，不能休息之意。刘殿爵认为"路"通"露"，将之翻译为"the Empire will be led along the path of incessant toil."（整个国家都会被引上无休止的辛劳之路）这一翻译前后逻辑关联紧密，将原文蕴含的所有意象都完整表达了出来。

　　[6] 在中国古代，"心"是思维和情感的统一体。理雅各和刘殿爵将之译为"mind"，赖发洛则翻译为"heart"。关于其中的区别，乔中哲曾给出了细致辨析："中文'心'的原始字形是心脏的图形。因此英语'heart'应该说是'心'的一种正确译法。可是古人相信我们现在作为器官看待的'心脏'也是情感和思维（或精神反映）的中心，因而在某些情况下将'心'（heart）理解为精神（mind）似乎更恰当。"

　　[7] 此处的"道"是中性词，指的是一种生活方式。杨伯峻说："'人之有道也'的句意和'民之为道也'（15.3）相同，则'有'犹'为'也。"刘殿爵的译文"the way of the common people"可以准确体现其含义。理雅各将之翻译为"a moral nature"不准确。

　　[8] 关于"振德"有两种不同的理解。一种以赵岐为代表，注解为"振其赢穷，加德惠"，即以"振"为救济，"德"为恩惠。刘殿爵的译文支持这种观点。一种以朱熹为代表，认为："德，犹惠也……提撕警觉以加惠焉，不使其放逸怠惰而或失之。"理雅各受其影响，将之翻译为"Then follow this up by stimulating them, and conferring benefits on them"（刺激他们，使之获得恩惠）。这段文字主要记载了尧对百姓无微不至的照顾和治理，因而刘殿爵对"振德"的翻译更符合文义。

　　[9] "鴃"是鸟名，又称"伯劳鸟"，用在此处比喻南方人说话难懂，就像伯劳鸟不停地聒噪鸣叫一样。理雅各将"南蛮鴃舌之人"直译为"this shrike-tongued barbarian of the south"，刘殿爵则选择将之意译为"the southern barbarian with the twittering tongue"（一个叽叽喳喳的南方野蛮人）。

这两种翻译皆能准确再现原文之意。

[10] 此处的"先王"指古代圣王，刘殿爵在翻译的时候将译文大写以突出其含义的特殊性，理雅各和赖发洛将之宽泛地翻译为"the ancient kings"（古代的王）和"bygone kings"（以往的王）不准确。关于"非先王之道"有两种理解：一种是刘殿爵的"非议先王之道"，一种是理雅各的"不是先王之道"。结合前文"陈相见孟子，道许行之言"，可知许行是不赞成先王之道的，因而刘殿爵的理解更准确。

[11] "戎"指的是我国西部的少数民族，"狄"是北方的少数民族。他们因居住在偏远地区，未接受中原文明而被称为野蛮人。刘殿爵直接将"戎狄"意译为"the barbarians"（野蛮民族），不如理雅各的"the barbarians of the west and the north"（西北部的野蛮民族）准确。"荆舒"是春秋时期的古国名，英语中没有对等词，译者多采用音译法。

[12] 对"巨屦小屦"有两种理解。一种观点以赵岐为代表。他指出："巨，粗屦也；小，细屦也。"显然他认为"巨屦小屦"指的是鞋子质量的好坏，刘殿爵的译文亦持这种观点。另外一种观点以朱熹为代表，他指出："若大屦小屦同价，则人岂肯为其大者哉？"显然他认为巨屦小屦指的是鞋子的大小。译者理雅各和赖发洛亦持这种观点。结合文意，许子认为，"屦大小同，则贾相若"，他只看重长短轻重、多寡大小而不论精粗美恶，因而孟子举精粗来反驳其观点的谬误，故"巨屦小屦"应指鞋子质量的精粗。如果"巨屦小屦"指大鞋和小鞋的话，由于孟子认为"巨屦小屦"的价格不应相等，那么他举的例子不能反驳许子"屦大小同，则贾相若"的观点。因而此处的"巨屦小屦"应指鞋子质量的好坏。

【原文】5.5 墨者夷之因徐辟而求见孟子[1]。孟子曰："吾固愿见，今吾尚病，病愈，我且往见，夷子不来！"他日，又求见孟子。孟子曰："吾今则可以见矣。不直，则道不见[2]；我且直之。吾闻夷子墨者，墨之治丧也，以薄为其道也；夷子思以易[3]天下，岂以为非是而不贵也？然而夷子葬其亲厚，则是以所贱事亲也。"徐子以告夷子。夷子曰："儒者之道，古之人'若保赤子[4]'，此言何谓也？之则以为爱无差等，施由亲始。"徐子以告孟子。孟子曰："夫夷子信以为人之亲其兄之子，为若亲其邻之赤子乎？彼有取尔也。赤子匍匐将入井，非赤子之罪也。且天之生物也[5]，使之一本[6]，而夷子二本故也。盖上世尝有不葬其亲者，其亲死，则举而委之于壑。他日过之，狐狸食之，蝇蚋姑嘬之。其颡有泚，睨而不视。夫泚也，非为人泚，中心达于面目，盖归反虆梩而掩之。掩之诚是也，则孝子仁人之掩其亲，亦必有道矣。"徐子以告夷子。夷子怃然为间，曰："命之矣。"

【译文】墨家的信徒夷之通过徐辟去见孟子。孟子说："我本来愿意见他，但是现在我病了，病好了我会去看他，不要让夷之来了。"过了几天，又来见孟子。孟子说："我现在可以见他了。不直接说清楚，真理就不能显现。我姑且直接给他说清楚了。我听说夷子是墨家信徒，墨家办理丧葬，以薄葬为原则。夷之想用薄葬来改革天下，难道是认为不薄葬就不珍贵吗？但是夷子厚葬了他的父母，这便是用他轻贱的东西侍奉父母。"徐子把这些话告诉了夷子。夷子说："儒家认为，'古人爱护百姓就像爱护婴儿一样'，这句话是什么意思？我以为是爱并没有区别，只是从父母亲开始罢了。"徐子又转告了孟子。孟子说："夷子真的认为人们爱自己兄弟的婴儿，和爱邻人的婴儿一样吗？他不过是抓住了这一点：婴儿爬到井边，快要掉下去了，这不是婴儿的过错。（不能因为每个人都有恻隐之心，就认为爱无等差）况且天生万物，只有一个根源，夷子却有两个根源的缘故。大概上古曾经有不埋葬父母的人，父母死了，抬着弃于山沟。过几天路过那里，看见狐狸在吃，苍蝇蚊子在咬，那个人额头上不由冒出汗，斜着眼睛不敢正视。流出的汗，不是别人看的，是内心的悔恨在面貌上的表现，大概他也回家去取了锄头筐子去埋葬尸体。埋葬当然是对的，那么，孝子仁人埋葬父母，自然有他的方式了。"徐子把这些话转告夷子。夷子颇为怅惘地停了一会儿，说：
"我学到了。"

【英译】The Mohist, Î Chih, sought, through Hsü Pî, to see
Mencius. Mencius said, 'I indeed wish to see him, but at present I am
still unwell. When I am better, I will myself go and see him. He need
not come here again.' Next day, Î Chih again sought to see Mencius.
Mencius said, 'To-day I am able to see him. But if I do not correct his
errors, the true principles will not be fully evident. Let me first correct
him. I have heard that this Î is a Mohist. Now Mo considers that in the
regulation of funeral matters a spare simplicity should be the rule. Î
thinks with Mo's doctrines to change the customs of the kingdom; —
how does he regard them as if they were wrong, and not honour
them? Notwithstanding his views, Î buried his parents in a sumptuous
manner, and so he served them in the way which his doctrines
discountenance.' The disciple Hsü informed Î of these remarks. Î said,
'Even according to the principles of the learned, we find that the
ancients acted towards the people "as if they were watching over an
infant." What does this expression mean? To me it sounds that we are
to love all without difference of degree; but the manifestation of love
must begin with our parents.' Hsü reported this reply to Mencius, who
said, 'Now, does Î really think that a man's affection for the child
of his brother is merely like his affection for the infant of a neighbour?
What is to be approved in that expression is simply this: —that if an
infant crawling about is likely to fall into a well, it is no crime in the
infant. Moreover, Heaven gives birth to creatures in such a way that
they have one root, and Î makes them to have two roots. This is the
cause of his error. And, in the most ancient times, there were some

who did not inter their parents. When their parents died，they took them up and threw them into some water—channel. Afterwards，when passing by them，they saw foxes and wild-cats devouring them，and flies and gnats biting at them. The perspiration started out upon their foreheads，and they looked away，unable to bear the sight. It was not on account of other people that this perspiration flowed. The emotions of their hearts affected their faces and eyes，and instantly they went home，and came back with baskets and spades and covered the bodies. If the covering them thus was indeed right，you may see that the filial son and virtuous man，in interring in a handsome manner their parents，act according to a proper rule.' The disciple Hsü informed Î of what Mencius had said. Î was thoughtful for a short time，and then said，'He has instructed me.'

【注释】

[1] 本章记载了孟子和墨家在爱和丧葬等问题上的不同看法。墨家是中国先秦时期最重要的学术派别之一。它代表小生产者的利益，针对儒家提出的"厚葬""爱有差等"等主张，明确提出了"薄葬""兼爱"等思想。其中，"兼爱"是墨家思想的核心，要求爱别人如同爱自己，爱别人的父母就如同爱自己的父母，从而使人类社会成为一个没有亲疏远近的完全平等的社会。

[2] "不直，则道不见"，朱熹注："直，尽言以相正也。"刘殿爵的译文受其影响，将之翻译为"If one does not put others right，on cannot hold the Way up for everyone to see"（如果一个人不能纠正别人，就不能让每个人都明白道）。他的译文体现出了儒家以使天下人明道为己任的普世关怀。陈器之则提出了另外一种理解："不直接说，道理就不明白。"赵甄陶的译文也持这一观点，将之翻译为"But if I do not say straight out what I think，truth will not be made clear."这两种理解皆可。

[3] 译者对"易"的翻译不同。理雅各和赖发洛都选择用"change"翻译，而刘殿爵、赵甄陶则选择"convert"。"Change"的含义是"使不同、使改变"，用来描述一种渐变的过程，而"convert"重在"转变"，指（某物）转变成另一种形式、物质、状态或结果。要确定哪种译文更能反映原文的神韵，首先要对汉语中变、易、化、迁的含义有所了解。虽然这几个字意思相近，但含义不同。安乐哲和罗思文曾对此做过详细论述："1）'变'，是在一段时期内的渐变；2）'易'，是将一物转变为另一物；3）'化'，是将 A 完全变为 B；4）'迁'，是从一地到另一地的位移；5）'改'，是在其他标准，或是 Y 的基础上，改变 X。"可见，"convert"（转变）更能体现原文的精髓。

[4] "若保赤子"引自《尚书·康诰》。朱熹指出："此儒者之言也。夷子引之，盖欲援儒而入于墨，以拒孟子之非己。"理雅各和赖发洛认为这儿的"儒者"泛指有学问的人，分别将之翻译为"the learned"和"the scholars"，刘殿爵则将"儒者"翻译为"Confucians"（儒家学者）。根据文意，"儒者之道，古之人若保赤子"是夷子对孟子批评的回应。在前文，孟子试图证明墨家学说在丧葬问题上存在自相矛盾之处，夷子借鉴这一方法，援引儒家学说"若保赤子"来证明"爱有差等"的谬误。理雅各和赖发洛的理解大大削弱了夷子的论据，使原文蕴含的针锋相对的辩论气氛消失殆尽。"赤子"指的是新生的婴儿。婴儿在刚出生时，因皮肤是红色的，故称之为赤子。理雅各将"赤子"翻译为"infant"，该词除有"婴儿"之意，还指未达到法定年龄的人，扩大了原文内涵，容易引起错误联想。赖发洛的"child"的含义更广泛，将婴儿、儿童和孩子气的成人都包含其中，与"赤子"的内涵相距甚远。刘殿爵将之翻译为"a new-born babe"（新出生的婴儿）。新生婴儿娇小柔弱，容易激发人们保护、呵护的欲望，很好地再现了原文的意境。

[5] 刘殿爵选择"Heaven"大写翻译"天"以突出其含义的独特性，但安乐哲和罗思文指出："当我们把天译为'Heaven'时，无论'H'是否大写，它都让西方读者联想到超越宇宙的造物主，以及精神、原罪和来世等

观念。"可见，用"Heaven"翻译孟子的"天之生物也"，会给孟子思想添加它本身不具备的形而上的东西。对"天"的翻译直接影响到对"天之生物"的理解。理雅各将之翻译为"Heaven gives birth to creatures"，即上帝产生了各种动物，这就将基督教上帝造人的传说移植到中国传统文化。赖发洛的译文是"every being begotten by Heaven"，即任何存在都是上帝产生的。这一翻译将西方哲学界耳熟能详的概念"存在"引入中国古典哲学。刘殿爵的译文"Heaven produces things"（上帝制造万物），也容易让人联想到基督造人的传说。

[6] 理雅各和赖发洛将"一本"翻译为"one root"（一个根源），刘殿爵翻译为"a single basis"（只有一个起源），译者基本能翻译出其字面含义。朱熹曾解释其蕴含的哲学含义："天之生物，有血气者本于父母，无血气者本于根，皆出于一而无二者也。其性本出于一，故其爱亦主于一焉。"朱熹进一步指出："且人物之生，必各本于父母而无二，乃自然之理，若天使之然也。故其爱由此立，而推以及人，自有差等。"林月惠区别了"同一本体"和"同为一体"的差异："'同一本体'意味着：人与万物皆源出于同一个'本体'，着重此'本体'的探究。而'同为一体'强调的是：人与天地、万物是'一体'的关系，偏重此'一体'之关系的探讨。……儒家一体观的讨论，是以'同为一体'之意为主。"可见，"一本"观体现了孟子对天、人和物关系的认识，包含着朴素的唯物主义思想。

卷　六

滕文公章句下

【原文】 6.1　陈代曰[1]："不见诸侯，宜若小然[2]；今一见之，大则以王，小则以霸。且《志》曰：'枉尺而直寻[3]'，宜若可为也。"孟子曰："昔齐景公田，招虞人以旌，不至，将杀之。'志士不忘在沟壑，勇士不忘丧其元[4]。'孔子奚取焉？取非其招不往也。如不待其招而往，何哉？且夫枉尺而直寻者，以利言也。如以利，则枉寻直尺而利，亦可为与？昔者赵简子使王良与嬖奚乘，终日而不获一禽。嬖奚反命曰：'天下之贱工也。'或以告王良。良曰：'请复之。'强而后可，一朝而获十禽。嬖奚反命曰：'天下之良工也。'简子曰：'我使掌与女乘。'谓王良。良不可，曰：'吾为之范我驰驱，终日不获一；为之诡遇，一朝而获十。诗云："不失其驰，舍矢如破。[5]"我不贯与小人乘，请辞。'御者且羞与射者比[6]；比而得禽兽，虽若丘陵，弗为也。如枉道而从彼，何也？且子过矣：枉己者，未有能直人者也。"

【译文】 陈代说："不去拜见诸侯，似乎过于拘泥小节了吧。如果去见，大则可以使诸侯成为统一天下的王，小则可以使诸侯称霸天下。况且《志》书上说：'弯曲一尺，伸直八尺'，似乎是可以去拜见的。"孟子说："以前齐景公打猎，用旌旗召唤猎场管理员，他不去，景公准备杀他。（孔子知道后说）'志士不怕弃尸山沟，勇士不怕掉脑袋。'孔子赞赏这个管理员哪一点呢？赞赏他不是召唤他的礼就不去。如果不等召见就去见诸侯，将会怎么样呢？况且你说弯曲一尺，伸直八尺，是就利而言。如果从利上说，弯曲八尺，伸长一尺也有利，也可以做吗？从前，赵简子命令王良和他宠幸的小臣奚驾车去打猎，一整天没有打到一只猎物。奚回来报告说：'王良是天下最差的驾车人。'有人把这话告诉了王良。王良说：'请让我再驾一次。'奚勉强同意，一个早晨就打中了十只猎物。奚又回报说：'王良是高明的驾车人。'赵简子说：'我命他专门替你驾车。'便同王良说，王良不肯，说道：'我按规矩驾车，整天打不到一只猎物，我违背规矩驾车，一个早晨便打中十只。《诗经》上说："按照规矩驾车去，箭一放出便中的。"我不习惯为小人驾车，请允许我辞掉这个差事。'驾车的人尚且以同不守规矩的射手合作为耻，合作得到的禽兽，纵是堆积如山，也不愿意做。如果我先屈就自己的正道而去追随诸侯，又会怎么样呢？而且你错了，自己不正直的人没有能使别人正直的。"

【英译】Ch'ǎn Tâi said to Mencius, 'In not going to wait upon any of the princes, you seem to me to be standing on a small point. If now you were once to wait upon them, the result might be so great that you would make one of them sovereign, or, if smaller, that you would make one of them chief of all the other princes. Moreover, the History says, "By bending only one cubit, you make eight cubits straight." It appears to me like a thing which might be done.' Mencius said, 'Formerly, the duke Ching of Ch'î, once when he was hunting, called his forester to him by a flag. The forester would not come, and the duke was going to kill him. With reference to this incident, Confucius said, "The determined officer never forgets that his end may be in a ditch or a stream; the brave officer never forgets that he may lose his head." What was it in the forester that Confucius thus approved? He approved his not going to the duke, when summoned by the article which was not appropriate to him. If one go to see the princes without waiting to be invited, what can be thought of him? Moreover, that sentence, "By bending only one cubit, you make eight cubits straight," is spoken with reference to the gain that may be got. If gain be the object, then, if it can be got by bending eight cubits to make one cubit straight, may we likewise do that? Formerly, the officer Châo Chien made Wang Liang act as charioteer for his favourite Hsî, when, in the course of a whole day, they did not get a single bird. The favourite Hsî reported this result, saying, "He is the poorest charioteer in the world." Some one told this to Wang Liang, who said, "I beg leave to try again." By dint of pressing, this was accorded to him, when in one morning they got ten birds. The favourite, reporting this result, said, "He is the best charioteer in the world." Chien said, "I will make him always drive your chariot for you." When he told Wang Liang so, however, Liang refused, saying, "I drove for him, strictly observing the proper rules for driving, and in the whole day he did not get one bird. I drove for him so as deceitfully to intercept the birds, and in one morning he got ten. It is said in the Book of Poetry, 'There is no failure in the management of their horses; the arrows are discharged surely, like the blows of an axe.' I am not accustomed to drive for a mean man. I beg leave to decline the office." Thus this charioteer even was ashamed to bend improperly to the will of such an archer. Though, by bending to it, they would have caught birds and animals sufficient to form a hill, he would not do so. If I were to bend my principles and follow those princes, of what kind would my conduct be? And you are wrong. Never has a man who has bent himself been able to make others straight.'

【注释】

[1] 通过举不以其道招，虞人不往；不以其道行，御者不乘的例子，孟子强调不同职业者都有自己所遵循的"道"，更不用说士之入仕了。贤者不论是否入仕，都必须循"道"而行，如果不按"道"的要求规范自己，既不可能"独善其身"，更无法"兼济天下"。孟子提出的不可"枉尺而直寻"的观点，成为历代志士仁人保持气节和原则的依据。

[2] 根据刘殿爵的译文，弟子陈代猜测，孟子不见诸侯似乎是因为觉得诸侯不重要。朱熹则指出，"小，谓小节也。"理雅各受其影响，将之翻译为"you seem to me to be standing on a small point."（我觉得这样似乎显得你太拘于小节了）结合下文，"'枉尺而直寻'，宜若可为也"可以看出，弟子是觉得孟子太拘泥于小节，因而理雅各的译文更准确。

[3] "尺"和"寻"是中国古代的长度单位，八尺为一寻。理雅各将"尺"翻译为"cubit"，即肘尺。肘尺等于从中指指尖到肘的前臂长度。理雅各将"寻"意译为"eight cubits"。赖发洛将"尺"和"寻"分别翻译为"foot"（英尺）和"fathom"（英寻）。根据英国的计量单位换算，一英寻约等于六英尺，这和"尺""寻"之间相差八倍的情况不符。刘殿爵将"尺"和"寻"分别翻译为"foot"（英尺）和"yard"（码），也不能准确体现古代中国计量单位"尺"和"寻"的关系。任俊华和赵清文指出："弯曲时长一尺，拉直了就可以长一寻了。"杨伯峻认为："所屈折的臂如只有一尺，而所伸直的却有八尺了。"刘殿爵的理解同杨伯峻，根据上文，"不见诸侯，宜若小然；今一见之，大则以王，小则以霸。"可以推断，陈代认为，如果孟子能放下身段，主动去见诸侯，可以成就王霸之大业。因而刘殿爵的译文更符合原文的意思。

[4] "志士不忘在沟壑，勇士不忘丧其元"鼓舞了一代代中华儿女为实现道义抛头颅、洒热血，形成了中华民族的脊梁。此处的"士"是古代对男子的称呼，而非特指知识分子，因而应将"志士"和"勇士"理解为"有

远大志向的人"和"大胆无畏的人"。刘殿爵的译文"A man of great resolve"（有巨大决心的人）和"a man of great valor"（有极大勇气的人）准确翻译出了其含义。理雅各将之分别翻译为"determined officer"（有决心的官员）和"brave officer"（勇敢的官员），译文缩小了原文的内涵。

[5]"不失其驰，舍矢如破"，赵岐注："言御者不失其驰驱之法，则射者必中之。顺毛而入，顺毛而出，一发贯臧，应矢而死者如破矣，此君子之射也。"理雅各的译文不仅准确再现了驾者遵循其道，和射者成功命中之间的关系，还完美展现了箭正中猎物时的速度、力度和精准度。

[6]"比"的含义有两种。颜师古注曰："比，合也。"刘殿爵亦将"比"理解为"in league with"（合作）。赵甄陶亦持此说，将之翻译为"lower himself to team up with such an archer"。朱熹给出另外一种解释："比，必二反，阿党也。"理雅各的译文与之相类，将之翻译为"Thus this charioteer even was ashamed to bend improperly to the will of such an archer."（因此，甚至驾车的人都羞于曲从这样一个射者）赖发洛也将之翻译为"Even a driver was ashamed to cringe to the bowman."（甚至驾车者都羞于阿谀奉承射者）从上文"我不贯与小人乘，请辞。"两种译文都能体现出孟子不愿违背本心，迎合不正当行为的态度。

【原文】6.2　景春曰[1]："公孙衍、张仪[2]，岂不诚大丈夫哉？一怒而诸侯惧，安居而天下熄。"孟子曰："是焉得为大丈夫乎？子未学礼乎？丈夫之冠也，父命之[3]；女子之嫁也，母命之，往送之门，戒之曰：'往之女家，必敬必戒，无违夫子！'以顺为正者，妾妇之道也[4]。居天下之广居，立天下之正位，行天下之大道[5]。得志，与民由之；不得志，独行其道。富贵不能淫，贫贱不能移，威武不能屈，此之谓大丈夫[6]。"

【译文】景春说："公孙衍和张仪难道不是真正的大丈夫吗？他们一发怒，诸侯都害怕，他们安定下来，天下便无战事。"孟子说："这怎么能是大丈夫呢？你没有学过礼吗？男子加冠礼的时候，父亲教导他，女子出嫁时，母亲训导她，将她送到门口，告诫说：'到了夫家，一定要恭敬、谨慎，不要违背丈夫。'以顺为最大原则的，是妇人之道。住在天下最宽广的住宅（仁），站在天下最正确的位置（礼），走在天下最宽广的大道（义）；能够实行志向，便和百姓一起实行；不能实行志向，就自己坚守，富贵不能乱我心，贫贱不能移我志，威武不能屈我节，这才是大大夫。"

【英译】Ching Ch'un said to Mencius, 'Are not Kung-sun Yen and Chang Î really great men? Let them once be angry, and all the princes are afraid. Let them live quietly, and the flames of trouble are extinguished throughout the kingdom.' Mencius said, 'How can such men be great men? Have you not read the Ritual Usages? — "At the capping of a young man, his father admonishes him. At the marrying away of a young woman, her mother admonishes her, accompanying her to the door on her leaving, and cautioning her with these words, 'You are going to your home. You must be respectful; you must be careful. Do not disobey your husband.'" Thus, to look upon compliance as their correct course is the rule for women. To dwell in the wide house of the world, to stand in the correct seat of the world, and to walk in the great path of the world; when he obtains his desire for office, to practise his principles for the good of the people; and when that desire is disappointed, to practise them alone; to be above the power of riches and honours to make dissipated, of poverty and mean condition to make swerve from principle, and of power and force to make bend: —these characteristics constitute the great man.'

【注释】

[1] 通过与景春的谈话，孟子给出了他对"大丈夫"的定义。大丈夫

是孟子所推崇的理想人格之一，其基本特征是"富贵不能淫，贫贱不能移，威武不能屈"。孟子的"大丈夫"标准鼓舞了一代又一代的中国人，形成了中国人的骨气和脊梁。

[2] 公孙衍和张仪都是魏国人。公孙衍是当时著名的说客，张仪是纵横家的代表，主张连横强秦。景春认为他们是大丈夫，因而译者在翻译时应对二人作注，否则不便于读者理解景春口中的"大丈夫"与孟子认可的有何不同，更不能使读者对在中国古代历史上曾发挥过重要影响的纵横家有一定的了解。理雅各在翻译时对景春、公孙衍和张仪的情况都作了简要介绍，为读者说明了景春推崇二人的原因，以及二人的主要主张和活动。他还为试图进一步了解二人情况的读者指明了参考书目。刘殿爵则是在附录中以检索的形势对文中出现的人名、地名作了简介，既保持了原文简洁的风格，又可以把原文出现的地名、人名介绍清楚，使译文体现了较强的学术性。

[3] "丈夫之冠也，父命之"一句包含了古代中国的一项重要礼仪，即加冠礼。在古代，男子到了二十岁即举行此礼，表明自己步入成年人的行列。据《中国礼仪大辞典》记载："古代行冠礼、须占卜择日，择主持人。加冠时，冠者要站在主人即其父亲陛（位置）上，以示其成年将代父而为家长。接着再请他坐到客位席上，向他敬酒。然后加冠三次；第一次加缁布冠，二次加皮弁服，三次加爵弁服，愈加冠服愈为贵重，三加弥尊。以勉励其未来有成，加冠行，不得再称其名，而称其号。冠者拜见母亲，母亲要答拜；冠者见兄弟，兄弟要再拜，以其成年，众人均须向其行礼。冠者再穿起玄冠玄端（黑色的冠及朝服）带上礼物去拜访国君，或拜访乡中有官位乃至已退休的老人，以表示其成年的身份。"理雅各将之翻译为"At the capping of a young man, his father admonishes him"，赖发洛翻译为"When a man is capped, his father instructs him"，二人的译文将"加冠礼"的核心内容"加冠于首"体现了出来，但未指出加冠礼需要在一定的年龄才能施行。

[4] 对文中的"顺"应当全面理解。在古代，妻道如臣道。妻子顺从丈夫，就如同臣子顺从君，即并非曲意顺从、阿谀奉承，而是以义为标准，

君、夫行义则顺之，不义则谏之。从本章的具体语境分析，孟子此处以"妾妇"之道来喻公孙衍、张仪非大丈夫，而是阿谀奉承的小人，因而，此处的"妾妇"特指那些不问是非、一味顺从之"妾妇"，也就是被人所鄙弃的"小老婆"之道。译者多将"妾妇"翻译为"women"，泛指所有妇女，容易引起读者对孟子的误解。

[5] 朱熹指出，"广居，仁也；正位，礼也，大道，义也。"结合"仁，人之安宅也；义，人之正路也"（《孟子·离娄上》）和"兴于诗，立于礼，成于乐"（《论语·泰伯》），可以推测朱熹的理解是准确的，探求到了孟子的本义。理雅各和刘殿爵在翻译时，都是按照字面意思翻译，给人一种模糊、似是而非的感觉。例如，理雅各将之翻译为"To dwell in the wide house of the world，to stand in the correct seat of the world，and to walk in the great path of the world"（居住在世界上最宽广的房子里，立足于世界上最正确的位置，走在世上最正确的道路上）。相比较而言，赵甄陶的译文"As for a man，he should live in the most spacious mansion of the world（benevolence—tr.），occupy the most proper position of the world（decorum—tr.），and walk down the broadest way of the world（righteousness—tr.）"，将原文主旨准确体现了出来。

[6] "富贵不能淫，贫贱不能移，威武不能屈"是孟子眼中大丈夫的体现，和景春眼中"一怒而诸侯惧，安居而天下熄"的大丈夫有本质区别。孟子认为，真正的大丈夫在任何环境下都能够坚守自己独立的人格，不因富贵改变自己的节操，不因贫贱改变自己的理想，更不会因武力威慑而放弃自己的追求。译者将之翻译为"a great man"基本能体现其含义。

【原文】6.3　周霄问曰[1]："古之君子仕乎？"孟子曰："仕。《传》曰：'孔子三月无君，则皇皇如也，出疆必载质[2]。'公明仪曰：'古之人三月无君，则吊。'""三月无君则吊，不以急乎？"曰："士之失位也，犹诸侯之失国家也。《礼》曰：'诸侯耕助[3]，以供粢盛；夫人蚕缫，以为衣服。牺牲不成，粢盛不洁，衣服不备，不敢以祭。惟士无田，则亦不祭。'牲杀、器皿、衣服不备，不敢以祭，则不敢以宴，亦不足吊乎?""出疆必载质，何也?"曰:"士之仕也，犹农夫之耕也;农夫岂为出疆舍其耒耜哉?"曰:"晋国亦仕国也，未尝闻仕如此其急。仕如此其急也，君子之难仕，何也?"曰:"丈夫生而愿为之有室，女子生而愿为之有家;父母之心，人皆有之。不待父母之命、媒妁之言，钻穴隙相窥，逾墙相从，则父母国人皆贱之。古之人未尝不欲仕也，又恶不由其道[4]。不由其道而往者，与钻穴隙之类也。"

【译文】周霄问道:"古代的君子外出做官吗?"孟子说:"做官。《传记》上说:'孔子如果三个月没有被君主任用，就会惶惶不安，离开一个国家，一定带上拜见别国君主的礼物。'公明仪说:'古代的人如果三个月没有君主任用，就要去安慰他。'"周霄说:"三个月没有君主任用就去安慰，太急了吧?"孟子说:"士失掉官位，就像诸侯失掉国家。《礼》说:'诸侯亲自耕种，用来祭祀;夫人亲自养蚕出丝，用来制作祭服。祭祀用的牲畜不肥，谷物不洁净，祭服不备好，都不敢祭祀。士如果没有供给祭祀的田，也不能祭祀。'牺牲、祭器、祭服不备好，也不敢去祭祀，也不敢举行宴会，这样还不该去安慰吗?"周霄又问:"离开国家一定带见面的礼物，为什么呢?"孟子说:"士做官，就像农夫耕田一样，农夫难道会为了离开国界便扔掉农具吗?"周霄说:"魏国也是一个可以做官的国家，我却从来没有听说过出来做官这样急迫的。出来做官这么急迫，君子又迟迟不肯出来做官，为什么呢?"孟子说:"男孩生下来，父母就希望他能找到妻室;女孩生下来，父母便希望能给她找到婆家。父母的心情，每个人都是这样。如果不等父母开口，经过媒人介绍，就钻洞扒门缝来相互偷看，爬墙私会，那么，爹娘和其他人都会轻贱他。古代的人没有不想做官的，但是又厌恶通过不符合礼义的方式去做官。通过不符合礼义的方式去做官，这和男女钻洞扒门缝差不多。"

【英译】Châu Hsiâo asked Mencius, saying, 'Did superior men

of old time take office?' Mencius replied, 'They did. The Record says, "If Confucius was three months without being employed by some ruler, he looked anxious and unhappy. When he passed from the boundary of a State, he was sure to carry with him his proper gift of introduction." Kung-ming ĭ said, "Among the ancients, if an officer was three months unemployed by a ruler, he was condoled with."' Hsiâo said, 'Did not this condoling, on being three months unemployed by a ruler, show a too great urgency?' Mencius answered, 'The loss of his place to an officer is like the loss of his State to a prince. It is said in the Book of Rites, "A prince ploughs himself, and is assisted by the people, to supply the millet for sacrifice. His wife keeps silkworms, and unwinds their cocoons, to make the garments for sacrifice." If the victims be not perfect, the millet not pure, and the dress not complete, he does not presume to sacrifice." And the scholar who, out of office, has no holy field, in the same way, does not sacrifice. The victims for slaughter, the vessels, and the garments, not being all complete, he does not presume to sacrifice, and then neither may he dare to feel happy." Is there not here sufficient ground also for condolence?' Hsiâo again asked, 'What was the meaning of Confucius's always carrying his proper gift of introduction with him, when he passed over the boundaries of the State where he had been?' 'An officer's being in office,' was the reply, 'is like the ploughing of a husbandman. Does a husbandman part with his plough, because he goes from one State to another?' Hsiâo pursued, 'The kingdom of Tsin is one, as well as others, of official employments, but I have not heard of anyone being thus earnest about being in office. If there should be this urgency, why does a superior man make any difficulty about taking it?' Mencius answered, 'When a son is born, what is desired for him is that he may have a wife; when a daughter is born, what is desired for her is that she may have a husband. This feeling of the parents is possessed by all men. If the young people, without waiting for the orders of their parents, and the arrangements of the go-betweens, shall bore holes to steal a sight of each other, or get over the wall to be with each other, then their parents and all other people will despise them. The ancients did indeed always desire to be in office, but they also hated being so by any improper way. To seek office by an improper way is of a class with young people's boring holes.'

【注释】

[1] 儒家虽然主张知识分子应积极"入世",实现自己的政治抱负和人生理想,但更强调入仕有道,认为必须坚持正确的原则和方法获得官位,如不由正道,犹"钻穴隙之类",是儒家不耻和鄙夷的。

[2] "出疆必载质"记载了古代中国的一种传统习俗。《古汉语常用字典》:"质,通贽,是古代初次拜见尊长时送的礼物。"赵岐注"质"为"臣所执以见君者也"。理雅各的译文将"质"的用途和特征准确体现了出来。

[3] 关于"诸侯耕助,以供粢盛"有不同的解释。焦循在《孟子正义》中指出:"是耕为躬耕,助,为民助。"理雅各的译文同焦循,将之翻译为"A prince ploughs himself, and is assisted by the people"(诸侯亲自参与耕种,百姓帮助他们一起劳动)。理雅各和赖发洛都认为"助"为帮助,和"耕"为并列动词,分属于不同的主语,即诸侯躬耕,而民帮助。而刘殿爵则把"耕助"理解为连绵动词:"耕即助,助即耕。"译为"lord takes part in the ploughing"(诸侯亲自耕种)。杨伯峻也持这一观点,认为:"耕助——此二字为连绵动词,和下文'蚕缫'相对成文。'助'即'籍'(《说文》作'耤',云,'帝耤千亩也。'经传多作'籍')。《滕文公上》已云:'助者,籍也。'故知《孟子》此处实假'助'为'籍'。……《国语·周语上》:'宣王即位,

不籍千亩'卢植曰：'籍，耕也。'《左传》昭公十八年云：'郮人籍稻。'《正义》引服虔《注》云：'籍，耕种于籍田也。'正是此'助'字之义。"

[4] 此处的"道"并非抽象的、形而上的东西，而是指获取官位的"合适的、可敬的方法和手段"。理雅各和刘殿爵的译文都将原文所蕴含之意准确传递出来：如果青年男女违背礼制，钻洞偷看，爬墙私会，他们的父母和百姓都会轻视他们。同样，如果君子通过不正当的手段谋求官位，也会受到人们的轻视。

【原文】 6.4 彭更问曰[1]："后车数十乘，从者数百人，以传食于诸侯，不以泰乎？"孟子曰："非其道，则一箪食不可受于人；如其道，则舜受尧之天下，不以为泰。子以为泰乎？"曰："否。士无事而食，不可也。"曰："子不通功易事，以羡补不足，则农有余粟，女有余布；子如通之，则梓匠轮舆，皆得食于子。于此有人焉，入则孝[2]，出则悌，守先王之道，以待[3]后之学者，而不得食于子；子何尊梓匠轮舆而轻为仁义者哉？"曰："梓匠轮舆，其志[4]将以求食也。君子之为道也，其志亦将以求食与？"曰："子何以其志为哉？其有功于子，可食而食之矣。且子食志乎？食功乎？"曰："食志。"曰："有人于此，毁瓦画墁[5]，其志将以求食也，则子食之乎？"曰："否。"曰："然则子非食志也，食功也。"

【译文】 彭更问道："后面跟随着几十辆车，随从几百人，从这国吃到那国，是不是太过分了？"孟子说："不符合道，那么一筐食物也不会从别人那里接受；如果符合道，那么舜从尧那里接受了天下，也不认为过分。你认为过分了吗？""不。读书人不做事，吃白饭，不可以。"孟子说："如果你不让不同行业的人互通成果，交换产品，用多余的补充不足的，那么农民有多余的粮食，织女有多余的布，如果能让他们互通有无，那么，木匠车工都能从你那里得到饭吃。假设这里有个人，在家孝顺父母，在外尊敬长辈，严守古代圣王的正道，用来培养向他学习的人，却不能从你这里获得食物，你为什么尊重木匠车工，却轻视有仁义的人呢？"彭更说："木匠车工，他的动机就是谋求饭食。君子追求道，也是有志于谋食吗？"孟子说："你为什么要论动机呢？他们有功于你，可以给吃的，便给吃的了。况且，你是依据动机给饭吃，还是依据功绩给吃的呢？"彭更说："依据动机。"孟子说："这里有个人，打碎屋瓦，还乱画墙壁，他的动机是为了找口饭吃，那么你给他吃吗？"彭更说："不。"孟子说："那么，你不是论动机给饭吃，而是论功绩。"

【英译】P'ǎng Kǎng asked Mencius, saying, 'Is it not an extravagant procedure to go from one prince to another and live upon them, followed by several tens of carriages, and attended by several hundred men?' Mencius replied, 'If there be not a proper ground for taking it, a single bamboo-cup of rice may not be received from a man. If there be such a proper ground, then Shun's receiving the kingdom from Yâo is not to be considered excessive. Do you think it was excessive?' Kǎng said, 'No. But for a scholar performing no service to receive his support notwithstanding is improper.' Mencius answered, 'If you do not have an intercommunication of the productions of labour, and an interchange of men's services, so that one from his overplus may supply the deficiency of another, then husbandmen will have a superfluity of grain, and women will have a superfluity of cloth. If you have such an interchange, carpenters and carriage-wrights may all get their food from you. Here now is a man, who, at home, is filial, and abroad, respectful to his elders; who watches over the principles of the ancient kings, awaiting the rise of future learners—and yet you will refuse to support him. How is it that you give honour to the carpenter and carriage-wright, and slight him who practises benevolence and righteousness?' P'ǎng Kǎng said, 'The aim of the carpenter and carriagewright is by their trades to seek for a living. Is it also the aim of the superior man in his practice of principles thereby to seek for a living?''What have you to do,'returned Mencius,'with his purpose? He is of service to you. He deserves to be supported, and should be supported. And let me ask—Do you remunerate a man's intention, or do you remunerate his service.'To this Kǎng replied, 'I remunerate his intention.'Mencius said,'There is a man here, who breaks your tiles, and draws unsightly figures on your walls;— his purpose may be thereby to seek for his living, but will you indeed remunerate him?''No,'said Kǎng;and Mencius then concluded, 'That being the case, it is not the purpose which you remunerate, but the work done.'

【注释】

[1] 本章集中体现了孟子的志功观。志功是中国传统哲学的重要概念，志是主观动机，功指实际效果。在志功观上，墨子提出"合其志功而观焉"（《墨子·鲁问》）的"志功统一"说，认为动机和效果不能偏废。对孟子的志功观，学界普遍流行的观点是孟子"尚志"，否定功利。刘鄂培指出："其实，这是一种误解。在中国先秦的'义利之辨'中，'义'指'公利'，'利'指'私利'。'义利之辨'实质上是公与私之辨，讨论公与私、社会和个人的关系问题。"联系《孟子·尽心上》"王子垫问曰：'士何事?'孟子曰：'尚志'"，结合本章"其有功于子，可食而食之矣"，可以看出，在志功观上，孟子持志功兼重论。

[2] 理雅各将"孝"翻译为"filial"，这一翻译更强调子女对父母的义务。"filial"虽不能包含儒家的孝观，但基本上能体现此处孝的含义。赖发洛将"孝"翻译为"pious"。它更强调宗教上的虔诚，并且含有虚伪的意思，和儿女发自内心的至真至切的孝敬之心相差甚远。刘殿爵将"孝"翻译为"obedient to his parents"（对父母唯命是从），这一翻译更符合秦汉以后变

异的儒家孝论，而非原生儒家孝论。曾振宇曾指出："注重自然亲情、追求人格独立与平等的原生儒家孝论，自秦汉以降便走向了它自身的反面。愚忠与愚孝一同诞生，强调子女对父母尊长绝对无条件的顺从是秦汉之后孝论最大的特点。"可见，刘殿爵的译文更侧重于阐发变异后的儒家孝论。

[3]"待"，焦循在《孟子正义》指出："赵氏读待为持，谓扶持后之学者。"刘殿爵的译文与之相类，翻译为"for the benefit of"（帮助、扶持）。一种观点取"待"的字面意思"等待"，如理雅各将之翻译为"awaiting"（等待）。从儒家积极入世的哲学取向来看，将"待"翻译为"等待"过于消极，不如"扶持、帮助"更全面体现儒家"穷则独善其身，达则兼善天下"的出世哲学。从孟子的总体思想来看，他"言必称尧舜"的目的是，宣扬先王之道，实践自己的仁政思想，因而更关注扶持、培养仁德之君，而非消极等待君主自觉向仁。

[4]理雅各和刘殿爵将"志"翻译为"intention"（计划、意图和目的），赵甄陶将之翻译为"motive"（产生行动的推动力），二者皆属于行为动机的范畴，基本上能体现"志"的含义。赖发洛将"志"翻译为"purpose"。它除了具有目的、意图的含义之外，还有效果、意义的含义，将"功"的部分内涵也包含其中，不利于此处的"志""功"之辩。

[5]刘殿爵取"墁"的本义"粉刷墙壁的工具"，将"毁瓦画墁"翻译为"makes wild movements with his trowel, ruining the tiles"（用铲子胡乱划，破坏了屋瓦）。赵岐的理解是："孟子言人但破碎瓦，画地则复墁灭之。"焦循指出："赵氏谓田地已有界画，而复将所界画之迹，用泥涂而灭去之。瓦破碎，则无能造屋。所画界坊灭，则等差无所验。是皆以有用为无用也。"杨伯峻则认为："这里似乎指新刷的墙壁而言。朱熹《集注》云：'墁，墙壁之饰也'可能亦是此意。"因而将之翻译为"把屋瓦打碎，在新刷的墙壁上乱画。"理雅各受朱熹影响，将本句翻译为"There is a man here, who breaks your tiles, and draws unsightly figures on your walls."（这儿有个人，他打碎了瓦，并在墙上画了一些丑陋的图案）这几种理解都言之有据，都能作为孟

子反驳彭更"食志"的论据。

【原文】6.5 万章问曰[1]:"宋,小国也;今将行王政,齐楚恶而伐之,则如之何?"孟子曰:"汤居亳,与葛为邻,葛伯放而不祀[2]。汤使人问之曰:'何为不祀?'曰:'无以供牺牲也。'汤使遗之牛羊。葛伯食之,又不以祀。汤又使人问之曰:'何为不祀?'曰:'无以供粢盛也。'汤使亳众往为之耕,老弱馈食。葛伯率其民,要其有酒食黍稻者夺之,不授者杀之。有童子以黍肉饷,杀而夺之。《书》曰:'葛伯仇饷。'此之谓也。为其杀是童子而征之,四海之内皆曰:'非富天下也,为匹夫匹妇复仇也。''汤始征,自葛载',十一征而无敌于天下。东面而征,西夷怨;南面而征,北狄怨,曰'奚为后我?'民之望之,若大旱之望雨也。归市者弗止,芸者不变,诛其君,吊其民,如时雨降。民大悦。《书》曰:'徯我后,后来其无罚!''有攸[3]不惟臣,东征,绥厥士女,篚厥玄黄,绍我周王见休[4],惟臣附于大邑周。'其君子实玄黄于篚以迎其君子,其小人[5]箪食壶浆以迎其小人;救民于水火之中,取其残而已矣。《太誓》曰:'我武惟扬,侵于[6]之疆,则取于残,杀伐用张,于汤有光。'不行王政云尔;苟行王政,四海之内皆举首而望之,欲以为君;齐楚虽大,何畏焉?"

【译文】万章问道:"宋是个小国,如果现在想实行仁政,招致齐楚两国的厌恶,出兵讨伐,该怎么办呢?"孟子回答说:"汤居住在亳地,和葛国相邻,葛伯非常放肆,而且不祭祀。汤派人去问:'为什么不祭祀?'回答说:'没有牛羊做祭品。'汤于是送给他牛羊。葛伯自己吃了牛羊,还是不祭祀。汤又派人去问:'为什么不祭祀?'答道:'没有用来祭祀的谷米。'汤派亳地百姓去替他们耕种,老弱的人负责给耕者送饭。葛伯却带领百姓去拦截、抢夺送酒菜饭食的人,不肯交出来的就杀掉。有个小孩去送饭和肉,竟被杀掉了,并且抢去了饭和肉。《书》

上说：'葛伯仇视送饭的人。'就是说的这个。汤因为葛伯杀了小孩而去讨伐，天下的人都说：'汤并不是贪图天下的财富，是为百姓报仇。''汤的征战，从葛国开始'，出征十一次，都没有与之匹敌的。向东方出征，西方的人抱怨；向南方出征，北方的人抱怨，说道：'为什么把我们放后面？'百姓盼望他，就像大旱年岁盼望下雨一样。经商的人不用停止，种地的人照常种地，杀暴君，安抚百姓，就像下及时雨一样，老百姓非常高兴。《书》上说：'等待我的王！王来了我们不再受罚！'又说：'攸国不臣服，周王向东讨伐，去安抚那里的男女百姓，他们也用筐子装好黑色、黄色的绸帛，请求介绍和周王相见，得到荣光，作大周国的臣民。'官员们用筐子装上黑色和黄色的绸束去迎接官员，百姓用竹筐盛食物，用壶盛浆液迎接士兵。周王出兵是救百姓于水火之中，只杀掉残暴的君主罢了。《太誓》说：'我们的威武要发扬，攻到邢国的疆土上，杀掉残暴的君王，攻伐得以伸张，功绩比成汤还伟大。'不行仁政便罢了；如果行仁政，天下的人都仰头盼望着，想要他成为君王，齐国楚国虽然强大，何必畏惧呢？"

【英译】Wan Chang asked Mencius，saying，'Sung is a small State. Its ruler is now setting about to practise the true royal government，and Ch'î and Ch'û hate and attack him. What in this case is to be done?' Mencius replied，'When T'ang dwelt in Po，he adjoined to the State of Ko，the chief of which was living in a dissolute state and neglecting his proper sacrifices. Tang sent messengers to inquire why he did not sacrifice. He replied，"I have no means of supplying the necessary victims."On this，T'ang caused oxen and sheep to be sent to him，but he ate them，and still continued not to sacrifice. Tang again sent messengers to ask him the same question as before，when he replied，"I have no means of obtaining the necessary millet."On this，T'ang sent the mass of the people of Po to go and till the ground for him， while the old and feeble carried their food to them. The chief of Ko led his people to intercept those who were thus charged with wine, cooked rice, millet, and paddy, and took their stores from them, while they killed those who refused to give them up. There was a boy who had some millet and flesh for the labourers, who was thus slain and robbed. What is said in the Book of History, "The chief of Ko behaved as an enemy to the provision-carriers," has reference to this. Because of his murder of this boy, T'ang proceeded to punish him. All within the four seas said, "It is not because he desires the riches of the kingdom, but to avenge a common man and woman." When T'ang began his work of executing justice, he commenced with Ko, and though he made eleven punitive expeditions, he had not an enemy in the kingdom. When he pursued his work in the east, the rude tribes in the west murmured. So did those on the north, when he was engaged in the south. Their cry was— "Why does he make us last." Thus, the people's longing for him was like their longing for rain in a time of great drought. The frequenters of the markets stopped not. Those engaged in weeding in the fields made no change in their operations. While he punished their rulers, he consoled the people. His progress was like the falling of opportune rain, and the people were delighted. It is said in the Book of History, "We have waited for our prince. When our prince comes, we may escape from the punishments under which we suffer." There being some who would not become the subjects of Châu, king Wû proceeded to punish them on the east. He gave tranquillity to their people, who welcomed him with baskets full of their black and yellow silks, saying— "From henceforth we shall serve the sovereign of our dynasty of Châu, that we may be made happy by him." So they joined themselves, as subjects, to the great city of Châu. Thus, the men of station of Shang took baskets full of black and yellow silks to meet the men of station of Châu, and the lower classes of the one met those of the other with baskets of rice and vessels of congee. Wû saved the people from the midst of fire and water, seizing only their oppressors, and destroying them. In the Great Declaration it is said, "My power shall be put forth, and, invading the territories of Shang, I will seize the oppressor. I will put him to death to punish him; —so shall the greatness of my work appear, more glorious than that of T'ang." Sung is not, as you say, practising true royal government, and so forth. If it were practising royal government, all within the four seas would be lifting up their heads, and looking for its prince, wishing to have him for their sovereign. Great as Ch'î and Ch'û are, what would there be to fear from them?'

【注释】

[1] 在这里孟子再次强调了"人和"在战争胜负和国家长治久安中的决定性影响。战国时期，各诸侯国纷纷寻求富国强兵之道，认为这是确保本国在诸侯征战中立于不败之地的决定性因素，而孟子则认为，实行仁政，争取民心才是确保国家立于不败之地的关键。孟子对民心的强调表明民本思想在先秦时期已经出现并得以蓬勃发展。

[2] 朱熹注曰："葛，国名。伯，爵也。放而不祀，放纵无道，不祀先祖也。"刘殿爵翻译"伯"为"Earl"不妥。葛国的首领被称为伯，与"chief"相似，但与英国"Earl"（伯爵）的含义不同，将二者简单对译，容易引起误解。祭祀祖先是中国古代国家的一项重要礼仪，但葛伯却沉溺享乐，对之置之不理，其统治的荒淫无道可窥一斑。理雅各和刘殿爵将"不祀"翻译为"neglecting his proper sacrifices"（忽视应有的祭祀）和"neglected his sacrificial duties"（忽略祭祀的义务）是准确的。赖发洛翻译为

"did not worship"。"worship"通常指对上帝的崇拜，尤其表明崇拜的盲目性。用它来翻译孟子认可的"祀"这一"国之大节"（《国语·鲁语上》）不合适。

[3] 朱熹将"攸"释为"所"，解为："有所不为臣，谓助纣为恶，而不为周臣者。"旧有注释多持此种观点，认为以"所"释"攸"是早期语法现象。理雅各的译文受朱熹影响，将之翻译为"There being some who would not become the subjects of Châu"。而杨伯峻则认为："旧注把'攸'字当'所'字解，恐误。根据甲文和晚商金文都有攸国之名，故译文作攸国。"刘殿爵亦将之翻译为"The state of Yu"（攸国）。

[4] "绍"，朱熹注曰："绍，继也，犹言事也。言其士女以筐盛玄黄之币，迎武王而事之也。"理雅各的翻译同朱熹，将本句译为"their people, who welcomed him with baskets full of their black and yellow silks, saying—"From henceforth we shall serve the sovereign of our dynasty of Châu, that we may be made happy by him."（他们把黑色、黄色的丝帛装满筐子来迎接他，并且说，"从今以后我们将服侍周王朝，他会给我们带来快乐"）任俊华和赵清文还总结出另外两种含义："一为介绍，引见；一说，绍为发语词，无义。"刘殿爵取"休"的"介绍，引见"之意，翻译为"They put bundles of black and yellow silk into baskets as gifts, seeking the honour of an audience with the King of Chou, and declared themselves subjects of the great state of Chou."（他们把成捆的黑色和黄色的丝帛放入筐子作为介绍礼，请求和周王相见得到荣耀，并且宣布他们是大周国的臣民）

[5] "小人"指的是普通百姓，和居上位的"君子"相对举而言。理雅各将"小人"翻译为"the lower classes"（下层人），基本上能体现出其含义。赖发洛用"small men"（年幼、心胸狭窄的人）翻译"小人"不妥。此处的"小人"更侧重身份地位，与年龄和道德无大关联。刘殿爵的"common people"（民众），可算是"小人"最恰当的翻译，体现了官民在身份上的对比。

[6] 旧有的注释多认为"于"是介词，如朱熹《集注》指出："言武王威武奋扬，侵彼纣之疆界。"理雅各和赖发洛的译文皆持此说。杨伯峻则认为"于"为古国名。他指出："这两个'于'字都是国名，陈梦家《尚书通论》云：'于即是邘。按《通鉴前编》，"纣有十八祀，西伯伐邘"，《注》引徐广曰"大传作于"。"于"疑即卜辞之盂方伯。'"刘殿爵的译文亦持此说。

【原文】 6.6　孟子谓戴不胜曰[1]："子欲子之王之善[2]与？我明告子。有楚大夫[3]于此，欲其子之齐语[4]也，则使齐人傅诸？使楚人傅诸？"曰："使齐人傅之。"曰："一齐人傅之，众楚人咻之[5]，虽日挞而求其齐也，不可得矣；引而置之庄岳之间数年，虽日挞而求其楚，亦不可得矣。子谓薛居州，善士也，使之居于王所。在于王所者，长幼卑尊皆薛居州也，王谁与为不善？在王所者，长幼卑尊皆非薛居州也，王谁与为善？一薛居州，独[6]如宋王何？"

【译文】 孟子对戴不胜说："你想要你的君主学好吗？我明白地告诉你。如果有位楚国的大夫，想要他的儿子会说齐国话，那么，是找齐国人教他呢？还是找楚国人教呢？"回答道："找齐国人教。"孟子说："一个齐国人教他，很多楚国人在干扰他，纵使每天用鞭打他，逼他学齐国话，也很难做到；如果把他放到临淄闹市住上几年，纵使每天鞭打他逼他说楚国话，也学不好。你说薛居州是个好人，让他住在王宫。如果王宫里不论年龄大小，还是地位高低的，都是薛居州那样的好人，宋王又能和谁一起干坏事呢？如果在王宫中，不论年龄大小，还是地位高低的，都不是好人，宋王又能和谁一起做好事呢？一个薛居州又能把宋王怎么样？"

【英译】 Mencius said to Tâi Pû-shǎng, 'I see that you are desiring your king to be virtuous，and will plainly tell you how he may be made so. Suppose that there is a great officer of Ch'û here，who wishes his son to learn the speech of Ch'î. Will he in that case employ a man of

Ch'ï as his tutor, or a man of Ch'û?' 'He will employ a man of Ch'î to teach him,' said Pû-shǎng. Mencius went on, 'If but one man of Ch'î be teaching him, and there be a multitude of men of Ch'û continually shouting out about him, although his father beat him every day, wishing him to learn the speech of Ch'î, it will be impossible for him to do so. But in the same way, if he were to be taken and placed for several years in Chwang or Yo, though his father should beat him, wishing him to speak the language of Ch'û, it would be impossible for him to do so. You supposed that Hsieh Chü-Châu was a scholar of virtue, and you have got him placed in attendance on the king. Suppose that all in attendance on the king, old and young, high and low, were Hsieh Chü-Châus, whom would the king have to do evil with? And suppose that all in attendance on the king, old and young, high and low, are not Hsieh Chü-Châus, whom will the king have to do good with? What can one Hsieh Chü-Châu do alone for the king of Sung?'

【注释】

[1] 孟子列举"楚大夫欲其子学齐语"的例子来说明好的学习环境非常重要，并由此论证，虽人性本善，但它容易受外界环境的影响，因而欲使王为善政，应确保他身边围绕着正人君子，以避免"陷溺其心"。环境对人的影响，古人在很早的时候就已经注意到了，例如孔子宣扬"里仁为美。择不处仁，焉得知？"（《论语·里仁》）孟子强调"富岁，子弟多赖；凶岁，子弟多暴"（《孟子·告子上》），以及荀子主张"蓬生麻中，不扶而直；白沙在涅，与之俱黑。"（《荀子·劝学》）

[2] "善"就是拥有高尚的品德，做对国家、对百姓有益之事。理雅各将之翻译为"be virtuous"。"virtuous"的含义是善良正直，品行端正，更侧重个人在道德修养上的成果。赖发洛用"well"翻译"为善"。"Well"更强调身体健康，没有疾病。刘殿爵选择用"Good"翻译，该词的含义非常广，

既可以指个人在道德修养上的成绩，也包含助人为乐，与人为善，相较而言，用它翻译更为准确。

[3]"大夫"是古代的官名，强调官员在等级上的高低，理雅各在翻译时用"great"修饰"officer"，模糊了"大夫"的特点，过于扩大了它的含义。楚至大认为："'大夫'不是 great officer，而应是 high-rank official，干脆译成 minister 亦无不可。"赖发洛直接把"大夫"翻译成"a great man"。他的译文有照字面硬译之嫌，不能体现大夫是"古代高级政府官员"的特点。刘殿爵将之翻译为"a Counsellor"。这一翻译既表明"大夫"作为君主的智囊团，有为君主献计献策的职能，同时用大写单词强调，它是中国古代特有的官职，在英语中没有对等词。这一翻译既有利于传播中国传统文化，又可以保留中国文化的特色。

[4]"齐语"，更确切地说，应当是齐国的方言。理雅各将之翻译为"the speech of Chʻî"，赖发洛翻译为"speak Chʻi"，刘殿爵的译文是"the language of Chʻi"，赵甄陶将之翻译为"the Qi dialect"。楚至大指出："齐语、楚语中的'语'恐怕也不是 speech 或 language，而应是 dialect。当时各诸侯国使用的语言文字大致相同，属于汉语的各种方言，彼此尚可交流。"虽然根据《美国传统词典双解》，"speech"也有"民族语言，地方方言"之意，但是这层含义不经常使用，因而要确保译文忠实于原文，应像楚至大和赵甄陶那样将"语"翻译成"dialect"（方言）。

[5]"众楚人咻之"是强调语言环境对语言学习的重要性。孟子认为，如果周围的人都说楚语，就会干扰孩子学习齐语。理雅各的译文是"a multitude of men of Chʻû continually shouting out about him"（众多的楚国人在他周围不断地大叫大喊）。赖发洛的译文是"all the Chʻu men shouting at him"（所有的楚国人都对他大喊大叫）。这两种翻译是对原文的硬译，容易让外国读者产生误解，不能明白为什么楚国人都要围着学齐国话的小孩大喊大叫。赵甄陶的译文是"many men from Chu talking incessantly around him"（很多楚国人围着他说个不停）。译者根据语境和篇章宗旨，将原文所表达的"楚

国人在学齐语的孩子周围用楚语讲个不停，不利于孩子学习语言"清楚地表达了出来。

[6]"独"，邓球柏给出三种理解："一说'岂，难道。副词。'一说'独犹将也。'一说'单独。'"理雅各、赖发洛和赵甄陶都将"独"翻译为"单独"（alone）。笔者认为，前文已经出现了"一薛居州"，"独"若再理解为"单独"，就会显得重复。刘殿爵采取意译法，没有单独表明对"独"的见解，但从译文看，似乎是理解为"将"，翻译为"What difference can one Hsüeh Chü-chou make to the King of Sung?"（仅凭薛居州一人将会给宋王带来什么不同的变化吗）此外，将"独"理解为"难道"，翻译为"难道仅凭薛居州一人能给宋王带来什么不同的变化吗?"也说得通。

【原文】6.7　公孙丑问曰[1]："不见诸侯何义[2]?"孟子曰："古者不为臣不见。段干木逾垣而避之，泄柳闭门而不纳，是皆已甚；迫，斯可以见矣[3]。阳货欲见孔子而恶无礼，大夫有赐于士，不得受于其家，则往拜其门。阳货瞰孔子之亡也，而馈孔子蒸豚；孔子亦瞰其亡也，而往拜之。当是时，阳货先，岂得不见[4]。曾子曰：'胁肩谄笑，病于夏畦。'子路曰：'未同而言，观其色赧赧然[5]，非由之所知也。'由是观之，则君子之所养，可知已矣。"

【译文】公孙丑问道："不去主动谒见诸侯，有什么道理吗?"孟子说："在古代，如果不是诸侯的大臣，就不去谒见。段干木翻墙躲开魏文侯，泄柳关着大门不见鲁穆公，这些都做得过分了；如果执意要见，也可以相见。阳货想要孔子来见他，又担心别人说他失礼。（当时的礼规定）大夫赠送礼物给士，如果士不在家，就应该亲自去大夫家答谢。阳货私下打听到孔子外出不在家，就赠送给孔子一个蒸小猪；孔子也私下打听到阳货不在家，才去登门答谢。如果那个时候，阳货先去看孔子，怎么会见不到? 曾子说：'耸起肩，装出讨好的笑脸，真比夏天在菜地里干活还累。'子路说：'拥有不同的志向，却还要交谈，看他说话脸上惭愧的样子，我真不能理解。'从这里可以看出，君子如何修养自己的品德，可以知道了。"

【英译】Kung-sun Châu asked Mencius, saying, 'What is the point of righteousness involved in your not going to see the princes?' Mencius replied, 'Among the ancients, if one had not been a minister in a State, he did not go to see the sovereign. Twan Kan-mû leaped over his wall to avoid the prince. Hsieh Liû shut his door, and would not admit the prince. These two, however, carried their scrupulosity to excess. When a prince is urgent, it is not improper to see him. Yang Ho wished to get Confucius to go to see him, but disliked doing so by any want of propriety. As it is the rule, therefore, that when a great officer sends a gift to a scholar, if the latter be not at home to receive it, he must go to the officer's to pay his respects, Yang Ho watched when Confucius was out, and sent him a roasted pig. Confucius, in his turn, watched when Ho was out, and went to pay his respects to him. At that time, Yang Ho had taken the initiative; —how could Confucius decline going to see him? Tsǎng-tsze said, "They who shrug up their shoulders, and laugh in a flattering way, toil harder than the summer labourer in the fields." Tsze-lû said, "There are those who talk with people with whom they have no great community of feeling. If you look at their countenances, they are full of blushes. I do not desire to know such persons." By considering these remarks, the spirit which the superior man nourishes may be known.'

【注释】

[1] 儒家重礼，在进退处事上都严格遵循礼的规定。孟子"不见诸侯"也是遵循"古者不为臣不见"的礼制规定而行。他虽重礼，但对礼的态度并不僵硬、教条，而是强调经与权，原则性与灵活性的统一。他认为在通常情

况下，应遵礼而行，但当情势所迫时，应学会变通。

[2] 公孙丑发问的前提是坚信孟子的行为是符合礼仪，但不清楚符合何种礼仪。因而从他的立场出发，可以看出此处的"义"并非中性词，而是询问孟子"不见诸侯"符合礼仪、道德，具有正当性和正义性的依据。理雅各将之翻译为"point of righteousness"（正义性、正当性），基本上能体现出原文的含义。赖发洛的"meaning"（意思，含义）过于中性，不能准确表达此句的含义。刘殿爵将"义"翻译为"significance"（重大意义、重要性）也是可以接受的。

[3] "迫，斯可以见矣。"省略了主语。理雅各根据上文"段干木逾垣而避之，泄柳闭门而不纳"，推断是君主强求要见贤者，因而翻译为"When a prince is urgent，it is not improper to see him."（当君主迫切要求见的时候，见他们是合适的）赖发洛将之翻译为"if pressed to see them"，他的译文没有表明"迫"这一行为的施力者，只是表明"如果迫切要见，他就可以见"这一含义。刘殿爵的译文也是如此。相较之下，理译本更便于读者理解，而赖译本和刘译本更能体现原文语言特点。

[4] "阳货先，岂得不见"，是孟子对阳货行为的批评。他认为，孔子是"圣之时者"，不会僵硬地固守礼制，如果他首先依礼去拜访孔子，孔子又怎会不见他。理雅各将本句翻译为"Yang Ho had taken the initiative；—how could Confucius decline going to see him?"（阳货已经主动了，孔子又怎能会拒绝见他呢）他认为孔子"往拜之"就是去见阳货。这种理解完全与原文之意相反。根据理雅各的理解，"馈孔子蒸豚"是阳货首先采取的主动行动，因而孔子不会拒绝见他，故"往拜之"是应该的，符合礼仪规定。但仔细阅读全篇文章，可以看出，阳货送孔子"蒸豚"是欲借助礼的规定逼迫孔子去见他，而孔子"瞰其亡也，而往拜之"表明，孔子其实不想见他，所以挑选他不在的时候去拜谢。从文意看，孔子是拒绝见他的。因而刘殿爵的译文用假设的语句指出，如果阳货首先依礼主动去拜访孔子，孔子又怎会拒绝见他呢？他的译文将孟子对阳货行为的批评之意准确传递了出来。

[5] 孟子假子路之口，表达了他对君子行为的态度。他认为君子入仕的目的是实现自己的政治抱负，"得志，与百姓由之"，而非遵循"妾妇之道"，放弃自己的正确观点，曲意顺从君主以取得荣华富贵，因而对那些"未同而言，观其色赧赧然"的人进行了批判。"未同"，赵岐注曰："志未合也。不可与之言而与之言谓之失言也。"理雅各将本句翻译为"There are those who talk with people with whom they have no great community of feeling. If you look at their countenances, they are full of blushes."（有些人和那些与他们没有共同志向的人谈话。如果看他们的表情，你会发现，他们因羞愧而面色通红）他的译文过于冗长，但便于读者理解。刘殿爵的译文是"To concur while not in agreement and to show this by blushing is quite beyond my understanding."（不同意却要假装同意，脸上却又显出惭愧的表情）他将"同"理解为"同意"而非"志同"，旨在表明这类人的虚伪和无原则性，和后文的"赧赧然"形成鲜明的对比。笔者更倾向于刘殿爵的翻译。

【原文】6.8　戴盈之曰[1]："什一，去关市之征，今兹未能，请轻之，以待来年，然后已，何如？"孟子曰："今有人日攘[2]其邻之鸡者，或告之曰：'是非君子[3]之道。'曰：'请损之，月攘一鸡，以待来年，然后已。'——如知其非义，斯速已矣，何待来年？"

【译文】戴盈之说："十分抽一的税率，免除关卡和市场上的赋税，今年还办不到，请先减轻一些，等到明年，然后完全执行，如何？"孟子说："现在有个人每天都偷邻居的鸡，有人告诉他说：'这不是君子应该做的。'他说：'请减少一些，一个月偷一只鸡，等到明年，完全不偷。'——如果知道行为不合义，应该赶紧停止，为何要等到明年？"

【英译】Tâi Ying-chih said to Mencius, 'I am not able at present and immediately to do with the levying of a tithe only, and abolishing the duties charged at the passes and in the markets. With your leave I will lighten, however, both the tax and the duties, until next year, and will then make an end of them. What do you think of such a course?' Mencius said, 'Here is a man, who every day appropriates some of his neighbour's strayed fowls. Some one says to him, "Such is not the way of a good man;" and he replies, "With your leave I will diminish my appropriations, and will take only one fowl a month, until next year, when I will make an end of the practice." If you know that the thing is unrighteous, then use all despatch in putting an end to it:—why wait till next year?'

【注释】

[1] 擅于运用浅显易懂的例子来说明深刻、抽象的道理是《孟子》的一大特点。孟子通过列举"攘鸡"的例子，来说明知错就改，不应拖沓，尤其是在国家治理上更应如此。国家的管理政策与百姓的生活休戚相关，在制定时应谨慎，对实施中出现的问题更应及时修正，切忌为错误寻找托词，人为延长错误的危害范围。

[2] 孟子举"今有人日攘其邻之鸡者"来说明，明年实行什一之法，取消关市之征是行不通的。陈襄民等指出："攘，与偷窃有所不同，古人称'凡六畜自来而取之曰攘'。"可见，"偷"有犯罪动机，是道德败坏的体现，而"攘"则是顺手牵羊，是道德缺陷所致。刘殿爵认识到了"攘"与"偷"的区别，翻译为"appropriate"。根据《简明英汉词典》，"appropriate"的含意为"挪用，窃用，为自己独自占有或使用，常未经许可"，能准确体现"攘"的暗含之意。而赖发洛和赵甄陶选择用"steal"翻译"攘"不准确。

[3] "君子"的内涵非常丰富，在不同语境下含义不同。理雅各用"a good man"（一个好人）来翻译此处的"君子"是准确的。笔者认为，试图以儒家的理想人格"君子"来说服一个道德存在缺陷，"攘其邻之鸡的人"不符合实际，未弄清自己的谈话对象。对于古代下层劳动人民来说，成为儒家所推崇的"君子"似乎遥不可及，他们更倾向于成为一个好人而已。赖发洛和刘殿爵用他们一贯翻译"君子"的单词翻译此处的"君子"不妥。

【原文】6.9　公都子曰[1]："外人[2]皆称夫子好辩[3]，敢问何也？"孟子曰："予岂好辩哉？予不得已也。天下之生久矣[4]，一治一乱。当尧之时，水逆行[5]，泛滥于中国，蛇龙居之，民无所定；下者为巢，上者为营窟。《书》曰：'洚水[6]警余。'洚水者，洪水也。使禹治之。禹掘地而注之海，驱蛇龙而放之菹；水由地中行，江、淮、河、汉是也。险阻既远，鸟兽之害人者消，然后人得平土而居之。尧舜既没，圣人之道衰，暴君代作，坏宫室以为污池，民无所安息；弃田以为园囿，使民不得衣食。邪说暴行又作，园囿、污池、沛泽多而禽兽至。及纣之身，天下又大乱。周公相武王诛纣，伐奄三年讨其君，驱飞廉于海隅而戮之，灭国者五十，驱虎、豹、犀、象而远之，天下大悦。《书》曰：'丕显哉，文王谟！丕承哉，武王烈！佑启我后人，咸以正无缺。'世衰道微，邪说暴行有作，臣弑其君者有之，子弑其父者有之。孔子惧，作《春秋》。《春秋》，天子之事也[7]；是故孔子曰：'知我者其惟《春秋》乎！罪我者其惟《春秋》乎！'圣王[8]不作，诸侯放恣，处士[9]横议[10]，杨朱、墨翟之言盈天下。天下之言不归杨，则归墨。杨氏为我，是无君也；墨氏兼爱，是无父也。[11]无父无君，是禽兽也。公明仪曰：'庖有肥肉，厩有肥马；民有饥色，野有饿莩，此率兽而食人也。'杨墨之道不息，孔子之道不著，是邪说诬民，充塞仁义也。仁义充塞，则率兽食人，人将相食。吾为此惧，闲[12]先圣之道，距杨墨，放淫辞，邪说者不得作。作于其心，害于其事；作于其事，害于其政。圣人复起，不易吾言矣。昔者禹抑洪水而天下平，周公兼夷狄、驱猛兽而百姓宁，孔子成《春秋》而乱臣贼子惧。《诗》云：'戎狄是膺，荆舒是惩，则莫我敢承。'无父无君，是周公所膺也。我亦欲正人心，息邪说，距诐行，放淫辞，以承三圣者；岂好辩哉？予不得已也。能言距杨墨者，圣人之徒也。[13]"

【译文】公都子说："外边的人都说您喜欢辩论，请问，为什么呢?"孟子说:"难道我喜欢辩论吗?我是不得已啊。天下存在了好长时间了,有时候太平,有时候混乱。在尧生活的时代,洪水横流,到处泛滥,蛇和龙居住在陆地上,百姓没有定居之地,住在低洼处的人在树上搭窝,住在高处的人便垒土建洞穴,《尚书》说:'大水警诫我们。'大水就是洪水。命令大禹治水,禹疏通河道,将水引入大海里,把蛇和龙驱逐到水草丛生的沼泽地。水顺着河道流,长江、淮河、黄河、汉水就是这样。危险既然已消除,害人的鸟兽也消失了,人们才能居住在平原上。尧舜死了之后,圣人之道衰微,暴君更替出现。毁坏民宅作深池,百姓无处安身;废弃农田去做园林,使百姓得不到衣服和食物。荒谬的学说、暴虐的行为又出现,园林、深池、草泽地增加,禽兽随之而来。到商纣王的时候,天下又大乱。周公辅助武王诛杀纣王,征伐奄国,并在三年后杀掉奄君,驱逐飞廉至海边,并且杀了他。总共灭掉五十个国家。把老虎、豹子、犀牛、大象驱赶到远方,天下的百姓非常高兴。《尚书》上说:'英明啊,文王的谋略!后继有人啊,武王的功业!护佑,启发我们后人,使大家都正确没有缺点。'太平之世衰落,仁义之道衰微,荒谬的学说、暴虐的行为又兴起,出现了臣杀君、子杀父的行为。孔子感到害怕,著《春秋》。著作《春秋》这种史书,是天子的职责,所以孔子说:'了解我,恐怕只有通过《春秋》吧!责骂我,恐怕也只是因为《春秋》吧!'圣王再未出现,诸侯放纵,隐居不仕的人乱发议论,杨朱、墨翟的学说在天下流行。天下流传的言论不是杨朱的学说就是墨翟的学说。杨朱主张人要为自己,是无君;墨翟主张对天下的人要有同等的爱,不分亲疏,这是无父。无父无君,那就是禽兽。公明仪说:'厨房里有肥肉,马厩里有肥马,老百姓却面黄肌瘦,野外有饿死的尸体,这就率领野兽吃人。'杨朱,墨翟的学说不破除,孔子的学说就不能发扬,荒谬的学说就会欺骗百姓,堵塞仁义。仁义被堵塞了,就是率领野兽吃人,人和人之间也会互相残杀。我为此感到忧虑,捍卫先王之道,反对杨墨的学说,驱逐淫辞邪说,使得邪说不能传播。因为邪说对心产生作用，就会对工作产生危害，对工作产生危害，就会危害政治。如果圣人再次兴起，也会同意我的这番话。从前大禹治水使得天下太平，周公兼并夷狄，赶走猛兽使得百姓安宁，孔子著《春秋》使得叛乱的大臣、不肖的儿子感到害怕。《诗》说：'攻打戎狄，惩罚荆舒，就没有人敢对抗我。'心中没有君主、父母的人是周公要惩罚的。我也想端正人心，消灭邪说，反对偏激的行为，驳斥荒唐的言论，从而继承三位圣人的事业；难道是喜欢辩论吗？我是不得已罢了。能够用学说反对杨墨的人，是圣人的门徒了。"

【英译】The disciple Kung-tû said to Mencius, 'Master, the people beyond our school all speak of you as being fond of disputing. I venture to ask whether it be so.' Mencius replied, 'Indeed, I am not fond of disputing, but I am compelled to do it. A long time has elapsed since this world of men received its being, and there has been along its history now a period of good order, and now a period of confusion. In the time of Yâo, the waters, flowing out of their channels, inundated the Middle Kingdom. Snakes and dragons occupied it, and the people had no place where they could settle themselves. In the low grounds they made nests for themselves on the trees or raised platforms, and in the high grounds they made caves. It is said in the Book of History, "The waters in their wild course warned me." Those "waters in their wild course" were the waters of the great inundation. Shun employed Yü to reduce the waters to order. Yü dug open their obstructed channels, and conducted them to the sea. He drove away the snakes and dragons, and forced them into the grassy marshes. On this, the waters pursued their course through the country, even the waters of the Chiang, the Hwâi, the Ho, and the Han, and the dangers and obstructions which they had occasioned were removed. The birds and beasts which had injured the people also disappeared, and after this men found the plains available for them, and occupied them. After the death of Yâo and Shun, the principles that mark sages fell into decay. Oppressive sovereigns arose one after another, who pulled down houses to make ponds and lakes, so that the people knew not where they could rest in quiet; they threw fields out of cultivation to form gardens and parks, so that the people could not get clothes and food. Afterwards, corrupt speakings and oppressive deeds became more rife; gardens and parks, ponds and lakes, thickets and marshes became more numerous, and birds and beasts swarmed. By the time of the tyrant Châu, the kingdom was again in a state of great confusion. Châu-kung assisted king Wû, and destroyed Châu . He smote Yen, and after three years put its sovereign to death. He drove Fei-lien to a corner by the sea, and slew him. The States which he extinguished amounted to fifty. He drove far away also the tigers, leopards, rhinoceroses, and elephants; —and all the people was greatly delighted. It is said in the Book of History, "Great and splendid were the plans of king Wăn! Greatly were they carried out by the energy of king Wu! They are for the assistance and instruction of us who are of an after day. They are all in principle correct, and deficient in nothing." Again the world fell into decay, and principles faded away. Perverse speakings and oppressive deeds waxed rife again. There were instances of ministers who murdered their sovereigns, and of sons who murdered their fathers. Confucius was afraid, and made the "Spring and Autumn." What the "Spring and Autumn" contains are matters proper to the sovereign. On this account Confucius said, "Yes! It is the Spring and Autumn which will make men know me, and it is the Spring and Autumn which will make men condemn me." Once more, sage sovereigns cease to arise, and the princes of the States give the reins to their lusts. Unemployed scholars indulge in unreasonable discussions. The words of Yang Chû and Mo Tî fill the country. If you listen to people's discourses throughout it, you will find that they have adopted the views either of Yang or of Mo. Now, Yang's principle is— "each one for himself," which does not acknowledge the claims of the sovereign. Mo's principle is "to love all equally," which does not acknowledge the peculiar affection due to a father. But to acknowledge neither king nor father is to be in the state of a beast. Kung-ming Î said, "In their kitchens, there is fat meat. In their stables, there are fat horses. But their people have the look of hunger, and on the wilds there are those who have died of famine. This is leading on beasts to devour men." If the principles of Yang and Mo be not stopped, and the principles of Confucius not set forth, then those perverse speakings will delude the people, and stop up the path of benevolence and righteousness. When benevolence and righteousness are stopped up, beasts will be led on to devour men, and men will devour one another. I am alarmed by these things, and address myself to the defence of the doctrines of the former sages, and to oppose Yang and Mo. I drive away their licentious expressions, so that such perverse speakers may not be able to show themselves. Their delusions spring up in men's minds, and do injury to their practice of affairs. Shown in their practice of affairs, they are pernicious to their government. When sages shall rise up again, they will not change my words. In former times, Yü repressed the vast waters of the inundation, and the country was reduced to order. Châu-kung's achievements extended even to the barbarous tribes of the east and north, and he drove away all ferocious animals，and the people enjoyed repose. Confucius completed the "Spring and Autumn，"and rebellious ministers and villainous sons were struck with terror. It is said in the Book of Poetry，"He smote the barbarians of the west and the north；He punished Ching and Shû；and no one dared to resist us." These father-deniers and king-deniers would have been smitten by Châu-kung. I also wish to rectify men's hearts，and to put an end to those perverse doctrines，to oppose their one-sided actions and banish away their licentious expressions；—and thus to carry on the work of the three sages. Do I do so because I am fond of disputing? I am compelled to do it. Whoever is able to oppose Yang and Mo is a disciple of the sages.'

【注释】

[1] 通过回应外人对自己好辩的指责，孟子提出了如下观点："予岂好辩哉？予不得已也。天下之生久矣，一治一乱。"这简单的两句话不仅表明了孟子对社会历史发展的认识，还表明了他身处乱世，以继承、捍卫孔子学说为己任，"距杨墨，放淫辞，邪说者不得作"的决心。"一治一乱"是孟子勾勒出的人类社会发展的大趋势。他认为人类社会产生以后，就进入了时治时乱的循环往复阶段。乱世需要像大禹、周公、孔子那样的"名世"的天才来治理，以进入治世阶段。他同时认为，自己生活的时代正处于乱世之中，邪说盛行，因而自己需要通过辩论来捍卫孔子学说，治理混乱之世。

[2] "外人"是孟门之外，对孟子不了解的人。他们指责孟子好逞口舌之利，试图在语言上胜过别人。理雅各的"the people beyond our school"（我们学派之外的人），赖发洛的"Men outside"（外面的人）以及刘殿爵的"Outsiders"（圈外的人）都能体现出"外人"的含义，但相比之下，理译本更准确，更便于读者理解。

[3] "好辩"，理雅各和刘殿爵选择用"dispute"（辩论、对……提出质疑）翻译是准确的。而赖发洛的"wrangling"（争吵）贬义性过强，与"辩"

的内涵不符。

[4]"天下之生",理雅各将之理解为"天下之生民",并将之翻译为"this world of men received its being",即"人类产生"。结合下文的例子可以看出,孟子讨论的是人类社会的发展趋势,因而这一翻译符合原文的意思。赖发洛按字面意思直译为"All below heaven was born"(天下万物的产生),刘殿爵翻译为"the world has existed"(世界已经存在),二人的译文皆扩大了原文内涵。

[5]"水逆行",朱熹注曰:"下流壅塞,故水倒流而旁溢也。"理雅各将之翻译为"the waters, flowing out of their channels"(水流出水道)。译文未能翻译出水汹涌而下,受到阻碍,倒转而行、四处横流的恐怖场景。赖发洛的译文是"the waters burst their banks"(水猛烈冲击着堤岸)。译文能体现水的来势凶猛,但不能表现水已冲破堤岸,在百姓居住区横冲直撞的场景。刘殿爵和赵甄陶的译文是"the water reversed its natural course"(水流倒转,一反常规)。他们的译文翻译出了"逆"的含义,但丧失了"逆"在汉语中所具备的大水来势凶猛、横冲直撞的意象。

[6]"洚水",理雅各将之翻译为"The waters in their wild course"(波涛汹涌的大水)。这一翻译准确体现了原文的意思。赖发洛则选择用"The waste water"(污水)翻译。刘殿爵选择用"Deluge"(诺亚时代的洪水)来翻译"洚水",虽便于西方读者理解,但将《圣经》中的内容移植到了中国传统文化。此外,《说文·水部》云:"洚,水不遵道。"这种理解可以很好呼应前文的"水逆行",因而将之翻译为"the water reversed its natural course"也是可以的。

[7]《春秋》是古代对编年史的通称,后专指相传由孔子根据鲁史修订而成的史书。当前学界对"《春秋》,天子之事也"大体有两种理解:一说认为编写《春秋》这样的史书是天子应做的事情;一说《春秋》记录了天子之事。刘殿爵的译文持第一种观点,认为编写《春秋》是君主的特权。理雅各和赖发洛皆持后种观点,认为《春秋》记载了君主的行为。理雅各和刘殿爵

分别将"天子"翻译为"sovereign"和"Emperor",基本上能体现孔孟时代的"天子"形象。赖发洛将"天子"翻译为"the Son of Heaven"。在英语世界中,大写的"Son"通常指"基督教的圣子,耶稣基督",将它与大写的"Heaven"连用,就将天堂、上帝等耶稣基督形象强加给中国文化,带来许多不必要,甚至是误导性的理解。

[8]孟子眼中的"圣王"是以尧、舜、禹等为代表的圣人君王。他们必须同时具备圣人和君主的双重身份。要想成为"圣王"必须首先是圣人。李娟指出:"圣人是孔子为世人设置的人生终极目标,他并不期望世人真的能成为具有圣人人格的人。"李娟还指出:"(孟子认为)圣人是一个集中了人类社会各种伦理道德标准的理想人物,是社会各阶层效法的榜样。"其次,要想成为"圣王"必须同时是君主。圣人虽然是人伦之至,但他必须是君主,能够借助君王的权力造福百姓,带领人民由乱世走向治世。理雅各和刘殿爵分别将"圣王"翻译为"sage sovereigns"和"sage kings",基本上能体现它的含义。赖发洛用"holy king"翻译"圣王"。"Holy"的基本词义是"神圣的、虔诚的",具有较强的宗教意味,与代表"人类社会各种伦理道德标准的"圣王的含义不符。

[9]"处士"指未做过官的士人。颜师古注《汉书异性诸侯王表》"处士横议"为:"处士,谓不官朝而居家者也。"理雅各用"Unemployed scholars"翻译"处士",而"unemployed"有"解雇、失业之意",容易让读者将"处士"和那些因失去工作而心怀怨恨,愤世嫉俗的失业者联系在一起。赖发洛将"处士"翻译为"idle knights",而"idle"通常用来形容那些游手好闲、无所事事的人。如果仅仅因为"处士"不愿在朝廷做官就将他们等同于游手好闲的懒惰之人不妥。刘殿爵的"people with no official position"(不担任官职的人)准确翻译出了"处士"的内涵,使读者能够对中国古代社会存在的这一特殊阶层有一个正确的认识。

[10]"横议"指放肆地发表违道、悖理的议论。焦循《孟子正义》载:"《列子皇帝篇》云:'横心之所念',《释文》云:'横,放纵也。'"理雅各将

之翻译为"unreasonable discussions"（无理的讨论），基本上能译出"横议"的含义。赖发洛用"argue foolishly"（愚蠢的辩论）翻译"横议"，仅能体现其违理的一面。刘殿爵的译文是"uninhibited in the expression of their view"（毫无节制地表达自己的观点），仅能体现"横议"放纵的一面。赖译本和刘译本结合起来，就可以全面展现"横议"的内涵。

[11] 墨子的学说由尚贤、尚同、兼爱、非攻、节用、节葬、天志、明鬼、非乐、非命、非儒等方面构成，其中"兼爱"是整个思想体系的核心，是"视人之国若视其国，视人之家若视其家，视人之身若视其身。"（《墨子·兼爱中》）可见，墨子强调的"兼爱"指爱在程度和性质上没有亲疏远近之别。刘殿爵的"love without discrimination"（没区别的爱）翻译出了"兼爱"的含义。理雅各将"兼爱"翻译为"love all equally"，侧重于爱在程度上的平等。孟子认为，墨家倡导"兼爱""是无父"的表现。理雅各采取解释性翻译的策略，将之翻译为"which does not acknowledge the peculiar affection due to a father"（不承认对父亲发自内心的特殊感情），这一翻译清楚表达了"无父"在此语境下的特殊含义。

[12] "闲"，焦循认为："孟子与杨墨辨，必原本于习先圣之道；习先圣之道，即讲习《六经》，不空凭心悟也。赵氏训闲为习，其义精矣。""习"的本意是鸟屡次拍着翅膀飞，可引申为张扬、宣讲。此外，"习"还有通晓熟悉之意。因而"闲先圣之道"可理解为"宣传先圣之道"，也可理解为"通晓先圣之道"。朱熹提出另外一种理解："闲，卫也"，即"捍卫先圣之道"。刘殿爵取"闲"的捍卫之意，但是和其他译者选择用"defend"不同，他则选用了语气更加强烈的、强调主动采取积极措施预防潜在危险的词"safeguard"翻译。

[13] "能言距杨墨者，圣人之徒也。"朱熹注曰："言苟有能为此距杨、墨之说者，则其所趋正矣，虽未必知道，是亦圣人之徒也。孟子既答公都子之问，而意有未尽，故复言此。"理雅各将本句翻译为"Whoever is able to oppose Yang and Mo is a disciple of the sages"（任何一个人，只要能够反对杨

墨，都是圣人的门徒）。他的译文和原文有出入，原文旨在强调"言"在抵制杨墨学说上的作用，以回应外人对孟子"好辩"的指责，而译文未能体现"好辩"在卫道上的作用。刘殿爵的译文"Whoever can，with words，combat Yang and Mo is a true disciple of the sages"体现了"言"的作用，并且选择用"combat"（战斗、争论）翻译"距"，准确再现了孟子的卫道之功。

【原文】6.10 匡章曰[1]："陈仲子岂不诚廉士哉[2]？居於陵，三日不食，耳无闻，目无见也。井上有李，螬食实者过半矣[3]，匍匐往，将食之，三咽[4]，然后耳有闻，目有见。"孟子曰："于齐国之士，吾必以仲子为巨擘焉[5]。虽然，仲子恶能廉？充仲子之操，则蚓而后可者也。夫蚓，上食槁壤，下饮黄泉。仲子所居之室，伯夷之所筑与？抑亦盗跖之所筑与[6]？所食之粟，伯夷之所树与？抑亦盗跖之所树与？是未可知也。"曰："是何伤哉？彼身织屦，妻辟纑，以易之也。"曰："仲子，齐之世家也。兄戴，盖禄万钟。以兄之禄为不义之禄而不食也，以兄之室为不义之室而不居也，辟兄离母，处于於陵。他日归，则有馈其兄生鹅者[7]，己频顣曰：'恶用是鶃鶃者为哉？'他日，其母杀是鹅也，与之食之。其兄自外至，曰：'是鶃鶃之肉也。'出而哇之。以母则不食，以妻则食之；以兄之室则弗居，以於陵则居之，是尚为能充其类也乎？若仲子者，蚓而后充其操者也。"

【译文】匡章说："陈仲子难道不是一个真正廉洁的人吗？住在於陵，三天不吃东西，耳朵听不见，眼睛看不到。井上有个李子，金龟子已经吃了大半个了，他爬过去，拿来就吃。吃了数口以后，耳朵才听到，眼睛才看见。"孟子说："在齐国的士人中，我肯定把仲子看作大拇指。但是，他怎能称作廉洁？要推广仲子的操守，那只有变成蚯蚓才能办到。蚯蚓，在地面上吃干土，在地下喝泉水。仲子住的房屋，是伯夷那样廉洁的人建的呢？还是盗跖那样的强盗建的呢？他吃的谷米，是伯夷那样廉洁的人种的呢？还是像盗跖那样的强盗种的呢？这也很难说。"
匡章说："这有什么关系呢？他亲自编草鞋，他的妻子绩麻练麻，交换
来的。"孟子说："仲子是齐国的世家大族。他的哥哥陈戴，在盖地享有
俸禄几万石。他认为哥哥的俸禄是不义之财，不吃；认为哥哥的房屋为
不义之室而不去住。躲避兄长，离开母亲，居住在於陵。有一天回去，
有人送给了他哥哥一只活鹅，他皱着眉头说：'要这种呃呃叫的东西干
什么啊？'过了几天，他的母亲杀了鹅，把肉给他吃。他的哥哥正好从
外面回来，说：'就是呃呃叫的东西的肉啊。'他赶紧跑出去呕吐了出
来。母亲做的食物不吃，妻子做的却吃；哥哥的房屋不住，於陵的房屋
就住，这能够在人类中推广吗？像仲子这样，只能把人变成蚯蚓才能做
到啊！"

【英译】K'wang Chang said to Mencius, 'Is not Ch'ǎn Chung a
man of true self-denying purity? He was living in Wû-ling, and for
three days was without food, till he could neither hear nor see. Over
a well there grew a plum-tree, the fruit of which had been more than
half eaten by worms. He crawled to it, and tried to eat some of the
fruit, when, after swallowing three mouthfuls, he recovered his sight
and hearing.' Mencius replied, 'Among the scholars of Ch'î, I must
regard Chung as the thumb among the fingers. But still, where is the
self-denying purity he pretends to? To carry out the principles which
he holds, one must become an earthworm, for so only can it be done.
Now, an earthworm eats the dry mould above, and drinks the yellow
spring below. Was the house in which Chung dwells built by a Po-î? or
was it built by a robber like Chih? Was the millet which he eats planted
by a Po-î? or was it planted by a robber like Chih? These are things
which cannot be known.' 'But,' said Chang, 'what does that matter?
He himself weaves sandals of hemp, and his wife twists and dresses

threads of hemp to sell or exchange them.' Mencius rejoined, 'Chung belongs to an ancient and noble family of Ch'î. His elder brother Tâi received from Kâ a revenue of 10, 000 chung, but he considered his brother's emolument to be unrighteous, and would not eat of it, and in the same way he considered his brother's house to be unrighteous, and would not dwell in it. Avoiding his brother and leaving his mother, he went and dwelt in Wû-ling. One day afterwards, he returned to their house, when it happened that some one sent his brother a present of a live goose. He, knitting his eyebrows, said, "What are you going to use that cackling thing for?" By-and-by his mother killed the goose, and gave him some of it to eat. Just then his brother came into the house, and said, "It is the flesh of that cackling thing," upon which he went out and vomited it. Thus, what his mother gave him he would not eat, but what his wife gives him he eats. He will not dwell in his brother's house, but he dwells in Wû-ling. How can he in such circumstances complete the style of life which he professes? With such principles as Chung holds, a man must be an earthworm, and then he can carry them out.'

【注释】

[1] 通过与匡章的谈话，孟子提出了他对"廉士"的认定。孟子肯定陈仲子是齐国的"巨擘"，但否认他是"廉士"。他认为，陈仲子只看重不食不义之禄，不居不义之室的小节，却舍弃了"人之大伦"，避兄离母，是困守小操守，而失去大操守的典型。胡广《四书大全》："南轩张氏曰：仲子徒欲洁身以为清，不知废大伦之为恶，原仲子本心亦岂不知母子之性重于妻兄之居愈于於陵乎？惟其私见所局，乱其伦类至此极也。众人惑于其迹以为清苦高介而取之，非矣。"

[2] "廉士"，庄子认为："众人重利，廉士重名，贤士尚志，圣人贵

精。"（《庄子·刻意》）刘向指出："义士不欺心，廉士不妄取。"朱熹亦认为："廉，有分辨，不苟取也。"可见，重视好名声、有节操、不苟取是"廉士"的重要特征。理雅各将"廉士"翻译为"a man of self-denying purity"（自我克制的纯洁之人），基本上能体现它的含义。赖发洛将之译为"honest knights"。他的译文强调诚实、正直，不能体现"廉士"的特征。刘殿爵用"a man of scruples"翻译"廉士"。"Scruples"的含义是"顾忌"，即认为错误而不愿做某事，能够对应"廉士""有分辨、不苟取"的特征。

[3]"李"究竟是李树还是果实，很难判断。刘殿爵认为是"李树"，将"井上有李，螬食实者过半矣"翻译为"By the well was a plum tree, more than half of whose plums were worm-eaten."（在井旁边长着一棵李树，它上面的果实大部分都被虫子吃掉了）理雅各、赵甄陶皆持此说。赵岐取"李"的"果实"之意，将之注为："李实有虫，食之过半，言仲子目不能择也。"即李树上的果实有一个正好在井的上方，已经被虫子吃掉了大半，但是由于陈仲子三天没吃饭，故"目无见"，不能选择好李，把被吃了多半个的坏李摘下来吃了。赖发洛的译文和赵岐相类，将之翻译为"Over the well was a plum, its flesh more than half eaten by maggots"。这样理解可以把"井上有李，螬食实者过半矣"和"目无见"紧密联系起来。

[4]"三咽"之"三"，刘殿爵将之理解为具体的数字，认为是吃了三口，理雅各和赖发洛皆持此意。《古代汉语常用字典》给出了另外一种理解："古代汉语里'三'和'九'往往不是具体的数字，而是泛指多次。"赵甄陶将之翻译为"swallowing several mouthfuls"（吞食了数口）也是可以的。

[5]"巨擘"，大拇指，在古代汉语文化语境下，它通常用来比喻有大才能的杰出人才。考虑到西方读者的文化背景和接受程度，刘殿爵将之意译为"I count Chung-tzu as the finest among Gentlemen in the state of Ch'i"（我认为仲子是齐国最优秀的士人）。理雅各的译本以直译著称，为了不影响读者的理解，在保持原文民族文化特征的基础上，他根据文意对译文进行了适当添加。他将本句翻译为"I must regard Chung as the thumb among the fingers"

（在齐国的士人中，我的确认为仲子是指中大者）。

　　[6]“伯夷”是中国历史上最为著名的洁行之士，而“盗跖”在先秦时期常被认为是典型的不守法礼之人。孟子举二人为例旨在说明仲子所坚守操行的偏执性和不可实现性。仲子认为他兄长的俸禄、房屋不义，故不食、不居。但他却无法断定自己所吃的粮食、所住的房屋是“伯夷”那样的廉洁之人，还是跖那样的大盗所为。显然，此处举二人实为指代和二人类似之人，并非特指二人，因而赵甄陶的译文“a scrupulous man like Boyi”（像伯夷那样廉洁的人）、“a robber like Zhi”（像跖那样的强盗）更准确。

　　[7]“则”，按《词诠》卷六：“承接连词，於初发现一事之已然状态时用之。”《古汉语纲要》也将之翻译为“原来，已经”。刘殿爵和理雅各的译文准确再现了“则”的内涵，即送他哥哥一个活鹅做礼物的事情已经发生。

卷　七

离娄章句上

【原文】7.1　孟子曰[1]："离娄之明，公输子之巧，不以规矩，不能成方圆；师旷之聪，不以六律，不能正五音[2]；尧舜之道，不以仁政，不能平治天下。今有仁心仁闻而民不被其泽，不可法于后世者，不行先王之道也。故曰，徒善不足以为政，徒法不能以自行。《诗》云：'不愆不忘，率由旧章。'遵先王之法而过者，未之有也。圣人既竭目力焉，继之以规矩准绳，以为方员平直，不可胜用也；既竭耳力焉，继之以六律正五音，不可胜用也；既竭心思焉，继之以不忍人之政，而仁覆天下矣。故曰，为高必因丘陵，为下必因川泽；为政不因先王之道，可谓智乎？是以惟仁者宜在高位。不仁而在高位，是播其恶于众也。上无道揆也，下无法守也，朝不信道，工不信度，君子犯义，小人犯刑，国之所存者，幸也[3]。故曰：城郭不完，兵甲不多，非国之灾也；田野不辟，货财不聚，非国之害也。上无礼，下无学，贼民兴，丧无日矣。《诗》曰：'天之方蹶，无然泄泄[4]。'泄泄犹沓沓也。事君无义，进退无礼[5]，言则非先王之道者，犹沓沓也。故曰，责难于君谓之恭[6]，陈善闭邪谓之敬[7]，吾君不能谓之贼。"[8]

【译文】孟子说："像离娄那么好的目力，像公输般那样好的技巧，如果不借助圆规和曲尺，也很难画出方形和圆形；像师旷那么好的听力，如果不用六律，也不能校正五音。虽然有尧舜之道，如果不实行仁政，也不能治理好天下。君主如果有仁爱的心和仁爱的名声，但是百姓却没有享受恩泽，也不能成为后世效法的榜样，因为他没有实行前代圣王之道。所以说：只有善心，不足以处理好政事；只有法律，法律自身不能很好地执行。《诗经》上说：'不偏差，不遗忘，一切都按照传统的规章。'遵循前代圣王的法度而犯错误的，是从来没有过的事。圣人在用尽目力之后，又用圆规、曲尺、水准器、绳墨，来做方的、圆的、平的、直的东西，这些东西就用之不尽了；圣人在用尽耳力之后，又用六律来校正五音，各种音阶也就用之不尽了；圣人在用尽心思后，又实行不忍心他人受苦的仁政，使得仁德遍布天下。所以说，想要建筑高台一定要借助山陵，想要挖深池一定要借助沼泽；如果管理国家不借助前代圣王之道，可以说是聪明吗？因此，只有仁人适宜处于统治地位。不仁的人占据统治地位，是把他的罪恶传播给百姓。在上的没有规矩可循，在下的没有法律可守，朝廷不信奉道义，工匠不相信尺度，君子触犯义理，小人触犯刑法，国家还能存在，那真是侥幸了。所以说，城墙不坚固，武器装备不多，不是国家的灾难；农田没开垦，货物和财产不聚集，不是国家的祸害。居上位的人不讲礼义，普通百姓不受教育，违法乱纪的人兴起，国家很快就会灭亡。《诗经》上说：'上天正在降灾难，不要多嘴多舌。'多嘴多舌即啰唆。侍奉国君不义，进退无礼，说话便诋毁前代圣王之道，这样就是'啰唆'。所以说，用仁政来严格要求君主叫作'恭'；向君主进善言，堵塞异端邪说叫作'敬'；说'我们君主做不到'叫作'贼'。"

【英译】Mencius said, 'The power of vision of Lî Lâu, and skill of hand of Kung-Shû, without the compass and square, could not form squares and circles. The acute ear of the music-master K'wang, without the pitch-tubes, could not determine correctly the five notes. The principles of Yâo and Shun, without a benevolent government, could not secure the tranquil order of the kingdom. There are now princes who have benevolent hearts and a reputation for benevolence, while yet the people do not receive any benefits from them, nor will they leave any example to future ages; —all because they do not put into practice the ways of the ancient kings. Hence we have the saying: — "Virtue alone is not sufficient for the exercise of government; laws alone cannot carry themselves into practice." It is said in the Book of Poetry, "Without transgression, without forgetfulness, following the ancient statutes." Never has any one fallen into error, who followed the laws of the ancient kings. When the sages had used the vigour of their eyes, they called in to their aid the compass, the square, the level, and the line, to make things square, round, level, and straight: —the use of the instruments is inexhaustible. When they had used their power of hearing to the utmost, they called in the pitch-tubes to their aid to determine the five notes: —the use of those tubes is inexhaustible. When they had exerted to the utmost the thoughts of their hearts, they called in to their aid a government that could not endure to witness the sufferings of men: —and their benevolence overspread the kingdom. Hence we have the saying: — "To raise a thing high, we must begin from the top of a mound or a hill; to dig to a great depth, we must commence in the low ground of a stream or a marsh." Can he be pronounced wise, who, in the exercise of government, does not proceed according to the ways of the former kings? Therefore only the benevolent ought to be in high stations. When a man destitute of benevolence is in a high station, he thereby disseminates his wickedness among all below him. When the prince has no principles by which he examines his administration, and his ministers have no laws by which they keep themselves in the discharge of their duties, then in the court obedience is not paid to principle, and in the office obedience is not paid to rule. Superiors violate the laws of righteousness, and inferiors violate the penal laws. It is only by a fortunate chance that a State in such a case is preserved. Therefore it is said, "It is not the exterior and interior walls being incomplete, and the supply of weapons offensive and defensive not being large, which constitutes the calamity of a kingdom. It is not the cultivable area not being extended, and stores and wealth not being accumulated, which occasions the ruin of a State." When superiors do not observe the rules of propriety, and inferiors do not learn, then seditious people spring up, and that State will perish in no time. It is said in the Book of Poetry, "When such an overthrow of Châu is being produced by Heaven, be not ye so much at your ease!" "At your ease;" —that is, dilatory. And so dilatory may those officers be deemed, who serve their prince without righteousness, who take office and retire from it without regard to propriety, and who in their words disown the ways of the ancient kings. Therefore it is said, "To urge one's sovereign to difficult achievements may be called showing respect for him. To set before him what is good and repress his perversities may be called showing reverence for him. He who does not do these things, saying to himself, —My sovereign is incompetent to this, may be said to play the thief with him."'

【注释】

[1] 孟子开篇利用三个意义相关、结构相同、语气相似的词组，论证了仁政在治理国家中的决定作用。离娄据说是黄帝时的人，有极强的目力，可以看见百步之外的秋毫之末；公输班，又称鲁班，是春秋末年鲁国人，为中国古代的能工巧匠；师旷是春秋时期著名的乐师。虽然他们三人分别在目

力、手艺和耳力上达到了极致，但要作出好的物品，也离不开外在的尺度和标准。同样，治理国家更不能抛弃仁政这一平治天下的法度。孟子在本章中反复强调因循先王之道的重要性，认为法先王之道可以避免过失，是智的表现。

[2]"六律"，即阳律六音。古代将音律分为阴律、阳律两部分，各有六种音。梁涛指出："相传黄帝时乐师伶伦截竹为筒，以筒的长短区别声音的清浊高下，乐器之音以此为标准。"可见，此处的"六律"实指中国古代用来定音的竹管。刘殿爵的译文"the six pipes"，不如理雅各和赵甄陶的"pitch-tubes"准确。

[3]"上无道揆也，下无法守也，朝不信道，工不信度，君子犯义，小人犯刑，国之所存者，幸也。"赵岐注曰："言君无道术可以揆度天意，臣无法度可以守职奉命，朝廷之士不信道德，百工之作不信度量，君子触义之所禁，谓学士当行君子之道也。小人触刑，愚人罹于密罔也，此亡国之政，然而国存者，侥幸耳，非其道也。"朱熹对此段话的理解是，"此言不仁而在高位之祸也。道，义理也。揆，度也。法，制度也。道揆，谓以义理度量事物而制其宜。法守，谓以法度自守。工，官也。度，即法也。君子小人，以位而言也。由上无道揆，故下无法守。无道揆，则朝不信道而君子犯义；无法守，则工不信度而小人犯刑。有此六者，其国必亡；其不亡者侥幸而已。"可见，两位注家的分歧一是体现在对句子逻辑关系的断定上。赵岐认为，"上无道揆""下无法守""朝不信道""工不信度""君子犯义"和"小人犯刑"之间是并列关系，是导致国家危亡的六种境况。译者赖发洛、刘殿爵、赵甄陶皆持这种理解。而朱熹则主张，"上无道揆也，下无法守也"导致"朝不信道，工不信度"，进而引起"君子犯义，小人犯刑"。显然，他认为这些境况之间是递进关系，最终导致国亡。理雅各的译文持此种逻辑。这两种对句子逻辑关系的界定都是可以接受的。分歧二体现在对"道揆""工"和"度"等的理解上。首先看译者对"上无道揆也，下无法守也"的理解，理雅各将之翻译为"When the prince has no principles by which he

examines his administration，and his ministers have no laws by which they keep themselves in the discharge of their duties"（当君主没有原则来审查他的政治，他的大臣没有法律来约束自己履行职责时）。显然他认为此处的"上"特指"君主"，"下"专指"大臣"，"道揆"为审查国家治理是否合宜的原则。刘殿爵和赵甄陶则认为"上"指"居上位者"，包含君主和大臣这些统治者。而"下"指"居下位者"，即普通百姓。"道揆"即规范原则。笔者认为，在本段话中，"上"与"下""君子"与"小人"是相对举而言，分别代指两个相互对立的阶层，因而将"下"理解为"居下位者"更准确。其次看译者对"工不信度"的翻译。"工"，既有官吏之意又有工匠之说。对它含义的界定直接影响到对"度"的解说。若将"工"理解为"官吏"，则"度"的含义就应是"法"；若认为是"工匠"，则"度"指尺度。杨伯峻就将"工"理解为"工匠"，认为"'度'字恐非法度之'度'，似宜读为韩非子'宁信度，毋自信也'之'度'，指尺码而言。"理雅各的译文受朱熹影响，将"工不信度"翻译为"in the office obedience is not paid to rule"。刘殿爵则将之翻译为"craftsmen have no faith in measures"（工匠不相信尺度）。在本段话中，"上"与"下""君子"与"小人"相对举而言，分别代指两个相互对立的阶层，因而"朝"和"工"也应是对立的关系。而"朝"的含义是确定的，指朝廷，若"工"指百官，二者就变成了相似的关系，所以将之理解为工匠更确切。再次看译者对"君子"和"小人"的理解。理雅各将之分别翻译为"Superiors"和"inferiors"，显然，他认为此处的"君子"和"小人"是就地位而非道德而言，强调的是尊卑的关系。赵甄陶亦持此种观点，将之翻译为"men of position"（有地位的人）和"the common people"（普通百姓）。刘殿爵则选择用"gentlemen"翻译"君子"，未能体现出此处"君子"的特殊含义。最后看译者对"幸也"的翻译。理雅各将之翻译为"a fortunate chance"，刘殿爵翻译为"good fortune"，赖发洛将之翻译为"luck"，这些翻译多强调运气，尤其是好运，往往含有成功或愉快之意。相比较而言，赵甄陶的"fluke"则强调侥幸、偶然、意外，更能体现此处"幸也"的含义。

[4]"泄泄"，朱熹注曰："怠缓悦从之貌。言天欲颠覆周室，群臣无得泄泄然，不急救正之。"理雅各将之翻译为"Be not ye so much at your ease!"赖发洛将之翻译为"Do not be so care-free"。显然二人都受朱熹影响，将之理解为"不要那么无忧无虑"。刘殿爵认为"泄泄"的含义是多言多语貌，将之翻译为"Do not chatter so"（不要那么喋喋不休）。赵甄陶也持这种观点，将之翻译为"Don't drivel on and on"（不要废话连篇）。将"泄泄"理解为多言多语貌更准确，任俊华曾对此做过详细解释，他指出："'泄泄'又作'呭呭'或'詍詍'。《说文·口部》说：'呭，多言也。从口世声。《诗》曰：'无然呭呭。'《说文·言部》则说：'詍，多言也。从言，世声。《诗》曰：'无然詍詍。'段玉裁注曰：'《口部》偁《诗》作呭呭，此作詍詍，盖四家之别也。'可见今本《诗经》中'无然泄泄'之'泄泄'，本来在不同的版本中就作'呭呭'或'詍詍'，而'呭呭'或'詍詍'都是喋喋多言的意思。下文孟子以'沓沓'释'泄泄'也可为证。"

[5]"进退无礼"，刘殿爵认为是担任官职和辞去官职时的行为不符合礼节规定。理雅各亦持此种观点，但赖发洛认为是拜见君主和退下时不遵守礼仪，并将之翻译为"neglect good form when you come in or withdraw"。赵甄陶则将之意译为"behaving himself without courtesy"，即"举止不礼貌"。这些理解皆可。

[6]"责难于君"，朱熹注："范氏曰：'人臣以难事责于君，使其君为尧舜之君者，尊君之大也。'"可见，"责难于君"的目的不是要为难君主，而是要使他像尧舜之君那样大有作为。理雅各将之翻译为"To urge one's sovereign to difficult achievements"，赵甄陶翻译为"To expect the highest possible achievement of one's ruler"，二位译者的译文将原文蕴含的言外之意完整地表达了出来。刘殿爵直接翻译为"To take one's prince to task"，不便于读者理解原文暗含之意。

[7]"闭邪"，朱熹注曰："开陈善道以禁闭君之邪心，惟恐其君或陷于有过之地者，敬君之至也"。理雅各翻译为"repress his perversities"（压制君

主的乖僻之心）。他的译文显然受朱熹的影响。这样理解虽能说通，但脱离原文语境，略显突兀。刘殿爵将"邪"理解为"异端"，将"闭邪"翻译为"keep out heresies"（将异端邪说阻隔在外）。这一翻译能和前文"言则非先王之道者，犹沓沓也"对应起来。孟子认为，为人臣应尽臣道，应让那些诽谤先王之道的异端邪说远离君主视听，这样才能保证君主行仁政。

[8] 朱熹将"吾君不能谓之贼"注解为："谓其君不能行善道而不以告者，贼害其君之甚也。"理雅各受其影响，将本句翻译为"He who does not do these things，saying to himself，—My sovereign is incompetent to this，may be said to play the thief with him"（不愿意作上述事情的人，肯定会说我们的君主不能胜任，这样的人是贼害君主的人）。他在翻译时做了适当添加，更便于读者理解。刘殿爵则选择意译为"to say 'My prince will never be capable of doing it' is to cripple him"（说"我的君主永远不会具备这样做的能力"是损害他）。这样翻译既能避免对原文做过多添加，又可将文意表达清楚。

【原文】7.2　孟子曰[1]："规矩，方圆之至也[2]；圣人，人伦之至也[3]。欲为君，尽君道；欲为臣，尽臣道。二者皆法尧舜而已矣。不以舜之所以事尧事君，不敬其君者也；不以尧之所以治民治民，贼其民者也。孔子曰：'道二，仁与不仁而已矣。'暴其民甚，则身弑国亡；不甚，则身危国削，名之曰'幽''厉'，[4]虽孝子慈孙，百世不能改也。《诗》云：'殷鉴不远[5]，在夏后之世。'此之谓也。"

【译文】孟子说："圆规和曲尺是方形和圆形的标准，圣人是做人的标准。作为君主，就要尽君主之道；作为臣子，就要尽臣子之道。不论是君道还是臣道只要效法尧和舜就行了。不用舜侍奉尧的方式侍奉君主，就是不尊敬君主；不用尧治理百姓的方式治理百姓，就是残害百姓。孔子说：'治国的方法有两种，行仁政和不行仁政罢了。'暴虐百姓太过分，就会被杀，国家也会灭亡；不过分，就会身危国削，死后的谥号被叫作'幽'、'厉',即使有孝顺的子孙,百代也不能改变。《诗经》说:'殷商的借鉴不远,就在前一代的夏朝。'说的就是这个意思。"

【英译】Mencius said, 'The compass and square produce perfect circles and squares. By the sages, the human relations are perfectly exhibited. He who as a sovereign would perfectly discharge the duties of a sovereign, and he who as a minister would perfectly discharge the duties of a minister, have only to imitate—the one Yâo, and the other Shun. He who does not serve his sovereign as Shun served Yâo, does not respect his sovereign; and he who does not rule his people as Yâo ruled his, injures his people. Confucius said, "There are but two courses, which can be pursued, that of virtue and its opposite." A ruler who carries the oppression of his people to the highest pitch, will himself be slain, and his kingdom will perish. If one stop short of the highest pitch, his life will notwithstanding be in danger, and his kingdom will be weakened. He will be styled "The Dark," or "The Cruel," and though he may have filial sons and affectionate grandsons, they will not be able in a hundred generations to change the designation. This is what is intended in the words of the Book of Poetry, "The beacon of Yin is not remote, it is in the time of the (last) sovereign of Hisâ." '

【注释】

[1] 孟子在本章再次重申了他理想的治国模式——"皆法尧舜而已矣"。尧舜之道其实是孟子一贯倡导的仁政思想的载体。他试图借前代圣王的权威来论证自己政治理想的合理性和可行性。与之相对并在当时受各诸侯国推崇的治国模式以商鞅为代表,他在"御前大辩论"时,曾说过:"治世不一道,便国不必法古。汤武之王也,不修古而兴;殷夏之灭也,不易礼而亡。然则反古者未可必非,循礼者未足多是也。"他认为,治理天下没有亘古不变的

法则，只要对天下有利就不必法先王。春秋战国时期是我国奴隶社会瓦解和封建社会逐步形成的时期，中国社会正经历着一场空前的大变革，因而以商鞅为代表的变革派更受诸侯青睐，而孟子的思想则被认为是"迂远而阔于事情"（《史记·孟子荀卿列传》）。

[2]"至"，朱熹注曰："极也"。理雅各、赖发洛和刘殿爵虽然选择用的单词不同，但基本上取"至"的"极也"的含义。赵甄陶则选择用"the standards"（标准）翻译，杨伯峻曾给出取"标准"之意的原因："《荀子·议兵篇》云：'所以不受命于主有三：可杀而不可使处不完，可杀而不可使击不胜，可杀而不可使欺百姓，夫是谓之三至。'杨倞《注》云：'至为一守而不变。'《孟子》此'至'意义固与'极'同，但与《荀子》此'至'之意义也不相违，所以译文以'标准'译出。"

[3]"人伦"，焦循注："即人事也。"刘殿爵将之翻译为"humanity"（人类、人性）。理雅各和赵甄陶则分别将之翻译为"human relations"和"the principles of human relationships"。结合《孟子》其它篇章对"人伦"的解释："教以人伦：父子有亲，君臣有义，夫妇有别，长幼有序，朋友有信。"（《孟子·滕文公》）可见，此处的"人伦"主要指人与人之间的各种关系。因而，理雅各和赵甄陶的译文更准确。

[4]"幽""厉"是周王的谥号。在古代，帝王、贵族、大臣、士大夫等具有一定地位的人死后，会根据他们的生前事迹与品德修养，给予一个或寓含善意评价，或带有评判、讽刺性质的称号。任俊华曾指出："《逸周书·谥法解》说：'蚤孤损位曰幽，雍遏不通曰幽，动静乱常曰幽'；'暴慢无亲曰厉，杀戮无辜曰厉'。朱熹《集注》曰：'幽，暗。厉，虐。皆恶谥也。'"可见，西周的幽王和厉王就因生前劣迹斑斑，而冠以不好的谥号。在翻译"幽""厉"时，刘殿爵首先对"幽""厉"做了解释，让读者明白这些称号是在他们死后人们对其生平的评价，接着选择对"幽"和"厉"进行音译，以突出其含义的特殊性，最后在附录中解释其含义。这样翻译既能保证译文的可读性和连贯性，又增强了译文的学术气息。理雅各和赖发洛将之

翻译为"The Dark"和"The Cruel"，译文将谥号的蕴含之意，即"暗"和"虐"翻译了出来。

[5]"殷鉴不远，在夏后之世"出自《诗经·大雅·荡》。"鉴"，最初指自戒用的刻有铭文的青铜镜。可见，"鉴"在中国古代文化语境下有借鉴、教训之意。理雅各将"鉴"翻译为"beacon"。"Beacon"的含义是灯塔，可引申为指引，用它来翻译"鉴"在表意上不如刘殿爵的"lesson"（经验教训）更准确。赖发洛将之直译为"mirror"（镜子），但"mirror"在西方语境下不能引起"鉴"在中国传统文化中本身所具备的文化联想。

【原文】7.3　孟子曰：[1]"三代之得天下也以仁，其失天下也以不仁[2]。国之所以废兴存亡者亦然。天子不仁，不保四海；诸侯不仁，不保社稷[3]；卿大夫不仁，不保宗庙[4]；士庶人不仁，不保四体。今恶死亡而乐不仁，是犹恶醉而强酒。"

【译文】孟子说："夏商周三代之所以能获得天下是因为仁，他们失去天下是因为不仁。国家之所以会出现衰败、兴盛、生存和灭亡的变化也都是因为这个道理。天子不仁，就不能保有四海；诸侯不仁，就不能保有社稷；卿大夫不仁，就不能保有祖庙；士人和普通百姓不仁，就不能保全身体。现在害怕死亡，却喜好不仁，就好像担心喝醉却强喝酒一样。"

【英译】Mencius said, 'It was by benevolence that the three dynasties gained the throne, and by not being benevolent that they lost it. It is by the same means that the decaying and flourishing, the preservation and perishing, of States are determined. If the sovereign be not benevolent, he cannot preserve the throne from passing from him. If the Head of a State be not benevolent, he cannot preserve his rule. If a high noble or great officer be not benevolent, he cannot preserve his ancestral temple. If a scholar or common man be not benevolent, he cannot preserve his four limbs. Now they hate death and ruin，and yet delight in being not benevolent；—this is like hating to be drunk，and yet being strong to drink wine.'

【注释】

[1] 虽然本章篇幅短小，但完美展现了孟子的论证和说理技巧。孟子在本章主要论证"仁"的重要性，认为它不仅是赢国、保国、治国的法宝，而且与个人的荣辱存亡休戚相关。为了证明这一观点，他先列举了夏商周三代兴亡的史实，反复重申了仁在三代历史中所起的作用，进而将这一作用上升为对国家兴亡规律的总结，并通过排比句式将这一规律层层推广，涵盖到所有的人。最后他又以"恶醉而强酒"为例，从反面论证了不仁的后果。

[2] "三代之得天下也以仁，其失天下也以不仁"是孟子对三代史实的评价，他强调的重点是突出"仁"在保有天下上的重要性。"三代"指夏、商、周三个朝代。理雅各将之翻译为"It was by benevolence that the three dynasties gained the throne，and by not being benevolent that they lost it. "（三个朝代是通过仁慈获得了王位，但同样是因为不仁而失去的它）译文用强调句型突出了"仁"的作用，达到了与原文同步的效果。刘殿爵的译文虽便于读者理解，但将"不仁"意译为"残暴"，与原文反复强调"仁"以突出"仁"的重要性不符。

[3] "社稷"，是土神和谷神。在古代，君主和诸侯都祭祀社稷，以求风调雨顺，五谷丰登，后来社稷就成了国家的象征。中国读者很容易理解社稷的象征意义，但如果逐字直译容易使外国读者疑惑。例如，赖发洛将"诸侯不仁，不保社稷"翻译为"without love, a feudal lord cannot ward the gods of land and grain"（如果诸侯不仁，就不能守护土神和谷神）。刘殿爵将之译为"a feudal lord cannot preserve the altars to the gods of earth and grain unless he is benevolent"（除非诸侯仁慈，否则他就不能保有祭祀谷神和土地神的祭坛）。译文仅仅做了些许添加，但在传情达意上远远胜过赖译本。理雅各的《孟子》译本虽以直译著称，但在翻译"社稷"时却选择了意译。他的译文

是 "If the Head of a State be not benevolent, he cannot preserve his rule." (如果诸侯不仁，就不能维持统治) 这一翻译避免了直译的缺陷，更便于读者接受。

[4] "宗庙"是卿大夫的家祠，和采邑密切相关。如果卿大夫失去了采邑就不能立宗庙。因而此处的"宗庙"同上文的"社稷"一样，也具有象征意义，实指卿大夫的封地。三位译者都将之直译为"ancestral temple"（祖庙），虽未能体现出其暗含的"封地"之意，但直译"宗庙"不会造成理解上的困惑。

【原文】7.4　孟子曰[1]："爱人不亲，反其仁；治人不治，反其智；礼人不答，反其敬——行有不得者皆反求诸己[2]，其身正而天下归之。《诗》云：'永言配命，自求多福。'"[3]

【译文】孟子说："爱别人，别人却不亲近，就要反省自己的仁；管理人，却没有管理好，就要反省自己的智慧；礼貌待人，却得不到相应的回应，就要反省自己的敬。所有行为如果达不到预期效果，都要从自身找原因。自身端正了，就会使天下人归附。《诗》上说：'永远配合天命，自己需求多福。'"

【英译】Mencius said, 'If a man love others, and no responsive attachment is shown to him, let him turn inwards and examine his own benevolence. If he is trying to rule others, and his government is unsuccessful, let him turn inwards and examine his wisdom. If he treats others politely, and they do not return his politeness, let him turn inwards and examine his own feeling of respect. When we do not, by what we do, realise what we desire, we must turn inwards, and examine ourselves in every point. When a man's person is correct, the whole kingdom will turn to him with recognition and submission. It is said in the Book of Poetry, "Be always studious to be in harmony with the ordinances of God，and you will obtain much happiness."'

【注释】

[1]"自省"是儒家修身的一项重要法宝，要求人要经常自我反省、自我省察以达到自我提高的目的。自省实际上是一种严于律己的精神，贯穿于儒家思想的始终。孔子在很早的时候就看到了"自省"的优点，宣称"躬自厚而薄责于人，则远怨矣。"(《论语·卫灵公》)受孔子的影响，曾子也将自己的修身方法概括为"吾日三省吾身"，孟子的"反求诸己"则是这一思想的延续和深化。

[2]孟子先从仁、智、礼三个具体德行的培养入手，强调自省在修德上的重要性，进而将其扩展到日常生活的一切行为中，提出"行有不得者皆反求诸己"这一普遍的修身、立命的原则。"皆"表明孟子把"反求诸己"看作是为人处世的不二法宝，具有普遍适用性，认为不论做什么事情，只要不能达到自己的预期目的，都要以此为手段检验自己的得失。刘殿爵的译文能清楚地表达这层含义。理雅各却认为"皆"是强调自我反省应该全面，不能拘泥一端，因而理雅各将之译为"When we do not，by what we do，realise what we desire，we must turn inwards，and examine ourselves in every point."(当我们做了一些事情，但是不能达到我们的期望时，我们必须转向内心，从各个方面省察自己)相比较而言，刘殿爵对"皆反求诸己"的理解更准确。

[3]"永言配命，自求多福。"引自《诗·大雅·文王》，这句话的意思是说，要长久地思念配合天命，自己寻求更多幸福。孟子引用此诗旨在强调，君主要推行仁政，就要未雨绸缪，在国家安定时修明政教，这样才能得到天命的垂青。理雅各的译文是"Be always studious to be in harmony with the ordinances of God，So you will certainly get for yourself much happiness"。理雅各的译文强调敬畏、顺服上帝的旨意，就会获得更多的幸福。他的翻译忽视了人的主观能动性。刘殿爵的译文则看到了配天命和自求福的并列关系，准确翻译出了原文之意。

【原文】 7.5   孟子曰[1]："人有恒言，皆曰，'天下[2]国[3]家[4]'，天下之本[5]在国，国之本在家，家之本在身。"

【译文】 孟子说："人们常讲一句话：'天下国家'。天下的基础是国，国的基础是家，家的基础是人本身。"

【英译】 Mencius said, 'People have this common saying, ——"The kingdom，the State，the family." The root of the kingdom is in the State. The root of the State is in the family. The root of the family is in the person of its Head.'

【注释】

[1] 虽然人们常说"天下国家"，但是天下、国、家和个人之间的关系又有几个人真正了解？孟子用简短的语言，概括出了他们之间的实质联系，那就是"天下之本在国，国之本在家，家之本在身。"这一认识是对《大学》倡导的"修身、齐家、治国、平天下"的个人修养目标的发展与深化。

[2] 赵岐注曰："天下，谓天子所主"。刘殿爵选择用"Empire"翻译"天下"，因为该词指一个拥有广大领土和众多民族的国家，并且由单一的最高权力者统治。这一含义和"天下"的含义非常相近，便于西方读者理解。他同时选择将"Empire"大写来提醒读者，虽然二者含义相近，但也有明显差别。理雅各将"天下"翻译为"The kingdom"（王国），虽然看到了二者的共同点，即在这片统一的领土上，有且仅有一人具有至高无上的绝对权力。但"kingdom"具有较强的宗教意味，用它来翻译"天下"，就将"天国""上帝的统治"等基督教意象强加给了中国文化。

[3] "国"，赵岐注曰："谓诸侯之国"。该词和西方的"state"有相似之处。"State"指统一国家内部拥有不同自治权的区域，和古代中国"诸侯之国"的含义具有相似性。但我们也应看到，古代诸侯和天子的关系以及诸侯国的权力和西方人熟悉的"state"也不完全一样。

[4] "家"，赵岐注曰："家谓卿大夫也。"杨伯峻则认为："从大学'治国'、'齐家'的解释看来，这一'家'字是一般的意义，未必是'大夫曰

家'的家。"《中庸》《大学》和《孟子》被学界公认为是思孟学派的代表作，它们的思想具有一脉相承性，因而杨伯峻将"家"字界定为一般意义的依据具有较强说服力。三位译者都认为此处的"家"泛指一般家庭，非专指卿大夫之家。赖发洛将之翻译为"house"（房子、住宅），不如刘殿爵的"family"（家庭）更准确。

[5]"本"的最初含义是草木的根或靠根的茎干，可引申为事物的基础或主体。水有源，木有本。无源之水不可能奔流不息，无本之木亦不可能长成参天大树。理雅各和赖发洛都将"本"翻译为"root"。它不论是在本义还是在引申义上都能较好地与"本"对应。但"root"的含义非常丰富，它的使用使译文具有较强的开放性，译者可以根据自己的理解程度选择"本"的不同含义。刘殿爵根据自己的理解，赋予了"本"明确的含义，即"basis"（基础）。他的翻译更便于读者准确把握原文的精髓。

【原文】7.6　孟子曰[1]："为政不难，不得罪于巨室[2]。巨室之所慕，一国慕之；一国之所慕，天下慕之；故沛然德教溢乎四海。"

【译文】孟子说："治理国家不难，只要不得罪于世家大族就行。世家大族所仰慕的，一国的人也都会仰慕，一国的人也都仰慕的，天下的人也都会仰慕。因此德教就会汹涌澎湃地充满天下。"

【英译】Mencius said, 'The administration of government is not difficult—it lies in not offending the great families. He whom the great families affect，will be affected by the whole State；and he whom any one State affects，will be affected by the whole kingdom. When this is the case，such an one's virtue and teachings will spread over all within the four seas like the rush of water.'

【注释】

[1] 孟子在本章中强调了"不得罪于巨室"在国家治理上的重要性。孟子看到了世家大族的影响力，认为如果世家大族能够向往仁政，那么推行

仁政、治理国家就非常容易了。

[2]"巨室"，赵岐注云："大家也，谓贤卿大夫之家"；朱熹解为"世臣大家也"。可见"巨室"指拥有较大影响力的世家大族。理雅各将之翻译为"the great families"。当"great"来修饰"family"时，可以指贵族的、有权力的家族；也可以指伟大的、崇高的家族。刘殿爵的译文是"noble families"，"noble"有"高尚的、贵族的"含义。赵甄陶则将之意译为"the families exercising great influence"（拥有巨大影响力的家族）。这三种翻译皆能体现出"巨室"的含义。

【原文】7.7　孟子说[1]："天下有道[2]，小德役大德，小贤役大贤；天下无道，小役大，弱役强。斯二者，天也。顺天者存[3]，逆天者亡。齐景公曰：'即不能令，又不受命，是绝物也[4]。'涕出而女于吴。今也小国师大国而耻受命焉，是犹弟子而耻受命于先师也。如耻之，莫若师文王。师文王，大国五年，小国七年，必为政于天下矣。《诗》云：'商之孙子，其丽不亿。上帝既命，侯于周服。侯服于周，天命靡常。殷士肤敏，裸将于京。'孔子曰：'仁不可为众也[5]。夫国君好仁，天下无敌。'今也欲无敌于天下而不以仁，是犹执热而不以濯也。《诗》云：'谁能执热，逝不以濯[6]？'"

【译文】孟子说："天下有道，道德不高的人被道德高的人所役使，不是很贤能的人被非常贤能的人役使；天下无道，小的被大的役使，弱的被强的役使。这两种情况是天所决定的。顺从天的存活，背天而行的灭亡。齐景公说：'既然不能命令别人，又不服从别人的命令，这是绝路一条。'流着眼泪把女儿嫁到吴国。现在小国以大国为师，却以接受命令为耻，这好比学生以接受老师的命令为耻。如果感到羞耻，最好以文王为师。以文王为师，大国需要五年，小国需要七年，定能统治天下。《诗经》说：'商代的子孙，人数何止十万。上天既有命令，都臣服周朝。都臣服周朝，可见天命不常。殷代的臣子也都漂亮聪敏，助祭于周京。'孔子说：'仁的力量不在于人的多少。君主如果爱好仁，就会无敌于天下。'如今一些诸侯想要无敌天下，却又不行仁政，这好比手拿热物而不用冷水冲手。《诗经》说过：'谁能手拿热物，却不用冷水冲手？'"

【英译】Mencius said, 'When right government prevails in the kingdom, princes of little virtue are submissive to those of great, and those of little worth to those of great. When bad government prevails in the kingdom, princes of small power are submissive to those of great, and the weak to the strong. Both these cases are the rule of Heaven. They who accord with Heaven are preserved, and they who rebel against Heaven perish. The duke Ching of Ch'î said, "Not to be able to command others, and at the same time to refuse to receive their commands, is to cut one's self off from all intercourse with others." His tears flowed forth while he gave his daughter to be married to the prince of Wû. Now the small States imitate the large, and yet are ashamed to receive their commands. This is like a scholar's being ashamed to receive the commands of his master. For a prince who is ashamed of this, the best plan is to imitate king Wăn. Let one imitate king Wăn, and in five years, if his State be large, or in seven years, if it be small, he will be sure to give laws to the kingdom. It is said in the Book of Poetry, "The descendants of the sovereigns of the Shang dynasty, are in number more than hundreds of thousands, but, God having passed His decree, they are all submissive to Châu. They are submissive to Châu, because the decree of Heaven is not unchanging. The officers of Yin, admirable and alert, Pour out the libations, and assist in the capital of Châu." Confucius said, "As against so benevolent a sovereign, they could not be deemed a multitude." Thus, if the prince of a state love benevolence，he will have no opponent in all the kingdom. Now they wish to have no opponent in all the kingdom，but they do not seek to attain this by being benevolent. This is like a man laying hold of a heated substance，and not having first dipped it in water. It is said in the Book of Poetry，"Who can take up a heated substance，Without first dipping it（in water）?"'

【注释】

[1] 本章集中记载了孟子关于人类社会发展规律的认识。他指出，天下有道，那么国家凭借德贤论关系；天下无道，国家直接凭借国力定高低。统治者应认清当前自己所处的天下无道的时代形势，敬畏、顺应天命。当然，顺应天命并非否定君主的个人主观努力，由于天命靡常，统治者只要师文王，行仁政，必定会得到天命的垂青，无敌于天下。

[2] 此处的"有道"和《孟子·尽心上》"天下有道，以道殉身；天下无道，以身殉道"中的"有道"含义相同。《孟子注疏》此章正义云："孟子言天下有治道之时。"即国家政治清明、得到很好治理的时期，故赵甄陶将之翻译为"When the world is well governed"。刘殿爵选择用"the Way"翻译不便于读者理解。

[3] "顺"的本义是沿着同一个方向，可引申为服从、不违背。理雅各将"顺"翻译为"accord with"（保持一致），虽能体现其字面意思，但不能重现原文所蕴含的对天命的敬畏和服从。刘殿爵选择用"obedient to"翻译，将"顺"的字面意思和蕴含之意都清楚地表达了出来。

[4] 朱熹注："物，犹人也。"受其影响，理雅各将"绝物"翻译为"cut one's self off from all intercourse with others"，即自己断绝同他人的一切交往。理雅各翻译出了"绝物"的字面意思。刘殿爵将之意译为"we are destined to be exterminated"（注定被消灭）。结合下文"涕出而女于吴"看，景公嫁女是天下无道，小国为求自保而臣服强国的无奈之举。刘殿爵的译文更突出了"即不能令，又不受命"的危害。

[5]"仁不可为众也"，赵岐注曰："行仁者，天下之众不能当也。"朱熹认为："有仁者则虽有十万之众，不能当之。故国君好仁，则必无敌于天下也。不可为众，犹所谓难为兄难为弟云尔。"结合下文"夫国君好仁，天下无敌"可以推测，"仁不可为众也"的含义应与"仁可无敌于天下"相类，因而赵岐和朱熹的注解基本上能够体现原文的意思。刘殿爵的译文"Against benevolence there can be no superiority in numbers"（在反对仁德的君主时，数量多并不占优势），准确再现了"仁不可为众也"的含义。

[6]"谁能执热，逝不以濯?"出自《诗经·大雅·桑柔》。赵岐注曰："谁能持热而不以水濯其手。"刘殿爵的译文持此种观点。而清代段玉裁《经韵楼集·〈诗〉"执热"解》则认为："寻诗意，'执热'犹触热、苦热，'濯'谓浴也。'濯'训涤，沐以濯发，浴以濯身，洗以濯足，皆得云'濯'。此《诗》谓谁能苦热而不澡浴以洁其体，以求凉快者乎? 乃常情常事。郑笺，《孟子》赵注、朱注，《左传》杜注，皆云'濯其手'，转使义晦，由泥于'执'字耳。"赵甄陶的译文持此说，将之翻译为"Who hates the broiling heat without taking a bath?"张觉教授在《"执热"新解》中提出了一种新的观点："据《孟子》、《左传》及《诗经》毛传，我以为此'执'字可训为'治'，其义证如:《诗·豳风·七月》:'上入执宫功。'《淮南子·主术训》:'故法律度量者，人主之所以执下。'也可解为'止'、'杜'，其义证如《左传·僖公二十八年》:'子玉使伯棼请战，曰:'非敢必有功也，愿以闲执谗慝之口。'执热，即治热，止热也。如此，则解《孟子》、解《诗经》皆文通字顺。"

【原文】7.8　孟子曰[1]:"不仁者可与言哉? 安其危而利其菑[2]，乐其所以亡者。不仁而可与言，则何亡国败家之有? 有孺子歌曰:'沧浪[3]之水清兮，可以濯我缨; 沧浪之水浊兮，可以濯我足。'孔子曰:'小子听之! 清斯濯缨，浊斯濯足矣。自取之也。'夫人必自侮，然后人侮之; 家必自毁，而后人毁之; 国必自伐，而后人伐之[4]。《太甲》曰:'天作孽，犹可违; 自作孽，不可活。'

此之谓也。"

【译文】孟子说："不仁的人可以向他谏言吗？把危险当作安全，把灾祸当作有利，把导致灭亡的事情当作快乐。不仁的人如果可以向他谏言，怎么会有亡国败家的事情发生呢？有小孩歌唱：'沧浪的水真清啊，可以洗我的帽缨；沧浪的水真浊啊，可以洗我的脚。'孔子说：'学生们快听，水清就可以洗帽缨，水浊就用来洗脚，这都是由水本身决定的。'所以人必定是先自取其辱，然后别人才会侮辱他；家必定是自己先毁坏，然后别人才毁坏它；国家必定是先自己招致讨伐，然后别人才会讨伐他。《太甲》说：'天造孽还可以逃，自己造孽，逃不掉，就是这个意思。'"

【英译】Mencius said，'How is it possible to speak with those princes who are not benevolent？Their perils they count safety，their calamities they count profitable，and they have pleasure in the things by which they perish. If it were possible to talk with them who so violate benevolence，how could we have such destruction of States and ruin of Families？There was a boy singing，"When the water of the Ts'ang-lang is clear，it does to wash the strings of my cap；When the water of the Ts'ang-lang is muddy，it does to wash my feet." Confucius said，"Hear what he sings，my children. When clear，then he will wash his cap-strings；and when muddy，he will wash his feet with it. This different application is brought by the water on itself." A man must first despise himself，and then others will despise him. A family must first destroy itself，and then others will destroy it. A State must first smite itself，and then others will smite it. This is illustrated in the passage of the T'âi Chiâ，"When Heaven sends down calamities，it is still possible to escape them. When we occasion the calamities ourselves，it is not possible any longer to live."'

【注释】

[1] 本章紧承上章，从反面论证了仁的重要性。孟子认为，人的安危祸福都是自己寻求的，亡国败家亦如此。君主之所以会面临亡国的危险，是因为他选择成为一个不仁之人，刚愎自用，不听劝谏，从而导致贤德之士不再同他讲述仁义道德。君主也将为自己的选择付出沉重的代价，失去了百姓的支持，最终走向亡国败家之路。

[2] “安其危而利其菑”，朱熹注：“不知其为危菑而反以为安利也”。刘殿爵的译文和朱熹相类，显然，他们认为，不仁的人丧失了辨别是非的能力，不能认清危险和灾难，反而认为它们对自己有利，安于现状，不求改进，从而最终面临亡国败家的危险。杨伯峻的理解与之迥然不同，他的译文是：“他们眼见别人的危险，无动于衷；利用别人的灾难来取利。”他的译文侧重于揭露不仁之人道德败坏，暴虐凶残的一面。相比之下，朱熹、刘殿爵等人强调不仁的危害，与下文“亡国败家”的联系更紧密，更能凸显本章的宗旨。

[3] “沧浪”，朱熹认为是“水名”。北魏郦道元《水经注·夏水》中说：“刘澄之著《永初山川记》云‘夏水，古文以为沧浪，渔父所歌也。’”理雅各和赖发洛皆持此种观点，将之音译为“Ts'ang-lang”。任俊华认为是“青苍色，或青苍色的水。如《文选·陆机〈塘上行〉》有：‘发藻玉台下，垂影沧浪泉。’李善注曰：‘《孟子》曰：“沧浪之水清。”沧浪，水色也。’卢文弨《钟山札记》云：‘仓浪，清色；在竹曰苍筤，在水曰沧浪’。”刘殿爵和赵甄陶持此种观点，将之翻译为“blue water”（碧水）。这两种翻译皆持之有据，故存疑以待来者。

[4] 孟子进一步强调祸福都是自己寻求的。理雅各严格按字面意思将本句翻译为“A man must first despise himself, and then others will despise him. A family must first destroy itself, and then others will destroy it. A State must first smite itself, and then others will smite it”（一个人必定首先轻视自己，然后别人才会轻视他；一个家庭必定首先自我毁坏，然后别人才会毁坏它；一

个国家必定首先自我攻伐，然后别人才会攻打它）。译者翻译出了原文所蕴含的先后关系，即自我轻视，自我毁灭在先，别人的轻视和攻伐紧随其后。但译文没有体现另外一层含义，即侮辱、毁灭和攻伐都是自己造成的，是"自取之也"。刘殿爵的译文"Only when a man invites insult will others insult him. Only when a family invites destruction will others destroy it. Only when a state invites invasion will others invade it."（只有当一个人自取侮辱的时候，别人才会侮辱他；只有当一个家庭自取毁灭时，别人才会摧毁它；只有当一个国家自取讨伐时，别人才会讨伐它）将原文包含的两层含义都准确体现了出来。

【原文】7.9　孟子曰[1]："桀纣之失天下也，失其民也；失其民者，失其心也。得天下有道：得其民，斯得天下矣；得其民有道：得其心，斯得民矣；得其心有道：所欲与之聚之[2]，所恶勿施，尔也[3]。民之归仁也，犹水之就下、兽之走圹也。故为渊驱鱼者，獭也；为丛驱爵者，鹯也；为汤武驱民者，桀与纣也。今天下之君有好仁者，则诸侯皆为之驱矣。虽欲无王，不可得已。今之欲王者，犹七年之病求三年之艾也[4]。苟为不畜，终身不得。苟不志于仁，终身忧辱，以陷于死亡。《诗》云：'其何能淑，载胥及溺[5]。'此之谓也。"

【译文】孟子说："桀和纣失去天下，是因为失去了百姓；他们失去百姓是因为失去了民心。得天下有方法：得到百姓，便获得天下了；得到百姓有方法：赢得民心，便是得到百姓了；赢得民心有方法：他们想要的，替他们聚积起来；他们厌恶的，不要强加给他们罢了。百姓归附仁，就像水向下流、兽向旷野奔跑一样。所以为深水赶鱼的是水獭；为丛林赶鸟雀的是鹯鹰；为商汤、周武赶来百姓的是夏桀与殷纣。现在如果有好仁的诸侯国主，那其他诸侯都会为他赶来百姓。虽然他不想当统一天下的王，也是做不到的。今天想要统一天下的人，就像得了七年的病要用三年的陈艾来治理。如果平时不储备，终身都得不到。如果不立志行仁，终身都会担忧受辱，以至于死亡。《诗》说：'他怎能办得好，只能一起落水罢了。'就是这个意思。"

【英译】Mencius said, 'Chieh and Châu's losing the throne, arose from their losing the people, and to lose the people means to lose their hearts. There is a way to get the kingdom:—get the people, and the kingdom is got. There is a way to get the people: get their hearts, and the people are got. There is a way to get their hearts:—it is simply to collect for them what they like, and not to lay on them what they dislike. The people turn to a benevolent rule as water flows downwards, and as wild beasts fly to the wilderness. Accordingly, as the otter aids the deep waters, driving the fish into them, and the hawk aids the thickets, driving the little birds to them, so Chieh and Châu aided T'ang and Wû, driving the people to them. If among the present rulers of the kingdom, there were one who loved benevolence, all the other princes would aid him, by driving the people to him. Although he wished not to become sovereign, he could not avoid becoming so. The case of one of the present princes wishing to become sovereign is like the having to seek for mugwort three years old, to cure a seven years' sickness. If it have not been kept in store, the patient may all his life not get it. If the princes do not set their wills on benevolence, all their days will be in sorrow and disgrace, and they will be involved in death and ruin. This is illustrated by what is said in the Book of Poetry, "How otherwise can you improve the kingdom? You will only with it go to ruin."'

【注释】

[1] 孟子从当时的社会现实出发，指出各诸侯国试图通过战争抢夺土

地和百姓以达到富国强兵的目的并非明智之举。他认为，仁政是争取民心，一统天下之本。统治者只有好仁义，行仁政才能获得民心，赢得百姓支持，从而最终成为统一天下的王。

[2] 孟子将得民心的方法概括为两点，即"所欲与之聚之，所恶勿施尔也。"这与孔子"己所不欲勿施于人"的思想一脉相承，不同的是孔子奉之为处世之道，孟子尊之为治国之法。"所欲与之聚之"，赵岐注曰："聚其所欲而与之"，即"给予他们，为他们聚积"。显然，他认为"与之"与"聚之"并列，此处的"与"字当解为动词。赖发洛的译文和赵岐相类，将之翻译为"gather for them and give them what they wish"。但杨伯峻认为，将"'与'字看为介词，较好"。他引王引之《经传释词》支持自己的观点："家大人曰：'与'，犹'为'也，'为'字读去声，'所欲与之聚之'，言所欲则为民聚之也。"刘殿爵的译文持后种观点，将之翻译为"amass what they want for them"（为他们积聚他们想要的东西）。从文意上看，这两种理解都能说得过去，不过从逻辑关系上看，应先"聚"再"与"，因而将"与"理解为介词更好。

[3] 赵岐注曰："尔，近也。勿施行其所恶，使民近，则民心可得矣。"但朱熹认为，此句的含义是："民之所恶，则勿施于民。"刘殿爵的译文同朱熹，虽能体现原文之意，但未翻译"尔也"的含义。杨伯峻引赵佑《温故录》指出："读'尔也'自为句"，认为"尔，如此；也，用法同耳。"赵甄陶的译文同杨伯峻，将之翻译为"There is a way to win the people's hearts: collect for them what they desire and do not force on them what they hate. That is all there is to it!"他将"尔也"自为句，用来修饰"所欲与之聚之，所恶勿施"，以凸显得民心、行仁政并不难。

[4] "艾"，赵岐注曰："可以为灸人病，干久益善，故以为喻。"可见，艾是一种草药，存放时间越久，疗效越好。"三年之艾"重在强调储备的必要性，如若平时不积累，奄奄一息的病人难以等到储备了三年的艾草来救命。理雅各将"三年之艾"翻译为"mugwort three years old"，他选择用

"mugwort"翻译"艾草"，但是根据《新牛津字典》，该词"尤指英国常见的树篱植物艾蒿，人们长期将之与魔法和迷信相联系"。显然用它翻译"艾"给原文增加了不必要的文化联想。不仅如此，他的译文也没说清楚到底是长了三年的艾，还是储备了三年的艾。刘殿爵选择将"艾"音译，以突出其含义的特殊性，并采用解释性翻译策略将之翻译为"ai that has been stored for three years"（储备了三年的艾草）。译文含义明确，而且突出了平常储藏的重要性，和下文的"苟为不畜，终身不得"相呼应，将原文严密的逻辑性准确传达给了读者。

[5]"其何能淑，载胥及溺"出自《诗经·大雅·桑柔》。郑玄《笺》云："淑，善；胥，相；及，与也。"刘殿爵的译文准确翻译出了诗句的字词之意。朱熹结合文意，将本句注解为："言今之所为，其何能善？则相引以陷于乱亡而已。"理雅各则结合文意探求所引诗句在原文中的含义。他受前文"苟不志于仁，终身忧辱，以陷于死亡"的影响，将之翻译为"How otherwise can you improve the kingdom? You will only with it go to ruin."（他认为如果君主不立志行仁政，不仅不能使国家富强，还会同国家一起灭亡）理雅各将引用的《诗经》里的句子和原文结合起来理解的方法，可以将诗句和孟子的观点紧密结合。

【原文】7.10　孟子曰[1]："自暴者，不可与有言也；自弃者，不可与有为也。言非[2]礼义，谓之自暴也；吾身不能居仁由义[3]，谓之自弃也。仁，人之安宅也[4]；义，人之正路也。旷安宅而弗居，舍正路而不由，哀哉！"

【译文】孟子说："自我损害的人，不能和他有什么好说的；自我放弃的人，不能和他一起有所作为。言语诋毁礼仪，叫作自我损害；认为自己不能以仁居心，由义而行，叫作自我放弃。仁是人安稳的住宅；义是人的正确道路。空着安稳的住宅而不去居住，舍弃正确的道路不走，真是可悲啊！"

【英译】Mencius said, 'With those who do violence to themselves, it is impossible to speak. With those who throw themselves away, it is impossible to do anything. To disown in his conversation propriety and righteousness, is what we mean by doing violence to one's self. To say— "I am not able to dwell in benevolence or pursue the path of righteousness," is what we mean by throwing one's self away. Benevolence is the tranquil habitation of man, and righteousness is his straight path. Alas for them, who leave the tranquil dwelling empty and do not reside in it, and who abandon the right path and do not pursue it?'

【注释】

[1] "自暴者"和"自弃者"是孟子批判、不屑与之交往的两类人。自暴者是诽谤诋毁仁义的人，自弃者虽不非议仁义，但却不能保有、行使自身固有的仁义。这两类人都没有看到仁义的重要性，因而孟子认为不应与这样的人商讨事情，共谋事业。

[2] "非"，朱熹认为"犹毁也"。杨伯峻指出："此处用及物动词，实是动词的意动用法，'以为不是'之意。"理雅各将"非"翻译为"disown"（否认），将"言非礼义"翻译为"To disown in his conversation propriety and righteousness"（在谈话中否认礼义），他的译文体现自暴者不认可礼义。刘殿爵选择用"attack"（抨击）翻译"非"，还将自暴者无知、极尽所能诋毁礼义的丑态刻画得入木三分。

[3] 朱熹注曰："由，行也。"可见"居仁由义"即守仁行义。刘殿爵用"abiding by benevolence"翻译"居仁"，"abide"的含义是"居住"，能够体现"居"的字面意思，而"abiding by"连用则取"遵守，依从"之意，这就将"居仁"的引申义也清楚地表达了出来。刘殿爵将"由义"翻译为"following rightness"（依义而行），再现了原文简洁的特点。

[4] 孟子以"安宅"和"正路"评价仁义，认为人只有居仁由义才能

确保内心的安静和行为的正确。在翻译"安宅"时，理雅各选择"tranquil habitation"，但"tranquil"通常形容环境安静，免受外界打扰。相比之下，刘殿爵的"peaceful abode"更侧重于内心的平静。同样，此处的"正路"是抽象意义上的路，指行动或行为的正确路线和方法，因而刘殿爵选择的"proper path"翻译优于赖发洛的"true road"。

【原文】7.11　孟子曰[1]："道在迩而求诸远[2]，事在易而求诸难：人人亲其亲，长其长[3]，而天下平。"

【译文】孟子说："道在近处却向远处寻求，事情本来容易却向难处做：人人都爱自己的父母，尊敬自己的长辈，天下就太平了。"

【英译】Mencius said, 'The path of duty lies in what is near, and men seek for it in what is remote. The work of duty lies in what is easy, and men seek for it in what is difficult. If each man would love his parents and show the due respect to his elders, the whole land would enjoy tranquillity.'

【注释】

[1] 孟子认为无论是做学问还是治理国家，最忌舍近求远、舍易求难，好高骛远，只要人人都能从自身做起，孝顺父母，尊敬兄长，并将之扩展到全天下，那么天下就太平了。

[2] "道"是儒家的一个重要的哲学概念，在《论语》中大约出现了一百次。孟子继承了孔子对"道"的论述，在《孟子》中"道"出现了一百四十八次。古人谈"道"并不详加界定，意义比较模糊。后世学者根据他们自己的理解诠释"道"，使它具备不同的特点。20世纪英国著名汉学家阿瑟·韦利（Arthur Waley）认为道是"一种永远正确的统治方法"（one infallible method of rule）。刘殿爵在他的英译《论语》中将"道"解释为"有关宇宙和人类真理的总和"。安乐哲认为："对于'道'的这种诠释，最充分、最细致和最持久的说明应当属于芬格莱特（Herbert Fingarette）。在对

'道'的解释中，芬格莱特将'道'定义为'没有十字路口的大道'。意思是说，'道'是一种唯一、确定的秩序。"综合三位学者对"道"的理解，可以将之概括为关于宇宙和人类社会的正确认识。理雅各将"道"翻译为"The path of duty"（当行之路），认为此处的"道"和《中庸》"率性之谓道"中"道"的含义一致。朱熹注曰："道，犹路也。人物各循其性之自然，则其日用事物之间，莫不各有当行之路，是则所谓道也。"理雅各指出，尽管有学者反对这一解释，但他认为这种注解似乎是正确的。理雅各的译文将"道"的字面意思和蕴含之意都清楚地表达了出来。赖发洛和刘殿爵都将之翻译为大写的"Way"，但未对其含义做出解释，任读者自己去揣摩、体会。"道在迩而求诸远"是对《中庸》"道不远人。人之为道而远人，不可以为道"继承和发展。朱熹注曰："道者，率性而已，固众人之所能知能行者也，故常不远于人。若为道者，厌其卑近以为不足为，而反务为高远难行之事，则非所以为道也。"朱熹认为，为道者，应在自身寻道，沿自己的本性去行道，不能好高骛远，因为事情简单卑微而不屑去做。刘殿爵将"道在迩"翻译为"The Way lies at hand"（道存在于近处），就是将《孟子》中"道"的含义放在整个儒家思想体系下去理解的。

[3] 在"亲其亲，长其长"中，第一个"亲"和"长"是动词，分别指"爱"和"尊敬"。第二个亲是"父母双亲"，"长"是"长辈"。理雅各准确翻译出了此句话的含义。

【原文】7.12　孟子曰[1]："居下位而不获于上，民不可得而治也。获于上有道，不信于友[2]，弗获于上矣。信于友有道，事亲弗悦，弗信于友矣。悦亲有道，反身不诚[3]，不悦于亲矣。诚身有道，不明乎善，不诚其身矣。是故诚者，天之道也；思诚者，人之道也[4]。至诚而不动者，未之有也；不诚，未有能动者也。"

【译文】孟子说："职位低下，而又得不到上级的信任，就不能把百姓治理好。得到上级的信任有方法，不能得到朋友的信任，就不能获得上级的信任。要从朋友那里取得信任有方法，侍奉父母不能使父母高兴，就不会得到朋友的信任。使父母高兴有方法，反躬自问，自己不真诚，就不能让父母高兴。要使自己真诚有方法，若是不明白什么是善，也不能使自己真诚。所以诚是天道，追求诚是人道。极端真诚而不能使别人感动的，是从来没有过的；不真诚，也不能感动别人。"

【英译】Mencius said，'When those occupying inferior situations do not obtain the confidence of the sovereign，they cannot succeed in governing the people. There is a way to obtain the confidence of the sovereign：—if one is not trusted by his friends，he will not obtain the confidence of his sovereign. There is a way of being trusted by one's friends：—if one do not serve his parents so as to make them pleased，he will not be trusted by his friends. There is a way to make one's parents pleased：—if one，on turning his thoughts inwards，finds a want of sincerity，he will not give pleasure to his parents. There is a way to the attainment of sincerity in one's self：—if a man do not understand what is good，he will not attain sincerity in himself. Therefore，sincerity is the way of Heaven. To think how to be sincere is the way of man. Never has there been one possessed of complete sincerity，who did not move others. Never has there been one who had not sincerity who was able to move others.'

【注释】

[1] 以"诚"为核心的工夫论是儒家思想的重要组成部分，在《中庸》中得以集中阐述。《中庸》把"诚"提升到"天道"的高度，认为"诚者，天之道也；诚之者，人之道也。"（《中庸》第二十章）孟子继承并发展了《中庸》对"诚"的论述，将思诚规定为人之道。他将信与诚对比使用，突出了二者的逻辑关系。在《说文解字》中，"信"与"诚"互相定义："诚，信也，从言成声。""信，诚也，从人言。"这表明，许慎亦认为二者内涵极其接近，

可互用。于民雄将二者的关系概括为："'诚'是内在的，'信'是'诚'的外在表现之一。它表现为两个方面，一是自己守信，二是得到他人的信任。故《中庸》说：'诚于中，形于外'。"

[2] 从词源上看，"信"由"人"和"言"构成，因而不少译者主张将"信"翻译为"living up to one's word"，即"遵守诺言"。这也是"信"最常用的含义，安乐哲指出："信不仅是指动机纯正意义上的可信赖，而且表示实际地具有一种力量，坚持实行和实现所许诺的事情。"在"信于友有道"中，"信"就取此种含义。刘殿爵选择用"trust"（得到他人信任）来翻译此处的"信"是准确的。

[3] "诚"，鲁芳以"真实无妄"和"诚实无欺"解释。她进一步指出："所谓'真实无妄'，意指'诚'就是客观存在的实理，它不仅是天之道，而且还存在于人性之中，所以人应该保持自身的本性，是其本来所是，真诚于善，而无任何私心杂念。……所谓'诚实无欺'是指人要真实地对待自己和他人，既要表里如一，不失其本心，又不欺骗他人。"美国学者安延明以中国古代经典为例证资源，指出："'诚'具有两个含义，即心理状态（信）与本质属性（实）。"理雅各和赵甄陶皆选择用"sincerity"翻译"诚"。刘殿爵将"诚"翻译为"be/being true"（真实的）。理雅各和赵甄陶对"诚"的翻译更侧重于指心理状态上的"信"，刘殿爵则强调本质属性上的"实"。

[4] 孟子的"思诚者"和中庸的"诚之者"含义一致。《中庸》云："诚者不勉而中，不思而得，从容中道，圣人也；诚之者，择善而固执之者也。"也就是说，"诚"是圣人天生自然的品格，他们可以不学而能，自然而诚。而一般人容易受私欲所碍，因而必须"择善而固执之"，也就是朱子所谓的"诚之者，未能真实无妄，而欲其真实无妄之谓，人事之当然也。"可见"思诚"的含义是"追求诚。"刘殿爵将"思诚"翻译为"reflect upon being true"（反思诚），不如赵甄陶的"striving for sincerity"（追求诚）准确。

【原文】7.13　孟子曰[1]："伯夷辟纣，居北海之滨，闻文王作，兴曰[2]：'盍归乎来！吾闻西伯[3]善养老者[4]。'太公辟纣，居东海之滨，闻文王作，兴曰：'盍归乎来！吾闻西伯善养老者。'二老者，天下之大老[5]也，而归之，是天下之父归之也。天下之父归之，其子焉往？诸侯有行文王之政者，七年之内，必为政于天下矣。"

【译文】孟子说："伯夷避开商纣王，居住在北海边，听说文王兴起，起身说：'何不去归附呢！我听说西伯善于养老人。'太公为躲避纣王，居住在东海边，听说文王兴起，便站起来说：'何不去归附呢！我听说西伯善于养老人。'这两位老人是天下最有声望的老人，都归附西伯，这等于天下的父亲都归附西伯了。天下的父亲都归附了，他们的儿子们还能去哪里呢？如果诸侯中有能行文王之政的，七年之内，一定能掌握天下的政权。"

【英译】 Mencius said, 'Po-î, that he might avoid Châu, was dwelling on the coast of the northern sea. When he heard of the rise of king Wǎn, he roused himself, and said, "Why should I not go and follow him? I have heard that the chief of the West knows well how to nourish the old." T'âi-kung, that he might avoid Châu, was dwelling on the coast of the eastern sea. When he heard of the rise of king Wǎn, he roused himself, and said, "Why should I not go and follow him? I have heard that the chief of the West knows well how to nourish the old." Those two old men were the greatest old men of the kingdom. When they came to follow king Wǎn, it was the fathers of the kingdom coming to follow him. When the fathers of the kingdom joined him, how could the sons go to any other? Were any of the princes to practise the government of king Wǎn, within seven years he would be sure to be giving laws to the kingdom.'

【注释】

[1] 孟子在本章继续强调法先王的重要性，认为诸侯如若能以文王为榜样，七年之内必能成为统一天下的王。不过孟子在此处强调的法先王是尊敬老人、善养老人。他对老人的重视不仅丰富了仁政的内容，而且形成了中华民族尊老、敬老的传统美德。

[2] 对"闻文王作兴曰"的断句有二：朱熹将之断为："闻文王作，兴曰。"赵岐则认为："作兴"为一词，将之断为"闻文王作兴，曰"。朱熹对"兴"的注释是"感动奋发之意"。显然，刘殿爵的译文同朱熹。理雅各将之翻译为"When he heard of the rise of king Wǎn, he roused himself"（他听说文王兴起，非常振奋地说）。显然，他的译文所持观点亦和朱熹一致。在汉语中，"作"与"兴"是近义词，理雅各用同源词"rise"和"rouse"翻译，更能体现原文的行文特色。赖发洛虽断句同朱熹，但将"兴"理解为"起身"，将这句话翻译为"When he heard of King Wen's doings, he rose"（他听说文王的所作所为后，站起来说）。

[3] "西伯"即周文王。邓球柏指出："周文王在早年时被纣王任命为西方诸侯之长，得以专征伐之权，故称为西伯。"刘殿爵将西伯音译为"His Po"，并在注释中对其含义作了解释。这样翻译既能保留古汉语的专有名词，又方便读者理解。理雅各将之翻译为"the chief of the West"（西方的首领）。他对西伯进行解释性翻译，便于读者理解。

[4] 对"善养老者"有两种理解，一种以理雅各为代表，认为其含义是"knows well how to nourish the old"（非常精通怎样照顾老人）。显然，他将"善"理解为"擅长、精通"。另一种以刘殿爵为代表，认为"善"的含义是"办好、弄好"，将"善养老者"理解为"takes good care of the aged"（把老人照顾得非常好）。这两种理解都能体现原文宗旨。

[5] "大老"，朱熹注曰："非常人之老者"，即不是一般的老人。"大老"的不一般体现在他们是"齿德皆尊"的"天下之父"。理雅各选择用"greatest old men"翻译"大老"。"Great"通常用来表示人的行为、品格等

伟大、崇高，基本上能体现其特征。刘殿爵选择用"grand old men"翻译
"大老"，"grand"除了形容建筑物的宏伟壮丽，还形容人年龄高和地位高，
亦能体现"大老"内涵。

【原文】7.14　孟子曰[1]："求也为季氏宰，无能改于其德[2]，
而赋粟倍他日。孔子曰：'求非我徒也，小子鸣鼓而攻之可也。'由
此观之，君不行仁政而富之，皆弃于孔子者也，况于为之强战？争
地以战，杀人盈野；争城以战，杀人盈城，此所谓率土地而食人
肉，罪不容于死。故善战者服上刑，连诸侯者次之，辟草莱、任土
地者次之。[3]"

【译文】孟子说："冉求做季康子的总管，不能改变他的德行，反
而把田赋增加了一倍。孔子说：'冉求不是我的学生，你们可以大张旗
鼓地攻击他。'从这里看，君主不行仁政却帮他聚财的人，都是被孔子
所唾弃的，何况那些为君主努力作战的人呢？为争夺土地而战，杀人
遍野；为争城池而战，杀人满城；这就是人们所说的率领土地来吃人肉，
死刑都不足以赎他们的罪过。所以好战的人应该受最重的刑罚，说服
诸侯合纵连横的人罪减一等，开垦荒地、尽地力的人该受再次一等的
刑罚。"

【英译】Mencius said, 'Ch'iû acted as chief officer to the head of
the Chî family, whose evil ways he was unable to change, while he
exacted from the people double the grain formerly paid. Confucius said,
"He is no disciple of mine. Little children, beat the drum and assail
him." Looking at the subject from this case, we perceive that when a
prince was not practising benevolent government, all his ministers who
enriched him were rejected by Confucius:—how much more would he
have rejected those who are vehement to fight for their prince! When
contentions about territory are the ground on which they fight, they

slaughter men till the fields are filled with them. When some struggle for a city is the ground on which they fight，they slaughter men till the city is filled with them. This is what is called "leading on the land to devour human flesh." Death is not enough for such a crime. Therefore，those who are skilful to fight should suffer the highest punishment. Next to them should be punished those who unite some princes in leagues against others；and next to them，those who take in grassy commons，imposing the cultivation of the ground on the people.'

【注释】

[1] 孟子在本章论证了他对臣属职责的看法。他认为大臣应首先帮助君主修德养性，使之明圣人之道，行先王之政。如果片面强调富国强兵，以战杀民，率土食人，不仅圣人弃之，最终也会成为国家和百姓的罪人。

[2] "改"，"更也"，本意是改变，理雅各将之翻译为"change"（改变），从语文学意义上看，它们的含义几乎完全一致，但结合上下文分析，此处的"改"更侧重于向好的方向改变，即改善、提高，因而刘殿爵的"improve"更准确。

[3] "任土地"，朱熹注曰："谓分土授民，使任耕稼之责，如李悝尽地方，商鞅开阡陌之类也。"开垦荒地、分民土地以尽地力本是好事，而孟子却反对，与理似乎说不通，对此杨伯峻是这样分析的："大概他认为诸侯之所以如此做，不是为人民，而是为私利。或者他认为当时人民之穷困，不是由于地力未尽，而是由于剥削太重，战争太多。"陈器之认为："今按：任，力役，见《荀子·议兵》注。任土地，谓为土地而役使百姓。"他的注解更便于解释孟子反对"任土地"者的原因。刘殿爵采取意译法，将"任土地"翻译为"increase the yield of the soil"（增加产量），这一翻译不便于读者理解为什么孟子反对"任土地"。理雅各将"任土地"翻译为"imposing the cultivation of the ground on the people"（强迫百姓耕种土地），他的译文更便于读者理解为什么孟子批判"任土地"者。

【原文】7.15 孟子曰[1]："存乎人者，莫良于眸子[2]。眸子不能掩其恶。胸中正，则眸子瞭焉；胸中不正，则眸子眊焉。听其言也，观其眸子，人焉廋哉？"

【译文】孟子说："观察一个人，没有比观察眼睛更好的。眼睛不能掩盖人心中的邪恶。内心正直，眼睛就会明亮；内心不正直，眼睛就会浑浊。听他说话，观察他的眼睛，这个人的善恶怎么能隐藏呢？"

【英译】Mencius said，'Of all the parts of a man's body there is none more excellent than the pupil of the eye. The pupil cannot be used to hide a man's wickedness. If within the breast all be correct，the pupil is bright. If within the breast all be not correct，the pupil is dull. Listen to a man's words and look at the pupil of his eye. How can a man conceal his character?'

【注释】

[1] 孟子认为一个人内心的善恶通常会在眼神中有所反映。眼睛在孟子的识人之道中也占有重要地位。他认为要认识一个人，不仅要听其言，还要仔细观察他的眼睛，因为"胸中正，则眸子瞭焉；胸中不正，则眸子眊焉"。

[2] "存"，《尔雅》曰："存在也"。理雅各取"存在"之意，将"存乎人者，莫良于眸子"翻译为"Of all the parts of a man's body there is none more excellent than the pupil of the eye"，即"人身上的所有部分，没有比瞳孔更好的"。他的译文表明孟子认为瞳孔是人身上最好的部分。刘殿爵根据下文"眸子不能掩其恶"认识到"眸子是人身上最纯真无伪"的东西，因而将之译为"There is in man nothing more ingenuous than the pupils of his eyes"（在人身上，没有任何部分比瞳孔更纯真无伪的）。他的译文能够准确地传达原文之意。《尔雅·释诂》给出了"存"的另外一种理解："存，察也。"赵甄陶亦取此意，将之翻译为"The best way to observe a man is to look at the pupils of his eyes"，即观察一个人最好的办法就是看他的眼睛。这几种理解

皆可。

【原文】7.16　孟子曰:[1]"恭者不侮人,俭者不夺人[2]。侮夺人之君,惟恐不顺焉,恶得为恭俭? 恭俭岂可以声音笑貌为哉?"

【译文】孟子说:"恭敬的人不欺侮别人,节俭的人不掠夺别人。欺侮和掠夺别人的君主只是担心别人不顺从自己,怎么能做到恭敬和节俭? 恭敬和节俭难道是靠声音和笑脸做出来的吗?"

【英译】Mencius said, 'The respectful do not despise others. The economical do not plunder others. The prince who treats men with despite and plunders them, is only afraid that they may not prove obedient to him: —how can he be regarded as respectful or economical? How can respectfulness and economy be made out of tones of the voice, and a smiling manner?'

【注释】

[1] "恭"和"俭"是儒家重要的修身标准。据《论语·学而》记载,孔子是凭借温、良、恭、俭、让取得诸侯国君信任,获悉各国政治的。孟子认为谦恭和节俭是长期修德的结果,它们植根于人的内心深处,通过人的行为举止自然而然地由内而发,并不是仅仅靠声音和笑貌等外在东西伪装而来。

[2] "俭",刘殿爵和理雅各认为是"节俭",将之分别译文"frugal"和"economical",梁涛则将之解读为"克制"。

【原文】7.17　淳于髡曰[1]:"男女授受不亲,礼与? [2]"孟子曰:"礼也。"曰:"嫂溺,则援之以手乎?"曰:"嫂溺不援,是豺狼也。男女授受不亲,礼也;嫂溺援之以手者,权也[3]。"曰:"今天下溺矣,夫子之不援,何也?"曰:"天下溺,援之以道;嫂溺,援之以手——子欲手援天下乎?"

【译文】 淳于髡问：“男女不亲自直接传递东西，是礼制吗？”孟子说：“是礼制。”淳于髡问道：“嫂子掉到水里，用手去救他吗？”孟子说：“嫂子掉到水里不伸手援救，是豺狼。男女之间不亲手传递东西，是礼制；嫂子掉到水里，用手去救，是权变。”淳于髡说：“现在天下人都掉入水里，您不伸手援救，为什么呢？”孟子说：“天下人都掉入水里，要用‘道’去援救；嫂子掉到水里，用手去援救。你想要我用手去救援天下人吗？”

【英译】 Shun-yü K'wǎn said, 'Is it the rule that males and females shall not allow their hands to touch in giving or receiving anything?' Mencius replied, 'It is the rule.' K'wǎn asked, 'If a man's sister-in-law be drowning, shall he rescue her with his hand?' Mencius said, 'He who would not so rescue the drowning woman is a wolf. For males and females not to allow their hands to touch in giving and receiving is the general rule; when a sister-in-law is drowning, to rescue her with the hand is a peculiar exigency.' K'wǎn said, 'The whole kingdom is drowning. How strange it is that you will not rescue it!' Mencius answered, 'A drowning kingdom must be rescued with right principles, as a drowning sister-in-law has to be rescued with the hand. Do you wish me to rescue the kingdom with my hand?'

【注释】

[1] “权”与“经”是古代哲学的一对重要范畴。冯用之在《权论》中指出：“夫权者，适一时之变，非悠久之用。然则适变于一时，利在于悠久者也。圣人知道德有不可为之时、礼义有不可施之时、刑名有不可威之时，由是济之以权。”可见“权”是在“经”不能发生作用时的变通方法，运用“权”是为了更好地遵循“经”。孟子重“经”但不否认“权”的作用。

[2] 孟子认为“男女授受不亲，礼也”是“经”，是具有普遍约束力的道德原则，是执中的外在标准。理雅各将之翻译为“For males and females

not to allow their hands to touch in giving and receiving is the general rule"（男女不亲手递接物品是普遍原则）。他认为此处的"礼"实际上就是与"权"对应的"经"，即普遍规律，因而将之翻译为"普遍原则"，以和下面的权宜之计相对应。这样翻译可以清楚表达孟子对"权"与"经"的态度，突出他对不偏不倚的"执中"原则的重视。刘殿爵采取直译法，直接将"礼"翻译为"prescribed by the rites"（礼的规定）。

[3] 孟子认为"嫂溺援之以手"是"权"，是具体问题具体分析，是执中的内在标准。若因循"男女授受不亲"之礼而"嫂溺不援"，就不是不偏不倚的"执中"，而是"犹执一也"的"无权"，是不知权的"禽兽""豺狼"。理雅各将"权"翻译为"peculiar exigency"（应急措施），认为"权"是危急关头、特殊情况下的非常手段，和"普遍原则"相呼应，能够体现"经"和"权"的关系。刘殿爵将"权"解释为"one uses one's discretion"（慎重斟酌后的灵活决定），也能够准确体现"权"的内涵。

【原文】7.18　公孙丑曰[1]："君子之不教子[2]，何也?"孟子曰："势不行也。教者必以正；以正不行，继之以怒。继之以怒，则反夷矣[3]。'夫子教我以正，夫子未出于正也。'则是父子相夷也。父子相夷，则恶矣。古者易子而教之，父子之间不责善[4]。责善则离，离则不祥莫大焉。"

【译文】公孙丑问："君子不亲自教育自己的孩子，为什么呢?"孟子说："情势不允许啊。教育的人一定用正道，用正道行不通，就会发怒，一发怒就会伤害感情。'父亲教我正道，自己却没有做到正道。'这是父子间互相伤害。父子间互相伤害是非常不好的。古时候人们相互交换儿子教育，父子间不相责以善。相责以善就会使父子间关系疏远，父子间关系疏远是最不好的事情。"

【英译】Kung-sun Ch'âu said，'Why is it that the superior man does not himself teach his son?' Mencius replied，'The circumstances of the case forbid its being done. The teacher must inculcate what is correct. When he inculcates what is correct，and his lessons are not practised，he follows them up with being angry. When he follows them up with being angry，then，contrary to what should be，he is offended with his son. At the same time，the pupil says，'My master inculcates on me what is correct，and he himself does not proceed in a correct path." The result of this is，that father and son are offended with each other. When father and son come to be offended with each other，the case is evil. The ancients exchanged sons，and one taught the son of another. Between father and son，there should be no reproving admonitions to what is good. Such reproofs lead to alienation，and than alienation there is nothing more inauspicious.'

【注释】

[1] "责善" 是朋友之道。孟子认为父子之间不能责善，否则就会伤害父子之间的天然亲情，因而古之人易子而教。

[2] "君子之不教子" 是君子不亲自教育儿子，而非不让孩子接受教育。理雅各和刘殿爵皆准确翻译出了 "教" 所蕴含的 "亲自教育" 的含义。

[3] "反夷矣"，朱熹注曰："夷，伤也。教子者，本为爱其子也，继之以怒，则反伤其子矣。" 可见，"反夷" 是父亲亲自教诲孩子，因发怒而对孩子造成的伤害。刘殿爵的译文 "father and son will hurt each other instead"（相反，父子会彼此伤害）。父亲对儿子发怒会伤害儿子，但他自己并没有受到伤害。儿子受伤后埋怨父亲，才伤害到了父亲，从而造成 "父子相夷" 的局面。刘殿爵将 "反夷" 翻译成了 "父子相夷"。赖发洛将 "反" 理解为 "返"，将 "反夷" 翻译为 "he becomes again a savage"（再次变成野蛮人）。他认为，父亲以正教育儿子，如果儿子不实行，父亲就会发怒，再次变成一个野蛮人。这样理解与原文之意不符。

[4] 父子主恩，朋友责善。如果父子相互责善就会伤恩，进而导致父

子隔阂，因而孟子反对父子之间彼此劝勉从善。因为"责善"绝非和风细雨的谆谆教导，而是严厉督促、责备，使之迁善改过。刘殿爵的译文"demand goodness from each other"虽能翻译出"责善"的含义，但在感情色彩的表达上不如理雅各的"reproving admonitions to what is good"（责备和劝诫为善）强烈。

【原文】7.19 孟子曰[1]："事，孰为大？事亲为大[2]；守，孰为大？守身为大[3]。不失其身而能事其亲者，吾闻之矣；失其身而能事其亲者，吾未之闻也。孰不为事？事亲，事之本也[4]；孰不为守？守身，守之本也。曾子养曾晳，必有酒肉；将彻，必请所与；问有余，必曰，'有。'曾晳死，曾元养曾子，必有酒肉；将彻，不请所与；问有余，曰，'亡矣。'——将以复进也。此所谓养口体者也。若曾子，则可谓养志也[5]。事亲若曾子者，可也。"

【译文】孟子说："侍奉谁最重要？侍奉父母最重要。守护什么最重要？守护自身最重要。自身无所失并且能侍奉父母的，我听说过；自身失守了还能够侍奉父母的，我没有听说过。什么侍奉的事不应该做？侍奉父母是侍奉的根本；什么守护的事不应该做？守护自身是根本。从前曾子奉养父亲曾晳，一定都有酒有肉。要撤除食物的时候，一定要问剩下的给谁；曾晳问还有没有剩余时，一定说：'有。'曾晳死后，曾元养曾子，也一定有酒有肉。要撤除食物的时候，不问剩下的给谁，曾子问还有没有剩余时，便说：'没有了。'准备留下以后给父亲吃。这个就是口体之养。至于曾子，那才叫顺从亲意之养。侍奉父母能够像曾子那样就可以了。"

【英译】Mencius said, 'Of services, which is the greatest? The service of parents is the greatest. Of charges, which is the greatest? The charge of one's self is the greatest. That those who do not fail to keep themselves are able to serve their parents is what I have heard. But

I have never heard of any, who, having failed to keep themselves, were able notwithstanding to serve their parents. There are many services, but the service of parents is the root of all others. There are many charges, but the charge of one's self is the root of all others. The philosopher Tsǎng, in nourishing Tsǎng Hsî, was always sure to have wine and flesh provided. And when they were being removed, he would ask respectfully to whom he should give what was left. If his father asked whether there was anything left, he was sure to say, "There is." After the death of Tsǎng Hsî, when Tsǎng Yüan came to nourish Tsǎng-tsze, he was always sure to have wine and flesh provided. But when the things were being removed, he did not ask to whom he should give what was left, and if his father asked whether there was anything left, he would answer "No;" —intending to bring them in again. This was what is called— "nourishing the mouth and body." We may call Tsǎng-tsze's practice— "nourishing the will." To serve one's parents as Tsǎng-tsze served his, may be accepted as filial piety.'

【注释】

[1] "孝"是中华民族的传统美德。儒家认为，上孝养志，下孝养体。孔子说："今之孝者，是谓能养。至于犬马，皆能有养；不敬，何以别乎？"（《论语·为政》）可见，赡养父母是为人子女的基本要求，而儒家强调的"孝"是发自内心对父母的恭敬和爱戴。

[2] "事亲"，焦循注曰："养亲也"。理雅各将之翻译为"The service of parents"（服侍父母，满足父母的需求），基本能体现"事亲"的含义。刘殿爵将之意译为"duty towards one's parents"（对父母的义务）。

[3] "守身"，赵岐注曰："使不陷于不义也"。此处的"守身"并不是字面上所体现的确保自己的身体免受伤害，而是说确保自己善良的本性免受外物蒙蔽，而陷于不义的境地。刘殿爵的译文强调对自己优秀品质的守护，

再现了"守身"的含义。

[4]"本"的本义是草木的根或靠根的茎干，可以引申为根源，也可以引申为根本和主体。理雅各取"本"的引申意"根源"，将"事亲，事之本也"翻译为"the service of parents is the root of all others"（侍奉父母是所有侍奉的源头）。刘殿爵将"本"理解为"首要的，最重要的"，认为"履行对父母应尽的义务是最重要的"。从上文"事亲为大"可以印证此处的"事亲，事之本也"应是侍奉父母是最重要的。

[5]孟子认为，事亲重在养志而非养口体。焦循指出了"养志"和"养口体"的区别："恐违亲意也，故曰养志。……不求亲意，故曰养口体。"可见，"养口体"是为父母提供赡养的物质条件，但不关注父母的意愿。如果仅仅做到这样离儒家倡导的孝还相差甚远。儒家更强调"养志"，即关注父母意愿的满足以及由此带来的精神的愉悦。赵甄陶将之翻译为"the gratification of his father's will"，强调心意满足后的快乐，很好地传递了"养志"的含义。刘殿爵的译文"solicitous of the wishes of his parents"则突出了"养志"的特征——对父母心意的关注。

【原文】7.20 孟子曰[1]："人不足与适也，政不足与间也[2]。唯大人为能格君心之非。君仁，莫不仁；君义，莫不义；君正，莫不正[3]。一正君而国定矣。"

【译文】孟子说："对于国君用人不当不值得谴责，为政也不值得非议；只有品德高尚的大人才能纠正国君不正确的思想。国君仁，没有人不仁；国君义，没有人不义；国君心正，没有人心不正。国君心正，国家也就安定了。"

【英译】Mencius said, 'It is not enough to remonstrate with a sovereign on account of the mal-employment of ministers, nor to blame errors of government. It is only the great man who can rectify what is wrong in the sovereign's mind. Let the prince be benevolent, and all his acts will be benevolent. Let the prince be righteous，and all his acts will be righteous. Let the prince be correct，and everything will be correct. Once rectify the ruler，and the kingdom will be firmly settled.'

【注释】

[1] 孟子在本章进一步强调了"格君心之非"的重要性。他看到了君主的表率作用，知道"上有好者，下必有甚焉者矣"（《孟子·滕文公》）。君主的好恶一旦端正了，通过他的表率作用，上行下效，整个国家就会形成好的社会风气，社会自然也就安定了。

[2] 对"人不足与适也，政不足与间也"的理解大体有两种，一种以赵岐为代表，认为"时皆小人居位，不足过责也。政教不足复非説"。一种以朱熹为代表，认为"言人君用人之非，不足过谪；行政之失，不足非间"。这两种理解的差别在于，前者认为"人"指的是君主所任用之人，后者认为"人"特指君主。前者更强调君主的表率作用，认为百官大臣都会效法君主，只有君主的思想端正，行为符合礼仪，即使小人在位，他们的行为和政治也会发生变化。因而品德高尚的大人根本不需要在评议百官行政上花费时间，只有他们能够改变君主，天下就会大治。后者则强调处理问题要看关键，不要在评议君主用人和政治得失上花费太多时间，要从根源抓起，借助具有高尚品格的大人来纠正君主的错误思想；思想端正了，不论用人还是行政都会发生变化。刘殿爵的译文同赵岐，认为此处的"人"是指君主所用之人。他的译文表明，君主任用的那些人不值得谴责，他们的政治也不值得非议。他的译文准确传达了孟子的哲学思想。理雅各的译文是"It is not enough to remonstrate with a sovereign on account of the mal-employment of ministers，nor to blame errors of government."（在任用大臣上劝诫君主，并且指责他们的政治过失是不够的）显然，他的译文受朱熹影响。这两种理解都能体现本章的宗旨："君仁，莫不仁；君义，莫不义；君正，莫不正。"

[3] "君仁，莫不仁；君义，莫不义；君正，莫不正"强调了君主的影响力，进一步突出了"正君心"的重要性。理雅各的译文前后有同义反复之

嫌。从孟子的整个思想体系看，他的译文不如刘殿爵的"When the prince is benevolent，everyone else is benevolent；when the prince is dutiful，everyone else is dutiful；when the prince is correct，everyone else is correct"（君主仁，没有人不仁；君主义，没有人不义；君主正，没有人不正）更突出篇章宗旨。

【原文】7.21　孟子曰[1]："有不虞之誉，有求全之毁[2]。"

【译文】孟子说："有出乎意料的赞扬，也有过于苛刻的诋毁。"

【英译】Mencius said，'There are cases of praise which could not be expected，and of reproach when the parties have been seeking to be perfect.'

【注释】

[1] 本章虽然短短一句话，但体现了孟子对荣辱的看法。他认为荣辱并不是自己本身就具有的仁义礼智诸端，只要去追求就一定能够得到，而是"求在外者也"，因而对待荣誉和耻辱要保持一颗平常心，不要因为这些我们不能掌控的东西而大喜大悲，更不要因为偶获一些意料不到的荣誉而得意忘形，因为求全责备者的苛刻而灰心丧气。

[2] 赵岐注曰："虞，度也。言人之行，有不度其将有名誉而得者，若尾生本与妇人期于梁下，不度水之卒至，遂至没溺，而获守信之誉。求全之毁者，若陈不瞻将赴君难，闻金鼓之声，失气而死，可谓欲求全其节，而反有怯弱之毁者也。"朱熹引吕氏曰："行不足以致誉而偶得誉，是谓不虞之誉。求免于毁而反致毁，是谓求全之毁。"可见，"不虞之誉"是不可预知的赞誉。赖发洛将之翻译为"Men are praised for want of forethought"（人们因为缺乏远见而受到表扬），显然错误理解了孟子的思想。刘殿爵将"不虞之誉"翻译为"unexpected praise"（难以预知的赞扬），准确翻译出了原文的意思。"求全之毁"，理雅各的理解和赵岐、朱熹的注解一致。刘殿爵则给出了另外一种理解："there is perfectionist criticism"（有求全责备者的批评）。他没有给出这样翻译的依据，我们可以在马有、敏春芳的《孟子解读献疑》

中寻求支撑。他们认为："赵注、朱注均非是。按句法……'求全'为'毁'之定语。……'求全之毁'，毁之由于求全责备者。"相比较而言，刘殿爵对"求全之毁"的翻译更准确。

【原文】7.22　孟子曰[1]："人之易其言也，无责耳矣。[2]"

【译文】孟子说："人们之所以轻易发表言论，是不用承担失言的责任罢了。"

【英译】Mencius said, 'Men's being ready with their tongues arises simply from their not having been reproved.'

【注释】

[1] 学者对此章的解释不尽相同，但总的来说，都认为孟子在警诫人们要慎言。

[2] 赵岐给出两种解释："人之轻易其言，不得失言之咎责也。一说人之轻易不肯谏正君者，以其不在言责之位者也。"朱熹同意前一种观点，指出："人之所以轻易其言者，以其未遭失言之责故耳。盖常人之情，无所惩于前，则无所警于后。非以为君子之学，必俟有责而后不敢易其言也。"杨伯峻则认为"赵岐及朱熹解此句都不好"。他认为俞樾的《孟子平义》"'乃言其不足责也'尚差强人意。"赵甄陶的译文受杨伯峻影响，将之翻译为"He who speaks lightly is beneath criticism"，即"什么话都轻易说出口的人，不足责备"。理雅各亦取"责"的"责备"之意，但理解为"人之所以轻易说话，这只是因为他们还没有因此受到过责备"。刘殿爵的译文"He who opens his mouth lightly does so simply because he has no responsibilities of office"则强调人们之所以未经思索，轻易发言，是因为他没有在言责之位，从而不用承担责任。从句意上看，此处的"责"训为"责任"更佳。

【原文】7.23　孟子曰[1]："人之患在好为人师[2]。"

【译文】孟子说："人的毛病在于喜欢做别人的老师。"

【英译】Mencius said, 'The evil of men is that they like to be teachers of others.'

【注释】

[1] 孟子批评的"好为人师"者是那些骄傲自满、处处喜欢以老师姿态彰显自己比别人高明却不虚心学习的人。正如王勉所说:"若好为人师,则自足而不复有进矣,此人之大患也。"

[2] "好为人师",理雅各的译文虽然翻译出了原文的字面意思,但不能传达孟子对"为人师"者的态度。实际上孟子不反对为人师,而是反对那些骄傲自满,认为自己无所不知的人。刘殿爵选择用"too eager to"的句型,将那些时刻都想着卖弄学问、认为自己无所不知,不虚心学习的人生动形象地刻画了出来。

【原文】7.24　乐正子[1]从于子敖之齐。乐正子见孟子。孟子曰:"子亦来见我乎?[2]"曰:"先生何为出此言也?"曰:"子来几日矣?"曰:"昔者。"曰:"昔者,则我出此言也,不亦宜乎?"曰:"舍馆未定。"曰:"子闻之也,舍馆定,然后求见长者乎?"曰:"克有罪。"

【译文】乐正子随从王子敖来到齐国。乐正子拜见孟子。孟子说:"你竟然也来看我吗?"乐正子问:"老师为什么这么说呢?"孟子说:"你来几天了?"乐正子答:"昨天。"孟子说:"昨天来的,我这么说,不应当吗?"乐正子说:"居住的地方没找好。"孟子说:"你听说过住所定了后,才拜见长辈的吗?"乐正子说:"我错了。"

【英译】The disciple Yo-chǎng went in the train of Tsze-âo to Ch'î. He came to see Mencius, who said to him, 'Are you also come to see me?' Yo-chǎng replied, 'Master, why do you speak such words?' 'How many days have you been here?' asked Mencius. 'I came yesterday.' 'Yesterday! Is it not with reason then that I thus speak?'

'My lodging-house was not arranged.''Have you heard that a scholar's lodging-house must be arranged before he visit his elder?'Yo-chǎng said,'I have done wrong.'

【注释】

[1] 虽然从表面上看，孟子责备乐正子是因为他没有及时拜见自己，其实是因为他和王子敖同游。王子敖因阿谀逢迎，得到齐王宠幸，但在行事的时候却自以为是，不守礼，孟子认为他不是君子，不愿与之为伍，但自己的爱徒却和他交游，因而孟子深责之，以警示他交友必须慎重。

[2] 根据古代礼制，学生去拜见老师是理所当然之事，而孟子却用一个疑问句"子亦来见我乎"发问，责备挖苦的口气溢于言表。刘殿爵的译文"It is very gracious of you to come to see me"将孟子的不满与责备之情传神地传达了出来。

【原文】7.25　孟子谓乐正子曰：[1]"子之从于子敖来，徒餔啜也[2]。我不意子学古之道[3]，而以餔啜也。"

【译文】孟子对乐正子说："你跟随王子敖来，只是为了吃喝。我绝对没有想到你学习了古人的道理，竟然是为了吃喝。"

【英译】Mencius, addressing the disciple Yo-chǎng, said to him, 'Your coming here in the train of Chî was only because of the food and the drink. I could not have thought that you，having learned the doctrine of the ancients，would have acted with a view to eating and drinking.'

【注释】

[1] 本章紧承上文，记载了孟子对乐正子跟从王子敖来齐的批评。孟子对王子敖没有好感，认为他不是君子，不能协助君主推行仁政。乐正子如果和他交往，不仅不能推行儒家倡导的古之道，还有可能使他为了富贵而放弃自己的所学。

　　[2] 对"徒餔啜也"的主语有两种理解。一种以朱熹为代表,认为"餔啜"的主语是乐正子:"言其不择所从,但求食耳。此乃正其罪而切责之。"即认为"乐正子跟随王子敖来,只是为着饮食罢了。"另一种以赵岐为代表,认为"餔啜"的主语是子敖。"子敖,齐之贵人右师王驩也。学而不行其道,徒食饮而已,谓之餔啜也。"笔者认为,朱熹的理解更准确。纵观孟子对王驩的态度,可以把"餔啜"看作是孟子对他的评价,但结合下文"我不意子学古之道,而以餔啜也。"即我没有料想到你跟我学习古人之道仅仅是为了谋求吃喝。这句话明确证明,"徒餔啜也"的主语应是乐正子。而且本章紧承上文,进一步表明孟子对乐正子"从于子敖来"的态度。他虽然在前章已经表明,责备乐正子是因为他没有及时拜见自己,但深层次原因是警示他如果择友不慎,自己苦修的道可能会沦落为谋求富贵的工具。孟子担心乐正子不能理解,因而在本章进一步说明。理雅各和刘殿爵的译文同朱熹,能准确翻译原文的意思。

　　[3] "意",应理解为"料想""测度",以体现出乎孟子意料之意。乐正子是孟子的得意门生,在鲁国要任命他为官时,孟子曾说过,"吾闻之,喜而不寐"。(《孟子·告子下》)显然,孟子认为乐正子深谙儒家之道,并可以践行之。当孟子发现他和子敖交往时,发出"我不意子学古之道,而以餔啜也"的感叹,以深警之。理雅各的译文将孟子当时的震惊、失望之情完美再现。

　　【原文】7.26　孟子曰[1]:"不孝有三[2],无后为大。舜不告而娶,为无后也,君子以为犹告也[3]。"

　　【译文】孟子说:"不孝的事情有三种,没有后代最严重。舜不禀告父母就娶妻,是因为担心没有后代,君子认为同禀告了一样。"

　　【英译】Mencius said, 'There are three things which are unfilial, and to have no posterity is the greatest of them. Shun married without informing his parents because of this, —lest he should have no posterity. Superior men consider that his doing so was the same as if he had informed them.'

【注释】

[1] 在本章，孟子再次强调了"经"与"权"的关系。传说舜娶尧的女儿时没有向父母禀告，因为他的父亲瞽瞍和后母是不会同意他娶妻生子的，如果这样就会没有后代，是最大的不孝，所以舜不告而娶是不得已的变通，是权。禀告父母，经父母同意后娶妻子是礼，是经。"权"是在"经"不能发生作用时的变通，运用"权"是为了更好地遵循"经"。

[2] "不孝有三"，赵岐注曰："于礼有不孝者三事，谓阿意曲从，陷亲不义，一不孝也。家贫亲老，不为禄仕，二不孝也。不娶无子，绝先祖祀，三不孝也。三者之中，无后为大。"刘殿爵用"a bad son"（不合格的儿子）翻译"不孝"，理雅各用"unfilial"翻译，基本能体现其内涵。

[3] "君子"，此处指品德高尚的人。赵甄陶将之翻译为"the men of virtue"，强调品德的高尚，可以准确体现其含义。理雅各将之翻译为"Superior men"，强调级别、职务上的高，不准确。

【原文】 7.27　孟子曰[1]："仁之实，事亲是也[2]；义之实，从兄是也；智之实[3]，知斯二者弗去是也；礼之实，节文斯二者是也；乐之实，乐斯二者，乐则生矣[4]；生则恶可已也，恶可已，则不知足之蹈之手之舞之。"

【译文】 孟子说："仁的实质是侍奉父母；义的实质是顺从兄长；智的实质是明白这两者的道理并且坚持下去；礼的实质是调节、修饰这二者；音乐的实质是对二者感到快乐，快乐由此而生。快乐一旦产生，就不可以遏制。快乐一旦不可遏制，就会不知不觉地手舞足蹈。"

【英译】 Mencius said, 'The richest fruit of benevolence is this, —the service of one's parents. The richest fruit of righteousness is this, —the obeying one's elder brothers. The richest fruit of wisdom is this，—the knowing those two things，and not departing from them. The richest fruit of propriety is this，—the ordering and adorning those two things. The richest fruit of music is this，—the rejoicing in those two things. When they are rejoiced in，they grow. Growing，how can they be repressed？When they come to this state that they cannot be repressed，then unconsciously the feet begin to dance and the hands to move.'

【注释】

[1] 在儒家学说中，乐实际上就是礼的一部分，因而可以说本章用简短的语言论述了仁、义、礼、智四德的实质及其关系。孟子指出，虽然四德包含的内容至广至深，似乎遥不可及，但其实质一致，即践行孝悌。因为孝悌是仁义的本质，是礼智的核心，做到孝悌，实际上就是在践行四德。在四德中，仁、义是核心，礼、智则影响仁、义的取舍。它们一起构成了儒者修身成德的主要内容。

[2] 儒家重孝，认为它是一切德行的根本和起点。据《孝经·开宗明义章第一》记载，"子曰：'夫孝，德之本也，教之所由生也。'"有子也认为，"君子务本，本立而道生。孝弟也者，其为仁之本与。"（《论语·学而第一》）可见，儒家认为，孝是一切德行的起点，是仁的实质和主要内容。因而孟子所谓的"仁之实，事亲是也"的含义是"孝顺父母是仁的主要内涵"。理雅各按字面意思将"实"翻译为"The richest fruit"，即认为"孝是仁的结果"，这与儒家对"孝"和"仁"的关系的认识不一致。赖发洛用"core"翻译"实"，认为孝是仁的核心，是仁最重要的部分，能够准确再现原文之意。刘殿爵认为，孝是仁的内容，将之翻译为"The content of benevolence"。显然他的译文受孟子"亲亲，仁也"的影响，认为仁就是亲亲，就是孝顺父母。

[3] "智"，刘殿爵和理雅各都将之翻译为"wisdom"（智慧），但郝大伟和安乐哲认为，"在早期中国文献中，'知'通'智'。这表明了理论和实践的不可分离；而在西方，理论和实践的分离，导致了'知识'和'智慧'的分离"。显然，"wisdom"和"智"在含义上并不完全等同。

[4] 孟子认为音乐的实质就是从仁义中得到快乐，这就将伦理道德范畴"仁""义"和审美情感"乐"联系起来。李颖指出："孟子实际上是将伦理道德的完善与精神情感的审美体验结合在一起，从而使他的'乐之实'在具有伦理学意义的同时，更具有美学的意义。""乐则生矣"，从下文"不知足之蹈之手之舞之"可以判断，是快乐在逐渐生长，以致手舞足蹈。刘殿爵的"the joy that comes of delighting in them"（快乐就会发生）能够准确体现原文的意思。

【原文】7.28　孟子曰：[1]"天下大悦而将归己，视天下悦而归己，犹草芥也，惟舜为然。不得乎亲，不可以为人；不顺乎亲，不可以为子[2]。舜尽事亲之道而瞽瞍厎豫，瞽瞍厎豫而天下化[3]，瞽瞍[4]厎豫而天下之为父子者定，此之谓大孝。"

【译文】孟子说："天下人都很高兴，要归附自己；把天下人都很高兴要归附自己，看作像草芥一样的，只有舜是这样的。不能让父母欢心，不可以做人；不能顺从父母，不可以做儿子。舜尽心竭力地侍奉父母，瞽瞍高兴了；瞽瞍高兴了，天下的人都受到感化；瞽瞍高兴了，天下父子的伦常也确定了，这就是大孝。"

【英译】Mencius said, 'Suppose the case of the whole kingdom turning in great delight to an individual to submit to him.—To regard the whole kingdom thus turning to him in great delight but as a bundle of grass；—only Shun was capable of this. He considered that if one could not get the hearts of his parents he could not be considered a man, and that if he could not get to an entire accord with his parents, he could not be considered a son. By Shun's completely fulfilling everything by which a parent could be served, Kû-sâu was brought to find delight in what was good. When Kû-sâu was brought to find that delight, the whole kingdom was transformed. When Kû-sâu was brought to find that delight, all fathers and sons in the kingdom were established in their respective duties. This is called great filial piety.'

【注释】

[1] 舜是儒家推崇的理想人格，以"孝德"著称。孔子称赞他"巍巍乎，舜、禹之有天下者也，而不与焉！"（《论语·泰伯》）他虽富拥四海，但坚信天下为公，不为自己谋半点私利。孟子认为舜是主张实行仁政的圣王，是道德的典范。尽管孔孟对大舜的各种优秀品质都推崇有加，但他们最为称赞的是舜的至孝、大德。

[2] 朱熹注曰："得者，因为承顺以得其心之悦而已。顺则有以谕之于道，心与之一而未始有违。"可见，"得亲"重在取悦父母，使父母高兴，"顺亲"则是儿女对父母心悦诚服的顺从。理雅各将"得乎亲"翻译为"get the hearts of his parents"（得到父母的喜爱），刘殿爵翻译为"please one's parents"（取悦父母），二人的译文基本上能体现"得亲"的含义。"顺亲"，理雅各选择用"accord with"翻译。"Accord"有自愿或主动保持一致之意，能准确体现"心悦诚服地顺从"。赖发洛将"顺"翻译为"get on with"（和睦相处），不能准确传达古代社会对合格子女标准的认定。刘殿爵选择用"obedient"翻译"顺"，"obedient"通常指对权威或控制自己的人的顺从，基本上能体现"顺亲"对子女的要求。"不可以"是说在伦理道德上不允许。它是"可以"的否定式，有三种语义，其中最重要的是"不能够"。刘利指出："'不能够'实际包含了客观上不许可和事理上不许可两种语义。"显然此处的"不可以"实际上取"事理上不许可"之意。理雅各和刘殿爵都选择用"cannot"翻译"不可以"，"cannot"更强调身体或精神上的能力不许可，不能完全对应此处"不可以"的含义。赖发洛选择用"be to do"句型来翻译，"be to do"有"根据义理应该"的含义，虽不能完全对应此处"不可以"的含义，但比"can"更恰当。

[3] "化"是先秦时期的一个重要哲学范畴，含义非常丰富。荀子对"化"的定义是："状变而实无别而为异者谓之化。"（《荀子·正名》）《中国

哲学史主要范畴概念简释》指出，荀子把"这种缓慢发生的只变形式不变实质的运动称之为'化'"。黄俊杰指出："先秦儒家在内、外两种语境脉络中使用'化'这个概念，既主张人的身体可以'化性起伪'（伪，为也），从'自然'走向'人文'；也可以'化民成俗'，以圣人（或谓'创造的少数'（creative minority）转化大众的生命。"显然，孟子使用的"天下化"取后者，即大舜践行孝道最终感化了自己的父亲和天下的百姓。理雅各和刘殿爵选择用"transform"翻译"化"，它既可以表示外形的改变，也可以指性质的转化，含义更宽泛。而且"transform"通常指骤然改变和神秘改变，这与古汉语"化"的渐变含义也不符合。赖发洛用"change"翻译"化"。它是表示变化的最普通、最常用的词，既表示变，又表示化，也不能准确对应"化"的含义。

[4]"瞽瞍"，理雅各和赖发洛都认为这是舜的父亲的名字，将之音译；而刘殿爵则认为它表明舜的父亲是盲人或者暗示舜父虽非盲人，但不能识别好坏，与盲人无异。他的译文显然受司马迁《史记》舜"盲者子。父顽，母嚚，弟傲，能和（之）以孝烝烝"和《书·尧典》"瞽子。传：无目曰瞽，舜父有目，不能分别好恶，故时人谓之瞽，配字曰瞍"的影响。今人翟满桂和蔡自新引用先秦文献系统论证了"舜父瞽叟无论从其家世，还是相关的一些记载中，都并不是一个盲者，而是一个乐师。"依据他们收集到的资料，可以认为瞽叟可能担任乐师职务，但在周代，乐官常用盲人担任，反推之，瞽叟是一个盲人乐师也不无可能。因而在翻译"瞽叟"时，不论将之音译还是翻译为"the Blind Man"，都言之有据。

卷 八

离娄章句下

【原文】 8.1　孟子曰[1]："舜生于诸冯，迁于负夏，卒于鸣条，东夷之人也。文王生于岐周，卒于毕郢，西夷之人也。地之相去也，千有余里；世之相后也，千有余岁。得志行乎中国[2]，若合符节[3]，先圣后圣，其揆一也[4]。"

【译文】 孟子说："舜出生在诸冯，迁居到负夏，死在鸣条，是东方人。文王生在岐周，死在毕郢，是西方人。两地相隔千里，生活的时代相距千年。他们得志时在中国的所作所为，几乎一模一样。古代的圣人与后代的圣人，他们的原则是一样的。"

【英译】 Mencius said, 'Shun was born in Chû-fǎng, removed to Fû-hsiâ, and died in Ming-tʻiâo;—a man near the wild tribes on the east. King Wǎn was born in Châu by mount Chʻî, and died in Pî-ying;—a man near the wild tribes on the west. Those regions were distant from one another more than a thousand lî, and the age of the one sage was posterior to that of the other more than a thousand years. But when they got their wish, and carried their principles into practice throughout the Middle Kingdom, it was like uniting the two halves of a seal. When we examine those sages, both the earlier and the later, their principles are found to be the same.'

【注释】

[1] 孟子认为，虽然圣人生活的时代不同，受到的环境熏陶各异，但当他们成为统一天下的王后，都能实行仁政，爱护百姓，成为后世君主效法的榜样。

[2] "中国"一词最早出现是在周代《诗经》中，如《大雅·民劳》"惠此中国"。李平指出："甲骨文字形，中像旗杆，上下有旌旗和飘带，旗杆正中竖立。本义是中心、当中，指一定范围内部适中的位置。"古代华夏族认为他们建国的黄河流域居天下之中，是"中央之国"，是政治、经济和文化中心，而四周的少数民族则被称为蛮夷之邦。理雅各和赖发洛选用"Middle Kingdom"翻译"中国"，"middle"多用作修饰空间或地方的形容词，表示"居于中间"。刘殿爵则选择用"Central Kingdom"翻译中国，"central"在表示方位时可以和"middle"互换，但它还能表示文化、商业、政治等中心，能准确体现此处"中国"的含义。

[3] "符节"是古代朝廷传达命令或调兵将时用的凭证，双方各执一半，合之以验真假。朱熹注曰："符节，以玉为之，篆刻文字而中分之，彼此各藏其半，有故则左右相合以为信也。"孟子在此处提到"符节"是为了证明前代圣人和后代圣人在为政上是一致的。刘殿爵选择用"tally"翻译"符节"，"tally"即符木，是英国中世纪的一种文件形式，类似于我国古代兵符，但内容为经济合同和协议。显然，从词义上看，它不是古代中国所谓"符节"的对等词。但从表意上看，孟子用"符节"作喻是为了表明圣人行为的一致，而符木是用来记账或记数来使彼此相吻合，因而用它来翻译"符节"也能体现原文的意思。

[4] "其揆一也"，孟子认为，尽管圣人们生活的时空不同，但他们奉行的标准和原则是一样的。理雅各和刘殿爵都准确翻译了这一含义。但赖发洛却将之翻译为"had one standard"（有一个标准）。显然，他的译文过于拘泥于原文的字面意思。

【原文】8.2　子产[1]听郑国之政[2]，以其乘舆济人于溱洧。孟子曰："惠而不知为政[3]。岁十一月，徒杠成；十二月，舆梁成，民未病涉也。君子平其政[4]，行辟人可也，焉得人人而济之？故为政者，每人而悦之，日亦不足矣。"

【译文】子产主持郑国的政治，用他的车子帮助人们渡过溱水和洧水。孟子说："他只是施展小恩小惠，并不懂政治。要是在十一月修成人行的小桥；十二月修成车行的大桥，百姓就不会为渡河发愁了。官员如果能把政治治理好，出行时可以让路人回避，哪用一个个帮着别人过河呢？所以说，为政的人如果要讨每个人的欢心，时间也不够用啊。"

【英译】When Tszu-ch'an was chief minister of the State of Chǎng, he would convey people across the Chǎn and Wei in his own carriage. Mencius said, 'It was kind, but showed that he did not understand the practice of government. When in the eleventh month of the year the foot-bridges are completed, and the carriage-bridges in the twelfth month, the people have not the trouble of wading. Let a governor conduct his rule on principles of equal justice, and, when he goes abroad, he may cause people to be removed out of his path. But how can he convey everybody across the rivers? It follows that if a governor will try to please everybody, he will find the days not sufficient for his work.'

【注释】

[1] 孟子通过评价春秋时期郑国著名贤相子产以惠为政的治国方略，阐述了他的治国思想。他认为统治者治理国家，要从大处着眼，要抓根本，解决主要问题，使所有老百姓都从国家政策中受益，而不是仅仅把目光局限在小恩小惠上。

[2]"听郑国之政"，赵岐注曰："为政，听讼也。"他认为"听政"与下文的"为政"都与审理诉讼案件有关。焦循支持赵岐将"听政"释为"听

讼"，并且提供了更多的证据作支撑。朱熹在注释"为政者，每人而悦之，日亦不足矣"时引用了诸葛亮的"治世以大德，不以小惠"。可见，朱熹认为孟子在此章主要讨论治国之道，而非仅仅局限在审理诉讼案件。笔者认为，朱熹的理解更准确。从孟子对子产"惠而不知为政"的评价可以看出，孟子对他的"听政"是不满的。如果此处的"听政"取"听讼"之意，孟子仅仅因为子产对人们施以小惠，载百姓过水，却没能修好桥，而责备他不懂得"听讼"之法，未免会给人"欲加之罪何患无辞"的感觉。相反，如果"听政"取执掌、处理国家政务之意，那么，作为负责掌管郑国政务的大臣，他却把主要精力放在每日载百姓渡河这样的小恩小惠上，确如孟子所说，他根本就不懂得如何治理国家。刘殿爵取治国之意，将之译为"the administration of the state of Cheng was in his hands"（子产处理郑国的政务）。理雅各根据史料记载，强调子产做郑国的卿相，也能体现管理政务之意。

[3] 孟子认为，作为治国大臣，子产仅仅以小恩小惠笼络百姓，给他们带来暂时的蝇头小利，却不能制定、颁布可以给百姓带来更大福祉的政策，让他们从根本上获利，因而评价他"惠而不知为政"。理雅各选择用"kind"（仁慈）翻译，显然受《说文解字》："惠，仁也"的影响。刘殿爵则选择用"generous"（慷慨大方）翻译。相比较而言，刘殿爵的译文更符合孟子对"惠"的定义。孟子认为，"分人以财谓之惠"（《孟子·滕文公上》）。那些能够把自己的钱财分给别人的人，应当具备慷慨大方的品质，因而刘殿爵的翻译更准确。

[4] 在儒家文献中，虽然"君子"在大多数时候是用来指代那些有道德的人，但有时也指居上位的统治者，例如在"君子平其政"中，"君子"就取其本义，指"有地位的男子"。理雅各的"governor"（统治者）准确体现了其含义。刘殿爵选择用"gentleman"翻译"君子"，虽有助于保持译文对"君子"翻译的一致性，但在传达原文之意上略显逊色。

【原文】8.3　孟子告齐宣王曰[1]："君之视臣如手足，则臣视君如腹心[2]；君之视臣如犬马，则臣视君如国人[3]；君之视臣如土芥，则臣视君如寇仇。"王曰："礼，为旧君有服，何如斯可为服矣？"曰："谏行言听，膏泽下于民[4]，有故而去；则君使人导之出疆，又先于其所往[5]；去三年不反，然后收其田里[6]。此之谓三有礼焉。如此，则为之服矣。今也为臣，谏则不行，言则不听，膏泽不下于民；有故而去，则君搏执之，又极之于其所往[7]；去之日，遂收其田里。此之谓寇仇。寇仇，何服之有？"

【译文】孟子告诉齐宣王说："君主把臣下看作如同自己的手足，那么臣下就会把君主看作如同自己的腹心；君主把臣下看作狗马，那么臣下也会把君主看作路人；君主把臣下看作泥土、草芥，那么臣下就会把君主看作强盗和仇敌。"王说："礼制规定，离职的臣下要对过去的君主服丧。君主怎样对待臣下，臣下才会为他服丧呢？"孟子说："劝谏能够听从，建议能够采纳，使君主的恩泽可以落到百姓身上；臣下因故离开，君主派人护送他出国境，并先派人到他要去的地方做一些安排；他离开三年不回来，君主才收回他的土地房屋。这个叫作三有礼。这样，臣下就会为君主服丧。如今的臣下，劝谏不被接受，建议不被听从，不能使君主的恩泽落到百姓身上；因故不得不离开，君主还要捉拿他，还要设法使他在要去地方陷入穷困；离开那一天，就收回他的土地房屋。这个叫作仇敌。对这样的旧君，臣下还会服丧吗？"

【英译】Mencius said to the king Hsüan of Ch'î, 'When the prince regards his ministers as his hands and feet, his ministers regard their prince as their belly and heart; when he regards them as his dogs and horses, they regard him as another man; when he regards them as the ground or as grass, they regard him as a robber and an enemy.' The king said, 'According to the rules of propriety, a minister wears mourning when he has left the service of a prince. How must a prince behave that his old ministers may thus go into mourning?' Mencius replied, 'The admonitions of a minister having been followed, and his advice listened to, so that blessings have descended on the people, if for some cause he leaves the country, the prince sends an escort to conduct him beyond the boundaries. He also anticipates with recommendatory intimations his arrival in the country to which he is proceeding. When he has been gone three years and does not return, only then at length does he take back his fields and residence. This treatment is what is called a "thrice-repeated display of consideration." When a prince acts thus, mourning will be worn on leaving his service. Now-a-days, the remonstrances of a minister are not followed, and his advice is not listened to, so that no blessings descend on the people. When for any cause he leaves the country, the prince tries to seize him and hold him a prisoner. He also pushes him to extremity in the country to which he has gone, and on the very day of his departure, takes back his fields and residence. This treatment shows him to be what we call "a robber and an enemy." What mourning can be worn for a robber and an enemy?'

【注释】

[1] 在君臣关系上，孔子提倡"君使臣以礼，臣事君以忠"（《论语·八佾》）。孟子主张"欲为君，尽君道；欲为臣，尽臣道。"（《孟子·离娄上》）可见，早期儒家并不强调君对臣单方面的支配，臣对君的绝对服从，而是认为君和臣各有自己的职责，并且他们的义务是对等的。

[2] "之"的含义是若、如果。正如熊浩莉所说："这是一个假设复句，且偏句和正句都是比喻句，这二句之间是一种假设关系，前者与后者匹配成双，前者处于从属地位，而后者占支配主导地位。前后两喻齐出，巧借关联词语'则'从中绾合，为相互比照创造了条件，因此前后为照，喻中藏比。"刘殿爵用"If"表假设，用"as"表"比喻"，准确翻译出了假设比喻句的

句型特点。但杨伯峻持反对意见："之，此处用以表示该句为主从复合句之从句。又王引之《经传释词》云：'之，犹'若'也。'恐非。"理雅各的译文也持这种观点，认为"之"并非表假设，将原文译为由关联词"When"引导的主从复合句。

[3]"国人"，朱熹注曰："犹言路人，言无怨无德也。"理雅各用"another man"（别人）翻译"国人"，"别人"有别于"自己"，"别人"对"我"无德，"我"也不需要对"别人"感恩。"别人"的疾苦与"我"无关，"我"不对"别人"承担任何责任和义务。因而用"别人"翻译"国人"基本上能体现其含义。刘殿爵根据上下文，将"国人"翻译为"a stranger"（陌生人）。国君如果像对待狗马一样对待臣属，那么百姓就会把他当作陌生人，也不会关注他的利益。因而刘殿爵的"陌生人"也能体现此处"国人"的内涵。

[4]"膏泽"，滋润土壤的雨水，常用来比喻恩惠。刘殿爵选择用"benefit"（恩惠）翻译"膏泽"，将原文之意清楚、准确地传递给了读者。理雅各虽然也看到此处应取"膏泽"的比喻义，但将"膏泽"翻译为"blessings"，该词具有较强的宗教意味，给中国文化增添了本身没有的耶稣基督的意象。

[5]"先于其所往"，按字面意思是"先派人去他要去的地方"。但如果按此翻译，就会使原文含义模糊，造成读者理解上的困难。派人先去那里干什么？为什么那样做就是有礼，就会受到臣属的感激，为之服孝？朱熹的注解有助于解除读者的疑惑："先于其所往，称道其贤，欲其收用之也。"君主先派人去他要去的地方，推荐他的才能，使别国君主能尊敬他、任用他。理雅各受朱熹影响，对原文作了补充，翻译为"提前去他要去的国家推荐他"。补充后的译文既便于读者理解，又增强了原文的逻辑性和说服力。

[6]"田里"，朱熹注曰："田禄里居"。理雅各将之翻译为"fields and residence"（土地和房屋），但刘殿爵认为仅仅指"土地"。在古代，"田里"既可以指百姓的田地和庐舍，也可以指卿大夫的封地和住宅。但不论取哪种

含义，"田里"都包含土地和房屋两部分。因而，理雅各的译文更准确。

[7]"极"，赵岐注曰："恶而困之也。"可见，"极"字是使动用法，取"使之穷困"之意。刘殿爵的"makes things difficult"（使诸事不顺）符合"极"在原文中的意思。理雅各选择用"pushes him to extremity"翻译"极之于其所往"。"Extremity"有极端、极度之意，可以对应"极"的字面意思；它还有困境之意，可以体现此处"极"的暗含之意。

【原文】 8.4　孟子曰[1]："无罪而杀士，则大夫可以去；无罪而戮民，则士可以徙。[2]"

【译文】 孟子说："士人没有犯罪却被杀死，那么大夫就可以离开了；百姓没有犯罪而惨遭杀戮，士人也可以离开了。"

【英译】 Mencius said, 'When scholars are put to death without any crime，the great officers may leave the country. When the people are slaughtered without any crime，the scholars may remove.'

【注释】

[1] 孟子倡导仁政，反对滥用刑罚，主张应尽早离开那些残暴无道、滥杀无辜的君主。他认为，如果一个国君随意杀害知识分子，则表明国君无道，不能尊贤使能，大夫在这样的国家任职也将难有作为，甚至惹来杀死之祸，故应见机而作，尽早离开。同理，如果一个国君随意杀害百姓，则显示国君暴虐、不得民心，这样的国家迟早会发生暴乱，士人应尽量避开这一是非之地，寻求更好的安身立命之所，这也是孔子所说的"危邦不入，乱邦不居"（《论语 泰伯》）。

[2]"民""士"和"大夫"是古代社会的重要阶层。"民"是下层百姓，是劳力者；关于"士"，王力指出，"春秋以前士是武士，有义务'执干戈以卫社稷'；春秋以后士是文士，士逐渐成了统治阶级知识分子的统称。"它是先秦时期贵族的最低等级，游离于贵族与庶民之间，通过自己的知识和才干求禄求爵。"大夫"，在先秦诸侯国中，在国君之下有卿、大夫和士三级，后

常以之泛指官员。理雅各将"士"翻译为"scholars"（知识分子），将"士"的首要特征准确体现了出来。赖发洛将"士"译为"knight"，即欧洲中世纪的骑士、武士。他的"士"重武，而孟子所谓的"士"尚文，二者存在明显的区别。刘殿爵将"士"译为"Gentleman"，看到了"士"是古代贵族的最低等级，有一定的社会身份这一特征，但这仅仅是"士"的一个方面，并不能代表其全部含义。此处的"大夫"泛指政府官员，理雅各将之译为"great officers"（高级官员）基本上能体现其含义。刘殿爵的译文是"Counsellors"（顾问）。相比之下，理雅各的译文更能体现"大夫"的含义。

【原文】8.5　孟子[1]曰："君仁，莫不仁；君义，莫不义。"

【译文】孟子说："君主仁，没有人不仁；君主义，没有人不义。"

【英译】Mencius said，'If the sovereign be benevolent，all will be benevolent. If the sovereign be righteous，all will be righteous.'

【注释】

[1] 此章强调君主以身作则的重要性，和《孟子·离娄上》重复，前文已详细论及，此处不再赘言。

【原文】8.6　孟子曰[1]："非礼之礼，非义之义，大人弗为。"

【译文】孟子说："具有礼的形式，却不符合礼的精神实质的礼；具有义的形式，却不符合义的精神实质的义，有德行的人是不会去做的。"

【英译】Mencius said，'Acts of propriety which are not really proper，and acts of righteousness which are not really righteous，the great man does not do.'

【注释】

[1] 孟子强调君子行礼守义要谨慎，不要做一些模棱两可，似是而非的事情。"非礼之礼，非义之义"，指那些貌似符合礼、义，而实际上与礼义的精神实质相差甚远的行为。赵岐注曰："若礼而非礼，陈质娶妇而长，拜

之也。若义而非义，藉交报仇是也。"焦循进一步指出："若，犹似也。似礼非礼，似义非义，皆似是而非者也"。刘殿爵将"非礼之礼"和"非义之义"分别翻译为"a rite that is contrary to the sprit of the rites"（与礼的精神相违的礼）和"a duty that goes against the spirit of dutifulness"（与义的实质相反的义）。译文将原文蕴含的似是而非、定要谨慎的含义准确传达了出来。

【原文】8.7　孟子曰[1]："中[2]也养[3]不中，才也养不才，故人乐有贤父兄也。如中也弃不中，才也弃不才，则贤不肖之相去[4]，其间不能以寸。[5]"

【译文】孟子说："道德品质高的人熏陶道德品质差的人，有才能的人熏陶没有才能的人，所以人们都乐于有贤能的父亲和兄长。如果道德品质高的人鄙弃道德品质差的人，有才能的人嫌弃没有才能的人，那么贤能和不肖者的差距就近得不能用寸来计量了。"

【英译】Mencius said, 'Those who keep the Mean，train up those who do not，and those who have abilities，train up those who have not，and hence men rejoice in having fathers and elder brothers who are possessed of virtue and talent. If they who keep the Mean spurn those who do not，and they who have abilities spurn those who have not，then the space between them—those so gifted and the ungifted—will not admit an inch.'

【注释】

[1] 孟子认为，那些德、才出众的人，应自觉担当起教育和培养普通人的责任，这样每个人都会希望自己能有才德兼备的父兄来帮助自己进步。相反，如果有才德的人置普通人于不顾，那么他也就称不上贤能之人了。

[2] 赵岐注曰："中者，履中和之气所生，谓之贤。"朱熹认为，"无过不及之谓中"。可见，"中"指的是那些有中和之气，守中庸之道，品德高尚的人。理雅各选择用"Mean"翻译"中"，取"中和、无过不及"之

意。《白虎通·五行篇》云："中，和也。中和居六德之首。"刘殿爵的译文是"morally well-adjusted"（品德好的），这和理雅各选择用"中和"翻译有异曲同工之妙。

[3]"养"，熏陶和培养。朱熹注曰："涵育熏陶，俟其自化也。"理雅各将之翻译为"train up"（教育、教养），赵甄陶翻译为"instruct"。这两种翻译看到了贤者通过言传身教对普通人的直接教育，忽视了他们靠自己的才德潜移默化地影响别人的能力。刘殿爵的译文是"look after"（照顾、照看），也不能完全体现"养"所蕴含的教化功能。

[4]"贤"和"不肖"在此处是以一对反义词的形式出现的。理雅各将之翻译为"so gifted and the ungifted"，他的译文表明，"中""才"指的是那些有天赋的"贤"者，而"不肖"则与"不中""不才"相对应，指的是那些没有天分的无才、无德的人。刘殿爵则在孟子的思想体系中理解本段，将之翻译为"the good"和"the depraved"，即那些保有人的善的本性的人和那些受外物蒙蔽的堕落的人。相比较而言，刘殿爵的翻译更符合孟子对"贤"与"不孝"的认识。

[5]刘殿爵和理雅各都将"其间不能以寸"理解为"近得不能用寸来计量"。他们认为此句旨在说明，如果德才兼备的人不去教育那些没有才德的人，那么他们也不能算是真正有德、有才的人，和那些普通人几乎没有什么区别。还有一种观点认为，如果有德、有才的人不去教育、熏陶那些没有天分的人，他们之间的差距会越来越大，根本不能用分寸来计算。

【原文】8.8　孟子曰："人有不为也，而后可以有为[1]。"

【译文】孟子说："人要有所不为，才能有所作为。"

【英译】Mencius said, 'Men must be decided on what they will not do，and then they are able to act with vigour in what they ought to do.'

【注释】

[1]孟子在本章讲了取舍之道。有学者认为，本章主要讲了取舍的标

准，如焦循认为："义可为乃为之，义所不可为则不为。"即符合礼义原则的就去做，不符合礼义原则的就不为。还有学者认为，本章是强调取舍的重要性，朱熹引程子曰："有不为，知所择也。惟能有不为，是以可以有为。无所不为者，安能有所为邪?"人的精力是有限的，如果事事都做，则事事难成。因而人们在做事之前，应当首先做一些取舍。刘殿爵和理雅各的译文同后者。刘殿爵译为"Only when a man will not do some things is he capable of doing great things"（只有当一个人决定放弃一些事情，他才能大有作所）。他和理雅各的译文将"有为"和"不为"的辩证关系清楚地展现在了读者面前。

【原文】8.9　孟子曰[1]："言人之不善，当如后患何?"

【译文】孟子说："说别人的坏话，因此招来后患怎么办?"

【英译】Mencius said, 'What future misery have they and ought they to endure, who talk of what is not good in others!'

【注释】

[1] 孟子在本章，再次强调慎言。对其理解，当前比较流行的观点有以下几种：一种观点认为，喜欢说别人坏话，当自己遇到忧患时怎么办? 这种认识发挥了孔子的"己所不欲勿施于人"（《论语·卫灵公》）的思想。理雅各的译文与之相类。还有一种观点认为，宣扬别人的不好，因此招来后患怎么办? 刘殿爵和赵甄陶的译文与之相类。这两种观点虽然强调的侧重点不同，但都主张人一定要慎言。陆象山给出另一种理解："今人多失其旨。盖孟子道性善，故言人无有不善。今若言人之不善，彼将甘为不善，而以不善向汝，汝将何以待之? 故曰：'当如后患何?'"他将本句放在孟子的思想体系下理解，而不仅仅局限在原文的字词之意，给原文增添了一些新的内涵。经无达诂，对《孟子》的各种理解只要言之有理，持之有据，都是可以接受的。

【原文】8.10　孟子曰："仲尼不为已甚者。"[1]

【译文】孟子说："仲尼不做过分的事情。"

【英译】Mencius said，'Chung-nî did not do extraordinary things.'

【注释】

[1] 这是孟子对孔子的评价，他认为孔子做事从不走极端，"无过无不及"。仲尼，是孔子的字。理雅各将之音译为"Chung-nî"，但对西方读者来说，他们更熟悉孔子"Confucius"，因而刘殿爵选择用它翻译"仲尼"。笔者认为，把"仲尼"译成"孔子"不会影响对文意的理解，而且可以减轻西方读者的陌生感，是一个不错的选择。"已甚者"，过分的事情。理雅各将之翻译为"extraordinary things"（非凡的事）不准确。孔子首创私学，打破学在官府，可以被称作"非凡的事"，但不能认为是"已甚"的事。相比较而言，刘殿爵的"beyond reasonable limits"（超越了合理的界限）更准确。

【原文】8.11　孟子曰[1]："大人者[2]，言不必信[3]，行不必果[4]，惟义所在。"

【译文】孟子说："德性完备的人，说话不用一定守信，做事也不用一定要贯彻始终，只是一切以义为标准。"

【英译】Mencius said，'The great man does not think beforehand of his words that they may be sincere，nor of his actions that they may be resolute；—he simply speaks and does what is right.'

【注释】

[1] 孟子在本章中指出，道德高尚的人，应该正确处理言、行、义的关系，将义作为言行的最终标准。

[2] "大人"也是儒家推崇的理想人格的代表，以德行的高尚为主要特征。理雅各和刘殿爵将之译为"great man"。"great"的内涵极其丰富，包含地位的高贵与品质的优秀，基本上能体现"大人"的特征。

[3] "信"的内涵是真诚守信，人们有时会把它和"诚实"等同起来。

李海霞指出了二者的区别："诚实是言行符合客观事实，它适用于人类生活的一切领域；真诚和守信指真心对人不怀他意，仅用于朋友间的交往。诚实必真诚守信，真诚守信则不必诚实。"理雅各将"信"翻译为"sincere"，"sincere"的一般词义是对人真诚，不口是心非，通常用在朋友之间，基本能体现"信"的含义。孟子在本句话中依"言"说"信"，因而刘殿爵将"信"翻译为"keep his word"（说话算话，守信用）更准确。

[4] 梁涛将"行不必果"注释为"做事不预期结果"。显然他的理解受朱熹"必，犹期也"的影响，认为大人做事都依义而行，因而在现实生活中根本不用预先考虑结果。刘殿爵则将"必"理解为"一定，必须"，将"行不必果"翻译为"nor does he necessarily see his action through to the end"（没必要将自己的行为贯彻始终）。显然，他认为，"义"是一切行为的准则，有时候为了符合义，可以不追求"果"。孟子在本章主要阐述"信""果"和"义"的关系，是在申明自己对言行进行价值判断的标准，因而刘殿爵的理解和主旨结合得更紧密。

【原文】8.12　孟子曰："大人者[1]，不失其赤子之心者也[2]。"

【译文】孟子说："德性完备的人，不会丧失婴儿般纯真无伪的心。"

【英译】Mencius said，'The great man is he who does not lose his child's-heart.'

【注释】

[1]"大人"，有两种理解，一说特指"国君"，一说泛指不失赤子之心的品德完备的人。理雅各和刘殿爵的译文同后者。从孟子的整个思想体系看，"赤子之心"是孟子在《尽心上》提到的"人之所不学而能"的"良能"和"所不虑而知"的"良知"，即自然而然、纯真无伪、不需经过后天的学习和修养的自然本性。保有良知、良能的人可以将人的四端充分扩充和发展，从而成为品德高尚的大人。因而，此处的"大人"应理解为品德完备的人。

[2] 焦循指出，关于"赤子之心"有两种理解："一说'赤子之心'谓'民心'；一说，赤子，婴儿。少小之心，专一未变化，人能不失其赤子时心，则为贞正大人也。"从孟子的整个思想体系看，将"赤子之心"理解为"少小之心"更准确。刘殿爵将之翻译为"the heart of a new-born babe"（新出生婴儿之心），但并未强调"赤子之心"的特征，而是让读者自己去体会。赵甄陶将之翻译为"one who keeps his heart as pure as a newborn baby's"。该译文将新出生婴儿未受外物蒙蔽、存一无伪的本然之心准确传递出来。

【原文】8.13　孟子曰[1]："养生者不足以当大事，惟送死[2]可以当大事。"

【译文】孟子说："奉养父母不算什么重大事情，只有送终才可以算是重大事情。"

【英译】Mencius said，'The nourishment of parents when living is not sufficient to be accounted the great thing. It is only in the performing their obsequies when dead that we have what can be considered the great thing.'

【注释】

[1] "养生"和"送死"共同构成了儒家孝论的重要内容。孟子在本章尤其强调"送死"，并非认为"养生"不重要，而是因为"送死"是人道之"大变"，是儿女对父母尽孝的最后一次机会，需要谨慎对待，才能使孝子之心得到少许宽慰。

[2] "送死"，送终。理雅各和赵甄陶直接翻译为"obsequies"（葬礼），刘殿爵则将之意译为"treating them decently when they die"（死后体面地对待他们），和前面"活着好好奉养"相对应，可以很好体现篇章宗旨。

【原文】8.14　孟子曰[1]："君子深造之以道[2]，欲其自得之也[3]。自得之，则居之安；居之安，则资之深[4]；资之深，则取之左右逢其原，故君子欲其自得之也。”

【译文】孟子说：“君子用正确的方法达到高深的造诣，就是想要他做到自觉地有所得。做到自觉地有所得，就会牢固地保有；牢固地保有，就会积蓄很深；积蓄很深，就能取之不尽，左右逢源，所以君子要自觉地有所得。”

【英译】Mencius said，'The superior man makes his advances in what he is learning with deep earnestness and by the proper course，wishing to get hold of it as in himself. Having got hold of it in himself, he abides in it calmly and firmly. Abiding in it calmly and firmly，he reposes a deep reliance on it. Reposing a deep reliance on it，he seizes it on the left and right，meeting everywhere with it as a fountain from which things flow. It is on this account that the superior man wishes to get hold of what he is learning as in himself.'

【注释】

[1] 本章集中论述了孟子的学习方法。

[2] “道”，朱熹注曰：“其进为之方也。”受其影响，理雅各将“道”翻译为“the proper course”（一种正确的深造方法）。刘殿爵则将“道”翻译为“Way”，他还将之大写以突出其含义的特殊性。不仅如此，理雅各认为“君子深造之以道”是说“君子通过正确的方法，满怀激情地推进学习上的进步”，而刘殿爵却理解为“A gentleman steeps himself in the Way”（君子沉溺于道）。二人的区别在于，理雅各强调的是正确的方法在学习上的重要性，而刘殿爵则强调学习“道”的重要性。

[3] “欲其自得之也”，赵岐注：“欲使己得其原本，如性自有之也。”刘殿爵将之翻译为“he wishes to find it in himself”（想要在自己身上发现它）。理雅各将之翻译为“wishing to get hold of it as in himself”（是为了能够掌握学习的内容，就像他本来就拥有那些内容一样）。虽然二人对“道”的理解不同，但对“自得之”的认识皆和赵岐相类。朱熹引程子曰：“学不言而自

得者，乃自得也。有安排布置者，皆非自得也。然必潜心积虑，优游餍饫于其间，然后可以有得；若急迫求之，则是私己而已，终不足以得之也。"赵甄陶的理解类程子，将之翻译为"he wants to attain his end consciously"（他想要自觉地实现自己的目标）。相比较而言，这种理解在逻辑关系上更紧密。

[4]"资"，段玉裁《说文解字注》说："资者，积也。旱则资舟，水则资车，夏则资皮，冬则资絺，皆居积之谓。"显然他认为"资"取积蓄的含义。赵甄陶的译文也持此意，将"资之深"翻译为"have a rich store of it"（就会积蓄得很深）。朱熹注："资，犹籍也。"显然，他认为此处的"资"有凭借，依靠之意。刘殿爵的译文类朱熹，将"资之深"翻译为"he can draw deeply upon it"（就能完全利用它）。

【原文】8.15　孟子曰："博学而详说之，将以反说约也[1]。"

【译文】孟子说："广博地学习，详细地解说，是为了达到简明扼要的目的。"

【英译】Mencius said, 'In learning extensively and discussing minutely what is learned, the object of the superior man is that he may be able to go back and set forth in brief what is essential.'

【注释】

[1]　孟子在本章继续阐述为学之道，他一针见血地指出了"博学"和"反约"的关系。博学是对知识的广泛占有，是反约的基础，而反约是将广博的知识融会贯通，提取出精华，是博学的更高境界。理雅各认为本章紧承上章，是在讨论君子的为学之道，因而在翻译上增加了主语"the superior man"。刘殿爵则认为孟子在此处论说的是一个放之四海而皆准的正确的学习方法，将之翻译为"Learn widely and go into what you have learned in detail so that in the end you can return to the essential"。和理雅各的翻译相比，他的译文也能准确再现"博""详"和"约"的关系，但仅突出了"扼要"，少了"in brief"（简明），降低了原文鲜明的对比色彩。

【原文】8.16　孟子曰[1]："以善服人者，未有能服人者也[2]；以善养人[3]，然后能服天下。天下不心服而王者，未之有也。"

【译文】孟子说："用善来使人服从，从来不能真正使人服从的；用善来养育人，才能使得天下服从。天下人不心悦诚服却能成为王者的，是从来没有过的事。"

【英译】Mencius said，'Never has he who would by his excellence subdue men been able to subdue them. Let a prince seek by his excellence to nourish men，and he will be able to subdue the whole kingdom. It is impossible that any one should become ruler of the people to whom they have not yielded the subjection of the heart.'

【注释】

[1] 孟子在本章强调"以善养人"的重要性。孟子推崇以德服人的王道，反对以力服人的霸道，但对"以德服人"应全面理解。孟子倡导的"以德服人"实际上包含"善政"和"善教"两个方面，"善政，民畏之；善教，民爱之。善政得民财，善教得民心"（《孟子·尽心上》）。因而要赢得人心，就需要"以善养人"，在善政和善教两个方面努力，让百姓既有恒产，又有恒心。

[2] "以善服人者，未有能服人者也"，孟子认为，仅仅依靠善政不能得民心。刘殿爵将本句翻译为"You can never succeed in winning the allegiance of men by trying to dominate them through goodness"（以善治人，是不可能得人心的）。他的译文准确体现篇章宗旨。

[3] "以善养人"实际上是指将善政和善教结合起来，用善政解决好民生问题，用善教熏陶、教育百姓。理雅各将之翻译为"Let a prince seek by his excellence to nourish men"（君主通过美德来滋养人们）。他的译文强调善教的重要性。刘殿爵的译文是"using this goodness for their welfare"（用善为他们谋福利），他的译文可以包含"善教"和"善政"双重含义。

【原文】8.17 孟子曰："言无实不祥。不祥之实，蔽贤者当之[1]。"

【译文】孟子说："推荐贤才的语言没有实际内容是不好的。这种不好的结果，应该由那些妨碍贤才被任用的人承担。"

【英译】Mencius said, 'Words which are not true are inauspicious, and the words which are most truly obnoxious to the name of inauspicious，are those which throw into the shade men of talents and virtue.'

【注释】

[1] 朱熹对"言无实不祥"持模棱两可的态度："或曰：'天下之言无有实不祥者，惟蔽贤为不祥之实。'或曰：'言而无实者不祥，故蔽贤为不祥之实。'二说不同，未知孰是，疑或有阙文焉。"朱熹提出的两种观点或许是当时比较流行的说法。今人梁涛认为："从下文'蔽贤者'一句看，应是推荐贤才之言。"他将本句注释为："推荐贤才没有说到点子上是不好的。这种不好的后果，要由那些埋没了贤才的人承担。"他认为"言"特指"举贤"的语言。刘殿爵则认为是泛指，并将之翻译为"Words without reality are ill-omened, and the reality of the ill-omened will befall those who stand in the way of good people"（没有实际内容的语言是不好的。这种不好的结果将会落到那些阻碍贤者进用的人身上）。从语意的前后关联度看，梁涛的理解更贴切。

【原文】8.18 徐子曰[1]："仲尼亟称于水，曰：'水哉，水哉！'何取于水也？"孟子曰："源泉混混[2]，不舍昼夜，盈科而后进，放乎四海。有本者如是[3]，是之取尔。苟为无本，七八月之间雨集，沟浍皆盈；其涸也，可立而待也。故声闻过情，君子耻之。"

【译文】徐子说："孔子几次称赞水，说：'水啊，水啊！'他看中水的哪方面了？"孟子说："有源头的泉水滚滚涌出，昼夜不停，把坑坑洼洼的地方灌满了继续前行，一直流入大海。有本源的都是这样，孔子就看中了这点。如果没有本源，七八月的时候雨水密集，把大小沟渠都灌满了；但是干枯得也很快。所以声望名誉超过了实际，君子会以之为耻辱。”

【英译】The disciple Hsü said, 'Chung-nî often praised water, saying, "O water! O water!" What did he find in water to praise? Mencius replied, 'There is a spring of water; how it gushes out! It rests not day nor night. It fills up every hole, and then advances, flowing on to the four seas. Such is water having a spring! It was this which he found in it to praise. But suppose that the water has no spring.—In the seventh and eighth months when the rain falls abundantly, the channels in the fields are all filled, but their being dried up again may be expected in a short time. So a superior man is ashamed of a reputation beyond his merits.'

【注释】

[1] “水”是中国文化中一种常见的象征意象，在先秦诸子的著作中均有尚水的言论。在儒家言论中，对水的推崇也屡见不鲜。孔子曾数次称赞水，并且认为乐水的人是智者。孟子在论辩中也数次以水作喻，并且宣称孔子尚水是因为水有本源。他借水来教导人们，做任何事情都要脚踏实地，要不断充实自己，不能沽名钓誉。

[2] “源泉”，指有本源的泉水。理雅各选择用“a spring of water”翻译，虽然二者在词义上能够对应，但本章主旨在突出“本源”的重要性，因而刘殿爵的“Water from an ample source”（拥有丰富源头的水），突出了水之源，更方便读者理解孟子强调的重点。“混混”，通滚滚。刘殿爵和理雅各的译文都突出了有源之水来势凶猛、奔流不息之貌。

[3] “有本者如是”，理雅各认为是针对水而发，将之翻译为“Such is water having a spring!”（有源头的水都是这样的）刘殿爵则认为，这句话是对有源之水特征的扩展和深化，即“Anything that has an ample source is like

this"（有本源的东西都会像有源之水这样）。从下文"声闻过情，君子耻之"可以看出，孟子是以水喻德，而非就水言水，因而刘殿爵的理解更准确。

【原文】8.19　孟子曰[1]："人之所以异于禽兽者几希，庶民去之，君子存之。舜明于庶物，察于人伦，由仁义行，非行仁义也[2]。"

【译文】孟子说："人和禽兽的差别只有一点点，百姓丢失它了，只有君子才保存了。舜明察事物，了解人类的常情，顺着仁义而行，而不是把仁义作为规范照着去做。"

【英译】Mencius said, 'That whereby man differs from the lower animals is but small. The mass of people cast it away, while superior men preserve it. Shun clearly understood the multitude of things, and closely observed the relations of humanity. He walked along the path of benevolence and righteousness; he did not need to pursue benevolence and righteousness.'

【注释】

[1] 孟子从人禽之辨出发谈论人性，认为人和动物的区别就在人先天地具备"仁义礼智四端"，如果人们不懂得扩而充之，让其为外物所蔽，最终会沦落到和禽兽没有什么区别。

[2] 朱熹注曰："由仁义行，非行仁义，则仁义已根于心，而所行皆从此出。非以仁义为美，而后勉强行之，所谓安而行之也。此则圣人之事，不待存之，而无不存矣。"可见，"由仁义行"是赵岐所谓的"仁义生于内，由其中而行"，即由内而外自觉地做仁义之事；"行仁义"则是"强力行仁义"，将仁义作为外在规范，根据其要求来约束自己的行为。理雅各的译文虽能在词义上准确对应原文，但不便于读者体会"由仁义行"和"行仁义"的实质区别。赵甄陶将之翻译为"He just followed the path of benevolence and righteousness, but did not use benevolence and righteousness as the means to an

end"。他在翻译的时候做了适当添加，更有利于读者理解二者的关系。

【原文】8.20　孟子曰[1]："禹恶旨酒而好善言[2]。汤执中，立贤无方[3]。文王视民如伤[4]，望道而未之见。武王不泄迩，不忘远。周公思兼三王，以施四事；其有不合者[5]，仰而思之，夜以继日；幸而得之，坐以待旦。"

【译文】孟子说："大禹厌恶美酒却喜欢有价值的话。商汤坚持中正之道，举用贤人不拘泥常规。文王对待百姓就好像他们受了伤，已经接近道就好像没看到一样。武王不特别亲近朝廷中的近臣，也不遗忘散在四方的远臣。周公想要兼学夏商周的君王，实践禹、汤、文王、武王的事业；如果有不合适的地方，就抬头思考，夜以继日，侥幸想通了，就会坐着等到天亮（马上去实行）。"

【英译】Mencius said,'Yü hated the pleasant wine, and loved good words. T'ang held fast the Mean, and employed men of talents and virtue without regard to where they came from. King Wăn looked on the people as he would on a man who was wounded, and he looked towards the right path as if he could not see it. King Wû did not slight the near, and did not forget the distant. The duke of Châu desired to unite in himself the virtues of those kings, those founders of the three dynasties, that he might display in his practice the four things which they did. If he saw any thing in them not suited to his time, he looked up and thought about it, from daytime into the night, and when he was fortunate enough to master the difficulty, he sat waiting for the morning.'

【注释】

[1] 孟子推崇禹、汤、文王、武王和周公，认为他们是圣王的代表，能践行仁政，因而列举了他们的优秀品质，希望后代君主能效仿。

[2]"善言"，有意义、有价值的话。理雅各将之翻译为"good words"。该词的含义是恭维的话、好听的话、赞扬的话，用它来翻译禹的优秀品质容易引起读者的误解，认为禹是一个肤浅之人，乐于接受别人的吹捧。但实际上，禹喜好的"善言"是对自己、对国家有益的建议和言论。刘殿爵将之翻译为"good advice"（好的建议），为我们再现了一个虚怀若谷、乐于接受别人建议的大禹形象。

[3]"无方"，一种观点主张以"方向"释"方"，认为"无方"即不问来自何方。赵岐注曰："惟贤速立之，不问其从何方来。"理雅各的译文持这一观点，将之译为"without regard to where they came from"（不论来自哪里）。一说以"常"释"方"，"无方"即不循常法，如《礼记·檀弓》"左右就养无方"，《礼记·内则》"博学无方"，郑玄注云："方，常也。"焦循结合文义，进一步指出"惟贤则立，而无常法，内申上'执中'之有权。"刘殿爵持这一观点，将之翻译为"no fixed formula"（没有固定的标准）。还有一种观点认为，"无方"即不问出身。朱熹《集注》曰："方，犹类也。立贤无方，惟贤则立之于位，不问其类也。"赖发洛支持这一观点，以"不问出身"解"无方"，将之翻译为"whoever they might be"（不管他是谁）。这三种理解皆有训诂资料作支撑，从词义和文义上讲，都能说得过去，因而都是可以接受的。但如焦循所示，"无方"似是对上文"执中"之意的进一步申明，因而相比较而言，刘殿爵以"无固定标准"译"无方"更确切。

[4]孟子认为，"视民如伤"是圣王爱民的表现。它源于儒家经典《春秋左氏传》，《左传·哀公元年》中有"臣闻国之兴也，视民如伤"。"视民如伤"就是对待百姓就像他们受了伤一样，只能爱抚让其静养，不能惊动打扰之。理雅各的译文体现了原文的字面意思，让读者自己去体味其内涵。

[5]"不合者"，朱熹注曰："时异势殊，故其事或有所不合。"理雅各将之翻译为"If he saw any thing in them not suited to his time"（当遇到不符合时代的情况）。根据他的译文孟子似乎支持世易时移，认为先王之法并不一定总是符合当代国情。但从孟子的整个思想体系看，他倡导法先王，认为

先王的治国之策即仁政是放之四海而皆准的真理，因而认为先王之法有不符合当代的情况与孟子的思想不符。刘殿爵将"不合者"翻译为"anything he could not quite understand"（并不完全理解的事）。这样翻译可以紧密呼应下文的"仰而思之，夜以继日"，即当遇到不理解的事，周公就会通宵达旦地思考，以寻求答案。

【原文】8.21　孟子曰[1]："王者之迹熄[2]而《诗》亡[3]，《诗》亡然后《春秋》[4]作。晋之《乘》，楚之《梼杌》，鲁之《春秋》，一也：其事则齐桓、晋文，其文则史。孔子曰：'其义则丘窃取之矣[5]。'"

【译文】孟子说："天子采诗的事情废止了，《诗》就不再被搜集；《诗》不再被搜集了，《春秋》等史书就出现了。晋国的《乘》，楚国的《梼杌》，鲁国的《春秋》，都是一样的：记载的齐桓公、晋文公的事情，用的笔法是史书的笔法。孔子说：'《诗》寓褒善贬恶的大义，我在《春秋》上借用了。'"

【英译】Mencius said, 'The traces of sovereign rule were extinguished, and the royal odes ceased to be made. When those odes ceased to be made, then the Ch'un Ch'iû was produced. The Shăng of Tsin, the Tâo-wû of Ch'û, and the Ch'un Ch'iû of Lû were books of the same character. The subject of the Ch'un Ch'iû was the affairs of Hwan of Ch'î and Wăn of Tsin, and its style was the historical. Confucius said, "Its righteous decisions I ventured to make."'

【注释】

[1] 本章虽短短几句话，却涵盖了孔子作《春秋》的时代背景，晋国史书《乘》、楚国史书《梼杌》和鲁国史书《春秋》的特点，以及孔子作《春秋》的原则。

[2] "王者之迹熄"，朱熹注曰："平王东迁，而政教号令不及于天下

也。"受其影响，理雅各将"迹"直译为"trace"（痕迹，迹象）。他在注解中对此作了如下解释："周朝王权衰落开始于公元前 769 年，周平王将国都从镐京迁往洛邑时。此后，周王的权力有名无实。"显然，理雅各认为"王者之迹熄"是王权衰落，天子号令天下的迹象消失了。刘殿爵将"迹"翻译为"wooden clappers"（木舌金铃）。他在注释中指出，"木舌金铃是四处采集民谣的官员使用的东西"。他的译文关注并突出中国文化的特殊性，使读者对中国古代采诗之人"以木铎记诗言"的特征有一个了解。朱骏声在《说文通训定声》中指出："'迹'即'迒'之误。"许慎在《说文解字·丌部》曰："迒，古之遒人以木铎记诗言。"程树德在《说文稽古篇》认为："考《左传》引夏书曰：'遒人以木铎徇于路。'杜注：'遒人，行人之官也。木铎，木舌金铃。徇于路，求歌谣之言。'"刘殿爵对古代传统习俗具有较强的敏感度，将"迹"中包含的古代圣王派使者去民间采集民谣、了解民情的传统介绍得较为清楚。

[3]"《诗》亡"，理雅各认为指的是《诗经》里的《雅》诗不再被创造出来。《雅》诗主要是奴隶主贵族上层社会举行各种典礼或宴会时演唱的乐歌，故理译为"royal odes"（王室颂）。刘殿爵则认为是"歌谣也不再被收集"。将"亡"与前文"迹"即"古代圣王派使者去民间采集民谣"的传统联系起来，使文义更加紧密。

[4]《春秋》含义有三：一是泛指各诸侯国编的史书，如《墨子·明鬼》："吾见百国《春秋》"；二是特指鲁国国史；三是指孔子根据鲁国国史编写的《春秋》。理雅各认为此处的《春秋》是特指，将之音译为"the Ch'un Ch'iû"。刘殿爵则认为是泛指各诸侯国的史书，将之翻译为"the Spring and Autumn Annals"。结合下文列举的三国史书可知，刘殿爵的译文更准确。

[5]"其义则丘窃取之矣"，清人皮锡瑞认为"孟子言鲁之《春秋》，止有其事其文而无其义，其义是孔子创立，非鲁《春秋》所有。"显然他认为孔子用义理裁定了鲁国的春秋。陈其泰也认为："孟子还强调《春秋》所重的不是史事，而是孔子加进去的义。"刘殿爵的译文是"I have appropriated

the didactic principles therein"（我把借用的道德判断原则用在了里面）。显然他支持董仲舒的"仲尼之作《春秋》也……引史记，理往事，正是非"，认为"其义"就是用来"正是非"之义。

【原文】8.22　孟子曰^[1]："君子之泽五世而斩，小人之泽五世而斩^[2]。予未得为孔子徒也，予私淑^[3]诸人也。"

【译文】孟子说："君子的影响，过了五代就断绝了；小人的影响，过了五代就断绝了。我没有成为孔子的学生，只是私下从别人那里学习孔子。"

【英译】Mencius said，'The influence of a sovereign sage termi- nates in the fifth generation. The influence of a mere sage does the same. Although I could not be a disciple of Confucius himself，I have endeavoured to cultivate my virtue by means of others who were.'

【注释】

[1] 孟子在本章表达了他以继承和发展孔子思想为己任的雄心壮志。

[2] 关于"君子"与"小人"的含义，存在争议。赵岐曾以"大德大凶"解之。焦循指出："近时通解以君子为圣贤在位者，小人为圣贤不在位者。"理雅各的译文类焦循，认为不论"君子"还是"小人"，都是圣人，区别在于是否担任官职，因而将之翻译为"a sovereign sage"和"a mere sage"。赵甄陶则认为"君子"和"小人"分别指担任官职的人和普通人，将之分别翻译为"men of position"和"commoners"。王鑫磊指出："到战国时代，'小人'一词在作'地位较低的人'解时，更多的是与'君子'同时出现，以表达在某一事情上居上位者与居下位者、有知识者和无知识者、有德者和无德者等一系列对立群体的区别，成为这些对立关系中处于低位一极的通称，而很少特指平民阶层了。"刘殿爵的译文表明他也认为"小人"是作为君子的对立群体而被提及。结合下文的"五世而斩"，将"君子"和"小人"理解为"圣贤在位者"和"圣贤不在位者"更准确。

[3]"私淑"的含义有两种，第一种以朱熹为代表，他认为，"私，犹窃也。淑，善也。"即私下用其善。理雅各的译文和朱熹相类。第二种观点以杨伯峻为代表，认为，"淑"应"借为'叔'，《说文》：'叔，取也。'"因而把"私淑"解释为私下拾取，即未能跟从本人直接学习，而是从别处私下获取。刘殿爵取第二种观点，将之译为"I have learned indirectly from him through others"（我通过别人间接地向他学习）。结合上文可知，孟子并未直接受业于孔子，因而刘殿爵的"私下学习"更确切。

【原文】 8.23　孟子曰[1]："可以取，可以无取，取伤廉[2]；可以与，可以无与，与伤惠；可以死，可以无死，死伤勇。"

【译文】 孟子说："可以拿，可以不拿，拿了就会伤害廉洁；可以给，可以不给，给了就会损害恩惠；可以死，可以不死，死了就会损害勇敢。"

【英译】 Mencius said，'When it appears proper to take a thing, and afterwards not proper，to take it is contrary to moderation. When it appears proper to give a thing and afterwards not proper，to give it is contrary to kindness. When it appears proper to sacrifice one's life，and afterwards not proper，to sacrifice it is contrary to bravery.'

【注释】

[1] 人在一生中肯定会面对各种选择，孟子主张在作出选择时应以是否符合道德为首要标准，坚持中庸之道，无过无不及。

[2] 朱熹认为："过取固害于廉，然过与亦反害其惠，过死亦反害其勇，盖过犹不及之意也。"理雅各将"廉"翻译为"moderation"（适度），受朱熹的"过犹不及"的影响。同时，他对"可以取，可以无取"的理解受"非礼之礼，非义之义，大人弗为"（《孟子·离娄章句下》）影响，将之理解为不去做一些模棱两可、似是而非、有损礼义的事。从孟子的整个思想体系来看，这种理解是可以接受的。刘殿爵则严格按照原文字面意思，将之翻

译为 "When it is permissible both to accept and not to accept, it is an abuse of integrity to accept."（当既可以接受也可以不接受的时候，接受就会损害廉洁）他的译文突出了"不苟取"的重要性。这两种理解皆可。

【原文】8.24　逢蒙学射于羿[1]，尽羿之道[2]，思天下惟羿为愈己，于是杀羿。孟子曰："是亦羿有罪焉。"公明仪曰："宜若无罪焉。"曰："薄乎云尔，恶得无罪？郑人使子濯孺子侵卫，卫使庾公之斯追之。子濯孺子曰：'今日我疾作[3]，不可以执弓，吾死矣夫！'问其仆曰：'追我者谁也？'其仆曰：'庾公之斯也。'曰：'吾生矣。'其仆曰：'庾公之斯，卫之善射者也；夫子曰"吾生"，何谓也？'曰：'庾公之斯学射于尹公之他，尹公之他学射于我。夫尹公之他，端人也，其取友必端矣。'庾公之斯至，曰：'夫子何为不执弓？'曰：'今日我疾作，不可以执弓。'曰：'小人学射于尹公之他，尹公之他学射于夫子，我不忍以夫子之道反害夫子。虽然，今日之事，君事也，我不敢废。'抽矢，扣轮，去其金，发乘矢而后反。"

【译文】古时候，逢蒙跟着羿学射箭，完全学会了羿的本领，便想，天下只有羿在射箭上比自己厉害，因此便杀死了羿。孟子说："这里羿也有错。"公明仪说："好像应该没有什么错误吧。"孟子说："错误不大罢了，怎么能说没有错呢？郑国曾经让子濯孺子侵犯卫国，卫国便派庾公之斯来追击他。子濯孺子说：'今天我的伤病发作，拿不了弓，我要死了。'问驾车的人：'是谁追我啊？'驾车的人说：'庾公之斯。'他便说：'能活命。'驾车的人说：'庾公之斯是卫国有名的射手，您说"能活命"，为什么呢？'回答说：'庾公之斯跟着尹公之他学射箭，尹公之他又跟我学射。尹公之他是个正派人，他选择的朋友也一定正派。'庾公之斯追上后，问道：'先生为什么不拿弓？'子濯孺子说：'今天我的伤病发作了，不能拿弓。'庾公之斯说：'我跟着尹公之他学射箭，尹公之他又跟着先生学射箭。我不忍心用您传授的技能来伤害您。但是，今天的事情是君主的命令，我不敢废弃。'于是抽出箭，向车轮敲打，磕掉箭头，射了四箭然后回去了。"

【英译】P'ang Măng learned archery of Î. When he had acquired completely all the science of Î, he thought that in all the kingdom only Î was superior to himself, and so he slew him. Mencius said, 'In this case Î also was to blame. Kung-ming Î indeed said, "It would appear as if he were not to be blamed," but he thereby only meant that his blame was slight. How can he be held without any blame?' The people of Chăng sent Tszu-cho Yü to make a stealthy attack on Wei, which sent Yü-kung Szu to pursue him. Tszu-cho Yü said, "To-day I feel unwell, so that I cannot hold my bow. I am a dead man!" At the same time he asked his driver, "Who is it that is pursuing me?" The driver said, "It is Yü-kung Szu," on which, he exclaimed, "I shall live." The driver said, "Yü-kung Szu is the best archer of Wei, what do you mean by saying 'I shall live?'" Yü replied, "Yü-kung Szu learned archery from Yin-kung T'o, who again learned it from me. Now, Yin-kung T'o is an upright man, and the friends of his selection must be upright also." When Yü-kung Szu came up, he said, "Master, why are you not holding your bow?" Yü answered him, "To-day I am feeling unwell, and cannot hold my bow." On this Sze said, "I learned archery from Yin-kung T'o, who again learned it from you. I cannot bear to injure you with your own science. The business of to-day, however, is the prince's business, which I dare not neglect." He then took his arrows, knocked off their steel points against the carriage-wheel, discharged four of them, and returned.'

【注释】

[1] 孟子在本章举了正反两个例子论证君子授徒和交友必须谨慎的道理。后羿是古代有名的射手，在收徒的时候未能关注学生的人品，结果被学生射死；子濯孺子则要求徒弟必须是正派人，因而可以转危为安。

[2] "尽羿之道"，即学会羿的技巧。刘殿爵将之译为"having learned everything Yi could teach"（学尽羿所教授的所有东西）。理雅各根据文义将"道"翻译为"science"（技巧），这两种翻译都准确且便于读者理解。

[3] "疾"字最早见于商代甲骨文，其字形像人腋下中箭，本义为受兵伤，后泛指疾病。"作"，表明该疾发作突然。刘殿爵将"疾作"翻译为"I have an attack of an old complaint"（我突然旧疾复发）。他选择用"complaint"翻译"疾"，该词多指那些不严重、但会对身体某部位产生影响的疾病，可以更好地呼应"不可以执弓"。理雅各将之翻译为"feel unwell"（生病了），过于平淡，不如刘殿爵的翻译生动形象地表明疾病来得突然，导致子濯孺子不能采取任何攻击和防御措施，只能束手就擒。

【原文】 8.25　孟子曰[1]："西子[2]蒙不洁[3]，则人皆掩鼻而过之；虽有恶人[4]，齐戒沐浴，则可以祀上帝。[5]"

【译文】 孟子说："如果西子沾染上污秽，那么别人都会捂着鼻子走过她身边；虽然是相貌丑陋的人，如果斋戒沐浴也可以祭祀上帝。"

【英译】 Mencius said, 'If the lady Hsî had been covered with a filthy head-dress, all people would have stopped their noses in passing her. Though a man may be wicked, yet if he adjust his thoughts, fast, and bathe, he may sacrifice to God.'

【注释】

[1] 本章强调修身的重要性。孟子认为真诚的心远比外貌更重要，虽然人的容貌是天生的，有美丑之分，但后天的修身努力更重要，它可以改变人的不足，使之成为有为之人。

[2]"西子",春秋时越国人,中国古代四大美女之一,后成为美女的代称。刘殿爵用音译翻译其名字,用"beauty"体现它所蕴含的文化内涵,这不失为翻译有中国特色文化词语的有效方法。

[3]"蒙不洁",赵岐注曰:"以不洁汗巾而蒙其头面。"即戴不干净的头巾,理雅各的译文持这一观点。而朱熹则认为:"蒙,犹冒也。不洁,污秽之物也。"即沾染了污秽之物,刘殿爵支持这一注解,将之翻译为"covered with filth"。结合下文"齐戒沐浴"可知,沾染了污秽之物更符合文义。

[4]"恶人",朱熹注曰:"丑貌者也。"《吕氏春秋·去尤篇》高诱《注》亦云:"恶,丑也。"刘殿爵和赵甄陶的译文亦持此观点。理雅各则认为是"坏人"。在本章中孟子将"西子"和"恶人"相对举而言,"西子"是美貌的代表,而与之对应的"恶人"也应指外貌丑陋的人。

[5]在中西方文化语境下,中国古代的"上帝"和西方的"God"存在着明显的不同。虽然1999年商务印书馆出版的《词源》指出,中国古代的"上帝"指"天帝,天神",冯友兰先生亦认为"主宰之天,即所谓皇天上帝",但是众多先秦古籍证明中国古代的上帝始终没有演变成西方的"God"那样万能的造物主。不仅如此,当前有不少学者指出,早期文献中的上帝虽和天关系密切,但并不等同于天,其内涵也出现由神到人(尧舜等圣王)的转变,沈顺福进一步指出,"中国先秦时期的上帝应该指先帝"。可见,用"God"翻译"上帝"不准确。纵观传教士编纂的汉英字典,马礼逊、麦都思、卫三畏等均未将"上帝"对译为"God",这亦从一个方面证明他们并不认为"God"可以作为汉语"上帝"的对应词。

【原文】8.26 孟子曰[1]:"天下之言性也,则故而已矣[2]。故者以利为本[3]。所恶于智者,为其凿也。如智者若禹之行水也,则无恶于智矣。禹之行水也,行其所无事也。如智者亦行其所无事,则智亦大矣。天之高也,星辰之远也,苟求其故[4],千岁之日至,可坐而致也。"

【译文】孟子说："天下的人讨论的性，只不过是习惯而已。习惯的培养要以顺应人性为根本。之所以厌恶聪明人，因为他们容易陷于穿凿附会。如果聪明人能像禹治水一样，就不会厌恶聪明的人了。禹治理水，（顺水之性）行其所无事。如果聪明的人也能行其所无事，那么聪明也就起很大的作用了。天很高，星辰很远，如果能顺其规律，一千年以内的冬至，都可以坐着推算出来。"

【英译】Mencius said, 'All who speak about the natures of things, have in fact only their phenomena to reason from, and the value of a phenomenon is in its being natural. What I dislike in your wise men is their boring out their conclusions. If those wise men would only act as Yü did when he conveyed away the waters, there would be nothing to dislike in their wisdom. The manner in which Yü conveyed away the waters was by doing what gave him no trouble. If your wise men would also do that which gave them no trouble, their knowledge would also be great. There is heaven so high; there are the stars so distant. If we have investigated their phenomena, we may, while sitting in our places, go back to the solstice of a thousand years ago.'

【注释】

[1] 古今学者对本章的注疏很多，理解亦不同。

[2] "故"，朱熹注曰："其已然之迹。"焦循指出："故为以往之事。"孙奭作《孟子注疏》云"盖故者事也"。杨伯峻在此基础上进一步指出，"故"是"'以往之事''既成事实'的根源、所以然"。赵甄陶即持此种观点，将之翻译为"seek into the whys and wherefores."理雅各在翻译时，将"故"理解为现象，将"天下之言性也，则故而已矣"翻译为"All who speak about the natures of things, have in fact only their phenomena to reason from"（所有谈论性的人实际上只是通过现象来推理）。很明显，理雅各在翻译此段时

受到了朱熹对"故"的认识的影响。理雅各还在注释中提出了他对本章的认识。他认为本章主要讲如何通过仔细研究现象来获得知识。他指出:"孟子主张现象是获得知识的正确途径的观点和培根的主张特别相似。遗憾的是,与世界上的其他国家相比,中国似乎更容易忽略现象在获取知识中的作用。"梁涛将郭店竹简《性自命出》与《孟子》的"天下之言性"联系起来给出了一种新的理解:"'天下之言性也,则故而已矣'是说,人们讨论的性不过是指积习、习惯而言。"赖发洛的理解与之相类,将"故"翻译为"habit"(习惯)。刘殿爵则将"故"翻译为"former theories"(先前的学说),认为在讨论人性的时候,世人仅仅遵循先前的学说。

[3] 梁涛曾指出,对"故者以利为本"向来有两种不同的理解:"一种是理解为孟子的正面言论,释'利'为有利,赵岐、朱熹、焦循等持这种看法;一种与此相反,是理解为孟子反对的言论,释'利'为自利,利害,陆九渊、黄彰健等持这种看法。"从文义上看,刘殿爵也认为是孟子的正面言论,但他延续其对"故"的理解,将此句创造性地翻译为"They do so because these theories can be explained with ease"(人们之所以要遵循先前的学说是因为这些学说解释起来比较容易)。

[4] "苟求其故",指如果认识到星辰固有的运行规律。刘殿爵继续其对"故"的理解,翻译为"if one seeks out former instances"(如果一个人查到了先前的实例)。结合下文"千岁之日至,可坐而致",将之理解为通过先前实例总结出来的星辰固有的运行规律更准确。

【原文】8.27 公行子有子之丧[1],右师[2]往吊。入门,有进而与右师言者,有就右师之位而与右师言者。孟子不与右师言,右师不悦曰:"诸君子皆与驩言,孟子独不与驩言,是简驩也。"孟子闻之,曰:"礼,朝廷不历位而相与言,不逾阶而相揖也。我欲行礼,子敖以我为简,不亦异乎?"

【译文】公行子为儿子办理丧事,右师去吊丧。他刚进门,就有人走过来和他说话，还有人走到他座位旁边和他说话。孟子却不和他说话。右师不高兴地说："各位大夫都和我讲话，只有孟子不和我说话，他不尊重我。"孟子听了后说："礼的规定是朝廷上不越位交谈，不能隔着台阶相互作揖。我想遵循礼制，王骧却认为我不尊重他，不也很奇怪吗？"

【英译】The officer Kung-hang having on hand the funeral of one of his sons, the Master of the Right went to condole with him. When this noble entered the door, some called him to them and spoke with him, and some went to his place and spoke with him. Mencius did not speak with him, so that he was displeased, and said, 'All the gentlemen have spoken with me. There is only Mencius who does not speak to me, thereby slighting me.' Mencius having heard of this remark, said, 'According to the prescribed rules, in the court, individuals may not change their places to speak with one another, nor may they pass from their ranks to bow to one another. I was wishing to observe this rule, and Tsze-âo understands it that I was slighting him：—is not this strange？'

【注释】

[1] 本章再现了孟子时刻不忘遵守礼制，不趋炎附势的高尚品质。孟子开篇为我们描述了右师入门后，众人趋炎附势、围着他巴结奉承的情景。虽然主动和别人打招呼貌似礼貌的表现，但不顾场合、不分形式，胁肩谄笑的行为是"非礼之礼"，君子是不会做的。

[2] "右师"，古代官名。赵岐注曰："齐之贵臣"。它在英语中没有对等词，刘殿爵将之音译为"yu shih"，既保留了中国传统文化的独特性，又可以避免因直译而引起的误解。理雅各将之翻译为"Master of the Right"，"Master"表明"右师"是一个官职，"Right"则是对"右"的词义对译，如此翻译基本上能体现"右师"的含义。赖发洛将之翻译为"Junior Tutor"。

"Junior"指职位低下，显然他认为在中国传统文化上以左为尊，以右为卑。但是他没有注意到孟子提到的"右师"是战国时代的官职，在秦汉以前我国是以"右"为尊的，直到东汉至隋、唐、两宋时期，我国才形成了左尊的传统，显然赖发洛的理解脱离了原文的时代背景。他将"师"翻译为"Tutor"（家庭教师），虽试图通过大写突出其含义特殊性，但容易让读者误解"右师"为"地位较低的家庭教师"。

【原文】8.28　孟子曰[1]："君子所以异于人者，以其存心也。君子以仁存心，以礼存心[2]。仁者爱人，有礼者敬人。爱人者，人恒爱之；敬人者，人恒敬之。有人于此，其待我以横逆[3]，则君子必自反[4]也：我必不仁也，必无礼也，此物奚宜至哉？其自反而仁矣，自反而有礼矣，其横逆由是也，君子必自反也：我必不忠。自反而忠矣，其横逆由是也，君子曰：'此亦妄人也已矣[5]。如此，则与禽兽奚择哉[6]？于禽兽又何难焉？'是故君子有终身之忧，无一朝之患也。乃若所忧则有之：舜，人也；我，亦人也。舜为法于天下，可传于后世，我由未免为乡人也，是则可忧也。忧之如何？如舜而已矣。若夫君子所患，则亡矣。非仁无为也，非礼无行也。如有一朝之患[7]，则君子不患矣。"

【译文】孟子说："君子同一般人不同的地方，在于存心不同。君子以仁存于心，以礼存于心。仁人爱别人，有礼的人尊敬别人。爱别人的人，别人也常爱他；尊敬别人的人，别人也常尊敬他。如果这里有个人，待我横暴无理，那么君子一定自我反省，我一定不仁，一定无礼，不然，为什么会遭遇这种态度？自我反省后，我确实仁，确实有礼，那人的横暴无理还是和以前一样，君子一定又自我反省，我一定没有尽心竭力。自我反省后，我确实尽心竭力了，那人的横暴无理还是和以前一样，君子就会说：'这不过是个狂妄的人罢了。像他这样，和禽兽有什么区别呢？对于禽兽又责备什么呢？'所以君子有长久的忧虑，却没有突发的忧患。至于他的忧虑是有的：舜是人，我也是人。舜可以成为天下人效仿的榜样，影响传于后代，我却不过是一个普通人，这个才是可忧虑的事。忧虑了怎么办？努力向舜学习罢了。至于君子其他的忧虑那是没有的。不符合仁爱的事不干，不符合礼的事不做。即使有突发的忧患，君子也不会放在心上。"

【英译】Mencius said, 'That whereby the superior man is distinguished from other men is what he preserves in his heart; —namely, benevolence and propriety. The benevolent man loves others. The man of propriety shows respect to others. He who loves others is constantly loved by them. He who respects others is constantly respected by them. Here is a man, who treats me in a perverse and unreasonable manner. The superior man in such a case will turn round upon himself— "I must have been wanting in benevolence; I must have been wanting in propriety; —how should this have happened to me?" He examines himself, and is specially benevolent. He turns round upon himself, and is specially observant of propriety. The perversity and unreasonableness of the other, however, are still the same. The superior man will again turn round on himself, — "I must have been failing to do my utmost." He turns round upon himself, and proceeds to do his utmost, but still the perversity and unreasonableness of the other are repeated. On this the superior man says, "This is a man utterly lost indeed! Since he conducts himself so, what is there to choose between him and a brute? Why should I go to contend with a brute?" Thus it is that the superior man has a life-long anxiety and not one morning's calamity. As to what is matter of anxiety to him, that indeed he has.—He says, "Shun was a man, and I also am a man. But Shun became an example to all the kingdom, and his conduct was worthy to be handed down to after ages，while I am nothing better than a villager."This indeed is the proper matter of anxiety to him. And in what way is he anxious about it？Just that he may be like Shun：—then only will he stop. As to what the superior man would feel to be a calamity，there is no such thing. He does nothing which is not according to propriety. If there should befall him one morning's calamity，the superior man does not account it a calamity.'

【注释】

[1] 孟子认为，君子应以仁礼存心，如若遇到不公平的待遇，也不要怨天尤人，而要从仁、礼和智三个方面自我反省。自省后发现自己没有错，君子就不要为这类琐事而忧虑分心，而要心存大志，学习大舜，以天下为己任。

[2]"存心"，朱熹注曰："以仁、礼存心，言以是存于心而不忘也。"理雅各的翻译与之相类，将之翻译为"what he preserves in his heart；—namely，benevolence and propriety"。刘殿爵的译文也持这一观点。梁涛则认为："存心：省察心。存：察。"

[3]"横逆"，赵岐注曰："以暴虐之道来加我也。"刘殿爵没有逐字翻译"横""逆"，而是将之意译为"outrageous"（蛮横的、残暴的），强调道德上的欠缺。理雅各将之翻译为"perverse and unreasonable"，"perverse"强调反对或对抗的情绪，而"unreasonable"则侧重于描绘不受理智控制的、荒唐的情绪和行为。译文将那些对言行举止符合仁、礼和智的君子采取"横逆"行为的人没有理智、行为荒唐的形象刻画得活灵活现。赖发洛选择用"cross"翻译"横"，"cross"既可以表现"横"的字面意思，又可以用来形容人的乖戾。"逆"，赖发洛将之翻译为"rude"（粗蛮）也能准确再现"横逆者"的粗暴无礼。

[4]"躬自厚而薄责于人"是孔子的处世之道，孟子将其继承发展，提出了他的"反求诸己"的自省方法，即"爱人不亲，反其仁；治人不治，反

其智；礼人不答，反其敬；行有不得者，皆反求诸己。"（《孟子·离娄上》）可见，孟子所谓的"自反"就是以仁、礼、忠等德目检省自己的行为，理雅各将之翻译为"turn round upon himself"（转向自己寻求）基本上能体现"自反"的特征。赖发洛的"question himself"（自我审问）和刘殿爵的"looking into himself"（自我审视）也能体现"自反"的基本意思。

[5]"妄人"指狂妄无知的愚人，刘殿爵选择用"savage"翻译，强调少教养、无礼貌、粗鲁的特点，基本上能体现"妄人"的内涵。理雅各将之翻译为"a man utterly lost"（一个迷途的人）。在基督教文化中，"迷途的羔羊"通常用来描述那些不信上帝、迷失自己人生方向的人，他将"妄人"翻译为"迷途的人"容易让读者产生不必要的联想。

[6]"择"，异也。赵岐注曰："无知者与禽兽何择异也。无异于禽兽，又何足难矣？"朱熹也认为："奚择，何异也。"刘殿爵的译文与之相类，把"择"翻译为"no different from"（没有什么不同）。从上下文看，这一理解非常恰当。理雅各取"择"的"选择之意"，将之翻译为"choose"，略显机械。

[7]"一朝之患"，指突如其来的、暂时的忧患，和前文的"终身之忧"相呼应。刘殿爵将之翻译为"unexpected vexations"（突如其来的苦恼），赵甄陶将之翻译为"a disaster that comes out of the blue"（突来的灾难），皆可。

【原文】 8.29 禹、稷[1]当平世[2]，三过其门而不入[3]，孔子贤之。颜子当乱世，居于陋巷，一箪食，一瓢饮，人不堪其忧，颜子不改其乐，孔子贤之。孟子曰："禹、稷、颜回同道。禹思天下有溺者，由己溺之也[4]；稷思天下有饥者，由己饥之也，是以如是其急也。禹、稷、颜子易地则皆然。今有同室之人斗者，救之，虽被发缨冠而救之[5]，可也；乡邻有斗者，被发缨冠而往救之，则惑也；虽闭户可也。"

【译文】 禹和稷处于政治清明的时代，三次经过自己的家门都不进去（稷没有），孔子称赞他们贤明。颜回处于政治昏乱的时代，住在狭窄的巷子里，一筐饭，一瓢水，别人都受不了那种苦生活，他却自得其乐，孔子称赞他贤能。孟子说："禹、稷和颜回是一个道理。禹想到天下的人有溺水的，好像自己使他溺水了一样；稷想到天下的人有挨饿的，好像自己使他挨饿一样，所以他们才这样急迫地拯救百姓。禹、稷和颜子如果互相交换位置也都是这样。如果同屋的人互相斗殴，为了阻止他们，纵是披着头发顶着帽子，连帽带子都不系，也是可以的。如果同乡的邻人打架，如果披着头发顶着帽子，不系帽带子去救，那就是糊涂了，纵使关上门都是可以的。"

【英译】Yü and Chî, in an age when the world was being brought back to order, thrice passed their doors without entering them. Confucius praised them. The disciple Yen, in an age of disorder, dwelt in a mean narrow lane, having his single bamboo-cup of rice, and his single gourd-dish of water; other men could not have endured the distress, but he did not allow his joy to be affected by it. Confucius praised him. Mencius said, 'Yü, Chî, and Yen Hûi agreed in the principle of their conduct. Yü thought that if any one in the kingdom were drowned, it was as if he drowned him. Chî thought that if any one in the kingdom suffered hunger, it was as if he famished him. It was on this account that they were so earnest. If Yü and Chî, and Yen-tsze, had exchanged places, each would have done what the other did. Here now in the same apartment with you are people fighting: —you ought to part them. Though you part them with your cap simply tied over your unbound hair, your conduct will be allowable. If the fighting be only in the village or neighbourhood, if you go to put an end to it with your cap tied over your hair unbound, you will be in error. Although you should shut your door in such a case, your conduct would be allowable.'

【注释】

[1] 孟子在本章强调，圣人处在不同的时代，遇到不同的事情，因而处理方式也各异，但他们所遵循的根本处世原则是一致的，"先圣后圣，其揆一也。"（《孟子·离娄下》）

[2] "平世"，即太平清明的时代，与下文的"乱世"相对。刘殿爵将之翻译为"a period of peace"（和平、安宁时期），和春秋战国时期诸侯混战的"乱世"相对。理雅各则用冗长的语言将之翻译为"in an age when the world was being brought back to order"（当世界归于有序之时），显然，他将"平世"和孟子对人类社会发展规律的认识，"天下之生久矣，一治一乱"联系在一起理解。两种翻译皆能体现"平世"的内涵。

[3] "稷"，后稷，舜时为农官。"三过其门而不入"是大禹治水的事迹，稷无此事。刘殿爵的译文按字面意思翻译，对于熟悉中国传统文化的读者来说，这样翻译不会引起误解，但是对于没有中国传统文化底蕴的外国读者来说，可能会认为禹和稷都"三过其门而不入"。赵甄陶在按字面意思翻译的基础上，做了编者注，即"Ji did not.—tr."这样更便于读者理解。

[4] "由"同"犹"，好像。"由己溺之也"，有两种理解。一种以理雅各的译文为代表，体现禹以天下为己任，看到有溺水者，觉得自己应该为之负责；一种以梁涛为代表，突出大禹对他人的痛苦感同身受，"想到天下还有人在溺水，就像自己在溺水一样。"下文"由己饥之也"同。

[5] 对"被发缨冠"有两种理解：一是披着头发，不结好帽带。朱熹注曰："不暇束发，而结缨往救，言急也。"杨伯峻进一步指出："缨本义是'冠系'（帽上带子，自上而下系在颈上的），此作动词用。"理雅各将之翻译为"with your cap simply tied over your unbound hair"（把帽子简单地系在披着的头发上）。二是披着头发，顶着帽子和帽带。焦循引《说文》曰，"缨，冠系也。"进一步指出，"急于戴冠，不及使缨摄于颈，而与冠并加于头。"刘殿爵的译文和焦循观点相类。结合文义，孟子举这个例子旨在强调面对同

室争斗的紧急情势，可以不顾穿着打扮是否符合礼仪，就匆忙上前去制止。刘殿爵的译文更能体现迫切之意。

【原文】 8.30 公都子曰[1]："匡章，通国皆称不孝焉，夫子与之游，又从而礼貌之，敢问何也？"孟子曰："世俗所谓不孝者五：惰其四支，不顾父母之养，一不孝也；博弈好饮酒[2]，不顾父母之养，二不孝也；好货财，私妻子[3]，不顾父母之养，三不孝也；从耳目之欲，以为父母戮，四不孝也；好勇斗很，以危父母，五不孝也。章子有一于是乎？夫章子，子父责善而不相遇也。责善，朋友之道也；父子责善，贼恩之大者。夫章子，岂不欲有夫妻子母之属哉？为得罪于父，不得近，出妻屏子，终身不养焉。其设心以为不若是，是则罪之大者，是则章子而已矣。"

【译文】 公都子说："匡章，全国的人都说他不孝，您却和他交往，而且对他很礼貌，请问这是为什么呢？"孟子说："世俗所说的不孝有五种：四肢懒惰，不养父母，是一不孝；喜好喝酒下棋，不养父母，是二不孝；好钱财，偏爱妻室儿女，不养父母，是三不孝：放纵耳目的欲望，使父母蒙羞辱，是四不孝；喜好勇猛爱好斗殴，使父母处于危险之境，是五不孝。章子有其中一种吗？章子不过是父子间以善相责而把关系弄坏了。以善相责，是朋友相处之道；父子之间以善相责，是最伤害感情的。难道章子不想有夫妻母子的关系吗？就因为得罪了父亲，不能亲近，因此把自己的妻子也赶出去，把自己的子女也赶到远方，终身不要他们侍奉。章子这样设想，不这样做，那罪过更大了。这就是章子呢。"

【英译】 The disciple Kung-tû said, 'Throughout the whole kingdom everybody pronounces Kʻwang Chang unfilial. But you, Master, keep company with him, and moreover treat him with politeness. I venture to ask why you do so.' Mencius replied, 'There are five things which are pronounced in the common usage of the age to be unfilial. The first is laziness in the use of one's four limbs, without attending to the nourishment of his parents. The second is gambling and chess-playing, and being fond of wine, without attending to the nourishment of his parents. The third is being fond of goods and money, and selfishly attached to his wife and children, without attending to the nourishment of his parents. The fourth is following the desires of one's ears and eyes, so as to bring his parents to disgrace. The fifth is being fond of bravery, fighting and quarrelling so as to endanger his parents. Is Chang guilty of any one of these things? Now between Chang and his father there arose disagreement, he, the son, reproving his father, to urge him to what was good. To urge one another to what is good by reproofs is the way of friends. But such urging between father and son is the greatest injury to the kindness, which should prevail between them. Moreover, did not Chang wish to have in his family the relationships of husband and wife, child and mother? But because he had offended his father, and was not permitted to approach him, he sent away his wife, and drove forth his son, and all his life receives no cherishing attention from them. He settled it in his mind that if he did not act in this way, his would be one of the greatest of crimes.—Such and nothing more is the case of Chang.'

【注释】

[1] 孟子在本章告诫公都子要准确判定一个人，需要做到以下几点：首先，要有准确的判断标准，同时要保持清醒的头脑，不能人云亦云；其次，要具体问题具体分析。匡章获不孝之名的原因不是有不孝之实，而是将朋友之间的责善之道错误地运用在了父子身上。对于自己的错误，他并非将错就错，而是积极采取补救措施，因而孟子会和匡章交游。

[2] "博弈"，有注释者认为是同一件事，赵岐注曰："弈，博也，或曰

围棋。"焦循则认为二者是有区别的。焦循征引《方言》、戴震《孟子字义疏证》、王念孙《广雅疏证》、宋翔凤《四书训纂》等有关博弈的解释后，又加己见："按谓博与弈异是也。博盖即今之双陆，弈为围棋，今仍此名矣。……盖弈但行棋，博以掷采而后行棋，后人不行棋而专掷采，遂称掷采为博，博与弈益远矣。赵氏以《论语》博、弈连言，故以博释弈，其实弈为围之专名，与博同类而异事也。"理雅各和刘殿爵也认为二者不同。理雅各将"博弈"翻译为"gambling and chess-playing"（赌博和围棋），但刘殿爵认为英语中没有"博弈"的对等词，采取音译的方法以突出其特殊性，并在注解中对其内涵作了解释说明，以便于理解。

[3]"私妻子"，就是与父母相比，更偏爱自己的妻儿，而懈怠对父母的赡养。刘殿爵将之翻译为"partiality toward one's wife"（偏爱妻子），但赵甄陶认为"私"的对象是"妻子和子女"，将之翻译为"affection on one's wife and children only"（只爱妻子和子女）。

【原文】8.31　曾子居武城[1]，有越寇。或曰："寇至，盍去诸？"曰："无寓人于我室，毁伤其薪木。"寇退，则曰："修我墙屋，我将反。"寇退，曾子反。左右曰[2]："待先生如此其忠且敬也[3]，寇至，则先去以为民望[4]；寇退，则反，殆于不可。"沈犹行曰："是非汝所知也。昔沈犹有负刍之祸[5]，从先生者七十人，未有与焉。"子思居于卫，有齐寇。或曰："寇至，盍去诸？"子思曰："如伋去，君谁与守？"孟子曰："曾子、子思同道。曾子，师也，父兄也；子思，臣也，微也。曾子、子思易地则皆然。"

【译文】曾子居住在武城，越国军队来侵犯。有人说："敌寇要来了，何不离开这里呢？"曾子说："不要让别人住在我家里，破坏那些树木。"敌寇退了后，曾子说："修理一下我的墙屋，我准备回来了。"敌寇撤退了，曾子回来。他旁边的人说："武城人对先生这样地忠诚恭敬，敌寇来了，就早早离开，给百姓做了个坏榜样；敌寇退了，马上就回来，恐怕不好吧。"沈犹行说："这个不是你们所能理解的。从前（先生住在我那里），有个名叫负刍的人作乱，跟随先生的七十个弟子也都早早走开了，没有一个参与平乱。"子思住在卫国，有齐国军队来侵犯。有人说："敌寇来了，为什么不离开呢？"子思说："如果我也离开，君主同谁来守城呢？"孟子说："曾子、子思所遵循的道是相同的。曾子是老师，是父兄；子思是臣子，地位低下。曾子和子思如果换一下位置，行为也会是这样的。"

【英译】When the philosopher Tsǎng dwelt in Wû-ch'ǎng, there came a band from Yüeh to plunder it. Someone said to him, 'The plunderers are coming: —why not leave this?' Tsǎng on this left the city, saying to the man in charge of the house, 'Do not lodge any persons in my house, lest they break and injure the plants and trees.' When the plunderers withdrew, he sent word to him, saying, 'Repair the walls of my house. I am about to return.' When the plunderers retired, the philosopher Tsǎng returned accordingly. His disciples said, 'Since our master was treated with so much sincerity and respect, for him to be the first to go away on the arrival of the plunderers, so as to be observed by the people, and then to return on their retiring, appears to us to be improper.' Ch'ǎn-yû Hsing said, 'You do not understand this matter. Formerly, when Ch'ǎn-yû was exposed to the outbreak of the grass-carriers, there were seventy disciples in our master's following, and none of them took part in the matter.' When Tsze-sze was living in Wei, there came a band from Ch'î to plunder. Some one said to him, 'The plunderers are coming; —why not leave this?' Tsze-sze said, 'If I go away, whom will the prince have to guard the State with?' Mencius said, 'The philosophers Tsǎng and Tsze-sze agreed in the principle of their conduct. Tsǎng was a teacher; —in the place of a father or elder brother. Tsze-sze was a minister；—in a meaner place. If the philosophers Tsăng and Tsze-sze had exchanged places，the one would have done what the other did.'

【注释】

[1] 孟子认为，君子在不同的时代环境下、居于不同的职位上，对同一事情可能会采取不同的态度。这些表面上相左的行为其实都符合道，都是完全合时宜的。

[2] "左右"，朱熹注曰："曾子之门人也"。理雅各受其影响，将之翻译为"His disciples"（他的弟子），即认为是追随曾子的门徒。刘殿爵则认为是武城侍奉曾子的仆从。从文意上看，不理解曾子行为的人应是那些见识短浅的仆人，而非常伴曾子左右、受圣人言行熏陶的学生。

[3] "忠"的含义大体有两种：一种是"中心为忠"，就是替人做事要真心实意、忠诚无私，这也是"忠"字的本义。另一种是"尽己之谓忠"，就是说尽心做好自己本分的事情。理雅各选择用"sincerity"（真诚）翻译"忠"，取其第一义。而刘殿爵将之翻译为"everything possible is done for him"（尽心竭力地满足他），显然他取"忠"的"尽己之谓忠"之意。"忠"是武城人对曾子的态度，即尽心竭力地给他提供好的居住环境，因而从文义上看，刘殿爵的译文更准确。

[4] "为民望"，朱熹注曰："言使民望而效之。"理雅各将之翻译为"observed by the people"（为百姓所效仿），准确翻译出了原文的意思。刘殿爵的译文是"taken the lead"（领先，带头），也能体现"民望"的意思。

[5] "负刍之祸"，赵岐注曰："时有作乱者曰负刍，来攻沈犹氏。"他认为"负刍"为人名，刘殿爵亦持此观点，将之翻译为"I had trouble in my place with a man by the name of Fu Chʻu"（在我居住的地方和一个叫负刍的人发生矛盾）。若仅仅因和一个叫负刍的人发生冲突，曾子就带七十个学生离开则有小题大做之嫌，因而赵甄陶将之翻译为"a riot led by the trouble-maker Fuchu"，即"由负刍领导的暴乱"更贴切。朱熹则认为："曾子尝舍于沈

犹氏，时有负刍者作乱，来攻沈犹氏，曾子率其弟子去之。"朱熹以"负刍"为背草之人，受其影响，理雅各将之翻译为"the outbreak of the grass-carriers"。从曾子和七十个学生都在沈犹氏家可以推测沈犹氏家资不菲，有专门为之背草的仆人并与之发生冲突也不足为怪。

【原文】8.32　储子曰[1]："王使人瞯[2]夫子，果有以异于人乎？"孟子曰："何以异于人哉？尧舜与人同耳[3]。"

【译文】储子说："齐王派人暗中观察先生，看您真有和别人不同的地方吗？"孟子说："哪有什么和别人不同的地方呢？尧舜也和一般人一样呢。"

【英译】The officer Ch'û said to Mencius, 'Master, the king sent persons to spy out whether you were really different from other men.' Mencius said, 'How should I be different from other men? Yâo and Shun were just the same as other men.'

【注释】

[1] 孟子宣称"人皆可以为尧舜"，认为圣人和普通人在外貌和天性上没有多少区别，他们的差别仅在于是否能保有和发展人天生的仁、义、理、智"四端"。

[2] "瞯"，窥视，偷看，并非光明磊落的君子行为。齐王想知道孟子在自处时的言谈举止是否和普通人不一样，又恐派人直接去观察，既违背礼仪，又不能看到孟子的真实状况，因而只好派手下去偷窥孟子的行为。理雅各翻译为"spy out"（暗中监视），准确再现了"瞯"所蕴含的趁人不备、悄悄察看之意。

[3] "尧舜与人同耳"，是对孟子性善论的进一步阐发。孟子认为，尧舜和普通人一样，都有天生的仁、义、礼、智"四端"，每个人通过扩而充之，都可以成为尧舜那样的圣人，因而尧舜和普通人没有什么区别。理雅各准确翻译出了原文之意。

【原文】 8.33　齐人[1]有一妻一妾而处室者，其良人出，则必餍酒肉而后反。其妻问所与饮食者，则尽富贵也。其妻告其妾曰："良人出[2]，则必餍酒肉而后反；问其与饮食者，尽富贵也，而未尝有显者来，吾将瞷良人之所之也[3]。"蚤起，施从良人之所之[4]，遍国中无与立谈者。卒之东郭墦间，之祭者，乞其余；不足，又顾而之他——此其为餍足之道也。其妻归，告其妾，曰："良人者，所仰望而终身也，今若此！"与其妾讪其良人，而相泣于中庭，而良人未之知也，施施从外来，骄其妻妾。由君子观之，则人之所以求富贵利达者[5]，其妻妾不羞也，而不相泣者，几希矣。

【译文】 齐国有个人，家里有一妻一妾，丈夫每次外出，一定会酒足肉饱地回来。妻子问他和谁一起吃喝，他说全是有钱有势的人。妻子便告诉他的妾说："丈夫外出，总是酒足肉饱地来；问他和谁一起吃喝，他说全是有钱有势的人，但是，从来没有显贵人物来我们家，我准备偷偷地看丈夫究竟去什么地方。"清早起来，她便尾随丈夫行走，走遍城中，没有一个人站着和她丈夫谈话。最后走到东郊外的墓地，她的丈夫走到祭扫坟墓的人那里，讨些剩下的饭菜；不够，又到处看，跑到别处去乞讨，这便是他酒足饭饱的办法。妻子回到家里，告诉他的妾自己的所见，并且说："丈夫，是我们仰望且终身倚靠的人，现在竟然这样！"于是她和妾一起在庭中咒骂丈夫并相对哭泣。丈夫并不知道，得意扬扬地从外面回来，在妻妾面前显摆威风。在君子看来，人们乞求升官发财的手段，能不让妻妾感到羞耻而相对哭泣的，实在太少了。

【英译】 A man of Ch'î had a wife and a concubine, and lived together with them in his house. When their husband went out, he would get himself well filled with wine and flesh, and then return, and, on his wife's asking him with whom he ate and drank, they were sure to be all wealthy and honourable people. The wife informed the concubine, saying, 'When our good man goes out, he is sure to come back having partaken plentifully of wine and flesh. I asked with whom he ate and drank，and they are all，it seems，wealthy and honourable people. And yet no people of distinction ever come here. I will spy out where our good man goes.'Accordingly，she got up early in the morning，and privately followed wherever her husband went. Throughout the whole city，there was no one who stood or talked with him. At last，he came to those who were sacrificing among the tombs beyond the outer wall on the east，and begged what they had over. Not being satisfied，he looked about，and went to another party；—and this was the way in which he got himself satiated. His wife returned，and informed the concubine，saying，'It was to our husband that we looked up in hopeful contemplation，with whom our lot is cast for life；—and now these are his ways！'On this，along with the concubine she reviled their husband，and they wept together in the middle hall. In the meantime the husband，knowing nothing of all this，came in with a jaunty air，carrying himself proudly to his wife and concubine. In the view of a superior man，as to the ways by which men seek for riches，honours，gain，and advancement，there are few of their wives and concubines who would not be ashamed and weep together on account of them.

【注释】

[1] 孔子宣称"不义而富且贵，于我如浮云。"（《论语·述而》）孟子继承了孔子的这一思想。他通过列举齐人乞讨墦间以满足口食之欲的寓言，讽刺了那些不择手段谋取富贵的人，表达了自己对富贵的态度。他不反对人们追求富贵显达，自己也积极入世，希望能施展自己的政治理想，但他更强调求富贵必须建立在遵循道义的基础之上。

[2] "良人"，丈夫。理雅各将之翻译为"our good man"，不如刘殿爵

的"our husband"（丈夫）便于读者理解。

[3]"瞷"，窥视，偷看。刘殿爵将之译为"find out"（查明），不如理雅各的"spy out"（秘密监视）准确。

[4] 赵岐注曰："施者，邪施而行，不欲使良人觉也。"焦循进一步指出："施与迆通。《淮南子·要略》云：'接经直施。'注云：'施，邪也。'故赵氏以邪释施。"故此处"施"指偷偷摸摸、躲躲藏藏地跟在后面。刘殿爵将之翻译为"follow"（跟踪），不如理雅各的"privately followed"（偷偷跟踪）传神。

[5]"则人之所以求富贵利达者"，朱熹注曰："孟子言自君子而观，今之求富贵者，皆如此人耳，使其妻妾见之，不羞而泣者少矣，言可羞之甚也。赵氏曰：'言今之求富贵者，皆以枉曲之道，昏夜乞哀以求之，而以骄人于白日，与斯人何以异哉？'"理雅各和赖发洛认为"以求富贵利达者"的"者"是"人们求富贵利达的方法"，刘殿爵则认为是"求富贵利达的人"。

卷 九

万章章句上

【原文】9.1 万章问曰[1]："舜往于田，号泣[2]于旻天[3]，何为其号泣也？"孟子曰："怨慕也[4]。"万章曰："'父母爱之，喜而不忘；父母恶之，劳而不怨。'然则舜怨乎？"曰："长息问于公明高曰：'舜往于田，则吾既得闻命矣；号泣于旻天，于父母[5]，则吾不知也。'公明高曰：'是非尔所知也。'夫公明高以孝子之心，为不若是恝，我竭力耕田，共为子职而已矣，父母之不我爱，于我何哉[6]？帝使其子九男二女，百官[7]牛羊仓廪备，以事舜于畎亩之中，天下之士多就之者，帝将胥天下而迁之焉。为不顺于父母[8]，如穷人无所归。天下之士悦之，人之所欲也，而不足以解忧；好色，人之所欲，妻帝之二女，而不足以解忧；富，人之所欲，富有天下，而不足以解忧；贵，人之所欲，贵为天子，而不足以解忧。人悦之、好色、富贵，无足以解忧者，惟顺于父母可以解忧。人少，则慕父母；知好色，则慕少艾；有妻子，则慕妻子；仕则慕君，不得于君[9]则热中[10]。大孝终身慕父母。五十而慕者，予于大舜见之矣。"

【译文】万章问道："舜去耕田的时候，一边哭泣一边哀诉于天，为什么一边哭泣一边哀诉呢？"孟子说："因为自己被父母厌弃而感到悲伤并且思慕父母啊。"万章问："（曾子说过）'父母爱我，高兴却不敢懈息；父母厌恶我，辛苦劳作不敢抱怨。'那么，舜是抱怨父母吗?"孟子回答说："长息曾经问公明高说：'舜去耕田，我已经听您教诲了；但他向天哭诉父母，这是我不懂的。'公明高说：'这不是你所能懂得的。'公明高以为孝子的心不能这样地满不在乎：我竭尽全力耕田，只是好好地做儿子该做的事情，父母不喜爱我，我又有什么办法呢? 帝尧让他的九个儿子和两个女儿，以及百官，带着牛羊、粮食，到田野中去服侍舜；天下也有很多士人到舜那里去，尧还把整个天下让给了舜。舜却只因为没有得到父母的欢心，就像穷苦的人无家可归一样。天下的士人都喜爱他，是谁都愿意的，却不足以消除忧愁；美丽的女子，是谁都爱慕的，他娶了尧的两个女儿，却不足以消除忧愁；财富，是谁都希望获得的，他富有天下，却不足以消除忧愁；尊贵，是谁都希望获得的，他贵为天下的君主，却不足以消除忧愁。大家都喜爱他、美丽的姑娘、财富和尊贵都不足以消除他的忧愁，只有得着父母的欢心才可以消除忧愁。人在小的时候，就依恋父母；情窦初开时，便喜欢年轻漂亮的姑娘；有了妻子，便迷恋妻室；做了官，便想着讨好君主，得不着君主的欢心，内心就焦急难受。只有最孝顺的人才终身依恋父母。到了五十岁还依恋父母的，我在伟大的舜身上看到了。"

【英译】Wan Chang asked Mencius, saying, 'When Shun went into the fields, he cried out and wept towards the pitying heavens. Why did he cry out and weep?' Mencius replied, 'He was dissatisfied, and full of earnest desire.' Wan Chang said, 'When his parents love him, a son rejoices and forgets them not. When his parents hate him, though they punish him, he does not murmur. Was Shun then murmuring against his parents?' Mencius answered, 'Ch'ang Hsî asked Kung-ming Kâo, saying, "As to Shun's going into the fields, I have received your instructions, but I do not know about his weeping and crying out to the pitying heavens and to his parents." Kung-ming Kâo answered him, "You do not understand that matter." Now, Kung-ming Kâo supposed that the heart of the filial son could not be so free of sorrow. Shun would say, "I exert my strength to cultivate the fields, but I am thereby only discharging my office as a son. What can there be in me that my parents do not love me?" The Tî caused his own children, nine sons and two daughters, the various officers, oxen and sheep, storehouses and granaries, all to be prepared, to serve Shun amid the channelled fields. Of the scholars of the kingdom there were multitudes who flocked to him. The sovereign designed that Shun should superintend the kingdom along with him, and then to transfer it to him entirely. But because his parents were not in accord with him, he felt like a poor man who has nowhere to turn to. To be delighted in by all the scholars of the kingdom, is what men desire, but it was not sufficient to remove the sorrow of Shun. The possession of beauty is what men desire, and Shun had for his wives the two daughters of the Tî, but this was not sufficient to remove his sorrow. Riches are what men desire, and the kingdom was the rich property of Shun, but this was not sufficient to remove his sorrow. Honours are what men desire, and Shun had the dignity of being sovereign, but this was not sufficient to remove his sorrow. The reason why the being the object of men's delight, with the possession of beauty, riches, and honours were not sufficient to remove his sorrow, was that it could be removed only by his getting his parents to be in accord with him. The desire of the child is towards his father and mother. When he becomes conscious of the attractions of beauty, his desire is towards young and beautiful women. When he comes to have a wife and children, his desire is towards them. When he obtains office, his desire is towards his sovereign: —

if he cannot get the regard of his sovereign, he burns within. But the man of great filial piety, to the end of his life, has his desire towards his parents. In the great Shun I see the case of one whose desire at fifty year's was towards them.'

【注释】

[1] 在本章孟子和万章就"舜往于田，号泣于旻天"这件事进行了讨论，从而引出了孟子对"孝"的深层次认识。万章首先问"舜号泣于旻天"的原因，在得到孟子答复后，二人就这一做法是否符合孝子行为展开了探讨，从而引出孟子对"大孝"的认识："大孝终身慕父母"。

[2] "号泣"，焦循注曰："《颜氏家训·风操篇》云：'礼以哭，有言者为号。'此云号泣，则是且言且泣。"刘殿爵的"wept and wailed"（哭泣和哀诉）准确翻译出了"号泣"所体现的"且言且泣"的特征。

[3] "旻天"，本义指秋天。《说文》曰："旻，秋天也。"《尔雅·释天》："秋为旻天。"郭璞注："旻犹愍也，愍万物彫落。"刘熙《释名释天》云："秋曰旻天，旻，闵也。物就枯落，可闵伤也。"可见，"旻天"有愁、悲伤、怜悯之意。理雅各取"旻天"的怜悯之意，将之翻译为"pitying heavens"。刘殿爵则取朱熹的"仁覆愍下谓之旻天"的注解，将之译为"merciful Heaven"（仁慈的天）。

[4] "怨慕"，赵岐注曰："言舜自怨遭父母见恶之厄而思慕也。"怨，虽有怨恨、仇恨、哀怨、悲痛诸意，但在此处更突出悲痛之情，而非怨恨不满之意。大孝的舜不可能对父母怨恨，因而最确切的理解应是舜因为不能得到父母的欢心而悲痛、难受。理雅各将"怨"翻译为"dissatisfied"，刘殿爵翻译为"complaining"，即诉苦、抱怨，二者都不能翻译出悲伤的含义。赵甄陶的"aggrieved"则很好切合此处"怨"的内涵。

[5] "号泣于旻天，于父母"，陈器之指出："于，等列连词，与也。"刘殿爵亦认为二者是并列关系。但笔者认为，这句话应理解为"对着上天边哭边叫父母啊，父母！"即认为"于父母"是"号泣于旻天"的补语，是

号泣的内容。赵甄陶在翻译时亦认为"于父母"是"号泣"的内容，将之翻译为"Shun should have wept and wailed to Heaven，grieving over his parents' dislike of him"。孟子在本章开篇交代了舜号泣的时间和地点，即在秋天去田地耕种的路上。在万物凋零、瑟瑟秋风中去耕作的舜，对自己不能获得父母的喜爱而悲伤不已，忍不住边哭边叫父母啊，父母。从文义上看，这样理解逻辑性更强。

[6]"与我何哉"，赵岐注云："与我之身，独有何罪哉。自求责于己而悲感焉。"理雅各受其影响，将之翻译为"What can there be in me that my parents do not love me?"（我身上到底有什么缺陷，令父母不喜欢）显然，他的译文是从正面论证大舜在乎父母是否喜爱自己，试图从自身寻找不被喜爱的根源。赵甄陶将之翻译为"that he need not worry whether his parents love him or dislike him"（不用担心父母是喜爱还是厌恶）。他的译文则是进一步解释前文的"为不若是恝"。

[7]"百官"，刘殿爵将之翻译为"the hundred officials"（各种官员）。杨伯峻指出："或云，与《论语·子张篇》'百官之富'的'百官'意义同，指宫室而不是官吏。'官'的本意指宫室屋宇。"

[8]"顺"，赵岐注："爱也。"赵甄陶亦取"爱"之意，将"不顺于父母"翻译为"win his parents' love"。杨伯峻提到另外一种理解："日本竹添进一郎《左传会笺》释襄公八年'唯子产不顺'云'顺亦悦也，孟子不顺于父母即不悦于父母也。'"刘殿爵的译文持此种观点，将之翻译为"please his parents"（使父母开心）。

[9]"不得与君"，朱熹和赵岐都认为是"失意于君"。理雅各的译文与之相类，翻译为"if he cannot get the regard of his sovereign"（得不到君主的认可）。刘殿爵则将之翻译为"if he is without one"（没有君主可以侍奉）。

[10]"热中"，朱熹注曰："躁急心热也。"理雅各将之翻译为"burn within"，形象生动地翻译出因得不到君主喜爱，内心所受到的煎熬。刘殿爵将"热中"意译为"restless"（烦躁不安），虽能体现原文的含义，但不如理

'The Tî also knew that if he informed them, he could not marry his daughters to him.' Wan Chang said, 'His parents set Shun to repair a granary, to which, the ladder having been removed, Kû-sâu set fire. They also made him dig a well. He got out, but they, not knowing that, proceeded to cover him up. Hsiang said, "Of the scheme to cover up the city-forming prince, the merit is all mine. Let my parents have his oxen and sheep. Let them have his storehouses and granaries. His shield and spear shall be mine. His lute shall be mine. His bow shall be mine. His two wives I shall make attend for me to my bed." Hsiang then went away into Shun's palace, and there was Shun on his couch playing on his lute. Hsiang said, "I am come simply because I was thinking anxiously about you." At the same time, he blushed deeply. Shun said to him, "There are all my officers:—do you undertake the government of them for me." I do not know whether Shun was ignorant of Hsiang's wishing to kill him.' Mencius answered, 'How could he be ignorant of that? But when Hsiang was sorrowful, he was also sorrowful; when Hsiang was joyful, he was also joyful.' Chang said, 'In that case, then, did not Shun rejoice hypocritically?' Mencius replied, 'No. Formerly, some one sent a present of a live fish to Tsze-ch'an of Chăng. Tsze-ch'an ordered his pond-keeper to keep it in the pond, but that officer cooked it, and reported the execution of his commission, saying, "When I first let it go, it embarrassed. In a little while, it seemed to be somewhat at ease, and then it swam away joyfully." Tsze-ch'an observed, "It had got into its element! It had got into its element!" The pond-keeper then went out and said, "Who calls Tsze-ch'an a wise man? After I had cooked and eaten the fish, he says, "It had got into its element! It had got into its element!" Thus a superior man may be imposed on by what seems to be as it ought to be，but he cannot be entrapped by what is contrary to right principle. Hsiang came in the way in which the love of his elder brother would have made him come；therefore Shun sincerely believed him，and rejoiced. What hypocrisy was there?'

【注释】

[1] 虽屡遭父母兄弟谋害，舜仍然以宽厚、仁慈的态度孝顺父母、友爱兄弟。万章难以理解，因而孟子举子产的例子作佐证，进一步论证了他的"君子可欺以其方，难罔以非其道"的著名观点。

[2] 赵甄陶将"信斯言也，宜莫如舜"翻译为"Shun should have been the first man to follow this instruction."即"舜应该是第一个遵循这一原则的人"。但实际上舜是"不告而娶"。如此理解这句话似乎存在逻辑上的矛盾。刘殿爵提出了一种创新性理解。他译为"If that were truly so, it would seem that Shun's example was not to be followed."（如果这句话是对的，似乎不应该学习大舜了）从逻辑上看，大舜"不告而娶"似乎和"必告父母"相矛盾。

[3] 赵岐注云："使舜浚井，舜入而即出，瞽瞍不知其已出，从而盖揜其井。"赵岐以"出"为舜出，"揜"为瞽瞍等掩。理雅各就持此说。另一说，以刘殿爵为代表，将之翻译为"set out after him and blocked up the well over him"（他们从舜后面出来，并把舜所在的井口堵上）。从上下文看，"出"当是瞽瞍等出，与下文"从而掩之"的"从而"相呼应，确保了主语的前后一致性，因而刘殿爵的翻译更确切。

[4] "谟盖都君咸我绩"，赵岐注曰："盖，覆也。"朱熹也认为，"盖，盖井也。"即策划用土盖井来杀害都君全是我的功劳。理雅各的译本亦持这种观点。还有一种观点认为，盖为"害"之假借字，焦循引阮元《释盖》曰："孟子'谟盖都君'，此兼井廪言之，盖亦当训为'害'也。若专以谟盖为盖井而不兼焚廪，则'咸我绩''咸'字无所著矣。"即认为所有谋害舜

的计划全是他做出的。刘殿爵就支持这一观点，将之翻译为"The credit for plotting against the life of Shun goes to me"（策划谋害舜的生命全是我一个人的功劳）。这两种理解都可以接受，但相比之下，刘殿爵的译文可以更好呼应上下文。

[5]"惟兹臣庶"，《尔雅·释诂》云："兹，此也。惟，思也。庶，众也。"即我想念这些臣下和百姓。理雅各的译文没有翻译出"惟"所体现的思念之意，只把"臣庶"翻译为"officers"（官员），缩小了原文的内涵。刘殿爵的译文"I am thinking of my subjects"准确翻译出了其含义。

[6]"校人"，赵岐注曰："主池沼小吏也"。理雅各选择用"pond-keeper"翻译，基本能体现其含义。刘殿爵的"fish-keeper"则有缩小其含义之嫌。

[7]朱熹注曰："欺以其方，谓诳之以理之所有，罔以非其道，谓昧之以理之所无。"他以"方""道"同义，并以"理"释之。刘殿爵受朱熹注解的影响，并根据自己的理解做了些许变通，将之翻译为"That only goes to show that a gentleman can be taken in by what is reasonable, but cannot be easily hoodwinked by the wrong method."（君子可以被合情合理的理由欺骗，但不容易被错误的方法蒙蔽）他的译文围绕朱熹的注解展开，符合孟子的本意。

【原文】9.3　万章问曰[1]："象日以杀舜为事，立为天子则放之，何也？"孟子曰："封之也；或曰放焉。"万章曰："舜流共工于幽州，放驩兜于崇山，杀[2]三苗[3]于三危，殛鲧于羽山[4]，四罪而天下咸服，诛不仁也。象至不仁，封之有庳。有庳之人奚罪焉？仁人固如是乎？在他人则诛之，在弟则封之。"曰："仁人之于弟也，不藏怒焉，不宿怨焉，亲爱之而已矣。亲之，欲其贵也；爱之，欲其富也。封之有庳，富贵之也。身为天子，弟为匹夫，可谓亲爱之乎？""敢问或曰放者，何谓也？"曰："象不得有为于其国，天子使吏治其国而纳其贡税焉，故谓之放。岂得暴彼民哉？虽然，欲常常

卷　九　363

而见之，故源源而来，'不及贡，以政接于有庳[5]。' 此之谓也。"

【译文】万章问："象每天把谋杀舜作为工作，等舜做了天子就流放了他，为什么呢？"孟子说："其实是封象为诸侯，有人说是流放罢了。"万章说："舜流放共工到幽州，把驩兜流放到崇山，把三苗的君主安置到三危，把鲧流放到羽山，惩处了这四个大罪犯，天下都归服了，因为他讨伐的是不仁的人。象是最不仁的人，却把他封到有庳。有庳的百姓有什么罪过啊？仁人难道就是这样做的吗？对别人就加以惩处，对弟弟，就封以国土。"孟子说："仁人对于弟弟，不把怒气藏在心中，不把怨恨留在心底，只是亲他、爱护他罢了。亲近他，就想要让他显贵；爱他，就想要他富有。把他封到有庳是使他富且贵啊。自己是天子，弟弟却是普通百姓，能说是亲近他、爱护他吗？"万章说："请问，为什么有人说是流放呢？"孟子说："象不能在他封国上为所欲为，天子派遣了官吏来治理国家，收取那里的贡税，所以说是流放。象怎么能够暴虐他的百姓呢？纵是如此，舜还是想常常看到象，所以象也不断地来和舜相见。这就是所谓的'不必等到朝贡的日子，平常也假借政事需要来接见有庳的国君'。"

【英译】Wan Chang said, 'Hsiang made it his daily business to slay Shun. When Shun was made sovereign, how was it that he only banished him?' Mencius said, 'He raised him to be a prince. Some supposed that it was banishing him?' Wan Chang said, 'Shun banished the superintendent of works to Yû-Châu; he sent away Hwan-tâu to the mountain Ch'ung; he slew the prince of San-miâo in San-wei; and he imprisoned K'wǎn on the mountain Yü. When the crimes of those four were thus punished, the whole kingdom acquiesced: —it was a cutting off of men who were destitute of benevolence. But Hsiang was of all men the most destitute of benevolence, and Shun raised him to be the prince of Yû-pî; —of what crimes had the people of Yû-pî been guilty? Does a benevolent man really act thus? In the case of other men, he cut them off; in the case of his brother, he raised him to be a prince.' Mencius replied, 'A benevolent man does not lay up anger, nor cherish resentment against his brother, but only regards him with affection and love. Regarding him with affection, he wishes him to be honourable: regarding him with love, he wishes him to be rich. The appointment of Hsiang to be the prince of Yû-pî was to enrich and ennoble him. If while Shun himself was sovereign, his brother had been a common man, could he have been said to regard him with affection and love?' Wan Chang said, 'I venture to ask what you mean by saying that some supposed that it was a banishing of Hsiang?' Mencius replied, 'Hsiang could do nothing in his State. The Son of Heaven appointed an officer to administer its government, and to pay over its revenues to him. This treatment of him led to its being said that he was banished. How indeed could he be allowed the means of oppressing the people? Nevertheless, Shun wished to be continually seeing him, and by this arrangement, he came incessantly to court, as is signified in that expression— "He did not wait for the rendering of tribute, or affairs of government, to receive the prince of Yû-pî."'

【注释】

[1] 舜对象的态度是儒家提倡的爱有差等思想在政治生活中的体现。对于共工、驩兜、三苗君主和鲧这些不仁之人，舜将其流放、驱逐，但对于"日以杀舜为事"的兄弟象，却富之贵之。

[2] "杀"，理雅各按字面意思翻译为"slew"（杀害），赵甄陶亦持此种观点，将之翻译为"killed"，但刘殿爵将之翻译为"banished"（流放）。陈器之指出："'杀'在《尚书·尧典》作'窜'，窜是驱逐的意思，故与'流''放'同义。"焦循亦认为："谓放之令自匿"。

[3]"三苗"，古国名。刘殿爵选择将之音译，但是将它和共工、驩兜和鲧这些人名连用，容易让读者误认为"三苗"是人而非国，因而理雅各做适当添加，将之翻译为"the prince of San-miâo"（三苗的君主）。

[4]"殛"有两种含义。一说是流放，理雅各持此观点，将之翻译为"imprisoned"（囚禁）；一说是诛杀，刘殿爵的译文持此观点。从句型上看，"流共工于幽州，放驩兜于崇山，杀三苗于三危，殛鲧于羽山"是由四个结构相似、意义相近的短句构成的排比句，"流""放""杀"和"殛"的含义应相同或相近，故取"殛"的"流放"之意更佳。

[5]"不及贡，以政接于有庳"疑是《尚书》逸文。朱熹注曰："谓不待及诸侯朝贡之期，而以政事接见有庳之君。"赵甄陶的译文与之相类，将之翻译为"When it was not time to pay tributes, the ruler of Youbi was often recalled to discuss state affairs."他的译文为我们展现了一个精通中庸之道，懂得权变的大舜形象。舜虽然希望能经常见到兄弟象，但又不能没有正当理由，随意召见封臣，因而以讨论政事为由屡屡召见有庳国君。这也可以很好地呼应前文的"源源而来"。刘殿爵的译文是"When it was time for tribute, Yu Pi was received on account of affairs of state."（在朝贡的时候，凭政事的名义接见有庳的国君）"不及贡"的意思是还未等到朝贡的时候，非在朝贡之时。理雅各将之翻译为"He did not wait for the rendering of tribute, or affairs of government, to receive the prince of Yû-pî."（不等到朝贡的日期和有政事时，才接见有庳的国君）他的译文表明，舜不顾礼制，不需要任何正当理由，随心所欲地接见有庳国君。这与儒家推崇的圣王形象不甚符合。

【原文】9.4 咸丘蒙问曰[1]："语云，'盛德之士，君不得而臣，父不得而子。'舜南面而立，尧帅诸侯北面而朝之，瞽瞍亦北面而朝之。舜见瞽瞍，其容有蹙。孔子曰：'于斯时也，天下殆哉，岌岌乎！'不识此语诚然乎哉？"孟子曰："否；此非君子之言，齐东野人[2]之语也。尧老而舜摄也。尧典曰：'二十有八载，放勋乃徂

落，百姓[3]如丧考妣，三年，四海遏密八音。'孔子曰：'天无二
日，民无二王。'舜既为天子矣，又帅天下诸侯以为尧三年丧，是
二天子矣。"咸丘蒙曰："舜之不臣尧，则吾既得闻命矣。《诗》云：
'普天之下，莫非王土；率土之滨，莫非王臣。'而舜既为天子矣，
敢问瞽瞍之非臣[4]，如何？"曰："是诗也，非是之谓也；劳于王事
而不得养父母也。曰：'此莫非王事，我独贤[5]劳也。'故说诗者，
不以文害辞，不以辞害志[6]。以意逆志，是为得之[7]。如以辞而已
矣，《云汉》之诗曰：'周余黎民，靡有孑遗。'信斯言也，是周无
遗民也。孝子之至，莫大乎尊亲；尊亲之至，莫大乎以天下养。为
天子父，尊之至也；以天下养，养之至也。《诗》曰：'永言孝思，
孝思维则。'此之谓也。《书》曰：'祇载见瞽瞍，夔夔斋栗，瞽瞍
亦允若。'是为父不得而子也。"

【译文】咸丘蒙问："古话说：'道德最高的人，君主不能够把他
当作臣，父亲不能够把他当作儿子。'舜做了天子，面南而立，尧便率
领诸侯向北朝见他，瞽瞍也面北朝见他。舜看见了瞽瞍，神色局促不
安。孔子说：'在这个时候，天下真是岌岌可危呀！'不知道这话真是如
此吗？"孟子回答说："不，这不是君子的话，而是齐国东面的乡野之人
的话。尧老年时，叫舜代理天子之职。《尧典》上说：'二十八年后，尧
死了，群臣好像死了父母一样，服丧三年，民间也停止一切音乐。孔子
说：'天上没有两个太阳，百姓没有两个天子。'假若舜已经做了天子，
又率领天下的诸侯为尧服丧三年，这便是有两个天子了。"咸丘蒙说：
"舜不以尧为臣，我已经接受您的教诲了。《诗经》上说：'天下没有不
是天子的土地；王土的四周，没有一人不是天子的臣民。'舜既然做了
天子，请问瞽瞍却不是臣民，为什么呢？"孟子说："这首诗，不是你所
说的那个意思，而是作者为国事辛劳不能够奉养父母。他说：'这些没
有一件不是天子之事呀，为什么只有我一人劳苦呢？'所以解说诗的人，
不要拘于文字而误解词句，也不要拘于词句而误解原意。读者用自己的

理解去推测作者的本意，这就对了。如果拘泥于词句，那《云汉》这首诗说：'周朝剩下的百姓，没有一个存留。'相信了这句话，是周朝没有留下一个人了。孝子最大的孝，没有比尊敬双亲更大的；尊敬双亲的最高境界，没有比拿天下奉养父母更大的。做了天子的父亲，是尊贵到了极点；以天下来奉养，是奉养的顶点。《诗经》上说：'永远地讲究孝道，孝道便是天下的法则。'就是这个意思。《书经》上说：'舜恭敬地来见瞽瞍，态度谨慎小心，瞽瞍也因之受到感化。'这难道是'父亲不能够以他为子'吗？"

【英译】Hsien-ch'iǔ Mǎng asked Mencius, saying, 'There is the saying, "A scholar of complete virtue may not be employed as a minister by his sovereign, nor treated as a son by his father. Shun stood with his face to the south, and Yâo, at the head of all the princes, appeared before him at court with his face to the north. Kû-sâu also did the same. When Shun saw Kû-sâu, his countenance became discomposed. Confucius said, At this time, in what a perilous condition was the kingdom! Its state was indeed unsettled." — I do not know whether what is here said really took place.' Mencius replied, 'No. These are not the words of a superior man. They are the sayings of an uncultivated person of the east of Ch'î. When Yâo was old, Shun was associated with him in the government. It is said in the Canon of Yâo, "After twenty and eight years, the Highly Meritorious one deceased. The people acted as if they were mourning for a father or mother for three years, and up to the borders of the four seas every sound of music was hushed." Confucius said, "There are not two suns in the sky, nor two sovereigns over the people." Shun having been sovereign, and, moreover, leading on all the princes to observe the three years' mourning for Yâo, there would have been in this case two sovereigns.' Hsien-ch'iŭ Măng said, 'On the point of Shun's not treating Yâo as a minister, I have received your instructions. But it is said in the Book of Poetry, "Under the whole heaven, every spot is the sovereign's ground; to the borders of the land, every individual is the sovereign's minister;" —and Shun had become sovereign. I venture to ask how it was that Kû-sâu was not one of his ministers.' Mencius answered, 'That ode is not to be understood in that way: — it speaks of being laboriously engaged in the sovereign's business, so as not to be able to nourish one's parents, as if the author said, "This is all the sovereign's business, and how is it that I alone am supposed to have ability, and am made to toil in it?" Therefore, those who explain the odes, may not insist on one term so as to do violence to a sentence, nor on a sentence so as to do violence to the general scope. They must try with their thoughts to meet that scope, and then we shall apprehend it. If we simply take single sentences, there is that in the ode called "The Milky Way," — "Of the black-haired people of the remnant of Châu, there is not half a one left." If it had been really as thus expressed, then not an individual of the people of Châu was left. Of all which a filial son can attain to, there is nothing greater than his honouring his parents. And of what can be attained to in the honouring one's parents, there is nothing greater than the nourishing them with the whole kingdom. Kû-sâu was the father of the sovereign; —this was the height of honour. Shun nourished him with the whole kingdom; — this was the height of nourishing. In this was verified the sentiment in the Book of Poetry, "Ever cherishing filial thoughts, those filial thoughts became an example to after ages." It is said in the Book of History, "Reverently performing his duties, he waited on Kû-sâu, and was full of veneration and awe. Kû-sâu also believed him and conformed to virtue."—This is the true case of the scholar of complete virtue not being treated as a son by his father.'

【注释】

[1] 在本章中，孟子和学生就如何理解诗词的内容展开讨论。孟子针对弟子在解诗中存在的误区，提出了"不以文害辞，不以辞害志。以意逆志，是为得之"的解诗法则。这一文学批评方法受到学者的普遍关注和广泛研究。理雅各在翻译儒家经典时就把孟子的这句名言作为解经的不二法门，印在了《中国经典》各卷扉页上。

[2] "齐东野人"，宋代以来，学者多将之解释为"齐国东边的野蛮人"。朱熹注曰："齐国之东鄙也。"理雅各亦持此种观点说，将之翻译为"an uncultivated person of the east of Ch'î"（齐国东边的野蛮人）。刘殿爵虽也认为，"齐东"为齐国之东，但认为"野人"是"乡下人"。由《说文》："野，郊外也。"可知，此种理解亦可。赵甄陶亦持此种观点。赵岐则给出另外一种理解："'平秩东作'，谓治农事也。"焦循则指出："赵氏以东为东作治农事，故引《书》《尧典》以证之，非东为东方之东也。"显然，他认为"齐东野人"是齐国从事耕作的农民或居住在郊野之人。

[3] "百姓"有百官和普通人两种含义。理雅各和刘殿爵取后者，将之译为"The people"，即"普通人"。但由赵甄陶主译的大中华文库版《孟子》却把之翻译为"All officials"（百官）。阎若璩在《四书释地又续》中指出："'百姓'义二，有指'百官'言者，书'百姓'与'黎民'对，礼大传'百姓'与'庶民'对是也。有指小民言者，'百姓不亲，五品不逊'是也。四书中'百姓'凡二十五见，惟'百姓如丧考妣'指'百官'，盖有爵士者为天子服斩衰三年，礼也。"阎若璩从词义和礼仪两个方面论证此处的"百姓"应为"百官"。

[4] 此处的"臣"是国君所统属的"臣民、百姓"，而非一般意义上的"官吏"。理雅各按字面意思将之翻译为"minister"（大臣）不准确。刘

殿爵的"subject"（臣民）准确体现了"臣"的含义。除了"臣"的区别之外，理雅各都将此句翻译为"Shun had become sovereign. I venture to ask how it was that Kû-sâu was not one of his ministers"（舜已经成了天子，瞽瞍怎么会不是臣（民）呢？）刘殿爵在翻译此句时，进行了创新。他认为，本句是"非X而何"句型，意谓"如果不是X它会是什么呢？"因而他将此句译为"Now after Shun became Emperor, if the Blind Man was not his subject，what was he?"（现在舜既然做了天子，如果瞽瞍不是臣民，他会是什么呢）

[5]"贤"并非指"才能"，而是指辛劳。杨伯峻引《毛传》云："贤，劳也。"宋翔凤《孟子赵注补正》云："《小尔雅》，'贤，多也。'《诗》，'大夫不均，我从事独贤'，'独贤'犹言'独多。'《孟子》说诗为'贤劳'，正是'多劳'之义。"刘殿爵的译文体现了"多劳"之意。理雅各在理解时，把"贤"翻译为"have ability"（多才能），而此处"贤劳"连用，旨在强调"劳"，与前文"劳于王事而不得养父母"相呼应。

[6]朱熹注曰："文，字也。辞，语也。""志"是作者在作品中表达出来的思想感情。如《尚书·尧典》记载："诗言志，歌永言。"郑玄注云："诗所以言人之志意也。"《毛诗序》的解释是："诗者，志之所之也，在心为志，发言为诗。"刘殿爵的译文强调不能让字词混淆句意，也不能让句子混淆已有之意。他将文、辞和志的关系准确体现了出来。

[7]古今注家对"意"和"逆"的理解不同。对"意"的理解大体有两种。一种认为"意"为作者之意。清代吴淇在《六朝诗选定论缘起》云："志古人之志，而意古人之意，故选诗中每每以古意命题是也？不知志者古人之心事，以意为与，载志而游，或有方，或无方，意之所到，即志之所在，故以古人之意求古人之志，乃就诗论诗，尤之以人治人也。"一种认为"意"指"读者之意"。朱熹指出："当以己意迎取作者之志，乃可得之。"刘殿爵、赵甄陶、理雅各等译者和古今注家多持此种观点。"逆"，朱熹理解是"迎也"。理雅各的理解同朱熹，将"以意逆志"翻译为"They must try with their thoughts to meet that scope"（他们必须试着让自己的想法迎合原意）。译

文看到了充分尊重作者创作意图的重要性，但是把读者置于被动接受原意的境地。《周礼》郑玄注云："逆，犹钩考也。"和"迎"强调被动地去迎接作者意图不同，"钩考"则强调读者的主动性，认为读者可以根据自己的经验和知识去主动感知、推测作者的意图。结合孟子后来举的几种关于诗歌内容的理解看，他更强调读者的主体性，因而后者更准确。刘殿爵将本句翻译为"meet the intention of the poet with sympathetic understanding"（通过心理同构的理解方式实现与作者意图的融合）。他的译文既强调对作者创作意图的尊重，又体现了读者的主动。

【原文】9.5　万章曰[1]："尧以天下与舜，有诸？"孟子曰："否；天子不能以天下与人。""然则舜有天下也，孰与之？"曰："天与之。""天与之者，谆谆然命之乎？"曰："否；天不言，以行与事示之而已矣[2]。"曰："以行与事示之者，如之何？"曰："天子能荐人于天，不能使天与之天下；诸侯能荐人于天子，不能使天子与之诸侯；大夫能荐人于诸侯，不能使诸侯与之大夫。昔者，尧荐舜于天，而天受之；暴之于民[3]而民受之；故曰，天不言，以行与事示之而已矣。"曰："敢问荐之于天，而天受之；暴之于民，而民受之，如何？"曰："使之主祭，而百神[4]享之，是天受之；使之主事，而事治，百姓安之，是民受之也。天与之，人与之，故曰，天子不能以天下与人。舜相尧二十有八载，非人之所能为也，天也。尧崩，三年之丧毕，舜避尧之子于南河之南，天下诸侯朝觐者，不之尧之子而之舜；讼狱者，不之尧之子而之舜；讴歌者[5]，不讴歌尧之子而讴歌舜[6]，故曰，天也。夫然后之中国，践天子位焉。而居尧之宫，逼尧之子，是篡也，非天与也。《泰誓》曰：'天视自我民视，天听自我民听。'此之谓也。"

【译文】万章问道："尧把天下授予舜，有这么回事吗？"孟子说："不。天子不能够把天下授予他人。"万章又问："那么，舜得到了天下，是谁给他的呢?"孟子答道:"是天授予他的。"又问道:"天授予,是反复告诫他的吗?"答道:"不是,天不说话,用行动和事情来表示罢了。"问道:"用行动和事情来表示,是怎样的呢?"答道:"天子能向天推荐人,却不能强迫天把天下授予他;诸侯能够向天子推荐人,却不能强迫天子把诸侯的职位授予他;大夫能够向诸侯推荐人,却不能强迫诸侯把大夫的职位给予他。从前,尧将舜推荐给天,天接受了;又把舜公开介绍给百姓,百姓也接受了。所以说,天不说话,拿行动和事情来表示罢了。"万章说:"请问推荐给天,天接受了;介绍给百姓,百姓也接受了,是怎样的呢?"孟子答道:"让他主持祭祀,所有神明都来享用,这就是天接受了他;叫他处理政事,政事治理得很好,百姓很满意他,这便是百姓接受了他。天授予他,百姓授予他,所以说,天子不能把天下授予他人。舜协助尧治理天下二十八年,这不是人的意志所能做到的,而是天意。尧死了,三年之丧完毕,舜为了使尧的儿子能够继承天下,自己便逃避到南河的南边去。可是,天下诸侯朝见天子时,不到尧的儿子那里,却到舜那里;诉讼的人,不到尧的儿子那里,却到舜那里;歌颂的人,不歌颂尧的儿子,却歌颂舜,所以说,这是天意。这样,舜才回到国都,做了天子。如果居住在尧的宫室,逼迫尧的儿子,这是篡夺,而不是天授予了。《泰誓》说:'上天看见的,来自百姓的眼睛;上天听到的,来自百姓的耳朵。'说的就是这个。"

【英译】Wan Chang said,'Was it the case that Yâo gave the throne to Shun?' Mencius said,'No. The sovereign cannot give the throne to another.''Yes;—but Shun had the throne. Who gave it to him?' 'Heaven gave it to him,' was the answer. '"Heaven gave it to him:"—did Heaven confer its appointment on him with specific injunctions?' Mencius replied,'No. Heaven does not speak. It simply showed its will by his personal conduct and his conduct of affairs.''"It showed its will by his personal conduct and his conduct of affairs:"—

how was this?' Mencius's answer was, 'The sovereign can present a man to Heaven, but he cannot make Heaven give that man the throne. A prince can present a man to the sovereign, but he cannot cause the sovereign to make that man a prince. A great officer can present a man to his prince, but he cannot cause the prince to make that man a great officer. Yâo presented Shun to Heaven, and Heaven accepted him. He presented him to the people, and the people accepted him. Therefore I say, "Heaven does not speak. It simply indicated its will by his personal conduct and his conduct of affairs."' Chang said, 'I presume to ask how it was that Yâo presented Shun to Heaven, and Heaven accepted him; and that he exhibited him to the people, and the people accepted him.' Mencius replied, 'He caused him to preside over the sacrifices, and all the spirits were well pleased with them; —thus Heaven accepted him. He caused him to preside over the conduct of affairs, and affairs were well administered, so that the people reposed under him; thus the people accepted him. Heaven gave the throne to him. The people gave it to him. Therefore I said, "The sovereign cannot give the throne to another." Shun assisted Yâo in the government for twenty and eight years; —this was more than man could have done, and was from Heaven. After the death of Yâo, when the three years' mourning was completed, Shun withdrew from the son of Yâo to the south of South river. The princes of the kingdom, however, repairing to court, went not to the son of Yâo, but they went to Shun. Litigants went not to the son of Yâo, but they went to Shun. Singers sang not the son of Yâo, but they sang Shun. Therefore I said, "Heaven gave him the throne." It was after these things that he went to the Middle Kingdom, and occupied the seat of the Son of Heaven. If he had, before these things, taken up his residence in the palace of Yâo, and had applied pressure to the son of Yâo, it would have been an act of usurpation, and not the gift of Heaven. This sentiment is expressed in the words of The Great Declaration, — "Heaven sees according as my people see; Heaven hears according as my people hear."'

【注释】

[1] 孟子是第一个全面系统地论述儒家"天人合一"思想的人，其中"天不言，以行与事示之而已矣"是重要表现。孟子认为，天通过民意来表达自己的意愿，因而"天与之"具体表现为"人与之"，民心就代表了天意，于是就达到了天与人的统一，实现了"天人合一"。这一天人关系体现在政治上就是以民为本，民贵君轻的仁政。

[2] 儒家的"天"有"自然之天""义理之天"和"主宰之天"等含义。在"天不言，以行与事示之而已矣"中，"天"取"主宰之天"的含义，但是这一具有超越性的天却不能言，而是内在于人，通过人的行事来表达，这就是所谓的"以行与事示之"。理雅各和赖发洛认为"行与事"的执行者是"天"，将之翻译为"his"，译文突出了"天"具有主宰性的特征。刘殿爵没有突出强调此处"天"的主宰性特征，用"its"作行与事的主语。但应看到，本章说"天"旨在强调人的重要性，因为"天视自我民视，天听自我民听"，故"行与事"的主语应是"men"（人）。

[3] "暴之于民"，朱熹注曰："暴，显也。"刘殿爵选择用"present"（介绍、引见、呈现）翻译，既能对应"暴"的词义，也符合原文之意。

[4] 古代中国是多神崇拜，"百神"是诸神的统称。理雅各将之翻译为"all the spirits"，而刘殿爵则翻译为"the hundred gods"。"spirits"有鬼神的含义，扩大了"百神"的内涵，相比较而言"gods"更贴切。

[5] 我国古代有编唱民谣讥讽或赞颂统治者、身居高位者的悠久传统。此处的"讴歌者"就是以民谣的形式歌颂大舜功绩的人。理雅各将之翻译为"Singers"（歌唱者）过于宽泛，不如刘殿爵的"ballad singers"（唱民谣者）

确切。

[6]"讴歌舜",理雅各将之翻译为"sang Shun","sang"既有歌颂舜的含义，也可以理解为唱与舜相关的歌，这样翻译容易引起读者的误解。因而刘殿爵的"sang the praises of Shun"（歌颂舜）更准确清楚地表达了原文的意思。

【原文】9.6　万章问曰[1]："人有言：'至于禹而德衰，不传于贤，而传于子。'有诸?"孟子曰："否，不然也；天与贤，则与贤；天与子，则与子。昔者，舜荐禹于天，十有七年，舜崩，三年之丧毕，禹避舜之子于阳城，天下之民从之，若尧崩之后不从尧之子而从舜也。禹荐益于天，七年，禹崩，三年之丧毕，益避禹之子于箕山之阴[2]。朝觐讼狱者不之益而之启，曰：'吾君之子也。'讴歌者不讴歌益而讴歌启，曰：'吾君之子也。'丹朱之不肖[3]，舜之子亦不肖。舜之相尧、禹之相舜也，历年多，施泽于民久[4]。启贤，能敬承继禹之道。益之相禹也，历年少，施泽于民未久。舜、禹、益相去久远，其子之贤不肖，皆天也，非人之所能为也。莫之为而为者，天也；莫之致而至者，命[5]也。匹夫而有天下者，德必若舜禹，而又有天子荐之者，故仲尼不有天下。继世以有天下，天之所废，必若桀纣者也，故益、伊尹、周公不有天下。伊尹相汤以王于天下，汤崩，太丁未立，外丙二年，仲壬四年，太甲颠覆汤之典刑，伊尹放之于桐，三年，太甲悔过，自怨自艾[6]，于桐处仁迁义[7]，三年，以听伊尹之训己也，复归于亳。周公之不有天下，犹益之于夏、伊尹之于殷也。孔子曰：'唐虞禅，夏后殷周继，其义一也。'"

【译文】万章问道："有人说：'到大禹的时候道德就衰微了，天下不传给贤者却传给自己的儿子。'是这样吗?"孟子说："不，不是这样的。天要授予圣贤的人，就授予圣贤的人；天要授予君主的儿子，便授予君主的儿子。从前，舜把禹推荐给天，十七年之后，舜死了，三年之丧完毕，禹为了让舜的儿子成为天子，自己便躲避到阳城去。天下的百姓追随禹，正好像尧死了以后不跟随尧的儿子却跟随舜一样。禹把益推荐给天，七年之后，禹死了，三年之丧完毕，益又为了让禹的儿子成为天子，自己便躲避到箕山之北去。朝见天子的人和诉讼的人，都不去益那里，而去启那里，他们说：'他是我们君主的儿子呀'。歌颂的人也不歌颂益，而是歌颂启，说道：'他是我们君主的儿子呀。'尧的儿子丹朱不贤，舜的儿子也不贤。而且，舜辅佐尧，禹辅佐舜，经过的年岁多，施与百姓恩泽的时间长。启很贤明，能够恭敬地继承禹的传统。益辅佐禹，经过的年岁少，施与百姓恩泽的时间短。舜、禹、益之间相距时间的长短，以及他们儿子的贤能与否，都是天意，不是人力所能做到的。没有人叫他们这样做，而竟这样做了的，便是天意；没有人叫他来，而竟这样来了的，便是命运。以一个老百姓能得到天下的，他的道德必然要像舜和禹一样，并且还要有天子推荐他，所以孔子没能拥有天下。世代相传而得到天下的，天若要废弃，一定有像夏桀、商纣那样的君主，所以益、伊尹、周公就没能拥有天下。伊尹辅助汤统一了天下，汤死了，太丁未立就死了，外丙在位二年，仲壬在位四年，太甲破坏了汤的典章制度，伊尹流放他到桐邑。三年之后，太甲悔过，自我怨恨，自我悔改，在桐邑，以仁居心，唯义是从，三年之后，听从伊尹对自己的教训了，又重新回到亳都做天子。周公不能得到天下，就好像益在夏朝、伊尹在殷朝一样。孔子说：'唐尧虞舜禅让天下，夏商周三代传于子孙，道理是一样的。'"

【英译】Wan Chang asked Mencius, saying, 'People say, "When the disposal of the kingdom came to Yû, his virtue was inferior to that of Yâo and Shun, and he transmitted it not to the worthiest but to his son." Was it so?' Mencius replied, 'No; it was not so. When Heaven gave the kingdom to the worthiest, it was given to the worthiest. When

Heaven gave it to the son of the preceding sovereign, it was given to him. Shun presented Yü to Heaven. Seventeen years elapsed, and Shun died. When the three years' mourning was expired, Yü withdrew from the son of Shun to Yang-ch'ǎng. The people of the kingdom followed him just as after the death of Yâo, instead of following his son, they had followed Shun. Yü presented Yî to Heaven. Seven years elapsed, and Yü died. When the three years' mourning was expired, Yî withdrew from the son of Yü to the north of mount Ch'î. The princes, repairing to court, went not to Yî, but they went to Ch'î. Litigants did not go to Yî, but they went to Ch'î, saying, "He is the son of our sovereign;" the singers did not sing Yî, but they sang Ch'î, saying, "He is the son of our sovereign." That Tan-chû was not equal to his father, and Shun's son not equal to his; that Shun assisted Yâo, and Yü assisted Shun, for many years, conferring benefits on the people for a long time; that thus the length of time during which Shun, Yü, and Yî assisted in the government was so different; that Ch'î was able, as a man of talents and virtue, reverently to pursue the same course as Yü; that Yî assisted Yü only for a few years, and had not long conferred benefits on the people; that the periods of service of the three were so different; and that the sons were one superior, and the other superior: —all this was from Heaven, and what could not be brought about by man. That which is done without man's doing is from Heaven. That which happens without man's causing is from the ordinance of Heaven. In the case of a private individual obtaining the throne, there must be in him virtue equal to that of Shun or Yü; and moreover there must be the presenting of him to Heaven by the preceding sovereign. It was on this account that Confucius did not obtain the throne. When the kingdom is possessed by natural succession, the sovereign who is displaced by Heaven must be like Chieh or Châu . It was on this account that Yî, Î Yin, and Châu-kung did not obtain the throne. Î Yin assisted T'ang so that he became sovereign over the kingdom. After the demise of T'ang, T'âi-ting having died before he could be appointed sovereign, Wâi-ping reigned two years, and Chung-zǎn four. T'âi-chiâ was then turning upside down the statutes of T'ang, when Î Yin placed him in T'ung for three years. There T'âi-chiâ repented of his errors, was contrite, and reformed himself. In T'ung he came to dwell in benevolence and walk in righteousness, during those three years, listening to the lessons given to him by Î Yin. Then Î Yin again returned with him to Po. Châu-kung's not getting the throne was like the case of Yî and the throne of Hsiâ, or like that of Î Yin and the throne of Yin. Confucius said, "T'ang and Yü resigned the throne to their worthy ministers. The sovereign of Hsiâ and those of Yin and Châu transmitted it to their sons. The principle of righteousness was the same in all the cases."'

【注释】

[1] 孟子在本章进一步指出无论是尧舜的禅让还是夏商周的父死子继，"其义一也"，都是顺从天意、服从民心的表现，符合天人合一的天命观。他还首次给出了具有哲理抽象意蕴的"天"和"命"的定义。

[2] "箕山之阴"，指箕山的北面。山的北面称阴，南面称阳，因而刘殿爵选择将"阴"翻译为"the northern slope"（山之北）。"箕山"是古代中国的山名，属于专有名词的范畴，因而刘殿爵选择对其进行音译。赖发洛按字面意思将"阴"翻译为"shade"（荫凉处），从文意上讲尚可，但将"箕山"按字面意思直译为"Sieve Hill"则不妥。

[3] "不肖"，子不似父也。《说文》："肖，骨肉相似也。从肉，小声。

不似其先，故曰不肖也。"可见"不肖"的本义是中性词，指儿子不像父亲，但后来它逐渐具备了不孝顺、不正派等贬义，而它的本义逐渐被人遗忘。理雅各取其本义，将"不肖"翻译为"not equal to his father"（不能像他父亲那样），准确翻译出了"不肖"的内涵。刘殿爵取其引申义，翻译为"depraved"（堕落、邪恶）。

[4] "施泽于民久"，刘殿爵选择用"rained down"翻译"施泽"，不仅能准确翻译出厚施恩惠之意，还传达了恩惠如雨水般大量降下，源源不断施与百姓的意象。

[5] 从词义上看，"命"的本义是"使""令"。在春秋前，它通常被看作是"天命"的缩写，后来逐渐具备了"命运"的含义。"命运"的显著特征是不受人力所控制，具有先定的不可改变性。郝大维和安乐哲根据孟子的定义，将"天"和"命"的区别定义为："'天'指称着自然与人间世界之自发产生的过程本身，而'命'代表着特殊现象的条件与可能性，那些特殊现象为其产生提供了依据。"刘殿爵选择用"decree"翻译"命"，从词义上看，"decree"可以在一定程度上对应"命"的内涵，但不能完全包含此处"命"的含义。

[6] "怨"，悔恨，"艾"，割草，"自怨自艾"比喻改正错误，故理雅各将之翻译为"repented of his errors, was contrite, and reformed himself"，即悔恨自己的过错并改正。古汉语的词义是不断发展变化的，"自怨自艾"也不例外。到了今天，"自怨自艾"只保留了悔恨之意，自我改正的意思逐渐消失。刘殿爵的译文就取"自怨自艾"的今天常用义"reproached himself"（自我悔恨）。下文的"处仁迁义"表明太甲不仅仅是消极悔过，还积极改正自己的错误。

[7] "处仁迁义"是太甲悔过、弃恶从善的表现，是一个变化的过程，而理雅各将之翻译为"dwell in benevolence and walk in righteousness"（居仁由义），仅展示了悔过后的成果。刘殿爵的"reformed and became a good and dutiful man"（改过自新，变成了一个善良、有责任心的人），将变化的过程

和成果完美呈现在了读者面前。

【原文】9.7 万章问曰[1]："人有言，'伊尹以割烹要汤'，有诸？"孟子曰："否，不然；伊尹耕于有莘之野，而乐尧舜之道焉。非其义也，非其道也，禄之以天下，弗顾也；系马千驷，弗视也。非其义也，非其道也，一介[2]不以与人，一介不以取诸人。汤使人以币[3]聘之，嚣嚣然[4]曰：'我何以汤之聘币为哉？我岂若处畎亩之中，由是以乐尧舜之道哉？'汤三使往聘之[5]，既而幡然[6]改曰：'与我处畎亩之中，由是以乐尧舜之道，吾岂若使是君为尧舜之君哉？吾岂若使是民为尧舜之民哉？吾岂若于吾身亲见之哉？天之生此民也，使先知觉后知[7]，使先觉觉后觉也。予，天民之先觉者也；予将以斯道觉斯民也。非予觉之，而谁也？'思天下之民匹夫匹妇有不被尧舜之泽者，若己推而内之沟中。其自任以天下之重如此，故就汤而说之以伐夏救民。吾未闻枉己而正人者也，况辱己以正天下者乎？圣人之行不同也，或远，或近；或去，或不去；归洁其身而已矣。吾闻其以尧舜之道要汤，末闻以割烹也。《伊训》曰：'天诛造攻自牧宫，朕载自亳。'"

【译文】万章问道："有人说：'伊尹通过切肉、烹饪获得汤的任用。'有这回事吗？"孟子说："不，不是这样的。伊尹在莘国的郊野种地，但喜好尧舜之道。如果不符合义，不合乎道，给他天下做俸禄，他也不会回头看一下；如果不符合义，不合乎道，一点点东西也不会给别人，一点点东西也不会拿别人的。汤派人拿礼物去聘请他，他毫不在乎地说：'我要汤的聘礼干什么？我还不如在田野中，就这样喜好尧舜之道呢？'汤几次派人去聘请，很快，他就完全改变了态度，说：'与其在田野中喜好尧舜之道，何不如使现在的君主成为尧舜那样的君主呢？何不如使现在的百姓成为尧舜时代的百姓呢？何不如使我自己亲眼看见尧舜的盛世呢？上天生育百姓，就是要让先知的人觉悟后知的人，使先悟的人觉醒后悟的人。我是承担天之使命的先觉者。我要拿尧舜之道使现在的百姓有所觉悟。不是我去使他们觉醒，又会有谁呢？'伊尹想到天下百姓中如果有一个男子或一个妇女，没有得到尧舜之道的惠泽，就好像自己把他们推进山沟中一样。他就是这样把天下的重担挑在自己肩上，所以到了汤那里，便说服汤讨伐夏桀、拯救百姓。我没有听说过，先使自己屈曲，却能够匡正别人的，更不用说先使自己遭受侮辱，却能够匡正天下的呢？圣人的行为各有不同，有的远离君主，有的接近君主，有的离开君主，有的留恋君主，归根到底都是为了使自己洁身自好罢了。我只听说过伊尹用尧舜之道向汤求取任用，没有听说过他用切肉做菜求取任用的事。《伊训》说：'上天的讨伐起自夏桀的宫室，我不过是从殷都亳邑开始谋划罢了。'"

【英译】Wan Chang asked Mencius，saying，'People say that Î Yin sought an introduction to T'ang by his knowledge of cookery. Was it so？' Mencius replied，'No，it was not so. Î Yin was a farmer in the lands of the prince of Hsin，delighting in the principles of Yâo and Shun. In any matter contrary to the righteousness which they prescribed，or contrary to their principles，though he had been offered the throne，he would not have regarded it；though there had been yoked for him a thousand teams of horses，he would not have looked at them. In any matter contrary to the righteousness which they prescribed，or contrary to their principles，he would neither have given nor taken a single straw. T'ang sent persons with presents of silk to entreat him to enter his service. With an air of indifference and self-satisfaction he said，"What can I do with those silks with which T'ang invites me？Is it not best for me to abide in the channelled fields，and so delight myself with the principles of Yâo and Shun？" T'ang thrice sent messengers to invite him. After this，with the change of resolution displayed in his countenance, he spoke in a different style, — "Instead of abiding in the channelled fields and thereby delighting myself with the principles of Yâo and Shun, had I not better make this prince a prince like Yâo or Shun, and this people like the people of Yâo or Shun? Had I not better in my own person see these things for myself? Heaven's plan in the production of mankind is this: —that they who are first informed should instruct those who are later in being informed, and they who first apprehend principles should instruct those who are slower to do so. I am one of Heaven's people who have first apprehended; — I will take these principles and instruct this people in them. If I do not instruct them, who will do so?" He thought that among all the people of the kingdom, even the private men and women, if there were any who did not enjoy such benefits as Yâo and Shun conferred, it was as if he himself pushed them into a ditch. He took upon himself the heavy charge of the kingdom in this way, and therefore he went to T‘ang, and pressed upon him the subject of attacking Hsiâ and saving the people. I have not heard of one who bent himself, and at the same time made others straight; —how much less could one disgrace himself, and thereby rectify the whole kingdom? The actions of the sages have been different. Some have kept remote from court, and some have drawn near to it; some have left their offices, and some have not done so: —that to which those different courses all agree is simply the keeping of their persons pure. I have heard that Î Yin sought an introduction to T‘ang by the doctrines of Yâo and Shun. I have not heard that he did so by his knowledge of cookery. In the "Instructions of Î," it is said, "Heaven destroying Chieh commenced attacking him in the palace of Mû. I commenced in Po."'

【注释】

[1] 伊尹是孟子称赞的圣人，他遵道守义，乐道轻财，行不违义，言不悖理，尚名节，不苟取，以安天下为己任。在他身上集中体现了修身、齐家、治国、平天下的圣人所具备的所有优秀品质，是后世学习效仿的榜样。

[2] "一介"，形容少，一点点。赵岐注曰："一介草。"王引之在《经义述闻·通说》中以"个"解之。理雅各的理解同赵岐，将"介"翻译为"straw"（稻草、麦秆），刘殿爵则取其比喻义"mite"（微小）。

[3] "币"，《说文》以"帛也"解之。郑玄注《聘礼记》云："币谓丝帛也。"可见"币"的本义是丝帛，后来泛指聘享的礼物。理雅各取其本义，将"币"翻译为"silk"（丝绸），刘殿爵取其引申义，翻译为"presents"（礼物）。这两种翻译都可以，但从上文的"禄之以天下"和"系马千驷"可以推测，刘殿爵将之翻译为"礼物"更确切。

[4] "嚣嚣然"，赵岐注曰："自得之志，无欲之貌也。"理雅各将之翻译为"indifference and self-satisfaction"，将伊尹自我满足、恬淡无欲的生活态度完整展现给了读者。刘殿爵的"calmly"（平静、安然）只体现了"嚣嚣然"的一个方面。

[5] "三使往聘之"，刘殿爵将之理解为确数，即"sent a messenger for the third time"（三次派人聘请他）。也有学者认为，古汉语中"三"多指概数，意为多次，因而此处的"三"和"三思而行""三缄其口"同义，指多次派人聘请他。

[6] "幡然"，朱熹注曰："变动之貌"。理雅各将之翻译为"with the change of resolution displayed in his countenance"（他脸上显出决心改变的表情），基本能体现其含义。但是值得注意的是在"幡然改"中，"幡"通"翻"即翻转，其实是强调很快而且彻底地改变。赖发洛的译文是"veered round"（彻底改变），和前文的"嚣嚣然"形成鲜明对比，更便于读者注意、体会到伊尹前后判若两人的变化。

[7] 朱熹注曰："知，谓识其事之所当然。觉，谓悟其理之所以然。觉

后知后觉，如呼寐者而使之寤也。""先知"，理雅各将之翻译为"who are first informed"（首先被告知的人）。在宗教和世俗世界中，先知是指对未来有较早了解或准确预言的人，但宗教中的先知对未来的描述来自于神，他们的预言是受到神的启示，是被神告知的，因而理雅各选择用被告知翻译"先知"宗教意味更浓一些。刘殿爵选择用"understanding"翻译。"Understand"的含义是对事物有彻底的认识，不仅了解其外在属性，还明白其内在规律，能准确再现此处"知"的含义。"觉"，悟也，通"寤"，醒也。理雅各将之意译为"instruct"（教导），基本上能体现"觉"在本章中的意义。刘殿爵选择用"awaken"翻译"觉"。"awaken"的本义是"醒来""弄醒"可以对应"觉"的字面意思。它们的比喻义是使觉醒、振奋，也能对应"觉"在本章中的含义。可见刘殿爵的译文不论在词义还是在文义上都能很好地对应"觉"的内涵。

【原文】 9.8　万章问曰[1]："或谓孔子于卫主痈疽[2]，于齐主侍人瘠环，有诸乎？"孟子曰："否，不然也；好事者为之也[3]。于卫主颜雠由。弥子之妻与子路之妻，兄弟也。弥子谓子路曰：'孔子主我，卫卿可得也。'子路以告。孔子曰：'有命[4]。'孔子进以礼，退以义，得之不得曰'有命'。而主痈疽与侍人瘠环，是无义无命也。孔子不悦于鲁卫，遭宋桓司马将要而杀之，微服而过宋。是时孔子当厄，主司城贞子，为陈侯周臣。吾闻观近臣，以其所为主；观远臣[5]，以其所主。若孔子主痈疽与侍人瘠环，何以为孔子？"

【译文】 万章问道："有人说，孔子在卫国住在卫灵公所宠幸的宦官痈疽家里，在齐国，住在齐景公崇信的宦官瘠环家里。有这回事吗？"孟子说："不，不是这样的，这是无事生非之人捏造出来的。孔子在卫国，住在颜雠由家中。弥子瑕的妻子和子路的妻子是姐妹。弥子瑕对子路说：'孔子住在我家中，可以作卫国的卿相。'子路把这话告诉了孔子。孔子说：'由命运决定。'孔子依礼进，依义退，所以他说是否得到官位是'由命运决定'。如果住在痈疽和宦官瘠环家中，便是无视礼义和命运了。孔子在鲁国和卫国不得志，又碰上了宋国的司马向魋预备拦截并杀死他，只得改变服装悄悄地走过宋国。这时候，孔子正处在困难的境地，便住在司城贞子家中，做了陈侯周的臣子。我听说过，观察在朝的臣子，看他所招待的客人；观察外来的臣子，看他所寄居的主人。如果孔子真的以痈疽和宦官瘠环为主人，还怎么能算'孔子'呢？"

【英译】Wan Chang asked Mencius，saying，'Some say that Confucius，when he was in Wei，lived with the ulcer-doctor，and when he was in Ch'î，with the attendant，Ch'î Hwan；—was it so？' Mencius replied，'No；it was not so. Those are the inventions of men fond of strange things. When he was in Wei，he lived with Yen Ch'âu-yû. The wives of the officer Mî and Tsze-lû were sisters，and Mî told Tsze-lû，"If Confucius will lodge with me，he may attain to the dignity of a high noble of Wei." Tsze-lû informed Confucius of this，and he said，"That is as ordered by Heaven." Confucius went into office according to propriety，and retired from it according to righteousness. In regard to his obtaining office or not obtaining it，he said，"That is as ordered." But if he had lodged with the attendant Ch'î Hwan，that would neither have been according to righteousness，nor any ordering of Heaven. When Confucius，being dissatisfied in Lû and Wei，had left those States，he met with the attempt of Hwan，the Master of the Horse，of Song，to intercept and kill him. He assumed，however，the dress of a common man，and passed by Song. At that time，though he was in circumstances of distress，he lodged with the city-master Ch'ǎng，who was then a minister of Châu，the marquis of Ch'ǎn. I have heard that the characters of ministers about court may be discerned from those whom they entertain，and those of stranger officers，from those with whom they lodge. If Confucius had lodged with the ulcer-doctor，and with the attendant Chî Hwan，how could he have been Confucius?'

【注释】

[1] 本章通过和学生的谈话，孟子驳斥了一些关于孔子的传言，重申了他认可的士人进退处世之道。

[2] "痈疽"有两种理解。一说是治疗痈疽的医生，如朱熹注曰："痈疽，疡医也"；二说是人名。理雅各和赖发洛持第一种观点，刘殿爵和赵甄陶持第二种观点。结合下文可知，孟子认为"主痈疽"是对孔子的污蔑，如果仅仅是因为孔子住在"治疗痈疽的医生"家里是"是无义无命"的话，有歧视社会分工之嫌，因而将之理解为人名更合理。

[3] "好事者"，终日无所事事，以造谣生事为己任的人。理雅各将之翻译为"men fond of strange things"（喜欢奇闻逸事的人）。爱好奇闻逸事并不可怕，可怕的是编造故事颠倒黑白、混淆视听、诽谤他人的人。因而刘殿爵的译文"These were fabrications by people with nothing better to do"更能体现"好事者"的特征。

[4] "命"，张岱年在《中国哲学史大纲》中指出："大致说来，可以说命乃指人力所无可奈何者。我们做一件事情，这件事情成功或失败，即此事的最后结果如何，并非做此事之个人之力量所能决定，但也不是以外任何个人或其他任何一件事情所能决定，而乃是环境一切因素之集聚的总和力量所使然。……做事者是个人，最后决定者却非任何个人。……这个最后的决定者，无以名之，名之曰命。"理雅各将"命"翻译为"ordered"，认为是否会获得官职都是事先预定的、安排好的。他的这一理解显然受基督教预定论的影响。刘殿爵将"命"翻译为"Decree"（神的谕旨），同理译本一样，这样翻译也具有较强的宗教意味，容易引起不必要的联想。

[5] 朱熹注曰："近臣，在朝之臣。远臣，远方来仕者。"可见"近臣"是本国在朝为官者，"远臣"指外来谋求官职之人，既包括已经为官者，也包括那些远道而来，寻求得到任用的普通人。赖发洛分别将"近臣"和"远

臣"直译为"a minister who is near"（附近的大臣）和"a minister from afar"（远道而来的大臣）。译文含义略显模糊，不便于读者理解。刘殿爵将"近臣"翻译为"courtiers who are natives of the state"（本国的朝臣），将"远臣"翻译为"come to court from abroad"（远道而来寻求入仕的人）。当地的朝臣不仅有实力为外来者提供住宿和饮食，还可以为君主推荐贤人，而外来求仕者初入一国也必定要寻求可以居住的地方和可以引荐他为官之人。刘殿爵的解释性翻译，有利于读者理解"近臣"和"远臣"的含义。

【原文】9.9　万章问曰[1]："或曰：'百里奚自鬻于秦养牲者五羊之皮，食牛以要秦穆公'，信乎？"孟子曰："否，不然，好事者为之也。百里奚，虞人也。晋人以垂棘之璧[2]与屈产之乘[3]，假道于虞以伐虢。宫之奇谏，百里奚不谏。知虞公之不可谏而去之秦，年已七十矣；曾不知以食牛干秦穆公之为污也，可谓智乎？不可谏而不谏，可谓不智乎？知虞公之将亡而先去之，不可谓不智也。时举于秦，知穆公之可与有行也而相之，可谓不智乎？相秦而显其君于天下，可传于后世，不贤而能之乎？自鬻以成其君，乡党自好者不为，而谓贤者为之乎？"

【译文】万章问道："有人说：'百里奚用五张羊皮的价格把自己卖给了秦国养牲畜的人，替人家饲养牛，以此来获得秦穆公的任用'。这话是真的吗？"孟子答道："不，不是这样的，这是喜欢无事生非的人捏造的。百里奚是虞国人，晋国人用垂棘所产的美玉和屈地所产的良马向虞国借道去攻打虢国。虞国的大夫宫之奇劝阻虞公，让他拒绝，百里奚却不去劝阻。他知道虞公是不可以劝阻的，因而离开虞国，搬到秦国时已经七十岁了，他竟不知道用饲养牛的方法来求见秦穆公是一种污浊的行为，能说他聪明吗？他能预见虞公不能被劝阻，便不去劝阻，可以说不聪明吗？他能预见虞公将要灭亡故而早早离开，不能说不聪明。当他在秦国被推举出来的时候，知道秦穆公是可以有所作为而去帮助他，能说他不聪明吗？做了秦国的卿相，使秦穆公名显天下，并且可以流传后世，如果不贤能怎么会做到呢？把自己卖掉来成就君主，乡里洁身自爱的人都不肯去做，难道说贤能的人会去这么做吗？"

【英译】Wan Chang asked Mencius, 'Some say that Pâi-lî Hsî sold himself to a cattle-keeper of Ch'in for the skins of five rams, and fed his oxen, in order to find an introduction to the duke Mû of Ch'in;—was this the case?' Mencius said, 'No; it was not so. This story was invented by men fond of strange things. Pâi-lî Hsî was a man of Yü. The people of Tsin, by the inducement of a round piece of jade from Ch'ûi-chî, and four horses of the Ch'ü breed, borrowed a passage through Yü to attack Kwo. On that occasion, Kung Chih-ch'î remonstrated against granting their request, and Pâi-lî Hsî did not remonstrate. When he knew that the duke of Yü was not to be remonstrated with, and, leaving that State, went to Ch'in, he had reached the age of seventy. If by that time he did not know that it would be a mean thing to seek an introduction to the duke Mû of Ch'in by feeding oxen, could he be called wise? But not remonstrating where it was of no use to remonstrate, could he be said not to be wise? Knowing that the duke of Yü would be ruined, and leaving him before that event, he cannot be said not to have been wise. Being then advanced in Ch'in, he knew that the duke Mû was one with whom he would enjoy a field for action, and became minister to him;—could he, acting thus, be said not to be wise? Having become chief minister of Ch'in, he made his prince distinguished throughout the kingdom, and worthy of being handed down to future ages;—could he have done this, if he had not been a man of talents and virtue? As to selling himself in order to accomplish all the aims of his prince, even a villager who had a regard for himself would not do such a thing；and shall we say that a man of talents and virtue did it？'

【注释】

[1] 孟子在为孔子辩解完后，继续为百里奚辟谣，强调贤者以仁、智存其心，非常重视洁身自好，坚信自己正方能正人，不会为了正天下而自辱其身。

[2] "璧"的本义是平而圆，中间有孔的玉，后成为美玉的通称。理雅各取其本义将之翻译为"a round piece of jade"（一块圆形的玉），刘殿爵则直接将之翻译为"jade"（玉）。

[3] "屈产之乘"，赵岐注曰："屈，产地，良马所生。乘，四马也。"即屈地盛产的良马。理雅各受其影响，将之翻译为"four horses of the Ch'ü breed"（屈地出产的四匹马）。古代中国常用"乘"来计算马的数量，虽然通常情况下，"乘"指四马，但在此处并非确数，因而刘殿爵翻译为"the horses"（马）。

卷　十

万章章句下

【原文】10.1　孟子曰[1]："伯夷，目不视恶色，耳不听恶声[2]。非其君，不事；非其民，不使。治则进，乱则退。横政之所出，横民[3]之所止，不忍居也。思与乡人处，如以朝衣朝冠坐于涂炭也。当纣之时，居北海之滨，以待天下之清也。故闻伯夷之风者，顽夫廉[4]，懦夫有立志。伊尹曰：'何事非君？何使非民？'治亦进，乱亦进。曰：'天之生斯民也，使先知觉后知，使先觉觉后觉。予，天民之先觉者也。予将以此道觉此民也。'思天下之民匹夫匹妇有不与被尧舜之泽者，若己推而内之沟中——其自任以天下之重也[5]。柳下惠不羞污君，不辞小官。进不隐贤，必以其道。遗佚而不怨，阨穷而不悯。与乡人处，由由然不忍去也。'尔为尔，我为我，虽袒裼裸裎于我侧，尔焉能浼我哉？'故闻柳下惠之风者，鄙夫宽，薄夫敦。孔子之去齐，接淅而行[6]；去鲁，曰：'迟迟吾行也，去父母国之道也。'可以速而速，可以久而久，可以处而处，可以仕而仕，孔子也。"孟子曰："伯夷，圣之清者也；伊尹，圣之任者也；柳下惠，圣之和者也；孔子，圣之时者[7]也。孔子之谓集大成。集大成也者，金声而玉振之也。金声也者，始条理也；玉振之也者，终条理也。始条理者，智之事也；终条理者，圣之事也。智，譬则巧也；圣，譬则力也。由射于百步之外也，其至，尔力也；其中，非尔力也。"

【译文】孟子说："伯夷眼睛不看不好的事物，耳朵不听不好的声音，不是理想的君主，不去侍奉，不是理想的百姓，不去使用。天下太平就出来做官，天下混乱就隐居田野。施行暴政的国家，有暴民居住的地方，他都不愿意去住。他认为和乡下人相处，好像穿着礼服戴着礼帽坐在泥涂或者炭灰之上。在商纣的时候，住在北海海边，等待天下的清平。所以听到伯夷的风范的人，贪得无厌的人都变得廉洁，懦弱的人也会立定意志。伊尹说：'什么君主，不可以侍奉？什么百姓，不可以使唤？'天下太平的时候也出来做官，天下混乱的时候也出来做官，并且说：'上天生育这些百姓，使先知的人觉醒后知的人，使先觉的人开导后觉的人。我是这些人中的先觉者。我将以尧舜之道来觉醒这些人。'他认为天下的百姓中只要有一个男子或一个妇女没有受到尧舜之道的润泽，就好像是自己把他推进山沟之中——他把天下的重担全部自己挑起来了。柳下惠不以侍奉坏君为羞，也不因官小就辞去。出仕不隐藏自己的才能，但必须按他的原则办事。被遗弃也不怨恨，陷入穷困也不忧愁。同乡下人相处，悠然自得地不忍离开。（他说）'你是你，我是我，纵使你在我身旁赤身露体，又怎能玷污我呢？'所以听到柳下惠的风节的人，胸襟狭小的人会变得宽容，刻薄的人也会变得厚道。孔子离开齐国的时候，不等把米淘完，捞起来就走；离开鲁国的时候说：'我们慢慢走吧，这是离开祖国的态度。'应该马上走就马上走，应该继续干就继续干，应该闲居就闲居，应该做官就做官，这便是孔子。"孟子又说："伯夷是圣人之中清高的人，伊尹是圣人之中尽责的人，柳下惠是圣人之中随和的人，孔子是圣人之中合时宜的人。孔子可以称作集大成者。'集大成'的意思，就好像奏乐时以敲钟开始，以击磬结尾。先敲钟，是节奏条理的开始：用磬结束，是节奏条理的终结。节奏条理的开始在于智，节奏条理的终结在于圣。智好比技巧，圣好比力气。就像在百步以外射箭，射到，是靠你的力气；射中，却不只是靠你的力气。"

【英译】Mencius said, 'Po-î would not allow his eyes to look on a bad sight, nor his ears to listen to a bad sound. He would not serve a prince whom he did not approve, nor command a people whom he did not esteem. In a time of good government he took office, and on the occurrence of confusion he retired. He could not bear to dwell either in a court from which a lawless government emanated, or among lawless people. He considered his being in the same place with a villager, as if he were to sit amid mud and coals with his court robes and court cap. In the time of Châu he dwelt on the shores of the North Sea, waiting the purification of the kingdom. Therefore when men now hear the character of Po-î, the corrupt become pure, and the weak acquire determination. Î Yin said, "Whom may I not serve? My serving him makes him my sovereign. What people may I not command? My commanding them makes them my people." In a time of good government he took office, and when confusion prevailed, he also took office. He said, "Heaven's plan in the production of mankind is this: —that they who are first informed should instruct those who are later in being informed, and they who first apprehend principles should instruct those who are slower in doing so. I am the one of Heaven's people who has first apprehended: —I will take these principles and instruct the people in them." He thought that among all the people of the kingdom, even the common men and women, if there were any who did not share in the enjoyment of such benefits as Yâo and Shun conferred, it was as if he himself pushed them into a ditch: —for he took upon himself the heavy charge of the kingdom. Hûi of Liû-hsiâ was not ashamed to serve an impure prince, nor did he think it low to be an inferior officer. When advanced to employment, he did not conceal his virtue, but made it a point to carry out his principles. When dismissed and left without office, he did not murmur. When straitened by poverty, he did not grieve. When thrown into the company of village people, he was quite at ease and could not bear to leave them. He had a saying, "You are you, and I am I. Although you stand by my side with breast and arms bare, or with your body naked, how can you defile me?" Therefore when men now hear the character of Hûi of Liû-Hsiâ the mean become generous, and the niggardly become liberal. When Confucius was leaving Ch'î, he strained off with his hand the water in which his rice was being rinsed, took the rice, and went away. When he left Lû, he said, "I will set out by-and-by": —it was right he should leave the country of his parents in this way. When it was proper to go away quickly, he did so; when it was proper to delay, he did so; when it was proper to keep in retirement, he did so; when it was proper to go into office, he did so: —this was Confucius. Mencius said, 'Po-î among the sages was the pure one; Î Yin was the one most inclined to take office; Hûi of Liû-Hsiâ was the accommodating one; and Confucius was the timeous one. In Confucius we have what is called a complete concert. A complete concert is when the large bell proclaims the commencement of the music, and the ringing stone proclaims its close. The metal sound commences the blended harmony of all the instruments, and the winding up with the stone terminates that blended harmony. The commencing that harmony is the work of wisdom. The terminating it is the work of sageness. As a comparison for wisdom, we may liken it to skill, and as a comparison for sageness, we may liken it to strength; —as in the case of shooting at a mark a hundred paces distant. That you reach it is owing to your strength, but that you hit the mark is not owing to your strength.'

【注释】

[1] 孟子以过犹不及为原则，对伯夷、伊尹、柳下惠和孔子这四位圣人的突出品质进行了详细描述，并用简洁的话语对他们进行了客观评价。他认为伯夷是"圣之清者"，伊尹是"圣之任者"，柳下惠是"圣之和者"，而孔子则集中了所有这些优点，无过无不及，是"圣之时者"。

[2] "目不视恶色，耳不听恶声"，赵岐注："谓行不正而有美色者，若夏姬之比也。耳不听恶声，谓郑声也。"夏姬是春秋时郑穆公之女，虽被公认为春秋时期的四大美女之一，但品德不好，与多位诸侯大夫通奸。"郑声"是郑国的音乐，与朝廷雅乐相对，因而遭到倡导雅乐的儒家批判，孔子曾说"恶郑声之乱雅乐也"。（《论语·阳货》）可见，赵岐认为，"恶色"和"恶声"都是和儒家倡导的礼仪不符合的声音、人和事物。刘殿爵的译文与之相类，他将之翻译为"improper sights"（不合适的事物）和"improper sounds"（不合适的声音），突出与礼不合。理雅各将之翻译为"a bad sight"和"a bad sound"。他的译文含义更广泛，可以包含一切不好的人、事物和声音。结合孟子对伯夷"隘"的评价，可以看出他认为伯夷做事过于绝对，不能很好奉行过犹不及的中庸之道，因而理雅各的翻译更贴切。

[3] 朱熹注曰："横，谓不循法度。"此处的"法度"既可以理解为法律制度，又可认为是规矩或行为准则。理雅各取第一种意思，更强调法的作用，将"横政"和"横民"分别翻译为"a lawless government"（不守法的国家）和"lawless people"（不守法的百姓）。刘殿爵则取后种，分别将之翻译为"the government took outrageous measures"（暴政横行的国家）和"unruly people"（暴民）。与鼓吹法治的法家相比，儒家更强调德治和教化的作用，因而刘殿爵的译文更确切。

[4] "顽夫廉"，赵岐注曰："顽贪之夫更思廉洁。"陈器之进一步指出："《孟子》'顽夫廉'，'顽'字古皆是'贪'字。"即贪婪的人变得清廉。刘殿爵的译文与之相类，将之翻译为"a covetous man will be purged"（贪婪的人

变得廉洁）。朱熹则认为："顽者，无知觉。廉者，有分辨。"即愚顽的人变得有辨别力。赖发洛的译文与之相类，将之翻译为"the fool grows honest"（愚人变得廉洁）。

　　[5]　对于"其自任以天下之重也"，刘殿爵认为，它"只由一个名词性语言单位构成，明显是不完整的"，因而援引《孟子·万章上》第七章"思天下之民匹夫匹妇有不被尧舜之泽者，若己推而内之沟中。其自任以天下之重如此"为依据，认为本句句末也应以"如此"作结，故将此句翻译为"This is the extent to which he considered the Empire his responsibility"（他以天下为己任是到了如此地步）。刘殿爵的译文既有事实依据作支撑，又将孟子对"伊尹"以天下为己任的赞扬之情准确地传递了出来。

　　[6]　"浙"有两种基本的词义。一是淘过的米，赵岐注曰："浙，渍米也。"朱熹进一步指出："接，犹承也。浙，渍米水也。渍米将炊，而欲去之速，故以手承水取米而行，不及炊也。"陈器之引《说文》"滰（jiàng 酱）字下引《孟子》作'滰浙而行'。一般用以指行色匆忙。"二是象声词，多形容风雨声。刘殿爵和理雅各对"浙"的理解基本持第一种观点，但译文略有差异。理雅各的译文是"he strained off with his hand the water in which his rice was being rinsed，took the rice，and went away"（他将米从淘米水中捞出，拿着滴水的米匆匆离开），刘殿爵将之翻译为"When he left Ch'i, Confucius started after emptying the rice from the steamer"（孔子从蒸笼中倒出米，接着离开）。赖发洛取第二种解释，将之翻译为"When Confucius left Ch'i, he faced the squall and went"（孔子迎着狂风暴雨离开齐国）。当前多数学者持第一种观点。

　　[7]　"时者"，指在正确的时间做正确的事情。赵岐注曰："孔子时行则行，时止则止。"赵甄陶的译文与之相类，将"圣之时者"翻译为"Confucius was the one who knew when to do what to do"（孔子知道什么时候该做什么）。刘殿爵选择用"actions were timely"翻译，表示"所有行为都符合时宜"，亦可。

did not amount to fifty lǐ, the chief could not have access himself to the Son of Heaven. His land was attached to some Hâu-ship, and was called a FÛ-YUNG. The Chief ministers of the Son of Heaven received an amount of territory equal to that of a Hâu; a Great officer received as much as a Pâi; and a scholar of the first class as much as a Tsze or a Nan. In a great State, where the territory was a hundred lǐ, square, the ruler had ten times as much income as his Chief ministers; a Chief minister four times as much as a Great officer; a Great officer twice as much as a scholar of the first class; a scholar of the first class twice as much as one of the middle; a scholar of the middle class twice as much as one of the lowest; the scholars of the lowest class, and such of the common people as were employed about the government offices, had for their emolument as much as was equal to what they would have made by tilling the fields. In a State of the next order, where the territory was seventy lî square, the ruler had ten times as much revenue as his Chief minister; a Chief minister three times as much as a Great officer; a Great officer twice as much as a scholar of the first class; a scholar of the first class twice as much as one of the middle; a scholar of the middle class twice as much as one of the lowest; the scholars of the lowest class, and such of the common people as were employed about the government offices, had for their emolument as much as was equal to what they would have made by tilling the fields. In a small State, where the territory was fifty lî square, the ruler had ten times as much revenue as his Chief minister; a Chief minister had twice as much as a Great officer; a Great officer twice as much as a scholar of the highest class; a scholar of the highest class twice as much as one of the middle; a scholar of the middle class twice as much as one of the lowest；scholars of the lowest class，and such of the common people as were employed about the government offices，had the same emolument；—as much，namely，as was equal to what they would have made by tilling the fields. As to those who tilled the fields，each husbandman received a hundred mâu. When those mâu were manured，the best husbandmen of the highest class supported nine individuals，and those ranking next to them supported eight. The best husbandmen of the second class supported seven individuals，and those ranking next to them supported six；while husbandmen of the lowest class only supported five. The salaries of the common people who were employed about the government offices were regulated according to these differences.'

【注释】

[1] 孟子在本章详细介绍了周朝的爵位和俸禄制度，他的记载和《礼记·王制》关于周朝爵禄制度的文字基本一致，有助于后世了解周代的政治制度。

[2] "班"，赵岐注曰："列也。""列"做名词，指等列，若用作动词，指划分等级。理雅各取其名词形式，将之翻译为"What was the arrangement of dignities and emoluments"，赖发洛则取其动词含义，将之翻译为"How were rank and pay allotted under the house of Chou?"这两种理解皆可。

[3] 此处孟子给出了两种周代的爵制，杜正胜在《编户齐民》中指出："五等是国际关系，六等是各国的内部秩序。"梁涛解读的《孟子》亦认为，"六个等级指诸侯国中的爵位划分"。但赵甄陶则认为划分的标准不同，六个等级是与五个等级相平行的官员等级，即"A parallel hierarchy of official ranks"。刘殿爵和理雅各的译文并没有明确提出五个等级和六个等级的区别，但是在翻译时采取了不同的策略。理雅各在翻译这五等爵禄时，采取大写音译的形式，将之分别翻译为"The SON of HEAVEN""KUNG""HAU""P

AI""TSZE""NAN"。译文采取这一方法便于提醒读者注意中西五等爵位的区别，避免混淆。刘殿爵则选择用西方人熟悉的单词"the duke，the marquis，the earl，the viscount and the baron"翻译。两位译者对"卿、大夫、上士、中士和下士"等古代爵位的翻译也是如此。

【原文】 10.3　万章问曰[1]："敢问友。"孟子曰："不挟长，不挟贵，不挟兄弟而友[2]。友也者，友其德也，不可以有挟也。孟献子，百乘之家也，有友五人焉：乐正裘、牧仲，其三人，则予忘之矣。献子之与此五人者友也。无献子之家者也。此五人者，亦有献子之家，则不与之友矣[3]。非惟百乘之家为然也，虽小国之君亦有之。费惠公曰：'吾于子思，则师之矣；吾于颜般，则友之矣；王顺、长息则事我者也。'非惟小国之君为然也，虽大国之君亦有之。晋平公之于亥唐也，入云则入，坐云则坐，食云则食；虽疏食菜羹，未尝不饱，盖不敢不饱也。然终于此而已矣。弗与共天位也，弗与治天职也，弗与食天禄也[4]，士之尊贤者也，非王公之尊贤也。舜尚见帝，帝馆甥于贰室，亦飨舜，迭为宾主，是天子而友匹夫也。用下敬上，谓之贵贵；用上敬下，谓之尊贤。贵贵、尊贤，其义一也。"

【译文】 万章问："请问怎么交朋友？"孟子说："不倚仗年纪大，不倚仗地位高，不倚仗兄弟交朋友。交朋友，要看重他的品德而去结交，不能因为有所倚仗。孟献子是拥有一百辆车马的大夫，他有五位朋友，乐正裘、牧仲，其他三位，我忘记了。献子和这五人交朋友，没有想到自己是大夫。这五人，如果也想着献子是大夫，也就不会和他交朋友了。并不是只有拥有百辆车马的大夫是这样，纵使小国的君主也有朋友。费惠公说：'我对子思，是以他为老师；对于颜般，是把他当朋友；王顺和长息只不过是侍奉我的人。'不仅小国的君主这样，纵使大国的国君也有朋友。晋平公对于亥唐，亥唐叫他进去，便进去，叫他坐，便坐，叫他吃饭，便吃饭。哪怕是糙米饭小菜汤，也没有不吃饱过，因为不敢不吃饱。然而他只是做到了这一点而已。不同他一起共有官位，不同他一起治理政事，不同他一起享受俸禄，这只是士人尊敬贤者的方式，不是王公尊敬贤者的态度。舜拜见尧，尧安排他的这位女婿住在另一处官邸中，设宴款待舜，俩人互为客人和主人，这是天子和老百姓交友啊。居下位的人尊敬高贵的人，叫作尊重贵人；高贵的人尊敬卑贱的人，叫作尊敬贤人。尊重贵人和尊敬贤人，道理是一样的。"

【英译】Wan Chang asked Mencius，saying，'I venture to ask the principles of friendship.' Mencius replied，'Friendship should be maintained without any presumption on the ground of one's superior age，or station，or the circumstances of his relatives. Friendship with a man is friendship with his virtue，and does not admit of assumptions of superiority. There was Măng Hsien，chief of a family of a hundred chariots. He had five friends，namely，Yŏ-chăng Chiû，Mû Chung，and three others whose names I have forgotten. With those five men Hsien maintained a friendship，because they thought nothing about his family. If they had thought about his family，he would not have maintained his friendship with them. Not only has the chief of a family of a hundred chariots acted thus. The same thing was exemplified by the sovereign of a small State. The duke Hûi of Pî said，"I treat Tsze-sze as my Teacher，and Yen Pan as my Friend. As to Wang Shun and Ch'ang Hsî，they serve me." Not only has the sovereign of a small State acted thus. The same thing has been exemplified by the sovereign of a large State. There was the duke P'ing of Tsin with Hâi T'ang：— when T'ang told him to come into his house，he came；when he told him to be seated，he sat；when he told him to eat，he ate. There might only be coarse rice and soup of vegetables，but he always ate his fill， not daring to do otherwise. Here, however, he stopped, and went no farther. He did not call him to share any of Heaven's places, or to govern any of Heaven's offices, or to partake of any of Heaven's emoluments. His conduct was but a scholar's honouring virtue and talents, not the honouring them proper to a king or a duke. Shun went up to court and saw the sovereign, who lodged him as his son-in-law in the second palace. The sovereign also enjoyed there Shun's hospitality. Alternately he was host and guest. Here was the sovereign maintaining friendship with a private man. Respect shown by inferiors to superiors is called giving to the noble the observance due to rank. Respect shown by superiors to inferiors is called giving honour to talents and virtue. The rightness in each case is the same.'

【注释】

[1] 在本章，万章向孟子请教交友之道。孟子认为交友标准首先是要确保双方人格平等，诚心诚意平等相交；其次交友要有选择，应与品德高尚的人为朋友。他指出，孟献子、费惠公和晋平公在交友时虽能做到乐人之贤忘己之势，但对待朋友的态度仅仅是一般士人尊贤的态度，而非诸侯国君应有的尊贤之道。

[2] "不挟长，不挟贵，不挟兄弟"。赵岐注曰："长，年长。贵，贵势。兄弟，兄弟有富贵者。"焦循又指出其他二种理解："江氏永《群经补义》云：'古人以婚姻为兄弟。'如张子之于二程，程允夫之于朱子，皆有中表之亲，既为友则有师道，不可谓我与彼为姻亲，有疑不肯下问也。挟兄弟而问，与挟故而问相似。俗解为不挟兄弟多人而友，兄弟多人有何可挟乎？须辨别之。'赵氏佑《温故录》云：'兄弟，等夷之称。必其人之与己等夷而后友之，则不肯与胜己处，不能不耻下问矣。兄弟有富贵者，则仍挟贵意耳。'"三种理解虽各有所依，但笔者更支持赵岐的观点。"不挟长，不挟贵，不挟兄弟"是由三个意义相关、结构相似、语气相同的短句组成的排比句。

既然各位注家对"不挟长"是"不挟己之长"的省略没有什么异议，那么将"不挟贵"理解为"不挟己之贵"，"不挟兄弟"理解为"不挟己之兄弟"亦无不妥。刘殿爵的译文同赵岐，他的翻译不仅体现了原文之意，还兼顾了外国读者的阅读和理解习惯。

[3] 孟子举献子的例子旨在说明，交友的双方要保持人格平等，以德行作为择友标准，而不应考虑和在乎外在的物质因素。"献子之与此五人者友也。无献子之家者也。此五人者，亦有献子之家，则不与之友矣。"就是要表达这一意思。理雅各将之翻译为"With those five men Hsien maintained a friendship，because they thought nothing about his family. If they had thought about his family，he would not have maintained his friendship with them."（献子和这五人交友是因为他们从不在意他的家庭背景。如果他们在乎他的家庭背景，他也不可能和他们交朋友）他的译文体现了孟子对"友其德也，不可以有挟也"的强调。但交友是两个人的事，而理雅各的译文则过于强调献子在交友上的谨慎与明智。相比之下，笔者更倾向杨伯峻的译文，他将之理解为："献子同这五位相交，心目中并不存有自己是大夫的观念。这五位，如果也存有献子是位大夫的观念，就不会同他交友了。"

[4] 孟子认为，王公尊贤，应与贤者共享"天位""天职"和"天禄"。从后面列举的尧待舜之道可知，此处的"天位""天职"和"天禄"皆是由上天赋予有德者，因而刘殿爵将之意译为"his position，his duties，or his revenue—all given to him by Heaven"（天赋予他的职务、责任和收入）。这样翻译更便于读者理解。理雅各选择逐字直译，分别译为"Heaven's places""Heaven's offices""Heaven's emoluments"，译文虽在字面意思上对应原文，但含义略显模糊，不便于读者理解。

【原文】10.4　万章问曰[1]："敢问交际[2]何心也?"孟子曰："恭也。"曰："'却之却之为不恭'，何哉?[3]"曰："尊者赐之，曰：'其所取之者义乎，不义乎?'而后受之，以是为不恭，故弗却也。"

曰："请无以辞却之，以心却之，曰：'其取诸民之不义也。'而以他辞无受，不可乎？"曰："其交也以道，其接也以礼，斯孔子受之矣。"万章曰："今有御人于国门之外者，其交也以道，其馈也以礼，斯可受御与？"曰："不可；《康诰》曰：'杀越人于货[4]，闵不畏死，凡民罔不譈。'是不待教而诛者也。殷受夏，周受殷，所不辞也，于今为烈[5]，如之何其受之？"曰："今之诸侯取之于民也，犹御也。苟善其礼际矣，斯君子受之，敢问何说也？"曰："子以为有王者作，将比今之诸侯而诛之乎？其教之不改而后诛之乎？夫谓非其有而取之者盗也，充类至义之尽也[6]。孔子之仕于鲁也，鲁人猎较，孔子亦猎较[7]。猎较犹可，而况受其赐乎？"曰："然则孔子之仕也，非事道与？"曰："事道也。""事道奚猎较也？"曰："孔子先簿正祭器[8]，不以四方之食供簿正。"曰："奚不去也？"曰："为之兆也。兆足以行矣，而不行，而后去，是以未尝有所终三年淹也。孔子有见行可之仕，有际可之仕，有公养之仕。于季桓子，见行可之仕也；于卫灵公，际可之仕也；于卫孝公，公养之仕也。"

【译文】万章问："请问与人交往应该保持什么样的态度呢？"孟子说："恭敬也。"万章问："'一再推辞不接受别人的礼物是不恭敬的。'为什么呢？"孟子说："尊者赠送礼物，你心里想：'他取得这种礼物的手段是合于义的呢？还是不合于义的呢？'想了以后才接受。这是不恭敬的，因此就不拒绝。"万章说："不用语言拒绝他的礼物，只是心里不接受，心里想：'这是他取自百姓的不义之财呀。'然后用其他理由拒绝，不可以吗？"孟子说："他依规矩和我交往，依礼节接待我，这样，孔子也会接受礼物的。"万章说："如果有人在城门外拦路抢劫，他也依规矩和我交往，也依礼节向我赠送礼物，这样也可以接受抢劫来的东西吗？"孟子说："不可以。《康诰》说：'杀人抢夺财物，强横不怕死的人，凡是百姓没有不痛恨的。'这是不需要先去教育就可以诛杀的人。殷商接受了夏朝的这条法律，周朝接受了殷商的这条法律，都没有更改。现在杀人抢劫更严重，怎样能够接受抢劫来的礼物呢？"万章说："现在这些诸侯，他们的财物取自百姓，也和拦路抢劫差不多。如果把交际的礼节搞好，君子也就接受了他们的礼物，请问这又如何解释呢？"孟子说："你认为如果有圣王兴起，对于今天的诸侯，会一律看待全部杀掉呢？还是先进行教化，对于那些不改过的，然后诛杀呢？而且，把不应归自己所有，而去取得它的行为称作是抢劫，这是把抢劫的含义扩大到了尽头。孔子在鲁国做官时，鲁国人争夺猎物，孔子也争夺猎物。争夺猎物都可以，何况接受赏赐呢？"万章说："那么，孔子做官，不是为了行道吗？"孟子说："为了行道。"万章说："为了行道，又为什么争夺猎物呢？"孟子说："孔子先用文书规定祭祀所用的器物和祭品，不用各处争夺来的猎物充当祭品。"万章说："为什么孔子不辞官离开呢？"孟子说："为了先验证一下自己的主张是否可以行得通。验证了他的主张可以行得通，但君主却不肯实行，然后才离开，所以孔子没有在一个地方停留满三年的。孔子有时因为可以行道而做官，有时因为君主礼遇周到而做官，有时因为国君养贤而做官。对于鲁国的季桓子，是因为可以行道而做官；对于卫灵公，是因为礼遇周到而做官；对于卫孝公，是因为国君养贤而做官。"

【英译】Wan Chang asked Mencius, saying, 'I venture to ask what feeling of the mind is expressed in the presents of friendship?' Mencius replied, 'The feeling of respect.' 'How is it,' pursued Chang, 'that the declining a present is accounted disrespectful?' The answer was, 'When one of honourable rank presents a gift, to say in the mind, "Was the way in which he got this righteous or not? I must know this before I can receive it;" —this is deemed disrespectful, and therefore presents are not declined.' Wan Chang asked again, 'When one does not take on him in so many express words to refuse the gift, but having declined it in his heart, saying, "It was taken by him unrighteously from the people," and then assigns some other reason for not receiving it; —is not this a proper course?' Mencius said, 'When the donor offers it on a ground of reason, and his manner of doing so is according to propriety; —in such a case Confucius would have received it.' Wan Chang said, 'Here now is one who stops and robs people outside the gates of the city. He offers his gift on a ground of reason, and does so in a manner according to propriety; — would the reception of it so acquired by robbery be proper?' Mencius replied, 'It would not be proper. In "The Announcement to K'ang" it is said, "When men kill others, and roll over their bodies to take their property, being reckless and fearless of death, among all the people there are none but detest them": —thus, such characters are to be put to death, without waiting to give them warning. Yin received this rule from Hsiâ and Châu received it from Yin. It cannot be questioned, and to the present day is clearly acknowledged. How can the gift of a robber be received?' Chang said, 'The princes of the present day take from their people just as a robber despoils his victim. Yet if they put a good face of propriety on their gifts, then the superior man receives them. I venture to ask how you explain this.' Mencius answered, 'Do you think that, if there should arise a truly royal sovereign, he would collect the princes of the present day, and put them all to death? Or would he admonish them, and then, on their not changing their ways, put them to death? Indeed, to call every one who takes what does not properly belong to him a robber, is pushing a point of resemblance to the utmost, and insisting on the most refined idea of righteousness. When Confucius was in office in Lû, the people struggled together for the game taken in hunting, and he also did the same. If that struggling for the captured game was proper, how much more may the gifts of the princes be received!'Chang urged, 'Then are we to suppose that when Confucius held office, it was not with the view to carry his doctrines into practice?''It was with that view,'Mencius replied, and Chang rejoined, 'If the practice of his doctrines was his business, what had he to do with that struggling for the captured game?'Mencius said, 'Confucius first rectified his vessels of sacrifice according to the registers, and did not fill them so rectified with food gathered from every quarter.''But why did he not go away?''He wished to make a trial of carrying his doctrines into practice. When that trial was sufficient to show that they could be practised and they were still not practised, then he went away, and thus it was that he never completed in any State a residence of three years. Confucius took office when he saw that the practice of his doctrines was likely; he took office when his reception was proper; he took office when he was supported by the State. In the case of his relation to Chî Hwan, he took office, seeing that the practice of his doctrines was likely. With the duke Ling of Wei he took office, because his reception was proper. With the duke Hsiâo of Wei he took office, because he was maintained by the State.'

【注释】

[1] 孟子在本章介绍了社会交往原则，认为在待人接物，尤其是授受礼物和接受官职时，首先要看交际方是否有诚意，是否怀有恭敬之心，其次要使自己的言行符合"道"和"礼"。

[2] "交际"，朱熹注云："谓人以礼仪币帛相交接也。"焦循指出："《尔雅释诂》云：'际，捷也。'捷与接通。《说文》手部云，'接，交也。'是际亦交也。谓诸侯以礼仪币帛与士相交接。"杨伯峻则认为："把'交际'的含义限于礼物的馈赠，大概因为下文所言都是指礼物的接受与否的缘故。我们

以为下文之所以只限于礼物的收拒者，盖由'却之却之为不恭'一问而引起，不关'交际'的含义。"理雅各的英译同朱熹，认为"交际"的内涵局限在授受礼物，因而将之翻译为"the presents of friendship"。刘殿爵同杨伯峻，将"交际"翻译为"social intercourse"（社会交往）。从文义上看，这两种理解都是可以接受的。

[3] 对于"'却之却之为不恭'，何哉"，理雅各将其译为'How is it,' pursued Chang, 'that the declining a present is accounted disrespectful?'"（为什么说拒绝别人的礼物是不恭敬的）他在注释中推测，"却之"重复出现可能由誊写者在抄录时的笔误造成，故在翻译时将重复的"却之"去掉，只译"却之为不恭"。理雅各表现出了学者敢于质疑原文，勇于提出自己见解的精神。刘殿爵认为"却之却之"重复使用是为了强调拒绝接受礼物的决心，将之意译为"Why is it said, 'Too insistent a refusal constitutes a lack of respect'?"（为什么一再拒绝别人的礼物是不恭敬的）

[4] 古今注家对"越"的词义在认识上存在差别。杨伯峻认为："'越'为虚词，无义。……'于货'，谓取其货也。"朱熹则认为："越，颠越也。"还有学者从"越"之字形分析，将之理解为抢夺。郑杰祥指出："卜辞越字，像人一手持钺、一手摆动往前急走之形……有强行夺取之义。"理雅各受朱熹影响，将"越"理解为"颠越"，将"杀越人于货"翻译为"When men kill others, and roll over their bodies to take their property"（杀死别人，翻转他的尸体拿着他的财产）。刘殿爵则取"越"的抢夺、抢劫之意，将之翻译为"He who murders and robs"（杀死别人，抢夺货物）。

[5] 朱熹认为："'殷受'至'为烈'十四字，语意不伦。李氏以为此必有断简或阙文者近之，而愚意其直为衍字耳。然不可靠，故阙之可也。"理雅各在注释中也指出，此句可能是衍文，他根据文义给出了他认为最有可能的理解"Yin received this rule from Hsiâ and Châu received it from Yin. It cannot be questioned, and to the present day is clearly acknowledged."（商朝从夏朝那里继承了这一准则，周朝又从商朝那里将之继承。这一准则不容置

疑，到了今天已经明显变成公认的了）他认为"于今为烈"指的是"凡民罔不譈"，即现在已经变成了大家公认的准则。而刘殿爵则认为，"This is a practice which the Yin took over from the Hsia and the Chou from the Yin without question. Such robbery flourishes more than ever today."（殷商从夏朝继承了这一惯例，周朝也毫不怀疑地从商朝继承了它。今天杀人抢劫行为变得更厉害）相比之下，刘殿爵的理解更能呼应前文的"杀越人于货"。

[6] 对于"充类至义之尽也"的断句有两种，一种认为是"充类至，义之尽也。"赵岐注曰："充，满。至，甚也。满其类大过至者，但义尽耳，未为盗也。诸侯本当税民之类者，今大尽耳，亦不可比于御。"一种断句是"充类，至义之尽也。"朱熹认为："乃推其类，至于义之至精至密之处而极言之耳。"杨伯峻指出："'充类'即'充其类'(6.10)，'至义'犹言'极其义'，其以'充类至'为一读者，误。"当前国内汉学界基本持这一观点。理雅各的译文同朱熹的注解相类，将之翻译为"pushing a point of resemblance to the utmost，and insisting on the most refined idea of righteousness."（举相似而推广到全类，并坚持对义作最完美的定义）刘殿爵将之意译为"pushing moral principles to the extreme"（把道德原则推到了极限），更便于读者理解。

[7] "猎较"，赵岐注曰："猎较者，田猎相较夺禽兽，得之以祭，世俗所尚，以为吉祥。"刘殿爵将之翻译为"fighting over the catch in a hunt to use as sacrifice"。他的译文准确翻译出了"猎较"的含义。

[8] "先簿正祭器"，赵岐注曰："孟子曰，孔子仕于衰世，不可卒暴改戾，故以渐正之。先为簿书，以正其宗庙祭祀之器。"朱熹认为："先簿正祭器，未详。徐氏曰：'先以簿书正其祭器，使有定数，不以四方难继之物实之。夫器有常数，实有常品，则其本正矣，彼猎较者，将久而自废矣。'"注家虽对"先簿正祭器"具体内涵的认识存在差异，但基本上认为是"先以簿书正其祭器"。理雅各和刘殿爵的译文亦支持这一观点，但理解略有差异。理雅各认为孔子是根据已有簿册调整祭器，因而将之翻译为"Confucius first rectified his vessels of sacrifice according to the registers"，而刘殿爵则认

为是孔子自己制定簿书以正祭器，即 "The first thing Confucius did was to lay down correct rules governing sacrificial vessels"（孔子首先制定了祭祀所用器物的正确原则）。

【原文】 10.5 孟子曰[1]："仕非为贫也，而有时乎为贫；娶妻非为养也[2]，而有时乎为养。为贫者，辞尊居卑，辞富居贫。辞尊居卑，辞富居贫，恶乎宜乎？抱关击柝[3]。孔子尝为委吏矣，曰：'会计当而已矣。'尝为乘田矣，曰：'牛羊茁壮长而已矣。'位卑而言高，罪也；立乎人之本朝，而道不行[4]，耻也。"

【译文】 孟子说："做官不是因为贫穷，但有时也因为贫穷。娶妻不是为了奉养父母，但有时也是为了奉养父母。因为贫穷而做官的，就应该辞去高官，接受小官；拒绝厚禄，只受薄俸。辞去高官，接受小官；拒绝厚禄，只受薄俸，那么居于什么位置才合宜呢？像守门打更的小吏就可以。孔子也曾经做过管理仓库的小吏，他说：'出入的数字都准确。'也曾经做过管理牲畜的小吏，他说：'牛羊都壮实地长大了。'官位低下而言论高远，这是罪过在君主的朝廷上做官，却不能实行自己的主张，这是耻辱。"

【英译】 Mencius said, 'Office is not sought on account of poverty, yet there are times when one seeks office on that account. Marriage is not entered into for the sake of being attended to by the wife, yet there are times when one marries on that account. He who takes office on account of his poverty must decline an honourable situation and occupy a low one; he must decline riches and prefer to be poor. What office will be in harmony with this declining an honourable situation and occupying a low one, this declining riches and preferring to be poor? Such an one as that of guarding the gates, or beating the watchman's stick. Confucius was once keeper of stores, and he then said, "My calculations must be all right. That is all I have to care about." He was once in charge of the public fields，and he then said，"The oxen and sheep must be fat and strong，and superior. That is all I have to care about." When one is in a low situation，to speak of high matters is a crime. When a scholar stands in a prince's court，and his principles are not carried into practice，it is a shame to him.'

【注释】

[1] 孟子主张积极入仕，但强调出来做官是为了实现自己的政治理想，如果政治主张不能实行，则应离去。但"家贫亲老，不为禄仕"是不孝的行为，在道不行但家境贫寒，不得不出来做官时应避高位，任小官。

[2] "娶妻非为养也"，朱熹注曰："娶妻本为继嗣，而亦有为不能亲操井臼，而欲资其馈养者。"刘殿爵的译文"To have someone to look after his parents does not constitute grounds for marriage"（结婚并不是为了能有人照顾自己的父母），基本上都能体现原文的意思。

[3] "抱关击柝"指看门守夜的人，常用来比喻地位低微的小官。赵岐注："抱关击柝，监门之职也。柝，门关之木也；击，椎之也。或曰：柝，行夜所击木也。"理雅各将之直译为"guarding the gates，or beating the watchman's stick"（守门或敲击巡夜人的门梆），译文虽略显僵硬，但也能使读者理解"抱关击柝"者的具体工作职责。刘殿爵的译文是"a gate-keeper or of a watchman"（守门人或巡夜者），更能清楚、准确地传达原文之意。

[4] "道不行"，即为官者不能实现自己的政治理想。译者们对"道"的内涵理解略有不同，刘殿爵认为是"take one's place at the court of a prince without putting the Way into effect"（做官者不能实践公认的道），赖发洛认为是"a man that does not follow the Way"（君主不能依道而行），理雅各认为是"his principles are not carried into practice"（为官者不能践行自己的原则），这三种理解都能很好地呼应孟子的"不遇故去"。

【原文】10.6　万章曰[1]："士之不托诸侯，何也？"孟子曰："不敢也。诸侯失国，而后托于诸侯，礼也；士之托于诸侯，非礼也。"万章曰："君馈之粟，则受之乎？"曰："受之。""受之何义也？"曰："君之于氓[2]也，固周之。"曰："周之则受，赐之则不受，何也？"曰："不敢也。"曰："敢问其不敢何也？"曰："抱关击柝者皆有常职以食于上。无常职而赐于上者，以为不恭也。"曰："君馈之，则受之，不识可常继乎？"曰："缪公之于子思也，亟问，亟馈鼎肉[3]。子思不悦。于卒也，摽使者出诸大门之外，北面稽首再拜而不受，曰：'今而后知君之犬马畜伋。'盖自是台无馈也。悦贤不能举，又不能养也，可谓悦贤乎？"曰："敢问国君欲养君子，如何斯可谓养矣？"曰："以君命将之，再拜稽首而受[4]。其后廪人继粟，庖人继肉，不以君命将之。子思以为鼎肉使己仆仆尔亟拜也，非养君子之道也。尧之于舜也，使其子九男事之，二女女焉，百官牛羊仓廪备[5]，以养舜于畎亩之中，后举而加诸上位，故曰，王公之尊贤者也。"

【译文】万章问："士不能寄居在诸侯那里生活，为什么呢？"孟子说："不敢啊！诸侯失去了国家，然后寄居在别的诸侯那里，是合乎礼的；士人寄居在诸侯那里，不合乎礼。"万章说："君主如果赠送给他谷米，能接受吗？"孟子说："接受。"万章问："接受是什么道理呢？"孟子答道："君主对于从外地来的人，原本就应该周济他。"万章问："周济他，就接受；赐予他，就不接受，为什么呢？"孟子回答道："因为不敢接受。"万章问道："请问不敢接受，又是为什么呢？"孟子答道："守门打更的人都有固定的职务，因而可以接受上面的供养。没有固定的职务，却接受上面的赏赐，这被认为是不恭敬。"万章接着问道："君王给他馈赠就接受，不知道可以经常这样吗？"答道："鲁缪公对于子思，就是多次问候，多次送给他肉食，子思很不高兴。最后，子思把来人驱逐出大门外，自己朝北面先稽首后作揖两次表示不接受，说道：'今天才知道国君把我当成犬马一样地豢养。'大概从此之后再不给子思馈赠了。喜爱贤人，却不能重用，又不能依礼照顾他的生活，可以说是喜爱贤人吗？"万章问道："请问如果君主要照顾君子的生活，怎样做才叫作有礼貌地照顾生活呢？"答道："先以君主的旨意赠送给他，他便先作揖两次然后磕头接受。此后管理仓库的人不断送去谷米，掌供膳食的人经常送去肉食，这些都不用说是君主的旨意了。子思认为为了一块肉便使自己屡次作揖行礼，这不是依礼照顾君子生活。尧对于舜，让自己的九个儿子向他学习，把自己的两个女儿嫁给他，而且各种官吏准备好牛羊、仓库，使舜在田野之中得到周到的照顾，然后推举他成为天子，所以说这才是王公尊贤啊！"

【英译】Wan Chang said, 'What is the reason that a scholar does not accept a stated support from a prince?' Mencius replied, 'He does not presume to do so. When a prince loses his State, and then accepts a stated support from another prince, this is in accordance with propriety. But for a scholar to accept such support from any of the princes is not in accordance with propriety.' Wan Chang said, 'If the prince send him a present of grain, for instance, does he accept it?' 'He accepts it,' answered Mencius. 'He accepts it,' answered Mencius. 'Why—the prince ought to assist the people in their necessities.' Chang pursued, 'Why is it that the scholar will thus accept the prince's help, but will not accept his pay?' The answer was, 'He does not presume to do so.' 'I venture to ask why he does not presume to do so.' 'Even the keepers of the gates, with their watchmen's sticks, have their regular offices for which they can take their support from the prince. He who without a regular office should receive the pay of the prince must be deemed disrespectful.' Chang asked, 'If the prince sends a scholar a present, he accepts it; —I do not know whether this present may be constantly repeated.' Mencius answered, 'There was the conduct of the duke Mû to Tsze-sze—He made frequent inquiries after Tsze-sze's health, and sent him frequent presents of cooked meat. Tsze-sze was displeased; and at length, having motioned to the messenger to go outside the great door, he bowed his head to the ground with his face to the north, did obeisance twice, and declined the gift, saying, "From this time forth I shall know that the prince supports me as a dog or a horse." And so from that time a servant was no more sent with the presents. When a prince professes to be pleased with a man of talents and virtue, and can neither promote him to office, nor support him in the proper way, can he be said to be pleased with him?' Chang said, 'I venture to ask how the sovereign of a State, when he wishes to support a superior man, must proceed, that he may be said to do so in the proper way?' Mencius answered, 'At first, the present must be offered with the prince's commission, and the scholar, making obeisance twice with his head bowed to the ground, will receive it. But after this the storekeeper will continue to send grain, and the master of the kitchen to send meat, presenting it as if without the prince's express commission. Tsze-sze considered that the meat from the prince's caldron, giving him the annoyance of constantly doing obeisance, was not the way to support a superior man. There was Yao's conduct to Shun:—He caused his nine sons to serve him, and gave him his two daughters in marriage; he caused the various officers, oxen and sheep, storehouses and granaries, all to be prepared to support Shun amid the channelled fields, and then he raised him to the most exalted situation. From this we have the expression, — "The honouring of virtue and talents proper to a king or a duke."'

【注释】

[1] 孟子指出，战国时期的诸侯虽争相礼贤下士，但不懂养君、悦贤之道。诸侯养君子应以尧养舜为榜样，首先要真心尊敬君子，设身处地为君子着想，尽其所能为君子提供一切便利条件，然后要相信君子、敢于任用君子。

[2] "氓"，焦循注曰："不言'君之于民也'而言'氓'者，'氓'是自他国至此国之民，与寄之义合。"刘殿爵将之翻译为"those who have come from abroad to settle"（外地迁入的人）。他的译文准确翻译出了"氓"的含义。理雅各将之翻译为"the people"（百姓），赖发洛翻译为"the destitute"（穷苦人）。

[3] "鼎肉"，《礼记·少仪》郑玄注云："谓牲体已解，可升于鼎。"刘殿爵的理解同郑玄，翻译为"meat for the tripod"（可以放到鼎里的肉）。朱熹注云："鼎肉，熟肉也。"理雅各的译文同朱熹，将之译为"cooked meat"（熟肉）。

[4] 杨伯峻认为"稽首再拜"和"再拜稽首"的区别是："拜头至地谓之稽首；既跪而拱手，而头俯至于手，与心平，谓之拜。再拜，拜两次。'再拜稽首'，谓之吉拜，表示接受礼物；'稽首再拜'，谓之凶拜，此处则表示拒绝礼物。"可见，"稽首"和"拜"是两种不同的礼节，出现的先后顺序不同，所表达的含义也有差异。理雅各将"稽首"和"再拜"分别翻译为"bowed his head to the ground"和"did obeisance twice"。他的译文基本上能体现二者的区别，刘殿爵则认为二者是一回事，将之翻译为"knocking his head twice on the ground"。

[5] "百官牛羊仓廪备"表现了尧养舜无微不至，尽最大所能为其提供便利。百官，焦循注曰："廪人、庖人之属。"理雅各将之翻译为"he caused the various officers, oxen and sheep, storehouses and granaries, all to be prepared to support Shun"（他为舜准备好了各种官员、牛羊和仓库）。他强调尧养舜的细心周到。而赖发洛的译文是"His hundred officers, his cows and

sheep，and his barns and storehouses were all made ready to feed Shun"（尧的百官、牛羊和仓库都准备好以奉养舜）。他侧重突出尧大公无私，以天下养贤者。刘殿爵的译文不同于理译本和赖译本，认为是"the hundred officials provided Shun with cattle and sheep and granaries for his use"（百官为舜准备好了牛羊和仓库以备用）。这几种理解皆可，相比之下，刘殿爵的译文更能呼应前文孟子推崇的国君养君子之道，即"以君命将之，再拜稽首而受。其后廪人继粟，庖人继肉，不以君命将之。"

【原文】10.7   万章曰[1]："敢问不见诸侯，何义也[2]？"孟子曰："在国曰市井之臣，在野曰草莽之臣，皆谓庶人。庶人不传质为臣，不敢见于诸侯[3]，礼也。"万章曰："庶人，召之役，则往役；君欲见之，召之，则不往见之，何也？"曰："往役，义也；往见，不义也。且君之欲见之也，何为也哉？"曰："为其多闻也，为其贤也。"曰："为其多闻也，则天子不召师，而况诸侯乎？为其贤也，则吾未闻欲见贤而召之也。缪公亟见于子思，曰：'古千乘之国以友士，何如？'子思不悦，曰：'古之人有言曰，事之云乎，岂曰友之云乎[4]？'子思之不悦也，岂不曰：'以位，则子，君也；我，臣也；何敢与君友也？以德，则子事我者也，奚可以与我友？'千乘之君求与之友而不可得也，而况可召与？齐景公田，招虞人以旌，不至，将杀之。志士不忘在沟壑，勇士不忘丧其元。孔子奚取焉？取非其招不往也。"曰："敢问招虞人何以？"曰："以皮冠，庶人以旃，士以旂，大夫以旌[5]。以大夫之招招虞人，虞人死不敢往；以士之招招庶人，庶人岂敢往哉？况乎以不贤人之招招贤人乎？欲见贤人而不以其道，犹欲其入而闭之门也。夫义，路也；礼，门也。惟君子能由是路，出入是门也。诗云：'周道[6]如底，其直如矢；君子所履，小人所视[7]。'"万章曰："孔子，君命召，不俟驾而行；然则孔子非与？"曰："孔子当仕有官职，而以其官召之也。"

【译文】万章问："请问士人不去拜见诸侯，这是为什么呢？"孟子说："没有职位的士人，居住在城市，叫作市井之臣；居住在田野，叫作草莽之臣，都是老百姓。老百姓没有送见面礼物给诸侯而成为臣属，就不敢去拜见诸侯，这是礼的规定。"万章说："老百姓，召唤他去服役就去服役；君主要见士人，召唤他，却不去谒见，这是为什么呢？"孟子说："去服役，是应该的；去拜见，是不应该的。况且君主想见他，为的是什么呢？"万章说："因为他见闻广博，因为他贤能。"孟子说："如果因为他见闻广博，那么天子还不能召见老师，何况诸侯呢？如果因为他贤能，那我也不曾听说过要见贤人却可以召唤的。鲁缪公多次去造访子思，说道：'古代拥有千辆兵车的国君和士人交友，是怎样做的呢？'子思不高兴，说：'古代人说的是国君把士人当老师吧，难道说的是和士人交友吗？'子思的不高兴，难道不是说'论地位，你是君主，我是臣下，我怎么敢同你交朋友呢？论道德，那你应该像对待老师那样侍奉我，怎么可以同我交朋友呢？'拥有一千辆兵车的国君想要和他交朋友都做不到，何况召唤他呢？齐景公田猎，用有羽毛装饰的旌旗召唤猎场管理员，他不来，要杀他。志士不怕弃尸山沟，勇士不怕丢掉脑袋。孔子对这一管理员赞许他哪一点呢？就是取不是召唤他的礼就不去。"问道："请问召唤猎场管理员用什么呢？"答道："用皮帽子。召唤老百姓用红色没有装饰的曲柄旗，召唤士用有铃铛的旗，召唤大夫才用有羽毛的旗。用召唤大夫的旗帜去召唤猎场管理员，猎场管理员死也不敢去；用召唤士人的旗帜去召唤老百姓，老百姓难道敢去吗？更何况用召唤不贤之人的礼节去召唤贤人呢？想见贤人，却不依循相应礼节，这就好像要请人家进来却关上大门。义好比是大路，礼好比是大门。只有君子能从义这条大路上行走，由礼这个大门出入。《诗经》说：'大路像磨刀石一样平，又像箭一样直；君子在上面走，百姓所效法。'"万章说："孔子，国君召唤他的时候，不等车马驾好就先走去。这样是孔子错了吗？"

孟子回答说："孔子正在做官，有职务在身，国君是按他担任的官职召见他。"

【英译】Wan Chang said, 'I venture to ask what principle of righteousness is involved in a scholar's not going to see the princes?' Mencius replied, 'A scholar residing in the city is called "a minister of the market-place and well," and one residing in the country is called "a minister of the grass and plants." In both cases he is a common man, and it is the rule of propriety that common men, who have not presented the introductory present and become ministers, should not presume to have interviews with the prince.' Wan Chang said, 'If a common man is called to perform any service, he goes and performs it; —how is it that a scholar, when the prince, wishing to see him, calls him to his presence, refuses to go?' Mencius replied, 'It is right to go and perform the service; it would not be right to go and see the prince.' 'And,' added Mencius, 'on what account is it that the prince wishes to see the scholar?' Because of his extensive information, or because of his talents and virtue,' was the reply. 'If because of his extensive information,' said Mencius, 'such a person is a teacher, and the sovereign would not call him; —how much less may any of the princes do so? If because of his talents and virtue, then I have not heard of any one wishing to see a person with those qualities, and calling him to his presence. During the frequent interviews of the duke Mû with Tsze-sze, he one day said to him, "Anciently, princes of a thousand chariots have yet been on terms of friendship with scholars; —what do you think of such an intercourse?" Tsze-sze was displeased, and said, "The ancients have said, 'The scholar should be served:' how should they have merely said that he should be made a friend of?"

When Tsze-sze was thus displeased, did he not say within himself, —
"With regard to our stations, you are sovereign, and I am subject.
How can I presume to be on terms of friendship with my sovereign?
With regard to our virtue, you ought to make me your master. How
can you be on terms of friendship with me?" Thus, when a ruler of a
thousand chariots sought to be on terms of friendship with a scholar,
he could not obtain his wish: —how much less could he call him to
his presence! The duke Ching of Ch'î, once, when he was hunting,
called his forester to him by a flag. The forester would not come,
and the duke was going to kill him. With reference to this incident,
Confucius said, "The determined officer never forgets that his end
may be in a ditch or a stream; the brave officer never forgets that he
may lose his head." What was it in the forester that Confucius thus
approved? He approved his not going to the duke, when summoned
by the article which was not appropriate to him.' Chang said, 'May I
ask with what a forester should be summoned?' Mencius replied, 'With
a skin cap. A common man should be summoned with a plain banner;
a scholar who has taken office, with one having dragons embroidered
on it; and a Great officer, with one having feathers suspended from
the top of the staff. When the forester was summoned with the article
appropriate to the summoning of a Great officer, he would have died
rather than presume to go. If a common man were summoned with
the article appropriate to the summoning of a scholar, how could
he presume to go? How much more may we expect this refusal to
go, when a man of talents and virtue is summoned in a way which is
inappropriate to his character! When a prince wishes to see a man of
talents and virtue, and does not take the proper course to get his wish,

it is as if he wished him to enter his palace, and shut the door against him. Now, righteousness is the way, and propriety is the door, but it is only the superior man who can follow this way, and go out and in by this door. It is said in the Book of Poetry, "The way to Châu is level like a whetstone, and straight as an arrow. The officers tread it, and the lower people see it." ' Wan Chang said, 'When Confucius received the prince's message calling him, he went without waiting for his carriage. Doing so, did Confucius do wrong?' Mencius replied, 'Confucius was in office, and had to observe its appropriate duties. And moreover, he was summoned on the business of his office.'

【注释】

[1] 儒家虽强调积极入仕，但更重视遵礼守身，始终把是否符合礼义作为为人处事和与人交往的首要原则。虽然接受君主召见有利于施展自己的政治抱负，但如果君主不以礼相招，以礼相待，君子也不会违礼相见。

[2] 本章针对万章的提问"不见诸侯，何义也"展开，理雅各认为这一提问主要指向那些未担任官职的知识分子，而刘殿爵则认为这一提问适用于所有人。从孟子的回答可以推测，二人的问答是针对士展开，因而理雅各的补充是准确和必需的。从文义上看，理雅各认为"不见诸侯"指"不主动去拜见诸侯"，因而将之翻译为"not going to see the princes"；而刘殿爵则认为是不接受君主的召见，将之翻译为"refuse to meet feudal lords"。从下文的"君欲见之，召之，则不往见之，何也"可以看出，刘殿爵的译文更准确。

[3] "庶人不传质为臣，不敢见于诸侯"是古代礼制对普通人谒见君主的规定，朱熹注曰："传，通也。质与贽同。质者，士执雉，庶人执鹜，相见以自通者也。国内莫非君臣，但未仕者与执贽在位之臣不同，故不敢见也。"因而刘殿爵翻译为"a Commoner does not dare present himself to a feudal lord unless he has handed in his token of allegiance."（普通人只有在呈交了臣服的信物后才能谒见诸侯）理雅各将之翻译为"it is the rule of propriety

that common men, who have not presented the introductory present and become ministers should not presume to have interviews with the prince."（根据礼的规定，士人只有在向君主赠送了见面礼，并因此成为其臣属时才能接受君主的召见）他们的译文都准确传达了这一古代传统礼仪。

[4] 古人说话言简意赅，其含义在汉语语境下比较容易理解，但翻译成英文时有时需要做一些必要的添加才能准确达意，如"古之人有言曰，事之云乎，岂曰友之云乎"就是一个例子。该句省略了主语和宾语，理雅各在翻译时做了适当的添加，将之译为"The ancients have said, 'The scholar should be served: how should they have merely said that he should be made a friend of?'"（古人说的是侍奉士人，他们怎么可能会说应当和士人交朋友）添加后的译文虽失去了原文简洁的风格，但更便于读者理解和传达子思不满的情绪。刘殿爵译为"What the ancients talked about was serving them, not making friends with them."（古人说的是侍奉他们，不是和他们交朋友）他的译文虽简洁，但改变了原文的句型特点，弱化了原文所蕴含的不满情绪。

[5] 孟子指出，根据礼的规定，对于不同身份的人，招呼的旗帜不同。朱熹注曰："皮冠，田猎之冠也。通帛曰旃……交龙为旂……析羽而注于旂干之首曰旌。"理雅各的译文同朱熹，将"皮冠、旃、旂、旌"分别翻译为"a skin cap""a plain banne""having dragons embroidered on it""one having feathers suspended from the top of the staff"，即"皮帽""没有装饰的旗""上面绣着龙的旗和上面装饰着羽毛的旗。""旃"，《说文》云："旗曲柄也。""旂"，《说文》云："旗有众铃。"刘殿爵的译文同《说文》，将之分别翻译为"a leather cap, a bent flag, a flag with bells and a pennon"（皮帽、曲柄旗、有铃铛的旗和有羽毛的旗）。二人的译文准确翻译出了招虞人的皮冠以及招大夫的旌的特征，但是对召庶人的旃和招士人的旂的翻译只是体现某个主要特征，将二者结合起来，才为其全貌，即"旃"是没有装饰的红色曲柄旗。"旂"是上面绣着双龙并在旗杆头上悬挂铃铛的旗。

[6] "周道"，焦循指出："按《毛诗》本意，'周道'谓周家贡赋赏罚

之道。……然则孟子引《诗》以'周道如底，其直如矢'，证义之为路，礼之为门，礼义即道也。"孟子也指出，"由义"是"行天下之大道"。因而刘殿爵选择用"highway"（大道）翻译"周道"。理雅各则采用音译法将之翻译为"The way to Châu"。

[7] 本章的论述均围绕"贤人"展开，因而在"君子所履，小人所视"中，"君子"和"小人"也是根据德行划分。"君子"是指道德高尚的人，"小人"指的是品德一般的普通百姓。理雅各将之分别翻译为"The officers"（为官者）和"the lower people"（下层百姓）不确切。刘殿爵选择用"gentleman"翻译"君子"，"gentleman"更强调身份等级的高贵，因而用之翻译也不准确。此处的"小人"指"common people"（普通百姓），他们通过效法贤人，也可以践行礼义，"虞人非其招不往"就是一个明显的例子。

【原文】 10.8　孟子谓万章曰[1]："一乡之善士斯友一乡之善士，一国之善士斯友一国之善士，天下之善士斯友天下之善士[2]。以友天下之善士为未足，又尚论古之人。颂其诗，读其书，不知其人，可乎? [3]是以论其世也。是尚友也。"

【译文】 孟子对万章说："一乡中的善士便和这一乡中的善士交朋友；一国中的善士和这一国中的善士交朋友；天下的善士和天下的善士交朋友。和天下的善士交朋友还不够，便又追论古代的人物。吟咏他们的诗，读他们的著作，不了解他们的为人，可以吗? 所以要讨论他们生活的时代。这就是追溯历史与古人交朋友。"

【英译】 Mencius said to Wan Chang, 'The scholar whose virtue is most distinguished in a village shall make friends of all the virtuous scholars in the village. The scholar whose virtue is most distinguished throughout a State shall make friends of all the virtuous scholars of that State. The scholar whose virtue is most distinguished throughout the kingdom shall make friends of all the virtuous scholars of the kingdom. When a scholar feels that his friendship with all the virtuous scholars of the kingdom is not sufficient to satisfy him, he proceeds to ascend to consider the men of antiquity. He repeats their poems, and reads their books, and as he does not know what they were as men, to ascertain this, he considers their history. This is to ascend and make friends of the men of antiquity.'

【注释】

[1] 孟子认为，学无止境，取善无穷。要想成为一个道德高尚的人，首先要同乡里、国中、天下的贤能之人交朋友，以友辅仁，通过学习他们的高尚品德和优秀品质来充实、提高自己。其次应向书本学习、向古代圣贤学习，不断丰富自己、深化自己，以达到修身养性，成就自我的目的。

[2] 对"一乡之善士斯友一乡之善士，一国之善士斯友一国之善士，天下之善士斯友天下之善士"的理解有二：一种以赵岐为代表，认为"各以大小来相友，自为畴匹也"。即强调交友的标准是双方善名的对等，即在乡里以品德高尚著称的人应和那些善名和他相同的人交友，不能和那些善名不如自己的人交友。刘殿爵的译文就持这一观点，他将本段翻译为"The best Gentleman of a village is in a position to make friends with the best Gentlemen in other villages；the best Gentleman in a state, with the best Gentlemen in other states；and the best Gentleman in the Empire, with the best Gentlemen in the Empire."（一个乡村里最优秀的人物应和其他乡村里最优秀的人物交朋友，一个国家里最优秀的人物应和其他国家里最优秀的人物交朋友，天下最优秀的人物应和天下最优秀的人物交朋友）另一种观点以朱熹为代表，指出"言己之善盖于一乡，然后能尽友一乡之善士。推而至于一国天下皆然，随其高下以为广狭也。"显然，他强调自我修身的重要性，认为只有自己的品德不断提升，交友的范围才会逐渐扩大。理雅各的译文基本上持这一观点。

[3] 虽然"颂其诗，读其书，不知其人，可乎？是以论其世也"论述

的是与古代圣贤交友的方法，但也为后世学者指明了读书的一种重要方法，即今人读古书，应在作者生活的时代背景和心路历程下理解作者所要传达的思想，而不应以读者生活的时代和价值标准对古书的字面内容妄加评论。刘殿爵的译文"When one reads the poems and writings of the ancients, can it be right not to know something about them as men?"既保留了原文的句型特点，又不执着于字词的逐个对应，用通俗易懂的语言准确传达了原文之意。

【原文】10.9　齐宣王问卿[1]。孟子曰："王何卿之问也？"王曰："卿不同乎？"曰："不同；有贵戚之卿，有异姓之卿[2]。"王曰："请问贵戚之卿。"曰："君有大过则谏；反复之而不听，则易位。"王勃然变乎色[3]。曰："王勿异也。王问臣，臣不敢不以正[4]对。"王色定，然后请问之卿。曰："君有过则谏，反复之而不听，则去。"

【译文】齐宣王问公卿的事情。孟子说："王，你问的是哪种类型的公卿？"王说："公卿还有不同的吗？"孟子说："不同；有与国君有血缘关系的公卿，有与国君无血缘关系的公卿。"王说："我问的是与国君有血缘关系的公卿。"孟子说："君王若犯有重大错误，就劝谏；反复劝谏还不听从，就把他废弃，另立国君。"王突然变了脸色。孟子说："王不要诧异。王问我，我不敢不拿实话回答。"王脸色正常了，然后又请问与国君无血缘关系的公卿。孟子说："君王若犯错，便劝谏，反复劝谏还不听从，就离职。"

【英译】The king Hsüan of Ch'î asked about the office of high ministers. Mencius said, 'Which high ministers is your Majesty asking about?' 'Are there differences among them?' inquired the king. 'There are,' was the reply. 'There are the high ministers who are noble and relatives of the prince, and there are those who are of a different surname.' The king said, 'I beg to ask about the high ministers who are noble and relatives of the prince.' Mencius answered, 'If the prince have great faults, they ought to remonstrate with him, and if he do not listen to them after they have done so again and again, they ought to dethrone him.' The king on this looked moved, and changed countenance. Mencius said, 'Let not your Majesty be offended. You asked me, and I dare not answer but according to truth.' The king's countenance became composed, and he then begged to ask about high ministers who were of a different surname from the prince. Mencius said, 'When the prince has faults, they ought to remonstrate with him; and if he do not listen to them after they have done this again and again, they ought to leave the State.'

【注释】

[1] 孟子根据血缘关系，将公卿分为贵戚之卿和异姓之卿，并详细论证了二类公卿不同的职责和权力。

[2] 赵岐认为："贵戚之卿，谓内外亲族也。异姓之卿，谓有德命为三卿也。"焦循进一步解释说："贵戚之卿，以亲而任，故云内外亲族也。异姓之卿，以贤而任，故云有德命为三卿也。"杨伯峻则认为，不包含异姓的外亲。他解释说："《孟子》此文以'贵戚之卿'与'异姓之卿'对文，则'贵戚'为同姓可知。核之儒家所传宗法制度，亦当如此解释，'外戚'不在'贵戚之卿'数内也。"可见，"贵戚之卿"是天子或诸侯有血缘关系的公卿，是君主亲亲的象征，而"异姓之卿"与君主没有血缘关系，是君主尊贤的产物。刘殿爵译为"ministers of royal blood and those of families other than the royal house"。他的译文表明二者的区别主要在于是否具备皇室血统，准确体现二者的区别。理雅各的译文类赵岐，将"贵戚之卿"翻译为"ministers who are noble and relatives of the prince"，扩大了其内涵。

[3] "勃然"表明变色的突然以及变色的表现是怒而惊。理雅各将"勃然变乎色"翻译为"The king on this looked moved, and changed countenance"

（王听到这里，显得有些激动，并且变了脸色）。译文未能传递出原文的感情色彩，也未体现变色的突然。赵甄陶的译文则凸显了变色的快，即"The king's face changed color at once"（君主的脸色立刻变了）。

[4]"正"，杨伯峻指出："《论语·述而篇》：'正唯弟子不能学也。'郑玄《注》云：'鲁读"正"为"诚"。'此处亦当读为'诚'。"理雅各将之翻译为"according to truth"，赵甄陶翻译为"be honest and outspoken"，二人皆翻译出了"正"所具备的实话、真实的含义。刘殿爵的译文"the proper answer"则形神兼备地译出了"正"的含义。

卷 十 一

告子章句上

【原文】11.1　告子曰[1]："性犹杞柳[2]也；义犹杯棬也；以人性为仁义[3]，犹以杞柳为杯棬。"孟子曰："子能顺杞柳之性而以为杯棬乎？将戕贼杞柳而后以为杯棬也？如将戕贼杞柳而以为杯棬，则亦将戕贼人以为仁义与？率天下之人而祸仁义者[4]，必子之言夫！"

【译文】告子说："人性好比杞柳树，义好比是杯盘；从人性中产生仁义，就好比用杞柳树制成杯盘。"孟子说："您是顺着杞柳树的本性去制成杯盘呢？还是残害杞柳树的本性来制作杯盘呢？如果是残害杞柳树的本性制作杯盘，那也要残害了人的本性去成就仁义吗？率领天下的人损害仁义的，一定是你这种学说！"

【英译】The philosopher Kâo said, 'Man's nature is like the ch'î-willow, and righteousness is like a cup or a bowl. The fashioning benevolence and righteousness out of man's nature is like the making cups and bowls from the ch'î-willow.' Mencius replied, 'Can you, leaving untouched the nature of the willow, make with it cups and bowls? You must do violence and injury to the willow, before you can make cups and bowls with it. If you must do violence and injury to the willow in order to make cups and bowls with it, on your principles you must in the same way do violence and injury to humanity in order

to fashion from it benevolence and righteousness！ Your words，
alas！ would certainly lead all men on to reckon benevolence and
righteousness to be calamities.'

【注释】

[1]《孟子·告子上》前四篇是一个整体，集中记载了孟子与告子关于
"性"的辩论。在"人性"上，孟子主张"人性善"，告子强调"人性无善无
不善"。在第一章，告子只是用类比的办法对自己"人性无善无不善"的观
点加以说明，而孟子也只是指出告子在使用类比时存在着自相矛盾的问题，
二人都未从内容上对自己的观点作出实质性的论证。

[2] 告子通过类比，首先表明了自己对人性的看法。他认为人性如杞
柳树，没有善与不善的区别。义就像杯棬，是独立于杞柳即性之外的。在这
里，告子用中国古代的一种树木来比喻人性，该树的特点是枝条柔软，可以
制作杯盘等器物。"杞柳"，刘殿爵采取音译、意译相结合的方法，将之翻
译为"ch'i-willow"。译者用意译表明这种树是柳树，用音译表明这种柳树
是中国古代特有的品种，将"杞柳"的音义都很好地传达给了读者。

[3] 告子认为，从人性中产生仁和义就如用杞柳制造杯子一样，会
对人性造成伤害。刘殿爵没有将"仁"和"义"分别译出，而是把它们合
译为"morality"（道德）。理雅各将之理解为"仁义"两种美德，翻译为
"benevolence and righteousness"。

[4] 孟子对告子的说法进行反驳，并指出告子的言论将会带来的祸
害——"率天下之人而祸仁义者"。理雅各将"祸仁义"理解为"以仁义
为祸"，译为"lead all men on to reckon benevolence and righteousness to be
calamities"（你的话注定要使所有的人都认为仁义是祸害）。刘殿爵则认为是
给仁义带来祸害，将之翻译为"bringing disaster upon morality"。二人强调的
侧重点不同，理雅各强调告子的言论会使天下人对仁义产生误解，刘殿爵则
强调告子的言论会使天下的人损害道德。

【原文】11.2　告子曰[1]："性犹湍水也，决诸东方则东流，决诸西方则西流。人性之无分于善不善也，犹水之无分于东西也。"孟子曰："水信无分于东西，无分于上下乎？人性之善也[2]，犹水之就下也。人无有不善，水无有不下。今夫水，搏而跃之，可使过颡；激而行之，可使在山。是岂水之性哉？其势则然也。人之可使为不善，其性亦犹是也。"

【译文】告子说："人性好比是急流水，从东面开缺口便向东流，从西面开缺口便向西流。人性没有善与不善的分别，就好像水没有东流还是西流的分别一样。"孟子说："水确实没有东流西流的分别，难道也没有向上或者向下的分别吗？人性表现为善，就像水性向下流一样。人没有不善良的，水没有不向下流的。水，拍打它使它飞溅起来，可以高过额角；阻挡使它倒流，可以引上高山。这难道是水的本性吗？是形势使它如此。人可以使他做坏事，他的本性的改变也如此。"

【英译】The philosopher Kâo said, 'Man's nature is like water whirling round in a corner. Open a passage for it to the east, and it will flow to the east; open a passage for it to the west, and it will flow to the west. Man's nature is indifferent to good and evil, just as the water is indifferent to the east and west.' Mencius replied, 'Water indeed will flow indifferently to the east or west, but will it flow indifferently up or down? The tendency of man's nature to good is like the tendency of water to flow downwards. There are none but have this tendency to good, just as all water flows downwards. Now by striking water and causing it to leap up, you may make it go over your forehead, and, by damming and leading it you may force it up a hill; —but are such movements according to the nature of water? It is the force applied which causes them. When men are made to do what is not good, their nature is dealt with in this way.'

【注释】

[1] 在此章中，孟子和告子继续用类比的方式对自己的人性论进行说明。告子以水喻性，认为人性没有善与不善的定性，就像激流的水，没有东流西流的定向一样。而孟子则认为人性的善良就像水要向下流一样，水之所以不向下流，人之所以会变恶主要是外在的影响。

[2] "之"，梁涛认为"犹'为'。是。"刘殿爵的理解与之相类，将"人性之善也"翻译为"Human nature is good"（人性是善良的）。理雅各把"之"作动词用，理解为"到、去，趋向"，将"人性之善也"翻译为"The tendency of man's nature to good"（人性趋向善）。理雅各将孟子的人性善理解为人性向善，并在他翻译的《中国经典》序言中提出"儒学的人性论与基督教思想是一致的，儒学主张人性向善与基督教的人必须弃恶向善的思想是相通的。孟子在这方面的思想与英国的巴特勒主教的学说是相同的。"

【原文】11.3 告子曰[1]："生之谓性[2]。"孟子曰："生之谓性也，犹白之谓白欤？"曰："然。""白羽之白也，犹白雪之白；白雪之白犹白玉之白欤[3]？"曰："然。""然则犬之性犹牛之性，牛之性犹人之性欤？"

【译文】告子说："生而具有的叫作性。"孟子说："生而具有的叫作性，好比白色的东西叫作白吗？"告子答道："是的。""白羽毛的白如同白雪的白，白雪的白如同白玉的白吗？"答道："是的。""那么，狗性如同牛性，牛性如同人性吗？"

【英译】The philosopher Kâo said, 'Life is what we call nature!' Mencius asked him, 'Do you say that by nature you mean life, just as you say that white is white?' 'Yes, I do,' was the reply. Mencius added, 'Is the whiteness of a white feather like that of white snow, and the whiteness of white snow like that of white jade?' Kâo again said 'Yes.' 'Very well,' pursued Mencius. 'Is the nature of a dog like the nature of an ox, and the nature of an ox like the nature of a man?'

【注释】

[1] 在此章中，孟子从告子的"生之谓性"的命题出发，运用类比推理的方法，推出犬之性与牛之性与人之性相同这样听起来荒谬绝伦的结论。

[2] 告子所谓的"生之谓性"是从与生俱来的角度言性，认为天生的本来状况就是性，即"生之然之谓性"，也就是《论衡·本性》所谓的"生而然者也"。刘殿爵的理解与之相类，将之翻译为"The inborn is what is meant by nature"（生来就具有的东西就是性）。朱熹注云："生，指人物之所以知觉运动者而言。"受其影响，理雅各将之翻译为"Life is what we call nature"（生命就是性）。

[3] 本章共出现了十个"白"字，赖发洛将之统一翻译为"white"，而理雅各和刘殿爵根据语境的变化，将之分别翻译为"white"和"whiteness"。前者保留了原文的行文特点，后者则更符合英文的表达习惯。

【原文】11.4 告子曰[1]："食色[2]，性也[3]。仁，内也，非外也；义，外也，非内也。"孟子曰："何以谓仁内义外也?"曰："彼长而我长之，非有长于我也；犹彼白而我白之，从其白于外也，故谓之外也。"曰："异于白马之白也[4]，无以异于白人之白也；不识长马之长也，无以异于长人之长欤？且谓长者义乎？长之者义乎？"曰："吾弟则爱之，秦人之弟则不爱也，是以我为悦者也[5]，故谓之内。长楚人之长，亦长吾之长，是以长为悦者也，故谓之外也。"曰："耆秦人之炙，无以异于耆吾炙，夫物则亦有然者也，然则耆炙亦有外欤？"

【译文】告子说："好美食美色是性。仁是内在的，不是外在的；义是外在的，不是内在的。"孟子说："为什么说仁是内在的，义是外在的呢？"告子答道："他年纪大，我就恭敬他；不是因为我预先就有恭敬他的心；就好比物品是白的，我便说它是白色的，这是根据它自身的白我才这么认为的，所以说义是外在的。"孟子说："白马的白和白人的白没有什么不同；不知道对老马的尊敬和对老者的尊敬，是不是也没有什么不同呢？而且，你说的义，是在于老者呢，还是在于恭敬老者的人呢？"答道："我的弟弟我便爱他，秦国人的弟弟我便不爱他，这是因我自己高兴这样，所以说仁是内在的东西。恭敬楚国的老人，也恭敬我自己的老人，这是因为他们是老者的关系，所以说义是外在的。"孟子说："喜欢吃秦国人的烤肉，和喜欢吃自己的烤肉没有什么不同，各种事物也有如此的情形。那么，难道喜欢吃烤肉也是外在的吗？"

【英译】The philosopher Kâo said, 'To enjoy food and delight in colours is nature. Benevolence is internal and not external; righteousness is external and not internal.' Mencius asked him, 'What is the ground of your saying that benevolence is internal and righteousness external?' He replied, 'There is a man older than I, and I give honour to his age. It is not that there is first in me a principle of such reverence to age. It is just as when there is a white man, and I consider him white; —according as he is so externally to me. On this account, I pronounce of righteousness that it is external.' Mencius said, 'There is no difference between our pronouncing a white horse to be white and our pronouncing a white man to be white. But is there no difference between the regard with which we acknowledge the age of an old horse and that with which we acknowledge the age of an old man? And what is it which is called righteousness? —the fact of a man's being old? Or the fact of our giving honour to his age?' Kâo said, 'There is my younger brother; —I love him. But the younger brother of a man of Ch'in I do not love: that is, the feeling is determined by myself, and therefore I say that benevolence is internal. On the other hand, I give honour to an old man of Ch'û, and I also give honour to an old man of my own people：that is，the feeling is determined by the age，and therefore I say that righteousness is external.’ Mencius answered him，‘Our enjoyment of meat roasted by a man of Ch‘in does not differ from our enjoyment of meat roasted by ourselves. Thus，what you insist on takes place also in the case of such things，and will you say likewise that our enjoyment of a roast is external?’

【注释】

[1] 本章孟子和告子主要围绕仁内义外展开辩论。

[2]《礼记·礼运篇》"饮食男女，人之大欲存焉"。在古代中国文化中，"食"和"色"通常连用，泛指人得以生存和繁衍的本能欲望，因而，"色"指"女色、性欲"，刘殿爵将之翻译为"sex"（性欲）。但是理雅各在注释中指出"食色也可以理解为沉迷情欲"，他根据熙周的注解，选择喜欢好的颜色这一翻译，因而将"色"译为"colours"（颜色）。

[3] 此处的"性"与孟子所谓"性"善的"性"概念不同。孟子在讨论人性时，是从人和动物的区别说起。但告子不同，正如张岱年所指出的：告子"认为人要生存、繁殖这就是人性。将人看成是'自然人'，把一切生物的共性当作了人性。"因而刘殿爵将之翻译为"nature"而非"human nature"。

[4]"异于"，朱熹《集注》引张氏曰："二字疑衍。"杨伯峻主张将"异于"二字删除，他在注释中指出，"按此说较是。焦循《正义》强加解释，无当于古代语法，故不从。"理雅各亦提出删掉第一个"异于"，将之译为"There is no difference between our pronouncing a white horse to be white and our pronouncing a white man to be white." 即"我们说一匹白马是白的，与说一个人是白的，在白上没有什么不同。"刘殿爵建议把原文修改为"异于白。白马之白无以异于白人之白也。"他将之翻译为"The case of rightness is different from that of whiteness. Treating as white is the same whether one is treating a horse as white or a man as white"（义的情形不同于白的情形。不管

是白马还是白人，白都是一样的）。显然，他的修改受下文"不识长马之长也，无以异于长人之长钦"的影响。修改后的译文不仅句意通顺，而且逻辑性更强。梁涛亦给出了另外一种理解："异。于白马之白也。"

[5] 学界对"悦"的含义和用法一直存在分歧。理雅各承认，自己没有弄明白"悦"的用法和含义，因而选择不翻译。虽然他曾试图引用《日讲四书义解》对"悦"的解释，即"吾弟则爱之，秦人之弟则不爱也，表明爱取决于我。悦乎我心，则爱之，不悦乎我心，则不爱。但是尊敬是由年龄决定的。凡遇长皆在所悦，不必产生于我们的心"来消除自己的困惑，但没有成功。刘殿爵则选择把"悦"当作"说"，将之翻译为"My brother I love, but the brother of a man from Chʻin I do not love. This means that the explanation lies in me."（我爱我的弟弟，但是不爱秦人的弟弟。这是就我的关系而说的）刘殿爵没有给出把"悦"当作"说"的依据。倪德卫指出："刘殿爵和葛瑞汉建议把'悦'字当作'说'字，是因为他们心里想的是后期墨家作为一种论辩之术的'说。'"后期墨家强调"以说出故"，即通过"说"的方式以明确"立辞"的根据和理由。赖发洛则按字面意思翻译"悦"为"pleased"。

【原文】11.5　孟季子问公都子[1]曰："何以谓义内也？"曰："行吾敬，故谓之内也。""乡人长于伯兄一岁，则谁敬？"曰："敬兄。""酌则谁先？"曰："先酌乡人。""所敬在此，所长在彼，果在外，非由内也。"公都子不能答，以告孟子。孟子曰："敬叔父乎？敬弟乎？彼将曰：'敬叔父'。曰：'弟为尸[2]，则谁敬？'彼将曰：'敬弟。'子曰：'恶在其敬叔父也？'彼将曰：'在位故也。'子亦曰：'在位故也。庸敬在兄，斯须之敬在乡人。'"季子闻之，曰："敬叔父则敬，敬弟则敬，果在外，非由内也。"公都子曰："冬日则饮汤，夏日则饮水[3]，然则饮食亦在外也？"

【译文】孟季子问公都子说："怎么说义是内在的呢？"回答说："义从我的内心发出，所以说是内在的。""本乡人比大哥大一岁，那你敬谁?"答道:"恭敬哥哥。""饮酒时,先给谁斟酒?"答道:"先给本乡长者斟酒。""内心恭敬的是大哥,却向本乡长者先行礼。可见义果真是外在的,不是发自内心。"公都子不能回答,便告诉了孟子。孟子说:"(你可以说)'恭教叔父呢?还是恭敬弟弟呢?'他将会说:'恭敬叔父。'你又说:'弟弟若做了祭祀时代替死者受祭的人,那又该恭敬谁呢?'他会说:'恭敬弟弟。'你便说:'那为什么又说恭敬叔父呢?'他会说:'这是因为弟弟在受恭敬之位的缘故。'那你也就说:'那是因为本乡长者在恭敬之位的缘故。平常恭敬哥哥,暂时的恭敬在于本地长者。'"季子听到了之后,说:"对叔父是恭敬,对弟弟是恭敬,义果真是外在的,不是由内心出发的。"公都子说:"冬天喝热水,夏天喝凉水,那么,难道饮食也是外在的吗?"

【英译】The disciple Măng Chî asked Kung-tû, saying, 'On what ground is it said that righteousness is internal?' Kung-tû replied, 'We therein act out our feeling of respect, and therefore it is said to be internal.' The other objected, 'Suppose the case of a villager older than your elder brother by one year, to which of them would you show the greater respect?' 'To my brother,' was the reply. 'But for which of them would you first pour out wine at a feast?' 'For the villager.' Măng Chî argued, 'Now your feeling of reverence rests on the one, and now the honour due to age is rendered to the other;—this is certainly determined by what is without, and does not proceed from within.' Kung-tû was unable to reply, and told the conversation to Mencius. Mencius said, 'You should ask him, "Which do you respect most,—your uncle, or your younger brother?" He will answer, "My uncle." Ask him again, "If your younger brother be personating a dead ancestor, to which do you show the greater respect,—to him or to your uncle?" He will say, "To my younger brother." You can go on,

"But where is the respect due, as you said, to your uncle?" He will reply to this, "I show the respect to my younger brother, because of the position which he occupies," and you can likewise say, "So my respect to the villager is because of the position which he occupies. Ordinarily, my respect is rendered to my elder brother; for a brief season, on occasion, it is rendered to the villager."' Mǎng Chî heard this and observed, 'When respect is due to my uncle, I respect him, and when respect is due to my younger brother, I respect him; the thing is certainly determined by what is without, and does not proceed from within.' Kung-tû replied, 'In winter we drink things hot, in summer we drink things cold; and so, on your principle, eating and drinking also depend on what is external!'

【注释】

[1] 本章是对前章"义外"之争的继续和补充，和前四章不同的是，这次争论是在孟季子和公都子之间展开的。

[2] 在本章中出现了一个具有丰富文化内涵的词语"尸"。郑玄注《仪礼·士虞礼》"祝迎尸，一人衰绖奉篚哭从尸"曰："尸，主也。孝子之祭，不见亲之形象，心无所系，立尸而主意焉。"何休注《春秋公羊传·宣公八年》"祭之明日也"曰："祭必有尸者，节神也。礼，天子以卿为尸，诸侯以大夫为尸，卿大夫以下以孙为尸。"可见，"尸"是古代祭祀时代替死者受祭的人，任何人只要处于尸位就会受到尊敬。刘殿爵将"尸"翻译为"impersonating an ancestor at a sacrifice"（在祭祀时扮演祖先的人）。这一翻译比较清楚地向读者传播了中国古代的祭祀传统。而理雅各的"personating a dead ancestor"（扮演已故祖先），传递的信息量过少，容易引起读者的疑问。

[3] "汤"的本义是热水、开水。《说文》云："汤，热水也。"因而"冬日则饮汤，夏日则饮水"应理解为"冬天喝热水，夏天喝凉水"。刘殿爵准

确翻译出了这一含义，但赖发洛照字面意思直译"汤"为"soup"，没有看到汤的古意，未能翻译出"冬与夏、汤与水（热与冷）"的鲜明对比关系。

【原文】 11.6　公都子曰[1]："告子曰：'性无善无不善也。'或曰：'性可以为善，可以为不善；是故文武兴，则民好善；幽厉兴，则民好暴。'或曰：'有性善，有性不善；是故以尧为君而有象；以瞽瞍为父而有舜；以纣为兄之子，且以为君，而有微子启、王子比干[2]。'今曰'性善'，然则彼皆非与？"孟子曰："乃若其情[3]，则可以为善矣，乃所谓善也。若夫为不善，非才[4]之罪也。恻隐之心，人皆有之；羞恶之心，人皆有之；恭敬之心，人皆有之；是非之心，人皆有之。恻隐之心，仁也；羞恶之心，义也；恭敬之心，礼也；是非之心，智也。仁义礼智，非由外铄[5]我也，我固有之也，弗思耳矣。故曰：'求则得之，舍则失之。'或相倍蓰而无算者，不能尽其才者也。《诗》曰：'天生蒸民[6]，有物有则。民之秉彝，好是懿德。'孔子曰：'为此诗者，其知道乎！故有物必有则；民之秉彝也，故好是懿德。'"

【译文】 公都子说："告子说：'性没有善和不善的区别。'有人说：'性可以使它善良，也可以使它不善良；所以文王、武王兴起，使得百姓好善；幽王、厉王在位，百姓爱好暴虐。'也有人说：'有的人性善，有的人性不善；所以尧做君主，也有象那样的百姓；瞽瞍这样坏的父亲，却有舜这样的好儿子；以纣为侄儿，而且为君王，却有微子启、王子比干这样的人。'现在说'性善'，那么，他们都错了吗？"孟子说："至于人性的实情，可以使它善良，这便是我所谓的善。至于有些人表现为不善，不能归罪于他的材质。同情心，每个人都有；羞耻心，每个人都有；恭敬心，每个人都有；是非心，每个人都有。同情心，属于仁；羞耻心，属于义；恭敬心，属于礼；是非心，属于智。仁义礼智，不是由外人给予我的，是我本来就具有的，只不过是没有意识到罢了。所以说：'探求便会得到，放弃便会失去。'人与人之间有相差一倍、五倍甚至无数倍的，就是不能充分实现他们的人性的本质的缘故。《诗经》说：'天生众民，每一样事物，都有它的法则。百姓把握住这些不变的法则，所以喜好这些品德。'孔子说：'写作这篇诗的人大概真懂的道呀！所以有事物便有它的法则；百姓把握住这些法则，所以喜好这些品德。'

【英译】The disciple Kung-tû said, 'The philosopher Kâo says, "Man's nature is neither good nor bad." Some say, "Man's nature may be made to practise good, and it may be made to practise evil, and accordingly, under Wǎn and Wû, the people loved what was good, while under Yû and Lî, they loved what was cruel." Some say, "The nature of some is good, and the nature of others is bad. Hence it was that under such a sovereign as Yâo there yet appeared Hsiang; that with such a father as Kû-sâu there yet appeared Shun; and that with Châu for their sovereign, and the son of their elder brother besides, there were found Ch'î, the viscount of Wei, and the prince Pî-kan. And now you say, "The nature is good." Then are all those wrong?' Mencius said, 'From the feelings proper to it, it is constituted for the practice of what is good. This is what I mean in saying that the nature is good. If men do what is not good, the blame cannot be imputed to their natural powers. The feeling of commiseration belongs to all men; so does that of shame and dislike; and that of reverence and respect; and that of approving and disapproving. The feeling of commiseration implies the principle of benevolence; that of shame and dislike, the principle of righteousness; that of reverence and respect, the principle of propriety; and that of approving and disapproving, the principle of knowledge. Benevolence, righteousness, propriety, and knowledge are not infused into us from without. We are certainly furnished with them. And a different view is simply owing to want of reflection. Hence it is said, "Seek and you will find them. Neglect and you will lose them." Men differ from one another in regard to them；——some as much again as others， some five times as much， and some to an incalculable amount：——it is because they cannot carry out fully their natural powers. It is said in the Book of Poetry，"Heaven in producing mankind， gave them their various faculties and relations with their specific laws. These are the invariable rules of nature for all to hold， and all love this admirable virtue." Confucius said，"The maker of this ode knew indeed the principle of our nature！" We may thus see that every faculty and relation must have its law， and since there are invariable rules for all to hold， they consequently love this admirable virtue.'

【注释】

[1] 孟子在本章中从正面阐述了他的人性观。

[2] 本章伊始，告子引用了诸多历史人物来作"性可善可不善""性无善无不善"以及"有性善，有性不善"的证据。文武是圣王，幽厉是暴君；尧舜是圣王，象是舜的同父异母的弟弟，整天想着谋杀舜，瞽瞍是舜的父亲，讨厌舜，经常欺辱甚至谋杀舜；纣王残暴不仁，微子启是他的庶兄，也是当时的贤者，王子比干是纣王的叔父。只有熟悉这些历史人物，才能更好理解当时流行的三种人性观。刘殿爵采取音译的方式进行翻译，并在文后索引中对这些人物进行了介绍，有助于读者理解原文。

[3] 关于"情"，有两种理解。一种以朱熹为代表，以性和情对言，解"情"为情感之情。朱熹注曰："性之动也。人之情，本但可以为善而不可以为恶，则性之本善可知矣。"理雅各和赖发洛的理解与之相类，把"情"翻译为"feelings"（情感）。另外一种观点解"情"为"实"。戴震的《孟子字义疏证》云："情犹素也，实也。"冯友兰在早期著作《中国哲学史》里，亦将"情"理解为"事之实也"。牟宗三也认为："情，实也，犹言实情（real

case)。"刘殿爵亦持此种观点，将之翻译为"what is genuinely"（实情、实际情况）。

[4]"才"字在《孟子》中最主要的含义是人的初生之质。《说文》解字谓"才"，"草木之初也。""才"还可以指才能，如朱熹注曰："才犹材质，人之能也。"在极少情况下，"才"特指有才能的人。结合上下文，此处的"才"应指人的初生之质，与前句的"其情"为"性之实情"相呼应。因而刘殿爵的"native endowment"（天生之质）准确翻译出了"才"的含义。

[5]"铄"，朱熹注曰："以火销金之名，自外以至内也。"理雅各将之翻译为"infuse"（灌输），取"铄"的"由外至内"之意。赖发洛翻译为"burnt into"（用火烧），取与"铄"的形似。刘殿爵将"铄"翻译为"weld"，"weld"的含义是使两个完全不同的东西，经过加热紧密地连接为一体。相比之下，刘殿爵对"铄"翻译是形神兼备。

[6]"蒸"今意指"用水蒸气的热力把东西加热"，在此处形容人数众多。理雅各省略了对"蒸"的翻译，赖发洛将之翻译为"seething"（火热的、川流不息的），既翻译出了"蒸"的字面意思，也体现了人数众多，奔流不息之意。刘殿爵的"teeming"翻译出了"人数众多"的意思。

【原文】11.7 孟子曰[1]："富岁，子弟多赖[2]；凶岁，子弟多暴，非天之降才尔殊也，其所以陷溺其心者然也。今夫麰麦，播种而耰之，其地同，树之时又同，浡然而生，至于日至[3]之时，皆熟矣。虽有不同，则地有肥硗，雨露之养、人事之不齐也。故凡同类者，举相似也，何独至于人而疑之？圣人，与我同类者。故龙子曰：'不知足而为屦，我知其不为蒉也。'屦之相似，天下之足同也。口之于味，有同耆也；易牙[4]先得我口之所耆者也。如使口之于味也，其性与人殊[5]，若犬马之与我不同类也，则天下何耆皆从易牙之于味也？至于味，天下期于易牙，是天下之口相似也。惟耳亦然。至于声，天下期于师旷[6]，是天下之耳相似也。惟目亦然。至于子都，天下莫不知其姣也；不知子都之姣者，无目者也。故曰，口之于味也，有同耆焉；耳之于声也，有同听焉；目之于色也，有同美焉。至于心，独无所同然乎？[7]心之所同然者何也？谓理也，义也。圣人先得我心之所同然耳。故理义[8]之悦我心，犹刍豢之悦我口。"

【译文】孟子说："丰年，少年子弟多懒惰；荒年，少年子弟多暴虐。不是天生的才有什么不同，是外部环境影响他们的心的缘故。就好比大麦，播了种，用土把种子盖好，如果土地一样，播种的时间一样，便会蓬勃生长，到了夏至，都会成熟了。即使有不同，那是由于土地的肥瘠、雨露的多少、人工的勤惰不同造成的。所以凡是同类的事物，都大体相同，为什么到了人便怀疑了呢？圣人和我是同类。所以龙子说：'即使不看脚样去编草鞋，我也知道不会编成筐子。'草鞋的外形相近，是因为脚大体相同。口对于味道，有相同的嗜好；易牙是先摸准了我们共同嗜好的人。如果口对于味道，人人生来不同，就好像狗马和我们不同类一样，那么，天下的人为什么都喜好易牙烹制出来的口味呢？说到口味，天下都期望做到易牙那样，这就说明天下人的味觉是相似的。耳朵也是这样。说到声音，天下的人都期望做到师旷那样，这说明天下人的听觉是相似的。眼睛也是这样。说到子都，天下没有人不知道他漂亮。不承认子都漂亮的，是不长眼睛的人。所以说，口对于味道，有相同的嗜好；耳对于声音，有相同的听觉；眼睛对于容貌，有相同的美感。说到心，就偏偏没有相同的地方了吗？心相同的地方是什么？是理，是义。圣人只不过是先摸准了我们内心的相同之处罢了，所以理义愉悦我的心，就像猪狗牛羊肉合乎我们的口一样。"

【英译】Mencius said, 'In good years the children of the people are most of them good, while in bad years the most of them abandon themselves to evil. It is not owing to any difference of their natural powers conferred by Heaven that they are thus different. The abandonment is owing to the circumstances through which they allow their minds to be ensnared and drowned in evil. There now is barley.— Let it be sown and covered up; the ground being the same, and the time of sowing likewise the same, it grows rapidly up, and, when the full time is come, it is all found to be ripe. Although there may be inequalities of produce, that is owing to the difference of the soil, as rich or poor, to the unequal nourishment afforded by the rains and dews, and to the different ways in which man has performed his business in reference to it. Thus all things which are the same in kind are like to one another; —why should we doubt in regard to man, as if he were a solitary exception to this? The sage and we are the same in kind. In accordance with this the scholar Lung said, "If a man make hempen sandals without knowing the size of people's feet, yet I know that he will not make them like baskets." Sandals are all like one another, because all men's feet are like one another. So with the mouth and flavours; —all mouths have the same relishes. Yî-yâ only apprehended before me what my mouth relishes. Suppose that his mouth in its relish for flavours differed from that of other men, as is the case with dogs or horses which are not the same in kind with us, why should all men be found following Yî-yâ in their relishes? In the matter of tastes all the people model themselves after Yî-yâ; that is, the mouths of all men are like one another. And so also it is with the ear. In the matter of sounds, the whole people model themselves after the music-master K'wang; that is, the ears of all men are like one another. And so also it is with the eye. In the case of Tsze-tû, there is no man but would recognise that he was beautiful. Any one who would not recognise the beauty of Tsze-tû must have no eyes. Therefore I say, —Men's mouths agree in having the same relishes; their ears agree in enjoying the same sounds; their eyes agree in recognising the same beauty: —shall their minds alone be without that which the similarly approve? What is it then of which they similarly approve? It is, I say, the principles of our nature, and the determinations of righteousness. The sages only apprehended before me that of which my mind approves along with other men. Therefore the principles of our nature and the determinations of righteousness are agreeable to my mind, just as the flesh of grass and grain-fed animals is agreeable to my mouth.'

【注释】

[1] 孟子虽强调人性善，但不否认环境的影响。他认为，人之所以会在道德水平上存在偏差，并非天生的材质不同，而是因为后天对善端的发扬程度相异，正如谷物的生长因土地和气候而异一样。他同时指出，人们之所以会自觉地选择理义，是因为他们具有基本类似的道德审美度，就像他们对声音、容貌和味道具有共同的偏爱一样。

[2] 学者对"赖"的理解大体有三种。一种以赵岐为代表，将之注为："赖，善。暴，恶也。"第二种以朱熹为代表，认为："赖，借也。丰年衣食饶足，故有所顾借而为善；凶年衣食不足，故以陷溺其心而为暴。"第三种是焦循在《孟子正义》引阮元曰："'赖'即'懒'。"理雅各受赵岐影响将"赖"翻译为"good"（好、善），赖发洛则翻译为"steady"（平和的），二人都认为此处的"赖"和后面的"暴"是对比而言。刘殿爵则将"赖"译为"lazy"（懒惰）。任俊华、赵清文对这三种注解进行了分析，并指出"直接将'赖'释为'善'未免有些牵强。虽然古人以'赢''利'释'赖'，但直接将其解释为'善'的却不多。……朱熹将'赖'释为'借'与下文'暴'字的对应不是非常贴切。"他们支持阮元的注解。杨伯峻等多数汉学家也都主张将"赖"释为"懒"。

[3] "日至"，夏至。刘殿爵直接将之翻译为"the summer solstice"（夏

至）。理雅各根据文义将之翻译为"when the full time is come"（当收获时节到来），赖发洛译为"midsummer"（仲夏、夏至）。三种翻译基本上能体现其含义。

[4]"易牙"，朱熹注曰："古之知味者也。"刘殿爵和其他译者皆选用音译。

[5]"与人殊"，杨伯峻指出："意盖谓人人不同。此宜云'人与人殊'，原文盖省一'人'字。"刘殿爵的译文也持此种观点，将之翻译为"If taste differed by nature from person to person"（人与人不同）。理雅各则提出了另外一种理解："Suppose that his mouth in its relish for flavours differed from that of other men"（假设他的口对于味道的品味和别人不同）。杨逢彬通过分析先秦文献的句型特点，反驳了杨伯峻的观点，亦支持将"与人殊"翻译为"假使口对于味道，他的体验和别人不同"。

[6]"师旷"是春秋时代晋国著名的乐师。在古代，地位最高的音乐家的名字前常被冠以"师"，因而理雅各将之翻译为"music-master K'wang"（音乐大家旷），刘殿爵则将之音译为"Shih K'uang"。

[7]焦循引毛氏奇龄《剩言补》云："'至于心，独无所同然'，承上'同耆'、'同听'言，谓同如是耳，与前'惟耳亦然'诸然字相应。"即认为"然"的含义是"这样"。刘殿爵的译文持此种观点。但朱熹认为，"然，犹可也。"理雅各受朱熹的影响，将之翻译为"approve"（认同、认可）。从上下文看，将"然"理解为"这样"逻辑性更强。

[8]在《孟子》中，"理义"连用仅在此处出现。杨泽波指出："'理'的本义为治玉，引申为纹理、条理，又引申为道理、规律。'理'与'义'相连，更加强了道理的含义，特指正确的道理、一般的道理。"联系上文，孟子是从人们有共同的味觉、听觉、视觉来论证人心有好"理义"这一共同爱好的，借此来宣扬他的性善说。因此，此处的"理义"其实就是"仁、义、礼、智"的统称。理雅各将之翻译为"the principles of our nature and the determinations of righteousness"，基本能涵盖其基本含义。刘殿爵则选择用

"Reason and rightness" 翻译，虽能体现其字面意思，但略显笼统。

【原文】11.8 孟子曰[1]："牛山之木尝美矣，以其郊于大国[2]也，斧斤伐之，可以为美乎？是其日夜之所息，雨露之所润，非无萌蘖之生焉，牛羊又从而牧之，是以若彼濯濯也。人见其濯濯也，以为未尝有材焉，此岂山之性也哉？虽存乎人者，岂无仁义之心哉？其所以放其良心者，亦犹斧斤之于木也，旦旦而伐之，可以为美乎？其日夜之所息，平旦之气，其好恶与人相近也者几希[3]，则其旦昼[4]之所为，有梏亡[5]之矣。梏之反复，则其夜气不足以存[6]；夜气不足以存，则其违禽兽不远矣。人见其禽兽也，而以为未尝有才焉者，是岂人之情也哉？故苟得其养，无物不长；苟失其养，无物不消。孔子曰：'操则存，舍则亡；出入无时，莫知其乡[7]。'惟心之谓与？"

【译文】孟子说："牛山的树木曾经长得很茂盛，因为它临近大都市，经常会用斧子去砍伐，还能够茂盛吗？当然，它日日夜夜在生长着，雨水露珠滋润着，不是没有新芽萌生出来，但是放羊牧牛紧随其后，所以变成那样光秃秃了。人们看见那样光秃秃，以为山上没有生长过大树木，这难道是山的本性吗？就说在人身上吧，难道没有仁义之心吗？之所以会丧失善良之心，也好像斧子砍树木一般，天天去砍伐它，能够茂盛吗？他在日夜所发出来的善心，在天刚亮时所接触到的清明之气，这激发出来的好恶和一般人相近的也有一点点。可是到了第二天白天，他的所行所为又将它扰乱、消灭了。这样反复地消灭，他夜间心里所发出的善念也不能保存；夜间心里所发出的善念也不能保存，便和禽兽相差不远了。别人看到他像禽兽，会以为他不曾有过善良的资质，这难道是人的本性吗？所以如果得到合适的照顾，没有东西不生；不能被合适照顾，没有东西不消亡。孔子说：'把握就存在，放弃就消亡；出入没定时，不知道它的去向。'这是指人心而言吧？"

【英译】Mencius said, 'The trees of the Niû mountain were once beautiful. Being situated, however, in the borders of a large State, they were hewn down with axes and bills; —and could they retain their beauty? Still through the activity of the vegetative life day and night, and the nourishing influence of the rain and dew, they were not without buds and sprouts springing forth, but then came the cattle and goats and browsed upon them. To these things is owing the bare and stripped appearance of the mountain, and when people now see it, they think it was never finely wooded. But is this the nature of the mountain? And so also of what properly belongs to man; —shall it be said that the mind of any man was without benevolence and righteousness? The way in which a man loses his proper goodness of mind is like the way in which the trees are denuded by axes and bills. Hewn down day after day, can it—the mind—retain its beauty? But there is a development of its life day and night, and in the calm air of the morning, just between night and day, the mind feels in a degree those desires and aversions which are proper to humanity, but the feeling is not strong, and it is fettered and destroyed by what takes place during the day. This fettering taking place again and again, the restorative influence of the night is not sufficient to preserve the proper goodness of the mind; and when this proves insufficient for that purpose, the nature becomes not much different from that of the irrational animals, and when people now see it, they think that it never had those powers which I assert. But does this condition represent the feelings proper to humanity? Therefore, if it receive its proper nourishment, there is nothing which will not grow. If it lose its proper nourishment, there is nothing which will not decay away. Confucius said, "Hold it fast, and it remains with you. Let it go，and you lose it. Its outgoing and incoming cannot be defined as to time or place."It is the mind of which this is said！'

【注释】

[1] 孟子在此处再次提到了"才"的问题。孟子在《告子上》"乃若其情"章就"情"讲"才"，在此处又据"气"言"才"。此处的"气"指的是人在不受外力作用时由初生之性所显露出的善心。他认为，当人们失掉良心，形同禽兽之时，并不能说明人的初生之性和禽兽无异，这如同牛山因过度砍伐和放牧而变成光秃秃，并不能说明山上本来没有木材。

[2] "大国"，大的国都，这里指临淄城。理雅各将之翻译为"in the borders of a large State"（大国的边界），不准确。刘殿爵认为是大都城的郊区，将之翻译为"the outskirts of a great metropolis"。国内学者也多持此观点，但梁涛认为："郊：此处用作动词。意为临近。"这两种理解皆可。

[3] "其好恶与人相近也者几希"是针对那些"放其良心者"而发，对他们来说，由初生之性所发出来的善心受平旦之气的影响，在好恶之情上与其他人也有一点点相近。理雅各将本句翻译为"the mind feels in a degree those desires and aversions which are proper to humanity，but the feeling is not strong"（虽然能在一定程度上感受到人类所特有的善恶之情，但是这种感觉并不强烈）。理雅各认为，"放其良心者"并非"未尝有才"，但因"夜气不足"，虽具备人共有的初生之性，但并不明显。显然，理雅各相信"几希"强调的是"相近的程度"。而刘殿爵认为是用来表明相近的内容。他将本句翻译为"scarcely any of his likes and dislikes resemble those of other men"（他的好恶和其他人几乎没有相近的地方）。孟子认为，人的初生之性都具备善端，但如果"失其养"，不能"扩而充之"，善端就会消亡。"放其良心者"的善端消亡后，在好恶内容上就会与他人存在差异，因而刘殿爵将"几希"理解为"内容上相似的很少"。

[4] "旦昼"连用，旨在强调"昼"。赵岐《注》曰："旦昼，昼日也。"理雅各和刘殿爵都将"旦昼"翻译为"the day"（在白天），而赖发洛将之翻

译为"the dawn and in the day-time"（在拂晓和白天）。从文义上看，前文已经指出在拂晓之时"放其良心者"可以接触到"平旦之气"来激发善心，若此处认为拂晓之时的行为会削减善心，就会和前文相矛盾。

[5] 古今注家对"梏亡"的理解有两种。一说因受束缚而致丧失。孙奭疏曰："梏，手械也。利欲之制善，使不得为，犹梏之制手也。"一说为因搅乱而丧失。焦循指出："捁牿梏同，赵氏读'牿'为'搅'故训为'乱'。"理雅各和赖发洛取前说，分别将"梏亡"翻译为"fettered and destroyed"（束缚和破坏）和"fetter and quell"（束缚和消亡）。刘殿爵根据上下文义，将"梏亡"意译为"dissipate"（驱散）。

[6] 根据文义，"夜气不足以存"省略的宾语是"才"，因而"夜气"指的是在夜晚不受外力影响时由人的初生之性显露出的善心。理雅各将本句翻译为"the restorative influence of the night is not sufficient to preserve the proper goodness of the mind"（晚上对本性的复原不足以保存人固有的善心）。孟子认为，人生而具备善性，因而对"本性的复原"实际上就是恢复"人的初生之性显露出的善心"。理雅各的译文可以准确体现"夜气"的内涵。赖发洛的译文是"the breath of night is too little to keep them alive"（夜晚的气息太少，不能保存他的好恶之情）。他过于直译，没有体现出"夜气"在此处的哲学内涵。刘殿爵翻译为"the influence of the air in the night will no longer be able to preserve what was originally in him"（晚上空气的感化力不再能保存他的初生之性）。刘殿爵的译文也能较为全面地译介"夜气"的内涵。

[7] "乡"有两种含义：赵岐《注》云："乡犹里，以喻居也。"一说见焦循《正义》曰："近读乡为向。"理雅各将"乡"理解为"居"，认为"莫知其乡"和"无时"都是用来形容"出入"的，他将本句翻译为"Its outgoing and incoming cannot be defined as to time or place"（它的来去没有固定的时间和地点）。赖发洛严格按照原文句型翻译为"none knows its home"（没有人知道它的居所）。虽然他也将"乡"理解为"居所"，但认为"出入无时"和"莫知其乡"是并列关系，分别指来去无定时和心的居所的神秘。

刘殿爵的译文是"neither does one know the direction"（也没有人知道它的方向）。"乡"的两种含义都能说得通，但是笔者认为将"乡"翻译为"方向"更符合心自由自在、不受约束的特性。

【原文】 11.9　孟子曰[1]："无或乎王之不智也。虽有天下易生之物也，一日暴之，十日寒之，未有能生者也。吾见亦罕矣，吾退而寒之者至矣[2]，吾如有萌焉何哉[3]？今夫弈之为数[4]，小数也；不专心致志，则不得也。弈秋，通国之善弈者也。使弈秋诲二人弈，其一人专心致志，惟弈秋之为听。一人虽听之，一心以为有鸿鹄将至，思援弓缴而射之，虽与之俱学，弗若之矣。为是其智弗若与？曰：非然也。"

【译文】孟子说："王不明智也不足为怪。即使有天下最容易生长的东西，如果晒它一天，冻它十天，也没有能生长的。我见王的次数也太少了，我离开，那些'冻'他的奸邪之人就到了，我虽然能使他有善良之心的萌芽，又能怎么样呢？现在围棋是技艺，是一个小技艺；不专心致志地学习，也学不好。弈秋是全国最擅长下棋的人。让他教两个人围棋，其中一人一心一意地学习，只听弈秋的讲解。一个人虽然在听，但一心认为有天鹅要飞来，想着要拿弓箭去射它。虽然是和那人一起学，肯定学的不如人家好。是因为他的聪明不如人家吗？当然不是了。"

【英译】Mencius said, 'It is not to be wondered at that the king is not wise! Suppose the case of the most easily growing thing in the world；—if you let it have one day's genial heat, and then expose it for ten days to cold, it will not be able to grow. It is but seldom that I have an audience of the king, and when I retire, there come all those who act upon him like the cold. Though I succeed in bringing out some buds of goodness, of what avail is it? Now chess-playing is but a small art, but without his whole mind being given, and his will bent, to it，a man cannot succeed at it. Chess Ch'iû is the best chess-player in all the kingdom. Suppose that he is teaching two men to play.—The one gives to the subject his whole mind and bends to it all his will，doing nothing but listening to Chess Ch'iû. The other，although he seems to be listening to him，has his whole mind running on a swan which he thinks is approaching，and wishes to bend his bow，adjust the string to the arrow，and shoot it. Although he is learning along with the other，he does not come up to him. Why？ —because his intelligence is not equal？ Not so.'

【注释】

[1] 孟子在本章举弈秋教人下棋的例子来说明，做任何事情都要一心一意，专心致志，否则很难取得成功，更不用说推行仁政这一国家大计。

[2] 对"吾退而寒之者至矣"有两种理解。一种以理雅各和刘殿爵为代表，认为是"寒之者"出现。理雅各将之翻译为，"when I retire，there come all those who act upon him like the cold"（我离开后，那些行为不良的人就来了，他们就像妨碍植物生长的冷空气）。他的译文将"寒之者"和"十日寒之"联系起来，既翻译出了原文的字面意思，又译出了原文所蕴含的言外之意，即"寒之者"是一些行为不良，诱其学坏之人。刘殿爵的译文也紧扣前文的"十日寒之"，但没有指明译文的暗含之意，而是让读者自己去体味。另一种理解以赵甄陶为代表，将之翻译为"leaving the king in the cold to the utmost degree"（把君主冷淡到了极点）。他认为"至"是修饰"寒"的，表示寒冷的程度。

[3] "吾如有萌焉何哉"，理雅各将之翻译为"Though I succeed in bringing out some buds of goodness，of what avail is it"（我即使能使他萌发一些善心，又有什么用啊）。他的译文紧扣篇章宗旨，将原文的暗含之意准确翻译了出来。刘殿爵的译文"What can I do with the few new shoots that come out"清楚地再现了原文的字面意思，而孟子所要表达的言外之意则让读者

自己去体味。

[4]"弈",是围棋最古老的称号,理雅各将之翻译为"chess-playing"（国际象棋），赖发洛将之翻译为"chequer"（西洋跳棋）。二人都选择用西方人熟悉的棋类翻译中国古代的"弈"，虽便于外国读者理解，但没有看到国际象棋、西洋跳棋和"弈"的区别，不利于传播中国传统文化，也不能让读者了解中国围棋的历史。刘殿爵用汉语拼音将"弈"翻译为"yi"，以凸显其内涵的独特性。

【原文】11.10 孟子曰[1]："鱼，我所欲也；熊掌亦我所欲也；二者不可得兼，舍鱼而取熊掌者也。生亦我所欲也，义亦我所欲也；二者不可得兼，舍生而取义者也。生亦我所欲，所欲有甚于生者，故不为苟得[2]也；死亦我所恶，所恶有甚于死者，故患有所不辟也。如使人之所欲莫甚于生，则凡可以得生者，何不用也？使人之所恶莫甚于死者，则凡可以辟患者，何不为也？由是则生而有不用也，由是则可以辟患而有不为也，是故所欲有甚于生者，所恶有甚于死者。非独贤者有是心也，人皆有之，贤者能勿丧耳。一箪食，一豆羹[3]，得之则生，弗得则死，呼[4]尔而与之，行道之人弗受；蹴尔而与之，乞人不屑也。万钟则不辩礼义而受之。万钟于我何加焉？为宫室之美、妻妾之奉、所识穷乏者得我与？乡为身死而不受，今为宫室之美为之；乡为身死而不受，今为妻妾之奉为之；乡为身死而不受，今为所识穷乏者得我而为之，是亦不可以已乎？此之谓失其本心[5]。"

【译文】孟子说："鱼是我想要的，熊掌也是我想要的；如果两者不能同时占有，便舍弃鱼，而要熊掌。生命是我想要的，义也是我想要的；如果两者不能同时占有，便舍弃生命，而要义。生命也是我想要的，但是想要的有比生命更重要的，所以我不干苟且偷生的事；死是我所厌恶的，但是有比死亡更让我厌恶的，所以有的祸害我不躲避。如果人们想要的没有超过生命的，那么，一切可以求得生存的方法，哪有不使用的？如果人们所厌恶的没有超过死亡的，那么，一切可以避免祸害的事情，哪有不做的？这样做就可以得到生存，然而有人却不做；这样做便可以避免祸害，然而有人却不去干。由此可知，人们想要的东西有比生命更重要的，所厌恶的东西有超过死亡的。并不仅仅是贤者有这种心，人人都有，贤者能不丧失而已。一筐饭，一碗汤，得到便能活下去，得不到便会饿死，呵斥着给予他，过路的人也不会接受；用脚踏过再给他，乞丐也不屑要。万钟的俸禄却不问是否合于礼义就接受了，万钟的俸禄对我有什么好处呢？为了住宅的华丽、妻妾的侍奉、我所认识的贫苦人感激我吗？过去宁肯死亡也不接受，今天却为住宅的华丽而接受了；过去宁肯死亡也不接受，今天却为了妻妾的侍奉而接受了；过去宁肯死亡也不接受，今天却为我所认识的贫苦人感激我而接受了，这些不可以停止吗？这就是所谓的丢掉了本性。"

【英译】Mencius said, 'I like fish, and I also like bear's paws. If I cannot have the two together, I will let the fish go, and take the bear's paws. So, I like life, and I also like righteousness. If I cannot keep the two together, I will let life go, and choose righteousness. I like life indeed, but there is that which I like more than life, and therefore, I will not seek to possess it by any improper ways. I dislike death indeed, but there is that which I dislike more than death, and therefore there are occasions when I will not avoid danger. If among the things which man likes there were nothing which he liked more than life, why should he not use every means by which he could preserve it? If among the things which man dislikes there were nothing which he disliked more than death, why should he not do everything by which he could avoid danger? There are cases when men by a certain course might preserve life, and they do not employ it; when by certain things they might avoid danger, and they will not do them. Therefore, men have that which they like more than life, and that which they dislike more than death. They are not men of distinguished talents and virtue only who have this mental nature. All men have it; what belongs to such men is simply that they do not lose it. Here are a small basket of rice and a platter of soup, and the case is one in which the getting them will preserve life, and the want of them will be death; —if they are offered with an insulting voice, even a tramper will not receive them, or if you first tread upon them, even a beggar will not stoop to take them. And yet a man will accept of ten thousand chung, without any consideration of propriety or righteousness. What can the ten thousand chung add to him? When he takes them, is it not that he may obtain beautiful mansions, that he may secure the services of wives and concubines, or that the poor and needy of his acquaintance may be helped by him? In the former case the offered bounty was not received, though it would have saved from death, and now the emolument is taken for the sake of beautiful mansions. The bounty that would have preserved from death was not received, and the emolument is taken to get the service of wives and concubines. The bounty that would have saved from death was not received, and the emolument is taken that one's poor and needy acquaintance may be helped by him. Was it then not possible likewise to decline this? This is a case of what is called—"Losing the proper nature of one's mind."'

【注释】

[1] 孟子指出，人在一生中会经常遇到需要选择的事，在两者不可兼得的情况下，人们通常会选择价值更高的东西，在面临生死抉择时也不例外。"无求生以害仁，有杀身以成仁"（《论语·卫灵公》）是孔子的生死观，

孟子将之继承和发展为"舍生取义"的人生观，强调"所欲有甚于生者，所恶有甚于死者"。他的人生观鼓舞了一代代的有志之士用青春热血和宝贵生命谱写了一曲曲舍弃生命，追求正义的正气歌。

[2]"苟得"是用不当的方法获得，《礼记·曲礼上》有"临财毋苟得"。孔颖达疏曰："非义而取，谓之苟得。"因而理雅各将"苟得"翻译为"use every means by which he could preserve it"（通过能想到的任何方法来占有它）。他的译文围绕篇章宗旨，突出强调"取义"的原因和重要性。刘殿爵的译文没有突出"苟得"方法非义的特点，将之意译为"That is why I do not cling to life at all costs"（不惜任何代价地保有生命）。他的译文也能体现原文宗旨。

[3]"箪"和"豆"都是古代盛食物的器皿。"箪"是古代用竹子编制的盛饭用的圆形竹器。"豆"形似高足盘，或有盖，盛食品，多为陶制，也有青铜制或木制涂漆。理雅各和刘殿爵分别将"箪"翻译为"a small basket"和"basketful"。"Basket"是编制而成的圆形盛器，和"箪"在外形和制作工艺上有共同之处。赖发洛将之翻译为"a dish"（一盘），取其和"箪"有相同的功能。"豆"，虽然理雅各和刘殿爵都看到了它作为盛器的功能，但对其外形的描述不同。理雅各认为它是"a platter"（大浅盘），而刘殿爵则认为是"a bowlful"（一满碗）。结合下文"豆"是作为"羹"的盛器而出现可以断定刘殿爵的翻译更准确。而赖发洛却将之误译为"bean soup"（豆汤）。

[4]"呼"，此处是动词，指带有侮辱性的招呼。理雅各将之翻译为"if they are offered with an insulting voice"（如果用侮辱的语气给他们）。他的译文既翻译出了原文的字面意思，又将"呼"所蕴含的轻蔑与不屑准确地传递了出来。赖发洛将之翻译为"given him with a shout"（呼喊着给他）。如果仅仅是因为别人大喊着叫他吃饭，他就宁愿饿死也不接受，这个行路之人也未免过于矫情。刘殿爵的译文"given with abuse"（辱骂着给他）。他的译文将路人坚守节操，为捍卫人格尊严不惜失去生命的气节准确表达了出来。

[5]"本心"，即人生而具备的四端之心。孟子强调人性善，认为"恻隐之心，仁之端也；羞恶之心，义之端也；辞让之心，礼之端也；是非之心，

智之端也。人之有是四端也，犹其有四体也。"可见此处的"本心"指的是人生而固有的仁、义、礼、智四端。刘殿爵的"original heart"（固有的、本来的心）基本能体现其含义。

【原文】11.11　孟子曰[1]："仁，人心也；义，人路也。舍其路[2]而弗由，放其心而不知求[3]，哀哉！人有鸡犬放，则知求之；有放心而不知求。学问之道无他，求其放心而已矣[4]。"

【译文】孟子说："仁是人的心，义是人的道路。舍弃了道路而不去行走，丢失了本心却不知道寻求，太悲哀了！人有鸡和狗走失了，就知道去寻找；善心丧失了，却不知道去寻求。学问知道没有别的，就是把丧失的善心找回来罢了。"

【英译】Mencius said, 'Benevolence is man's mind, and righteousness is man's path. How lamentable is it to neglect the path and not pursue it, to lose this mind and not know to seek it again! When men's fowls and dogs are lost, they know to seek for them again, but they lose their mind, and do not know to seek for it. The great end of learning is nothing else but to seek for the lost mind.'

【注释】

[1] 心是孟子学说的一个重要范畴，含义非常丰富。根据上下文，此处的"心"主要指"良心、本心"。因而本章旨在强调保持、涵养和发展人生来固有的善良之心的重要性。

[2] "舍其路"，理雅各将之翻译为"neglect the path"（忽视道路），认为它并非人的有意行为，而是无意中偏离了正义之路。赖发洛的译文是"To leave the road unfollowed"（远离大道不遵循），他强调有意识地避开大道，不去执行。而刘殿爵的译文"gives up the right road"（放弃正路）则突出"舍其路"者自甘堕落，自愿抛弃正道不遵循的愚昧无知。"路"，理雅各将之翻译为"path"（途径），更强调抽象之意，而赖发洛和刘殿爵则将之译为

"road"，指现实中的道路。从孟子的论证特色看，他在说理时习惯将抽象的事理具体化，以便于读者形象地把握其内涵，因而刘殿爵和赖发洛取现实的"路"的含义，以突出其直观性亦可。

[3]"不知求"，理雅各和刘殿爵的译文表明"放其心"者愚昧无知，不知道应该找回失去的本心，而赖发洛则认为虽知道应该找回，但由于个人能力有限，"not know where to seek it"（不知道应去何处寻找）。相比较而言，理雅各和刘殿爵的理解更准确。

[4]应将"求其放心而已矣"放到孟子的整个思想体系下去理解。理雅各将之翻译为"The great end of learning is nothing else but to seek for the lost mind."（学习的伟大目标仅仅是寻求丧失的心），显然他认为孟子把寻求丧失的本心当作学习、修身的最高境界和目标。刘殿爵的译文是"The sole concern of learning is to go after this strayed heart."（做学问唯一关注的是追求迷失的心）。二人不拘泥于原文字面意思，在孟子的整个思想体系下解读孟子思想，都将"求其放心"作为修养身心的首要目标和唯一归宿。

【原文】11.12　孟子曰[1]："今有无名之指[2]屈而不信，非疾痛害事也，如有能信之者，则不远秦楚之路，为指之不若人也[3]。指不若人，则知恶之；心不若人，则不知恶，此之谓不知类[4]也。"

【译文】孟子说："现在有人无名指弯曲不能伸直，虽然不痛也不影响做事，但是只要有人能使它伸直，就是到秦国、楚国也不会嫌弃远，因为手指比不上别人。手指比不上别人，就知道厌恶；心比不上别人，却不知道厌恶，这就是不懂得轻重。"

【英译】Mencius said, 'Here is a man whose fourth finger is bent and cannot be stretched out straight. It is not painful, nor does it incommode his business, and yet if there be any one who can make it straight, he will not think the way from Ch'in to Ch'û far to go to him; because his finger is not like the finger of other people. When a man's finger is not like those of other people，he knows to feel dissatisfied，but if his mind be not like that of other people，he does not know to feel dissatisfaction. This is called—"Ignorance of the relative importance of things.''

【注释】

[1] 孟子擅从浅显易懂的事例类比引申出深奥难懂的义理。无名指在手指中的地位最低，作用最小，尽管如此，如果它不能伸直，人们也会千方百计地寻找治疗它的方法，因为任何人都不会容忍自己不如别人。但是普通人通常只会看到形体上的差距，却不明白人和人最根本、最重要的差别在内心。能否保有和发展善良的本心，是圣人、普通人和禽兽的首要区别。

[2] "无名之指"，赵岐注曰："手之第四指也。盖以其余指皆有名。无名指者，非手之用指也。"可见，古人认为，无名指作用不大。理雅各将之译为 "fourth finger"（第四个手指），但刘殿爵却认为是 "third finger"（第三个手指）。赖发洛将之译为 "nameless finger"（无名指）。无名指是小拇指旁的手指已成为共识，因而理雅各的译文是准确的。在欧洲，"无名指"通常被认为是 "ring finger" 而不叫 "nameless finger"，但是 "ring finger" 一般特指左手的无名指。相比较而言，理雅各的翻译更清楚明白。

[3]《词诠》指出"若"多用于否定句和反问句，为"外动词，及也。《礼记·檀弓上》云：'丧礼，与其哀不足而礼有余也，不若礼不足而哀有余也。'"因而刘殿爵译为 "finger is inferior to other people's"（手指比不上别人）。理雅各和赖发洛则认为"不若人"是和别人不一样。

[4] "不知类"，赵岐注曰："心不若人，可恶之大者也。而反恶指，故曰不知其类也。"可见，"不知类"就是舍大取小，舍本逐末，因而朱熹将之解为："不知轻重之等也。"理雅各的理解与之相类，将之翻译为 "Ignorance of the relative importance of things"（不知道事情的轻重），而刘殿爵则认为是 "failure to see that one thing is the same in kind as another"（不知道这一事物和其他事物是一类）。

【原文】 11.13　孟子曰^[1]：“拱把之桐梓^[2]，人苟欲生之，皆知所以养之者。至于身，而不知所以养^[3]之者，岂爱身不若桐梓哉？弗思甚也。”

【译文】 孟子说：“一两把粗的桐树、梓树，人们如果想让它们生长，都知道要去培养。对于自己，却不知道如何去培养，难道是爱自己不如桐树、梓树吗？真是太不用脑子思考了。”

【英译】 Mencius said, 'Anybody who wishes to cultivate the t'ung or the tsze, which may be grasped with both hands, perhaps with one, knows by what means to nourish them. In the case of their own persons, men do not know by what means to nourish them. Is it to be supposed that their regard of their own persons is inferior to their regard for a t'ung or tsze? Their want of reflection is extreme.'

【注释】

[1] 生活在农耕社会的人虽然擅养动物、植物，明白若要它们苗壮成长，就应费尽心思去照料，但却往往忽视自身的道德修养。这并不是因为人们不爱护自己的身体，而是未能认识到修身养性的重要性。

[2] “拱”，赵岐注曰：“合两手也。把，以一手把之也。”理雅各将之翻译为 “the t'ung or the tsze, which may be grasped with both hands, perhaps with one”（两手或一手可以抓得过来的桐树和梓树）。他的译文将古汉语“拱把”的含义准确翻译了出来。刘殿爵则选择用西方人比较熟悉的测量单位 “span” 翻译“拱把”。“桐梓”，理雅各和刘殿爵选择用音译法翻译中国古代专有名词，而赖发洛则将之翻译为 “tallow trees”（乌桕）和 “lindens”（椴树）。

[3] 本章“养”的含义非常丰富，既可指给人或动物提供食物，又可指给植物以养料，还包括用仁义美德修养身心。理雅各选择用 “feed” 翻译“养”，“feed” 的含义非常广泛，指给人、动物或植物以食物或养料来促进其生长。赖发洛的译文 “nourish” 则强调为生物提供生存所必需的食物或养

料，尤指用营养品促其生长。而刘殿爵的"tend"既可以指照料身体，也可以指修养心性。

【原文】11.14 孟子曰^[1]："人之于身也，兼所爱^[2]。兼所爱，则兼所养也。无尺寸之肤不爱焉，则无尺寸之肤不养也。所以考其善不善者，岂有他哉？于己取之而已矣。体有贵贱，有小大。无以小害大，无以贱害贵。养其小者为小人，养其大者为大人。今有场师，舍其梧槚^[3]，养其樲棘，则为贱场师焉。养其一指而失其肩背，而不知也，则为狼疾^[4]人也。饮食之人，则人贱之矣，为其养小以失大也。饮食之人无有失也，则口腹岂适为尺寸之肤哉？"

【译文】孟子说："人们对于身体，每一部分都爱护。都爱护便都会保养。没有一尺一寸的皮肤不爱护，便没有一尺一寸的皮肤不保养。考察他保养得好或者不好，难道有别的方法吗？只是看他看重身体的哪一部分就可以了。身体有重要的部分，也有次要的部分：有小的部分，也有大的部分。不要因为小的部分损害大的部分，不要因为次要的部分损害重要的部分。保养小的部分的就是小人，保养大的部分的便是大人。如果园艺师放弃梧桐、槚树，却去培养酸枣、荆棘，那就是位差劲的园艺家。如果一个人只保养他的一个手指，却遗忘了肩头、背脊，自己还不知道，那就是一个糊涂透顶的人了。只讲究吃喝的人，人们都会轻视他，因为他保养了小的部分，丧失了大的部分。如果说只讲究吃喝的人没有丢失什么，那么，吃喝的目的难道仅仅是为了保养尺寸的肌肤吗？"

【英译】Mencius said, 'There is no part of himself which a man does not love, and as he loves all, so he must nourish all. There is not an inch of skin which he does not love, and so there is not an inch of skin which he will not nourish. For examining whether his way of nourishing be good or not, what other rule is there but this, that he determine by reflecting on himself where it should be applied? Some parts of the body are noble，and some ignoble；some great，and some small. The great must not be injured for the small，nor the noble for the ignoble. He who nourishes the little belonging to him is a little man，and he who nourishes the great is a great man. Here is a plantation-keeper，who neglects his wû and chiâ，and cultivates his sour jujube-trees；—he is a poor plantation-keeper. He who nourishes one of his fingers，neglecting his shoulders or his back，without knowing that he is doing so，is a man who resembles a hurried wolf. A man who only eats and drinks is counted mean by others；—because he nourishes what is little to the neglect of what is great. If a man，fond of his eating and drinking，were not to neglect what is of more importance，how should his mouth and belly be considered as no more than an inch of skin？'

【注释】

[1] 孟子在本章继续强调养身的重要性，并对如何养身作了详细论述。他认为，人的身体的各个部分有贵贱大小之分，人应当认清他们之间的区别，把主要精力放在心性的修养之上，将养身修心有机统一起来，不要成为舍本逐末、因小失大的糊涂之人。

[2] "兼所爱"，理雅各认为是爱身体上的所有部分，将之翻译为"There is no part of himself which a man does not love"，而刘殿爵则认为是没有差别地爱身上的所有部分。从下文"体有贵贱，有小大"可以断定，孟子在告诫人们不能因小失大，因贱害贵，对身体的爱应有差等，有选择，因而理雅各的翻译更准确。

[3] "梧槚"，是中国古代的树木名称，理雅各选择用汉语拼音将之译为"wû and chiâ"，并选择用斜体排版以突出其含义的特殊性。赖发洛则选择用西方人熟悉的"tallow trees"（乌桕）和"lindens"（椴树）翻译。刘殿爵认为孟子引用"梧槚"主要是为了突出树木的珍贵，至于具体是什么树

木对理解文义无甚影响，因而直接将之意译为"the valuable ones"（珍贵的树木）。

[4]"狼疾"，赵岐注曰："谓医养人疾，治其一指，而不知其肩背之有疾，以至于害之，此为狼藉乱不知治疾之人也。"焦循解曰："赵氏读'狼疾'为'狼藉'，而以乱解之。"可见，此处的"狼疾"是说人太糊涂，不明智。理雅各过于拘泥于原文的字面意思，将之翻译为"a man who resembles a hurried wolf"（像一个疾驰的狼一样的人），显然这与原文之意不符合。刘殿爵根据上下文将"狼疾"翻译为"a muddled man"（一个糊涂透顶的人）。他的译文准确翻译出了孟子的原意。

【原文】11.15　公都子问曰[1]："钧是人也，或为大人，或为小人[2]，何也？"孟子曰："从其大体为大人，从其小体为小人。"曰："钧是人也，或从其大体，或从其小体，何也？"曰："耳目之官[3]不思，而蔽于物。物交物，则引之而已矣。心之官则思，思则得之[4]，不思则不得也。此天之所与我者。先立乎其大者，则其小者不能夺也。此为大人而已矣。"

【译文】公都子问道："同样是人，有些人成为君子，有些人成为小人，是什么原因？"孟子回答道："看重满足身体中重要器官需求的是君子，看重满足身体中次要器官需求的是小人。"问道："同样是人，有人重满足身体中重要器官的需求，有人看重满足身体中次要器官的需求，为什么呢？"回答道："耳朵、眼睛这类的器官不会思考，容易为外物所蒙蔽。一旦与外物相接触，便容易被引诱过去。心这个器官能思考，一思考便得着，不思考便得不着。这是上天赋予我们的。先把心这个重要器官树立起来，那么耳目这类的次要器官便不容易被引诱。这样就可以成为君子了。"

【英译】The disciple Kung-tû said, 'All are equally men, but some are great men, and some are little men; —how is this?' Mencius replied, 'Those who follow that part of themselves which is great are great men; those who follow that part which is little are little men.' Kung-tû pursued, 'All are equally men, but some follow that part of themselves which is great, and some follow that part which is little;—how is this?' Mencius answered, 'The senses of hearing and seeing do not think, and are obscured by external things. When one thing comes into contact with another, as a matter of course it leads it away. To the mind belongs the office of thinking. By thinking, it gets the right view of things; by neglecting to think, it fails to do this. These—the senses and the mind—are what Heaven has given to us. Let a man first stand fast in the supremacy of the nobler part of his constitution, and the inferior part will not be able to take it from him. It is simply this which makes the great man.'

【注释】

[1] 公都子向孟子提问说，既然人性本善，那么为什么有的人后来成了品德高尚的君子、圣人，而有的人却是品德一般、甚至卑劣的普通人？孟子通过对这一问题的回答，进一步强调了修养心性的重要性。他指出，心是天赋与人的大体，具备思维功能。人若能够不断用仁义之道修养心性，就不会被外物蒙蔽而丧失人的本性。因而要想成为"大人"就要重视对心的修养，"先立乎其大者，则其小者不能夺也。"

[2] 孟子在本章将"大人"和"小人"相对举而言，以突出二者的区别。孔子曰："君子喻于义，小人喻于利。"（《论语·里仁》）孟子继承和发展了这一思想，指出大人"从其大体"，而小人则"从其小体"。理雅各将"大人"和"小人"分别翻译为"great men"和"little men"，赖发洛则翻译为"great man"和"small man"。正如在前面章节所指出的，"great"内涵非常丰富，既表示地位上的高贵显著，也表示个性或品质上的优秀，用它来翻译"大人"，基本上能体现出"大人"的特征。虽然"small"和"little"

都可以用来修饰人，但在原文中"大人"和"小人"是对举出现的，如果"great man"可以作为"大人"的对等词，那么就应该用"great"的对应词"little"来翻译小人，以突出二者的对应关系。刘殿爵将"大人"意译为"some men greater than others"（有些人比其他人更伟大），虽在含义上能讲通，但本章旨在说明何为"大人"，何为"小人"以及怎样成为"大人"，因而应突出而非淡化二者的对应关系，并保持译文对"大人"和"小人"的翻译前后一致。

[3]"耳目之官"，赵岐注曰："官，精神所在也。谓人有五官六府。"朱熹亦认为："官之为言司也。耳司听，目司视，各有所职而不能思，是以蔽于外物。"可见，"官"是器官、官能之意。理雅各将"官"翻译为"sense"（官能），赖发洛翻译为"office"（职责），刘殿爵则将之翻译为"organs"（器官）。这三种理解都可以接受。

[4]"思则得之"，杨伯峻认为："此'之'字何所指，古今注释家都未能明确指出，宋元理学家竟以为指'理'而言。按之第六章'求则得之，舍则失之'两句，与此立意相同，彼处是指'我固有之'的'仁义礼智'的'才'而言，则此亦当同。"他把这句话放到孟子的整个思想体系之下去理解，分析有理有据，能准确译出"思则得之"的暗含之意。理雅各将之翻译为"By thinking, it gets the right view of things"（通过思考，就能正确认识事物）。他的译文紧扣前文，即由于耳朵、眼睛不能思考，容易为外物所蒙蔽，而被引向歧途，而心能够思考，故能正确认识事物。从文义上看，他这一理解也是恰当的。刘殿爵的译文是"it will find the answer only if it does think"（如果它确实进行了思考，就能找到正确的答案）。他也是结合前后文理解"之"的含义。

【原文】11.16 孟子曰[1]："有天爵者，有人爵者[2]。仁义忠信，乐善[3]不倦，此天爵也；公卿大夫，此人爵也。古之人修其天爵，而人爵从之。今之人修其天爵，以要人爵；既得人爵，而弃其天爵，则惑之甚者也，终亦必亡而已矣[4]。"

【译文】孟子说："有天赐的爵位，有人授予的爵位。仁义忠信，喜好善不感到疲倦，这是天赐的爵位；公卿大夫是人授予的爵位。古代的人修养天赐的爵位，人授予的爵位就会随之而来。现在的人修养天赐的爵位是为了追求人授予的爵位；已经得到了人授予的爵位，就抛弃了天赐的爵位，那真是太糊涂了，最终也会丧失人授予的爵位。"

【英译】Mencius said, 'There is a nobility of Heaven, and there is a nobility of man. Benevolence, righteousness, self-consecration, and fidelity, with unwearied joy in these virtues; —these constitute the nobility of Heaven. To be a kung, a ch'ing, or a tǎ-fǔ; —this constitutes the nobility of man. The men of antiquity cultivated their nobility of Heaven, and the nobility of man came to them in its train. The men of the present day cultivate their nobility of Heaven in order to seek for the nobility of man, and when they have obtained that, they throw away the other: —their delusion is extreme. The issue is simply this, that they must lose that nobility of man as well.'

【注释】

[1] 孟子认为，爵位有天爵、人爵之分。仁义忠信是上天赋予人的天爵，由人的善良本性发展而来，经过后天的道德修养而成。人获得了天爵，公卿大夫等人爵就会紧随而来。这也是孟子说的"先立乎其大者，则其小者不能夺也"。（《孟子·告子上》）但今人目光短浅，获得高官厚禄后就会沉迷其中，放弃了对仁义的追求，最终会落得天爵、人爵双双消亡的恶果。

[2] 赵岐注曰："天爵以德，人爵以禄。"他的注解简洁地对二者进行了区分。"天爵"指仁义忠信这些内在的善性以及对善性的喜好，"人爵"则是指公卿大夫等官职。理雅各将"天爵"和"人爵"分别翻译为"a nobility of Heaven"（上天赋予的高贵身份）和"a nobility of man"（人给予的贵族身份）。赖发洛的译文是"titles given by Heaven"（天赐予的头衔）和

"titles given by man"（人授的头衔）。刘殿爵将之译为"honours bestowed by Heaven"（天授予的荣誉）和"honours bestowed by man"（人授予的荣誉）。三位译者虽遣词造句各异，但基本上能体现出"天爵"和"人爵"的主要区别。

[3] "乐善"，刘殿爵认为它和"仁义忠信"一起构成了天爵的内涵。理雅各则认为所乐之善仅仅是"仁义忠信"四种美德，将之翻译为"with unwearied joy in these virtues"，即"丝毫不感到厌倦地喜欢这四种美德"。

[4] 对于"终亦必亡而已矣"究竟是什么，理雅各和刘殿爵有不同的理解。理雅各认为"they must lose that nobility of man as well"（他们也肯定会丧失人爵）。在这里他将"人爵"用斜体字表示，为了说明这个词在原文中没有，为了方便读者理解，译者根据文意所加。他的补充性翻译可以很好地呼应篇章主旨。刘殿爵则认为"in the end are sure only to perish"（最终必定会招致灭亡）。本段主要讨论"人爵"和"天爵"的关系，"人爵丧失"比"人灭亡"更符合文义。

【原文】11.17　孟子曰[1]："欲贵者，人之同心也。人人有贵于己者，弗思耳矣。人之所贵者，非良贵也[2]。赵孟[3]之所贵，赵孟能贱之。《诗》云：'既醉以酒，既饱以德。'言饱乎仁义也，所以不愿人之膏粱之味也；令闻广誉施于身，所以不愿人之文绣也。"

【译文】孟子说："希望尊贵，这是人们共同的心愿。每人都有可尊贵的东西，只是不去思考罢了。别人所给予的尊贵，不是真正的尊贵。赵孟可以使他尊贵，赵孟同样也可以使他下贱。《诗经》说：'酒已经醉了，德已经饱了。'就是说仁义之德很富足了，所以不羡慕别人的美味佳肴了；众所周知的好名声加在身上，也就不羡慕别人的绣花衣裳。"

【英译】Mencius said, 'To desire to be honoured is the common mind of men. And all men have in themselves that which is truly honourable. Only they do not think of it. The honour which men confer is not good honour. Those whom Châo the Great ennobles he can make mean again. It is said in the Book of Poetry，"He has filled us with his wine，he has satiated us with his goodness.""Satiated us with his goodness，"that is，satiated us with benevolence and righteousness，and he who is so satiated，consequently，does not wish for the fat meat and fine millet of men. A good reputation and far-reaching praise fall to him，and he does not desire the elegant embroidered garments of men.'

【注释】

[1] 孟子在本章旨在强调树立正确价值观的重要性。获得尊贵是人们普遍的心理，本无可厚非，但人们往往会忽略自身所固有的良贵，而一味地去追求高官厚禄等外在的物质享受。殊不知"饱乎仁义也，所以不愿人之膏粱之味也；令闻广誉施于身，所以不愿人之文绣也"。

[2] 关于"人之所贵者，非良贵也"的理解大体有两种。一种以刘殿爵为代表，译为"What man exalts is not truly exalted."（人人都觉得最可贵的东西，不一定是真正最可贵的东西）另一种观点以杨伯峻为代表，认为"别人所给予的尊贵，不是真正值得尊贵的"。理雅各、赖发洛的译文与此观点相类。相比较而言，"别人所给予的尊贵，不是真正值得尊贵的"可以很好地呼应下文的"赵孟之所贵，赵孟能贱之"。

[3] "赵孟"是春秋时期晋国的正卿赵盾，他的字是孟，因而后来他的子孙也称赵孟。这里代指有权势，可以决定普通人社会地位的官员。刘殿爵直接选择音译，在传意上略逊于赵甄陶的译文。赵甄陶则将之翻译为"Men as distinguished as Zhao Meng（Chief Minister of Jin—tr.）"，即"像赵孟一样显赫的人物"，并进一步解释了赵孟的身份地位，便于读者理解。

【原文】 11.18 孟子曰[1]："仁之胜不仁也，犹水胜火。今之为仁者，犹以一杯水救一车薪之火也[2]；不熄，则谓之水不胜火，此又与于不仁之甚者也[3]，亦终必亡而已矣。"

【译文】孟子说："仁胜过不仁就像水可以扑灭火一样。如今行仁的人就好像用一杯水来救一车燃烧的柴火；火焰不熄灭，就说水不能扑灭火，这又和那些很不仁的人相同了，最终一定会连这一点点仁都会消失的。"

【英译】Mencius said, 'Benevolence subdues its opposite just as water subdues fire. Those, however, who nowadays practise benevolence do it as if with one cup of water they could save a whole waggon-load of fuel which was on fire, and when the flames were not extinguished, were to say that water cannot subdue fire. This conduct, moreover, greatly encourages those who are not benevolent. The final issue will simply be this—the loss of that small amount of benevolence.'

【注释】

[1] 孟子认为，仁定能胜不仁，就如水定能胜火一样是亘古不变的真理。但在世道衰微，不仁之至的战国时期，仁与不仁的力量相差悬殊，因而君主如欲行仁政，就要有坚定的决心和毅力，不能因遇到暂时的困难就怀疑仁的作用，否则他们就会失去仁。

[2] 今天被广泛运用的成语"杯水车薪"就取自"今之为仁者，犹以一杯水救一车薪之火也"。孟子以"水"喻"仁"，以"火"比"不仁"，一方面表明水定能胜火，仁必能胜不仁，以增强人们对"仁"的信心；另一方面也暗示在当时的社会中，仁与不仁力量相差悬殊，因而施行仁政、推行仁义非一朝一夕之事，需要有持之以恒的毅力。刘殿爵将之译为"Those who practise benevolence today are comparable to someone trying to put out a cartload of burning firewood with a cupful of water."（今天行仁的人，就好像用一杯水来救一车燃烧的木材）他的译文表明行仁者所遇到的困难和艰险，鼓励他们

要不畏艰险，坚持行仁。而理雅各的译文"Those, however, who nowadays practise benevolence do it as if with one cup of water they could save a whole waggon-load of fuel which was on fire."（今天行仁的人，和那些认为自己能用一杯水救一车燃烧的木柴的人一样）他的译文则表明那些行仁之人不自知。这显然和原文要表达的意思有出入。

[3] 对"此又与于不仁之甚者也"有两种理解。"与"，焦循指出，"近解作助"。朱熹注曰："与，犹助也。"即这又助长了那些非常不仁的人。理雅各的译文同朱熹，将之翻译为"This conduct, moreover, greatly encourages those who are not benevolent."即认为"行仁半途而废，承认水不胜火，仁难以战胜不仁，会助长不仁之风"。而刘殿爵则认为"与"的含义是"同"，将之译为"Those who practise benevolence today are comparable to someone trying to put out a cartload of burning firewood with a cupful of water."（那些开始行仁的人，和那些最不仁的人是一样的）。从文义上看，这两种理解都说得通。

【原文】11.19   孟子曰："五谷者，种之美者也；苟为不熟，不如荑稗[1]。夫仁，亦在乎熟之而已矣。"

【译文】孟子说："五谷是庄稼中的好品种；如果不能成熟，比不上稊米和稗子。仁，也在于使它成熟罢了。"

【英译】Mencius said, 'Of all seeds the best are the five kinds of grain, yet if they be not ripe, they are not equal to the tî or the Pâi. So, the value of benevolence depends entirely on its being brought to maturity.'

【注释】

[1] "荑稗"在古代社会被认为是不利于庄稼生长的杂草，果实比谷小，虽可食，但味不美，可作为家畜饲料。朱熹注曰："荑稗，草之似谷者，其实亦可食，然不能如五谷之美也。"理雅各用汉语拼音将之音译为"tî or

the Pâi"。刘殿爵则将之意译为"wild varieties"（野生的谷物变种），他的译文清楚再现了"莨莠"和"五谷"的关系。

【原文】 11.20　孟子曰[1]："羿之教人射，必志于彀；学者亦必志于彀[2]。大匠[3]诲人必以规矩；学者亦必以规矩。"

【译文】 孟子说："羿教人射箭，一定要拉满弓；学习的人也一定要努力拉满弓。高明的木匠教人一定要用好规矩，学习的人一定要学好规矩。"

【英译】 Mencius said, 'Î, in teaching men to shoot, made it a rule to draw the bow to the full, and his pupils also did the same. A master-workman, in teaching others, uses the compass and square, and his pupils do the same.'

【注释】

[1] 孟子举羿和大匠诲人的例子，指出做任何事情都要遵循一定的规矩准则。为人师长，应有明确的教育目标，以高标准严格要求向自己求学的人。而学习的人也要理解和明白师长的良苦用心，努力向自己行业的规矩靠拢。

[2] 两个"必志于彀"重复使用旨在突出教者和学者都严格遵守本行业的规矩的决心。刘殿爵严格按照原文结构将之翻译为英文。这一反复结构翻译成英文后虽有啰唆之嫌，但本章旨在强调遵守规矩准则对于教者和学者都很重要，重复强调的价值即在于此。理雅各将之翻译为"Î, in teaching men to shoot, made it a rule to draw the bow to the full, and his pupils also did the same"，即"（羿）把拉满弓作为准则，他的学生也这样做。"他的译文改变了原文反复强调的特点，更符合英文的表达习惯。

[3] "匠"是一个会意字。从匚，盛放工具的筐器，从斤（斧）。工具筐里放着斧头等工具，表明从事木工。因而"匠"的本义是木工，后泛指工匠。由于"规矩"是画圆成方的器具，是木工常用之物，因而此处"大匠"

的准确含义是"有名的木工"。刘殿爵将之翻译为"the master carpenter"非常确切。理雅各选择用"a master workman"（有名的工匠）翻译"大匠"，虽在词义上亦通，但不确切。

卷 十 二

告子章句下

【原文】12.1　任人有问屋庐子曰[1]："礼与食孰重？"曰："礼
重。""色与礼孰重？"曰："礼重。"曰："以礼食，则饥而死；不以
礼食，则得食，必以礼乎？亲迎[2]，则不得妻；不亲迎，则得妻，
必以礼乎？"屋庐子不能对，明日之邹以告孟子。孟子曰："于答
是也，何有？不揣其本，而齐其末，方寸之木可使高于岑楼[3]。金
重于羽者，岂谓一钩金[4]与一舆羽之谓哉？取食之重者与礼之轻
者而比之，奚翅食重？取色之重者与礼之轻者而比之，奚翅色重？
往应之曰：'绐兄之臂而夺之食，则得食；不绐，则不得食，则将
绐之乎？逾东家墙而搂其处子，则得妻，不搂，则不得妻；则将搂
之乎？'"

【译文】有个任国人问屋庐子说："礼和食哪个重要？"回答说："礼
重要。"

又问："娶妻和礼哪个重要？"答道："礼重要。"问道："如果按着
礼法去找吃的，就会被饿死；不按着礼法去找吃的，就会有吃的，那一
定要按着礼法行事吗？如果遵守亲迎礼，便娶不到妻子；如果不奉行亲
迎礼，便会娶到妻子，那一定要奉行亲迎礼吗？"屋庐子不能回答，第
二天便去邹国，把这话告诉孟子。孟子说："回答这个问题，有什么困
难呢？如果不衡量基地的高低，而只比较其顶端，那一寸厚的木块，可

以高过尖角的高楼。金子比羽毛重，难道是说一丁点的金子比一大车的羽毛还重吗？拿饮食的重要方面和礼的细枝末节相比较，何止是饮食重要？拿娶亲的重要方面和礼的细枝末节相比较，何止是娶妻重要？你这样去答复他吧：'扭住哥哥的胳膊，抢夺他的食物，就可以得到吃的；不扭，便得不着吃的，那会去扭吗？爬过东邻的墙去搂抱人家的姑娘，便能得到妻子；不去搂抱，便得不着妻子，那会去搂抱吗？'"

【英译】A man of Zǎn asked the disciple Wû-lû, saying, 'Is an observance of the rules of propriety in regard to eating, or eating merely, the more important?' The answer was, 'The observance of the rules of propriety is the more important.' 'Is the gratifying the appetite of sex, or the doing so only according to the rules of propriety, the more important?' The answer again was, 'The observance of the rules of propriety in the matter is the more important.' The man pursued, 'If the result of eating only according to the rules of propriety will be death by starvation, while by disregarding those rules we may get food, must they still be observed in such a case? If according to the rule that he shall go in person to meet his wife a man cannot get married, while by disregarding that rule he may get married, must he still observe the rule in such a case?' Wû-lû was unable to reply to these questions, and the next day he went to Tsâu, and told them to Mencius. Mencius said, 'What difficulty is there in answering these inquiries? If you do not adjust them at their lower extremities, but only put their tops on a level, a piece of wood an inch square may be made to be higher than the pointed peak of a high building. Gold is heavier than feathers;—but does that saying have reference, on the one hand, to a single clasp of gold, and, on the other, to a waggon-load of feathers? If you take a case where the eating is of the utmost importance and the observing the rules of propriety is of little importance, and compare the things together, why stop with saying merely that the eating is more important? So, taking the case where the gratifying the appetite of sex is of the utmost importance and the observing the rules of propriety is of little importance, why stop with merely saying that the gratifying the appetite is the more important? Go and answer him thus, "If, by twisting your elder brother's arm, and snatching from him what he is eating, you can get food for yourself, while, if you do not do so, you will not get anything to eat, will you so twist his arm? If by getting over your neighbour's wall, and dragging away his virgin daughter, you can get a wife, while if you do not do so, you will not be able to get a wife, will you so drag her away?"'

【注释】

[1] 本章起于任人和屋庐子的对话。任人在对话时有偷换概念之嫌。他在发问时,问的是一般情况下礼和食、礼和色孰轻孰重,但在反驳屋庐子的回答时却拿"食之重者与礼之轻者"相比较,驳得屋庐子哑口无言,从而向孟子请教。儒家认为,礼、食和色相比较而言,礼最重,这是一般规律,毋庸置疑。但礼有大小,食有轻重,以礼之小者与食之大者相比较时,则应具体问题具体分析,不能一概而论,以偏概全,这一思想也符合儒家过犹不及的中庸之道和权变思想。

[2] "亲迎"是中国古代婚礼"六礼"之一。所谓"六礼"指纳采、问名、纳吉、纳徵、请期和亲迎。根据古代礼制,夫婿需亲自到女家迎娶新娘入室。理雅各采取解释性翻译策略,将"亲迎"翻译为"he shall go in person to meet his wife"(亲自去迎娶新娘),基本上能体现原文之意。同时,理雅各还在译文中明确指出,"亲迎"是中国古代礼制的规定,以表明任人认为有时候色比礼更重要,虽违反"亲迎"之礼,但可以娶到妻子。刘殿爵

在翻译时选择对"亲迎"进行音译,以表明它是中国古代的一种特殊礼仪,在西方语言中没有对等词。

[3] "方寸之木可使高于岑楼",朱熹注曰:"本,谓下。末,谓上。方寸之木至卑,喻食色。岑楼,楼之高锐似山者,至高,喻礼。若不取其下之平,而升寸木于岑楼之上,则寸木反高,岑楼反卑矣。"理雅各和刘殿爵认为"可使高于岑楼"指"比尖角高楼还要高",而赖发洛认为是"you can make a stick an inch thick as high as a mountain tower!"(你可以使一寸长的木棍和高楼一样高)从文义看,孟子认为任人之所以会得出食、色重于礼的结论,就在于他比较的起点不同,因而采取"以子之矛,攻子之盾"的方法,来推论其结论的荒谬,指出若按照他的比较方法,一寸长的木板甚至会比尖角高楼还要高。故理雅各和刘殿爵的译文更确切。

[4] 朱熹注曰:"钩,带钩也。金本重而带钩小,故轻。"可见,"一钩金"是做成一个衣带钩所需要的金子,比喻数量很少。孔广森在《经学卮言》中指出:"然则带钩金半钩,才重三分两之一。"刘殿爵将之翻译为"gold in a clasp"(一个衣带扣大的金子),赵甄陶将之翻译为"a gold buckle"(金带扣),基本都能体现其含义。

【原文】12.2 曹交问曰[1]:"人皆可以为尧舜,有诸?"孟子曰:"然。""交闻文王十尺,汤九尺,今交九尺四寸以长,食粟而已,如何则可?"曰:"奚有于是?亦为之而已矣。有人于此,力不能胜一匹雏[2],则为无力人矣;今曰举百钧[3],则为有力人矣。然则举乌获之任,是亦为乌获而已矣。夫人岂以不胜为患哉?弗为耳。徐行后长者谓之弟,疾行先长者谓之不弟。夫徐行者,岂人所不能哉?所不为也。尧舜之道,孝弟而已矣。子服尧之服,诵尧之言,行尧之行,是尧而已矣[4]。子服桀之服,诵桀之言,行桀之行,是桀而已矣。"曰:"交得见于邹君,可以假馆,愿留而受业于门。"曰:"夫道[5]若大路然,岂难知哉?人病不求耳。子归而求之，有余师。"

【译文】曹交问道："人人都可以成为尧舜那样的人，有这话吗？"孟子答道："有的。"曹交问："我听说文王身高十尺，汤身高九尺，如今我有九尺四寸高，只会吃饭罢了，怎么做才可以呢？"孟子说："这有什么关系呢？只要去做就可以了。如果这儿有个人，他的力气连一只小鸡都提不起来，就是一个毫无力气的人；如果说能够举起三千斤，那便是有力气的人了。那么，如果能举得起乌获所能举的重量，也就成为乌获那样的人了。难道人要担心不能胜任吗？只是不去做罢了。慢慢地走在长者后，便是悌；快步走到长者前，便是不悌。慢慢走，难道是人做不到的吗？只是不去做罢了。尧舜之道，也不过就是孝和悌罢了。你穿尧穿的衣服，说尧说的话，做尧做的事，便是尧了。你穿桀穿的衣服，说桀说的话，做桀做的事，便是桀了。"曹交说："我准备去谒见邹君，向他借个住的地方，想要留在您门下学习。"孟子说："道就像大路一样，难道难于知晓吗？只怕人不去寻求罢了。你回去自己寻求，老师有很多呢。"

【英译】Chiâo of Tsâo asked Mencius，saying，'It is said，"All men may be Yâo s and Shuns；"—is it so？'Mencius replied，'It is.' Chiâo went on，'I have heard that king Wǎn was ten cubits high，and T'ang nine. Now I am nine cubits four inches in height. But I can do nothing but eat my millet. What am I to do to realize that saying？'Mencius answered him，'What has this—the question of size—to do with the matter？ It all lies simply in acting as such. Here is a man，whose strength was not equal to lift a duckling：—he was then a man of no strength. But to-day he says，"I can lift 3，000 catties'weight，" and he is a man of strength. And so，he who can lift the weight which Wû Hwo lifted is just another Wû Hwo. Why should a man make a want of ability the subject of his grief？ It is only that he will not do the thing.

To walk slowly, keeping behind his elders, is to perform the part of a younger. To walk quickly and precede his elders, is to violate the duty of a younger brother. Now, is it what a man cannot do—to walk slowly? It is what he does not do. The course of Yâo and Shun was simply that of filial piety and fraternal duty. Wear the clothes of Yâo, repeat the words of Yâo, and do the actions of Yâo, and you will just be a Yâo. And, if you wear the clothes of Chieh, repeat the words of Chieh, and do the actions of Chieh, you will just be a Chieh.' Chiâo said, 'I shall be having an interview with the prince of Tsâu, and can ask him to let me have a house to lodge in. I wish to remain here, and receive instruction at your gate.' Mencius replied, 'The way of truth is like a great road. It is not difficult to know it. The evil is only that men will not seek it. Do you go home and search for it, and you will have abundance of teachers.'

【注释】

[1] 孟子认为，尧舜之道无他，孝悌而已矣。一个人只要能孝顺父母，尊敬兄长，他就是在行尧舜之道，因而可以成为尧舜那样的人。孟子亦认为，"孩提之童，无不知爱其亲者，及其长也，无不知敬其兄也。"（《孟子·尽心上》）可见，孝悌是人生而具备的品德，因而人人可以成为尧舜那样的人。至于有些人不能成为尧舜，是他"不为也，非不能也。"

[2] "一匹雏"，朱熹注曰："匹，字本作鸥，鸭也，从省作匹。礼记说'匹为鹜'是也。"理雅各的译文与朱熹的注解相类，认为"一匹雏"指的是"a duckling"（一只小鸭子）。但杨伯峻则认为："'一匹雏'之语例与'一钧金'、'一舆羽'同，'钧'与'舆'皆作量词，则匹亦为量词。……此则借以计雏。'一匹雏'犹今言一只小鸡。"刘殿爵也认为"匹"是量词，将之翻译为"a chicken"（小鸡）。

[3] "钧"，古代的重量单位，三十斤为一钧。理雅各将"百钧"换算

为"3000 catties"（3000 斤）翻译，刘殿爵则将之翻译为"a ton"（1 吨）。

[4] 中国古代思想家和统治者都十分重视榜样的作用，鼓励"见贤思齐焉"。至于如何"思齐"，孟子为人们指明了效仿的方向和道路，即"子服尧之服，诵尧之言，行尧之行，是尧而已矣。"他主张人们不仅仅要在言行举止上效仿尧舜等圣人，还要在穿衣打扮、生活习惯上向圣人靠拢。此处的"子"仅仅是对男子的统称，而非含有尊敬之意。

[5] 至于此处的"道"，根据文义可以推测是"尧舜之道"，即孝悌仁义之道，理雅各将之翻译为"The way of truth"（真理之路），刘殿爵则选择用大写的"Way"翻译，让读者自己去揣摩其确切内涵。

【原文】 12.3　公孙丑问曰[1]："高子曰：'《小弁》[2]，小人[3]之诗也。'"孟子曰："何以言之？"曰："怨。"曰："固哉，高叟之为诗也！有人于此，越人关弓而射之，则己谈笑道之[4]；无他，疏之也。其兄关弓而射之，则己垂涕泣而道之；无他，戚之也。《小弁》之怨，亲亲也。亲亲，仁也。固矣夫，高叟之为诗也！"曰："《凯风》何以不怨？"曰："《凯风》，亲之过小者也；《小弁》，亲之过大者也。亲[5]之过大而不怨，是愈疏也；亲之过小而怨，是不可矶[6]也。愈疏，不孝也；不可矶，亦不孝也。孔子曰：'舜其至孝矣，五十而慕。'"

【译文】 公孙丑问："高子说：'《小弁》是小人作的诗。'"孟子说："为什么那么说？"公孙丑答道："因为诗里透着怨恨。"孟子说："高老先生讲诗真是太呆板了！这里有个人，越国人拉开弓去射他，他可以有说有笑地讲这事，没有别的原因，因为关系疏远。若是他哥哥拉开弓去射他，他会哭哭啼啼地讲述这事，没有别的原因，因为哥哥是关系亲近的人。《小弁》的怨恨，正是亲爱亲人的缘故。亲爱亲人，是合乎仁的。高老先生讲诗真是太呆板了！"公孙丑说："《凯风》这一篇诗为什么没有怨恨呢？"孟子回答道："《凯风》是由于母亲的过错小，《小弁》是由于父亲的过错大。父母过错大，却不抱怨，是更加疏远父母的表现；父母的过错小，却抱怨，是不能受一点委屈啊。更加疏远父母是不孝，自己不能受一点委屈也是不孝。孔子说：'舜是最孝顺的人吧，五十岁还依恋父母。'"

【英译】Kung-sun Ch'âu asked about an opinion of the scholar Kâo, saying, 'Kâo observed, "The Hsiâo P'ân is the ode of a little man."' Mencius asked, 'Why did he say so?' 'Because of the murmuring which it expresses,' was the reply. Mencius answered, 'How stupid was that old Kâo in dealing with the ode! There is a man here, and a native of Yüeh bends his bow to shoot him. I will advise him not to do so, but speaking calmly and smilingly; —for no other reason but that he is not related to me. But if my own brother be bending his bow to shoot the man, then I will advise him not to do so, weeping and crying the while; —for no other reason than that he is related to me. The dissatisfaction expressed in the Hsiâo P'ân is the working of relative affection, and that affection shows benevolence. Stupid indeed was old Kâo's criticism on the ode.' Ch'ǎu then said, 'How is it that there is no dissatisfaction expressed in the K'âi Fǎng?' Mencius replied, 'The parent's fault referred to in the K'âi Fǎng is small; that referred to in the Hsiâo P'ân is great. Where the parent's fault was great, not to have murmured on account of it would have increased the want of natural affection. Where the parent's fault was small, to have murmured on account of it would have been to act like water which frets and foams about a stone that interrupts its course. To increase the want of natural affection would have been unfilial, and to fret and foam in such a manner would also have been unfilial. Confucius said, "Shun was indeed perfectly filial! And yet, when he was fifty, he was full of longing desire about his parents.'"

【注释】

[1] 孟子通过和公孙丑讨论他对《小弁》和《凯风》这两首诗的看法表达了他对亲亲和孝的看法。他认为如果父母有大过错，却不抱怨，这不是孝顺父母，而是疏远父母的表现。相反，如果父母有了小过错，就去抱怨不停，不让自己受一点委屈，也是不孝的表现。

[2]《小弁》是《诗经·小雅》中的篇章。《毛诗》以为是周幽王太子宜臼的老师所作；一说是宜臼所作。内容是指责周幽王废除申后及太子宜臼，改立宠爱的褒姒的儿子伯服为太子。理雅各和刘殿爵在翻译时选择用汉语拼音音译。

[3] 从文义上看，高子认为《小弁》之诗含有怨意，因而将之贬为"小人"之诗。可见，此处的"小人"作为贬义词，指那些道德水平低下、见识短浅的人。刘殿爵将之翻译为"a petty man"（小心眼的人），基本上能体现原文的意思。

[4] "道之"，朱熹注曰："语也"。理雅各认为"语"的内容是劝说、劝告，将之翻译为"I will advise him not to do so"（我会劝他不要这样做）。刘殿爵则认为"语"仅仅是向别人叙述发生过的事情，不含有劝诫越人不要射箭之意，将之译为"recounting the incident"。

[5] "亲"指父母双亲。《凯风》是《诗经·邶风》中的篇章。《凯风》通篇都是七个儿子自责以感悟母亲不要改嫁。可见，《小弁》和《凯风》皆是与父亲或母亲的过错相关，因而赖发洛的"kinsman"（同族者）不如刘殿爵的"parent"（父亲或母亲）准确。

[6] "不可矶"，朱熹注曰："矶，水激石也。不可矶，言微激之而遽怒也。"理雅各将之翻译为"like water which frets and foams about a stone that interrupts its course"（就像水冲激阻挡其道路的岩石而出现沉沉波浪一样）。他的译文将"矶"所包含的意象准确传递给了读者，但没有指明比喻义后的暗含之意，即没有将作者选择用"矶"作喻所要表达的真实含义传递给读

者。赖发洛根据文义将"不可矶"翻译为"不宽容"（to be unforgiving），刘殿爵的译文是"react too violently"（反而激怒自己），这两种翻译基本上体现出"不可矶"的内涵。

【原文】12.4　宋牼将之楚[1]，孟子遇于石丘，曰："先生[2]将何之？"曰："吾闻秦、楚构兵[3]，我将见楚王说而罢之。楚王不悦，我将见秦王说而罢之。二王我将有所遇焉。"曰："轲也请无问其详，愿闻其指。说之将何如？"曰："我将言其不利也。"曰："先生之志则大矣，先生之号则不可。先生以利说秦、楚之王，秦、楚之王悦于利，以罢三军之师，是三军之士乐罢而悦于利也。为人臣者怀利以事其君，为人子者怀利以事其父，为人弟者怀利以事其兄，是君臣、父子、兄弟终去仁义，怀利以相接，然而不亡者，未之有也。先生以仁义说秦、楚之王，秦、楚之王悦于仁义，而罢三军之师，是三军之士乐罢而悦于仁义也。为人臣者怀仁义以事其君，为人子者怀仁义以事其父，为人弟者怀仁义以事其兄，是君臣、父子、兄弟去利，怀仁义[4]以相接也，然而不王者，未之有也。何必曰利？"

【译文】宋牼要到楚国去。孟子在石丘遇到了他，孟子问道："先生要往哪里去？"答道："我听说秦、楚两国交战，我打算去拜见楚王，劝说他罢兵。如果楚王不听，我打算再去拜见秦王，劝他罢兵。两位君主中，总会有位投合的。"孟子说："我不想问得太详细，只想知道你的主要观点。你将怎样去劝说呢？"答道："我打算告诉他们交战是不利的。"孟子说："先生的志向很大，可是先生的主张却不行。先生用利来劝说秦王、楚王，秦王、楚王因为有利而高兴，于是停止军事行动，这将使军队的官兵因为喜欢利而停战。做臣属的心里想着利去服事自己的君主，做儿子的心里想着利去奉养自己的父亲，做弟弟的心里想着利来侍奉自己的哥哥，这就会使君臣、父子、兄弟之间都完全抛掉仁义，心里想着利来互相对待，如此而不灭亡的，是从来没有过的。先生用仁义来劝说秦王、楚王，秦王、楚王因仁义而高兴，于是停止军事行动，这将使军队的官兵因为喜欢仁义而停战。做臣属的心里想着仁义去服事自己的君主，做儿子的心里想着仁义去奉养自己的父亲，做弟弟的心里想着仁义来侍奉自己的哥哥，这就会使君臣、父子、兄弟之间都完全抛掉利，心里想着仁义来互相对待，如此而不能成为统一天下的王，是从来没有过的。何必要说利呢？"

【英译】Sung K'ang being about to go to Ch'û, Mencius met him in Shih-ch'iû. 'Master, where are you going?' asked Mencius. K'ang replied, 'I have heard that Ch'in and Ch'û are fighting together, and I am going to see the king of Ch'û and persuade him to cease hostilities. If he shall not be pleased with my advice, I shall go to see the king of Ch'in, and persuade him in the same way. Of the two kings I shall surely find that I can succeed with one of them.' Mencius said, 'I will not venture to ask about the particulars, but I should like to hear the scope of your plan. What course will you take to try to persuade them?' K'ang answered, 'I will tell them how unprofitable their course is to them.' 'Master,' said Mencius, 'your aim is great, but your argument is not good. If you, starting from the point of profit, offer your persuasive counsels to the kings of Ch'in and Ch'û, and if those kings are pleased with the consideration of profit so as to stop the movements of their armies, then all belonging to those armies will rejoice in the cessation of war, and find their pleasure in the pursuit of profit. Ministers will serve their sovereign for the profit of which they cherish the thought; sons will serve their fathers, and younger brothers will serve their elder brothers, from the same consideration: —and the issue will be, that, abandoning benevolence and righteousness, sovereign and minister, father and son, younger brother and elder, will carry on all their intercourse with this thought of profit cherished in their breasts. But never has there been such a state of society, without ruin being the result of it. If you, starting from the ground of benevolence and righteousness, offer your counsels to the kings of Ch'in and Ch'û, and if those kings are pleased with the consideration of benevolence and righteousness so as to stop the operations of their armies, then all belonging to those armies will rejoice in the stopping from war, and find their pleasure in benevolence and righteousness. Ministers will serve their sovereign, cherishing the principles of benevolence and righteousness; sons will serve their fathers, and younger brothers will serve their elder brothers, in the same way: — and so, sovereign and minister, father and son, elder brother and younger, abandoning the thought of profit, will cherish the principles of benevolence and righteousness, and carry on all their intercourse upon them. But never has there been such a state of society, without the State where it prevailed rising to the royal sway. Why must you use that word "profit."'

【注释】

[1] 孟子在本章再次详细阐述了自己重义轻利的义利观。孟子认为要避免战争，确保国家长治久安，就要说服君主重义轻利，通过榜样的作用，上行下效，君臣、父子、兄弟皆去利行仁，那么整个国家就会大兴仁义之风，君主也定能成为统一天下的王。

[2] "先生"，赵岐注曰："学士年长者，故谓之先生。"焦循解曰："《齐策》云：'孟尝君宴坐谓三先生'，注云：'先生，长老先己以生者也。'轻盖年长于孟子，故孟子以先生称之而自称名。"但杨伯峻引某氏云："今按其时孟子年已逾七十，而轻欲历说秦楚，意气犹健，年未能长于孟子。先生自

是稷下学士先辈之通称，孟子亦深敬其人，故遂自称名为谦耳。"理雅各和赖发洛选择用"Master"（名家、大师），刘殿爵选择用"sir"翻译"先生"，基本都能体现孟子对宋轻的尊敬之情。

[3]"构兵"，焦循指出："交、结、连、构四字义同，构兵即交兵也。"刘殿爵认为宋轻是去说服正在交战的秦楚两国停战，将之译为"hostilities had broken out"（战争爆发了）。赖发洛将之翻译为"moving troops"（调动军队）。他认为两国正准备发动战争而尚未交战。相比较而言，刘殿爵的译文更确切。

[4]孟子在本章通过正反两个例子，进一步强调了他重义轻利的义利观。他首先从反面指出，如果一个国家的君臣百姓都"去仁义，怀利以相接"，这个国家必定灭亡。接着孟子从正面进一步强调了以"仁义"为名去劝服秦楚停战的重要性，认为如果"去利，怀仁义以相接"，不仅能说服秦楚两国停止战争，还能使践行仁义的君主成为天下的王。刘殿爵认为"仁义"并非特指，而是泛指儒家推崇的一切美德，将之翻译为"morality"。他的译文扩大了原文的内涵，没有突出孟子对仁义的重视。

【原文】 12.5　孟子居邹[1]，季任[2]为任处守，以币交，受之而不报。处于平陆，储子为相，以币交，受之而不报。他日，由邹之任，见季子；由平陆之齐，不见储子。屋庐子喜曰："连得间[3]矣。"问曰："夫子之任，见季子；之齐，不见储子，为其为相与？"曰："非也，《书》曰：'享多仪，仪不及物曰不享，惟不役志于享[4]。'为其不成享也。"屋庐子悦。或问之，屋庐子曰："季子不得之邹，储子得之平陆。"

【译文】 孟子在邹国的时候，季任留守任国，代理国政，送礼物来和孟子结交，孟子接受了礼物，并没有回谢。孟子住在平陆的时候，储子做齐国的卿相，也送礼物和孟子交友，孟子接受了礼物，并没有回谢。过了一段时间，孟子从邹国到任国，去拜访了季子；从平陆到齐国，却不去拜访储子。屋庐子高兴地说："我找到了可乘之机了。"便问道："老师到任国，拜访了季子；到齐都，不拜访储子，是因为他只是卿相吗？"答道："不是，《尚书》说：'进献礼物注重的是仪节，仪节不够，礼物虽多，只能叫作没有进献，因为心意并没有用在进献上面。'这是因为他没有完成进献的缘故。"屋庐子听了很高兴。有人问他。他说："季子不能够亲自去邹国，储子可以去平陆。"

【英译】When Mencius was residing in Tsâu, the younger brother of the chief of Zǎn, who was guardian of Zǎn at the time, paid his respects to him by a present of silks, which Mencius received, not going to acknowledge it. When he was sojourning in P'ing-lû, Ch'û, who was prime minister of the State, sent him a similar present, which he received in the same way. Subsequently, going from Tsâu to Zǎn, he visited the guardian; but when he went from P'ing-lû to the capital of Ch'î, he did not visit the minister Ch'û. The disciple Wû-lû was glad, and said, 'I have got an opportunity to obtain some instruction.' He asked accordingly, 'Master, when you went to Zǎn, you visited the chief's brother; and when you went to Ch'î, you did not visit Ch'û. Was it not because he is only the minister?' Mencius replied, 'No. It is said in the Book of History, "In presenting an offering to a superior, most depends on the demonstrations of respect. If those demonstrations are not equal to the things offered, we say there is no offering, that is, there is no act of the will in presenting the offering." This is because the things so offered do not constitute an offering to a superior.' Wû-lû was pleased, and when some one asked him what Mencius meant, he said, 'The younger of Zǎn could not go to Tsâu, but the minister Ch'û might have gone to P'ing-lû.'

【注释】

[1] 中国自古就是一个礼仪之邦，礼的内容纷繁复杂，涉及社会生活的各个方面，已经成为规范人们行为的普遍准则。儒家尤其重礼，强调"非礼勿视，非礼勿听，非礼勿言，非礼勿动"（《论语·颜渊》），要求人们的言行举止都要符合礼仪的要求。礼仪之所以重要，在于它包含了敬贤尊长等道德观念，有助于人们形成高尚的道德情操。子思拜而不受缪公所馈鼎肉，孟子受储子币但不见出储子都表明，对于那些有礼之名但无礼之实的"非礼之礼"，君子不认可，也不屑接受。

[2] "季任"，赵岐注曰："任君季弟也。任君朝会于邻国，季任为之居守其国也。"理雅各受其影响，采取解释性翻译策略，将之译为"the younger brother of the chief of Zǎn"（任国国君的弟弟）。在古代伯、仲、叔、季是长幼之称，相当于现在的长子、次子、三子和四子。他认为"季任"是用来表明赠孟子礼物的人和任国国君的关系。刘殿爵则认为"季任"为人名，因而对之采取音译。

[3] "得间"，本义是找到机会或有机可乘。朱熹注曰："屋庐子知孟子之处此必有义理，故喜得其闲隙而问之。"理雅各持第一种观点，将"得间"翻译为"got an opportunity to obtain some instruction"（找到受教的机会）。杨伯峻却认为是"找到了老师的岔子"。他认为"得间"在此处指发现孟子在待人接物上存在的差错和漏洞。赖发洛的理解与之相类，将之翻译为"found a flaw"（找到缺陷）。从孟子和弟子的谈话可以推测孟子在教学中推崇怀疑精神，强调"尽信书，则不如无书"。受其影响，他的学生在学习时也相信"尽信师不如无师"，会对孟子的行为提出质疑，这在《孟子·公孙丑下》中体现得尤为明显。孟子的弟子陈臻认为他不接受齐王赠送的黄金，却接受宋和薛国的馈赠，如果"前日之不受是，则今日之受非也今日之受是，则前日之不受非也。"显然，认真观察老师的行为，并敢于提出质疑是孟子的弟子增加才干的重要手段，因而赖发洛将"得间"翻译为"找到缺陷"更确切。

[4] "享多仪，仪不及物曰不享，惟不役志于享"引自《尚书·洛诰

篇》。孟子引之来证明自己不见储子的原因。朱熹注曰："享，奉上也。仪，礼也。物，币也。役，用也。言虽享而礼意不及其币，则是不享矣，以其不用志于享故也。"理雅各的翻译准确体现了进献礼物的精髓。儒家重礼，看重的是礼节所体现的尊敬和心意，而非繁杂的仪式和框架。

【原文】 12.6　淳于髡曰[1]："先名实[2]者，为人也；后名实者，自为也。夫子在三卿[3]之中，名实未加于上下而去之，仁者固如此乎？"孟子曰："居下位，不以贤事不肖者，伯夷也；五就汤，五就桀者，伊尹也；不恶污君，不辞小官者，柳下惠也。三子者不同道，其趋一也。一者何也？曰：仁也。君子亦仁而已矣。何必同？"曰："鲁缪公之时，公仪子为政，子柳、子思为臣，鲁之削也滋甚，若是乎，贤者之无益于国也！"曰："虞不用百里奚而亡，秦穆公用之而霸。不用贤则亡，削何可得欤？"曰："昔者王豹处于淇，而河西善讴；绵驹处于高唐，而齐右善歌；华周、杞梁之妻善哭其夫，而变国俗[4]。有诸内，必形诸外。为其事而无其功者，髡未尝睹之也。是故无贤者也，有则髡必识之。"曰："孔子为鲁司寇，不用[5]；从而祭，燔肉[6]不至，不税冕而行[7]。不知者以为为肉也，其知者以为为无礼也。乃孔子则欲以微罪行，不欲为苟去[8]。君子之所为，众人固不识也。"

【译文】 淳于髡说："重视名誉功业是为着经世救民，轻视名誉功业是为了洁身自好。您为齐国三卿之一，名誉和功业既没有上达君主，也没有下及百姓，您现在就离开，仁人原来是这样吗？"孟子说："处在卑贱的职位，不拿自己贤人的身份去服事不肖的人，这是伯夷；五次去汤那里，五次去桀那里，这是伊尹；不厌恶污秽的君主，不拒绝卑微的职位，这是柳下惠。三个人的行为不相同，但方向是一致的。一致的是什么呢？应该说是仁。君子只要实行仁就行了，为什么一定要相同呢？"淳于髡说："鲁缪公的时候，公仪子主持国政，泄柳和子思也都在朝廷担任大臣，鲁国的削弱却更严重，贤人对国家没有好处，竟像这样呀！"
孟子说："虞国不用百里奚而灭亡，秦缪公用了他而称霸。不用贤人就
会灭亡，只是被削弱能做到吗？"淳于髡说："从前王豹住在淇水边，河
西的人因此都会吟唱；绵驹住在高唐，齐国西部的人都会唱歌；华周、
杞梁的妻子痛哭她们的丈夫，因而改变了国家的风俗。里面存在什么，
一定会表现在外面。如果干了某件事，却见不到功绩，我还没见过。所
以想着是没有贤人，如果有，我一定会知道。"孟子说："孔子做鲁国司
寇的时候，不被信任，跟随着去祭祀，祭肉不按规定送来，于是还没来
得及脱下祭帽就匆忙地离开。不了解孔子的人以为他是因为祭肉离开，
了解孔子的人认为他是因为鲁国失礼而离去。至于孔子，则是想要自己
背一点小罪名离开，不想随便离去。君子的作为，一般人本来就是不知
道的。"

【英译】Shun-yü K'wǎn said, 'He who makes fame and meritorious services his first objects, acts with a regard to others. He who
makes them only secondary objects, acts with a regard to himself.
You, master, were ranked among the three chief ministers of the
State, but before your fame and services had reached either to the
prince or the people, you have left your place. Is this indeed the way of
the benevolent?' Mencius replied, 'There was Po-î; —he abode in an
inferior situation, and would not, with his virtue, serve a degenerate
prince. There was Î Yin; —he five times went to T'ang, and five times
went to Jie. There was Hûi of Liû-Hsiâ; —he did not disdain to serve a
vile prince, nor did he decline a small office. The courses pursued by
those three worthies were different, but their aim was one. And what
was their one aim? We must answer— "To be perfectly virtuous."
And so it is simply after this that superior men strive. Why must they
all pursue the same course?' K'wǎn pursued, 'In the time of the duke

Mû of Lû, the government was in the hands of Kung-î, while Tszu-liû and Tszu-sze were ministers. And yet, the dismemberment of Lû then increased exceedingly. Such was the case, a specimen how your men of virtue are of no advantage to a kingdom!' Mencius said, 'The prince of Yü did not use Pâi-lî Hsî, and thereby lost his State. The duke Mû of Chin used him, and became chief of all the princes. Ruin is the consequence of not employing men of virtue and talents; — how can it rest with dismemberment merely?' K'wǎn urged again, 'Formerly, when Wang P'âo dwelt on the Ch'î, the people on the west of the Yellow River all became skilful at singing in his abrupt manner. When Mien Ch'ü lived in Kâo-t'ang, the people in the parts of Ch'î on the west became skilful at singing in his prolonged manner. The wives of Hwa Châu and Ch'î Liang bewailed their husbands so skilfully, that they changed the manners of the State. When there is the gift within, it manifests itself without. I have never seen the man who could do the deeds of a worthy, and did not realize the work of one. Therefore there are now no men of talents and virtue. If there were, I should know them.' Mencius answered, 'When Confucius was chief minister of Justice in Lû, the prince came not to follow his counsels. Soon after there was the solstitial sacrifice, and when a part of the flesh presented in sacrifice was not sent to him, he went away even without taking off his cap of ceremony. Those who did not know him supposed it was on account of the flesh. Those who knew him supposed that it was on account of the neglect of the usual ceremony. The fact was, that Confucius wanted to go away on occasion of some small offence, not wishing to do so without some apparent cause. All men cannot be expected to understand the conduct of a superior man.'

【注释】

[1] 本章详细记载了孟子和淳于髡关于贤者应有什么作为的争论。淳于髡认为孟子等儒者过于清高，不去行建功立业、造福百姓，是"自为者"的代表。孟子举伯夷、伊尹和柳下惠的例子指出，虽然贤人的行为有很大差别，但他们都是仁者。仁者以推行仁义、实践自己的政治主张为目标。如果不能实现自己的主张，名誉、功利都是毫无意义的。

[2] "名实"，朱熹注曰："名，声誉也。实，事功也。"理雅各将之翻译为"fame"（名誉）和"meritorious services"（造福于人的事业），基本能体现"名实"的含义。原文中，淳于髡不嫌啰唆，反复强调"先名实"和"后名实"的区别。理雅各没有遵循原文的行文特点，而是根据英文的表达习惯，将第二个"名实"翻译为"them"，这样翻译虽不影响文义的表达，但不能突出"名实"在本章中的地位。刘殿爵不仅准确翻译出了"名实"的含义，还保持了原文反复强调的特点。

[3] "三卿"，全祖望《经史问答》云："大抵三卿者，上卿、亚卿、下卿而言。……或曰一卿是相，一卿是将，其一为客卿，而上下本无定员，亦通。"理雅各、赵甄陶选择用"the three chief ministers"翻译，显然不能完全再现此处三卿的含义。刘殿爵亦看到了这一点，选择用大写的"Ministers"翻译，以突出其含义的特殊性。

[4] 华周、杞梁是齐国大夫，朱熹注曰："二人皆齐臣，战死与莒。其妻哭之哀，国俗化之，皆善哭。"《说苑·善说》亦载，他们战死后，妻子痛苦哀悼，把城墙都哭倒了。因而赵甄陶将"华周杞梁之妻善哭其夫而变国俗"翻译为"The wives of Hua Zhou and Qi Liang bemoaned the death of their husbands in such a way as to change the national custom."（华周、杞梁的妻子因为各自丈夫的离世而恸哭，影响了整个国家的风俗）他的译文强调华周、杞梁的妻子非常悲伤，刘殿爵的译文"being supreme in the way they wept for their husbands"则强调华周、杞梁的妻子擅长哭夫。

[5] "不用"，赵岐注曰："不能用其道也。"刘殿爵将之译为"his

advice was not followed"（君主不能按照他的建议行事）。但赖发洛按字面意思将之翻译为 "they made no use of him"（不能使用他）。朱熹注曰："按史记：孔子为鲁司寇，摄行相事。齐人闻而惧，于是以女乐遗鲁君。季桓子与鲁君往观之，怠于政事。"既然鲁君让孔子摄行相事，并引起齐国恐惧，这就表明鲁君能使用孔子，但他后来"怠于政事"，不能践行孔子的良策，因而刘殿爵的译文更确切。

[6]"燔肉"，即祭肉。根据古礼，宗庙社稷的祭祀，要把祭肉分给同姓之国以及有关诸人，表示同"福禄"。刘殿爵将之翻译为 "the meat of the sacrificial animal"（用于祭祀的动物的肉），准确体现了其含义。

[7]"不税冕而行"，表明孔子离开得匆忙、迫切，连祭祀时戴的帽子都没来得及脱下。刘殿爵根据文义将"冕"翻译为 "ceremonial cap"（祭祀时戴的帽子），而赖发洛仅仅将之翻译为 "cap"（帽子）。其实"冕"并不是普通的帽子，它只是用于祭祀，平时不戴，因而刘殿爵的译文更准确。

[8]孟子指明孔子离开鲁国的真正原因是"乃孔子则欲以微罪行，不欲为苟去。"朱熹注曰："孟子言以为为肉者，固不足道；以为为无礼，则亦未为深知孔子者。盖圣人于父母之国，不欲显其君相之失，又不欲为无故而苟去，故不以女乐去，而以膰肉行。其见几明决，而用意忠厚，固非众人所能识也。"理雅各将之翻译为 "The fact was, that Confucius wanted to go away on occasion of some small offence"（孔子宁愿因为（君主）小的过错而离开）。刘殿爵却认为 "Confucius preferred to be slightly at fault in thus leaving"（孔子宁愿背一点小罪名走）。焦循曾对此做过进一步的解释："乃孔子之意，则欲以己不税冕之罪行，不欲为苟去。"这两种理解皆通。

【原文】12.7　孟子曰[1]："五霸[2]者，三王[3]之罪人[4]也；今之诸侯，五霸之罪人也；今之大夫，今之诸侯之罪人也。天子适诸侯曰巡狩，诸侯朝于天子曰述职。春省耕而补不足，秋省敛而助不给。入其疆，土地辟，田野治，养老尊贤，俊杰在位，则有庆；庆以地。入其疆，土地荒芜，遗老失贤，掊克在位，则有让。一不朝，则贬其爵；再不朝，则削其地；三不朝，则六师[5]移之[6]。是故天子讨而不伐，诸侯伐而不讨[7]。五霸者，搂诸侯以伐诸侯者也，故曰，五霸者，三王之罪人也。五霸，桓公为盛。葵丘之会[8]，诸侯束牲载书而不歃血。初命曰，诛不孝，无易树子，无以妾为妻。再命曰，尊贤育才，以彰有德。三命曰，敬老慈幼，无忘宾旅。四命曰，士无世官，官事无摄，取士必得[9]，无专杀大夫。五命曰，无曲防[10]，无遏籴，无有封而不告。曰：凡我同盟之人，既盟之后，言归于好。今之诸侯皆犯此五禁，故曰，今之诸侯，五霸之罪人也。长君之恶其罪小，逢君之恶其罪大。[11]今之大夫皆逢君之恶，故曰，今之大夫，今之诸侯之罪人也。"

【译文】孟子说："五霸是三王的罪人；现在的诸侯是五霸的罪人；现在的大夫，是现在的诸侯的罪人。天子去诸侯的国家叫巡狩，诸侯去朝见天子做述职。春天视察耕种的情况，补助穷苦的人；秋天视察收获的情况，救济缺粮的人。进入诸侯的疆界，如果土地已经开垦，田野里也治理得很好，老人得到赡养，贤人得到尊敬，杰出的人才在朝廷任职，那么就会有赏赐；赏赐给土地。进入诸侯的疆界，如果土地荒废，老人被遗弃，贤者不被任用，贪官在朝廷任职，那么就会有责罚。诸侯有一次不朝见，就降低爵；两次不朝见，就削减他的封地；三次不朝见，就派军队过去。所以天子是'讨'不是'伐'，诸侯是'伐'不是'讨'。五霸是挟持一部分诸侯去攻伐另一部分诸侯的人，所以说，五霸是三王的罪人。五霸中齐桓公最强大。在葵丘盟会中，诸侯们捆绑了牺牲，把盟约放在它身上，但是没有歃血盟誓。第一条盟约说：诛杀不孝的人，不要废立太子，不要立妾为妻。第二条盟约说：尊敬贤人，养育人才，来表彰有德的人。第三条盟约说：尊敬老人，慈爱幼小，不要怠慢贵宾和旅客。第四条盟约说：士人的官职不世袭，公务不兼任，选用士子一定要得当，不要擅自杀戮大夫。第五条盟约说：不要编设堤防，

不要禁止邻国来采购粮食，不要封赏而不报告（盟主）。最后说，所有
参与盟会的人，订立盟约以后，都要恢复往日的友好。现在的诸侯都违
犯了这五条禁令，所以说现在的诸侯，是五霸的罪人。助长君主的恶
行，这罪行还算小；逢迎君主的恶行，这罪行就大了。现在的大夫，都
逢迎君主的恶行，所以说，现在的大夫，都是现在的诸侯的罪人。"

【英译】Mencius said, 'The five chiefs of the princes were sinners
against the three kings. The princes of the present day are sinners against
the five chiefs. The Great officers of the present day are sinners against
the princes. The sovereign visited the princes, which was called "A
tour of Inspection." The princes attended at the court of the sovereign,
which was called "Giving a report of office." It was a custom in the
spring to examine the ploughing, and supply any deficiency of seed;
and in autumn to examine the reaping, and assist where there was a
deficiency of the crop. When the sovereign entered the boundaries of
a State, if the new ground was being reclaimed, and the old fields
well cultivated; if the old were nourished and the worthy honoured;
and if men of distinguished talents were placed in office: then the
prince was rewarded, —rewarded with an addition to his territory. On
the other hand, if, on entering a State, the ground was found left
wild or overrun with weeds; if the old were neglected and the worthy
unhonoured; and if the offices were filled with hard taxgatherers: then
the prince was reprimanded. If a prince once omitted his attendance at
court, he was punished by degradation of rank; if he did so a second
time, be was deprived of a portion of his territory; if he did so a third
time, the royal forces were set in motion, and he was removed from
his government. Thus the sovereign commanded the punishment, but
did not himself inflict it, while the princes inflicted the punishment,

but did not command it. The five chiefs, however, dragged the princes to punish other princes, and hence I say that they were sinners against the three kings. Of the five chiefs the most powerful was the duke Hwan. At the assembly of the princes in K'wei-ch'iû, he bound the victim and placed the writing upon it, but did not slay it to smear their mouths with the blood. The first injunction in their agreement was, — "Slay the unfilial; change not the son who has been appointed heir; exalt not a concubine to be the wife." The second was, — "Honour the worthy, and maintain the talented, to give distinction to the virtuous." The third was, — "Respect the old, and be kind to the young. Be not forgetful of strangers and travellers." The fourth was, — "Let not offices be hereditary, nor let officers be pluralists. In the selection of officers let the object be to get the proper men. Let not a ruler take it on himself to put to death a Great officer." The fifth was, — "Follow no crooked policy in making embankments. Impose no restrictions on the sale of grain. Let there be no promotions without first announcing them to the sovereign." It was then said, "All we who have united in this agreement shall hereafter maintain amicable relations." The princes of the present day all violate these five prohibitions, and therefore I say that the princes of the present day are sinners against the five chiefs. The crime of him who connives at, and aids, the wickedness of his prince is small, but the crime of him who anticipates and excites that wickedness is great. The officers of the present day all go to meet their sovereigns' wickedness, and therefore I say that the Great officers of the present day are sinners against the princes.'

【注释】

[1] 孟子推崇王政，主张恢复三王的政治传统。他认为五霸破坏了王

道政治的原则，建立的霸政主张虽不能与王道媲美，但仍能维护孝悌忠信等美好品德。但后起诸侯为争夺土地和人口的无义战又破坏了五霸建立的霸道政治。孟子进一步指出，是在诸侯担任官职的大夫造成了战国时期诸侯混战的政治局面。他们不能劝君行仁政，反而为了讨君主欢心，阿谀奉承，曲意迎合君主的过错，陷君于不义。

[2]"五霸"是春秋时期先后称霸的五个诸侯。一说指齐桓公、晋文公、宋襄公、楚庄王、秦缪公（《吕氏春秋·当务》高诱注）；一说齐桓公、晋文公、楚庄王、吴王阖闾、越王勾践（《荀子·王霸》）；一说齐桓公、宋襄公、晋文公、秦穆公、吴王夫差（《汉书·诸侯王表》颜师古注）。刘殿爵的译文是"诸侯的五个首领"。他的译文传递的信息较为丰富，能体现春秋时期诸侯林立，并有五个诸侯首领领导众多诸侯小国的社会现实。赖发洛的"The five powers"则过于笼统，不能再现"五霸"所引起的文化联想。可见这种包涵着丰富的历史文化内涵的名词，在翻译的时候应该对其进行详细的解释，否则原文中的丰富意义将会缺失。

[3]"三王"，赵岐注曰："夏禹、商汤和周文王。"理雅各和赖发洛直接用"the three kings"翻译，刘殿爵和赵甄陶则将之大写，以突出其含义的特殊性。

[4]"罪人"，理雅各和赵甄陶将之翻译为"sinners"，"sinners"更强调宗教或道德上的罪人，具有较强的宗教意味，通常是指那些不信神的人。赖发洛将之翻译为"transgressors"，"transgressors"通常指违背规则、法律、条约的人。刘殿爵将"罪人"翻译为"offenders"，"offenders"尤指那些违反公共法规的人。"五霸"违反了"三王"所制定的仁政条款，而诸侯又背离了"五霸"的盟约，因而赖发洛和刘殿爵对"罪人"内涵的认识更贴切。

[5]"六师"，即六军。根据周代的军队编制只有天子可以保有"六师"。理雅各将之意译为"the royal forces"（王家的军队），刘殿爵则选择直译"六师"，并将之大写以突出其含义的特殊性。

[6]"移之"，赵岐注曰："不朝至三，讨之以六师。移之，就之也。"

刘殿爵取"移之，就之也"之意，将之翻译为"move into his state"（开进他的封地）。朱熹则认为："移之者，诛其人而变置之也。"理雅各的译文与之相类，将之翻译为"he was removed from his government"。

[7] 在今天"讨"和"伐"含义相近，但在三王时期所代表的意义相差甚远。赵岐注曰："讨者，上讨下也。伐者，敌国相征伐也。"朱熹进一步指出："讨者，出命以讨其罪，而使方伯连帅帅诸侯以伐之也。伐者奉天子之命，声其罪而伐之也。"可见，"讨"的发起对象是天子，他对诸侯罪行进行裁定，而"伐"则是诸侯对天子裁定的执行。理雅各将之翻译为"the sovereign commanded the punishment，but did not himself inflict it，while the princes inflicted the punishment，but did not command it"（下达处罚命令，但自己不亲自执行，诸侯执行惩罚命令但不能下达命令）。他的译文体现了二者的区别。

[8] "葵丘"是古代地名，春秋时属宋，在今河南考城县东三十里。公元前 651 年，齐桓公邀请宋、卫、郑、鲁等诸侯于此地会盟，并签订了盟约。葵丘之会确立了齐桓公的霸主地位。刘殿爵和理雅各选择对"葵丘"进行音译，赖发洛则逐字对译"Mallow Knoll"。

[9] "取士必得"是省略句，朱熹将其解为"必得其人也"。理雅各的译文受朱熹影响，将之翻译为"In the selection of officers let the object be to get the proper men"（在选择官员时，应选择合适的人）。刘殿爵则保持了原文简洁的风格，将之译为"the selection of Gentlemen should be appropriate"（对士的选择应当适当）。

[10] "无曲防"，朱熹注曰："不得曲为堤防，壅泉激水，以专小利，病邻国也。"他的注解强调在筑堤时不得损人利己，牺牲他国利益。理雅各的译文与之相类，将之翻译为"Follow no crooked policy in making embankments"（在筑堤时不要采取欺诈的政策）。但杨伯峻认为，"曲是副词，与《易·系词》'曲成万物而不遗'、《荀子·非相篇》'曲得所谓焉'、《荀子·礼论篇》'曲容备物之谓道矣'诸'曲'字同义，有'无不''遍'之

义",因而将"无曲防"翻译为"不要到处筑堤"。赵甄陶的译文与之相类,翻译为"dykes are not to be built everywhere"。

[11] 朱熹言简意赅地概括了"长君之恶"和"逢君之恶"的特征:"君有过不能谏,又顺之者,长君之恶也。君之过未萌,而先意导之者,逢君之恶也。"可见"长君之恶"是助长君主已有的过错,"逢君之恶"是将君子未发之恶心催发,变为现实行动。理雅各分别将之翻译为"connives at,and aids,the wickedness of his prince"(纵容并协助君主的罪行)和"anticipates and excites that wickedness"(促进和激起君主的邪恶)。译文准确再现了二者的区别。

【原文】12.8 鲁欲使慎子为将军[1]。孟子曰:"不教民而用之[2],谓之殃民。殃民者,不容于尧舜之世。一战胜齐,遂有南阳,然且不可。"慎子勃然不悦曰:"此则滑厘所不识也。"曰:"吾明告子。天子之地方千里,不千里,不足以待诸侯。诸侯之地方百里,不百里,不足以守宗庙之典籍。周公之封于鲁,为方百里也,地非不足,而俭于百里[3]。太公之封于齐也,亦为方百里也,地非不足也,而俭于百里。今鲁方百里者五,子以为有王者作,则鲁在所损乎,在所益乎?徒取诸彼以为此,然且仁者不为,况于杀人以求之乎?君子之事君也,务引其君以当道,志于仁而已。"

【译文】 鲁国想要任命慎子做将军。孟子说:"不先教导百姓便用他们打仗,这叫作祸害百姓。祸害百姓的人,在尧舜生活的时代是容不下的。即使只打一次仗就可以战胜齐国,收回南阳,仍然是不可以的。"慎子突然变脸,不高兴地说:"这是我所不明白的。"孟子说:"我明白地告诉你吧。天子的土地方圆一千里,不到一千里,便不能接待诸侯。诸侯的土地方圆一百里,不到一百里,便不够奉守宗庙的典章制度。周公被封于鲁,是方圆一百里,土地并不是不够,却仅限于百里。太公被封于齐,也是方圆一百里,土地并不是不够,却仅限于百里。如今鲁国的土地有五个方圆一百里，你认为假如有圣王兴起，鲁国的土地是在减少之列呢？还是在增加之列呢？不费力气，白白地取来那里的土地并入这里，仁人尚且不干，何况杀人来求得土地呢？君子服事君主，只是努力地引导他趋向正道，有志于仁罢了。"

【英译】The prince of Lû wanted to make the minister Shǎn commander of his army. Mencius said, 'To employ an uninstructed people in war may be said to be destroying the people. A destroyer of the people would not have been tolerated in the times of Yâo and Shun. Though by a single battle you should subdue Ch'î, and get possession of Nan-yang, the thing ought not to be done.' Shǎn changed countenance, and said in displeasure, 'This is what I, Kû-lî, do not understand.' Mencius said, 'I will lay the case plainly before you. The territory appropriated to the sovereign is 1,000 lî square. Without a thousand lî, he would not have sufficient for his entertainment of the princes. The territory appropriated to a Hâu is 100 lî square. Without 100lǐ, he would not have sufficient wherewith to observe the statutes kept in his ancestral temple. When Châu-kung was invested with the principality of Lû, it was a hundred lî square. The territory was indeed enough, but it was not more than 100 lǐ. When T'âi-kung was invested with the principality of Ch'î, it was 100 lî square. The territory was indeed enough, but it was not more than 100 lǐ. Now Lû is five times 100 lî square. If a true royal ruler were to arise, whether do you think that Lû would be diminished or increased by him? If it were merely taking the place from the one State to give it to the other, a benevolent man would not do it; —how much less will he do so, when the end is to be sought by the slaughter of men! The way in which a superior man serves his prince contemplates simply the leading him in the right path, and directing his mind to benevolence.'

【注释】

[1] 孟子反对抢占土地、争夺百姓的不义战争，主张君主应当教民以德、保民而王。他同时劝诫臣子应劝导国君实行仁政，爱惜百姓，让人民免于战争之苦。他鄙视那些为君主争夺土地、抢占百姓的大臣，认为"善战者服上刑，连诸侯者次之，辟草莱、任土地者次之。"（《孟子·离娄章句上》）

[2] "不教民而用之"，赵岐注曰："不教民以仁义而用之战斗。"朱熹亦认为："教民者，教之礼义，使知入事父兄，出事长上也。""教民"是孟子仁政思想的重要组成部分。他认为实行仁政首先要确保百姓衣食无忧，其次要以人伦教育百姓，因为"饱食、暖衣、逸居而无教，则近于禽兽"。尧舜之世，以仁义教民，而战国之时，君主不但不养民、教民，反而驱使百姓参加争夺土地的战争，这显然是祸害百姓。赵甄陶将之翻译为"To send the people to fight without training them first is to plunge them into disasters"（不首先经训练百姓，就把他们送去打战，会使他们陷入灾难）。他的译文则强调训练人们作战技能的重要性，刘殿爵的译文与之相类，认为不先教育、训练百姓就让他们参战是祸害百姓。这和孟子一贯的反战主张不一致。

[3] "俭"，朱熹注曰："止而不过之意也。二公有大勋劳于天下，而其封国不过百里。"理雅各和刘殿爵持这一观点，将"俭"理解为"限于"。焦循指出："《说文》：'俭，约也。'《淮南子主术训》，'所守甚约'。高诱《注》云：'约，少也。'"杨伯峻的译文取这一观点，将之翻译为"但实际上少于一百里"。赵甄陶的英译本亦持此观点，将之翻译为"was actually less than that"。结合前文，"不百里，不足以守宗庙之典籍"看，取"俭"的"限于"之意逻辑性更强。

【原文】12.9　孟子曰[1]："今之事君者皆曰：'我能为君辟土地[2]，充府库。'今之所谓良臣，古之所谓民贼也。君不乡道，不志于仁，而求富之，是富桀也。'我能为君约与国，战必克[3]。'今之所谓良臣，古之所谓民贼也。君不乡道，不志于仁，而求为之强战，是辅桀也。由今之道，无变今之俗，虽与之天下，不能一朝居也。"

【译文】 孟子说："今天侍奉君主的人都说：'我能为君主开拓土地，充实府库。'今天所谓的'良臣'正是古代的所谓'民贼'。君主不向往道德，不立志于仁，却想着为他谋求财富，这是为夏桀谋财富啊。'我能为君主邀结盟国，每战必胜。'今天所谓的'良臣'正是古代的所谓'民贼'。君主不向往道德，不立志于仁，却想着为他努力作战，这是辅助夏桀啊。沿着现在的道路，不改变现在的风俗习气，即使把天下都给他，也不能坐稳一天。"

【英译】 Mencius said, 'Those who now-a-days serve their sovereigns say, "We can for our sovereign enlarge the limits of the cultivated ground, and fill his treasuries and arsenals." Such persons are now-a-days called "Good ministers," but anciently they were called "Robbers of the people." If a sovereign follows not the right way, nor has his mind bent on benevolence, to seek to enrich him is to enrich a Chieh. Or they will say, "We can for our sovereign form alliances with other States, so that our battles must be successful." Such persons are now-a-days called "Good ministers," but anciently they were called "Robbers of the people." If a sovereign follows not the right way, nor has his mind directed to benevolence, to seek to enrich him is to enrich a Chieh. Although a prince, pursuing the path of the present day, and not changing its practices, were to have the throne given to him, he could not retain it for a single morning.'

【注释】

[1] 孟子指责战国时期的大臣不懂为臣之道，以扩充土地、增加财富、发动战争来献媚君主，以求高官厚禄。今天那些被称作良臣的人，实际上是

那些在古代圣王时期被称作民贼的人。因为他们不能引导君主走正道，行仁义，成明君，却要为这些不顾百姓死活的嗜战君主扩充土地，增加财富，陷百姓于水深火热之中。

[2]"辟土地"，赵岐注曰："侵邻国也。"侵犯邻国必引起战争，荒废耕地，死伤百姓；搜刮百姓定陷人们于贫苦潦倒之地，因而孟子认为擅长这些的大臣是"民贼"。刘殿爵将之翻译为 "extend the territory of my prince"（扩充君主的疆土）。孟子时期，各国的疆域基本上都已经划定，要扩充疆域，就要侵犯他国领土。因而他的译文和赵岐的注解相类。朱熹认为，"辟"是"开垦也"。理雅各受其影响，将"辟土地"翻译为 "enlarge the limits of the cultivated ground"（扩充耕地）。显然，他认为这里说的是那些为君主"辟草莱、任土地者"，他的译文更能呼应下文的"富之"。

[3]"约与国，战必克"有两种理解。一种以理雅各为代表，认为"约与国"是"战必克"的前提，将之翻译为 "form alliances with other States, so that our battles must be successful"（签订合约，建立联盟，以此来确保战争的胜利）。第二种理解以刘殿爵为代表，认为二者是并列关系，"我"既具备外交能力，可"约与国"，又懂得作战技术，逢战必胜。他的译文是 "I am able to gain allies and ensure victory in war for my prince"（我能建立联盟，也能确保战争的胜利）。从行文上看，"今之事君者皆曰"的两段内容，在句法、句式上基本一致，能够相互对应，因而可结合前文"辟土地，充府库"推断，此处的"约与国，战必克"也应是两个独立的行为。

【原文】12.10　白圭曰[1]："吾欲二十而取一，何如？"孟子曰："子之道，貉[2]道也。万室之国，一人陶，则可乎？"曰："不可，器不足用也。"曰："夫貉，五谷不生，惟黍生之；无城郭、宫室、宗庙、祭祀之礼，无诸侯币帛饔飧[3]，无百官有司，故二十取一而足也。今居中国，去人伦，无君子[4]，如之何其可也？陶以寡，且不可以为国，况无君子乎？欲轻之于尧舜之道者，大貉小貉也；欲重之于尧舜之道者，大桀小桀也[5]。”

【译文】白圭说：“我想定二十抽一的税率，怎么样？”孟子说：“你的办法是貉国的办法。假若有一万户的国家，一个人制作陶器，可以吗？”答道：“不可以，陶器会不够用。”孟子说：“貉国，五谷不生，只长黍；没有城墙、宫室、宗庙和祭祀的礼节；没有诸侯国之间互相送礼物和宴请；没有各种衙门和官吏，所以二十抽一就够了。现在居住在中原，废弃人伦，不要各种官吏，那怎么能行呢？做陶器的人少，尚且不能够把一个国家搞好，更何况没有官吏呢？想要比尧舜的十分抽一的税率还轻的，是大貉小貉；想要比尧舜的十分抽一的税率还重的，是大桀、小桀。”

【英译】Pâi Kwei said，‘I want to take a twentieth of the produce only as the tax. What do you think of it?’ Mencius said，‘Your way would be that of the Mo. In a country of ten thousand families，would it do to have only one potter?’ Kwei replied，‘No. The vessels would not be enough to use.’ Mencius went on，‘In Mo all the five kinds of grain are not grown；it only produces the millet. There are no fortified cities，no edifices，no ancestral temples，no ceremonies of sacrifice；there are no princes requiring presents and entertainments；there is no system of officers with their various subordinates. On these accounts a tax of one-twentieth of the produce is sufficient there. But now it is the Middle Kingdom that we live in. To banish the relationships of men，and have no superior men；—how can such a state of things be thought of? With but few potters a kingdom cannot subsist；—how much less can it subsist without men of a higher rank than others? If we wish to make the taxation lighter than the system of Yao and Shun，we shall just have a great Mo and a small Mo. If we wish to make it heavier，we shall just have the great Chieh and the small Chieh.’

【注释】

[1] 孟子认为，最合适的税收制度是尧舜时期奉行的十分之一税率。如果超过了这一税率就会给百姓带来巨大负担，是陷百姓于水深火热之中的夏桀暴政。如果低于这一税率，就会影响国家的正常运作。

[2] "貉"是古代北方少数民族创立的国家。理雅各和赖发洛在翻译时选择音译法，将之翻译为"Mo"，而刘殿爵则选择将之意译为"Northern barbarians"（北方少数民族）。孟子举"貉"并非要介绍这个少数民族的习俗和特点，而是取它和其他生活在北方少数民族的共性，因而是否将之音译为"貉"并不影响对文意的理解。

[3] "币帛"是天子与诸侯或诸侯国之间在交往时互赠的礼物。"饔飧"，朱熹注曰："以饮食馈客之礼也。"可见，此处孟子是在强调貉国不注重国家间交往的礼仪。 刘殿爵将之翻译为"They do not have diplomacy with its attendant gifts and banquets"（在对外交往时，没有礼物和宴会）。他的译文表明，貉国不注重国与国之间这些交往的礼仪。赖发洛将之翻译为"no feudal lords，or gifts of silk，or breakfasts and suppers"（没有诸侯、没有丝织品的礼物，没有早晚饭）。他的译文给读者塑造了一个穷困潦倒，连最基本的生活都难以保障的貉国形象。貉国虽贫苦，但亦有黍生长，不可能没有维持生存所必需的饭食，因而强调貉国缺乏交往的礼义，更贴切。

[4] 虽然孟子提到的"君子"通常指那些道德高尚的人，是儒家的理想人格，但在本章"君子"指的是那些居上位的统治阶层，以对应前文提到的"无诸侯""无百官有司"。刘殿爵将之翻译为"men in authority"（当权者），赵甄陶翻译为"officials in authority"，都突出了其含义的特殊性。

[5] 孟子认为尧舜确立的税率最符合中原的实际，欲轻于尧舜的税率，就难以维持正常的礼仪交往，那么他们就像貉一样不知礼仪。偏离得多就是大貉，偏离得少就是小貉。同理，如果诸侯规定的税率重于尧舜的十分抽一，那他们就像夏桀一样残暴，不顾百姓的死活。因而孟子发出如是感叹："欲轻之于尧舜之道者，大貉小貉也。欲重之于尧舜之道者，大桀小桀

也。"刘殿爵的译文就持这一观点，认为"大貉小貉"和"大桀小桀"的称谓是根据对尧舜之道的偏离程度而定。但赵岐指出："尧、舜以来，什一而税，足以行礼，故以此为道。今欲轻之二十税一者，夷貉为大貉，子为小貉也。欲重之过十一，则夏桀为大桀，子为小桀也。"理雅各的译文与赵岐的注解相类，认为古有"大貉、大桀"，今天偏离尧舜之道的诸侯国就是"小貉、小桀。"

【原文】12.11　白圭曰[1]："丹[2]之治水也愈于禹。"孟子曰："子过矣[3]，禹之治水，水之道也，是故禹以四海为壑。今吾子以邻国为壑[4]。水逆行谓之洚水[5]——洚水者，洪水也——仁人之所恶也。吾子过矣。"

【译文】白圭说："我治理水患强过大禹。"孟子说："你错了。大禹治理水患，是顺着水的本性进行疏导，所以大禹是把水引入四海。你却把水引到附近的国家去。水逆流而行叫作洚水——泽水就是洪水——是仁人所最憎恶的。你错了！"

【英译】Pâi Kwei said，'My management of the waters is superior to that of Yü.' Mencius replied，'You are wrong，Sir. Yü's regulation of the waters was according to the laws of water. He therefore made the four seas their receptacle，while you make the neighbouring States their receptacle. Water flowing out of its channels is called an inundation. Inundating waters are a vast waste of water，and what a benevolent man detests. You are wrong，my good Sir.'

【注释】

[1] 白圭向孟子夸耀自己的治水功绩，认为自己的功劳已经超过了大禹。孟子对他的自夸行为进行了批评，并指出，大禹的治水之功之所以能被后人牢记和推崇，是因为他能顺水之性治水，以四海为壑，把天下苍生放在心中，而白圭却以邻国为壑，虽能治理本国水患，却给别国人民带来灾难。

[2]"丹",是白圭的名。古人通常有名有字。自称名表自谦,称对方的字,以表示尊重。翻译时通常直接用"I"(我)代替。

[3] 白圭自诩治水之功超过了大禹,孟子认为他这种看法是错误的。理雅各将"过"翻译为"wrong"(错误),而赖发洛和刘殿爵则译为"mistaken"。这两个词虽都表示错误,但侧重点不同。"Wrong"侧重强调事物本身错误、不正当,而"mistaken"则强调对事件的判断和看法错误。相比较而言,赖发洛和刘殿爵的译文更确切。

[4]"以邻国为壑",据《韩非子·喻老》记载,白圭治水不是疏通河道,将水引入江海而是建筑堤防,让水流入邻国。理雅各选择直译为"you make the neighbouring States their receptacle"(把邻国当作水的容器)。他的译文略显僵硬,相比较而言,刘殿爵的译文"you empty the water into the neighbouring states"(将水注入邻国)更便于读者理解。

[5] 从"水逆行谓之洚水"可以推测,"洚水"的一大特征是水逆流倒行。刘殿爵的译文"water goes counter to its course"准确体现了其含义。理雅各将之翻译为"flowing out of its channels"(溢出河道的水),他的译文也翻译出了"洚"的一个特征,但没有体现"逆行"的特点。

【原文】12.12　孟子曰:"君子不亮,恶乎执?[1]"

【译文】孟子说:"君子没有诚信,哪能有什么操守?"

【英译】Mencius said,'If a scholar have not faith, how shall he take a firm hold of things?'

【注释】

[1] 孟子在本章强调了诚信的重要性。赵岐解此章为:"亮,信也。《易》曰:'君子履信思顺。'若为君子之道,舍信将安执之。"赵甄陶的译文与之相类,将之翻译为"If a gentleman is not sincere, how can he adhere to his honorable conduct?"这也是当前比较流行的翻译。虽然刘殿爵取"亮"的诚信的含义,但选择将"执"理解为"固执"。他将本句话翻译为"Other

than by adherence to his word，in what respect can a gentleman be guilty of inflexibility?"（除了坚持守信外，君子在哪些方面会因为固执而受到指责）显然，他的理解受孔子"言必信，行必果，硁硁然小人哉"（《论语·子路》）的影响。理雅各将本句翻译为"If a scholar have not faith，how shall he take a firm hold of things?"他选择用"faith"翻译"亮"，但是该词的常用义是"信仰"，容易让读者认为孟子在强调"信仰"在保持人的道德操守上的重要性。他对"执"的翻译受朱熹"言凡事苟且，无所执持也"的影响。李葆华认为："'君子不亮，恶乎执'中的'恶'字，应解作'厌恶'的'恶'，而非疑问代词。……此章意谓'君子之所以不太强调和讲究信，是因为厌恶对信的理解与实践的固执和偏执'。"

【原文】 12.13　鲁欲使乐正子为政[1]。孟子曰："吾闻之，喜而不寐。"公孙丑曰："乐正子强[2]乎?"曰："否。""有知虑乎?"曰："否。""多闻识乎?"曰："否。""然则奚为喜而不寐?"曰："其为人也好善。""好善足乎?"曰："好善优于天下，而况鲁国乎? 夫苟好善，则四海之内皆将轻千里而来告之以善；夫苟不好善，则人将曰：'讪讪，予既已知之矣。[3]'讪讪之声音颜色距人于千里之外。士[4]止于千里之外，则谗谄面谀之人至矣。与谗谄面谀之人居，国欲治，可得乎?"

【译文】 鲁国打算任用乐正子治理国家。孟子说："我听说后，高兴得睡不着。"公孙丑说："乐正子很坚强吗?"答道："不。""很聪明，有主意吗?"答道："不。""见多识广吗?"答道："不。""那你为什么高兴得睡不着呢?"答道："他为人好善。""好善就够了吗?"答道："好善，用来治理天下都绰绰有余，何况仅仅一个鲁国呢? 如果好善，那四处的人都会不远千里来告诉他善，如果不好善，他会说'嗯嗯! 我早就知道了。'嗯嗯的声音和面色就会把别人拒绝在千里之外了。士人在千里之外停止不来，那些进谗言、当面奉承的人就会来了。和进谗言、当面奉承的人在一起，想要治理好国家，做得到吗？"

【英译】The prince of Lû wanting to commit the administration of his government to the disciple Yo-chǎng, Mencius said, 'When I heard of it, I was so glad that I could not sleep.' Kung-sun Ch'âu asked, 'Is Yo-chǎng a man of vigour?' and was answered, 'No.' 'Is he wise in council?' 'No.' 'Is he possessed of much information?' 'No.' 'What then made you so glad that you could not sleep?' 'He is a man who loves what is good.' 'Is the love of what is good sufficient?' 'The love of what is good is more than a sufficient qualification for the government of the kingdom; —how much more is it so for the State of Lû! If a minister love what is good, all within the four seas will count 1,000 lî but a small distance, and will come and lay their good thoughts before him. If he do not love what is good, men will say, "How self-conceited he looks? He is saying to himself, I know it." The language and looks of that self-conceit will keep men off at a distance of 1,000 lî. When good men stop 1,000 lî off, calumniators, flatterers, and sycophants will make their appearance. When a minister lives among calumniators, flatterers, and sycophants, though he may wish the State to be well governed, is it possible for it to be so?'

【注释】

[1] 孟子认为，就治理国家而言，性格坚强、深谋远虑和见多识广并非必要标准。真正的治国栋梁必须好善言，行善行，能够广泛听取不同的建议，善于招徕四方贤才，为己所用。

[2] 公孙丑不明白为什么孟子会因听说乐正子要治理鲁国就高兴得睡不着觉，并质疑乐正子是否具备当时普遍认为的管理者应该具备的品质。可见，此处的"强"并非身体是否强壮，而是问他是否具备强有力的领导性格。理雅各将之翻译为"a man of vigour"（有气魄），刘殿爵的译文是

"great strength of character"（性格坚强），二人的译文都能准确体现"强"的含义。

[3]"呫呫，予既已知之矣"为我们刻画了一个不好善言，自以为是的小人之貌。"呫呫"，赵岐注："自足其智不嗜善言之貌。"即听别人意见时，不耐烦的声音。通常用来形容人自以为很聪明，而不愿意接受别人的建议。理雅各将之翻译为"How self-conceited he looks？He is saying to himself, I know it."（他看起来太自负了吧？他在自言自语地说："我知道。"）理雅各在翻译"呫呫"时选择将之意译，准确翻译出来原文的意思。刘殿爵的译文"He seems to say 'I know it all'"，虽然没有专门翻译"呫呫"，但是也再现了说话者不耐烦的自满之态。

[4]三位译者都能翻译出"士止于千里之外"的含义，但对"士"的翻译不同。理雅各将"士"翻译为"good men"（优秀、善良的人），赖发洛翻译为"knights"（骑士、武士），刘殿爵则翻译为"Gentlemen"。虽然"士"在春秋末期主要是指知识分子阶层，但此处的"士"则指那些能"告之以善"的人，因而理雅各的翻译更确切。

【原文】12.14 陈子曰[1]："古之君子何如则仕？"孟子曰："所就三，所去三[2]。迎之致敬以有礼；言，将行其言也，则就之；礼貌未衰，言弗行也，则去之。其次，虽未行其言也，迎之致敬以有礼，则就之；礼貌衰，则去之。其下[3]，朝不食，夕不食，饥饿不能出门户。君闻之，曰：'吾大者不能行其道，又不能从其言也，使饥饿于我土地，吾耻之。'周之，亦可受也，免死而已矣。"

【译文】陈子说："古代的君子怎么样才出来做官？"孟子说："就职的情况有三种，离职的情况也有三种。有礼貌恭敬地接待，对他的进言，准备实行，便就职。礼貌虽未衰减，但对他的进言不再去实行，便辞职。再次一等，虽然没有实行他的进言，但是有礼貌恭敬地接待，便就职。礼貌衰减了，便离开。最下一等，早晨没有饭吃，晚上也没有饭吃，饿得出不了门，君主听说了便说：'从国家大政上看，我不能实行他的主张，又不能听从他的进言，使他在我的国土上饿着肚皮，我感到耻辱。'于是周济他，这也可以接受，不过是为了免于死亡罢了。"

【英译】The disciple Ch'ǎn said, 'What were the principles on which superior men of old took office?' Mencius replied, 'There were three cases in which they accepted office, and three in which they left it. If received with the utmost respect and all polite observances, and they could say to themselves that the prince would carry their words into practice, then they took office with him. Afterwards, although there might be no remission in the polite demeanour of the prince, if their words were not carried into practice, they would leave him. The second case was that in which, though the prince could not be expected at once to carry their words into practice, yet being received by him with the utmost respect, they took office with him. But afterwards, if there was a remission in his polite demeanour, they would leave him. The last case was that of the superior man who had nothing to eat, either morning or evening, and was so famished that he could not move out of his door. If the prince, on hearing of his state, said, "I must fail in the great point, —that of carrying his doctrines into practice, neither am I able to follow his words, but I am ashamed to allow him to die of want in my country;" the assistance offered in such a case might be received, but not beyond what was sufficient to avert death.'

【注释】

[1] 孟子在本章主要是谈了士人的出仕之道。他将出来做官的情况概括为"所就三，所去三"。朱熹解释说："所谓'见行可'之仕，若孔子于季桓子是也。受女乐而不朝，则去之矣。所谓'际可'之仕，若孔子于卫灵公是也。故与公游于圃，公仰视蜚雁而后去之。所谓'公养'之仕，君之于

民，固有周之之义，况此又有悔过之言，所以可受。然未至于饥饿不能出门户，则犹不受也。其曰免死而已，则其所受亦有节矣。"

[2] "所就三，所去三"是对陈子"何如则仕"问题的回应，因而"就"和"去"并非其字面意义上的"靠近"和"离去"，而是指"任职"和"离职"。刘殿爵将之翻译为"There were three cases in which they accepted office，and three in which they left it."（在三种情况下君子会担任官职，同样在三种情况下他会辞官）他的译文能更清楚、准确地体现原文的意思。

[3] 孟子在本章归纳的三种情况，地位并非平等，而是逐级下降的。孟子最推崇的是第一种情况，即能够实践自己的政治抱负。至于第二种情况，则是伺机而动，希望潜移默化地影响国君采纳自己的建议。而第三种情况则是不得已而为之的情况。君子在摆脱了生命之忧后，应立刻结束不能施展自己政治才能的官位。因而原文中的"其次"和"其下"并非表并列关系的"二"和"三"，而是"再次一等"和"最次一等"。因而理雅各用"The second case"（第二种情况）和"last case"（最后一种情况），刘殿爵用"Second"（第二）和"Third"（第三）翻译，不甚妥当。

【原文】12.15　孟子曰[1]："舜发于畎亩之中，傅说举于版筑之间，胶鬲举于鱼盐之中，管夷吾举于士，孙叔敖举于海，百里奚举于市[2]。故天将降大任于是人也，必先苦其心志，劳其筋骨，饿其体肤，空乏其身，行拂乱其所为，所以动心忍性，曾益其所不能[3]。人恒过，然后能改；困于心，衡[4]于虑，而后作；征于色，发于声，而后喻。入则无法家拂士[5]，出则无敌国外患者。国恒亡。然后知生于忧患而死于安乐也。"

【译文】孟子说："舜兴起于田野之中，傅说从筑墙的工作中被提举出来，胶鬲被提举于鱼盐的工作，管夷吾从狱官的手里被提举出来，孙叔敖从海边被提举出来，百里奚被从市场提举出来。所以天要把重任落到某人身上，一定先要磨砺他的心志，劳累他的筋骨，饥饿他的身体，穷困他的身子，扰乱他的行为，这样，便可以震动他的心志，坚韧他的性情，增加他的能力。一个人常常犯错误，才能改正；心意困苦，思虑不通，才能奋发有为；表现在面色上，抒发在言语中，才能被人了解。一个国家，国内没有通晓法度的大臣和辅助君主的士人，国外没有相与抗衡的国家和外在的忧惧，国家常常会灭亡。由此可以知道，忧愁患害使人生存，安逸享乐使人死亡。"

【英译】Mencius said, 'Shun rose from among the channelled fields. Fû Yüeh was called to office from the midst of his building frames；Chiâo-ko from his fish and salt；Kwan Î-wû from the hands of his gaoler；Sun-Shû Ao from his hiding by the sea-shore；and Pâi-lî Hsî from the market-place. Thus, when Heaven is about to confer a great office on any man, it first exercises his mind with suffering, and his sinews and bones with toil. It exposes his body to hunger, and subjects him to extreme poverty. It confounds his undertakings. By all these methods it stimulates his mind, hardens his nature, and supplies his incompetencies. Men for the most part err, and are afterwards able to reform. They are distressed in mind and perplexed in their thoughts, and then they arise to vigorous reformation. When things have been evidenced in men's looks, and set forth in their words, then they understand them. If a prince have not about his court families attached to the laws and worthy counsellors, and if abroad there are not hostile States or other external calamities, his kingdom will generally come to ruin. From these things we see how life springs from sorrow and calamity, and death from ease and pleasure.'

【注释】

[1] "舜发于畎亩之中"一章是《孟子》中较为著名的篇章。它通过列举一些著名人物在艰难环境中成功的例子说明了一个深刻的道理：生于忧

患，死于安乐。逆境虽然会给人带来困苦，但可以磨炼人的意志，增益人的才干，促人成功。

[2] 本章开篇列举了六位生于忧患的贤人，他们分别是舜、傅说、胶鬲、管夷吾、孙叔敖、百里奚。传说舜耕于历山，傅说因罪服刑，在筑墙时被武丁提拔，胶鬲在民间贩卖鱼盐时被武王发现提拔，管夷吾因帮助公子纠争夺君位失败入狱，后被桓公提拔为相，孙叔敖被楚庄王在海滨提拔，百里奚则是在集市上被提拔。了解历史上这六位历史人物的经历，可以深刻地认识到艰苦的环境有助于磨砺人们的心志，促人成才。

[3]"必先苦其心志，劳其筋骨，饿其体肤，空乏其身，行拂乱其所为，所以动心忍性，曾益其所不能"是孟子总结的要担当大任的人所面临的种种磨难。对于这些磨难，刘殿爵采取意译法，只关注将原文的意思表达清楚，不求完全对译原文字词。理雅各在翻译时采用直译法，逐一列举，反复说明。

[4]"衡"，赵岐注："横也。横塞其虑于胸臆之中。"可见，此处的衡通"横"，指横塞。理雅各将之翻译为"perplexed in their thoughts"（心中产生疑虑），刘殿爵翻译为"frustrated in mind"（思虑阻塞）皆可。

[5] 赵岐注："法度大臣之家，拂（弼）之士。"理雅各将"法家"翻译为"families attached to the laws"（有法度的世家），将"拂士"翻译为"worthy counsellors"（令人敬畏的谏臣）；刘殿爵翻译为"law-abiding families"（遵守法律的世家）和"reliable Gentlemen"（可依靠的君子）。二人基本上都能翻译出"法家"和"拂士"的含义。

【原文】12.16　孟子曰[1]："教亦多术[2]矣，予不屑之教诲也者[3]，是亦教诲之而已矣。[4]"

【译文】孟子说："教育也有多种方式，我不屑于去教诲，也是在教诲啊。"

【英译】Mencius said, 'There are many arts in teaching. I refuse,

as inconsistent with my character, to teach a man, but I am only
thereby still teaching him.'

【注释】

[1] 孟子在此处论述了自己的教育思想。孟子认为教育有多种方法，
"不屑之教诲"即通过拒绝教育的方式来激发受教育者的羞耻心，使之自我
反省，有所领会。孔子在教学中，也运用过这一教育方法。

[2] "术"，方式方法。郑玄注《礼记·祭统》"惠术也，可以观政矣"
曰："术犹法也。"刘殿爵的理解与之相类，将"教亦多术矣"译为"There
are more ways than one of instructing others"（教育的方法有多种），理雅各则
取"术"的技艺的含义，将之翻译为"art"，赖发洛则翻译为"secrets"（奥
秘）。孟子在此处主要论证教育的方法，刘殿爵的翻译更贴切。

[3] "予不屑之教诲也者"，赵岐注曰："屑，洁也。我不洁其人之行，
故不教诲之。"朱熹亦认为："不以其人为洁而拒绝之。"理雅各的译文与之
相类，但陈器之认为："予不屑之教诲即予不屑教诲之。也者，语气词连用，
用在句中，表示停顿与提示，可译为'啊'。"显然，他认为"予不屑之教诲
也者"的含义是"我认为他不值得教诲。"赖发洛的译文是"If I do not deign
to teach a man"（我不愿意屈尊教育一个人）。他的译文传达的意思和刘殿爵
相类，即"My disdain to instruct a man"（我不屑于教育这个人）。从文义上
看，这两种理解都可以。

[4] "是亦教诲之而已矣"，朱熹注曰："其人若能感此，退自修省，则
是亦我教诲之也。"理雅各的译文和朱熹的注解相类。赖发洛将之翻译为"I
teach him a lesson too"（我这也是给了他一个教训），基本也能体现原文之意。
相比较而言，刘殿爵的"one way of instructing him"（这也是一种教育方法）
更能呼应前文。

卷 十 三

尽心章句上

【原文】13.1　孟子曰[1]：“尽其心者，知其性也[2]。知其性，则知天矣。存其心，养其性，所以事天也。夭寿不贰[3]，修身以俟之，所以立命也。”

【译文】孟子说：“充分扩充自己的本心，就能知道自己的性。知道了自己的性，就懂得天命了。保持自己的本心，养护自己的性，这就是对待天命的方法。短命也好，长寿也好，我都不会三心二意，只是修养身心等待天命，这就是立命的方法。”

【英译】Mencius said, 'He who has exhausted all his mental constitution knows his nature. Knowing his nature, he knows Heaven. To preserve one's mental constitution, and nourish one's nature, is the way to serve Heaven. When neither a premature death nor long life causes a man any double-mindedness, but he waits in the cultivation of his personal character for whatever issue; this is the way in which he establishes his Heaven-ordained being.'

【注释】

[1] 孟子在本章将“心”“性”和“命”放在一起讨论，通过论述三者之间的关系，给出了对待天命的方法。

[2] 孟子即心言性，要了解心和性的关系首先要把握心的内涵。在孟

子那里，心的内涵极其丰富，一方面，心具备道德功能，由人人都生而具备
的四心组成，即恻隐之心、羞恶之心、辞让之心和是非之心；另一方面，心
还具有思考的功能，孟子曾明确指出，"心之官则思"（《孟子·告子上》）。
可见，"尽其心者，知其性也"，强调充分扩充四端之心，就可以认识人性。
理雅各将之翻译为"He who has exhausted all his mental constitution knows
his nature"，根据他的译文，人只有付出很大的努力，穷尽心志，才能认识
自己的性。赵甄陶将之翻译为"To fully develop the kindness of the heart is to
understand human nature"，即"充分扩充人的善良本心，就是懂得了人的本
性"。他将对心性关系的认识放到孟子的整个心性学说下去理解，更能突出
篇章宗旨。

[3]"夭寿不贰"，朱熹注曰："贰，疑也。不贰者，知天之至，修
身以俟死，则事天以终身也。"可见，本句是强调信心的坚定，不论是长
寿还是短命，都要毫不动摇地修身以待天命。理雅各受其影响，将之直
译为"When neither a premature death nor long life causes a man any double-
mindedness"（不论是短命还是长寿都不会让人三心二意）。刘殿爵采取解释
性翻译的策略，将之译为"Whether he is going to die young or to live to a ripe
old age makes no difference to his steadfastness of purpose."（不论长寿还是短
命都没有什么区别，他会专一不变地坚定自己的目标）两种译文皆可，相比
较而言，刘殿爵的译文更便于理解。

【原文】13.2　孟子曰[1]："莫非命也[2]，顺受其正[3]，是故知
命者[4]，不立乎岩墙之下。尽其道而死者，正命也；桎梏死者，非
正命也。"

【译文】孟子说："没有一样不是命，但要接受正命；所以懂得命的
人不站在可能倾倒的危墙下。尽力行道而死的人，是正命；犯罪而死的
人，不是正命。"

【英译】Mencius said, 'There is an appointment for everything.

A man should receive submissively what may be correctly ascribed thereto. Therefore，he who has the true idea of what is Heaven's appointment will not stand beneath a precipitous wall. Death sustained in the discharge of one's duties may correctly be ascribed to the appointment of Heaven. Death under handcuffs and fetters cannot correctly be so ascribed.'

【注释】

[1] 孟子在本章继续谈命。他将命分为正命和非正命两种，指出人应该接受正命，同时在人力可及的范围内，发挥能动性，争取好的结果，尽可能远离危险，摆脱非正命。

[2] "命"，张岱年在《中国哲学史大纲》指出："可以说命乃指人力所无可奈何者。我们作一件事情，这件事情之成功或失败，即此事的最后结果如何，并非作此事之个人之力量所能决定，但也不是以外任何个人或任何其它一件事情所能决定，而乃是环境一切因素之积聚的总和力量所使然。如成，既非完全由于我一个人的力量；如败，亦非因为我用力不到，只是我一个因素，不足以抗广远的众多因素之总力而已。作事者是个人，最后决定者却非任何个人。这是一件事实。儒家所谓命，可以说即由此种事实而导出的。这个最后的决定者，无以名之，名之曰命。"理雅各则将"莫非命也"翻译为"There is an appointment for everything"（任何事情都是预定的），显然，他将基督教的预定论思想移植到了孟子的思想中，否定了任何其他外部因素的作用。刘殿爵将"命"翻译为"destiny"（命运），认为所有发生的事情都是由命运决定的。"destiny"所表达的意象是不以人的意志为转移的必然趋势，和"命"的含义最为接近。

[3] "顺受其正"，理雅各将之翻译为"A man should receive submissively what may be correctly ascribed thereto."他认为"莫非命也"和"顺受其正"是因果关系，正是因为所有的事情都是预定的，所以人要顺从地接受那些正确的、提前预定的东西。刘殿爵将之翻译为"one accepts willingly only

what is one's proper destiny"。他认为这两个句子之间是转折关系，即尽管所有的事情都是由命运决定的，但是人们只愿意接受正命。对那些非正命的事情，人们会千方百计地避免。他的译文突出了人的能动性，联系下文，刘殿爵的理解更确切。

[4]"知命者"，朱熹注曰："命，谓正命。……知正命，则不处危地以取覆压之祸。"理雅各将之翻译为"he who has the true idea of what is Heaven's appointment"，即"真正理解上帝预定思想的人"。译文增加了原文不具备的宗教意向。相比较而言，刘殿爵的"he who understands destiny"（懂得命运的人）更准确。

【原文】13.3　孟子曰[1]："求则得之，舍则失之[2]，是求有益于得也，求在我者[3]也。求之有道，得之有命，是求无益于得也，求在外者也。[4]"

【译文】孟子说："追求便会得到，放弃，便会失掉，这种追求有益于得到，是追求我身上本来就存在的东西。探求有一定的方式，得到由命运决定，这种追求不益于得到，是追求我本身之外的东西。"

【英译】Mencius said, 'When we get by our seeking and lose by our neglecting—in that case seeking is of use to getting，and the things sought for are those which are in ourselves. When the seeking is according to the proper course，and the getting is only as appointed；—in that case the seeking is of no use to getting，and the things sought are without ourselves.'

【注释】

[1] 孟子认为人生有"求在我者"和"求在外者"两种追求。前者可以通过个人的追求得到，后者则受各种因素的制约，因而人们应努力追求"求在我者"，不要过分关注"求在外者"。

[2]"舍则失之"，刘殿爵认为"舍"是人有意识的行为，主动放手、

放弃，就会失去，而理雅各则认为是人因疏忽而失去。相比较而言，理雅各的译文更能体现心性"操则存，舍则亡；出入无时，莫知其乡"（《孟子·告子上》）的特点。

[3]"求在我者"，朱熹注曰："谓仁、义、礼、智，凡性之所有者。"可见，求在我者是人身固有的东西，即人的善性。如果扩充发展，就会保有；如果忽视，就会失去。理雅各将之翻译为"When we get by our seeking and lose by our neglecting—in that case seeking is of use to getting, and the things sought for are those which are in ourselves"（如果寻求我们就会得到，忽视就会失去，在这种情况下，寻求有助于得到，而我们寻求的东西就是我们内心的东西）。他的译文准确体现了"求在我者"的内涵。

[4]朱熹注曰："在外者，谓富、贵、利、达，凡外物皆是。"孟子认为，对于这些身外之物的寻求，首先要方法得当，其次，是否能得到，非人力所能决定，由"命"安排，个人的努力追求对最终结果并不能起任何作用。理雅各将"得之有命"翻译为"the getting is only as appointed"（能否得到却是预定的），他的翻译掺杂了耶稣基督的预定论思想。刘殿爵的译文准确翻译出了求在外者的特点，但将"命"翻译为"destiny"，增强了孟子思想的宿命性。

【原文】13.4 孟子曰："万物皆备于我矣[1]。反身而诚[2]，乐莫大焉。强恕[3]而行，求仁莫近焉。"

【译文】孟子说："万物与我为一体。反省自己做到了真诚，没有比这更快乐的了。努力实践推己及人的恕道，没有比这更容易达到仁了。"

【英译】Mencius said, 'All things are already complete in us. There is no greater delight than to be conscious of sincerity on self-examination. If one acts with a vigorous effort at the law of reciprocity, when he seeks for the realization of perfect virtue, nothing can be closer than his approximation to it.'

【注释】

[1]"万物皆备于我"章的含义较难理解,古往今来的学者对其认识也不尽相同。东汉赵岐注曰:"物,事也。我,身也。普谓人为成人已往,皆备知天下万物,常有所行矣。"他认为万事万物皆备于我身之中,人具备认识万事万物的能力。宋朱熹认为:"此言理之本然也。大则君臣父子,小则事物细微,其当然之理,无一不具于性分之内也。"显然,他认为是"万物之理皆备于我"。陆象山则把"万物皆备于我"解释为万物皆备于"我心"或"我之本心"。即客观世界的一切事物都存在于人的内心中。张岱年指出:"这个'心'是论者强加于孟子的。这称之为'增字解经',乖离了孟子原意。"结合"反身而诚"和"强恕而行"的修身方法,可以看出"万物皆备于我"并不是在回答物质与精神何为第一性的问题,而是在彰显通过这些修身方法,人们所能达到的"物我合一"的最高的精神境界。理雅各将"万物皆备于我"翻译为"All things are already complete in us"(所有的事情都已经完备于我之中),他的译文具有明显的主观唯心主义色彩。赖发洛的译文是"Ten thousand living things are all found within us"(一万种生物都可以从我们身上找到)。显然,他也认为,孟子的这一论述是典型的唯心主义命题,主张万物都存于"我"之中。他在注释中还援引托马斯·布朗的《一个医生的宗教信仰》来帮助读者理解这句话,认为孟子的这一思想和"我们跑到外面去找的奇异,我们身里其实都具有;整个非洲和它的怪物都可以从我们身里找出……"显然他们的译文都具有典型的唯心主义倾向,没有结合文义体会篇章宗旨。

[2]"诚",是儒家重要的哲学概念,内涵非常丰富。理雅各将之翻译为"sincerity","sincerity"侧重强调真诚地对待他人,不口是心非。而赖发洛的"true"和刘殿爵的"true to myself"则主张回归真实无妄的本性。理雅各的译文强调如何待人接物,而赖发洛和刘殿爵的译文则是针对保有人性而言。结合前文的"反身",可以判定此处的"诚"应取保持自身的本性之

意，因而赖发洛和刘殿爵的译文更能体现"诚"的含义。

[3]"恕"，朱熹注曰："推己以及人也。"可见，"恕"的基本含义是在要求别人做某事前，首先要想想自己是否愿意做，如果自己不想做，那么就不要强迫别人去做。理雅各将之翻译为"law of reciprocity"（互惠法则）。他的译文虽与"恕"的某些含义有相通之处，但不能传达这一重要哲学概念的基本特征。赖发洛翻译为"feelings for others"（体谅他人）。他的译文能准确体现"恕"的重要特征，但不如刘殿爵的"Try your best to treat others as you would wish to be treated yourself"（想要别人如何待你，就如何对待别人）更全面。

【原文】13.5 孟子曰[1]："行之而不著焉，习矣而不察焉[2]，终身由之而不知其道者，众[3]也。"

【译文】孟子说："如此做去，却不明白其当然，习以为常却不能深知其所以然，一生都在遵循却不知道它的道理，这是一般的人。"

【英译】Mencius said, 'To act without understanding, and to do so habitually without examination, pursuing the proper path all the life without knowing its nature; —this is the way of multitudes.'

【注释】

[1] 孟子倡导知行统一，主张对于要做事情要明白其当然，对于习惯做的事情要深知其所以然，只有这样才能做到知行统一，成为一个清醒、明智的人。

[2]"习"，最早见于商代甲骨文，其字形像鸟在日光下练习飞行，此处引申为习惯，经常做。理雅各将"习矣而不察焉"翻译为"to do so habitually without examination"（习惯了这么做却没有细查原因）。赖发洛的译文是"practising it without asking why"（经常这么做，却没有问过为什么）。虽然二人都能准确翻译出原文的意思，但赖发洛对"习"的翻译略胜一筹。他将"习"翻译为"practising"，这个单词既能体现"习"的字面意思"练

习"，又有"惯做，常做"之意，能够形神兼备地翻译出古汉语"习"字的含义。

[3]"众"，杨伯峻指出是"'众庶'之意。《文选·幽通赋》：'斯众兆之所惑。'曹大家《注》云：'众，庶也。'"理雅各和刘殿爵选择用"multitude"，赖发洛选择用"the many"翻译，皆取"民众"之含义。

【原文】13.6　孟子曰[1]："人不可以无耻，无耻之耻，无耻矣[2]。"

【译文】孟子说："人不可以没有羞耻，对没有羞耻而感到羞耻，那就真不会有羞耻了。"

【英译】Mencius said,'A man may not be without shame. When one is ashamed of having been without shame，he will afterwards not have occasion to be ashamed.'

【注释】

[1]孟子在本章强调了羞耻心的重要性。

[2]关于本句大体有三种理解。一种以赵岐为代表，认为："人能耻己之无所耻，是为改行从善之人，终身无复有耻辱之累也。"即人能把没有羞耻作为一种耻辱，就不会再有耻辱了。陈器之也同意这样理解，他在《孟子通译》中指出："人不可以没有羞耻，以没有羞耻是羞耻，便没有羞耻之事了。"理雅各和赖发洛的译文也都支持这一观点。第二种以杨伯峻为代表，认为，这句话应理解为："人不可以没有羞耻，不知羞耻的那种羞耻，真是不知羞耻呀。"在杨伯峻那里，"无耻"是"不知羞耻"而非"没有羞耻"，他强调不知羞耻是可耻的。刘殿爵的译文与杨伯峻的理解相同。杨伯峻同时指出第三种理解，即"有人把这个'之'字看为动词，适也。那么'无耻之耻，无耻矣'便当如此翻译：由没有羞耻之心到有羞耻之心，便没有羞耻之事了。"他同时指出，这一理解存在的问题："'之'字用作动词，有一定范围，一般'之'下的宾语多是地方、地位之词语，除了如在'遇观之否'等

卜筮术语中'之'字后可不用地方、地位之词语以为，极小见其他用法，因此不取。"

【原文】13.7　孟子曰^[1]："耻之于人大矣，为机变之巧者，无所用耻焉。不耻不若人，何若人有^[2]？"

【译文】孟子说："羞耻对于人来说关系重大，精于算计，老于权谋的人是用不着羞耻的。不把比不上别人看作是羞耻，怎样能比得上别人呢？"

【英译】Mencius said, 'The sense of shame is to a man of great importance. Those who form contrivances and versatile schemes distinguished for their artfulness, do not allow their sense of shame to come into action. When one differs from other men in not having this sense of shame, what will he have in common with them?'

【注释】

[1] 孟子在本章继续强调羞耻心的重要性。人只有认识到自己的不足，并因此感到耻辱，才能改正错误，提升自我。

[2] 学界对"不耻不若人，何若人有"的理解存在多样性。一种以赵岐为代表，认为："不耻不如古之圣人，何有如贤人之名也？"即不以自己不如古代圣人为耻辱，怎么能做成圣人那样呢。朱熹则给出了另外一种理解："但无耻一事不如人，则事事不如人矣。"他同时给出了第三种理解："或曰：'不耻其不如人，则何能有如人之事。'其义亦通。"刘殿爵的译文同第三种理解，译为"If a man is not ashamed of being inferior to other men, how will he ever become their equal?"（如果一个人不以比不上别人为羞耻，又怎么能赶上别人）他指出此处的"若"为外动词，多用于否定句和反问句，和"丧礼，与其哀不足而礼有余也，不若礼不足而哀有余也"的含义相类，取"及，比得上"之意。理雅各则给出了第四种认识。他取"若"的"同，相当"之意，将之翻译为"When one differs from other men in not having this

sense of shame, what will he have in common with them?"（当一个人因没有羞耻心而和别人不同时，他和别人还有什么共同点吗）他的译文突出强调了羞耻心是人类的共性。相比较而言，刘殿爵的译文更能突出原文宗旨，与孟子的思想体系更为接近。

【原文】13.8 孟子曰[1]："古之贤王好善而忘势；古之贤士何独不然？乐其道而忘人之势[2]，故王公不致敬尽礼[3]，则不得亟见之。见且由不得亟，而况得而臣之乎？"

【译文】孟子说："古代的贤君喜好善而忘记自己的富贵权势，古代的贤士何尝不是这样？他们喜好自己的道而忘记了别人的富贵权势，所以王公贵族不对他恭敬尽礼，就不能够多次见到他。多次见到他都不能，更何况让他成为臣子呢？"

【英译】Mencius said, 'The able and virtuous monarchs of antiquity loved virtue and forgot their power. And shall an exception be made of the able and virtuous scholars of antiquity, that they did not do the same? They delighted in their own principles, and were oblivious of the power of princes. Therefore, if kings and dukes did not show the utmost respect, and observe all forms of ceremony, they were not permitted to come frequently and visit them. If they thus found it not in their power to pay them frequent visits, how much less could they get to employ them as ministers?'

【注释】

[1] 本章介绍了贤君明主和俊杰良才的交往之道。孟子认为，君王应礼贤下士，尊重人才，而士人也应洁身自好，不枉道求利。这一议论是针对当时上骄下谄之风而提，同时也表明了孟子洁身自好，不愿牺牲自己的人格和政治抱负来寻求取富贵的傲气。

[2] "乐其道而忘人之势"是孟子对古代贤士的评价。刘殿爵认为

"道"是"普遍存在的大道","人"是"他人"。理雅各和赖发洛认为"乐其道"是"乐于坚持他们自己的原则"。理雅各认为"人之势"是"古之贤王之势",赖发洛则认为是泛指"大人物"。此处的"人"并非特指,而是囊括了所有有权势的人,这也体现了古代贤人待人接物重德不重权势的原则,因而刘殿爵的译文更确切。

[3]"致敬尽礼",理雅各将之翻译为"if kings and dukes did not show the utmost respect, and observe all forms of ceremony"(显示最崇高的敬意和遵守所有的礼节),赖发洛的译文是"if they did not treat him with the highest respect and the greatest courtesy"(最高的尊敬和最隆重的礼仪)。二人的译文虽能体现原文的字面意思,但容易引起读者,尤其是那些对中国传统文化不甚了解的外国读者的误解。他们会误认为只要有足够的敬意和最隆重的礼节就能经常见到贤者,其实不然。中国自古就是一个礼仪之邦,礼制规定非常复杂,君、臣、父、子、夫、妇各有其应循之礼,所谓守礼,并非礼仪越隆重越好,而是礼节适合各人的身份、地位。因而刘殿爵的"due respect and observing due courtesy"(应有的尊敬和合适的礼遇),更符合中国传统文化和原文之意。

【原文】13.9　孟子谓宋勾践曰[1]:"子好游[2]乎?吾语子游。人知之,亦嚣嚣;人不知,亦嚣嚣[3]。"曰:"何如斯可以嚣嚣矣?"曰:"尊德乐义,则可以嚣嚣矣。故士穷不失义,达不离道[4]。穷不失义,故士得己[5]焉;达不离道,故民不失望焉。古之人,得志,泽加于民;不得志,修身见于世。穷则独善其身,达则兼善天下[6]。"

【译文】孟子对宋人勾践说:"你喜欢游说吗?我告诉你游说的态度。别人理解我,我安然自得;别人不理解我,我也安然自得。"问道:"要怎样才能够安然自得呢?"答道:"崇尚德,喜好义,就可以安然自得了。所以,士人穷困时不失掉义;得意时,不离开道。穷困时不失掉义，所以能保持自己的操守；得意时不离开道，所以百姓不会失望。古代的人，得志时，恩惠普施百姓；不得志时，修身立于世。穷困时便独善其身，显达时便兼善天下。"

【英译】Mencius said to Song Kâu-ch'ien, 'Are you fond, Sir, of travelling to the different courts? I will tell you about such travelling. If a prince acknowledge you and follow your counsels, be perfectly satisfied. If no one do so, be the same.' Kâu-ch'ien said, 'What is to be done to secure this perfect satisfaction?' Mencius replied, 'Honour virtue and delight in righteousness, and so you may always be perfectly satisfied. Therefore, a scholar, though poor, does not let go his righteousness; though prosperous, he does not leave his own path. Poor and not letting righteousness go;—it is thus that the scholar holds possession of himself. Prosperous and not leaving the proper path;—it is thus that the expectations of the people from him are not disappointed. When the men of antiquity realized their wishes, benefits were conferred by them on the people. If they did not realize their wishes, they cultivated their personal character, and became illustrious in the world. If poor, they attended to their own virtue in solitude; if advanced to dignity, they made the whole kingdom virtuous as well.'

【注释】

[1] 孟子在本章既说明了游说君主之道，又为知识分子安身立命指明了方向。他认为士人在劝说君主实行自己的政治主张时，要尊德乐义，保持自得无欲的状态。他同时提出了"穷则独善其身，达则兼善天下"的人生观。这一人生观千百年来一直是知识分子的安身立命之道，影响了一代又一代的读书人。

[2] 朱熹注云："游，游说也。"孟子在此章提到的"游"并非一般

意义上的"游玩、旅行",而是指"通过游说不同的君主来宣传、实践自己的政治主张"。理雅各将之翻译为"travelling to the different courts"(去不同的朝廷游历),基本上能体现"游"的含义。赖发洛将之简单翻译为"travelling"(游玩、行走)不妥。刘殿爵将之翻译为"traveling from state to state,offering advice"(游走于不同的国家,向君主提供建议)。他的译文将"游"的文化内涵清楚、准确地传递给了读者。

[3] "嚣嚣",赵岐注:"自得无欲之貌。""人知之,亦嚣嚣;人不知,亦嚣嚣"是孟子推崇的士人在游说诸侯时应当具备的道德情操。理雅各将之翻译为"If a prince acknowledge you and follow your counsels,be perfectly satisfied. If no one do so,be the same."(如果一个君主认可你,并且遵循你的建议,你应当自得其乐;如果君主不这样做,你也应该如此)他的译文略微修改了原文的行文特点,更符合英语的表达习惯。虽然译文不能和原文保持形似,但能将原文所蕴含之意非常准确地表达出来。他将"人"翻译为"君主",并将"知"和"游"结合起来翻译,使原文的宗旨和逻辑性更加突出。赖发洛的译文是"Be blithe and happy if men know you,and if they do not know you,be blithe and happy too"(如果别人明白你,要高兴快乐;如果别人不了解你,也要高兴快乐)。他的译文再现了原文反复强调"嚣嚣"重要性的特点,但在传递原文所蕴含之意时略显不足。

[4] 本章是针对游说诸侯而发,"穷"和"达"相对举而言,故"穷"并非泛指"穷困",而是特指"不得志,不能实现自己的政治抱负"。"达"则特指"政治理想得到君主的认可,能够在国家推行,可以惠及百姓。"理雅各将"穷"和"达"分别翻译为"poor"(贫穷)和"prosperous"(富裕),赖发洛翻译为"poor"(贫穷)和"succeeds"(成功)。虽然译者都能翻译出原文的字面意思,但不能完全再现"穷"和"达"在本章的独特含义。

[5] "得己",赵岐注曰:"得己之本性也。"朱熹则解为"言不失己也"。理雅各受朱熹《集注》的影响,将"得己"翻译为"holds possession of himself"(把持住自己)。杨伯峻指出了赵岐和朱熹在理解上的不足,并

提出了自己对"得己"的看法："犹言'自得'。赵岐《注》解为'得己之本性'，增字为训，恐误。朱熹《集注》谓'言不失己也'，虽可通，但与'嚣嚣'之义关连不密，恐亦不确。"正如杨伯峻所说，这与孟子对"嚣嚣"的强调联系不密。刘殿爵将"得己"翻译为"finds delight in himself"（自得其乐）。他的译文同杨伯峻的理解一致，能够密切呼应"嚣嚣"，更能突出篇章宗旨。

[6]"穷则独善其身，达则兼善天下"，千百年来一直是中国知识分子安身立命之本。理雅各认为，"善其身"强调"they attended to their own virtue in solitude"（修养自身的道德品德），但赖发洛认为是"bettered his own life only"（让自己的一生更加完备）。显然他认为孟子在宣扬应当使生命更加有价值。刘殿爵则认为孟子主张"makes perfect his own person"（身心俱修），既要重视道德修养，也要加强对身体的爱护。儒家重视道德修养是毋庸置疑的，至于身体，早在孔子时代就曾强调过"身体发肤，受之父母，不敢毁伤，孝之始也。"（《孝经》）可见，儒家注重身心俱养，因而刘殿爵的译文最确切。"达则兼善天下"的"天下"也并非指世界上的所有地区，而是指整个中国的版图。因而理雅各和刘殿爵的"整个国家"比赖发洛的"all below heaven"（天下所有的地方）更准确。

【原文】13.10　孟子曰[1]："待文王而后兴者，凡民也。若夫豪杰之士[2]，虽无文王犹兴。"

【译文】孟子说："等待文王出现后奋起的，是一般百姓。至于出色的人才，即使没有文王，也能奋起。"

【英译】Mencius said, 'The mass of men wait for a king Wăn, and then they will receive a rousing impulse. Scholars distinguished from the mass, without a king Wăn, rouse themselves.'

【注释】

[1] 孟子认为普通人和豪杰之士的区别在于前者过于依赖他人的教化

和督促，不懂得个人努力，而后者具有较强的主动学习的能力，即使身处逆境，也能奋发图强，成就一番伟业，造福四方百姓。

[2]"豪杰之士"，朱熹注曰："有过人之才智者。"理雅各的理解与之相类，将之翻译为"Scholars distinguished from the mass"（不同于普通人的知识分子）。赖发洛翻译为"the best and bravest knights"（最优秀最勇敢的骑士），刘殿爵和赵甄陶则将之译为"outstanding man"（杰出的人）。"士"的本义是古代中国对人，尤其是男子的美称。可见，刘殿爵的译文侧重于取"士"的本义。由于"士"是封建社会中最基层的贵族，同欧洲的骑士、日本的武士具有相似的社会地位，因而赖发洛选择用西方人熟悉的"骑士"翻译"士"。这样翻译虽便于外国读者理解，但模糊了二者的区别。中国的"士"这一称谓后演变为对知识分子的泛称，因而理雅各将之翻译为"知识分子"。三个译文分别从不同的角度突出了"士"的某些特征。

【原文】13.11　孟子曰[1]："附之以韩魏之家，如其自视欿然，则过人远矣[2]。"

【译文】孟子说："把韩、魏两家的财富都来送给他，如果他并不自满，那就远远超过一般人了。"

【英译】Mencius said，'Add to a man the families of Han and Wei. If he then look upon himself without being elated，he is far beyond the mass of men.'

【注释】

[1] 虽然安贫乐道、重义轻利是儒家的人生追求，但儒家并不反对物质上的富足，认为那些富而不骄，谦虚谨慎的人在品德修养上已经大大超过了一般人。

[2]"自视欿然"，赵岐认为，本章"言人既自有家，复益韩、魏百乘之家，其富贵已美矣。而其人欿然不以足，自知仁义之道不足也，此则过人甚远矣。"刘殿爵的理解与之相似，将"自视欿然"翻译为"To look upon

oneself as deficient"（知道自己的缺点和不足）。朱熹引"尹氏曰：'言有过人之识，则不以富贵为事'。"理雅各的理解与之相类，翻译为"If he then look upon himself without being elated"（他自己并不自满）。这两种理解都是可以的。

【原文】13.12　孟子曰[1]："以佚道使民，虽劳不怨。以生道杀民，虽死不怨杀者[2]。"

【译文】孟子说："用使百姓获得安逸的方式去役使百姓，他们虽然劳苦但不怨恨。用使百姓获得生存的方式杀死百姓，百姓虽然被杀死，也不会怨恨那些导致他们被杀的人。"

【英译】Mencius said, 'Let the people be employed in the way which is intended to secure their ease, and though they be toiled, they will not murmur. Let them be put to death in the way which is intended to preserve their lives, and though they die, they will not murmur at him who puts them to death.'

【注释】

[1] 圣明的君主在治理国家时，虽然也役使百姓，杀戮恶人，但却能使百姓劳而不怨，死而无憾，因为贤君一心为民，故能赢得百姓的支持和谅解。

[2] 程子曰："以佚道使民，谓本欲佚之也，播谷、乘屋之类是也。以生道杀民，谓本欲生之也，除害去恶之类是也。"理雅各在翻译本章时注重强调政策执行者的动机，认为动机而非结果是判定统治者功过是非的标准。他认为统治者如果怀着善良的愿望，欲施恩于民，结果虽适得其反，但不会遭到百姓的怨恨。赖发洛的译文是"Lead the people on the way to ease, and they will not even grumble at hard work. Kill them on the way to life, and even as they die, they will not grumble against the slayer."（要带领百姓走上安逸之路，即使非常辛苦，他们也不会怨恨。在追求生存时杀害了百姓，他们即使死

了，也不会怨恨杀他们的人）他认为只要目标崇高，即使有所牺牲，也会得到百姓的谅解和拥护。刘殿爵将这段话翻译为"If the services of the common people were used with a view to sparing them hardship，they would not complain even when hard driven. If the common people were put to death in pursuance of a policy to keep them alive，they would die bearing no ill-will towards the man who put them to death"（如果役使百姓是为了让他们免于劳苦，即使非常劳累，他们也不会抱怨。如果因为要执行让百姓生存的政策而杀死百姓，他们即使死了也不会怨恨杀他们的人）。他也认为，如果统治者真心为百姓谋福利，即使结果不尽如人意，也不会遭到百姓的怨恨。

【原文】13.13　孟子曰[1]："霸者之民欢虞如也，王者之民皞皞如也[2]。杀之而不怨，利之而不庸，民日迁善而不知为之者。夫君子[3]所过者化，所存者神，上下与天地同流，岂曰小补之哉?"

【译文】孟子说："霸主的百姓欢喜快乐，统一天下的王者的百姓怡然自得。百姓被杀了，也不怨恨；得到好处，也不认为应该感谢；每日里向善发展，却不知道谁使他如此。君子经过之处，人们受到感化，停留之处，所起的作用，更是神秘莫测，上与天、下与地同时流动，难道说只是小小的补益吗?"

【英译】Mencius said，'Under a chief，leading all the princes，the people look brisk and cheerful. Under a true sovereign，they have an air of deep contentment. Though he slay them，they do not murmur. When he benefits them，they do not think of his merit. From day to day they make progress towards what is good，without knowing who makes them do so. Wherever the superior man passes through，transformation follows；wherever he abides，his influence is of a spiritual nature. It flows abroad，above and beneath，like that of Heaven and Earth. How can it be said that he mends society but in a small way！'

【注释】

[1] 孟子宣扬仁政王道，因而更重视道德的教化作用。他认为能够实行王道者都是君之圣人，他们可以通过自己的行动和高尚的道德情操潜移默化地影响民众，使他们日迁善而不自知。百姓的气质和道德修养提高后，国家才能长治久安。因而王道政治才是统治者应该遵循的永久治国方略。

[2] 为了突出王道的重要性，孟子首先指明了在王道和霸道统治下百姓的不同状态。霸道统治下的百姓是"欢虞如也"，即欢喜快乐，而王道统治下的百姓是"皞皞如也"，即怡然自得。"欢虞"和"皞皞"貌似相近，其实质相差甚远。霸道虽能给百姓带来暂时的快乐，但不能改变他们的气质。他们的心情会随着外界境遇的变化而或喜或悲，起伏不定。而王道统治下的百姓身受圣人潜移默化的影响，品质有了极大提高，能不以物喜不以己悲，始终处于一种怡然自得的状态。理雅各和刘殿爵将"欢虞"理解为"高兴，快乐"，认为"欢虞"同"欢娱"。而赖发洛则将之翻译为"restless and anxious"（烦乱、焦虑）。显然，他将"欢虞"分开理解，认为"欢"就是好动，"虞"就是"焦虑"。根据上下文和训诂资料，理雅各和刘殿爵的译文更确切，而赖发洛的翻译过于机械。"皞皞"，朱熹注曰："广大自得之貌。"理雅各和刘殿爵的译文同朱注，而赖发洛则将之翻译为"shine with light"（像被光照着一样明亮）。赖译本过于拘泥于按原文字面意思对译原文，不利于文意的传达。

[3] 朱熹《集注》曰："君子，圣人之通称也。"杨伯峻进一步指出，"这一'君子'的意义和一般有德者谓之君子以及有位者谓之君子的意义不同，故朱熹《集注》云'君子，圣人之通称也。'不但指'王者'，可能也指非王者之'圣人'，如孔子等，所以此处不用'王者'字样而改用'君子'两字。"理雅各和刘殿爵在翻译此处的"君子"时，都采取一贯译法，将之翻译为"the superior man"和"a gentleman"，未能体现"君子"内涵的丰富性。

【原文】13.14　孟子曰[1]："仁言不如仁声之入人深也，善政不如善教之得民也[2]。善政，民畏之；善教，民爱之。善政得民财，善教得民心。"

【译文】孟子说："仁德的语言比不上仁德的音乐那样深入人心，好的政令不如好的教育赢得民众。好的政令，百姓怕它；好的教育，百姓爱它。好的政令得到百姓的财富，好的教育得到百姓的心。"

【英译】Mencius said, 'Kindly words do not enter so deeply into men as a reputation for kindness. Good government does not lay hold of the people so much as good instructions. Good government is feared by the people, while good instructions are loved by them. Good government gets the people's wealth, while good instructions get their hearts.'

【注释】

[1]"善政"和"善教"实质上代表了法治和德治两种不同的治国方略。孟子通过对比、类比指出德治的优越性在于它能够赢得民心，而法治虽可使百姓心存畏惧，顺从一时，但最终会引来他们的反抗。

[2] 在本章"仁言"和"仁声"相对举而言，结合下文可知，"仁言"指"善政"，"仁声"指"善教"。赵岐注曰："仁言，政教法度之言也。仁声，乐声雅颂也。仁言之政虽明，不如雅颂感人心之深也。"朱熹引程子曰："仁言，谓以仁厚之言加于民。仁声，谓仁闻，谓有仁之实而为众所称道者也。"理雅各的理解类朱熹，亨顿的译文则兼取朱熹对"仁言"的注解，以及赵岐对"仁声"的理解，将之翻译为"It's Humane music that goes deep inside people, not Humane words."刘殿爵的译文亦兼取朱熹和赵岐的注解，认为仁德的语言不如仁德的音乐那样深入人心。这几种理解皆可。

【原文】13.15　孟子曰[1]："人之所不学而能者，其良能也；所不虑而知者，其良知也[2]。孩提之童无不知爱其亲者，及其长也，无不知敬其兄也。亲亲，仁也；敬长，义也；无他，达之天下也[3]。"

【译文】孟子说："人不用学习就能做到的，是良能；不用思考就知道的，是良知。两三岁的小孩儿没有不知道爱父母的，等到他长大后，没有不知道尊敬兄长的。亲爱父母是仁，尊敬兄长是义；没有别的，只是把这两种品德推行于天下。"

【英译】Mencius said, 'The ability possessed by men without having been acquired by learning is intuitive ability，and the knowledge possessed by them without the exercise of thought is their intuitive knowledge. Children carried in the arms all know to love their parents，and when they are grown a little，they all know to love their elder brothers. Filial affection for parents is the working of benevolence. Respect for elders is the working of righteousness. There is no other reason for those feelings；—they belong to all under heaven.'

【注释】

[1] "良知""良能"是孟子性善论的重要概念，可以为他的性善论和道德修养说提供支撑。

[2] "良"，赵岐注曰："不学而能，性所自能。良，甚也。"赖发洛和刘殿爵的译文与之相类，认为"良能良知"就是"所最能，所最知"。朱熹则认为"良者，本然之善也。程子曰：'良知良能，皆无所由，乃出于天，不系于人。'"理雅各的理解与之相类，分别将之翻译为"intuitive ability"（与生俱来的能力）和"intuitive knowledge1"（与生俱来的知识）。正如李鉴所说："良知之知是一种直觉之知，是不待思辨而直接明觉得，所以见父兄知孝悌，即是良知。良知一旦呈现，便一定会引发道德的行为，因良知本身便有沛然莫之能御的要求实践道德的力量，这力量便是良能。"孟子主张人性善，认为亲亲（仁）、敬长（义）是生而具有的良知、良能。因而"良"取"与生俱来"之意更佳。

[3]"无他，达之天下也"，赵岐注曰："人，仁义之心少而皆有之。欲为善者无他，达，通也。但通此亲亲敬长之心，推之天下人而已。"刘殿爵的译文就持这种观点，将之译为"What is left to be done is simply the extension of these to the whole Empire"（仅仅需要把它们推广到天下就够了）。他的译文可以很好地呼应儒家的推恩思想。理雅各将之理解为"这些情感的出现没有其他理由，天下所有的人都有"。他的译文可以更好地呼应人生而具备四端之心。这两种理解皆可。

【原文】13.16　孟子曰[1]："舜之居深山之中，与木石居，与鹿豕游，其所以异于深山之野人者几希；及其闻一善言，见一善行，若决江河，沛然莫之能御也[2]。"

【译文】孟子说："舜住在深山之中时，和树、石头相处，与麋鹿和野猪往来，他和深山之中居住的野人不同的地方极少；等到他听到一句善言，看到一种善行，他的善性就好像江河决了口，浩浩荡荡没有什么力量可以阻挡。"

【英译】Mencius said，'When Shun was living amid the deep retired mountains，dwelling with the trees and rocks，and wandering among the deer and swine，the difference between him and the rude inhabitants of those remote hills appeared very small. But when he heard a single good word，or saw a single good action，he was like a stream or a river bursting its banks，and flowing out in an irresistible flood.'

【注释】

[1] 舜居住在深山之时，和普通人不同的地方很少。但他虚心好学，看到外在的善行，听到外在的善言，就会激发内在的善性，最终成为道德高尚的人。可见，人生而具备的善性的实现离不开后天的培养。

[2]"若决江河，沛然莫之能御也"形象生动地表明舜的善性被激发后

的充沛气势。"江河"，理雅各和赖发洛都认为这是泛指任何一条河流，将之翻译为 "a stream or a river"，而刘殿爵则认为是特指"长江、黄河"。长江是中国第一大河，在古时简称江；黄河仅次于长江，是中国第二大河，简称河。"长江和黄河"总会让人联想到水量充沛、澎湃汹涌、势不可挡等词语，用它们比喻舜激发出来的善性，比普通河流更具说服力。

【原文】13.17　孟子曰："无为其所不为，无欲其所不欲，如此而已矣[1]。"

【译文】孟子说："不干我不该干的事，不要我不该要的物，这样就行了。"

【英译】Mencius said，'Let a man not do what his own sense of righteousness tells him not to do，and let him not desire what his sense of righteousness tells him not to desire；—to act thus is all he has to do.'

【注释】

[1] 在《孟子》一书中有许多在理解上存在争议的地方，本章就是其中之一。虽然仅仅十几个字，但是翻译家或者是注释者们对其含义尚未达成一致。对于本句话的含义，当前比较流行的认识有两种。一种认为，孟子在这里发挥了孔子"己所不欲、勿施于人"的思想，强调人要推己及人。如赵岐注："无使人为己所不欲为者，无使人欲己之所不欲者。"另一种观点认为，孟子强调一个人要始终依据内心本有的善性来引导自己的行为，不想、不做违背善心的事情。第一种观点从学术渊源上谈起，看到了孟子对孔子思想的继承与发挥。第二种观点从孟子自身的哲学体系出发，认为所不为、所不欲皆出于心，而心之所以不愿，是因为先天具备的四心不允许。从儒家传统和孟子的哲学体系看，这两种认识都是可以的。理雅各的译文同第二种观点。刘殿爵和赖发洛还给出了另外一种解释。刘殿爵认为这句话的含义是 "Do not do what others do not choose to do；do not desire what others do not

desire"（不要做别人不愿意做的事，不追求别人不想要的东西）。赖发洛将之翻译为"Do nothing they do not do, wish nothing they do not wish"（不做他们不做的事情，不希望获得他们不希望的东西）。他认为孟子的这一思想，和现代西方保守主义之父柏克"让我们一致，让我们自己与别人一体化"的思想具有一致性。

【原文】13.18 孟子曰[1]："人之有德慧术知者，恒存乎疢疾。独孤臣孽子[2]，其操心也危[3]，其虑患也深，故达。"

【译文】孟子说："人之所以有道德、智慧、本领、才智，往往是由于他们生活在忧患之中。那些被疏远的大臣和贱妾所生的儿子，他们的内心总是忧虑不安，考虑的祸害也非常深远，所以才能通达事理。"

【英译】Mencius said, 'Men who are possessed of intelligent virtue and prudence in affairs will generally be found to have been in sickness and troubles. They are the friendless minister and concubine's son, who keep their hearts under a sense of peril, and use deep precautions against calamity. On this account they become distinguished for their intelligence.'

【注释】

[1] 孟子主张"生于忧患，死于安乐"，认为艰苦的环境更能磨炼人的意志，那些道德高尚、能力超群的人通常都是在逆境中奋起的人，因而他发出"人之有德慧术知者，恒存乎疢疾"的感叹。

[2] "孤臣孽子"，朱熹注曰："孤臣，远臣。孽子，庶子。皆不得于君亲，而常有疢疾者。"刘殿爵的译文与之相类，将之翻译为"The estranged subject or the son of a concubine"（被疏远的大臣或小妾生的儿子）。理雅各译为"the friendless minister and concubine's son"（无依无靠的大臣和小妾生的儿子）亦通。赖发洛的"A fatherless liege or a bastard son"（没有父亲的大臣或私生子）不妥。

[3] "其操心也危"，焦循正义引《战国策》高诱注："危，不安也。"理雅各将之翻译为 "keep their hearts under a sense of peril"（他们的心始终处于危险焦虑的状态）。刘殿爵将之意译为 "he conducts himself with the greatest of caution"（他时常提高警惕）。二人都取"危"的"畏惧、忧虑"之意。正因为有忧患，有畏惧，人们才能在逆境中奋发崛起。赖发洛将之译为 "has a dauntless hold on his heart"（无所畏惧地把持着自己的心），这一翻译和宗旨关联不甚紧密。

【原文】13.19　孟子曰[1]："有事君人者，事是君则为容悦者也；有安社稷臣者，以安社稷为悦者也；有天民[2]者，达可行于天下而后行之者也；有大人者[3]，正己而物正者也。"

【译文】孟子说："有侍奉君主的人，那是侍奉某一位君主，就为了讨他喜欢的人；有安定国家的大臣，那是以安定国家为快乐的人；有天民，那是他的道能行于天下时，然后去推行的人；有在朝廷为官的道德高尚的圣人，那是端正了自己也能使外物端正的人。"

【英译】Mencius said, 'There are persons who serve the prince;—they serve the prince, that is, for the sake of his countenance and favour. There are ministers who seek the tranquillity of the State, and find their pleasure in securing that tranquillity. There are those who are the people of Heaven. They, judging that, if they were in office, they could carry out their principles, throughout the kingdom, proceed so to carry them out. There are those who are great men. They rectify themselves and others are rectified.'

【注释】

[1] 孟子根据人品的不同，将人臣分为四种：第一种人，以侍奉君主、讨君主欢心为己任，一味地阿谀奉承，这是人臣中的最下一品。第二种人，以安定国家，富国强民为己任，终身致力于扶持君主，建功立业，他们是忠

臣良将，国之栋梁。但他们的眼界和恩惠仅仅局限在一国之内。第三种人品行高洁，志向远大，以安天下人为己任。他们不屑污君，只在圣明君主出现并能践行他的理想的时候才出来做官。这类人目光远大，不为功名累其心，因而又高于社稷之臣。第四种人是德行盛大的圣人，他们对百姓的影响虽潜移默化，但能从根本上正民风，规民行，从而实现天下大治。

[2]"天民"，朱熹注曰："民者，无位之称。以其全尽天理，乃天之民，故谓之天民。"可见，所谓"天民"是指明乎天理，合乎天性之人。"天民"虽以"济天下"为己任，但他在确定"道"能行于天下后，才出来实践它。所以"天民"指的是那些达则兼济天下，穷则独善其身的人。理雅各和赖发洛将之翻译为"the people of Heaven"（天之民），刘殿爵将之翻译为"subjects of Heaven"，基本能体现其字面含义。

[3]"大人"是四类人中最高的一品，朱熹注曰："大人，德盛而上下化之，所谓'见龙在田，天下文明'者。"他认为"大人"是德高志远的圣人，通过自己的高尚品格潜移默化地影响百姓。杨伯峻则认为："孟子数言'大人'，涵义不一。《史记索隐》引向秀《易乾卦注》云：'圣人在位，谓之大人。'或者是此'大人'之义。"他将"大人"理解为在朝廷为官的圣人。孟子根据道德、志趣和节操的差异将人归为四类。很明显，前两类人是在朝廷为官者。而"天民"虽是"民"，但以"济天下"为己任，在政治理想可以实行时也会出来做官，因而也可以把他归为官员的一种，故此处的"大人"也应理解为在朝廷为官的圣人。理雅各、赖发洛和刘殿爵都将"大人"翻译为"great men"。"Great"不仅可以指品质优秀，还指地位崇高、有权力，基本上能涵盖其含义。

【原文】13.20　孟子曰[1]："君子有三乐，而王天下不与存焉[2]。父母俱存，兄弟无故[3]，一乐也；仰不愧于天，俯不怍于人，二乐也；得天下英才而教育之，三乐也。君子有三乐，而王天下不与存焉。"

【译文】孟子说："君子有三种快乐，但是统治天下并不在其中。父母都健康，兄弟没灾患，是第一种快乐；抬头无愧于天，低头无愧于人，是第二种快乐；得到天下优秀人才而对他们进行教育，是第三种快乐。君子有三种快乐，但是统治天下并不在其中。"

【英译】Mencius said, 'The superior man has three things in which he delights, and to be ruler over the kingdom is not one of them. That his father and mother are both alive, and that the condition of his brothers affords no cause for anxiety；—this is one delight. That, when looking up, he has no occasion for shame before Heaven, and, below, he has no occasion to blush before men；—this is a second delight. That he can get from the whole kingdom the most talented individuals, and teach and nourish them；—this is the third delight. The superior man has three things in which he delights, and to be ruler over the kingdom is not one of them.'

【注释】

[1] 虽然孟子一生都在为他的"王道"政治奔波，但未把它包含在"君子三乐"中。他的三乐，虽看似平淡，但蕴含着丰富的人生哲理。他将第一乐定为"家庭"之乐，认为能有兄弟相依，并能够为父母尽孝是人生的一大乐事，是朱熹所谓的"人所深愿而不可必得者"。"子欲养而亲不待"的悲剧曾让多少人抱憾终生。"仰不愧于天，俯不怍于人"说的是"为人"之乐。人具有是非观，只有当自己的行为符合理义时，才能做到内心的平静，享受做"人"的快乐。"得天下英才而教育之"是"为人师"之乐，也是圣人、君子对社会应尽的责任。

[2]"王天下"，即结束当时诸侯分裂格局、战乱不断的局面，实现国家的统一，因而刘殿爵将之翻译为"being ruler over the Empire"（成为这个国家的统治者）。赖发洛将之翻译为"be king of all below heaven"（成为全天下的君主），赵甄陶翻译为"being the unifier of the world"（统一世界），则

扩大了其内涵。

[3]"故",郑玄注《礼记·曲礼》"君无故,玉不去身"云:"故,灾患丧病也。"理雅各的译文与之相类,将之翻译为"no cause for anxiety",即"没有焦虑的理由"。赖发洛则将之翻译为"have no trouble with his brethren",即"和兄弟之间没有什么纠纷,和睦相处"。刘殿爵的译文则侧重取"well"(身体健康)之意。

【原文】13.21 孟子曰[1]:"广土众民,君子欲之,所乐不存焉;中天下而立,定四海之民,君子乐之,所性不存焉。君子所性,虽大行不加焉,虽穷居不损焉,分定故也[2]。君子所性,仁义礼智根于心,其生色也睟然,见于面,盎于背,施于四体,四体不言而喻[3]。"

【译文】孟子说:"拥有广阔的土地、众多的百姓,是君子想要的,但是乐趣不在这儿;居于天下的中央,安定四方的百姓,君子以此为乐,但是本性不在这儿。君子的本性,纵使他的理想通行于天下也不会增加,纵使穷困隐居也不会减少,因为本分已经固定了的缘故。君子的本性,仁义礼智之根植于心,表现出来的神色是温润和顺的,表现在颜面上,充溢于肩背上,延伸到手足四肢,体现在手足四肢的动作上,不必言语,别人就一目了然。"

【英译】Mencius said, 'Wide territory and a numerous people are desired by the superior man, but what he delights in is not here. To stand in the centre of the kingdom, and tranquillize the people within the four seas;—the superior man delights in this, but the highest enjoyment of his nature is not here. What belongs by his nature to the superior man cannot be increased by the largeness of his sphere of action, nor diminished by his dwelling in poverty and retirement;—for this reason that it is determinately apportioned to him by Heaven. What belongs by his nature to the superior man are benevolence, righteousness, propriety, and knowledge. These are rooted in his heart; their growth and manifestation are a mild harmony appearing in the countenance, a rich fullness in the back, and the character imparted to the four limbs. Those limbs understand to arrange themselves, without being told.'

【注释】

[1] 孟子在本章强调了君子保持本性的重要性。君子虽然有所欲、所乐，但所性才是最珍贵的。君子的所性是仁义礼智，它们可以通过君子的音容笑貌、举手投足体现出来。

[2] "分定故也"，朱熹注曰："分者，所得于天之全体，故不以穷达而有异。"也就是说，他认为"分"字为"本分"之义，相信"仁义礼智"是本分中固定的东西，不会随着外界环境的变化而有所增损。刘殿爵的理解与之相类，认为"本分是固定的"。理雅各则将之翻译为"it is determinately apportioned to him by Heaven"。大写的"Heaven"在英语世界里通常指"上帝"，因而这句话可以回译为"这是因为上帝分配给他的（本性）是固定的"。从孟子的整个思想体系看，他宣扬人性本善，相信人生来就具备四心，它们是仁、义、礼、智的四端。因而仁、义、礼、智是人的本分中固定的东西，不会因为君子穷达而有所改变。而理雅各却将耶稣基督的绝对权威强加给中国文化，认为君子的本性配额是由上帝决定和分配的。赖发洛的译文是"it is his fixed share"（因为份额是固定的）。"分定故也"是针对"君子所性"而言，如果理解为君子本性的份额是固定的，显然和孟子对性善的认识不符。

[3] "四体不言而喻"，朱熹注曰："言四体不待吾言，而自能晓吾意也。"理雅各将其翻译为"Those limbs understand to arrange themselves, without being told"（四肢不用被告知就知道怎样摆放）。由于仁义礼智根植于君子之心，会自然而然地表现在形体动作上，因而不需要告诉四肢应当如

何摆放。在古代汉语中有一种"受事名词＋动词"的句式，即用主动的形式来表示被动的意义。他认为，孟子在此处就使用了这一句式。刘殿爵则认为，虽然仁义礼智根植于君子心中，但能够"体现在君子的四肢动作上，因而不需要言语，别人就一目了然"。理雅各和刘殿爵强调的侧重点不同，但都是在孟子的思想体系下理解本句之意。

【原文】13.22　孟子曰[1]："伯夷辟纣，居北海之滨，闻文王作，兴曰：'盍归乎来，吾闻西伯善养老者。'太公辟纣，居东海之滨，闻文王作，兴曰：'盍归乎来，吾闻西伯善养老者。'天下有善养老，则仁人以为己归矣。五亩之宅，树墙下以桑，匹妇蚕之，则老者足以衣帛矣。五母鸡，二母彘，无失其时，老者足以无失肉矣。百亩之田，匹夫耕之，八口之家足以无饥矣。所谓西伯善养老者，制其田里，教之树畜，导其妻子使养其老。五十非帛不暖，七十非肉不饱。不暖不饱，谓之冻馁。文王之民无冻馁之老者，此之谓也。"

【译文】孟子说："伯夷避开商纣王，居住在北海边，听说文王兴起，起身说：'何不去归附呢，我听说西伯善于养老人。'太公为躲避纣王，居住在东海边，听说文王兴起，便站起来说：'何不去归附呢，我听说西伯善于养老人。'天下有善于养老人的人，仁人便把他当作自己的依靠了。五亩地的宅院，在墙下栽培桑树，妇女养蚕缫丝，老年人足以有丝织品穿了。五只母鸡，两头母猪，不要让它们丧失繁殖的时机，老年人足以有肉吃了。百亩的土地，男子去耕种，八口人的家庭足以吃饱了。所谓西伯善于养老，就在于他制定土地制度，教育人民栽种畜牧，引导百姓奉养他们的老人。五十岁，没有丝棉便穿不暖；七十岁，没有肉便吃不饱。穿不暖，吃不饱，叫作挨冻受饿。文王的百姓没有挨冻受饿的老人，就是这个意思。"

【英译】Mencius said, 'Po-î, that he might avoid Châu, was

dwelling on the coast of the northern sea when he heard of the rise of king Wǎn. He roused himself and said, "Why should I not go and follow him? I have heard that the chief of the West knows well how to nourish the old." Tʿâi-kung, to avoid Châu, was dwelling on the coast of the eastern sea. When he heard of the rise of king Wǎn, he said, "Why should I not go and follow him? I have heard that the chief if the West knows well how to nourish the old." If there were a prince in the kingdom, who knew well how to nourish the old, all men of virtue would feel that he was the proper object for them to gather to. Around the homestead with its five mâu, the space beneath the walls was planted with mulberry trees, with which the women nourished silkworms, and thus the old were able to have silk to wear. Each family had five brood hens and two brood sows, which were kept to their breeding seasons, and thus the old were able to have flesh to eat. The husbandmen cultivated their farms of 100 mâu, and thus their families of eight mouths were secured against want. The expression, "The chief of the West knows well how to nourish the old," refers to his regulation of the fields and dwellings, his teaching them to plant the mulberry and nourish those animals, and his instructing the wives and children, so as to make them nourish their aged. At fifty, warmth cannot be maintained without silks, and at seventy flesh is necessary to satisfy the appetite. Persons not kept warm nor supplied with food are said to be starved and famished, but among the people of king Wǎn, there were no aged who were starved or famished. This is the meaning of the expression in question.'

【注释】

[1] 孟子在本章重申了"养老"的重要性，认为这是文王能够招徕天

下贤人为己所用的关键。孟子借文王之政详细描绘了自己的政治、经济主张。由于本章出现的绝大部分文字在前文已经出现，故此处不再赘言，详见《离娄上》第十三章，《梁惠王上》第三章、第七章。

【原文】13.23　孟子曰[1]："易其田畴[2]，薄其税敛，民可使富也。食之以时，用之以礼，财不可胜用也。民非水火不生活，昏暮叩人之门户求水火，无弗与者，至足矣。圣人治天下，使有菽粟如水火。菽粟如水火，而民焉有不仁者乎？"

【译文】孟子说："耕种好田地，减轻税收，可以使百姓富足。按时饮食，依礼消费，财物便用不完。百姓没有水和火便不能生存，黄昏夜晚敲人的门窗求水火，没有人会不给的，因为水火极多的缘故。圣人治理天下，要使百姓的粮食像水火那样多。粮食像水火那样多了，百姓哪有不仁爱的呢？"

【英译】Mencius said, 'Let it be seen to that their fields of grain and hemp are well cultivated, and make the taxes on them light；— so the people may be made rich. Let it be seen to that the people use their resources of food seasonably, and expend their wealth only on the prescribed ceremonies：—so their wealth will be more than can be consumed. The people cannot live without water and fire, yet if you knock at a man's door in the dusk of the evening, and ask for water and fire, there is no man who will not give them, such is the abundance of these things. A sage governs the kingdom so as to cause pulse and grain to be as abundant as water and fire. When pulse and grain are as abundant as water and fire, how shall the people be other than virtuous？'

【注释】

[1] 先富后教是孟子仁政思想的重要组成部分。他认为要培养百姓的

道德，需要有足够的物质财富作保障。"让生于有余，争起于不足"（《论衡·治期篇》），只有老百姓生活富裕，财务充足，才会相互谦让，乐于助人。正像水火充足，所以向别人索要时都会得到慷慨馈赠一样，如果百姓拥有的粮食像水火一样充足，就不会对别人不仁爱了。

　　[2] 朱熹注曰："易，治也。畴，耕治之田也。"可见，朱熹认为，"易其田畴"的含义是耕种好田地。理雅各将之翻译为"'Let it be seen to that their fields of grain and hemp are well cultivated"（搞好谷田和麻田的耕种）。虽然"畴"的本义是已耕作的田地，但也可特指种麻的田，因而理雅各的理解也是准确的。赖发洛将之翻译为"If the crops in the fields are changed"（改变土地上种植的谷物），认为这是富民的重要方法之一。土地上种植的农作物一般是由当地的气候、土质和水源决定的，并不能随意改变，更不可能被认为是富民的通行方法，因而他的理解是错误的。刘殿爵将"易其田畴"翻译为"Put in order the fields of the people"（治理好百姓的耕地），他的理解是针对君主治国而言，可以很好地呼应下文的"薄其税敛"，因而也是准确的。

【原文】13.24　孟子曰[1]："孔子登东山而小鲁，登泰山而小天下[2]，故观于海者难为水，游于圣人之门者难为言。观水有术，必观其澜。日月有明，容光必照焉[3]。流水之为物也，不盈科不行；君子之志于道也，不成章不达[4]。"

【译文】孟子说："孔子登上了东山，便觉得鲁国小了；登上了泰山，便觉得天下都变小了，所以，看过大海的人，就很难被别的水所吸引；在圣人门下学习过的人，就很难被别的议论所吸引。观赏水有方法，一定要看它的波澜。太阳月亮都有光辉，凡是能容纳光线的地方就一定能照到。流水这个东西不把坑洼流满，就不再向前流；君子有志于道，不到一定的程度，也就不能通达。"

【英译】Mencius said, 'Confucius ascended the eastern hill, and Lû appeared to him small. He ascended the T'âi mountain, and all beneath the heavens appeared to him small. So he who has contemplated the sea，finds it difficult to think anything of other waters，and he who has wandered in the gate of the sage，finds it difficult to think anything of the words of others. There is an art in the contemplation of water.—It is necessary to look at it as foaming in waves. The sun and moon being possessed of brilliancy，their light admitted even through an orifice illuminates. Flowing water is a thing which does not proceed till it has filled the hollows in its course. The student who has set his mind on the doctrines of the sage，does not advance to them but by completing one lesson after another.'

【注释】

[1] 孟子认为人要树立远大的志向，在制定目标时，要把视点放得高一些，把视野放得宽一些，把要求提得高一些，但在追求和实践理想时则要脚踏实地、循序渐进。

[2] "小鲁"和"小天下"，是孔子处在不同的位置，在不同的视点上对"鲁"和"天下"的感觉，并非"鲁国"和"天下"真的变小了。可见，这个"小"是孔子的一种心理活动，一种判断性的认识。刘殿爵将之分别翻译为 "felt that Lu was small"（觉得鲁国变小了）和 "felt that the Empire was small"（觉得天下变小了）。赖发洛的 "Lu grew small"（鲁国变小了）和 "all below heaven grew small"（天下变小了）则略显机械。

[3] "容光必照焉"，赵岐注曰："容光，小郤也。"焦循进一步指出："苟有丝发之隙可以容纳，则光必入而照焉，容光非小隙之名，至于小隙，极言其容之微者，以见其照之大也，故以小郤明容光。"理雅各将之翻译为 "their light admitted even through an orifice illuminates"（即使非常小的缝隙，只要能进入，他们也能照亮）。译文虽略显冗长，但能体现原文意思。赖发洛将之译为 "wheresoever their rays enter there is light"（他们的光线不论什么地方都能照亮），刘殿爵的译文是 "the light shows up the least crack that will

admit it"（他们的光亮能把任何一点缝隙照亮）。二人用简明的语言准确传递了原文的意思。

[4] 朱熹注曰："成章，所积者厚，而文章外见也。"杨伯峻指出："《说文》：'乐竟为一章。'按由此引申，事物达到一定阶段，具一定规模，即可曰成章，《国语·周语》'得以讲事成章'，《吕氏春秋·大乐篇》'阴阳变化，一上一下，合而成章'，都是此义。"本章的宗旨是教育人们既要目光长远、目标远大，又要循序渐进，脚踏实地。理雅各将"不成章不达"翻译为"does not advance to them but by completing one lesson after another." 即"如果不一节一节地完成，就不能实现（圣人之道）"。赖发洛的译文是"he will not pass on before each stage is mastered."（不熟练掌握每一章，就不能前进下去）二人的译文体现了逐渐积累的重要性。

【原文】13.25　孟子曰[1]："鸡鸣而起，孳孳为善者，舜之徒也；鸡鸣而起，孳孳为利者[2]，跖之徒也。欲知舜与跖[3]之分，无他，利与善之间也。"

【译文】孟子说："鸡叫便起来，孜孜行善的人，是舜一类的人；鸡叫便起来，孜孜谋利的人，是跖一类的人。想要知道舜和跖的不同，没有别的，只是利和善的不同罢了。"

【英译】Mencius said, 'He who rises at cock-crowing and addresses himself earnestly to the practice of virtue, is a disciple of Shun. He who rises at cock-crowing, and addresses himself earnestly to the pursuit of gain, is a disciple of Chih. If you want to know what separates Shun from Chih, it is simply this, —the interval between the thought of gain and the thought of virtue.'

【注释】

[1] 孟子通过举舜与跖的例子进一步重申了他重义轻利的义利观。他认为判断一个人是圣人还是盗贼的主要依据是看他孜孜不倦、一心追求的东

西是什么。他把努力不懈追求公义和良善的人称为圣人，把一心追求个人私利、危害他人的人等同于盗贼。

[2]"孳孳"，朱熹注曰："勤勉之意。"理雅各将"孳孳"翻译为"addresses himself earnestly to"（热心投入），表明"为善"和"为利"完全出于个人的兴趣爱好和价值追求，是自己选择的结果。赖发洛将"孳孳"翻译为"toil and toil"（非常辛劳），认为不论"为善"还是"为利"都非常辛苦，这显然偏离了原文的宗旨。刘殿爵的译文是"never tires"（从来不感觉到疲倦），就是因为发自内心的喜欢，所以能一直追求，从不厌倦。"孳孳为善"和"孳孳为利"实际上体现了圣人和盗贼的不同价值取向和判断标准。理雅各和刘殿爵的译文能将这一取向和标准完整地传达给读者。

[3]在中国古代文化中"舜"是圣人的代表，"跖"则代指暴徒、盗贼。对中国文化和传统略有常识的人都知道"舜"是古代圣王，但人们对"跖"的了解并不多，因而刘殿爵和理雅各在翻译"舜"和"跖"时皆采用音译法，并在译本的注释中做了解释和说明。

【原文】13.26　孟子曰[1]："杨子取为我，拔一毛而利天下，不为也。墨子兼爱，摩顶放踵[2]利天下，为之。子莫执中[3]。执中为近之。执中无权，犹执一也。所恶执一者，为其贼道也，举一而废百也。"

【译文】孟子说："杨子主张为我，拔一根毫毛而有利于天下，他都不愿意做。墨子主张兼爱，摩秃头顶，走破脚跟，只要对天下有利，他都去干。子莫主张中道，主张中道便接近正确了。但是主张中道如果没有权变，就好像执着一点了。之所以厌恶执着一点，因为它损害正道，只是抓住一点而废弃了其余的缘故。"

【英译】Mencius said, 'The principle of the philosopher Yang was— "Each one for himself." Though he might have benefited the whole kingdom by plucking out a single hair, he would not have done it. The philosopher Mo loves all equally. If by rubbing smooth his whole body from the crown to the heel，he could have benefited the kingdom，he would have done it. Tsze-mo holds a medium between these. By holding that medium，he is nearer the right. But by holding it without leaving room for the exigency of circumstances，it becomes like their holding their one point. The reason why I hate that holding to one point is the injury it does to the way of right principle. It takes up one point and disregards a hundred others.'

【注释】

[1] 孟子在此处强调了"权"的重要性。孟子批评固执一端，也反对不知变通，强调在坚持"中"道的基础上灵活变通，根据实际情况处理问题。

[2] "摩顶放踵"，赵岐注："摩秃其顶，下至于踵。"朱熹亦持此意。理雅各的理解与之相类，将之直译为"rubbing smooth his whole body from the crown to the heel"（从头到脚都磨平），赵甄陶则将之意译为"he wore himself out from top to toe"（从头到脚都累得筋疲力尽）。二人的译文皆取"放"的"至"之意。刘殿爵将之译为"shaving his head and showing his heels"（剃了头和露出脚跟）。他的译文和杨伯峻提出的另一种观点类似，即"放者犹谓放纵"。

[3] 对"子莫执中"大体有两种理解。一种观点认为"子莫"是人名，如赵岐注曰："子莫，鲁之贤人也。其性中和专一者也。"刘殿爵、理雅各、赖发洛都取此观点，认为"子莫"是人名。另外一种观点认为，"子"代指"杨子""墨子"，是说他们二人都不能执中。焦循引《音义》云："陆云：言子等无执中。"从文义上看，这两种理解都可说得通。"中"，刘殿爵根据文义，将之翻译为"holds on to the middle, half way between the two extremes"（介于两个极端的中间）。他认为子莫既不极端为我，也不过分兼爱。赖发洛按字面意思将"中"翻译为"the middle ground"（中间立场），认为子莫坚

持处于中间立场。这两种翻译皆可。

【原文】13.27　孟子曰[1]："饥者甘食，渴者甘饮，是未得饮食之正[2]也，饥渴害之也。岂惟口腹有饥渴之害？人心亦皆有害。人能无以饥渴之害为心害，则不及人不为忧矣[2]。"

【译文】孟子说："饥饿的人觉得什么食物都香甜，口渴的人觉得什么饮料都好喝，这是因为没有尝到饮食的正常滋味，是由于受到饥饿干渴的损害的缘故。难道仅仅口腹会受到饥饿干渴的损害吗？人心也会受到这种损害。如果人们能够使心不受到饥饿干渴那样的损害，那就不会为赶不上别人忧虑了。"

【英译】Mencius said, 'The hungry think any food sweet, and the thirsty think the same of any drink, and thus they do not get the right taste of what they eat and drink. The hunger and thirst, in fact, injure their palate. And is it only the mouth and belly which are injured by hunger and thirst? Men's minds are also injured by them. If a man can prevent the evils of hunger and thirst from being any evils to his mind, he need not have any sorrow about not being equal to other men.'

【注释】

[1] 利用浅显易懂的例子作类比，来说明深刻的道理是孟子惯用的说理技巧。孟子先举人们比较熟悉的口腹因饥渴所害而丧失正常的味觉功能的例子，来说明人心也常会为贫贱所害，而丧失了对道德和仁义的追求。

[2] "饮食之正"是省略句，含义需读者自己体会。理雅各和赖发洛在翻译时做了适当补充，认为"饮食之正"是"饮食之正味"的缩写，而刘殿爵则认为是"对饮食的正确评价标准"。结合上下文，这两种理解都可以。

[3] "则不及人不为忧矣"，理雅各将之翻译为"he need not have any sorrow about not being equal to other men"（不需要因为不如别人而感到悲伤）。显然他取"忧"的"忧伤"之意，而刘殿爵、赖发洛和赵甄陶则取"担忧"

之意，认为没有必要担心自己不如别人。不论是忧伤还是担忧，都是动心的表现，正如朱熹所言："人能不以贫贱之故而动其心，则过人远矣。"三位译者都翻译出了原文暗含之意，即那些不允许饥渴等外界因素而干扰内心修养的人，不是不如别人，而是远远超过了一般人。

【原文】13.28　孟子曰[1]："柳下惠不以三公[2]易其介[3]。"

【译文】孟子说："柳下惠不会为做高官而改变他的操守。"

【英译】Mencius said, 'Hûi of Liû-Hsiâ would not for the three highest offices of State have changed his firm purpose of life.'

【注释】

[1] 孟子赞美了柳下惠不因高官厚禄而改变自己特立独行的节操，同时也表明自己不会为了物质利益的满足而放弃政治理想和做人原则。

[2] "三公"是古代三种最高官衔的合称，理雅各将之翻译为"the three highest offices of State"（国家的三个最高官职）。他还在注释中对"三公"做了介绍。他的译文便于那些对中国古代官职不甚了解的读者理解"三公"的基本内涵和原文宗旨。刘殿爵将"三公"翻译为"the three ducal offices"（三个公爵职位）。他用西方人熟悉的"公爵"来反向格义"三公"，虽便于读者理解，但容易让读者将二者等同起来，不利于传播中国传统文化。

[3] "介"，赵岐注："大也。柳下惠执宏大之志，不耻污君，不以三公荣位易其大量也。"朱熹则解为："介，有分辨之意。柳下惠进不隐贤，必以其道，遗佚不怨，阨穷不悯，直道事人，至于三黜，是其介也。"此外，"介"还有独特、耿直、特异之意。陆云："介，谓特立之行。"从文义上看，上述解释都可以说得通，但从孟子的整个思想体系出发，将"介"理解为"操守"更确切。理雅各将"介"翻译为"firm purpose of life"（人生理想），赖发洛翻译为"his course"（自身的原则），刘殿爵的译文是"his integrity"（耿直品格）。这三个译文都含"操守"之意，因而都能体现孟子的原意。

【原文】13.29　孟子曰[1]："有为者辟若掘井，掘井九轫[2]而不及泉，犹为弃井也。"

【译文】孟子说："做一件事情就像掏井，掏到六七丈深还挖不到泉水，仍然是一个废井。"

【英译】Mencius said，'A man with definite aims to be accomplished may be compared to one digging a well. To dig the well to a depth of seventy-two cubits，and stop without reaching the spring，is after all throwing away the well.'

【注释】

[1] 孟子以"掘井"譬喻，指出做任何事情，都要有孜孜不倦、持之以恒的精神，不能因为暂时的困难而放弃正确的目标，否则一切努力将会功亏一篑。

[2] "轫"同"仞"，为古代的长度单位。赵岐注曰："轫，八尺也。"而郑玄注《仪礼·乡射礼》曰："七尺曰仞。"可见，古代关于"仞"这一长度单位的认识不固定，但此处九轫强调很深。理雅各受赵岐影响，认为一轫为八尺，故将"九轫"翻译为"seventy-two cubits"（七十二腕尺）。赖发洛和刘殿爵认为"轫"和西方人熟悉的长度单位"fathom"（英寸）相类，将"九轫"翻译为"九英寸"，回避了七尺或者八尺的长度换算。孟子在本章旨在说明持之以恒的重要性，并非要准确说明所挖井的深度，因而不必细究"轫"所代表的长度。不过，笔者仍支持在翻译古代计量单位时采取音译加注的翻译方法。

【原文】13.30　孟子曰[1]："尧舜，性之也；汤武，身之也；五霸，假之也。久假而不归，恶知其非有也[2]？"

【译文】孟子说："尧舜实行仁义，是本性自然；商汤和武王便是亲身努力推行仁义；五霸便是假借仁义来谋利。借得长久了，总不归还，又怎能知道他们不是自己真有了呢？"

【英译】Mencius said, 'Benevolence and righteousness were natural to Yâo and Shun. T'ang and Wû made them their own. The five chiefs of the princes feigned them. Having borrowed them long and not returned them, how could it be known they did not own them?'

【注释】

[1] 孟子将实行仁政的君主分为三类，第一类是像尧、舜那样本性好仁爱，自然而然地施行仁道的圣君；第二类是汤、武那样身体力行，践行仁义的君主；第三类是齐桓公、晋文公等假借仁义之名、行霸业之实的霸主。

[2] "久假而不归，恶知其非有也"是孟子对五霸假借仁义之名的行为评价。关于孟子对五霸的态度，存在赵岐和朱熹两种不同的理解。赵岐注曰："五霸若能久假仁义，譬如假物，久而不归，安知其不真有也。"显然，他对"五霸"假仁义持乐观态度，认为如果能长时间借用仁义之名，约束自己的行为，久而久之就可以真正执行仁义之政。朱熹则持批判态度，认为："有，实有也。言窃其名以终身，而不自知其非真有。或曰：'盖叹世人莫觉其伪者。'亦通。旧说，久假不归，即为真有，则误矣。"笔者以为，赵岐注解更符合孟子之意。孟子虽然明白战国时期混战的诸侯既不是能身行仁义之君，更不是发自内心的爱好仁义、自觉行仁政的圣王，但仍积极游说各国，希望能遇到一个有见识的君主欣赏他的仁义学说，推行他的仁政主张。他之所以这样做，就是因为从五霸身上得到启发，相信虽然这些君主不能像尧舜和汤武那样"性之""身之"，但若能像"五霸"那样假之，仍能成就一番大业，造福天下百姓。如果孟子在此对五霸假借仁义持批判态度，感叹世人不知道他们是伪有仁政，就不会积极向那些甚至连"假之"都不愿意做的诸侯国君宣扬他的政治主张了。理雅各的理解和朱熹的后一种解释"盖叹世人莫觉其伪者"相近，认为百姓被五霸所蒙蔽，不知道他们在伪装仁义。刘殿爵的译文是"But if a man borrows a thing and keeps it long enough, how can one be sure that it will not become truly his"（如果一个人借了一件东西，保存了很久但没有归还，谁又能说这个东西没有真正变成他的）。他的译文同赵岐，

更能体现孟子的原意。

【原文】 13.31　公孙丑曰[1]："伊尹曰：'予不狎于不顺[2]。'放太甲于桐，民大悦。太甲贤，又反之，民大悦。贤者之为人臣也，其君不贤，则固可放欤？"孟子曰："有伊尹之志，则可；无伊尹之志，则篡也。"

【译文】 公孙丑说："伊尹说过：'我不愿亲近违背德行的人。'把太甲放逐到桐邑，百姓非常高兴。太甲变好了，又将他接回来，百姓非常高兴。贤人是臣属，他的君王不贤，就可以放逐吗？"孟子说："有伊尹那样的志向就可以；如果没有伊尹那样的志向，就是篡夺了。"

【英译】 Kung-sun Chʻâu said, 'Î Yin said, "I cannot be near and see him so disobedient to reason," and therewith he banished Tʻâi-chiâ to Tʻung. The people were much pleased. When Tʻâi-chiâ became virtuous, he brought him back, and the people were again much pleased. When worthies are ministers, may they indeed banish their sovereigns in this way when they are not virtuous?' Mencius replied, 'If they have the same purpose as Î Yin, they may. If they have not the same purpose, it would be usurpation.'

【注释】

[1] 孟子认为，如果为人臣属能有伊尹那样的忠心，一心为百姓谋福利，就可以流放违背礼义、不贤不肖的君主，但如果没有那样的心胸和道德修养，则容易将旨在教育君主的流放转变为犯上作乱的篡位。

[2] "不顺"，朱熹注曰："言太甲所为，不顺义理也。"理雅各的理解与之相类，将之翻译为 "disobedient to reason"（不服从义理）。赖发洛翻译为 "the unruly"（不受控制），刘殿爵的译文是 "one who is intractable"（难以驾驭）。伊尹是一心为民的忠臣，不可能会因为"太甲"不受他的控制，难以驾驭就流放他，否则和谋权篡位的犯上作乱者没有什么区别。结合下文

"太甲贤，又反之"可以断定，太甲被流放的原因应是不明事理，胡作非为。因而理雅各的译文更符合孟子的原意。

【原文】13.32　公孙丑曰[1]："《诗》曰：'不素餐兮[2]。'君子之不耕而食，何也？"孟子曰："君子居是国也，其君用之，则安富尊荣；其子弟从之，则孝弟忠信。'不素餐兮'，孰大于是[3]？"

【译文】公孙丑说："《诗经》说：'不白吃饭啊。'君子不种庄稼也能获得食物，为什么呢？"孟子说："君子居住在一个国家，君主用他，就会安定、富足、尊贵、荣耀；少年子弟跟随他，就会孝父母、敬兄长、忠心而守信。'不白吃饭啊'，还有比这更大的吗？"

【英译】Kung-sun Ch'âu said, 'It is said, in the Book of Poetry, "He will not eat the bread of idleness!" How is it that we see superior men eating without labouring?' Mencius replied, 'When a superior man resides in a country, if its sovereign employ his counsels, he comes to tranquillity, wealth and glory. If the young in it follow his instructions, they become filial, obedient to their elders, true-hearted, and faithful.——What greater example can there be than this of not eating the bread of idleness?'

【注释】

[1] 孟子将劳动分为劳力和劳心两种，认为劳心也是劳动，甚至比劳力更重要。因为劳心者不仅可以凭借自己的知识，给国家带来和平、富足和荣誉，还能成为这个国家年轻人效仿的榜样，教导他们成为孝顺、敬长、忠心和诚信的人。

[2] "不素餐兮"出自《诗·魏风·伐檀》："彼君子兮，不素餐兮。"理雅各将之翻译为"He will not eat the bread of idleness"（他不会不劳而食）。赖发洛的译文是"Be no idle eater!"（不要吃闲饭）二人都按照原文的字面意思翻译，体现了原文的句式特点，而刘殿爵则结合《诗·魏风·伐檀》

"彼君子兮，不素餐兮"，将之意译为"enjoys only food he has earned"（君子只吃他自己挣得的东西）。

[3]"孰大于是"是反问句表肯定，理雅各的译文在句型、语气和含义上都能准确对应原文。赖发洛的译文是"What could be further from an idle eater than that!"（有什么能比它更能说明不要吃闲饭啊）他选择用感叹句翻译这句话，表达了孟子强烈的肯定态度。刘殿爵的译文"Is there a truer case of 'enjoying only food he has earned'?"（还有比这更确切的只享受自己劳动所得的例子吗）他的译文不拘泥于原文的句型结构，更关注译文准确传递原文的含义。

【原文】13.33 王子垫问曰[1]："士[2]何事?"孟子曰："尚志。"曰："何谓尚志?"曰："仁义而已矣。杀一无罪非仁也;非其有而取之非义也。居恶在? 仁是也;路恶在? 义是也。居仁由义,大人之事备矣。"

【译文】齐国王子垫问道："士做什么事情呢?"孟子答道："士要使自己的心志高尚。"问道："怎样才算使自己的心志高尚?"答道："行仁和义罢了。杀一个无罪的人是不仁,不是自己的东西却取了过来,是不义。所居住之处在哪里呢? 仁便是;所行之路在哪里呢? 义便是。居住于仁,行走由义,大人的事情便完备了。"

【英译】The king's son, Tien, asked Mencius, saying, 'What is the business of the unemployed scholar?' Mencius replied, 'To exalt his aim.' Tien asked again, 'What do you mean by exalting the aim?' The answer was, 'Setting it simply on benevolence and righteousness. He thinks how to put a single innocent person to death is contrary to benevolence; how to take what one has not a right to is contrary to righteousness; that one's dwelling should be benevolence; and one's path should be righteousness. Where else should he dwell? What other path should he pursue? When benevolence is the dwelling-place of the heart, and righteousness the path of the life, the business of a great man is complete.'

【注释】

[1] 孟子认为高尚的志向对知识分子来说是非常重要的。知识分子应当树立崇高的志向，时刻以仁义观念存心，居仁由义，这样才能成为一个道德高尚、受人尊敬的人。

[2] "士"，理雅各将之翻译为"the unemployed scholar"（尚未担任政府官职的知识分子）。他认为"士"和"君子"具有明显的区别，不能用同一个单词翻译。而赖发洛选择将"士"和"君子"都翻译为"knight"，正如前文所说，不论是"士"还是"君子"，和西方的"骑士"在含义上都有显著差异，选择用它反向格义具有浓重中国文化气息的词语不妥。虽然刘殿爵也选择用同一个单词"gentlman"翻译"君子"和"士"，但为了提醒读者二者的区别，他选择用大写的"Gentleman"翻译"士"。从文义看，理雅各对"士"的翻译更准确。

【原文】 13.34　孟子曰[1]："仲子，不义与之齐国而弗受，人皆信之[2]，是舍箪食豆羹之义也。人莫大焉，亡亲戚、君臣、上下。以其小者信其大者，奚可哉？"

【译文】 孟子说："陈仲子，如果用不合理的方式把齐国都给他，他都不会接受，别人都相信这一点，不过这也只是拒绝一筐饭、一碗汤的义。人没有比不要父兄、君臣、尊卑还大的罪过。因为他有小节操，就相信他有大节操，怎么可以呢？"

【英译】 Mencius said, 'Supposing that the kingdom of Ch'î were offered, contrary to righteousness, to Ch'ǎn Chung, he would not receive it, and all people believe in him, as a man of the highest worth. But this is only the righteousness which declines a dish of rice or a plate of soup. A man can have no greater crimes than to disown his parents and relatives，and the relations of sovereign and minister，superiors and inferiors. How can it be allowed to give a man credit for the great excellences because he possesses a small one?'

【注释】

[1] 孟子认为"义"有"大义"和"小义"的区别，不能为了保有饮食方面的小义而丧失人伦大义。在评价一个人的时候，更不应该因为他在小的事情上保有节操就相信他在大事上能坚守美德。

[2] "人皆信之"，朱熹注曰："齐人皆信其贤。"理雅各将之翻译为"all people believe in him，as a man of the highest worth."（所有人都相信他是一个具有极大美德的人）。他采取补充性翻译策略，用增添字词做解释的方法，使文义更加明确。对于原文没有词语，他都用斜体字标出，以提示读者这是译者自己添加的东西。刘殿爵的译文是"Everyone believes that Ch'eh Chung would refuse the state of Ch'i were it offered to him against the principles of rightness"（所有的人都相信如果不符合道义，把整个齐国给仲子，他都会拒绝）。他认为"之"指代前文的"不义与之齐国而弗受"这件事，而理雅各则认为指代的是"仲子"这个人。从下文"以其小者信其大者"可以推测，将"之"理解为"具有极大美德"更贴切。

【原文】13.35　桃应问曰[1]："舜为天子，皋陶为士[2]，瞽瞍杀人，则如之何？"孟子曰："执之而已矣。""然则舜不禁与？"曰："夫舜恶得而禁之？夫有所受之也[3]。""然则舜如之何？"曰："舜视弃天下犹弃敝蹝也。窃负而逃，遵海滨而处，终身欣然，乐而忘天下[4]。"

【译文】桃应问道："舜做天子，皋陶做法官，如果瞽瞍杀了人，那怎么办？"孟子答道："逮捕他就是了。""那么，舜不阻止吗？"答道："舜怎么能阻止呢？他去逮捕是有法律依据的。""那么，舜又怎么办呢?”答道:"舜把抛弃天子之位看得像抛弃破草鞋一样。偷偷地背着父亲逃走,沿着海边住下来,一辈子快乐得很,把做过天子的事情都忘了。"

【英译】T'âo Ying asked, saying, 'Shun being sovereign, and Kâo-Yâo chief minister of justice, if Kû-sâu had murdered a man, what would have been done in the case?' Mencius said, 'Kâo-Yâo would simply have apprehended him.' 'But would not Shun have forbidden such a thing?' 'Indeed, how could Shun have forbidden it? Kâo-Yâo had received the law from a proper source.' 'In that case what would Shun have done?' 'Shun would have regarded abandoning the kingdom as throwing away a worn-out sandal. He would privately have taken his father on his back, and retired into concealment, living some where along the sea-coast. There he would have been all his life, cheerful and happy, forgetting the kingdom.'

【注释】

[1] 弟子桃应通过假设向孟子提出了一个问题:在亲情和法律发生矛盾时,圣人应当如何做?孟子的答案是"窃负而逃",虽看似两者兼顾,但最终还是选择了亲情,因而也必将付出"弃天下"的重大代价。

[2] 在"皋陶为士"中,"士"特指上古掌刑狱之官。理雅各将之翻译为"chief minister of justice"(司法部部长),刘殿爵的译文是"judge"(法官),基本上能体现"士"的内涵。赖发洛坚持他的一贯作风,试图用同一个英语词语翻译原文中常用概念,不过他也注意到此处的"士"具有明显不同的含义,因而选择用大写的"Knight"翻译。他的译文虽能确保对重要概念翻译的前后一致性,但牺牲了中国文化负载词含义的丰富性和语义的不确定性。

[3] "夫有所受之也",朱熹注曰:"言皋陶之法,有所传受,非所敢私,虽天子之命亦不得而废之也。"理雅各受其影响,对原文做了适当添加,

将之翻译为"Kâo-Yâo had received the law from a proper source"（皋陶所执行的法律是正当合适的）。赖发洛按字面意思直译为"he had authority for it"（他有权这样做）。理雅各的译文侧重突出皋陶所执之法的正当性，赖发洛的译文旨在强调皋陶权力的正当性。

[4]"终身欣然，乐而忘天下"是本章的宗旨，表明了舜，更确切地说是孟子的价值取向，即对父母尽孝是最重要也是最快乐的事情，帝王之权或荣华富贵对孝而言是微不足道的。理雅各将"乐而忘天下"翻译为"forgetting the kingdom"，赖发洛翻译为"all below heaven would have been forgotten"。"forget"的含义主要是指"忘记"，更强调粗心和疏忽，并非主体有意识的选择，而刘殿爵的"never giving a thought to"更侧重因认为某物微不足道而不去考虑和计较。显然"乐而忘天下"是孟子权衡"天下"和"孝顺父亲"后做出的选择，因而刘殿爵的译文更贴切。

【原文】13.36　孟子自范之齐[1]，望见齐王之子[2]，喟然叹曰："居移气，养移体，大哉居[3]乎！夫非尽人之子与？"孟子曰："王子宫室、车马、衣服多与人同，而王子若彼者，其居使之然也。况居天下之广居者乎？鲁君之宋，呼于垤泽之门。守者曰：'此非吾君也，何其声之似我君也？'此无他，居相似也。"

【译文】孟子从范邑到齐国都城，远远看见齐王的儿子，长叹一声说道："环境改变气质，奉养改变体质，环境真是重要啊！他难道不也是人的儿子吗？"孟子说："王子的宫室、车马、衣服多半和别人相同，但是王子却能那样，是因为他的环境使他这样；更别说那些居住在天下最广阔的房子（仁）的人了。鲁国君主去宋国，在宋国城门下呼喊，守门的人说：'这不是我们的君主，为什么他的声音和我们的君主那么像呢？'这没有别的原因，环境相似罢了。"

【英译】Mencius, going from Fan to Ch'î, saw the king of Ch'î's son at a distance, and said with a deep sigh, 'One's position alters the air，just as the nurture affects the body. Great is the influence of position！Are we not all men's sons in this respect？'Mencius said，'The residence，the carriages and horses，and the dress of the king's son，are mostly the same as those of other men. That he looks so is occasioned by his position. How much more should a peculiar air distinguish him whose position is in the wide house of the world！When the prince of Lû went to Sung，he called out at the T'ieh-châi gate，and the keeper said，"This is not our prince. How is it that his voice is so like that of our prince？"This was occasioned by nothing but the correspondence of their positions.'

【注释】

[1] 孟子在本章以齐王之子和鲁君为例，强调了环境对人言谈举止的影响。他所说的环境不仅仅是居住环境和身份地位，还包括道德环境。他认为，虽然人的地位和生活条件不能选择，但人们可以选择居住在"仁"这一天下最舒适的住宅里，以提高自身的道德修养和气质。

[2] "望"的本义是从远处看，因而"望见齐王之子"指远远看见齐王的儿子。理雅各和刘殿爵都准确翻译出了"远远看见"这一含义，而赖发洛的"look up"则有仰望、尊敬之意，用在此处不确切。

[3] "居"指大的生活环境，不仅包括身份地位和衣食住行等物质条件，还包含仁、义、礼、智等道德环境的熏陶。理雅各将"居"翻译为"position"，更强调身份地位对人气质的影响。赖发洛选择用"place"翻译"居"，突出居住场所对人言谈举止的影响。这两种翻译强调的侧重点不同，但基本上都能体现原文的意思。不过，从准确性上看，刘殿爵的"surroundings"（环境）最全面，不仅可以囊括理雅各和赖发洛的译文，还可以将道德影响力纳入其中。

【原文】 13.37　孟子曰[1]："食而弗爱，豕交之也；爱而不敬，兽畜之也。恭敬者，币之未将者也[2]。恭敬而无实，君子不可虚拘。"

【译文】 孟子说："养活但不爱护，那就像养猪一样；爱护但不尊敬，就像养牲畜一样。恭敬的心，在送礼物之前就应该具备了。如果只有表面恭敬，但没有恭敬的诚心实意，君子是不会被这种虚假的礼数留住的。"

【英译】 Mencius said, 'To feed a scholar and not love him，is to treat him as a pig. To love him and not respect him，is to keep him as a domestic animal. Honouring and respecting are what exist before any offering of gifts. If there be honouring and respecting without the reality of them，a superior man may not be retained by such empty demonstrations.'

【注释】

[1] 战国之时，诸侯竞相礼遇贤士，以达到富国强兵的目的，但是他们却不懂得应该如何与君子结交。孟子针对当时诸侯虚情假意礼贤下士的现象，提出了结交君子应持的态度。他指出，仅仅靠提供优越的物质条件不能得到治国之才。要想结交君子，不仅要有发自内心的喜爱，更要有实质的尊敬行为和态度。

[2] "将"，杨伯峻引"《尔雅·释言》云：'送也。'《仪礼·少仪》郑注云：'将，犹奉也。'"结合前文，"恭敬者，币之未将者也"应当理解为"恭敬之心在礼物送出之前就已经具备了"。理雅各和刘殿爵的译文准确翻译出了这一含义。而赖发洛却将之翻译为"Honour and respect are the ungiven gift"（恭敬是未送出的礼物）。孟子在本章旨在说明应当如何结交君子。他先指出了两种错误的结交之道，以突出恭敬的重要性，接着指出恭敬无实的危害。可见，存有"恭敬"之心是与君子结交的关键，也是本章论述的重点。因而理雅各和刘殿爵的译文更符合篇章之意。此外，"恭"和"敬"虽含义相近，但略有不同。所谓"在貌为恭，在心为敬"，也就是说，"恭"更

强调外在身体的恭态，而"敬"突出内在心理的敬意。理雅各和赖发洛看到了二者的差异，选择用"honour"和"respect"翻译"恭敬"。刘殿爵只选择用"respect"翻译，仅突出了内心的敬意，没有体现恭敬的言行举止对于结交君子同样重要。

【原文】13.38　孟子曰："形色，天性也[1]；惟圣人然后可以践形[2]。"

【译文】孟子说："形体和容貌是天生的，只有圣人才能充分实现他的形体和容貌。"

【英译】Mencius said，'The bodily organs with their functions belong to our Heaven-conferred nature. But a man must be a sage before he can satisfy the design of his bodily organization.'

【注释】

[1]"形色，天性也"，朱熹注曰："人之有形有色，无不各有自然之理，所谓天性也。"理雅各将之翻译为"The bodily organs with their functions belong to our Heaven-conferred nature"（我们的身体器官及其功能是上天赋予我们的天性）。赖发洛的译文是"Our shape and hue are the nature given us by Heaven"（我们的身体和外貌是上天赋予的天性）。虽然两位译者对"形色"的翻译不同，但都认为他们属于人性的范畴。"形色"虽具备孟子所谓"性"的与生俱来的特征，但孟子的人性旨在说明人与动物的区别在于人生来就具备善性。因而将"形色"纳入人性的范畴与孟子对性善的论述相冲突。在古代，"性"和"生"互通，通常会混用，因而此处的"性"不妨可以理解为"生"，即认为"人的身体容貌是天生的"。杨伯峻的今译本，以及赵甄陶的翻译皆持这一观点。

[2]"惟圣人然后可以践形"，孟子认为，只有圣人能发展人性中的四端而不受外物的蒙蔽，故能够践行人性善的本质。理雅各的译文基本上能体现本句话的含义。赖发洛的译文"None but the holy man can attain his full

shape"（只有圣人才能完全具备人的形体外貌）过于机械，不如刘殿爵的
"Only a sage can give his body complete fulfillment"（只有圣人才能完全践行
人的形体特征）准确。人具备与其他动物不同的形体外貌，因而也应体现其
他动物所不具备的言行举止和行为规范。只有圣人才能将人的本质和人的外
形结合起来，体现人性善的实质。

【原文】13.39　齐宣王欲短丧。公孙丑曰："为期之丧，犹愈
于已乎？"孟子曰："是犹或绐其兄之臂，子谓之姑徐徐云尔，亦教
之孝悌[1]而已矣。"王子有其母死者，其傅为之请数月之丧。公孙
丑曰："若此者何如也？"曰："是欲终之而不可得也。虽加一日愈
于已，谓夫莫之禁而弗为者也。"

【译文】齐宣王想要缩短服丧的时间。公孙丑说："服丧一年，总
比完全不服丧强些吧？"孟子说："这就像有一个人在扭他哥哥的胳膊，
你却对他说，姑且慢慢地扭吧。应该教导他孝父母、敬兄长就可以了。"
王子有死了母亲的，王子的师傅替他请求服丧几个月。公孙丑问道：
"像这样的事，怎么样？"孟子答道："这是王子想要服丧三年而办不到。
纵使多服丧一天也比不服好，是对那些没有人禁止他服丧自己却不去服
丧的人说的。"

【英译】The king Hsüan of Ch'î wanted to shorten the period of
mourning. Kung-sun Ch'âu said, 'To have one whole year's mourning
is better than doing away with it altogether.' Mencius said, 'That is
just as if there were one twisting the arm of his elder brother, and you
were merely to say to him— "Gently, gently, if you please." Your
only course should be to teach such an one filial piety and fraternal
duty.' At that time, the mother of one of the king's sons had died,
and his tutor asked for him that he might be allowed to observe a
few months' mourning. Kung-sun Ch'ǎu asked, 'What do you say

of this?'Mencius replied,'This is a case where the party wishes to complete the whole period, but finds it impossible to do so. The addition of even a single day is better than not mourning at all. I spoke of the case where there was no hindrance, and the party neglected the thing itself.'

【注释】

[1] "孝悌",理雅各将之翻译为"filial piety and fraternal duty"。正如前文所说,在英语世界里,"piety"主要指宗教中人对上帝的爱和尊敬,有明显的基督教味道,用它和"filial"连用翻译"孝"不合适。他将"悌"翻译为"fraternal duty"(兄弟间的义务),扩大了"悌"的适用范围。正如朱熹所说:"善事兄长为悌。"可见"悌"是针对弟弟而言,是弟对兄的义务,而非兄弟双方的共同义务。赖发洛将"孝"译为"piety"不妥。他选择用"modesty"(谦虚)来翻译"悌"也过于笼统。刘殿爵将"孝悌"翻译为"the duties of a son and a younger brother."(子女和弟弟应尽的义务)。他通过解释性翻译准确传递了"孝悌"之义。

【原文】13.40 孟子曰[1]:"君子之所以教者五:有如时雨化之者[2],有成德者,有达财者,有答问者,有私淑艾者[3]。此五者,君子之所以教也。"

【译文】孟子说:"君子的教育方式有五种:有像及时雨那样滋润感化万物的,有成全品德的,有培养才能的,有解答疑问的,还有靠学问品德使那些没能直接接触的人私下受益的。这五种便是君子的教育方法。"

【英译】Mencius said,'There are five ways in which the superior man effects his teaching. There are some on whom his influence descends like seasonable rain. There are some whose virtue he perfects,and some of whose talents he assists the development. There are some whose inquiries he answers. There are some who privately cultivate and correct themselves. These five ways are the methods in which the superior man effects his teaching.'

【注释】

[1] 同孔子一样，孟子也是一位伟大的教育家。他根据学生的不同潜能，提出了"如时雨化之者，成德者，达财者，答问者和私淑艾者"五种教育方式。

[2] "如时雨化之者"，朱熹注曰："及时之雨也。草木之生，播种封殖（培养而使生长），人力已至，而未能自化，所少者雨露之滋耳，及此时而雨之，则其化速矣。"可见，"时雨"适应万物的需要，能够化生万物，对万物的成长具有重要作用。君子的这一教人方法如"时雨"一样，也是根据受教育者的需要，促进受教者成人、成才。理雅各在翻译这一教育方法的时候，直接翻译成"like seasonable rain"（像及时雨），让读者自己去体会。赖发洛译为"Like rain in season it may bring new life"（就像能够化生新生命的及时雨）。刘殿爵认为这一教育方法"a transforming influence like that of timely rain"就像能够产生决定性作用的及时雨。赖发洛的"化生新生命"以及刘殿爵的"决定性作用"都翻译出了时雨对受教育者产生的影响，使读者能够更清晰明白地了解孟子的这一教育方法。

[3] 学界对"有私淑艾者"的理解可谓见仁见智。李鎏指出："'私淑艾'者即'私拾取'也。亲为门徒，面相授受，直也。未得为孔子之徒，而拾取于相传之人，故为私，'私淑'犹云'窃取'也。彼言私淑诸人，不必又叠'艾'字，其义自足。此叠'艾'字以足其句，其实'私淑艾'犹'私淑'也。"理雅各翻译为"There are some who privately cultivate and correct themselves"（有些人私下纠正和培养自己）。他在注释中对此做了说明："这一类人从来没有真正和他们的老师接触过，但从别处听说并学习过他们的理论。因而老师虽然没有亲自教育过他们，但是确实影响了他们。"理雅各的注释准确传递了"私淑艾"的含义。但结合文意，孟子在本章列举的是五个

教育方法，而理雅各却将"私淑艾"翻译为学习方法，偷换了主语。因而他的译文不如刘殿爵的译文"by setting an example others not in contact with him can emulate."（为那些不能直接和他接触的人树立榜样，让他们效仿）确切。刘殿爵的译文受赵岐"君子独善其身，人法其仁，此亦与教法之道无差也"的影响，能保持译文前后主语的一致性。

【原文】13.41　公孙丑曰[1]："道则高矣[2]，美矣，宜若登天然，似不可及也；何不使彼为可几及而日孳孳也[3]？"孟子曰："大匠不为拙工改废绳墨，羿不为拙射变其彀率。君子引而不发，跃如也。中道而立，能者从之。"

【译文】公孙丑说："道很高很美，就好像登天一般，似乎不可企及；为什么不使它变成有可能达到，因而叫人们每天去努力追求呢？"孟子说："高明的工匠不会为笨拙的工人改变或者废弃绳墨，羿也不因为笨拙的射手改变拉弓的标准。君子（教导别人好比射手）张满了弓，却不发箭，作出跃跃欲试的样子。他站在正确的道路中间，有能力的人便跟随着来。"

【英译】Kung-sun Ch'âu said, 'Lofty are your principles and admirable, but to learn them may well be likened to ascending the heavens, ——something which cannot be reached. Why not adapt your teaching so as to cause learners to consider them attainable, and so daily exert themselves！' Mencius said, 'A great artificer does not, for the sake of a stupid workman, alter or do away with the marking-line. Î did not, for the sake of a stupid archer, charge his rule for drawing the bow. The superior man draws the bow, but does not discharge the arrow, having seemed to leap with it to the mark；and he there stands exactly in the middle of the path. Those who are able, follow him.'

【注释】

[1] 孟子在此处提出了自己对道的见解。道是儒家的最高理想和追求，是君子所以安身立命之本。君子在任何时候都应坚守道，不能因为别人达不到而降低自己的准则。

[2] "道"是儒家哲学的最高概念，在西方语言中没有与它完全对等的词。因而理雅各在翻译"道"时，往往根据文义翻译。他认为公孙丑的这段感慨是针对孟子而发。孟子游说诸侯君主，试图施行他的仁政和王道主张，但不能取得这些国君的信任和支持。公孙丑认为，这是因为孟子的政治理想对那些君主来说似乎遥不可及，不如霸道来得实在。因而理雅各主张将"道"翻译为"your principles"（你的准则）。而赖发洛和刘殿爵则选择用"The Way"翻译"道"。他们认为此处的"道"泛指儒家追求的最高理想，并非特指孟子的政治理想。这两种翻译强调的侧重点不同，但都能符合原文之意。

[3] "何不使彼为可几及而日孳孳也"，理雅各认为，这是公孙丑在劝说孟子改变自己的学说，使它更符合普通人的接受能力。刘殿爵的理解与之相类，译为"Why not substitute for it something which men have some hopes of attaining so as to encourage them constantly to make the effort"（为什么不把它变成有希望达到的，因而鼓励人们每天都努力呢）。二人的译文能很好呼应下文，点明宗旨。

【原文】 13.42　孟子曰[1]："天下有道，以道殉身[2]；天下无道，以身殉道；未闻以道殉乎人者也[3]。"

【译文】 孟子说："天下有道，道从身上得以施行；天下无道，用生命捍卫道；没有听说过牺牲道来屈从人的。"

【英译】 Mencius said, 'When right principles prevail throughout the kingdom, one's principles must appear along with one's person. When right principles disappear from the kingdom, one's person must vanish along with one's principles. I have not heard of one's principles being dependent for their manifestation on other men.'

【注释】

[1] 孟子将道和人的关系概括为"以道殉身""以身殉道"和"以道殉人"。他认为，天下有道，政治清明之时，道会随着人的活动而实施，即"以道殉身"。但在天下无道，政治黑暗之时，就会出现为了捍卫道而献出生命的事情，也就是孟子所说的"以身殉道"。上述两种情况在人类社会发展史上交替出现，但孟子否认"以道殉人"，声称自己从未听说过。"以道殉人"并非未出现过，只是孟子鄙视这一做法，认为这不是对待道的正确态度。

[2] "以道殉身"，朱熹注曰："殉，如殉葬之殉，以死随物之名也。身出则道在必行，道屈则身在必退，以死相从而不离也。"即道为人所用，随人的活动而得以施行。刘殿爵的译文与之相类，将之翻译为"it goes where one's person goes"（道随着人的活动得以施行）。理雅各的译文"one's principles must appear along with one's person"（道必须和人一同显现）则略显僵硬，但也能体现原文的意思。赖发洛的译文"the Way is devoted to life"（道献身于生命），过于拘泥于原文的字面意思，不关注文义的表达。

[3] "以道殉乎人者"，朱熹《集注》云："以道从人，妾妇之道。"即歪曲破坏道以逢迎当世王侯。刘殿爵的译文与之相类，将之翻译为"making the Way go where other people are going"（牺牲道以迎合他人）。理雅各译为"one's principles being dependent for their manifestation on other men"（依赖他人实现自己的道）。孟子并不否认依靠君主来实践他的王道主张，他反对的是歪曲、破坏自己的道来讨好，迎合他人。因而理雅各的译文并不准确。

【原文】 13.43　公都子曰[1]："滕更之在门[2]也，若在所礼，而不答，何也？"孟子曰："挟贵而问，挟贤而问，挟长而问，挟有勋劳而问，挟故而问，皆所不答也。滕更有二焉。"

【译文】 公都子说:"滕更在您门下的时候,似乎该在礼遇之列,可是您却不回答他,为什么呢?"孟子说:"倚仗着自己的地位发问,倚仗着自己的才能发问,倚仗着自己年长发问,倚仗着自己有功劳发问,倚仗着自己是老交情发问,都是我所不回答的。滕更占了其中两条。"

【英译】 The disciple Kung-tû said, 'When Kǎng of T'ǎng made his appearance in your school, it seemed proper that a polite consideration should be paid to him, and yet you did not answer him. Why was that?' Mencius replied, 'I do not answer him who questions me presuming on his nobility, nor him who presumes on his talents, nor him who presumes on his age, nor him who presumes on services performed to me, nor him who presumes on old acquaintance. Two of those things were chargeable on Kǎng of T'ǎng.'

【注释】

[1] 孟子认为,学生在向师长请教问题时,应保持虚心的态度,不能依仗自己位高权重,或年长有功就无视师道尊严,显出不应有的傲慢与懈怠。

[2] "滕更",赵岐注曰:"滕君之弟,来学者也。"滕更曾就学于孟子,但他凭借自己特殊的身份和小聪明向孟子请教,孟子不愿意回答他的问题。"在门",在古代指就学于某一个学术思想派别。理雅各的"made his appearance in your school"(就学于你的学派)和刘殿爵的"studying under you"(就学于你),基本能体现其含义。赖发洛按字面意思翻译为"at the door"(在门口),他的译文过于模糊,不能体现出孟子和滕更的关系。

【原文】 13.44 孟子曰[1]:"于不可已而已者,无所不已。于所厚者薄,无所不薄也[2]。其进锐者,其退速。"

【译文】 孟子说:"对于不可以放弃的却放弃了,那就没有什么不可以放弃了。对于应该厚待的人却去薄待他,那就没有什么不可以薄待了。前进太快的人，后退也会快。"

【英译】Mencius said, 'He who stops short where stopping is acknowledged to be not allowable, will stop short in everything. He who behaves shabbily to those whom he ought to treat well, will behave shabbily to all. He who advances with precipitation will retire with speed.'

【注释】

[1] 孟子在本章进一步强调了坚守中庸之道，无过无不及的重要性。对于那些无视中庸之道这一原则，在不该放弃的事情上放弃的人来说，没有什么事情是不可以放弃的。同样，对于应该厚待人时却冷漠对待的人来说，没有什么人不可以冷漠对待。当人丧失了应该坚守的原则和应当保有的亲情时，人所以异于禽兽者的"几希"也会荡然无存。

[2] "于所厚者薄，无所不薄也"，理雅各和刘殿爵认为此句话是针对人而发，旨在说明处理人与人关系的误区。二人认为，如果一个人对他应该厚待的人冷漠对待的话，他会冷漠对待所有的人。当前学术界基本上也持这一观点。赖发洛却独辟蹊径，将之理解为"He that makes light of things of weight, makes light of anything"（轻视重要事情的人，会轻视所有的事情）。前文的"于不可已而已者，无所不已"显然是针对事物而发，因而将"于所厚者薄，无所不薄也"理解为事物，在逻辑上也能说得通。

【原文】13.45　孟子曰[1]："君子之于物也，爱[2]之而弗仁；于民也，仁[3]之而弗亲。亲亲[4]而仁民，仁民而爱物。"

【译文】孟子说："君子对于万物，爱惜它，却不用仁爱对待它；对于百姓，用仁爱对待他们，却不亲爱他们。君子亲爱亲人，因而仁爱百姓，仁爱百姓，因而爱惜万物。"

【英译】Mencius said, 'In regard to inferior creatures, the superior man is kind to them, but not loving. In regard to people generally, he is loving to them，but not affectionate. He is affectionate to his parents，and lovingly disposed to people generally. He is lovingly disposed to people generally，and kind to creatures.'

【注释】

[1] 孟子在本章集中论述了仁的基本内容。

[2] "爱"，朱熹将之解为"取之有时，用之有节。"他用言简意赅的话语道出了君子"爱"物的真谛，即爱惜，不浪费。理雅各将"爱"翻译为"kind to"（仁慈），赖发洛翻译为"likes"（喜欢）。这两个译文都未翻译出"爱"在此处的确切含义。刘殿爵认为，君子对物的"爱"有爱惜和节俭两层含义，因而选择用"sparing"翻译。他的译文准确道出了君子"爱"物的内涵。

[3] "仁"，焦循指出："《说文·人部》云：'仁，亲也。'亲即是仁，而仁不尽于亲。仁之在族类者为亲，其普施于民者，通谓仁而已。仁之言人也，称仁以别于物；亲之言亲也，称亲以别于疏。"可见，"仁"通常用来处理人与人之间的关系，"亲"则是血缘家族关系中出现的天生的亲近、依恋之情。在翻译"仁"时，理雅各和赖发洛受孔子"仁者爱人"的影响，选择用"love"（爱）翻译。刘殿爵则坚持他对《孟子》中"仁"的一贯译法，将之翻译为"benevolence"（仁爱）。

[4] "亲"是对父母、亲人天生的亲近和依恋。理雅各将"亲亲"翻译为"affectionate to his parents"（对父母发自内心的强烈的爱）。刘殿爵将之翻译为"attached to his parents"（对父母的深深依恋）。二人的译文都能体现此处"亲亲"的内涵。赖发洛则认为"仁人"和"亲亲"的区别是"loves the people"（爱一般人）和"loves his kinsmen"（爱亲人）的区别。

【原文】 13.46　孟子曰[1]："知者无不知也，当务之为急；仁者无不爱也，急亲贤之为务[2]。尧舜之知而不遍物，急先务也；尧舜之仁不遍爱人，急亲贤也。不能三年之丧，而缌、小功[3]之察；放饭流歠，而问无齿决[4]，是之谓不知务。"

【译文】孟子说："智者没有不想知道的，但是应以当前重要的工作为急；仁者没有不想爱的，但是应以先爱亲人和贤者为先。尧舜的智慧不能完全知道一切事物，因为他急于知道重要事务；尧舜的仁德不能遍爱一切的人，因为他们急着爱亲人和贤者。不能服丧三年，却讲究缌麻三月、小功五月；在尊长之前大吃大喝，却讲求不要用牙齿啃断干肉，这叫作不识大体。"

【英译】Mencius said, 'The wise embrace all knowledge, but they are most earnest about what is of the greatest importance. The benevolent embrace all in their love, but what they consider of the greatest importance is to cultivate an earnest affection for the virtuous. Even the wisdom of Yâo and Shun did not extend to everything, but they attended earnestly to what was important. Their benevolence did not show itself in acts of kindness to every man, but they earnestly cultivated an affection for the virtuous. Not to be able to keep the three years' mourning, and to be very particular about that of three months, or that of five months; to eat immoderately and swill down the soup, and at the same time to inquire about the precept not to tear the meat with the teeth; such things show what I call an ignorance of what is most important.'

【注释】

[1] 孟子认为，面对纷繁复杂的事物，首先要分清轻重缓急，把眼下最紧要、最关键的事情办好，不要因小失大，舍本逐末。

[2] 对"急亲贤之为务"有两种认识。一种观点认为"亲"是名词，和"贤"是并列关系，将"亲贤"理解为"先爱亲人和贤者"。赵甄陶的译文与之相类，将"亲贤"翻译为"his relatives and the virtuous"。另外一种观点认为"亲"是动词，和"贤"是动宾关系，将"急亲贤之为务"翻译为

"把亲近贤人看作是最重要的事情"。刘殿爵、理雅各和赖发洛的译文都持这种观点。如果仅从文义上看，这两种理解都是可以的。但结合上章孟子对"仁"和"亲"的论述，以及孟子的爱有等差思想，将"亲"理解为和"贤"并列的名词更确切。

[3] "缌"和"小功"是古代丧服的名称。其中"缌"是五服中最轻的一服，以细麻布为孝服，服丧三个月。而"小功"是五服中的第四等，以熟麻布为孝服，服丧五个月。理雅各和刘殿爵以服丧时间为主线，选择用"三个月"和"五个月"的丧礼来翻译"缌"和"小功"。而赖发洛则以丧服的材质"sackcloth"（麻布）来翻译"缌"和"小功"。两种译文分别从不同的方面再现了"缌"和"小功"的重要特征。但相比较而言，以服丧时间来翻译"缌"和"小功"更确切，因为前文的"三年之丧"也是针对丧期而非丧服材质而发。

[4] 孟子认为，"放饭流歠，而问无齿决"的人不懂得事情的轻重缓急，犯了因小失大的错误。要想理解孟子的这一感叹，首先要对古代的礼仪制度有所了解。朱熹注曰："放饭，大饭。流歠，长歠，不敬之大者也。齿决，啮断干肉，不敬之小者也。"正如朱熹所指出的，根据古代礼制的规定，年轻人在尊长面前大口吃饭、大口喝汤是非常不礼貌的行为，而用牙齿啮断干肉虽也是无礼行为，但较之前者，错误就非常小了。译者在翻译这句话时，基本上都是按字面意思翻译，但未能体现其暗含之意。

卷 十 四

尽心章句下

【原文】14.1　孟子曰[1]："不仁哉，梁惠王也！仁者以其所爱及其所不爱，不仁[2]者以其所不爱及其所爱。"公孙丑问曰："何谓也？""梁惠王以土地之故，糜烂其民而战之，大败，将复之，恐不能胜，故驱其所爱子弟[3]以殉之，是之谓以其所不爱及其所爱也。"

【译文】孟子说："不仁啊，梁惠王！仁人把他所喜爱的推及于他所不喜爱的人，不仁的人把他所不喜爱的推及于他所喜爱的人。"公孙丑问道："这是什么意思呢？""梁惠王因为土地的缘故，摧残百姓，驱使他们作战，大败后，又想再战，担心不能得胜，所以又驱使他所喜爱的子弟去送死，这就是所谓的把所不喜爱的推及于他所喜爱的人。"

【英译】Mencius said, 'The opposite indeed of benevolent was the king Hûi of Liang! The benevolent, beginning with what they care for, proceed to what they do not care for. Those who are the opposite of benevolent, beginning with what they do not care for, proceed to what they care for.' Kung-sun Ch'âu said, 'What do you mean?' Mencius answered, 'The king Hûi of Liang, for the matter of territory, tore and destroyed his people, leading them to battle. Sustaining a great defeat, he would engage again, and afraid lest they should not be able to secure the victory, urged his son whom he loved till he sacrificed him with them. This is what I call—"beginning with what they do not care for，and proceeding to what they care for."'

【注释】

[1] 通过批判梁惠王，孟子提出了他的战争观。他反对诸侯国为争夺土地和人口而进行的战争，认为这些战争都是不义之战，给百姓的生命和生活造成了巨大的灾难。

[2] "仁"是孟子思想的一个核心概念，在其思想体系中占据重要地位。在本章，"仁"和"不仁"相对举而言，突出了"仁"在孟子思想中的地位。理雅各选择将"不仁"翻译为"the opposite of benevolent"。赖发洛的译文与之相类，选择用"without love"翻译。这两个译文表明"仁"是孟子价值判断的一大标准，孟子对君主和事件的评价往往以"仁"为依据。刘殿爵将"不仁"译为"ruthless"（残忍），虽也能体现原文的字面意思，但不如前两个译文更能突出"仁"的重要性。

[3] "子弟"，朱熹注曰："谓太子申也。"理雅各受其影响，将之翻译为"his son"（他的儿子）。赖发洛和刘殿爵则认为是泛指"青年男子"。从词义上看，这两种解释都是可以的。但从文义看，孟子举梁惠王的例子是为了说明"以其所不爱及其所爱"。而"子弟"是其"所爱"，那么前面的"糜烂其民而战"中的"民"就是他所不爱的。正因为对百姓没有发自内心的爱，所以他才会驱使百姓为自己争夺土地。百姓战败后，为了确保再次发动战争能取得胜利，他不惜让自己心爱的儿子也投入战争。如此理解，更符合行文逻辑。如果将"子弟"理解为"青年男子"，在含义上就会和前面的"民"相重叠。

【原文】 14.2　孟子曰[1]："春秋无义战。彼善于此，则有之矣。征者，上伐下也，敌国[2]不相征也。"

【译文】 孟子说："春秋时代没有正义的战争。那一国的君主比这一国的君主好一点，那是有的。所谓征讨，是上级讨伐下级，同等级的国家不能互相征讨。"

【英译】Mencius said, 'In the "Spring and Autumn" there are no righteous wars. Instances indeed there are of one war better than another. "Correction" is when the supreme authority punishes its subjects by force of arms. Hostile States do not correct one another.'

【注释】

[1] 孟子认为，春秋时期诸侯之间发动的战争没有一个是正义的，尽管有的战争会比其他战争稍微好点。之所以认为这些战争非正义，是因为征讨是天子讨伐有罪诸侯的行为，诸侯之间不能互相征讨。他通过评价春秋时期诸侯的战争，表明了自己对战国时期诸侯征战的看法，即坚决反对这些为了争城夺地而置百姓生死于不顾的无义战。

[2] "敌国"，理雅各和赖发洛认为"敌"是"敌对、仇视"，因而将之翻译为"Hostile States"（敌对的国家）和"Rival lands"（相互对抗的国家）。他们认为，孟子主张两个相互对抗的国家不能彼此征伐。但刘殿爵认为此处的"敌"取"匹敌，对等"之义，将之翻译为"peers"（两个地位相同的国家）。前文的"征者，上伐下也"，是针对国家的地位高低而言，孟子认为，只有天子才能征讨有罪诸侯，地位相同的诸侯不得彼此相互征伐，否则就是无义之战，因而刘殿爵的译文更确切。

【原文】14.3　孟子曰[1]："尽信《书》[2]，则不如无《书》。吾于《武成》[3]，取二三策而已矣。仁人无敌于天下，以至仁伐至不仁，而何其血之流杵也。"

【译文】孟子说："完全相信《尚书》，那不如没有《尚书》。我对于《武成》一篇只相信其中两三简罢了。仁人在天下没有对手，以周武王这样的至仁者去讨伐商纣这样的至不仁的人，何至于血流成河，连舂米的长木棒都漂起来了呢？"

【英译】Mencius said, 'It would be better to be without the Book of History than to give entire credit to it. In the "Completion of the War," I select two or three passages only, which I believe. The benevolent man has no enemy under heaven. When the prince the most benevolent was engaged against him who was the most the opposite, how could the blood of the people have flowed till it floated the pestles of the mortars?'

【注释】

[1] 虽然本章仅论述了读《尚书》之法，但为后世学者的求学之路指明了正确的方向。

[2] 此处的《书》特指《尚书》，是孟子针对读《尚书》时遇到的问题而发表感叹。因而理雅各和刘殿爵将之翻译为"the Book of Histor"，而赖发洛却认为此处的"书"是对所有的"书籍"而言，将之翻译为"books"。赖发洛的译文扩大了原文的内涵。

[3]《武成》是《尚书》中的一篇，孟子举它是为了进一步说明为什么不能完全相信《尚书》的内容。东汉王充在《论衡·艺增》中指出："夫《武城》之篇，言武王伐纣，血流浮杵。"理雅各和赖发洛分别将《武成》翻译为"Completion of the War"和"The End of the War"，译文没有说明它和《尚书》的关系，容易让读者产生疑惑：为什么孟子开篇说不能完全相信《尚书》，接着却论述了为什么不能完全相信《武成》？刘殿爵将《武成》翻译为"Wu ch'eng chapter"（《武成》这一章），能让读者明白孟子是举《尚书》中的《武成》篇为例，来说明为什么不能完全相信《尚书》。

【原文】 14.4　孟子曰[1]："有人曰：'我善为陈，我善为战。'大罪也。国君好仁，天下无敌焉。南面而征，北狄怨；东面而征，西夷怨，曰：'奚为后我?'武王之伐殷也，革车三百两，虎贲三千人。王曰：'无畏！宁尔也，非敌百姓也。'若崩厥角稽首[2]。征之为言正也，各欲正己也，焉用战?"

【译文】孟子说："有人说：'我擅长布阵，我擅长作战。'这是大罪。国君爱好仁德，在天下没有对手。（商汤）征讨南方，北方便埋怨；征讨东方，西方便埋怨，说：'为什么把我放到后面？'周武王讨伐殷商，兵车三百辆，勇士三千人。武王说：'不要害怕，我是来安抚你们的，不是和百姓为敌的。'百姓便都额头触地叩起头来。征是正的意思，各人都想着端正自己，那又何必要战争呢？"

【英译】Mencius said，'There are men who say——"I am skilful at marshalling troops，I am skilful at conducting a battle！"——They are great criminals. If the ruler of a State love benevolence，he will have no enemy in the kingdom. When Tʻang was executing his work of correction in the south，the rude tribes on the north murmured. When he was executing it in the east，the rude tribes on the west murmured. Their cry was——"Why does he make us last？" When king Wû punished Yin，he had only three hundred chariots of war，and three thousand life-guards. The king said，"Do not fear. Let me give you repose. I am no enemy to the people！ On this，they bowed their heads to the earth，like the horns of animals falling off." "Royal correction" is but another word for rectifying. Each State wishing itself to be corrected，what need is there for fighting？'

【注释】

[1] 孟子反对战国时期诸侯彼此征战的局面，认为那些善于为君主摆阵、布兵的人都是国之罪人，会造成生灵涂炭。他举武王伐殷的例子说明，如果君主好仁，就会无敌于天下，根本不需要战争。

[2] "若崩厥角稽首"，朱熹注曰："于是商人稽首至地，如角之崩也。"孔颖达疏《尚书·泰誓中》"百姓懔懔，若崩厥角"曰："以畜兽为喻，民之怖惧，若似畜兽崩摧其角然。"理雅各的译文与之相类，将之翻译为"they bowed their heads to the earth，like the horns of animals falling off."（他们俯首

在地，就好像禽兽的角脱落了一样）杨伯峻则认为："厥，同'蹶'，顿也。《说文》云：'顿，下首也。'角，额角。'厥角'之意即'顿首'。"刘殿爵的译文与之相类，认为是"the people knocking their heads on the ground was like the toppling of a mountain"（百姓以额触地，就像山倒了一样）。"若崩厥角"取"像野兽折了头角"之意时，通常用来比喻危惧不安的样子。百姓对武王是心悦诚服地归顺，而非因恐惧而顺从。因而刘殿爵和杨伯峻的理解更贴切。

【原文】14.5　孟子曰[1]："梓匠轮舆能与人规矩[2]，不能使人巧。"

【译文】孟子说："木工以及车工能够把制作的规矩准则传授给别人，却不能够使别人做到巧妙。"

【英译】Mencius said, 'A carpenter or a carriage-maker may give a man the circle and square, but cannot make him skilful in the use of them.'

【注释】

[1] 孟子认为认识了规矩法则并不代表能够熟练运用它们，要想实现技艺的巧妙，离不开后天的努力钻研。

[2] "规矩"，朱熹注曰："法度可告者也。"理雅各将之译为"the circle and square"（校正圆形和方形的工具），他认为"规矩"是具体的工具。孟子在告诫教育者不仅要传授给受教育必要的工具，还要教授他们如何使用这些工具。刘殿爵则认为，此处的"规矩"指"rules"（规矩法则），即木工和做车子的人虽然能够教给别人制作东西的规矩准则，却不能使他们变得灵巧。显然，他认为孟子是在告诫求学者，前人的经验和知识虽有助于人们掌握技艺，但要熟练掌握和运用这些理论知识，还要靠求学者的主观努力。这两种理解强调的重点不同，但都言之有理，持之有据，因而都是可以接受的。

【原文】 14.6　孟子曰[1]："舜之饭糗[2]茹草也，若将终身焉；及其为天子也，被袗衣[3]，鼓琴，二女果，若固有之。"

【译文】 孟子说："舜吃干粮和野菜的时候，好像准备终身如此。等他作了天子，穿着华贵的衣服，弹着琴，尧的两个女儿侍候着，又好像他本来就有这些一样。"

【英译】 Mencius said, 'Shun's manner of eating his parched grain and herbs was as if he were to be doing so all his life. When he became sovereign, and had the embroidered robes to wear, the lute to play, and the two daughters of Yâo to wait on him, he was as if those things belonged to him as a matter of course.'

【注释】

[1] 孟子以舜为例，指出修身之道贵在修心。只有当内心有了高尚的道德操守，才能不以物喜不以己悲，正如朱熹所说："不以贫贱而有慕于外，不以富贵而有动于中，随遇而安，无预于己，所性分定故也。"

[2] "糗"，炒熟的米麦，泛指干粮。理雅各将之翻译为"parched grain"（炒干的谷物），能准确体现"糗"的含义。赖发洛将之翻译为"porridge"（粥），但粥和干饭有明显区别，用它翻译不甚妥帖。刘殿爵的译文是"dried rice"（干米），基本上能再现"糗"的含义。

[3] "袗衣"，朱熹注曰："画衣也。"即绘有文采的华丽衣服，理雅各的译文与之相类，翻译为"embroidered robes"（绣花的衣服）。刘殿爵则将之译为"precious robes"（讲究的衣服），和前文舜吃干饭、野菜形成对比。杨伯峻则认为"画衣"不准确，应该是"麻葛单衣"。

【原文】 14.7　孟子曰[1]："吾今而后知杀人亲[2]之重也：杀人之父，人亦杀其父；杀人之兄，人亦杀其兄。然则非自杀之也，一间耳[3]。"

【译文】 孟子说："我现在才知道杀害别人的亲人的严重性了：杀了

别人的父亲，别人也会杀自己的父亲；杀了别人的哥哥，别人也就会杀自己的哥哥。那么，虽然不是自己杀了他们，但相差也不远了。”

【英译】Mencius said, "From this time forth I know the heavy consequences of killing a man's near relations. When a man kills another's father, that other will kill his father; when a man kills another's elder brother, that other will kill his elder brother. So he does not himself indeed do the act, but there is only an interval between him and it.'

【注释】

[1] 孟子本章旨在警告人们要多行善，勿作恶。他曾经引用曾子的话"戒之戒之，出乎尔者，反乎尔者也"来说明为什么百姓会"疾视其长上之死而不救"。在本章，他再次说明了"出乎尔者，反乎尔者"的严重后果："杀人之父，人亦杀其父；杀人之兄，人亦杀其兄。"

[2] 虽然在孟子一书中，提到"亲"处多指"父母双亲"，但在此处指所有的家庭成员。因为"亲"后孟子所举的例子既包括"父"，又包含"兄"。理雅各将"亲"翻译为"a man's near relations"（近亲），赖发洛翻译为"a man's kinsman"（同族），刘殿爵翻译为"a member of the family"（家庭成员）。这三种译文基本都能体现此处"亲"的含义。

[3] "一间耳"是孟子对"杀人亲"和"自杀之"之间差距的认识。朱熹注曰："一间者，我往彼来，间一人耳，其实与自害其亲无异也。"即杀害别人的亲人而招致的血腥报复，和亲手杀害自己的亲人没有什么不同。理雅各将之翻译为"an interval between him and it"（仅仅是他和它的间隔），他的译文过于机械僵硬，不如刘殿爵的"one step removed"（仅仅只有一步之遥）更通俗易懂。

【原文】14.8　孟子曰[1]："古之为关[2]也，将以御暴；今之为关也，将以为暴。"

【译文】孟子说:"古代设立关卡是为了抵御暴行;今天设立关卡却是打算实行暴行。"

【英译】Mencius said, 'Anciently, the establishment of the frontier-gates was to guard against violence. Nowadays, it is to exercise violence.'

【注释】

[1] 以小见大是孟子在说理时惯用的手法。此处他以"关卡"为例,抨击时政,指责当时的诸侯国君不行仁政,将古代圣王用来保护、方便百姓的政策变成盘剥、残害百姓的工具。

[2] "关",古代在险要地方或国界处设立的守卫处所,朱熹注曰:"讥察非常。"理雅各将之翻译为"the frontier-gates",赖发洛翻译为"barriers",刘殿爵翻译为"a border station",基本上都能体现"关"的某个特征。

【原文】14.9 孟子曰[1]:"身不行道,不行于妻子;使人不以道,不能行于妻子[2]。"

【译文】孟子说:"自己不依道而行,就无法使妻子儿女也依道而行;使唤别人不合于道,连妻子儿女也使唤不了。"

【英译】Mencius said, 'If a man himself do not walk in the right path, it will not be walked in even by his wife and children. If he order men according to what is not the right way, he will not be able to get the obedience of even his wife and children.'

【注释】

[1] 孟子本章是对孔子"其身正,不令而行;其身不正,虽令不从"(《论语·子路》)的进一步论述。正所谓"正人先正己",只有自身端正,身体力行,才能要求别人按照自己的主张去做,否则就连自己的妻子儿女都不会顺从。

[2] 朱熹注曰:"身不行道,以行言之。……使人不以道者,以事言

之。"理雅各认为本章出现的两个"道"字内涵不完全相同，因而根据文义将之分别翻译为"right path"和"right way"。他认为此处的"道"暗含正确、正义之意。赖发洛和刘殿爵则选择将"道"统一翻译为"Way"。

【原文】14.10　孟子曰[1]："周于利者凶年不能杀[2]，周于德者邪世不能乱。"

【译文】孟子说："财利富足的人，荒年都不会窘困；道德富足的人，乱世都不会迷惑。"

【英译】Mencius said, 'A bad year cannot prove the cause of death to him whose stores of gain are large; an age of corruption cannot confound him whose equipment of virtue is complete.'

【注释】

[1] 君子要居安思危，注重平时的物质积累和道德修养，只有这样，在遇到不虞之祸时才能从容应对。

[2] "杀"，赵岐注曰："虽凶年不能杀之。"显然他认为此处的"杀"取"使失去生命"之意。但任俊华、赵清文认为"杀""指歉收。如郑玄注《礼记·礼器》'是故年虽大杀，众不匡惧'曰：'杀，谓谷不孰也。'"杨伯峻的理解与之相似，将之解为"缺乏，有窘困意"。理雅各、赖发洛和刘殿爵对"杀"的理解与赵岐一致，将之翻译为"kill"（杀死）。赵甄陶的理解同杨伯峻，将"杀"翻译为"suffer from want"（窘困）。从文义上看，这两种理解都可以。

【原文】14.11　孟子曰[1]："好名之人，能让千乘之国。苟非其人，箪食豆羹见于色。"[2]

【译文】孟子说："好名的人能够把拥有千辆兵车的国家让给别人。若不是这种人，一箪饭、一盆汤，也会使他显出不高兴的神色。"

【英译】Mencius said, 'A man who loves fame may be able to

decline a State of a thousand chariots；but if he be not really the man to do such a thing，it will appear in his countenance，in the matter of a dish of rice or a platter of soup.'

【注释】

[1] 孟子在本章讨论了好名之人的特点。

[2] 赵岐注曰："好不朽之名者，轻让千乘，伯夷、季札之类是也。诚非好名者，争箪食豆羹变色，讼之致祸。"根据他的注解，孟子在本章列举了"好名之人"和"不追求名声的人"在赠送给别人物质财富时的两种表现。前者视物质财富为草芥，而后者却把很小的物质利益都看得很重。中国古典诗词和哲学翻译家大卫·亨顿（David Hinton）在 1998 年出版的英译本《孟子》就将本句翻译为"If you love renown，you can give away a nation of a thousand war-chariots. If you don't，you can't give away a basket of rice or bowl of soup without looking pained."（如果你爱好名声，你可以把拥有一千辆兵车的国家给别人。如果你不爱好名声，即使给别人一筐饭、一碗汤你也会显得很不乐意）但朱熹对本章持另一种看法："好名之人，矫情干誉，是以能让千乘之国；然若本非能轻富贵之人，则于得失之小者，反不觉其真情之发见矣。盖观人不于其所勉，而于其所忽，然后可以见其所安之实也。"根据他的理解，孟子在本章旨在讽刺那些沽名钓誉之人。他们并非真正轻视富贵，仅仅是为了获得好的名声而假装慷慨。但若从小处细察，可以看出，如果不是为了好名声，他们甚至连最小的物质利益都不会放过，显然，这些人并非是看淡富贵之人。理雅各的翻译与之相类，认为一个追求好名声的人，可以把拥有千辆兵车的国家让给别人；如果他不是真正能看轻富贵的人，把一筐饭、一碗汤让给别人，他都会把不乐意表现在脸上。今人杨伯峻又提出了另外一种看法，即"好名的人可以把有千辆兵车国家的君位让给别人，但是，若不是那受让的对象，就是要他让一筐饭，一碗汤，他那不高兴神色都会在脸上表现出来。"赵甄陶的英译本与之相类。这三种理解皆可。

【原文】14.12　孟子曰[1]："不信仁贤，则国空虚[2]；无礼义，则上下乱；无政事，则财用不足。"

【译文】孟子说："不信任仁人、贤人，国家就会人才空虚；没有礼义，上下的关系就会混乱；没有好的政治措施，国家就会用度不足。"

【英译】Mencius said, 'If men of virtue and ability be not confided in, a State will become empty and void. Without the rules of propriety and distinctions of right, the high and the low will be thrown into confusion. Without the great principles of government and their various business, there will not be wealth sufficient for the expenditure.'

【注释】

[1] 孟子认为仁贤在位，恪守礼仪和善政惠民是治理好国家的三大措施。

[2] "不信仁贤，则国空虚"，焦循注曰："不亲信仁贤，仁贤去之，国无贤人，则空虚也。"朱熹注曰："空虚，言若无人也。"受其影响，理雅各认为"如果不信任贤能之人，国家就会空虚。"刘殿爵的译文与之相类，强调"仁德之人"和"贤能之人"对国家的重要性。赖发洛则认为"不信仁贤"指"Without faith in love and worth the land is empty and hollow"（不信仰仁爱和价值，国家就会空虚）。他的译文强调信仰对治理国家的重要性。古代中国是一个重视人治的国家，孟子更是推崇圣王治世、能者在位，因而理雅各和刘殿爵的理解更确切。

【原文】14.13　孟子曰[1]："不仁而得国者，有之矣；不仁而得天下者，未之有也[2]。"

【译文】孟子说："不仁却能得到一个国家，是有的；不仁能得到天下，从未有过。"

【英译】Mencius said, 'There are instances of individuals without benevolence, who have got possession of a single State, but there has been no instance of the throne's being got by one without benevolence.'

【注释】

[1] 孟子在此又重申了仁对于王天下的重要性。他认为，战国时期各诸侯国试图通过战争来统一中国的做法是错误的。在人类历史上，或许存在过不仁之人取得诸侯国政权的情况，但从来没有一个不施行仁政的君主，可以仅仅通过战争就能成为统一天下的王者。

[2] 在本章"国"和"天下"相对举而言。只有将二者的区别体现出来，才便于读者理解为什么"仁"对王天下非常重要。"国"的本义是邦国，邦、国、天下的关系可以概括为大曰邦，小曰国，邦国合称为"天下"。即在古代，王、侯的封地称为"国"，但相对于天子统治的"天下"而言，它仅仅是下属单位或组成部分。"天下"则包含中国范围内的全部土地，类似于现在的全国。理雅各将"国"翻译为"a single State"（一个国家），将"天下"翻译为"throne"（王权）。赖发洛将之分别译为"Lands"（国土）和"all below heaven"（天下），刘殿爵则选择用"state"（国家）和"the Empire"（帝国）翻译。三位译者的翻译未能完全体现"国"和"天下"的区别。

【原文】14.14　孟子曰[1]："民为贵，社稷次之，君为轻。是故得乎丘民[2]而为天子，得乎天子为诸侯，得乎诸侯为大夫。诸侯危社稷，则变置。牺牲既成，粢盛既絜，祭祀以时，然而旱干水溢，则变置社稷[3]。"

【译文】孟子说："百姓最重要，土神、谷神为次，君主为轻。所以得到百姓的拥护便能做天子，得到天子的信任便能做诸侯，得到诸侯的信任便能做大夫。诸侯危及土神、谷神，那就改立。牺牲肥壮，祭品洁净，也依一定时令祭祀，但是还遭受旱灾水灾，那就改立土神、谷神。"

【英译】Mencius said, 'The people are the most important element in a nation；the spirits of the land and grain are the next；the sovereign is the lightest. Therefore to gain the peasantry is the way to become sovereign；to gain the sovereign is the way to become a prince of a State；to gain the prince of a State is the way to become a great officer. When a prince endangers the altars of the spirits of the land and grain，he is changed，and another appointed in his place. When the sacrificial victims have been perfect，the millet in its vessels all pure，and the sacrifices offered at their proper seasons，if yet there ensue drought，or the waters overflow，the spirits of the land and grain are changed，and others appointed in their place.'

【注释】

[1] 本章集中体现了孟子的民本思想。孟子认为人民最为重要，是天下的根本。其次才是社稷，君主最轻。君主要想统一天下，并且确保国家的长治久安，就应该把行仁政、得民心放在首位。

[2] "丘民"的内涵大体有两种，一种如朱熹所注："丘民，田野之民。"理雅各的译文和朱熹相类，将"丘民"翻译为"the peasantry"（农民）。另一种观点认为，"丘民"即众人，泛指国中所有的人。焦循注："《周礼·地官·小司徒》：'九夫为井，四井为邑，四邑为丘。'一邑四井，四邑故为十六井。然则丘民犹言邑民、乡民、国民也。"王念孙也在《广雅疏证》中指出："丘，众也。《孟子·尽心篇》：'得乎丘民而为天子'。《庄子·则阳篇》云：'丘里者，合十姓百名，以为风俗也。'《释名》云：'四邑为丘，丘，聚也'，皆众之义也。"赖发洛和刘殿爵则认为此处的"丘民"并非特指农民，分别将之翻译为"country folk"（国民）和"the multitudinous people"（众人）。这两种理解都可以接受，但将"丘民"理解为"全体国民"更确切。

[3] "变置社稷"即改立土神和谷神。朱熹注曰："社，土神。稷，谷神。……祭祀不失礼，而土谷之神不能为民御灾捍患，则毁其坛墠而更置之。"理雅各将"变置社稷"翻译为"the spirits of the land and grain are changed"（改立土谷之神），基本能体现其含义。相比较而言，刘殿爵的

"the altars should be replaced"（改立土谷之神的祭坛）更确切。

【原文】 14.15　孟子曰[1]："圣人[2]，百世之师也，伯夷、柳下惠是也。故闻伯夷之风者，顽夫廉，懦夫有立志；闻柳下惠之风者，薄夫敦，鄙夫宽。奋乎百世之上，百世之下，闻者莫不兴起也。非圣人而能若是乎？而况于亲炙之者[3]乎？"

【译文】 孟子说："圣人是百代的老师，伯夷和柳下惠就是这样的人。所以听到伯夷的高风亮节，贪得无厌的人会变得清廉，懦弱的人也会立定志向；听到柳下惠的高风亮节，刻薄的人也变得厚道，狭隘的人会变得心胸宽广。他们在百代以前发奋而为，百代而后的人没有不为之感动发奋的。不是圣人，能够像这样吗？更何况那些亲自接受熏陶的人呢？"

【英译】 Mencius said, 'A sage is the teacher of a hundred generations：—this is true of Po-î and Hûi of Liû-Hsiâ. Therefore when men now bear the character of Po-î, the corrupt become pure, and the weak acquire determination. When they hear the character of Hûi of Liû-Hsiâ the mean become generous, and the niggardly become liberal. Those two made themselves distinguished a hundred generations ago, and after a hundred generations, those who hear of them, are all aroused in this manner. Could such effects be produced by them, if they had not been sages？ And how much more did they affect those who were in contiguity with them, and felt their inspiring influence！'

【注释】

[1] 孟子在本章高度赞扬了圣人的影响力，认为他们的言行不仅能感召和熏陶同时代的人提高道德素质和自身修养，而且也为百世之后的人树立了效仿的榜样，鼓励他们奋发有为。

[2] "圣人"是儒家的最高理想人格，指那些才德兼备、知行完备的至

善之人。理雅各和刘殿爵选择用"sage"翻译它。"Sage"在英语里指"贤明、睿智的贤人或哲人",虽不能完全代表儒家理想人格"圣人"的内涵,但比较符合其主要特征。赖发洛则将之翻译为"A holy man","holy"的基本意思是"神圣的、虔诚的、供神用的",具有强烈的宗教色彩,用它来翻译儒家的最高理想人格"圣人"不妥当。

[3]"亲炙",朱熹注曰:"亲近而熏炙之也",即亲身接受教育和熏陶。理雅各将"亲炙之者"翻译为"those who were in contiguity with them, and felt their inspiring influence"(和他们接触,并亲自感受他们的熏陶和教育的人)。他的译文虽能体现出原文之意,但略显冗长、僵硬。赖发洛将之翻译为"the men whom they themselves fired"(他们亲自唤起热情的人),刘殿爵翻译为"those who were fortunate enough to have known them personally"(亲身接触过他们的人),二人的译文将原文之意准确、清楚地表达了出来。

【原文】 14.16　孟子曰[1]:"仁也者,人也[2]。合而言之,道也。"

【译文】 孟子说:"仁的意思就是人。合并起来讲,便是道。"

【英译】 Mencius said, 'Benevolence is the distinguishing characteristic of man. As embodied in man's conduct, it is called the path of duty.'

【注释】

[1] 本章主要讲了仁、人和道的关系。

[2] 朱熹注曰:"仁者,人之所以为人之理也。"理雅各的理解与之相类,将"仁也者,人也"翻译为"Benevolence is the distinguishing characteristic of man"(仁是人的本质属性)。如果这样理解,应当指明此处的"人"不是一般人,而是通过道德实践而达到的人。余纪元指出:"这句话的真正含义在于,'仁'是使一个人真正成其为人的品质。"即只有真正具备"仁"这一品质的人,才能成为真正意义上的人。赖发洛则按字面意思直

译为"Love is man"（仁是人），译文按字面意思翻译，不便于读者理解。刘殿爵译为"Benevolence means man"（仁的意思就是人）。在古代，"人"和"仁"不但读音相同，而且可以互训。他从自己丰富的训诂学知识出发，指出了"仁"和"人"在词义和语音上的关系。

【原文】 14.17　孟子曰[1]："孔子之去鲁，曰：'迟迟吾行也，去父母国之道也。'去齐，接淅而行，去他国之道也。"

【译文】 孟子说："孔子离开鲁国时，说：'我们慢慢走吧，这是离开祖国的态度。'离开齐国时，便不等把米淘完，沥干水分再走，这是离开别国的态度。"

【英译】 Mencius said, 'When Confucius was leaving Lû, he said, "I will set out by-and-by；"—this was the way in which to leave the State of his parents. When he was leaving Chʻî, he strained off with his hand the water in which his rice was being rinsed, took the rice, and went away；—this was the way in which to leave a strange State.'

【注释】

[1] 本章在《万章章句下》已经出现过，此处不再赘言。

【原文】 14.18　孟子曰[1]："君子[2]之厄于陈、蔡之间，无上下之交也。"

【译文】 孟子说："孔子被困在陈国、蔡国之间，是因为和两国的君臣都没有交往的缘故。"

【英译】 Mencius said, 'The reason why the superior man was reduced to straits between Chʻǎn and Tsʻâi was because neither the princes of the time nor their ministers sympathized or communicated with him.'

【注释】

[1] 孟子在此发表了他对孔子"陈蔡之困"的看法。

[2] "君子",指孔子。根据《史记·孔子世家》记载:"孔子迁于蔡三岁,吴伐陈。楚救陈,军于城父。闻孔子在陈、蔡之间,楚使人聘孔子。孔子将往拜礼,陈蔡大夫谋曰:'孔子贤者,所刺讥皆中诸侯之疾。今者久留陈蔡之间,诸大夫所设行皆非仲尼之意。今楚,大国也,来聘孔子。孔子用于楚,则陈蔡用事大夫危矣。'于是乃相与发徒役围孔子于野。不得行,绝粮。从者病,莫能兴。"《论语·卫灵公》亦记载,"在陈绝粮,从者病,莫能兴。子路愠见曰:'君子亦有穷乎?'孔子曰:'君子固穷,小人穷斯滥矣。'"理雅各、赖发洛和刘殿爵在译文中没有注明此处的"君子"是"孔子",不便于读者理解"君子"困于陈蔡之间的原因。赵甄陶将之翻译为"The gentleman (i.e. Confucius—tr.)",他通过编者注的形式指出了此处"君子"的特殊含义。

【原文】 14.19 貉稽曰[1]:"稽大不理于口[2]。"孟子曰:"无伤也。士憎兹多口[3]。诗云:'忧心悄悄,愠于群小。'孔子也。'肆不殄厥愠,亦不殒厥问。'文王也。"

【译文】 貉稽说:"我口碑很不好。"孟子说:"没有关系。士人总会遭到很多非议。《诗经》说:'忧愁沉沉压在心,小人对我怨又恨。'孔子就是这样的人。'别人的怨恨不消除,自己的名声也不倒。'文王就是这样的人。"

【英译】 Mo Ch'î said, 'Greatly am I from anything to depend upon from the mouths of men.' Mencius observed, 'There is no harm in that. Scholars are more exposed than others to suffer from the mouths of men. It is said, in the Book of Poetry, "My heart is disquieted and grieved, I am hated by the crowd of mean creatures." This might have been said by Confucius. And again, "Though he did not remove their wrath, he did not let fall his own fame."This might be said of king Wăn.'

【注释】

[1] 孟子举孔子和文王的例子劝告貉稽不要太在意别人的非议。孔子和文王是儒家推崇的圣人，是至善之人，但他们也不能摆脱流言蜚语的中伤。因而孟子劝诫貉稽不要过于在意别人的非议，而应该加强自身的道德修养，努力成为一个品德高尚的人。

[2]"不理于口"，赵岐注曰："为众口所训。理，赖也。"焦循进一步指出："不理于口，犹云不利于人口也。"杨伯峻指出："《广雅·释诂》云：'理，顺也。'王念孙《疏证》曾引《易经·说卦传》'和顺于道德而理于义'及《周礼·考工记·匠人》'永属不理孙谓之不行'以相印证，此'理'字亦可训'顺'，则'不理于口'犹言'不顺于人口。'"可见，基本上古今注家都认为"不理于口"指被人说的很坏。理雅各受赵岐、朱熹释"理"为"赖"的影响，将"理"翻译为"depend upon"（依赖），这样翻译过于机械，不便于读者理解。尽管他在注释中指出"理"的含义是"人们不光不夸他，还说他坏话"。赖发洛将"不理于口"翻译为"I am much ill used by men's mouths"（人们把我说的很坏）。他的译文能准确体现原文之意。刘殿爵对"不理于口"提出了创新性理解，将之翻译为"'I am not much of a speaker"（不擅长说话）。但他在书中没有给出这一创新性理解的依据。

[3]"憎"，朱熹指出："赵氏曰：'为士者，益多为众口所训'按此则'憎'当从'土'，今本皆从心，盖传写之误。"理雅各同意此说，把"士憎兹多口"翻译为"Scholars are more exposed than others to suffer from the mouths of men"（士人会比别人更多地遭受别人议论）。刘殿爵则根据原文字面意思将之翻译为"A Gentleman dislikes those who speak too much"（士人讨厌多嘴多舌）。下文的"诗云：'忧心悄悄，愠于群小。'孔子也。"可以看作是对"士憎兹多口"的举例说明。孟子先说士人更容易被小人中伤，接着举孔子的例子作说明，因而理雅各的翻译更符合文义。

【原文】14.20　孟子曰[1]："贤者以其昭昭使人昭昭[2]，今以其昏昏使人昭昭。"

【译文】孟子说："贤者用自己的彻底明白去使别人彻底明白，现在的人自己还稀里糊涂，却想让别人彻底明白。"

【英译】Mencius said, 'Anciently, men of virtue and talents by means of their own enlightenment made others enlightened. Nowadays, it is tried, while they are themselves in darkness, and by means of that darkness, to make others enlightened.'

【注释】

[1] 孟子认为，要教育和影响别人，首先要让自己彻底明白，才有可能说服别人，使别人信服。如果试图用一些自己还似懂非懂的思想观点去改变别人，只会劳而无功，适得其反。

[2] "昭昭"，朱熹注曰："明也。"理雅各将之翻译为"enlightenment"（觉悟），刘殿爵翻译为"clear understanding"（很明白），基本能体现其含义。赖发洛的理解则过于拘泥于原文的字面意思。他将"昭"翻译为"sunlight"（日光）。显然他的理解受《说文》"昭，日明也"的影响。但用"sunlight"翻译"昭昭"，不便于读者理解原文究竟要说什么。

【原文】14.21　孟子谓高子曰[1]："山径之蹊间，介然用之而成路[2]；为间不用，则茅塞之矣。今茅塞子之心矣。"

【译文】孟子对高子说："山间的小径阻隔不通，一直走的话就会变成路；隔一段时间不走，就会被茅草堵塞。现在茅草也把你的心堵塞了。"

【英译】Mencius said to the disciple Kâo, 'There are the footpaths along the hills;—if suddenly they be used, they become roads; and if, as suddenly they are not used, the wild grass fills them up. Now, the wild grass fills up your mind.'

【注释】

[1] 孟子在本章以山间小径譬喻，强调修身要持之以恒的道理。

[2] 对于本句有多种断句方式。赵岐注曰："山径，山之岭，有微蹊介然，人遂用之不止，则蹊成为路。"显然，他将本句断为"山径之蹊间介然，用之而成路。"孔广森在《经学卮言》说："间介，盖隔绝之意。径，路也。蹊，足迹也。"他将本句断为"山径之蹊间介，然用之而成路。"杨伯峻指出："《荀子·修身篇》云：'善在身，介然必以自好也。'此'间介然'当于荀子之'介然'同义，都是意志专一而不旁骛之貌。"因而他将本句断为："山径之蹊，间介然用之而成路。"梁涛则以"阻隔"释"间"，以"专一"释"介然"，并将本句断句为："山径之蹊间，介然用之而成路。"但朱熹认为，"介然，倏然之顷也"，即强调变化快。刘殿爵的理解与朱熹相类，将之翻译为"A trail through the mountains, if used, becomes a path in a short time"（山间小道，如果有人走，很快就会变成路）。赖发洛亦持此观点，将之翻译为"If a track across the hills is used, it soon grows to be a road"（如果山间小路有人走，它很快就会变成路）。理雅各亦持此观点。结合下文"为间不用，则茅塞之矣"，即短时间不走，就会被茅草堵塞可知，孟子是在论证"意志专一，持之以恒"的重要性，因而将"介然"理解为持之以恒更准确。

【原文】14.22 高子曰[1]："禹之声尚文王之声。"孟子曰："何以言之？"曰："以追蠡[2]。"曰："是奚足哉？城门之轨，两马之力与[3]？"

【译文】高子说："禹的音乐胜过文王的音乐。"孟子说："这样说的根据是什么？"答道："因为禹的钟钮都快断了。"孟子说："这个怎么足以证明呢？城门下的车迹那样深，难道是几匹马的力量吗？"

【英译】The disciple Kâo said, 'The music of Yü was better than that of king Wǎn.' Mencius observed, 'On what ground do you say so?' And the other replied, 'Because at the pivot the knob of Yü's bells is nearly worn through.' Mencius said, 'How can that be a sufficient proof? Are the ruts at the gate of a city made by a single two-horsed chariot?'

【注释】

[1] 孟子告诫高子看待问题要全面、透彻，不要被事物的表面现象所迷惑，盲目妄下结论。

[2] 邓球柏指出，古今注家对"追蠡"的理解大体有三："一说，为钟钮欲断貌；一说，为器物剥蚀貌；一说，为击钟留下的痕迹。"理雅各、赖发洛和刘殿爵皆取磨损严重之意，赵甄陶还进一步解释"The metallic ropes of the bells handed down from Yu are worn thin, almost to the point of breaking"（尧时传下来的钟钮都磨细了，快要断了）。

[3] "两马"，赵岐以"国马""公马"解之；朱熹注曰："一车所驾也。"理雅各的理解与朱熹相类，将之翻译为"a single two-horsed chariot"（一辆双马战车）。赖发洛和刘殿爵的译文亦持此说。梁涛认为："犹言'车马'。两：'辆'之古字，指车。"

【原文】 14.23　齐饥[1]。陈臻曰："国人皆以夫子将复为发棠，殆不可复?"孟子曰："是为冯妇也。晋人有冯妇者，善搏虎，卒为善士。则之野，有众逐虎[2]。虎负嵎，莫之敢撄。望见冯妇，趋而迎之。冯妇攘臂下车。众皆悦之，其为士者笑之。"

【译文】 齐国发生饥荒。陈臻说："齐国人都认为先生会再次请求齐王打开棠邑的粮仓救济百姓，或许不会那么做了吧?"孟子说："那样做就和冯妇一样了。晋国人冯妇，善打老虎，后来成为善人。有次去野外，很多人在追逐老虎。老虎背靠山角，没有人敢靠近。他们远远看见冯妇，忙跑过去迎接。冯妇也撸起袖子，伸出胳膊，走下车来。大家都很高兴，可是士人都讥笑他。"

【英译】 When Ch'î was suffering from famine, Ch'ǎn Tsin said to

Mencius，'The people are all thinking that you，Master，will again ask that the granary of T'ang be opened for them. I apprehend you will not do so a second time.' Mencius said，'To do it would be to act like Fǎng Fû. There was a man of that name in Tsin，famous for his skill in seizing tigers. Afterwards he became a scholar of reputation，and going once out to the wild country，he found the people all in pursuit of a tiger. The tiger took refuge in a corner of a hill，where no one dared to attack him，but when they saw Fǎng Fû，they ran and met him. Fǎng Fû immediately bared his arms，and descended from the carriage. The multitude were pleased with him，but those who were scholars laughed at him.'

【注释】

[1] 孟子曾苦口婆心地劝说齐王实行仁政，成为大有作为之君，但后来发现，齐王不能实践他的政治理想，因而举冯妇的例子表明自己离开齐国的决心。他同时告诫陈臻，人要懂得审时度势、进退合宜，否则就会贻笑大方。

[2] 古往今来，有不少学者对本句如何断句展开争论。本文所标注的标点在当前比较流行，受东汉赵岐和宋人朱熹的影响。东汉赵岐注曰："善士者，以善搏虎有勇名也，故进之以为士。"朱熹注云："卒为善士，后能改行为善也。"虽然二人对"卒为善士"的内涵理解不同，但都认为"善士"应连读。理雅各、赖发洛、刘殿爵、亨顿以及赵甄陶等的《孟子》英译本皆持这种断句方法，认为"善士"应连读，"则"字连下。他们对文义的理解也和朱熹相类，认为善于打虎的冯妇最后成为善士，不再打虎了。宋人刘昌诗的《芦蒲笔记》和周密的《志雅堂杂抄》则提出了第二种断句方法，即将"善"和"士"分开，以"卒为善，士则之"断句。今人秦桦林、凌瑜则提出了第三种断句方法："卒为善士则。之野，有众逐虎。"

【原文】14.24 孟子曰[1]："口之于味也，目之于色也，耳之于声也，鼻之于臭也[2]，四肢之于安佚也，性也，有命焉，君子不谓性也。仁之于父子也，义之于君臣也，礼之于宾主也，知之于贤者也，圣人之于天道也，命也。有性焉，君子不谓命也[3]。"

【译文】孟子说："口对于美味，眼对于美色，耳对于好听的声音，鼻子对于好闻的气味，四肢对于舒服安逸的喜好，都是天性。但是是否能得到，却属于命运，所以君子不会把它们当作天性而去强求它们。仁对于父子，义对于君臣，礼对于宾主，智慧对于贤者，圣人对于天道，能够实现与否，属于命运，但也是天性的必然，所以君子不把他们当作命运使然。"

【英译】Mencius said, 'For the mouth to desire sweet tastes，the eye to desire beautiful colours，the ear to desire pleasant sounds，the nose to desire fragrant odours，and the four limbs to desire ease and rest；—these things are natural. But there is the appointment of Heaven in connexion with them，and the superior man does not say of his pursuit of them，"It is my nature." The exercise of love between father and son，the observance of righteousness between sovereign and minister，the rules of ceremony between guest and host，the display of knowledge in recognising the talented，and the fulfilling the heavenly course by the sage；—these are the appointment of Heaven. But there is an adaptation of our nature for them. The superior man does not say，in reference to them，"It is the appointment of Heaven."'

【注释】

[1]"性"和"命"是孟子哲学思想的两个重要概念，二者既有区别又有联系。针对时人"性""命"不分，"性""命"混用的现实，孟子提出了他的"性""命"观。他认为，耳目之欲等自然属性，虽可称为性，但属于"求在外者也"（《孟子·尽心上》），所以孟子不称之为性，而宁谓之命。仁

义理智等美德"求则得之，舍则失之"（《孟子·告子上》），是"求在我者也"。（《孟子·尽心上》）因而孟子认为它们属于性而不应称之命。

[2] 从本义上看，"味""色"和"声"指的是一切味道、颜色和声音，没有美丑、香臭之分，但从文义看，它们都是人类天生的各种物质欲望，是人对美好事物的本能追求。正如杨伯峻所说："'味''色''声'都是中性词（不含美恶之义），但用在此处，则指'美味''美色''乐声'，此种用法，以前诸章不乏其例。'臭'字亦如此。'臭'的本义是'气味'，不论香臭都叫'臭'，此则专指芬香之气。"理雅各的译文和杨伯峻的理解相类似，而刘殿爵则将它们全部翻译为"tastes"（味道）、"colours"（颜色）、"sounds"（声音）和"smells"（气味）。相比较而言，理雅各的译文更符合原文之意。

[3] 关于性和命的关系，徐复观解释说："'生而即有''主宰在人之自身'是性的含义；'莫之致而至''不能操之在己'是命的含义。'生而即有'与'莫之致而至'的意思是一样的，所以性与命相通的含义就是'生而即有，莫之致而至'。命与性的不同之处在于，称为命的不能操之在己，称为性的主宰在人之自身。"可见，普通人和孟子对"性"和"命"的认识主要区别是：前者认为凡是"生而即有"的东西都属于"性"的范畴，凡是"莫之致而至"者皆是"命"。他们只看到"性"与"命"相通的一面，但忽视了二者的区别，故常将之混用。而孟子强调、君子认可的"性"，必须具备"生而即有"和"求在我者"两个条件。因而君子所谓的"性"则是将人和动物区别看的"性"，也就是孟子所谓的人性善的"性"。

孟子对"性"和"命"的论述主要集中在"性也。有命焉，君子不谓性也"和"命也。有性焉，君子不谓命也"两句。理雅各认为，耳目之欲是天生的，但有天命与之相关，君子不说追寻这些欲望的满足是自己的本性。仁义理智天道是天命，但是人性与之相适应，因而君子不认为它们是天命。他根据孟子思想体系对原文做了一些必要的补充，使译文更便于读者理解。赖发洛过于拘泥于原文字面意思，分别译为"these are our nature. But when the Bidding comes to him, a gentleman does not plead his nature."（这些耳目之欲等都是人性。但是，当命降临到他身上，君子不声称那些是他的性）和 "these are the Bidding. But what is nature in him a gentleman does not plead is the Bidding"（仁义理智天道都是命。但是对于那些他天生就具备的东西，君子不会称为命）。这样翻译显然和孟子的思想体系不符合。刘殿爵的译文强调"性"与"命"的联系，即"性"中有"命"，"命"中有"性"。时人所谓的"性"通常是耳目之欲等自然属性，君子看到在生而即有这一点上，固可称之为性，但它们同时含有"命"的因素在里面，因而君子认为不能称之为"性"。同样，仁义理智天道等虽可被称为"命"，但其中又包含"性"的因素在里面，因而君子也不称之为"命"。他的译文能较为清楚地表达原文意思。三位译者对"性"和"命"的内涵把握不确切。第一个"性"主要强调人的自然属性，是普通人对"生而即有"的事物的统称，而赖发洛和刘殿爵却将之翻译为 "our nature"（我们的本性）和 "human nature"（人性）不妥。相比较而言，理雅各的 "natural"（天生的）虽改变了词性，但能准确表达第一个"性"的内涵。第二个"性"和第三个"性"是孟子在突出人和动物的区别的基础上提出，是人性而非泛指一切"生而即有"的东西，理雅各和赖发洛都准确将之翻译为 "our nature"（人性），但刘殿爵却将之泛泛译为 "nature"（本性），扩大了其内涵。同"性"一样，三个"命"的含义也不同。理雅各将之统一翻译为 "appointment of Heaven"，赖发洛翻译为 "Bidding"，刘殿爵翻译为 "Decree"（天命）。大写的 "Heaven" 和 "Decree" 通常会让人联想到基督教的上帝、天堂以及基督教的教义或纪律法令，与孟子之意不符。而 "Bidding" 虽在字义上能对应"命"，但与孟子强调的"命"的内涵相距甚远。

【原文】14.25 浩生不害问曰[1]："乐正子何人也？"孟子曰："善人也，信人也。""何谓善？何谓信？"曰："可欲之谓善[2]，有诸己之谓信[3]，充实之谓美，充实而有光辉之谓大，大而化之之谓圣，圣而不可知之之谓神[4]。乐正子，二之中、四之下也。"

【译文】浩生不害问："乐正子是什么样的人？"孟子说："善人，信人。""怎么叫善？怎么叫信呢？"回答说："值得我们追求的便叫作'善'；值得追求的善存在于他本身，便叫作'信'；那些善充满他的本身叫作'美'；充满并且光辉地展现出来便是'大'；展现出来了，又能融会贯通，便是'圣'；圣到了神妙不可预测的境界，便是'神'。乐正子处于善和信之间，其它四者之下。"

【英译】Hâo-shǎng Pû-hâi asked, saying, 'What sort of man is Yo-chǎng?' Mencius replied, 'He is a good man, a real man.' 'What do you mean by "A good man," "A real man?"' The reply was, 'A man who commands our liking is what is called a good man. He whose goodness is part of himself is what is called a real man. He whose goodness has been filled up is what is called beautiful man. He whose completed goodness is brightly displayed is what is called a great man. When this great man exercises a transforming influence, he is what is called a sage. When the sage is beyond our knowledge, he is what is called a spirit-man. Yo-chǎng is between the two first characters, and below the four last.'

【注释】

[1] 孟子将道德修养的境界分为善、信、美、大、圣和神六个层次，并指出它们之间的关系是逐级递增的，因而要想成为圣人、神人，就不能好高骛远，要立足当下，努力奋进，逐渐提高自身境界。

[2] "可欲之谓善"，焦循指出："可欲即可好，其人善则可好，犹其人不善则可恶。其人可恶，即为恶人；其人可好，即为好人。"理雅各将之翻译为 "A man who commands our liking is what is called a good man."（值得我们喜欢的人，我们称之为善人）他认为此句话是针对人而发，旨在说明"善人"的标准。戴明玺批判焦循"善恶依好恶转移，纯乎情感中事，而无客观之标准。此与李卓吾'以吾之是非为是非'同趣，而与孟子原意相违。"他

认为焦循过分夸大了孟子对个人"好""恶"的强调，没有看到孟子的"可好"与"可恶"以"善"和"不善"为依据。理雅各所谓的"值得我们喜欢的人"就暗含着"善"这一判断标准。赖发洛将"可欲之谓善"翻译为"Whatever we like we call good"（我们称自己喜欢的所有东西为善）。他的译文才是以"我"的好恶作为判断善恶的依据，从而使善恶失去了客观标准。刘殿爵从孟子的整个思想体系出发，将之翻译为"The desirable is called 'good'"（我们称悦人心意的人为善人）。孟子认为"理义之悦我心，犹刍豢之悦我口"，可见"悦人心意的人"必是具备和践行"理义"的人，因而可以称其为善人。

[3] "有诸己之谓信"，朱熹注曰："凡所谓善，皆实有之，如恶恶臭，如好好色，是则可谓信人矣。"显然，他认为善真正存在于人身上就是信。理雅各和刘殿爵的译文与之相似，认为"身上的确存在善的人就是信人"。而赖发洛认为"when it is inborn we call it truth"（我们生而具备的善就是信）。"善"是道德修养的第一个层次，以之为基础继续提升自己就可以成为信人。可见善和信的关系是递进而非并列，因而理雅各和刘殿爵的理解更确切。

[4] "神"是会意字，从示申。"申"是天空中闪电形，古人因闪电变化莫测，威力无穷，故称之为神。孟子对"神"的定义是"圣而不可知之"，显然取"神"的神妙不可测度之意。理雅各将之翻译为"spirit-man"，具有较强的宗教色彩。赖发洛将之翻译为"inspiration"，"inspiration"的常用义是灵感，还可以指宗教上的神灵启示，与此处"神"的含义不甚符合。刘殿爵将之翻译为"divine"，虽然它也是宗教常用词，但有"超凡的，完美的"之意，能体现孟子所谓"神"的重要特征。

【原文】 14.26 孟子曰[1]："逃墨必归于杨，逃杨必归于儒[2]。归，斯受之而已矣。今之与杨、墨辩者，如追放豚，既入其苙，又从而招之[3]。"

【译文】孟子说："离开墨家必定会归向杨朱一派，离开杨朱一派必定会归向儒家。归向儒家，接受他就是了。现在和杨朱、墨家辩论，就好像追赶走失的猪一样，已经关进猪圈了，还要用绳子把它们的脚困住。"

【英译】Mencius said，'Those who are fleeing from the errors of Mo naturally turn to Yang，and those who are fleeing from the errors of Yang naturally turn to orthodoxy. When they so turn，they should at once and simply be received. Those who nowadays dispute with the followers of Yang and Mo do so as if they were pursuing a stray pig，the leg of which，after they have got it to enter the pen，they proceed to tie.'

【注释】

[1] 孟子认为墨家主张兼爱，无亲疏之别，是最错误的学说。信奉者很容易认识到其缺陷，从而转向与之相对的杨朱学说。杨朱主张为我、贵己、重生，否认个人对君主的义务，也是错误的。认识到二家的缺陷，人们开始体会到儒家学说的正确性，最终必然归附儒家。对于这些归附者，要持一种宽容的态度，反对大力打击和限制。

[2] "儒"，指的是孔子首创的儒家学派，前代译者各自选择他们自以为相近的英语单词翻译它。例如，理雅各将之翻译为"orthodoxy"（正统派学说），赖发洛将之翻译为"scholarship"（学问）。他们的译文从不同方面体现了"儒"的一些重要特征，但不全面。随着孔子地位的提升以及儒家文化在国外的广泛传播，学者们对"儒家"的翻译也逐渐统一和固定。现在，绝大多数汉学家和译者都选择用"Confucianist"来翻译"儒家"。"Confucianist"不仅已经逐渐被国内外学者所接受，甚至对西方普通读者来说，它也不再是什么陌生的术语了。刘殿爵将"儒"翻译为"Confucianist"就是这一趋势的体现。

[3] "招"，朱熹注曰："罥也，羁其足也。言彼既来归，而又追咎其既往之失也。"理雅各和刘殿爵的译文与之相似，取"绑住它的脚"之意。而

赖发洛取"招"的本义，将之翻译为"keep beckoning to him"（继续向他招手）。相比较而言，理雅各和刘殿爵的理解更贴切。

【原文】14.27　孟子曰[1]："有布缕之征，粟米之征，力役之征。君子[2]用其一，缓其二。用其二而民有殍，用其三而父子离[3]。"

【译文】孟子说："有征收布帛的赋税，有征收粮食的赋税，还有征发人力的。君子采用其中的一项，就暂时不用其他两项了。同时用两种，百姓就会有饿死的，如果同时用三种，父子就会骨肉离散。"

【英译】Mencius said, 'There are the exactions of hempen-cloth and silk, of grain, and of personal service. The prince requires but one of these at once, deferring the other two. If he require two of them at once, then the people die of hunger. If he require the three at once, then fathers and sons are separated.'

【注释】

[1] 民为国之本，取之无度，则国危。孟子并不反对为了维持国家的正常运转而向百姓征收赋税，他强调取之有度，反对君主为一己私利，横征暴敛，置百姓生死于不顾。

[2] "君子"，理雅各认为特指"君主"，因而将之翻译为"The prince"，而赖发洛和刘殿爵则选择用"gentleman"翻译。本章旨在说服国君行仁政，取民有度。结合文义，理雅各的理解更确切。

[3] "用其二而民有殍，用其三而父子离"，朱熹注曰："征赋之法，岁有常数，然布缕取之于夏，粟米取之于秋，力役取之于冬，当各以其时。"孟子认为这三种赋税形式可根据实际情况，选择一种，不能同时使用两种，更不能同时使用三种，赖发洛将之翻译为"If two are levied the people die of hunger；if all three are levied fathers and sons are parted."（如果征收两种，百姓就会饿死；如果征收三种，父子就会分离）他的译文不如理雅各的"如

果同时使用两种，就有百姓会饿死；如果同时使用三种，父子就会离散"准确。

【原文】 14.28 孟子曰[1]："诸侯之宝[2]三：土地、人民、政事。宝珠玉者，殃必及身。"

【译文】 孟子说："诸侯有三样宝：土地、人民和政事。以珍珠、美玉为宝贝的，祸害一定会降到他身上。"

【英译】 Mencius said, 'The precious things of a prince are three；—the territory，the people，the government and its business. If one value as most precious pearls and jade，calamity is sure to befall him.'

【注释】

[1] 土地、人民和政事是构成国家的最重要因素，理应是君主最珍贵、最爱惜的东西。如果君主以它们为宝，就会实现国家的长治久安。相反，如果君主不珍视土地，爱惜百姓，劳于政事，而去一味追求珠玉，就会变得贪得无厌，酿成国危身亡的悲剧。

[2] "宝"，指珍爱、珍视的东西，是就人而言，因人的珍爱才使其获得价值。理雅各将之翻译为 "precious things"（珍爱的东西）。赖发洛和刘殿爵将之翻译为 "treasures"（珍爱之物）。这两种翻译都可以将人对物发自内心的珍惜和喜爱之情表达出来。

【原文】 14.29 盆成括仕于齐[1]，孟子曰："死矣，盆成括[2]！"盆成括见杀，门人问曰："夫子何以知其将见杀？"曰："其为人也小有才[3]，未闻君子之大道也，则足以杀其躯而已矣。"

【译文】 盆成括在齐国做官，孟子说："盆成括要死了！"盆成括被杀，学生问道："老师怎么会知道他将会被杀？"答道："他这个人有点小聪明，但是没有听说过君子的大道，那就足够杀害自己的身体罢了。"

【英译】 P'an-ch'ǎng Kwo having obtained an official situation in

Ch'î, Mencius said, 'He is a dead man, that P'an-ch'ǎng Kwo!' P'an-ch'ǎng Kwo being put to death, the disciples asked, saying, 'How did you know, Master, that he would meet with death?' Mencius replied, 'He was a man, who had a little ability, but had not learned the great doctrines of the superior man.—He was just qualified to bring death upon himself, but for nothing more.'

【注释】

[1] 孟子认为，人贵闻道。只有真正习得君子之道，谦虚待人，才会避免恃才妄作，招人怨恨。

[2] "死矣，盆成括"是孟子的预言和猜测，而非孟子在陈述盆成括已经死了这一客观事实。理雅各将之翻译为"He is a dead man"（他死定了），刘殿爵翻译为"He is certain to meet his death"（盆成括肯定会死的）。译文将原文的暗含之意准确传达了出来。

[3] "小有才"，即有小聪明。理雅各将之翻译为"a man，who had a little ability"（有点能力的人），赖发洛翻译为"a man of small wiles"（一个只会耍阴谋诡计的人），刘殿爵翻译为"a man with limited talent"（能力有限的人）。从文义上看，"其为人也小有才"和"未闻君子之大道也"之间是转折关系，因而理雅各和刘殿爵的翻译似乎更能体现孟子在评价人上的公正和全面。

【原文】 14.30　孟子之滕[1]，馆于上宫[2]。有业屦于牖上，馆人求之弗得。或问之曰："若是乎从者之廋也？"曰："子以是为窃屦来与？"曰："殆非也。夫子之设科也[3]，往者不追，来者不拒。苟以是心至，斯受之而已矣。"

【译文】 孟子在滕国，居住在上宫。有一双没有织好的草鞋放在窗台上，旅馆的人找不到了。有人问孟子说："是跟随您的人把它藏起来了吧？"孟子说："你以为他们是为了偷草鞋而来吗？"答道："大概不是。

（不过）您开设课程，（对于学生）去的不追问，来的不拒绝。只要他们怀着学习的心来，便接受了。"

【英译】When Mencius went to T'ǎng, he was lodged in the Upper palace. A sandal in the process of making had been placed there in a window，and when the keeper of the place came to look for it，he could not find it. On this，some one asked Mencius，saying，'Is it thus that your followers pilfer?' Mencius replied，'Do you think that they came here to pilfer the sandal?' The man said，'I apprehend not. But you，Master，having arranged to give lessons，do not go back to inquire into the past，and you do not reject those who come to you. If they come with the mind to learn，you receive them without any more ado.'

【注释】

[1] 同孔子一样，孟子也是一位著名的教育家，"往者不追，来者不拒"是他所遵循的重要教育理念。

[2] "上宫"，赵岐注云："楼也。"朱熹认为："上宫，别宫名。"焦循指出："此'上宫'当如'上舍'，谓上等之馆舍也。"刘殿爵的理解同朱熹，认为"上宫"指宫室之名，将之音译，而理雅各和赖发洛翻译为"the Upper palace"，显然他们二人也认为上宫是宫殿之名。

[3] "夫子"，杨伯峻认为是别人对"孟子"的尊称，即"你老人家"。理雅各的译文与之相似，将之翻译为"you, Master"（老先生）。但赵岐注曰："孟子曰：'夫我设教授之科，教人以道德也。'"根据他的注解，他所依据的《孟子》版本中，"夫子"实际上是"夫予"。"夫"是发语词，"予"是孟子自称。赖发洛和刘殿爵的译文与之相类，梁涛也持这种观点，将本句录为"夫予之设科也"。

【原文】14.31　孟子曰[1]："人皆有所不忍，达之于其所忍，仁也；人皆有所不为，达之于其所为，义也。人能充无欲害人之心，而仁不可胜用也；人能充无穿逾[2]之心，而义不可胜用也；人能充无受尔汝[3]之实，无所往而不为义也。士未可以言而言，是以言餂之也，可以言而不言，是以不言餂之也，是皆穿逾之类也。”

【译文】孟子说：“每个人都有不忍心干的事，把它扩充到他所忍心的事上便是仁；每个人都有不耻做的事，把它扩充到耻于做的事上，便是义。人能够扩充不想害人的心，仁就用不尽了；人能扩充不愿挖洞跳墙的心，义就用不尽了；人能够扩充不受别人轻蔑的言行，无论到哪里都会合于义了。对于不可以言谈的士人，却同他言谈，这是用言语来诱取别人的想法，可以同他言谈却不去同他言谈，这是用沉默来诱取别人的想法，这些都是属于挖洞跳墙这一类型的。”

【英译】Mencius said, "All men have some things which they cannot bear; —extend that feeling to what they can bear, and benevolence will be the result. All men have some things which they will not do; —extend that feeling to the things which they do, and righteousness will be the result. If a man can give full development to the feeling which makes him shrink from injuring others, his benevolence will be more than can be called into practice. If he can give full development to the feeling which refuses to break through, or jump over, a wall, his righteousness will be more than can be called into practice. If he can give full development to the real feeling of dislike with which he receives the salutation, "Thou," "Thou," he will act righteously in all places and circumstances. When a scholar speaks what he ought not to speak, by guile of speech seeking to gain some end; and when he does not speak what he ought to speak, by guile of silence seeking to gain some end; —both these cases are of a piece with breaking through a neighbour's wall.'

【注释】

[1] 孟子在本章首先用浅显易懂的语言对"仁"和"义"下了定义，接着教导人们应当如何扩充生而具备的"恻隐之心"和"羞恶之心"以达到仁义的境界。

[2] "穿逾"的字面意思是挖墙洞和爬墙头，代指偷窃行为。赵岐注曰："穿墙逾屋，奸利之心也。"朱熹亦认为："穿，穿穴。逾，逾墙。皆为盗之事也。"《论语·阳货》有："色厉而内荏，譬诸小人，其穿窬之盗也与。"可见，在中国古代，"穿逾"代指偷窃行为，因而在翻译的时候，应当体现这一含义，否则不便于那些对中国传统文化知之甚少的外国读者理解。刘殿爵按字面意思将"穿逾"翻译为"boring holes and climbing over walls"（挖墙洞和爬墙头），赵甄陶则将之意译"stealing"（偷东西），都不如赖发洛的"stealing through or climbing over"（通过挖墙洞和爬墙头偷东西）更清楚易懂。

[3] "尔汝"，朱熹注曰："盖尔汝人所轻贱之称，人虽或有所贪昧隐忍而甘受之者，然其中心必有惭忿而不肯受之之实。人能即此而推之，使其充满无所亏缺，则无适而非义矣。"可见，"尔汝"是轻蔑的称呼，表示对别人的鄙视和不尊敬。理雅各选择用两个重复的"Thou"来翻译"尔汝"，赖发洛则选择用"thou"及其宾格形式"thee"翻译，二人的译文未能体现轻蔑之意。虽然刘殿爵也选择用"thou"和"thee"翻译"尔汝"，但是他在译文中指明了这种称呼是"the actual humiliation"（实际的耻辱）。相比较而言，刘殿爵的译文能将"尔汝"的字面意思和所蕴含的鄙视之意都清楚地表达出来。

【原文】 14.32 孟子曰[1]："言近而指远者，善言也；守约而施博[2]者，善道也。君子之言也，不下带[3]而道存焉；君子之守，修其身而天下平。人病舍其田而芸人之田——所求于人者重，而所以自任者轻。"

【译文】孟子说："言语浅近，意义却深远，这是善言；操持简约，恩施广大，是善道。君子的言语，讲的是常见之事，却蕴含着深刻的道理；君子的操守，修养自己而使天下太平。人的毛病就在于舍弃自己的田地不耕，却去耕别人的田——要求别人的很多，自己承担的却很少。"

【英译】Mencius said, "Words which are simple, while their meaning is far-reaching, are good words. Principles which, as held, are compendious, while their application is extensive, are good principles. The words of the superior man do not go below the girdle, but great principles are contained in them. The principle which the superior man holds is that of personal cultivation, but the kingdom is thereby tranquillized. The disease of men is this:—that they neglect their own fields, and go to weed the fields of others, and that what they require from others is great, while what they lay upon themselves is light.'

【注释】

[1] 大道至简，简以至用。修身虽然是儒者终生力求的事情，但修身的方法却简单明了。孟子认为修身应从善言和善道两个方面展开。所谓善言就是言语浅近而意义深远的语言，而善道则指所坚守的原则简单，而产生的效果广大。善言、善道所追求的就是用最简单的途径达到修身这一伟大目标。

[2] "施博"，刘殿爵、理雅各和赖发洛认为是"应用范围广阔"。但杨伯峻认为："《易乾》：'见龙在田，德施普也。'《疏》云：'道德恩施能普遍也。'《左传》僖公二十四年云：'报者倦矣，施者未厌。'杜《注》云：'施，功劳也。有劳则望报过甚。'此'施'字之义与上两'施'字同，'恩惠'之意。"因而，他指出"施博"应理解为"效果广大"。赵甄陶的译文与之相类，将之翻译为"achieving a wide-spread effect"。从前后文的逻辑呼应看，将"施博"理解为"效果广大"更能呼应前文的"指远"，即意义深远。

[3] "不下带"，朱熹注曰："古人视不下于带，则带之上，乃目前常见至近之处也。举目前之近事，而至理存焉，所以为言近而指远也。"可见，"不下带"比喻眼前常见之事。刘殿爵将"不下带"直译为"never go as far as below the sash"（不会在束腰带以下），但未进一步解释说明其比喻义。理雅各和赖发洛虽然也是直译，但是为了便于读者理解，他们在注释中引用《礼记》内容对此项规定作了简要介绍。

【原文】14.33　孟子曰[1]："尧舜，性者也；汤武，反之也[2]。动容周旋中礼者，盛德之至也。哭死而哀，非为生者也。经德不回[3]，非以干禄也。言语必信，非以正行也。君子行法，以俟命而已矣。"

【译文】孟子说："尧舜是出于本性，汤武是经过努力回复本性的结果。动作容貌无不合于礼，是德性的最高表现。为死者悲哀地哭泣，不是做给活着的人看的。遵从道德而不违背，不是为了谋求官职。说话一定守信用，不是为了让别人知道自己行为端正。君子依法度而行，以等待天命。"

【英译】Mencius said, 'Yâo and Shun were what they were by nature; T'ang and Wû were so by returning to natural virtue. When all the movements, in the countenance and every turn of the body, are exactly what is proper, that shows the extreme degree of the complete virtue. Weeping for the dead should be from real sorrow, and not because of the living. The regular path of virtue is to be pursued without any bend, and from no view to emolument. The words should all be necessarily sincere, not with any desire to do what is right. The superior man performs the law of right, and thereby waits simply for what has been appointed.'

【注释】

[1] 本章是对孔子"古之学者为己，今之学者为人"（《论语·宪问》）思想的展开与发展。孟子认为尧、舜、汤、武的举止仪容、进退揖让全都符合礼节是他们圣德的自然体现，而非为了获得美名、爵禄和别人的赞扬。

[2]"反之也"，朱熹注曰："反之者，修为以复其性而至于圣人也。"即通过努力修身使得善良的本性重新返还自身。赵甄陶将之翻译为"recovered it through self-cultivation"（通过修身重新获得），他的译文准确体现了"反之也"的特点。刘殿爵和理雅各仅强调"returned to"（重新回归），但没有指明通过什么方式回归。

[3]"经"，行也。"回"，违逆，违背。如《诗经·大雅·常武》有："徐方不回，王曰还归。"郑玄笺曰："回，犹违也。"可见，"经德不回"即遵从道德而不违背。赵岐则以"回邪"或"曲"释此"回"字，理雅各的理解同赵岐，将"回"翻译为"bend"（弯曲），赖发洛则取"回"的返回之意，将之翻译为"turning back"，相比较而言，刘殿爵的译文"follows unswervingly the path of virtue"（坚定不移地遵循道德）更准确。

【原文】 14.34 孟子曰[1]："说大人[2]，则藐之，勿视其巍巍然。堂高数仞[3]，榱题数尺，我得志，弗为也。食前方丈，侍妾数百人，我得志，弗为也。般乐饮酒，驱骋田猎，后车千乘，我得志，弗为也。在彼者，皆我所不为也；在我者，皆古之制也，吾何畏彼哉？"

【译文】 孟子说："游说达官显贵，就要藐视他，不要把他高高在上的地位放在眼里。殿堂几丈高，屋檐几尺宽，我如果得志，不追求这些。食物堆满桌，服侍的姬妾有几百，我如果得志，不追求这些。饮酒作乐，驰驱打猎，跟随的车子上千辆，我如果得志，不追求这些。他们所追求的，都不是我所追求的；我所追求的，都符合古代的制度，我为什么要怕他们呢？"

【英译】Mencius said，'Those who give counsel to the great should despise them，and not look at their pomp and display. Halls several times eight cubits high，with beams projecting several cubits；—these，if my wishes were to be realized，I would not have. Food spread before me over ten cubits square，and attendants and concubines to the amount of hundreds；—these，though my wishes were realized，I would not have. Pleasure and wine，and the dash of hunting，with thousands of chariots following after me；—these，though my wishes were realized，I would not have. What they esteem are what I would have nothing to do with；what I esteem are the rules of the ancients.—Why should I stand in awe of them？'

【注释】

[1] 游说达官显贵，最重要的是保持自己的气节和自信，不要畏惧他们的位高权重。他们喜好的仅仅是华美的宫室、奢侈的物质享受以及纵情享乐的生活，这些都是士人所鄙弃的荒芜之事。士人精通古代制度，言行举止符合礼制，因而根本不需要在他们面前卑躬屈膝。

[2] "说大人"，即劝说权贵听从自己的建议。刘殿爵将之翻译为"speaking to men of consequence"（和诸侯交谈），不如理雅各的"give counsel to the great"（为诸侯出谋划策）准确。

[3] "堂高数仞"，焦循注曰："经传称堂高者，皆指堂阶而言。"理雅各、赖发和刘殿爵都选择用"hall"翻译"堂"。虽然"hall"也有礼堂、走廊之意，但古代建筑物的"堂阶"是外在于殿堂之外的台阶，而非内包于建筑物之内，译文未能再现其特点。

【原文】 14.35　孟子曰[1]："养心[2]莫善于寡欲。其为人也寡欲，虽有不存焉者，寡矣[3]；其为人也多欲，虽有存焉者，寡矣。"

【译文】孟子说："养心的方法没有比减少欲望更好的。他的为人欲望不多，虽然善心有所丧失，也不会太多；他的为人欲望很多，虽然善心有所保存，也是极少的了。"

【英译】Mencius said, 'To nourish the mind there is nothing better than to make the desires few. Here is a man whose desires are few：—in some things he may not be able to keep his heart，but they will be few. Here is a man whose desires are many：—in some things he may be able to keep his heart，but they will be few.'

【注释】

[1] 通过对比寡欲者和多欲者在养心上产生的不同效果，孟子论证了"养心莫善于寡欲"的主张。孟子主张的"寡欲"是少欲而非灭欲。他认为减少物质上和精神上的各种欲望是保有和发展人固有善性的最好办法。

[2] 根据文义和孟子的身心观，"养心"就是培养和发展人固有的善心。理雅各选择用"nourish the mind"翻译"养心"。"Nourish"侧重向人或动植物提供必需的食物以确保其健康，用它翻译"养心"不妥。赖发洛将"养心"理解为给心提供"food"，"food"的基本含义是养料、食物，与保养和发展人之善端也不甚符合。相比较而言，刘殿爵的"nurturing of the heart"更妥帖。"Nurturing"的基本含义是助长某种情绪、观点等的形成和发展，更符合此处"养心"的含义。

[3] 理雅各和刘殿爵认为，"虽有不存焉者，寡矣"是说"欲望不多的人，虽然可能会在一些事上不能保持其心，但这样的事情并不多"，而赖发洛则认为，"Men of few desires may lose their heart，but few are they that do"（虽然在欲望少的人中，可能也有人会失去本心，但是这样的人很少）。这两种理解都可以接受，但赖发洛的理解在说理的力度上明显逊色于理雅各和刘殿爵的译文。孟子推崇寡欲，认为它是养心的最好办法。为了证明这一点，他举"寡欲"和"多欲"在"养心"上的不同效果作说明，试图从正反两个方面来论证这一观点。理雅各和刘殿爵的译文紧紧围绕这一宗旨，更能突出"寡欲"的作用。

【原文】 14.36　曾晳嗜羊枣[1]，而曾子不忍食羊枣[2]。公孙丑问曰："脍炙与羊枣孰美?"孟子曰："脍炙哉!"公孙丑曰："然则曾子何为食脍炙而不食羊枣?"曰："脍炙所同也，羊枣所独也。讳[3]名不讳姓，姓所同也，名所独也。"

【译文】 曾晳喜欢吃羊枣，因而曾子不忍吃羊枣。公孙丑问道："烤肉同羊枣哪个好吃?"孟子答道："烤肉啊!"公孙丑问："那么，曾子为什么吃烤肉却不吃羊枣?"孟子答道："烤肉是大家都喜欢吃的，羊枣只是曾子父亲一个人喜欢吃的。这好像父母之名应被避讳，姓却不避讳一样，因为姓是大家共有的，名却是他一个人独有的。"

【英译】 Mencius said, 'Tsǎng Hsî was fond of sheep-dates, and his son, the philosopher Tsǎng, could not bear to eat sheep-dates.' Kung-sun Ch'âu asked, saying, 'Which is best, ——minced meat and broiled meat, or sheep-dates?' Mencius said, 'Mince and broiled meat, to be sure.' Kung-sun Ch'âu went on, 'Then why did the philosopher Tsǎng eat mince and broiled meat, and would not eat sheep-dates?' Mencius answered, 'For mince and broiled meat there is a common liking, while that for sheep-dates was peculiar. We avoid the name, but do not avoid the surname. The surname is common; the name is peculiar.'

【注释】

[1] 曾子以孝闻名，但普通人仅仅能看到他孝行的表面现象，不能理解孝行背后所蕴含的深意。孟子和公孙丑的对话就是一个最好的例子。曾子在父亲去世后就不再忍心吃父亲爱吃的羊枣，公孙丑仅看到了这一现象，但不明白曾子为什么这么做，孟子举"讳名不讳姓，姓所同也，名所独也"这一浅显易懂的例子来解释曾子不食羊枣背后所蕴含的对父亲恩情的深深思念。

[2] "曾子不忍食羊枣"，朱熹注曰："羊枣，实小黑而圆，又谓之羊

矢枣。曾子以父嗜之，父殁之后，食必思亲，故不忍食也。"刘殿爵按字面意思将之翻译为"Because Tseng Hsi was fond of eating jujubes，Tseng Tzu could not bring himself to eat them."（因为曾皙喜欢吃羊枣，所以曾子不吃它们）他的译文不便于读者理解曾子不喜欢吃的原因，理雅各做了一些补充，将之翻译为"Tsǎng Hsî was fond of sheep-dates，and his son，the philosopher Tsǎng，could not bear to eat sheep-dates."（曾皙喜欢吃羊枣，因而他的儿子、哲学家曾子不忍心吃羊枣）他的译文能够体现二者的关系，但不能让读者明白为什么父亲喜欢吃的东西，儿子却不忍心吃。赵甄陶的译文做了进一步的解释说明，将之翻译为"Zeng Xi was fond of jujubes. After his death his son Zengzi could not bear to eat any jujubes."（曾皙喜欢吃羊枣，他去世后，儿子曾子再也不忍心吃羊枣了）赵甄陶的译文能将原文暗含之意表达出来。

[3]"讳"，即避讳，也就是避免直接写出或说出父母和君主的名字以示尊敬。刘殿爵将"讳"翻译为"taboo"，它的基本含义是"因社会习俗或感情上的反感而导致的禁忌或忌讳"。因为出于对父母和尊长的爱和尊敬，所以反感直说或书写他们的名字，故刘殿爵的译文确切体现了其含义。理雅各将之翻译为"avoid"，赖发洛翻译为"shun"。"Avoid"的突出含义是"努力逃离被认为是困难和危险的根源"，而"shun"源自古英语"scunian"（憎恶），有"故意与厌恶或不想要的事物划清界限"之意。这两种翻译都不如刘殿爵的"taboo"准确。

【原文】 14.37　万章问曰[1]："孔子在陈曰：'盍归乎来！吾党之士狂简，进取，不忘其初。'孔子在陈，何思鲁之狂士？"孟子曰："孔子'不得中道而与之，必也狂狷乎！狂者进取，狷者有所不为也'。孔子岂不欲中道哉？不可必得，故思其次也。""敢问何如斯可谓狂矣？"曰："如琴张、曾皙、牧皮者，孔子之所谓狂矣。""何以谓之狂也？"曰："其志嘐嘐然，曰'古之人，古之人。'夷考其行，而不掩焉者也。狂者又不可得，欲得不屑不洁之士而与之，是獧也，是又其次也。孔子曰：'过我门而不入我室，我不憾焉者，其惟乡原乎！乡原，德之贼也。'"曰："何如斯可谓之乡原矣？"曰："'何以是嘐嘐也？言不顾行，行不顾言，则曰，古之人，古之人。行何为踽踽凉凉？生斯世也，为斯世也，善斯可矣[2]。'阉然媚于世也者，是乡原[3]也。"万子曰："一乡皆称原人焉，无所往而不为原人，孔子以为德之贼，何哉？"曰："非之无举也，刺之无刺也，同乎流俗，合乎污世，居之似忠信，行之似廉洁，众皆悦之，自以为是，而不可与入尧舜之道，故曰'德之贼'也。孔子曰：'恶似而非者：恶莠，恐其乱苗也；恶佞，恐其乱义也；恶利口，恐其乱信也；恶郑声，恐其乱乐也；恶紫，恐其乱朱也；恶乡原，恐其乱德也。'君子反经而已矣[4]。经正，则庶民兴，庶民兴，斯无邪慝矣。"

【译文】万章问道："孔子在陈国时，说道：'为什么不回去呢，我家乡的那些学生志向远大而处世简单，进取而不忘本。'孔子在陈国时，为什么思念鲁国这些狂放之人？"孟子答道："孔子说过：'找不到中道的人同他相交，那只能找狂放之人和狷介之士吧。狂放的人向前进取，狷介之士有所不为。'孔子难道不想与中道的人交往吗？不一定能得到，所以只想次一等的了。""请问，怎么样的人才能叫作狂放的人？"答道："像琴张、曾皙、牧皮这类人就是孔子所说的狂放的人。""为什么称他们是狂放的人呢？"答道："他们志大而言夸，总是说'古人呀，古人呀。'可是一考察他们的行为，却不和言语相吻合。狂放的人结交不到，便找不屑于同流合污的人来交友，这就是狷介之士，这又是次一等的。孔子说：'从我门口经过，却不进我屋里，我也并不遗憾的，那只有好好先生吧。好好先生，是贼害道德的人。'"问道："怎样的人才可以叫好好先生呢？"答道："（这种人认为）为什么这样志气高大呢？言语不能和行为符合，行为也不能同言语符合，就只说'古人呀，古人呀。'（又认为）为什么落落寡合呢？生在这个世界上，为这个世界做事，只要过得去就可以了。'事事迎合，处处讨好的人就是好好先生。"万章说："全乡的人都说他是老好人，他也处处表现出是一个老好人，孔子竟把他当作贼害道德的人，为什么呢？"答道："这种人，要指责他，却又举不出什么大错误来；要责骂他，却找不到责骂的理由。他只是同流合污，为人好像忠诚老实，行为好像清正廉洁，大家也都喜欢他，他自己也以为自己不错，但实际上却与尧舜之道完全违背，所以说他是贼害道德的人。孔子说：'厌恶那种似是而非的东西：厌恶狗尾草，因为怕它混淆了禾苗；厌恶不正当的才智，因为怕它把义搞乱了；厌恶夸夸其谈，因为怕它把信扰乱了；厌恶郑国的乐曲，因为怕它把雅乐搞乱了；厌恶紫色，因为怕它混淆了红色；厌恶好好先生，因为怕它把道德搞乱了。'君子只不过是使一切回到正道罢了。回到正道，百姓就会振奋；百姓振奋了，也就没有邪恶了。"

【英译】Wan Chang asked, saying, 'Confucius, when he was in Ch'ǎn, said: "Let me return. The scholars of my school are ambitious, but hasty. They are for advancing and seizing their object, but cannot forget their early ways." Why did Confucius, when he was in Ch'ǎn, think of the ambitious scholars of Lû?' Mencius replied, 'Confucius not getting men pursuing the true medium, to whom he might communicate his instructions, determined to take the ardent and the cautiously-decided. The ardent would advance to seize their object; the cautiously-decided would keep themselves from certain things. It is not to be thought that Confucius did not wish to get men pursuing the true medium, but being unable to assure himself of finding such, he therefore thought of the next class.' 'I venture to ask what sort of men they were who could be styled "The ambitious?"' 'Such,' replied Mencius, 'as Ch'in Chang, Tsǎng Hsî, and Mû P'ei, were those whom Confucius styled "ambitious."' 'Why were they styled "ambitious?"' The reply was, 'Their aim led them to talk magniloquently, saying, "The ancients!" "The ancients!" But their actions, where we fairly compare them with their words, did not correspond with them. When he found also that he could not get such as were thus ambitious, he wanted to get scholars who would consider anything impure as beneath them. Those were the cautiously-decided, —a class next to the former.' Chang pursued his questioning, 'Confucius said, "They are only your good careful people of the villages at whom I feel no indignation, when they pass my door without entering my house. Your good careful people of the villages are the thieves of virtue." What sort of people were they who could be styled "Your good careful people of the villages?"' Mencius replied, 'They are those who say, "Why are they so magniloquent? Their words have not respect to their actions and their actions have not respect to their words, but they say, —The ancients! The ancients! Why do they act so peculiarly, and are so cold and distant? Born in this age, we should be of this age, to be good is all that is needed." Eunuch-like, flattering their generation;—such are your good careful men of the villages.' Wan Chang said, 'Their whole village styles those men good and careful. In all their conduct they are so. How was it that Confucius considered them the thieves of virtue?' Mencius replied, 'If you would blame them, you find nothing to allege. If you would criticise them, you have nothing to criticise. They agree with the current customs. They consent with an impure age. Their principles have a semblance of right-heartedness and truth. Their conduct has a semblance of disinterestedness and purity. All men are pleased with them, and they think themselves right, so that it is impossible to proceed with them to the principles of Yâo and Shun. On this account they are called "The thieves of virtue." Confucius said, "I hate a semblance which is not the reality. I hate the darnel, lest it be confounded with the corn. I hate glib-tonguedness, lest it be confounded with righteousness. I hate sharpness of tongue, lest it be confounded with sincerity. I hate the music of Chǎng, lest it be confounded with the true music. I hate the reddish blue, lest it be confounded with vermilion. I hate your good careful men of the villages, lest they be confounded with the truly virtuous." The superior man seeks simply to bring back the unchanging standard, and, that being correct, the masses are roused to virtue. When they are so aroused, forthwith perversities and glossed wickedness disappear.'

【注释】

[1] 孟子对"狂简"之士、"狷介"之士、"中道"之士和"乡原"进行了评价，并重点揭露了表面上道貌岸然、容易被错认为是"中道"之士的"乡原"的丑恶嘴脸。

[2] 关于"何以是嘐嘐也？……为斯世也，善斯可矣"，有以下理解。一种以朱熹为代表，认为："乡原讥狂者曰：'何用如此嘐嘐然，行不掩其言，而徒每事必称"古人"邪？'又讥狷者曰：'何必如此踽踽凉凉，无所亲厚哉？人既生于此世，则但当为此世之人，使当世之人皆以为善，则可矣。'此乡原之志也。"理雅各和刘殿爵的译文与朱熹的注解一致，认为是乡原对狂者和狷者的讥讽。一说为孟子描述乡原之辞。焦循《正义》曰："何以是嘐嘐以下皆论乡原。嘐嘐，乡原之嘐嘐也。言何以是嘐嘐若有大志，谓乡原之言何以嘐嘐若有大志也，非如狂者之真有大志也。言不顾行，行不顾言，乡原之言行不顾也。狂者曰古之人古之人，乡原则亦曰古之人。但狂者之称古人，是欲之、幕之；乡原之称古人，则大言以讥剌之，谓古之人行何为踽踽凉凉，无所用于世。此乡原之大言，非如狂者之大言也。"显然，焦

循将后一句"古之人"属下文，读为"古之人行何为踽踽凉凉？"而赖发洛的译文提出了一种新的见解："何以是嘐嘐也？言不顾行，行不顾言"是乡原讥狂者的话，而"古之人，古之人。行何为踽踽凉凉？"则是乡原批判古人的话。他将之翻译为："He says, 'How loud they crow! Their words do not answer to their deeds, their deeds do not answer to their words.' Then he says, 'The men of old, the men of old! Why be so distant and aloof, so cold and chill? Born of the times, be of the times! Be good, that is enough.'"

[3]"乡原"，"原"通"愿"，本义为"谨慎、老实、质朴"，但孔子和孟子认为他们表面上道貌岸然，而实际上为满足一己私欲与流俗合污，是十足的伪君子，因而被孔子指责为"德之贼"，并成为孟子重点批判的对象。理雅各将"乡原"翻译为"your good careful people of the villages"（村里面小心谨慎的好人），赖发洛翻译为"the plain townsmen"（坦率、质朴的市民），刘殿爵翻译为"village honest men"（村里面诚实正直的人）。三位译者都是按照"乡原"的本义翻译，不便于读者理解为什么孔子称其为"德之贼"。译者若将"乡原"翻译为"goody-goodies"（伪善的人）或"whited sepulcher"（伪君子）会更便于读者理解。

[4]"君子反经而已矣"，朱熹注曰："反，复也。经，常也，万世不易之常道也。"理雅各的理解与之相类，将之翻译为"The superior man seeks simply to bring back the unchanging standard"（君子只要重新恢复不变的标准就行了）。刘殿爵译为"A gentleman goes back to the norm"（君子使一切回归标准）。这两种理解都可以体现其含义。赖发洛从"经"的字源出发，指出"经"的本意是织物的纵线，与"纬"相对，因而将之翻译为"A gentleman turns back to the warp, that is all."。虽然"warp"能对应"经"的本义，但显然，并非此处"经"之意。而且"warp"还有"使歪曲，反常"之意，容易引起误解。

【原文】14.38　孟子曰[1]："由尧舜至于汤，五百有余岁，若禹、皋陶[2]，则见而知之；若汤，则闻而知之。由汤至于文王，五百有余岁，若伊尹、莱朱则见而知之[3]；若文王，则闻而知之。由文王至于孔子，五百有余岁，若太公望、散宜生，则见而知之；若孔子，则闻而知之。由孔子而来至于今，百有余岁，去圣人之世若此其未远也，近圣人之居若此其甚也，然而无有乎尔，则亦无有乎尔[4]。"

【译文】孟子说："从尧舜到汤，经历了五百多年，像禹、皋陶那样的人，是亲眼看见尧舜之道而了解其道理的；像汤，是听说尧舜之道而了解其道理的。从汤到文王，经历了五百多年，像伊尹、莱朱，是亲眼看见而了解其道理的；像文王，是听说而了解其道理的。从文王到孔子，经历了五百多年，像太公望、散宜生那样的人，是亲眼看见而了解其道理的；像孔子，是听说而了解其道理的。从孔子到今天，一百多年了，离开圣人的年代如此地不远，距离圣人的家乡如此地接近，但是已经没有承继的人了，已经没有承继的人了！"

【英译】Mencius said, 'From Yâo and Shun down to T'ang were 500 years and more. As to Yü and Kâo Yâo, they saw those earliest sages，and so knew their doctrines，while T'ang heard their doctrines as transmitted，and so knew them. From T'ang to king Wăn were 500 years and more. As to Î Yin，and Lâi Chû，they saw T'ang and knew his doctrines，while king Wăn heard them as transmitted，and so knew them. From king Wăn to Confucius were 500 years and more. As to T'âi-kung Wang and San Î-shăng，they saw Wăn，and so knew his doctrines，while Confucius heard them as transmitted，and so knew them. From Confucius downwards until now，there are only 100 years and somewhat more. The distance in time from the sage is so far from being remote，and so very near at hand was the sage's residence. In these circumstances，is there no one to transmit his doctrines? Yea，is there no one to do so?'

【注释】

[1] 唐代韩愈在《原道》中所标示的尧舜禹汤文武周公孔子的圣人道统，在本章中已经大备。孟子通过列举在古代历史上出现的杰出政治领袖，描绘了一个从尧舜到孔子的圣贤道统，表达了自己继承孔子之志，传播圣贤之道的决心。

[2] 孟子在本章集中列举了一系列圣贤之士，对于他们名字的英译，起初没有固定的规定，译者往往根据自己所处时代通用的注音系统和自己的翻译习惯翻译，这就使汉语人名的英译出现严重混乱现象。理雅各、赖发洛和刘殿爵的译本都选择用威妥玛式拼音翻译，但译文也有明显不同。理雅各的译本早在 1861 年就已经出版，当时用威妥玛式拼音翻译中国的地名、人名在中国和国际上都很流行，因而他的译文体现了威妥玛式拼音保持接近英文拼法，但是并不完全迁就英文的拼写习惯，并沿袭了前人使用送气符号来表示声母的办法。英国人赖发洛的《孟子》译本出现于 1932 年。他的译文显然受 1867 年来华的翟理斯的影响。翟理斯对威妥玛的标音系统加以改良，并于 1892 年出版了《华英字典》。1906 年春在上海举行的"帝国邮电联席会议"决定，基本上以翟理斯所编的《华英字典》中的拉丁字母拼写法为依据，也就是威妥玛—翟理斯式拼音。为了适合打电报的需要，会议还决定不采用任何附加符号（例如送气符号等）。此种拼音被称为"邮政式拼音"，是 20 世纪上半叶西方国家拼写中国地名时最常用的系统。刘殿爵的《孟子》译本出版于 1970 年，当时我国规定用汉语拼音方案作为汉语人名罗马字拼写法的正式规定（1978 年）尚未出台，而且他长期在伦敦大学任教，在翻译汉语地名和人名时亦深受威妥玛—翟理斯式拼音影响。例如，三人将"皋陶"分别翻译为"Kâo Yâo""Kao-yao"和"Kao Yao"，体现了译者的时代特征。

[3] 纵观全文，可以看出孟子虽罗列了上述圣贤，但并非特指这些人，而是用他们代指他们所生活时代的一类贤人。正如焦循《正义》所说："在

汤时举一伊尹莱朱，则当时贤臣如女鸠、女房、义伯、仲伯、咎单等括之矣。在文王时举一太公望、散宜生，则虢叔、泰颠、闳夭、召公、毕公、荣公等括之矣。非谓见知者，仅此一二人也。"理雅各和赖发洛在翻译的时候，都严格按照字面意思音译。他们的译文给读者传递的信息是，孟子所说的"见而知之"者和"闻而知之"者仅指罗列的这些人。而刘殿爵则翻译为"Men like Yi Yin and Lai Chu"（像伊尹莱朱那些人），他的译文则表明，孟子实际上是说和所列举人相似的贤能之人都是"见而知之"者和"闻而知之"者。

[4]"然而无有乎尔，则亦无有乎尔"，杨伯峻指出："当时和孔子出生地最近的有名望的儒者，除了孟子，更无他人。孟子说'无有乎尔'，正和'夫圣，孔子不居'一样，是不能明说的。"赵岐亦认为："乎尔者，叹而不怨之辞也。"因而这句话应理解为"但是如果没有继承圣人之道的人，那么以后也就没有继承圣人之道的人了。"这句话实际上体现了孟子继承圣人之道，"舍我其谁"的气概。理雅各将之翻译为"In these circumstances, is there no one to transmit his doctrines? Yea, is there no one to do so?"（在这种环境下，难道没有人传播他的学说吗？是的，会没有人这么做吗）他的译文貌疑实肯，与赵岐的"言则亦者，非实无有也"有异曲同工之妙。赖发洛译为"yet if it is not in thee, then it is not in thee!"（然而如果没有在你身上，那么真是没有在你身上）和理雅各不同的是，他把"尔"理解为第二人称代词"你"。他的译文不便于传递孟子的真实含义。刘殿爵译为"yet if there is no one who has anything of the sage, well then, there is no one who has anything of the sage."（如果没有人继承圣人之道，那么以后也不会有人继承圣人之道了）他对"乎尔"的理解与陈器之相似，即认为"乎尔，语气词连用，重点在'尔'上，表示断定，可译为'了''呢'。"刘殿爵选择用肯定句传递孟子继承圣人之道的决心和信心。

后　记

　　为了更好地解读《孟子》思想，本书不仅广泛借鉴、引用了古代学者的诸多研究成果，如宋朱熹的《四书章句集注》（中华书局 1983 年版）、清焦循的《孟子正义》（中华书局 1987 年版），还广泛吸收了当代学者的研究成果，如杨伯峻的《孟子译注》（中华书局 1960 年版），任俊华、赵清文的《大学·中庸·孟子正宗》（华夏出版社 2008 年版），梁涛的《孟子》（国家图书馆出版社 2017 年版）以及学界关于《孟子》思想和英译研究的最新期刊文章。

　　为了彰显《孟子》多维度诠释的可行性，本书还重点关注了其他代表性的英译者对《孟子》中核心概念和思想的理解和译介。本书中的英文译文选用的是理雅各的《孟子》英译本（James Legge，*The Works of Mencius*，New York：Dover Pub.，Inc，1970.），试图通过将该译本和刘殿爵（D. C. Lau）的《孟子》英译本（London：Penguin Books，1970.）、伦纳德·赖发洛（Leonard A. Lyall）的 *Mencius*（London：Longmans，Green and Co，1932）以及赵甄陶、张文庭、周定之的汉英对照版《孟子》（湖南人民出版社、外文出版社 1999 年版）进行对比研究，以凸显《孟子》内涵的丰富性。